W9-ACS-874

INFERRING: The mental process a person goes through when he observes facts and tries to *explain* what they mean. For example: The children observe that paper clips stick to a magnet. Possible inference: The magnet must have a force. Example: Plants bend toward the light source (fact); therefore, there must be some change in the way the tissue of the plant grows in response to light (inference).

INQUIRY OR ENQUIRY: (Authors vary in their spelling of this word.) The process of investigating a problem. Inquiry differs from problem solving in that an individual may originate the problem and develop his own strategies for obtaining information. Unlike problem solving there is no set pattern to inquiry. An individual may be involved in many methods of obtaining information and he may take intuitive approaches to the problem. The end product of inquiry may result in a discovery.

INVENTION: The process whereby children suggest or modify an object so that it may be used for a purpose other than that for which it was originally intended. Dr. Karplus of SCIS also uses the word to refer to situations in which the teacher gives a name to a phenomenon the children are observing. For example: the teacher invents the *magnetic field concept* to describe what happens when two magnets approach each other.

INVESTIGATION: A careful search or gathering of information. It may involve observing such as looking at cells, making inferences, reading. It differs from experimenting by not having a control.

MICROTEACHING: A short teaching period which is observed and then evaluated. The teacher's total performance or a portion of it may be examined by others or by himself on video tape. For example: The teacher's ability to question. The results of the evaluation may be used by the teacher to improve his teaching ability.

PROBLEM SOLVING: In science, refers to all those mental and experimental activities a person goes through in attempting to resolve some problem. A student involved in scientific problem solving formulates hypotheses, experiments to test the hypotheses, and draws conclusions from the experiments.

PROCESSES (critical thinking): The cognitive abilities the mind is capable of performing, such as hypothesizing, comparing, inferring, controlling variables, classifying, etc.

PSYCOMOTOR OBJECTIVES: Involve muscular motor skills such as manipulation of scientific apparatus.

RESOURCE UNIT: Instructional materials usually limited to one scientific topic such as seeds, plants, animals, weather, or a conceptual scheme.

SCIENTIFIC PRINCIPLE: A generalization of science involving several related concepts. For example: Cells arise from only cells; Gases expand when heated. Principles are sometimes called conceptual statements or simply concepts by some authors.

TEACHING UNIT: A group of lessons, audio visual aids, and tests selected from the resource materials to teach a particular class.

TERMINAL BEHAVIOR: The behavior an individual is to acheive by the time the teacher's work with him ends.

THEORY: A generalization or body of related principles that explains some scientific phenomena. Examples of theories are evolution, and the molecular nature of the matter.

The definitions listed above are given to aid the reader of this text. We have tried to present definitions encompassing a consensus of science educators. It should be mentioned, however, that other authors may differ in their use of these terms.

P. 306
P. 450

880
gan

TEACHING SCIENCE THROUGH DISCOVERY

Second Edition

Arthur A. Carin
Queens College

Robert B. Sund
Northern Colorado University

CHARLES E. MERRILL PUBLISHING COMPANY
A Bell & Howell Company
Columbus, Ohio 43216

Copyright © 1970, 1964 by Charles E. Merrill Publishing Company, Columbus, Ohio. All rights reserved. No
part of this book may be reproduced in any form, electronic or mechanical, including photocopy, recording,
or any information storage and retrieval system, without permission in writing from the publisher.

ISBN:0-675-09348-1

Library of Congress Catalog Card Number: 73-122523

2 3 4 5 6 7 8 9 10 / 75 74 73 72 71 70

Printed in the United States of America

Hilda Graham Cooper
406 E. Arch St.
Lancaster, S. C.

. . . who shall kindle others
must himself glow . . .

Italian Proverb

PREFACE

The objective of this book is to prepare prospective and experienced teachers to teach science in the elementary schools utilizing the discovery approach. This approach is emphasized because it follows more closely the investigative patterns of science, excites children more than some other methods, characterizes the philosophical foundation of the modern national elementary curriculum efforts, and applies what we know about children from developmental psychology.

Elementary science education has made great strides since the first edition of this book was published. Many groups have been established to bring about change. All of these groups stress the importance of the child's discovery of science concepts and principles through being involved in the use of science processes. One of the major movements has been in the number and variety of inquiry or discovery approach science projects such as AAAS, COPES, ESS, SCIS, etc. This revision retains the well-received original format, but has expanded in the following ways in order to amplify and illustrate the most current ideas and trends in the teaching of science in the elementary school.

Part I—Shaping Science Education in the Elementary School. A framework is presented in this section for modern, future-oriented science education. The latest research and proven classroom practices are applied to such fundamental questions as "What is modern science?" "Why should science be taught to children?" and "How do children best learn science?" Two new chapters have been added to update this section: Chapter Three, "The Nature of Discovery in Science Teaching-Learning," presents the work of Jean Piaget, Jerome Bruner, Robert Karplus, and others and their implications for guiding children's discoveries in science. The research presented reinforces the need for active involvement of children in process oriented problem solving. Chapter Four, "Innovation, Experimentation, and Reform in Elementary School Science," presents a cogent historical look at the past developments as well as a description and analysis of several major science projects. Possible trends in science are shown by means of an analysis of the similarities in the major science projects.

Part III—Enrichment Activities for Discovery Teaching-Learning. The revised Chapters Ten and Eleven offer an increased number of enrichment activities for meeting individual differences of students in science programs and for encouraging creativity. More specific classroom-tested experiences are also presented for working in science with the "slow" learner and the "exceptional" student. A new chapter has been added in which the integration of mathematics into the elementary science program is discussed. The chapter on "Evaluation: Another Discovery Teaching-Learning Experience" takes cognizance of the pros and cons of the role of behavioral obectives and presents specific examples of cognitive, affective, and psychomotor evaluative devices.

Part IV—Discovery Laboratory Activities. The lessons in this section have undergone extensive revision through further elementary classroom testing and the inclusion of updated materials (behavioral objectives, Piaget's levels of learning, Bruner's discovery theory, etc.). The discovery activities employ a new feature: discovery questions are included in each lesson as resource possibilities for teachers to use. The type of student thinking process for each question is noted beside the question in this way:

Student Thinking Process	Teacher Discovery-type Question
Designing an investigation	How would you find out . . .
Hypothesizing	What do you think will happen if . . .

The discovery laboratory activities are offered as the foundation upon which the teacher can structure the science program. Teachers may wish to use them in their own groups before using them with children in order to better master the discovery process. Micro-teaching sessions will also prove helpful. Teachers will be able to expand and improve upon the lessons and be more creative as they further understand the purpose and effectiveness of this approach.

Student teachers as well as beginning and experienced teachers have assisted the authors in improving upon the already well-received lesson plans. Only the most effective of these lessons are presented here. The addition of needed artwork as well as modification of existing artwork has resulted in greater clarity and directions for teachers to follow.

The authors gratefully acknowledge the support and suggestions of their colleagues at Queens College and Northern Colorado University, especially Professors James McClurg, Leslie Trowbridge, and Kenneth Olson. Acknowledgment is also due to Dr. Anthony Picard for his many comments on the role of mathematics and science discoveries and to our students for various kinds of help and enlightenment relevant to production of this book.

Thanks are due to the following organizations and governmental agencies for providing information and other data: The American Association for the Advancement of Science; National Science Foundation; The Department of Health, Education, and Welfare; the Elementary Science Study; Educational Services, Inc.; The University of California, Science Curriculum Improvement Study; The Elementary School Science Project; the University of Illinois Elementary School Science Project; The National Foundation of the Princeton Study; the Coordinated Science and Mathematics Curriculum; University of Minnesota; the School Mathematics Study Group.

Sincere gratitude is again extended to Terry, Jill, Amy, and Jon Carin, without whose patience, inspiration, and sacrifice this revision never would have been written.

Arthur A. Carin

Robert B. Sund

March, 1970

PHOTO CREDITS

The authors and the publisher gratefully acknowledge all those who generously and graciously supplied the photographs which appear in this book. The numbers following the credit indicate the pages upon which the photos appear.

Baton Rouge Parish School Board, Baton Rouge, La.: 276

Bell & Howell Company, Chicago, Ill.: 165, 169

Dr. Arthur Carin: 10, 27, 29, 32, 34, 42, 140, 207, 223, 257

Ray Cicero, Inc.: 208

Cincinnati, Ohio, Public Schools: 150, 220

Commission on Science Education, American Association for the Advancement of Science: 58, 248

A. Devaney, Inc.: 36

Geoffrey Dubrowsky, Flushing, N.Y.: 4, 174, 176

Elementary Science Advisory Center, University of Colorado: 45, 90, 206, 225, 267, 321

Elementary Science Study of Educational Services, Inc., Watertown, N.J.: 75, 115

Flint Hills Science Project, Emporia, Kan.: 51, 63, 64, 87, 92, 141, 143, 152, 184, 239, 262, 264, 273, 280, 285, 286

Guttenberg Comes to Film, *Media & Methods,* © 1967: 171

Jefferson County School District: 252

Jewell Aquarium Co., Chicago, Ill.: 191, 193, 200, 201

Learning Center, Princeton, N.J.: 40, 74, 211

Bob Lehker Photos, Cincinnati, Ohio: 116

Marsh Photographers, Cincinnati, Ohio: 240

Minnesota School Mathematics and Science Center, from the MINNEMAST project, supported by the National Science Foundation: 122, 180, 181

National Education Association: Frontispiece, 230, 103, 242

National Science Teachers Association—Equipment by E. H. Sheldon Equipment Co., Muskegon, Mich.: 79, 112, 131, 186, 187, 231, 275, 314

H. Armstrong Roberts: 2, 24, 97, 192

Savannah, Ga., Board of Public Education: 26, 128, 305

School District No. 241, Mobile Science Laboratory Program, Albert Lea, Minn.: 156, 172, 178, 212

Science Curriculum Improvement Study, University of California: 20, 22, 52, 55, 60, 68, 82, 99, 118, 164, 218, 228, 234, 236, 250, 270, 272, 284, 316, 319, 322

Warren Shepler, University of Pittsburgh Learning R & D Center: 158, 216, 222

United States Department of Agriculture: 142

Bob Waters, Photographer, Colorado State College: 201

Xerox Corporation, Rochester, N.Y. by George Platteter: 9, 227, 251, 269, 278

CONTENTS

TEACHING SCIENCE
THROUGH
DISCOVERY

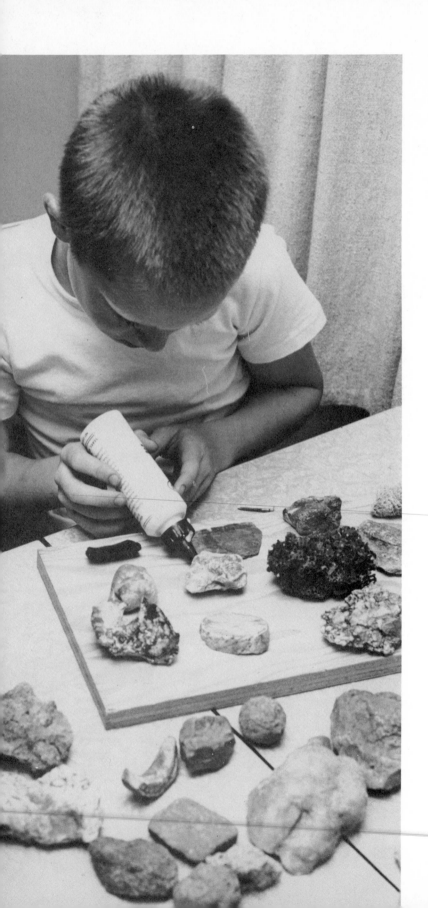

PART
ONE

SHAPING SCIENCE EDUCATION IN THE ELEMENTARY SCHOOL

The creative artist seeks to encompass in a single poem, in a painting, in a musical composition, a certain segment of human experience. In much the same way the scientist seeks for unity amid the variety of nature.[1]

CHAPTER 1

WHAT IS MODERN SCIENCE?

What you want your children to gain from your science program should come from what you believe is the true spirit, structure, and function of modern science.

A Working Definition of Science

It is difficult to write a short, simple, universally-accepted definition of anything so complex as science, but many attempts have been made.[2] A working definition of *science*, reflecting the approaches generally accepted today in science education, is:

> Science is an accumulated and systematized learning, in general usage restricted to natural phenomena. The progress of science is marked not only by an *accumulation of fact*, but by the emergence of *scientific method* and of the *scientific attitude*.[3]

Science, then, is a combination of both *processes* and *products*, related to and dependent upon each other. When used in this way, science offers methods of inquiry useful in learning more about the universe and its workings. The *processes* of *science* are scientific attitudes and methods of inquiry. As a result of these processes we derive the *products* of science which are the accumulated and systematized bodies of knowledge.

Figure 1 shows the interrelated and expanding nature of the processes and products of science. As man uses scientific processes to investigate the phenomena of nature, he gains increasing tested, scientific products: of facts, concepts, principles, generalizations, theories, and laws. These newly acquired products are then used to broaden and increase his scientific investigations which involve further use of processes resulting in more tested scientific products, ad infinitum.

---

[1] J. Darrell Barnard, "The Role of Science in Our Culture," *The Fifty-ninth Yearbook of the National Society for the Study of Education*, Part I (Chicago: University of Chicago Press, 1960), Chapter 1, p. 5.

[2] The reader will find insight into the problem by reading how one science educator arrived at an operational definition of science in this brief, well-written journal article: John H. Woodburn, "Science Defined Versus Indefinable. A Personal Attempt to Define Science," *The Science Teacher*, Vol. 34, No. 8 (November 1967), pp. 27-30.

[3] "Science," *The Columbia Encyclopedia*, (3rd ed. 1963), p. 1990.

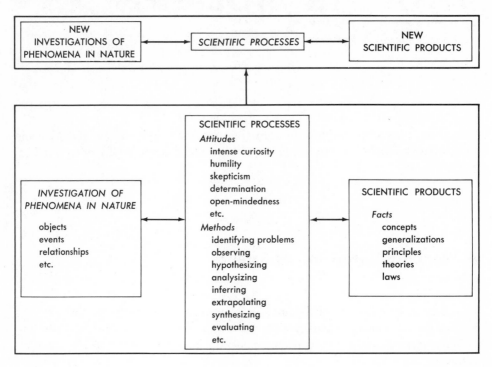

FIGURE 1. Interrelationship Between Scientific Processes and Products

Processes of Science

Scientific Attitudes

Science stems from human urges and needs which drive people to seek rational answers to their many questions. It is much the same motivation as the mountain climber who climbs mountains "Because they're there." Just as the young child enjoys discovering the texture, color, size, weight, and taste of sand at the seashore or in the sandbox because it intrigues him, the scientist studies the wonders of nature because he delights in them. This dynamic—almost compulsive—involvement of child or adult investigator searching for answers provides the fuel for the vehicle of investigation. Without this attitude of discovery for discovery's sake there would not be scientific inquiry. It is not important that practical applications be found for the results of investigations, for the scientist often is not concerned with nor even aware of the uses for his findings. The sheer joy of discovery and determining knowledge for its own sake is justification and reward enough for studying something. This motivation has been well expressed by Charles P. Snow, who says:

Anyone who has ever worked in any science knows how much esthetic joy he has obtained. That is, in the actual activity of science, in the process of making a discovery, however humble it is, one can't help feeling an awareness of beauty.[4]

The scientist because of his unquenchable thirst for knowing becomes a perpetual learner: free to seek, free to be curious, free to inquire. There is a zest for knowing, and as he knows more and more he discovers that he knows so little. This fosters other scientific attitudes—*humility* and *skepticism.*

Humility and Skepticism. Humility, freedom from pride and arrogance, comes to the scientist partly as a result of his exposure to everbroadening horizons and partly from his observations of human beings and the ways in which they tend to behave. He must constantly guard against his own tendencies to be dogmatic and try to avoid accepting things blindly and unquestioningly. A healthy skepticism is also a vital ingredient for the scientist. He tries not to have his mind so imprinted with static thoughts that alternative ideas do not occur to him, or if alternatives are pointed out he attempts to objectively evaluate them. Authoritarianism is the enemy of skepticism and therefore anti-scientific. Opinionated, categorical, and pedantic individuals are not scientific because their minds are sealed to new information. On the other hand, a scientist cannot be gullible and easily fall for the latest fad or idea. The scientist builds safeguards into his methods of research against these human tendencies. These safeguards have evolved from the work of hundreds of scientists. They have gradually, through the hundreds of years of scientific history, been molded and formed into the processes of science which have collectively become known as *the scientific method.* On the methods of science it has been said:

> One of the great achievements of science is to have developed a method which works almost independently of the people whom it is operated on.

Positive Approach to Failure. A human tendency is to become discouraged, especially when months of study end with little progress or fail to resolve a problem. Scientists have attempted to overcome this problem by adopting a very realistic and healthy approach to their work. They view their efforts on a never-ending continuum. At any given point in their work they see the results as incomplete because later on they will know more about the subject as a result of further work. "Failure" as thought of by the layman really is not failure at all to a scientist. All revealed knowledge has value. "Failure" in laymen's terms is really a step along a path in research because it says, "This is not the right answer you are seeking, but at least you now know this is not the answer. Try another route to resolve the problem." From this perspective, failure becomes a type of success because it tells the scientist his hunch was not the correct one. Actually the failure can be interpreted as an addition to the great storehouse of cumulative scientific information.

An example of success stemming from failure can be observed in the work of Dr. Paul Ehrlich, 1908 Nobel Prize winner in medicine and physiology. Dr. Ehr-

---

[4] Charles P. Snow "Appreciations in Science," *Science,* 133 (January 27, 1961), pp. 256-259.

lich developed Salvarsan for the treatment of syphilis after 605 unsuccessful experiments. As a matter of fact, Salvarsan was called "606" by Dr. Ehrlich because of the numerical order in his experimental series. The 605 "failures" experienced by Paul Ehrlich contributed *positively* to medical research by providing all the information that lead to the development of the 606th formula.

The historical records of scientific endeavor abound with numerous stories of this kind. A more recent example can be found in the modern-day quest for sixty-second color pictures developed by the Polaroid Camera Company. Howard Rogers, a chemist, spent fifteen years searching for just the right chemical compound needed for instant color pictures. It took experimentation with 5000 different chemical compounds before Rogers actually invented an entirely new chemical molecule. His 5000 "failures" added to the knowledge in chemistry.[5]

Failures enable scientists to know what has been tried, to avoid repeating errors, and to advance in new directions. The Ehrlichs and the Rogerses have enabled us to reap the inheritance of a vast, cumulative body of tested information from which our investigations advance. It can be said then, that the scientist comes to know a kind of success in the long run from daily, intelligent failure.

The Only Certainty Is Uncertainty. Most career scientists discover there is a light shining through the dark haze of frustration and weariness of daily failures in their work. The light is the knowledge that the only certainty in scientific study is uncertainty. This discovery usually follows the awareness that failure is just one place on the continuum of research. The scientist then accepts his work as being continually unfinished. His current research may arrive at a point where he is able to make certain conclusions from his collected data. However, in the process of investigating a problem other unanswered questions arise. As one scientist put it: "I'm in a wonderful profession. I'll always have a job to do because of the revealing nature of the scientific enterprise. Problems are solved and in the process others become uncovered."

These scientific attitudes—curiosity, humility, skepticism, open-mindedness, avoidance of dogmatism or gullibility, and a positive approach to failure—have become rules of behavior for scientists to follow in scientific investigations. The degree to which these scientific attitudes are manifested by the scientist as he carries out his investigations determines how well he will be able to utilize the processes of science to make significant discoveries.

Scientific Inquiry

Scientific inquiry broadly defined is a search for truth or knowledge. Emphasis is placed upon the aspects of *search*, rather than on the mere acquisition of knowledge. Joseph J. Schwab laments the absence of this search element of scientific inquiry in much of current science education with this astute observation:

> It is the almost total absence of this portrayal of science which marks the greatest disparity between science as it is and science as seen through most text-

---

[5] For an absorbing and colorful story of the search for a new chemical molecule see: "Instant Color Pictures," *Life* (January 25, 1963), pp. 74-88.

books. We are shown conclusions of enquiry as if they were certain or nearly certain facts. Further, we rarely see these conclusions as other than isolated, independent "facts." Their coherence and organization—the defining marks of *scientific* knowledge—are underemphasized or omitted. And we catch hardly a glimpse of the other constituents of scientific enquiry—organizing principles, data, and the interpretation of data.[6]

What would you guess the value of this activity to be?

Science educators are beginning to see that the most crucial kinds of activities to which the scientists give their attention are embodied in these constituents of inquiry. For this reason, newer science education programs involve students *directly* in activities similar to how scientists operate in discovering new knowledge. The objective is to have students imitate as closely as is possible the scientists and their methods of inquiry. This application of the scientists' methods of inquiry to teaching science is referred to as *the discovery approach to teaching*, and a fuller description of this approach is presented in Chapter 3.

---

6 Joseph J. Schwab, "The Teaching of Science as Enquiry," in Joseph J. Schwab and Paul F. Brandwein, *The Teaching of Science* (Cambridge, Mass.: Harvard University Press, 1962), p. 31.

By the time this youngster is old enough for formal science classes, he will already have made his first scientific observations. How can a teacher build on this early experience?

Inquiry is launched with inherent problems existing and all the processes usually associated with science to find solutions are called upon. Some of the processes used are observing, questioning, measuring, guessing, controlling variables, inferring, evaluating, and hypothesizing. There are attitudes that are also part of the scientific inquiry, such as questioning of authority, viewing knowledge as dynamic rather than static, and cautiousness and humility when evaluating, synthesizing, and interpreting data. But above all, scientific inquiry is concerned with asking the *right kinds* of questions, so that the *right things* are investigated.

The Right Kinds of Questions. "What?" "How?" "Why?"—heard so frequently all the way from toddlers exploring their sensory worlds to scientists working on profound intellectual activities—are the foundations of science. These three types of questions are the essence of science inquiry for they form the bulk of questions asked by scientists.

"What?" questions generally ask for *descriptions* and are the simplest type, such as "What kind of rock is that?" or "What bird is that on the fence?" The answers to these questions are usually brief and often monosyllabic.

The "How?" questions require greater inquiry because they usually are concerned with some *process*. The ways to approach the answering of this type of question frequently are suggested by the question. Answering it, however, may be very taxing. For example, consider the question: "How is heat energy conducted through a piece of iron?" In order to answer it, the *process* of heat conduction must be understood. The answer is more involved than describing that the end of the bar feels hot, even though heat was applied to the other end. It involves these factors: knowledge of molecular structure of matter, action of heat on molecules, interaction of "stimulated" molecules, transfer of energy from molecule to molecule.

The most difficult questions to answer are the "Why?" ones. These questions rarely have final answers. Each successive answer to a "Why?" question usually leads to another, more fundamental question. This is observable in the young child asking "Dad, why is grass green?" The father answers, "Because it has chlorophyll," to which the child immediately asks, "Well—why is *chlorophyll* green?" This could go on almost indefinitely because the question pushes back each time to more basic conceptual information. Because questioning is the heart of the scientific inquiry, Chapter 5 is devoted entirely to the specifics of questioning techniques in science education.

Some people, perhaps partly in frustration and partly in ignorance, respond to "Why?" questions with anthropomorphic or teleological answers. Anthropomorphic explanations give human qualities to nonhuman things. *Anthropomorphism* comes from two Greek words: *anthropos* (man) and *morphos* (form). The word therefore means attributing human form or qualities to nonhuman things. An example of this is the way Lassie's action and qualities are described in the movies and on television. Lassie is made to appear as if she can think, reason, and act like a human. *Teleology* attributes purpose, design, or will to nonhuman things. An example would be to say, "Chemical bonding takes place because the material *wants* to share its electrons with another material." Both anthropomorphic and teleological explanations are scientifically unsatisfactory because they are vague, lead to dead ends, and grind the processes of inquiry to a nonproductive halt. How then do scientists structure their studies so that they have better opportunities to find productive answers to questions?

Strategies of Inquiry. Once a scientist is aware of a problem or question he wants to answer, it is mistakenly assumed by some that all he needs to do is apply *the* scientific method. After analyzing *the* method it is assumed his answers will come pouring forth by some mysterious process. This common misconception stems from the memorization in our high school or college days of the steps scientists are supposed to follow in problem solving:

1. State problem
2. Suggest hypothesis
3. Experiment.
4. Observe

5. Collect and analyze data
6. Re-experiment to verify data
7. Draw conclusions from data

These steps are the way a scientist *reports* his work in giving a paper at a science conference or preparing it for distribution.

When a scientist investigates a problem, he may follow all of these steps, but he may not follow them in the exact sequence given here. He may actually spend a considerable amount of time defining the problem and then move from defining the problem to making several hypotheses many times. He may devise several experimental approaches and test all of them before he makes any conclusions. Processes of scientific inquiry are idiosyncratic and creative. Paul F. Brandwein has emphasized this illusiveness of trying to standardize the processes of inquiry:

> It follows that in attempting to define the artist's, the musician's, the poet's, or the scientist's way, one experiences a sense of failure. Rightly so. Creativeness is both its own cause and its own result. Creativeness, the most essential attribute of a scientist's approach, will at present not yield to definition except in the most general term; creativity is an art of an individual. One can see the fire of creativeness, but one doesn't know the terminology of its incandescence. The term "Scientific Method" is perhaps useful only in historiography.[7]

---

[7] Paul F. Brandwein, "Elements in a Strategy for Teaching Science in the Elementary School," in Joseph J. Schwab and Paul F. Brandwein, *The Teaching of Science* (Cambridge, Mass.: Harvard University Press, 1962), p. 115-116.

The fact that a precise description cannot be applied to the processes of inquiry does not mean that structures do not exist in scientific research. On the contrary, three important aspects built into all scientific processes of inquiry are relentless testing of data, application of scientific reasoning, and search for cause and effect.

Relentless Testing of Data. The questions constantly confronting a scientist in his relentless search for meaning out of natural phenomena are:

> *How do you know what you know?* (Checking validity of observation.)
> *How well do you know it?* (Checking validity of assertion.)

By applying these two questions constantly, the scientist tries to minimize his errors in making his observations and in recording his data. He knows that unless his data can be replicated by anyone who repeats his work under similar conditions, it cannot be considered scientifically trustworthy. The fact that scientific results must be reported in such a way that they can be replicated by another investigator makes the scientist constantly on his guard as to the accuracy of his data. This ability to test an experimenter's data is a safeguard and the cornerstone of science. Precision in the observation and recording of data has improved rapidly as scientific instruments have become more sophisticated. In most scientific experiments scientists try to rely less upon their feelings, observations, and senses, in favor of more objective devices such as photography, electronic computers, and data processors. In spite of the superiority of electronic gadgets for data gathering there is no substitute at this stage for man's greatest ability—his scientific reasoning.

Scientific Reasoning. Just as it is impossible to describe completely a single process of scientific inquiry, so too is it impossible to define easily man's reasoning processes. Several types of reasoning are valuable when a man thinks. Two broad classes of reasoning, however, are invaluable in the processes of inquiry: *inductive reasoning* and *deductive reasoning*.

The *inductive reasoning* process starts with the specific and moves toward the general. It tries to pull together small bits of data into some type of "Gestalt," or whole, or generalization.

The *deductive reasoning* process starts with generalization and tries to make predictions based upon these generalizations. One of the problems in using this type of reasoning comes from the fact that the basic assumptions underlying the generalizations may be faulty. If this occurs then the resulting conclusions may be logical, but false.

The use of relentless testing combined with inductive and deductive reasoning makes up the heart of the process of inquiry—the search for cause and effect.

Search for Cause and Effect. Scientists are basically interested in finding cause and effect relationships between the seemingly independent and fragmented data they collect. Whenever possible, scientists use their greatest device for testing their ideas of cause and effect—the controlled experiment. In controlled experiments each separate condition is isolated and controlled as accurately as possible. The isolated and controlled conditions are called the *variables* of an experiment.

Variables may be conditions of temperature, light, moisture, or any aspect to be tested. By setting up two identical experiments and precisely varying one variable in one of the experiments, differences can be observed, recorded, and analyzed. In this way the cause and effect of the changed variable can be observed. For young children a controlled experiment could be as simple as:

> *Wet* one sponge thoroughly, put it in dish, and sprinkle it with some grass seeds. Label dish "WITH WATER." Take an identical sponge, put it *dry* in dish and sprinkle grass seed on it. Label dish "WITHOUT WATER." Keep the wet sponge moist by adding water when needed. Keep both dishes in same spot in room to assure as identical temperature and light conditions as possible.

In this experiment the dry sponge is called the *control*. Moisture is called the *variable.* The experiment establishes some cause-effect relationship between water and germination of grass seed. If left for a few days, it is very probable the grass seed on the wet sponge will germinate. The children then can be helped to see some cause-effect relationship between water and grass seed germination if other conditions of temperature and light are suitable and constant.

The controlled experiment is one of the most important contributions of science to man's search for reliable, repeatable data. However, to control *all* variables precisely at *all* times is extremely difficult if not impossible. Even slight changes in conditions may yield significant differences in findings. Scientists try to account for these slight changes in conditions and build degrees of accuracy, tolerance, and measurement into the standards of scientific work. However, it is not always possible to use precisely controlled experiments due to the inability to duplicate natural conditions, the largeness of the sample needed, or the effect on the subjects of the experiments, especially with humans or wild animals in their natural habitat.

Through the controlled experiment, science has amassed a huge store of *tested* knowledge. This store of knowledge is increasing at a phenomenal rate. In fact, it has been estimated our fund of *tested* scientific knowledge doubles every ten years. This tested knowledge is the *product of science*.

Products of Science

Accumulated and Systematized Tested Bodies of Knowledge

Scientists have found it convenient and efficient to divide their work into manageable fields and sub-fields. A scientist, for example, may decide to work in the broad field of astronomy which limits itself to the scientific study of the heavenly bodies. While working in astronomy, his interest may be keenly sharpened by a particular aspect of astronomy. Due to many factors, he may decide to delimit his efforts to investigating the *physics* of astronomy. He then is said to have become involved in the sub-field called astrophysics which includes studies of the composition of the heavenly bodies (for which the spectroscope is essential), radiation, light, etc. The science of astronomy includes the body of tested knowledge arranged systematically to show the facts, generalizations or concepts, theories, and laws of the universe. Similar organization is true for other scientific disciplines such as biology, geology, chemistry, etc.

Scientific Facts.   Facts are very important in the process of scientific inquiry. Ivan Pavlov pointed this out when he said:

> Perfect as the wing of a bird may be, it will never enable the bird to fly if unsupported by the air. Facts are the air of science. Without them the men of science can never rise. Without them your theories are vain surmises.

What is a scientific fact? James B. Conant has supplied a definition of *scientific fact* that is widely accepted. It contains two essential identifying criteria:

1. A fact must be directly observable (observed).
2. A fact must be directly demonstrable (repeated).[8]

Although these criteria are severe and confining, they give a degree of objectivity to what would otherwise be subjective judgment. There are exceptions to the two criteria, but they are rare and are almost always suspect because of some subjective element included.

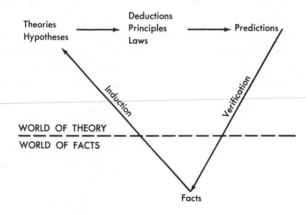

FIGURE 2. Delineation of Scientific Terms

Occasionally scientists themselves violate the definition by confusing a conclusion with a fact. An astrophysicist may say the sun contains helium, even though his information was gathered by a spectroscope and not observed directly. The *fact* would be: lines in the sun's spectrum correspond to lines in spectrum of helium—this is both criterion 1. (a fact must be *directly* observed) and criterion 2. (a fact must be repeatable). However, to say that the sun contains helium is a conclusion based on the facts. Facts are the building blocks of science *upon* which generalizations are made. Figure 2 is an attempt to show the relationships between facts, principles, theories, and laws.[9]

---

[8] James B. Conant, *Science and Common Sense* (New Haven, Conn.: Yale University Press, 1951).

[9] Louis J. Kuslan and A. Harris Stone, *Teaching Children Science: An Inquiry Approach* (Belmont, Calif.: Wadsworth Publishing Company, 1968), p. 24.

Generalization or Concept.   When a series of facts seem to fit together and show some pattern of relationship, scientists call this a *generalization or concept.* The term *concept* is somewhat more vague than generalization and is used more to describe mental processes than scientific definitions. For instance, Brandwein defines concept as "a reduction of events to a recognizable configuration."[10] The term *molecule* as used in the molecular theory is a concept. Molecule as used there describes many phenomena such as pressure, volume changes, states of matter, diffusion, etc.

Generalizations come in all different varieties. Often they are used by scientists interchangeably with facts because they are based upon so many direct observations and repeatable demonstrations. When this happens, these generalizations are called *principles* by scientists. Several scientific generalizations, or principles, are:

Heated metals expand.
Light is refracted when it passes from less dense to more dense media.
Robins migrate southward in autumn.
Coastal regions generally experience one high tide daily.

Generalizations and principles enable man to construct broader, more inclusive explanations for the phenomena he observes.

What percepts and concepts might be gained from observing plants and animals in their natural environment?

Theories: Science's Broad Explanations.   One of the major goals of science is to devise broad explanations that wed many seemingly related and/or isolated facts, generalizations, and principles into more inclusive or theoretical models or conceptual schemes. Put another way by the National Science Teachers Association: "The essence of science lies not so much in seeking out the detailed structure of nature as in trying to understand it."[11]

---

10 Paul F. Brandwein, *op. cit.* p. 111.
11 *Theory Into Action—in Science Curriculum Development*, National Science Teachers Association (Washington, D. C., 1964), p. 43.

These broad attempts at understanding are called *theories*. A theory is general in its approach rather than specific in nature like facts and principles. It is of a higher order of abstraction than a fact or principle. Theories relate, explain, and predict wide varieties of experimental and observational findings in the simplest and most efficient way. The great British physicist, J. J. Thomson, has given this definition of scientific theory:

> From the point of view of the physicist, a theory of matter is a policy rather than a creed; its object is to connect or coordinate apparently diverse phenomena and above all to suggest, stimulate, and direct experiment.[12]

Sometimes a theory may broaden as new observational and experimental data suggest more application and interrelationships with the data than originally conceived. The electron theory is an example of this. Not only does the electron theory help us explain phenomena in the area of electricity, but it has now expanded into explanations of chemical reactions such as chemical bonding, electrovalence, and co-valence, etc.

Sometimes a theory may become narrower in its scope than originally conceived. The molecular theory of matter is of this nature. Originally the theory held that all matter was made up of molecules. Recent studies using X-ray diffraction have shown that most (if not all) inorganic crystals have an ionic rather than a molecular structure.[13]

From the examples here the reader can see that a theory is not a simple, all encompassing statement. In fact, theories exist in hierarchies. In this hierarchy, a simple theory often is a component of more comprehensive theories. An example of this would be:

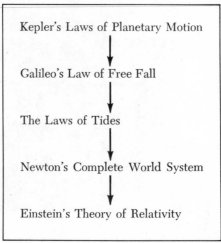

Kepler's Laws of Planetary Motion

↓

Galileo's Law of Free Fall

↓

The Laws of Tides

↓

Newton's Complete World System

↓

Einstein's Theory of Relativity

There is much division of opinion among scientists on many aspects of theory development. Although the ultimate goal is complete verification of theories, some scientists feel this is impossible, some feel a theory can never be proven, while

---

[12] J. J. Thompson in James B. Conant, *Modern Science and Modern Man* (New York: Columbia University Press, 1952), p. 91.

[13] W. L. Bragg, "British Achievements in X-Ray Crystallography," *Science*, 131 (1960), p. 1870.

many if not most accept certain theories as proven when supported by what appears to them as overwhelming indirect evidence. An example of the latter is the acceptance by many biologists today of evolution as a *fact* rather than a *theory.*

Scientific Laws.   This hierarchy of theories leads to a frequent source of controversy and confusion in many science textbooks over the definition and use of the term *law*. Often a scientific law is defined as a theory which has been exhaustively tested and found to be valid with few or no exceptional cases. This definition leads many students to believe a law is a theory that has been tested and found to be "true." Students begin to think that if a theory hangs around long enough and stands the test of time, it will become a law. Actually, a law is a description of a regularly occurring phenomenon, which makes prediction highly possible.
    Scientific laws are derived from and explained by theories. For example:

> "Boyles' Law" (relating pressure of a gas to its volume) is derived from and explained by the Kinetic-Molecular Theory (molecules in motion and forces acting upon molecules).

There are and have been many scientific "schools" which champion different theories and laws: heliocentric *vs.* geocentric schools of cosmology; stimulus-response *vs.* phenomenological schools of psychology; "Big Bang" *vs.* "Continuous Creation" schools of astronomy; quantum theory *vs.* wave-particle schools of physics; etc. These controversies are the healthy signs of science because they stimulate scientists to critically examine and compare their work constantly. Scientific progress comes from these controversies over new ways to verify or validate theories and laws which are promoted.
    Theories and laws are constantly changing as they are modified, discarded, and new ones take their place. This is the essence of science: *The only constant in science is change.*

a process of enquiry

Implications of Scientific Inquiry for Teaching Science

The basic direction for your science teaching becomes clear if you regard science not merely as a body of information to be memorized but as processes of inquiry about the world. If you look at the scientist as a perpetual learner, then you as a science teacher must also be so oriented. In the same way, you must encourage the child to be free to seek, to be continually curious, and to inquire. You must set the stage so that you *expect* and encourage persistent learning. For want of a better term we refer to this involvement of children in inquiring as the *discovery approach* to teaching science.
    Teaching science through discovery is harder, but more rewarding, than teaching by memorization. However, you must become familiar with the processes of science as they relate to teaching your class and learn techniques for helping children develop skills in learning to "discover" answers to the questions they have about their world. These science processes of science and discovery skills

may be foreign to you, but this book can help you "discover" answers to your questions, too.

Above all you will realize that the interest, enjoyment, and satisfactions gained by your children from your efforts to teach through discovery are well worth your investment.

Summary

Science is a combination of processes and products. The processes of science consist of attitudes and methods of inquiry. Scientific attitudes—including humility, skepticism, avoidance of dogmatism, willingness to consider new data, and a positive approach to failure—influence the methods used in scientific inquiry. Three kinds of questions form the basis of scientific inquiry: "What?" questions (descriptive answers), "How?" questions (process answers), and "Why?" questions (rarely final answers).

The next processes of scientific inquiry are idiosyncratic and difficult to describe, but they usually include relentless testing of data, scientific reasoning, and the use of controlled experimentation for searching for cause and effect.

The products of scientific processes are the accumulated and systematized tested body of knowledge of the fields of science. Facts, concepts, generalizations, and principles are the results of constant scientific testing of data. These then become the raw materials scientists use in their search for broad conceptual schemes for answers to questions, which they call theories and laws. These theories and laws are perennially scrutinized to see if they are valid.

Too often in science teaching, elementary school teachers have stressed the *products* rather than the *processes* of science. Teaching science through discovery in elementary schools is consistent with science as both processes and products.

SELF-EVALUATION AND FURTHER STUDY

1. Select several everyday problems in your personal life from such areas as economic, social, scholastic, or professional fields. Analyze the processes by which you arrived at some solutions to these problems.
2. Ask children in an elementary school class to write on the following topics: *What is science? Describe and/or draw a picture of a scientist.* Analyze and categorize results. Compare the findings with *your* image of a scientist.
3. Serendipity (chance happenings), the hunch, the brilliant flash of imagination, the educated guess, or intuition have all played some part in the methods of inquiry

of some research scientists. Of course, sometimes these are given undue weight. It would be profitable for you to read about these from research scientists themselves in the following enjoyable, well-written articles:

Beveridge, W. B., *The Art of Scientific Investigation.* New York: W. W. Norton & Company, Inc., 1957, Chapters 5, 6.

Conant, James B., *Science and Common Sense.* New Haven, Conn.: Yale University Press, 1951, p. 48.

Sayvetz, Aaron, *Scientists at Work: Case Studies in the Physical Sciences.* Chicago: Center for the Study of Liberal Education for Adults, 1954.

Wolf, Abraham, "Scientific Method," *Encyclopaedia Britannica*, Vol. 20 (1955), pp. 125-31.

4. Discuss whether the statement that "the earth rotates" is a fact, a generalization, or a theory.

5. A scientist discussing scientific inquiry said of cancer research, "What *does not* cure cancer is as much scientific as what *does* cure cancer." What did he mean?

6. Many well-qualified scientists and scholars have rejected the idea that there is *a* scientific method. Select from the following references and read about the ever-widening controversy over the scientific method and the question of the existence of one general method.

Ashford, Theodore Askounes, *From Atoms to Stars.* New York: Holt, Rinehart and Winston, Inc., 1960, Chapter 1.

Brandwein, Paul F., Fletcher G. Watson, and Paul E. Blackwood, *Teaching High School Science; A Book of Methods.* New York: Harcourt, Brace & World, Inc., 1958, Chapter 1.

Bright, Wilson E., Jr., *An Introduction to Scientific Research.* New York: McGraw-Hill Book Company, 1952, Chapter 3.

Conant, James B., *Science and Common Sense.* New Haven, Conn.: Yale University Press, 1951, Chapters 1-3, 11-12.

Conant, James B., ed. *Harvard Case Histories in Experimental Science.* Cambridge, Mass.: Harvard University Press, 1957, Introduction.

Kemeny, John G., *A Philosopher Looks at Science.* Princeton, N.J.: D. Van Nostrand Co., Inc., 1959, Chapters 5, 10.

7. Explain the quotation by J. Darrell Barnard on the first page of this chapter in relation to the role theory development plays in science.

8. Why should a scientist make a thorough survey of the literature on a problem before starting research on it?

9. Explain this statement: *Scientific research aimed solely at practical ends is the most impractical scientific research.*

10. Describe the advantages to teacher and learner of teaching science through a discovery or inquiry approach rather than by memorization. What similarities are there between learning or teaching science through discovery and scientific processes?

Probably no child will study science without having his ideas and attitudes on such matters as health and citizenship modified; conversely, his growing understanding of their significance to him will help to motivate his study of science and to make it more meaningful.[1]

CHAPTER 2

WHY SHOULD YOU TEACH SCIENCE IN THE ELEMENTARY SCHOOL?

Because of their inquisitive nature, children are fascinated with their environment, animals, plants, rocks, the heavens, their bodies, how they are growing, and numerous physical situations which appear as magic to them. In fact, many scientific phenomena are as mysterious and hold as much fascination for children as a magic show. It is this innate interest of children in natural phenomena that helps to make the teaching of science relatively easy.

Science Contributes to the General Objectives of the School

Because of this interest, science instruction is utilized to contribute to the general objectives of the school such as reading, writing, spelling, and such cognitive skills as observing, comparing, classifying, predicting, measuring, hypothesizing, inferring, interpreting data, and creating, plus many others.

An objective is a goal a teacher endeavors to help children attain. A primary goal of education is the development of good citizens. But what does it mean to be a good citizen? Most individuals would agree a good citizen must be a rational, critical thinking, creative human. He should have a wealth of knowledge, problem-solving skills, desirable attitudes, appreciation for the contributions of others, and broad interests.

Science Objectives Stated in Behavioral Terms ✓

Science teaching, as with all areas of instruction, contributes to these general goals; but in addition it has specific objectives which scientists, science educators, and teachers believe contribute to the development of the individual. If objectives are to influence instruction, they should be stated in a practical teaching framework. Dr. Robert F. Mager in his book *Preparing Instructional Objectives* outlines such a framework. He suggests three questions need to be answered in designing a good educational experience.

---

[1] "Science Education in American Schools," Part F, Forty-sixth Yearbook of the National Society for the Study of Education (Chicago: University of Chicago Press, 1947).

What relationships do these charts help children discover?

What is it you wish to teach?
How will you know when you have taught it?
What materials and procedures will work best to teach what you wish to teach?[2]

Mager believes a teacher really cannot answer these questions with any degree of certainty unless the objectives are phrased in *behavioral terms*. His viewpoint is accepted today by many educators. To write objectives behaviorally means they should be stated in terms of some behavior a student will be able to perform after having completed the learning period. For example: a non-behavioral objective might be as follows:

The child develops a liking for science.

The trouble with this statement is it does not suggest how it can be evaluated. The objective might be modified in behavioral terms as follows:

At the completion of the study of science, the child should demonstrate an interest in it by selecting more science books to read in his free time, outlining or carrying out additional scientific investigations, making collections, participating voluntarily in science fairs and other science activities.

The attainment of these objectives can be determined by observation. Other examples of behavioral objectives might be stated as follows:

The child should be able to:	*Behaviors Required*
1. Group leaves by size, shape, color and type, such as evergreen or deciduous.	(classifying)
2. State how a population of organisms will develop when introduced into a new environment.	(hypothesizing)

---

[2] Robert F. Mager, *Preparing Instructional Objectives* (Palo Alto, Calif.: Fearon Publishers, Inc., 1962).

3. Interpret data from a bar graph of material new to him.   (interpreting data)
4. Suggest ways to design an experiment to determine the effect of an acid soil on plants.   (designing an experiment)
5. Suggest what the control should be in an experiment.   (controlling variables)
6. Complete a bar graph when the information is given.   (communicating and translating information from verbal to graph form)
7. Interpolate and extrapolate from plotted data.   (interpreting data)

Refer to this list and study how the objectives vary. Which of them do you think requires the most intellectual sophistication? How would you use them to construct a test? How would you use them to help you improve your teaching ability?

Which of the following types of words is the key word in writing a behavioral objective: verb, noun, adjective, pronoun? It should be obvious to you from this brief analysis that the key word is a *verb*. When you ask a person to do something, you have to use an action word, a verb, in the sentence. By performing this action you can observe his behavior.

Examples of some of the verbs you might use in science are:

predict	state the problem	identify
compare	estimate	control variables
group	organize	infer
classify	extrapolate	hypothesize
interpret	integrate	evaluate
compute	analyze data	create
design an experiment		

A problem you might encounter in writing behavioral objectives is that you may use a verb which will not elicit any behavior you can observe or test. For example, the following words are often used in statements of objectives:

appreciate	understand
become aware	feel
be receptive	be sensitive

These do not give you any clue as to what behavior you would expect a child to demonstrate. How would you know, for example, whether or not a child "appreciates the contributions of science." The secret to altering this statement is to describe some behavior you accept as illustrating a child "appreciates" scientific contributions or give the conditions of performance that you would accept as indicating the attainment of the objective.

To state objectives clearly in behavioral terms is a sophisticated activity particularly if the teacher realizes there are hierarchies of objectives and levels of competency in their attainment. An instructor, however, who teaches without any clearly stated purpose of instruction is like a person stepping into the street of an unfamiliar metropolitan city without a map. He wanders—he knows not where. A teacher can also wander without knowing where.

General Objectives of Science Instruction

Although many learned individuals and groups have struggled with the problem of outlining objectives for science, their views probably can best be summarized by the following material. This information combines objectives from the Forty-

How is this boy's curiosity being encouraged? In what ways can you encourage children to discover on their own?

sixth Yearbook of the National Society for the Study of Education entitled "Science Education in American Schools," published in 1947,[3] and the more recent report of the Commission on Science Education of the American Academy for the Ad-

---

[3] "Science Education in American Schools, *loc. sit.*

vancement of Science.[4] Some liberty has been taken in modifying the original statements so that they are expressed in behavioral terms. The objectives are grouped into six main categories:

1. *Knowledge*   4. *Scientific Attitudes*
2. *Instrumental Skills*   5. *Appreciations*
3. *Problem-Solving Skills*   6. *Interests*

A pupil after having a science course should be better able to achieve these objectives:

1. *Knowledge*

   Read and state the meaning of certain scientific facts and concepts.
   Show that he can apply scientific principles. When a problem situation is stated requiring the application of some scientific principle, a child has learned that he should be able to apply the principle.

2. *Instrumental Skills*

   Manipulate basic science equipment, interpret and prepare maps, graphs, charts, and tables appropriate to problems.

3. *Problem-Solving Skills*

   Demonstrate problem-solving skills such as: observing, inferring, sensing and defining problems, making hypotheses, outlining scientific procedures to test hypotheses, carrying out an investigation, controlling and manipulating variables, formulating models, making valid conclusions, recognizing and using space and time relations, recognizing and using number and number relations, classifying, measuring, communicating, and making operational definitions.

4. *Scientific Attitudes*

   Demonstrate such scientific attitudes as open-mindedness by being willing to consider new facts in making judgments, withholding conclusions until all available facts are in, using controls, generalizing with sufficient evidence.

5. *Appreciations*

   Describe the uses, benefits, and limitations of science to society.

6. *Interests*

   Indicate interest by reading, collecting, studying, or becoming involved in some scientific activity as a leisure time pursuit.

Science Instruction Contributes to Critical Thinking

It is apparent from looking at these objectives that the problem-solving skills and scientific attitudes objectives correlate with one of the main purposes of school,

---

[4] *Commission on Science Education, Newsletter,* Vol. I, No. 1, American Association for the Advancement of Science, Washington, D.C., 1964.

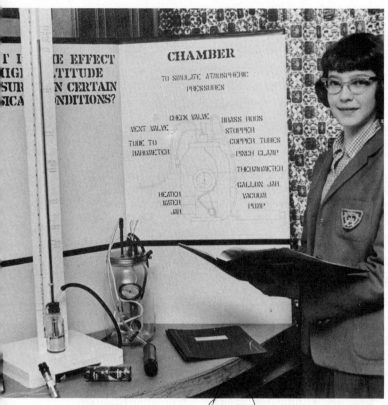

How can the selection of a problem and following it through to a conclusion help this student develop sound habits for all areas of study?

the development of critical thinking. The Educational Policies Commission of the National Education Association has stressed the importance of this function for the school in the following statement:

> The purpose which runs through and strengthens all other educational purposes—the common thread of education—is the development of the ability to think. This is the central purpose to which the school must be oriented if it is to accomplish either its traditional tasks or those newly accentuated by recent changes in the world.[5]

Science instruction of an investigative-experimental type demands sensory-motor involvement. When science is taught through discovery, lessons are structured so that the child, in addition to learning science concepts and principles, also learns how to use his mind. This is done by structuring the learning activities so the child is forced to use his mind to formulate hypotheses, control variables, design experiments, make operational definitions, formulate models, interpret data, plus many more cognitive processes. The child in performing these processes is required to make many mental operations. It is only by the performance of such operations that the mind learns to function and evolve into a mature, adult, critical thinking entity. The development of such a mind is one of the most worthy objectives of the school and discovery science teaching contributes significantly to its attainment.

---

[5] *The Central Purpose of American Education* (Washington, D.C.: National Education Association, 1961), p. 12.

Elementary Science Teaching May Contribute to the Development of Creative Ability

Science instruction can also be structured to give the child opportunities to manifest his creative potential. This can be done by allowing him to outline and carry out scientific investigations on his level of maturity.

A major manpower problem today concerns the development of highly creative individuals. American industry is built on competition which is not unique to the continental United States. American products must compete with foreign merchandise on world markets, but because of our standard of living, we cannot compete on a labor basis. Then, on what basis are we competing? We are selling our creative genius. We must always be on the frontier with newly developed industrial products. This requires creative minds, minds that see and produce scientific and technical products not yet realized by foreign market. Maintenance of our standard of living depends upon nurturing creative individuals of tomorrow's generation.

Learning Science Helps to Prepare Children for the Future

One aspect of any school instruction is to prepare children for the world in which they are going to live. A child enters formal education and starts on a long

How will this child be able to more readily understand the medical advances taking place daily as a result of his science study?

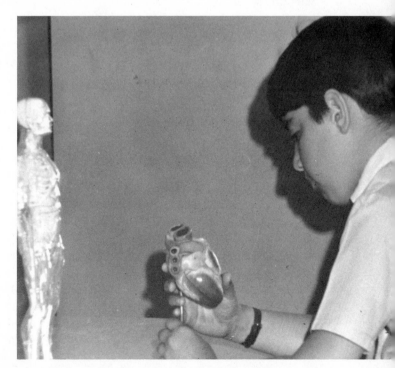

process of unique experiences contributing to the development of his tastes, mind, and body. The school, therefore, is faced with the problem of preparing today an individual who is going to live in a world far into the future.

The American society is an industrial society. An industrial complex grows and develops with technology, and technology is based upon discoveries made in the sciences. Over the last decades there has been an explosion of scientific and technical knowledge, the affect of which has permeated the entire society.

Think for a moment of the many things you use that were not around twenty years ago: miracle drugs, plastics, synthetic fibers, commercial jet flights. By such reflection you soon get some idea of the rapidity of change in our industrial complex. The atomic age, the space age, are titles given to this period of history, and our society continues to become even more scientifically and technologically oriented. The computer, for example, is likely to modify our ways of living in manners we can little dream of. George B. Leonard says of the future:

> Education in a new sense will be the main purpose of life. Learning is what human life is. Humanity has traveled a long way to arrive at that essential truth. Man in the past may have been a hunting animal, a fighting animal or a working animal. Future man will be a learning animal, not just during what we now think of as the school years, but during all of life. To go on learning, to go on communicating that learning to others will be considered a purpose worthy of man's enormous and ever-expanding capacity.[6]

Because the world described by Leonard will be characterized even more by science and technology, his learner will of necessity require an excellent background in the sciences in order to take advantage of all educational pursuits.

Scientific Literacy

No citizen today is truly educated unless he is scientifically literate. The layman is surrounded by scientific words: radio, electronics, floridation, penicillin, polio vaccine, virus, missile, radiation, isotope. He must make intelligent decisions based on his understanding of these words and concepts. An example of this decision making on scientific matters can be seen in state and national life. Most senators and representatives are trained as lawyers with only a bare minimum of scientific training or background. Yet, these politicians must sit in judgment of the value of expenditures for space research, public health, atomic energy, the National Science Foundation, and military preparedness programs. The wisdom of their decisions is dependent upon their understanding of science. Because of a continually accelerated growth of scientific knowledge and its influence on society, education for science literacy must start in the elementary grades.

To be scientifically literate an individual must know and understand basic sciences concepts and principles. These are the *Specific Subject Matter Objectives* of science which are a part of any science teaching unit. These concepts and principles are really included under category 1. *Knowledge* of the general objectives previously stated. Children, after completing the study of science, will be better able to explain the meaning of such concepts as cells, friction, gravity, in-

---

clined plane, momentum, heat, germination, reproduction, temperature, etc. They would also be better able to apply science principles, the generalizations of science, such as: Metals when heated expand; Life only comes from life; Disease can be caused by microorganisms; Traits may be inherited, etc.

Science Instruction Can Lead to Better Use of Leisure Time

In spite of the demands of population growth, leisure time will undoubtedly increase. Today a considerably shortened work week in many fields already indicates this trend. One can but wonder what workers will do with all their free time. Leisure to the Greeks meant time when citizens fulfilled their civic responsibilities and family duties, improved their minds, and refreshed their souls. It was not a time only for play or licentiousness. The Greek concept of leisure is useful and culturally desirable. Citizens of the future should look upon leisure as a wonderful opportunity, a time to contribute to the cultural enrichment of the community and family. Leisure should be a blessing and not a curse to be wasted in raucousness or simple diversions in hopes that "it too shall pass away."

What effect do interested parents have upon children's curiosity?

Science because of its investigative quality offers a wealth of leisure time activities. What boy or girl has not been fascinated with exploring a river, slough, or beach. What a thrill and what fun it is to discover some creature scurrying about its natural environment. Children are fascinated with crayfish, tadpoles, young frogs, mosquito larvae, cocoons, spiders, and burrowing animals. This is substantiated by the popularity of animated creatures in cartoons. Children's love for adventure is bountiful. They enjoy collecting rocks, leaves, and flowers.

Picture a fourth grade class visiting a pond to study the life there. Jo Ann runs to the teacher, Mrs. Johnson, and shows her three leaves she collected from different plants near the water. Mark has captured a small insect that can walk on the surface of the water. He asks, "How can it walk on the water when I can't?" What fun it will be finding the answer to this question. Jerry has found some mosquito larvae and runs to the teacher and asks, "Why do they wiggle? Are they going to die?"

Mrs. Johnson is building a lasting foundation in kindling a thrill for inquiry. Her pupils will one day leave, but she has left an imprint, a love for exploring the world. If these experiences are nurtured and reinforced in other grades and by parents, the children as adults will have the ability to use their leisure time wisely. They will be rock hounds, photographers, hikers, natural history addicts, readers, and collectors. For many children this will become a way of life. The leisure aspects of science are endless. Elementary teachers can open a world of excitement and adventure in leisure pursuits for their pupils and themselves.

Scientific and Technical Professions Present Great Opportunities

What will be the vocational world of the future? In what jobs will your pupils be employed? The scientific and engineering demands are among the fastest growing areas of manpower supply. In 1960 there were 1.4 million scientists and engineers. By 1970 this figure swelled to over 2.5 million. Needs in sciences and engineering increase on an average of six per cent per year of the manpower in the fields, and the demands for individuals with graduate training accelerates at a

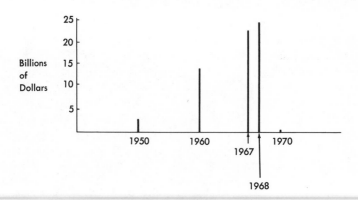

FIGURE 3. Increase of Expenditures in Scientific Research and Development in the United States, 1950-1968.

more rapid rate. Until recently the population of the United States roughly doubled about ever fifty years while the demands for technical manpower doubled about every ten years. Expenditures in scientific research and development in the United States increased as follows: 3.5 billion dollars in 1950, 14 billion dollars in 1960, 23.8 billion dollars in 1967, and 25 billion dollars in 1968 (*see* Figure 3).

Who carries out this research and development? Obviously it requires highly trained technical and scientific manpower. Figure 4 points out this trend. Even today one has only to look at the want-ad section of a large metropolitan newspaper to realize how great the demand is for technicians. It is reasonable to think almost every citizen in the labor force in the next decade will work in some position involving technical tasks. The best employment opportunities in the future will be in the scientific and technical fields. The schools can prepare the individual to take advantage of these opportunities.

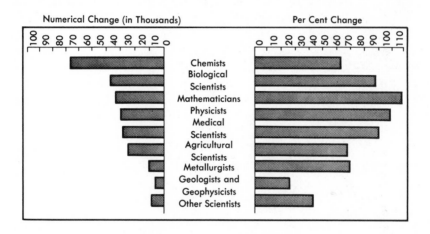

FIGURE 4. Projected Growth in Requirements for Scientists,
by Occupation, 1960-70

Source: National Science Foundation, *Scientists, Engineers, and Technicians in the 1960's, Requirements and Supply* (NSF 63-34).

The elementary school has a significant role to play in preparing for future vocations. Dr. Robert M. Gagné suggests if children in the primary grades are not involved in learning certain competencies in science, such as hypothesizing, predicting, and measuring, their vocational decisions later in life may be detrimentally affected. He says of the college student: "If he has missed some of the important competencies at the earliest level (elementary school), the chances are very good that he has some time previously decided to major in some field other than science.[7]

The implication of Dr. Gagné's statement is that the lack of the development of scientific competencies in the early elementary grades contributes to the individual's feelings of inadequacy to such an extent that he does not think he could

---

[7] Robert M. Gagné, "The Learning Requirements for Enquiry," *Journal of Research in Science Teaching,* Vol. I, Issue 2, 1963.

succeed in a scientific profession. The individual's lack of early training in the sciences, in other words, restricts his freedom of vocational choice.

Women: A Resource of Scientific Manpower.   A country is as rich as its resources. It once was thought that land was the ultimate basis of wealth. However, modern economic theory denies this tenet and states that manpower is at least equally important. Consider the small country of Switzerland. Even though it has little land area, the country maintains a high standard of living. This is possible because the educational background of its populace has enabled the Swiss to utilize science and technology to produce an industrialized economy.

How is this classroom display making science more real and interesting for these girls?

The Swiss demonstrate the importance of manpower in a developing nation. Any nation which does not utilize its manpower reservoir to its maximum potential suffers. American society has been wantonly wasteful in not using effectively one of its greatest resources—women. National concern has recently been generated in the United States by the realization that Russia employs a far greater proportion of its women in science and engineering than does our country. In 1961, for example, 37 per cent of the Russian engineering students were women. This compares to less than seven per cent in the United States. Similar comparisons are true in other areas of the scientific manpower pool.

One reason for this disparity between the United States and Russia is that many Americans consider some professions masculine and others feminine. Anne Roe has suggested that an effort should be made to change this viewpoint.[8] Our culture generally starts early to mold the child's attitudes toward professions.

---

[8] Anne Roe, "The Psychology of the Scientist," *Science*, 134 (Aug. 18, 1961), pp. 56-59.

Witness parents' attitudes toward children's toys. A father will buy a baseball bat for a baby boy who can barely hold a spoon. Mechanical toys and science kits are thought to be mainly for boys, and girls are not supposed to be interested in these. What an absurd idea! Elementary teachers can help to change this pattern enabling girls with ability to manifest their intellectual potential so valuable to our country's survival.

Teachers should plan to discuss the various types of technical occupations emphasizing the roles women play in them. By so doing the teacher begins to build in the minds of girls the idea that they can be doctors, chemists, biologists, or technicians.

Dr. Dorothy Crowfoot Kodgkin, Nobel Prize Laureate in Science, and Dr. Marie Goeppert Mayer, Professor of Physics, University of California, San Diego, prominent women of science.

Teachers should further point out the many advantages of these fields for women. Through her professional training she makes many desirable contacts and is prepared for a rewarding career. When marriage precludes full-time employment, part-time opportunities in the sciences are manifold if desired. After raising a family, when she might feel a lack of purpose in her life, her profession and the compensation it offers is there to keep her a dynamic and zestful person. Madame Curie certainly presented a desirable model of such a woman—a wife, mother, and scientist who richly savored the fruits of living.

Opportunities for Minority Groups in Science. The United States presently is involved in a racial, ethnic, and religious revolution. Minority groups long silent and reticent about obtaining opportunities within our society have exerted power and pressure for change. These groups seek opportunities to enhance their economic and social status. Because the scientific enterprise does not tolerate bias within its own framework and respects truth regardless of its source, its workers—scientists—are undoubtedly one of the least biased professional groups. The judgment of the value of a man in science is truly democratic since it is based solely on his contribution to scientific knowledge. For this reason, religious, ethnic, and racial minorities are more likely to obtain the goals they seek in scientific fields. Because of greater national efforts to develop the potentials of minority groups, the opportunities of these groups in the technical vocations daily become brighter. It may well be members of minority groups who will solve such problems as the cure for cancer, the cold, tissue transplantation, or air pollution as they have done in such areas as polio vaccine, hybredization of plants, and a theory of relativity. When these problems are solved, all Americans will reap the rewards regardless of the origin of the scientist. Elementary teachers should make an effort

What are these children learning about living things that they cannot learn from reading or filmed aids?

to help children become aware of the opportunities in the scientific and technical fields regardless of their backgrounds.

Children Love to Investigate

Although there are many practical reasons for including science instruction in the school, the most important one is that children love to investigate nature. If you watch a young child confronted with a new phenomenon in his environment you will see him investigate it. He will not be inclined to sit silently for a long period and not inquire.

Discovery oriented science instruction better fits the natural inclination of the investigative nature of children. They love science taught through discovery, and in the process of such involvement they learn to reason, create, read, write, and perform mathematical skills.

Summary

A main reason why science should be taught in the elementary school is that children are interested in it, and this interest can be utilized to contribute to the attainment of the general objectives of the school. When children are involved in scientific investigation, they are learning to read, write, spell, and develop such cognitive abilities as observing, comparing, classifying, hypothesizing, inferring, collecting data, and creating.

In addition to contributing to the general objectives of the school, science instruction also has specific objectives. These include the understanding of basic scientific facts, concepts, principles; the ability to use instrumental and problem-solving skills; the development of scientific attitudes such as open-mindedness; the ability to describe the benefits and limitations of science; and the development of an interest in science. Educators are of the opinion that these objectives should be stated in behavioral terms so that their attainment can be assessed in determining the effectiveness of the instruction.

The teaching of science may involve children in creative activities, suggest leisure time pursuits, and make *all* children more aware of the opportunities for employment in the scientific and technical fields.

SELF-EVALUATION AND FURTHER STUDY

1. If you were going to appeal to the board members of a new school for modern science instruction in the curriculum starting at the kindergarten level, what arguments would you use?
2. What are the specific objectives of science?
3. Which objective do you consider the most important to try to teach and why?
4. Why should the objectives of science be stated in behavioral terms?
5. What relevance do objectives have to preparing tests for science?
6. Write five behavioral objectives for science.
7. Describe in a classroom situation how science instruction could contribute to the development of critical thinking behaviors of children.
8. Describe some problem-solving skills in behavioral terms.
9. How would you teach science to contribute to the development of children's creative ability?
10. How does science learning prepare the individual for the future?
11. What is meant by the term *scientific literacy* and how would you go about testing to see whether you were increasing the literacy of your children?
12. Why are the opportunities in the scientific and technical professions likely to broaden in the future?
13. Why should a greater effort be made to interest those women with potential in the scientific and professional fields?
14. Why do we have fewer women in the scientific and technical fields than Russia?
15. What advantages are there for a person from a minority group in the scientific and technical fields?

Children should be led to make their own investigations and draw their own inferences. They should be told as little as possible and induced to discover as much as possible.[1]

CHAPTER 3

THE NATURE OF DISCOVERY IN SCIENCE TEACHING-LEARNING

As you make the professional decisions of selecting, planning, and conducting science experiences with your children, you want to know if these experiences are consistent with how children learn and if they achieve the goals of teaching science processes and products effectively and efficiently.

Science teachers and prospective science teachers have been exposed to the fundamentals of educational psychology. The following sections of this chapter will review the highlights of the latest information on how children learn within a framework of how this data influences science teaching. As you read, try to view the material presented in terms of your own current or prospective teaching assignment and the curriculum decisions you make in connection with it, your students, and how the materials can enhance your teaching. The ideas are valuable to you if they have some impact upon your teaching.

How Do Children Learn?

What is known about how learning takes place? Very little, if anything, if we think in terms of "scientific truths" beyond the possibilities of revision. However, evidence is mounting and gaining acceptance in psychological circles for the following ideas which are built on data rather than the shifting sands of opinion or sentiment.

It is axiomatic to say that learning is idiosyncratic. However, more of us pay lip service to the fact that everyone learns differently than actually practice it. As teachers we become acutely sensitive to this as we try to teach a whole class of children, all of whom are unique in some ways. Psychologists have determined that although children learn in different patterns and rates, a generalized process of learning can be charted. This process can be diagrammed as in Figure 5 to show the interrelationships and direction of the different aspects of learning.

---

1 Herbert Spencer, *Education: Intellectual, Moral, and Physical* (London: Hurst and Co., 1860).

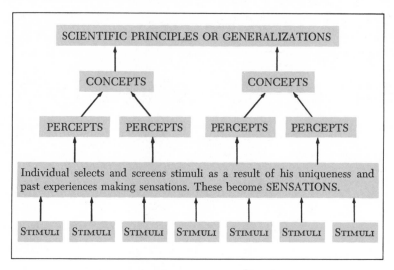

FIGURE 5. Learning Ladder[2]

From Figure 5 we see that:

1. The learner selects and screens stimuli making sensations.
2. Sensations help produce percepts.
3. Percepts form concepts.
4. Many concepts shape principles or generalizations.

Diagramatically it can be read:

STIMULI → SENSATIONS → PERCEPTS → CONCEPTS → PRINCIPLES

Importance of Percepts

Percepts develop from impressions or awareness of sensations caused by environmental stimuli. They require little interpretation by the learner. For example, the infant reacts to the sight of his nursing bottle (stimulus) with sensations of pleasure, of warmth, and of good taste (percepts). The next time the nursing bottle is brought near, previous experience will influence how the infant "sees" (perceives) the bottle. "Bottle" begins to mean warmth and good taste (concepts). From many percepts and concepts the child generalizes that some objects are warm and some are cold (principle).

Children learn about their environment through their perceptions. Their readiness for new learning experiences depends to a great degree upon the type and accuracy of their perceptions. Research has shown that our perceptions are influenced by many factors:

1. We tend to perceive what we have learned or were taught to perceive. Put another way by John M. Culkins, we can see the influence of culture on perceptions:

---

[2] Chart modified from Charlotte Crabtree and Fannie Shaftel, "Fostering Thinking," *Curriculum for Today's Boys and Girls*, Robert S. Fleming, ed. (Columbus, Ohio: Charles E. Merrill Publishing Company, 1963), p. 259.

Each culture develops its own balance of the senses in response to the demands of its environment. The most generalized formulation of the theory would maintain that the individual's modes of cognition and perception are influenced by the culture he is in, the language he speaks, and the media to which he is exposed. Each culture, as it were, provides its constituents with a custom-made set of goggles. The differences in perception are a question of degree. Some cultures are close enough to each other in perceptual patterns so that the differences pass unnoticed. Other cultural groups, such as the Eskimo and the American teen-ager, are far enough away from us to provide esthetic distance.[3]

2. We tend to perceive what we want to perceive. (Picture the children you know who "tune out" things that don't interest them.)
3. We tend to perceive accurately when our observations fit into a pattern that has meaning to us.
4. We tend to perceive what others around us perceive.
5. We can reduce, but not entirely prevent, errors in our perceptions.[4]

The evidence from the research here shows that daily sensory experiences must be provided early in a child's life so that he develops proper percepts and concepts for further learning. Project Head Start, a program for children mainly from poverty areas, bases its program on this sensory approach. These early sensory experiences are vital for learning. Evidence shows that high school students who are bright in physics and mathematics more likely have engaged in such sensory experiences as tinkering with toys, manipulating things, and inquiring through their senses as young children.[5] This also is true for college freshmen whose differences in ability to learn science and mathematics have been partially traced to variances in the amount of their earlier direct sensory experiences.[6]

Jean Piaget and his associates have studied extensively the relationship of direct sensory experiences to learning. They state that children's ability to deal with the broad concepts of space, time, matter, and causality depends upon a type of learning that slowly develops from the direct sensory experiences of children.[7]

Each direct sensory experience then gives more fibers to the child for him to weave the fabric of perception. The child responds to many sensory experiences in combination. Simple percepts are usually part of a pattern of percepts influenced by all these sensory experiences. An example of such a pattern of intersensory percepts may involve a rabbit: *feeling* the soft, warm, furry body; *smelling* its odors; *seeing* the whiteness, darting eyes, twitching nose; *hearing* the crunching, nibbling of the food.

---

[3] John M. Culkins, "A Schoolman's Guide to Marshall McLuhan," *Saturday Review*, March 18, 1967, p. 53.

[4] Harry W. Sartain, "Percepts and Concepts," Paper of the 17th Annual Conference on Reading at the University of Pittsburgh, ed. Donald L. Leland (Pittsburgh: University of Pittsburgh Press, 1961).

[5] Celia B. Stendler, "Cognitive Development of Children and Readiness for High School Physics," *American Journal of Physics*, 12 (December, 1961), pp. 832-835.

[6] *Ibid.*

[7] Jean Piaget, "Development and Learning," *Journal of Research in Science Teaching*, Vol. 2, Issue 3 (1964), pp. 176-185.

How does raising chicks from eggs provide opportunities for developing observational skills through sensory experience?

Another excellent example to illustrate the value of many senses concerns the development of the concept of "water" by the blind, deaf, and mute child, Helen Keller, with the assistance of her remarkable teacher, Anne Sullivan. Although the accounts vary, the story reportedly follows these general lines:

Miss Sullivan took one of Helen's hands, put it in a bowl, and poured cold water over it while holding Helen's other hand to her own mouth repeating "water, water, water, water," over and over. After countless, painfully frustrating repetitions, Miss Keller finally uttered, "water." Miss Keller relates that her concept of water at that moment was "cold" because the water was cold. The alert teacher sensed the partial concept formation and repeated the procedure substituting warm water for the cold. For a long time after that, Miss Keller had the feeling that water was anything liquid. In an attempt to broaden Helen's concept of water, Anne Sullivan began introducing other liquids to Helen such as oils and kerosene for comparison. Eventually using the multi-sensory technique and utilizing the senses available to them (unfortunately only smell, taste, and touch), Miss Keller and Anne Sullivan developed what to us is a simple concept—*water.*

Percepts Shape Concepts

Paul Brandwein considers a concept as the simplest pattern which helps us to order the events around us.[8] Percepts in the form of images and stored sensory experiences or memories help develop this pattern or ordering of events. The concept is organized as a result of many related sensations, percepts, and images with verbal symbols added. David Butts goes even further:

[8] Paul F. Brandwein, *Elements in a Strategy for Teaching Science in the Elementary School* (Cambridge, Mass.: Harvard University Press, 1962), p. 6.

A concept is more than a merging of percepts; it is a dynamic part of the cognitive structure that helps direct the attention of a student in a new situation: it helps organize the new perceptions into new meaningful configurations or new concepts.[9]

TIME ⟶	EARLY	PRE-SCHOOL	LOWER ELEMEN-TARY	SECOND-ARY SCHOOL
EXPERIENCE	Bottle always full of milk (large volume).	Sand on the beach ("infinite" quantity).	Water in lakes and oceans ("infinite" volume).	Matter in universe ("infinite" volume).
	Crib is big; room is very big.	House is big; doll house is small.	Cities are large; states are larger.	Some stars are much larger than the sun.
	Walk to chair (long distance).	School is close; grandma lives far away.	New York is "closer" than London.	The nearest star is 8 light years away.
	Many beads on the string.	There are "many" children in the school.	There are many shrubs and trees in a forest.	The number of protons and electrons in the universe is "infinite."
			INCREASED CONCEPTUALIZATION	

FIGURE 6. Formation of Concept of Magnitude or Relative Size[10]

When a child can identify dogs from other furry animals—whether large or small, collie or beagle, black or brown—he has applied the verbal symbol "dog" to a pattern of percepts and has developed a concept—*dog*. In the same way, the

---

[9] David P. Butts, "The Degree to Which Children Conceptualize from Science Experiences," *Journal of Research in Science Teaching*, Vol. 1, Issue 2 (1963), p. 135.

[10] Chart modified from Joseph D. Novak, "Concepts in Science Are Broad Generalizations Regarding Some Aspect of the Physical or Biological World. They Are a Composite of Problem Solving Experiences, Emotional Experiences, and Individual Facts and Observations." An abstract of a paper presented at the thirty-fifth annual meeting of the National Association for Research in Science Teaching, Washington, D.C., Feb. 21-24, 1968.

older child can develop the concept of *vertebrate* for a robin, a toad, and a hamster. However, the child by building this order of animals will expect the robin to have feathers (not the toad and hamster), as well as to have a warm body, and to lay hard-shelled eggs. The latter characteristics—feathers, warm body, and hard-shelled eggs—will help him formulate still another concept—*bird*. As individuals mature they constantly reconstruct previous concepts on greater levels of abstraction. This constant reconstruction can be seen by referring to Figure 6. The chart shows the formation of one of our most important concepts—relative size or magnitude. Think in terms of your own experiences with the four examples presented and you will be able to understand the long range of time and experiences required for this concept to develop.

Formation of Scientific Principles

The term *concept* has been applied to patterns of organizing new perceptions into new, meaningful configurations. What then are scientific principles and what relationship is there between concepts and principles? Laurence Frank insists that we derive our generalizations inductively from analysis and synthesis of data.[11]

To which scientific principles are these children being exposed?

In effect, then, generalizations or principles are concepts; however, they differ from simple concepts in that they state some kind of relationship between two or more concepts, abstractions, objects, or events. Newton's Third Law, "For every action there is an equal and opposite reaction," is an example of a scientific principle. The relationships between the concepts "action," "equal," and "opposite" are involved in this principle. Often in textbooks the words *concepts* and *principles* are used interchangeably; they should not be, due to their own unique aspects. Refer again to Figure 3 to see the graphic representation and relationship between STIMULI → SENSATIONS → PERCEPTS → CONCEPTS → PRINCIPLES. Although this is the general direction for development of scientific principles in children, there are many *levels* of learning in each of these.

---

[11] Laurence K. Frank, *The School as Agent for Cultural Renewal* (Cambridge, Mass.: Harvard University Press, 1960).

Learning Levels. There is a growing body of knowledge that says children develop intellectually in stages from pre-school to post-adolescence. Each stage of learning is vital for the development of the succeeding stages. You can't jump over one stage, as each stage integrates the one before, and paves the way for the next one. One of the foremost and widely heralded exponents of this approach to understanding children's learning is the Swiss psychologist Jean Piaget. Some psychologists are convinced that his work will become as influential as Freud's. His impact on science education programs has been great, as indicated in this chapter. Basically, Piaget sees the four stages of growth and learning as the:[12]

1. *Sensory-Motor Stage* (Birth to 2 years)

    a. Child learns through his muscles and senses and he develops certain habits for dealing with external objects and events.
    b. Language begins to form.
    c. Child begins to understand that things exist even when beyond his sight or touch.
    d. Child begins to represent things by word or gesture.
    e. Child mainly directed by outside stimuli.
    f. Child can't imagine an act or think an act before carrying it out.
    g. No time other than the present.
    h. No space other than immediate and what he sees.
    i. By the end of this period he distinguishes animals, activities, and things.

2. *Preoperational or Representational Stage* (2 to 6 years)

    a. Period of greatest language growth; he operates in a plane of representation.
    b. Through the use of these newly acquired words and symbols (concepts), child can represent outside world and his own inner world of feeling.
    c. Child finds many magical explanations make sense to him ("God pushes the sun around"; "Stars go to bed when He does").
    d. Child begins to gain a sense of symmetry.
    e. Child depends upon trial and error.
    f. Child has difficulty seeing that an object can have more than one property.
    g. Child uses intuitive approach; he makes judgments in terms of how a thing *looks* to him.
    h. Child centers on one variable only—the one that stands out *visually*.
    i. Time is limited to days, hours, seasons.
    j. Space is limited to a map of the neighborhood.
    k. Can't form genuine concepts of chance or probability.
    l. Child uses animistic and artificial explanations for phenomena.
    m. Child has problems with: time, causality, measurement, number, quantity, velocity.

3. *Concrete Operations* (7 to 11 years)

    a. Child can move things around and make them fit properly.
    b. Child acquires fine motor skills.

---

[12] Abstracted from: Jean Piaget, *Psychology of Intelligence* (Paterson, N.J.: Littlefield, Adams & Co.), 1963.

     c. Child can organize his thinking into system with inner rules.
     d. Child has mental activity oriented toward concrete objects and events.
     e. As a result of d. above, child knows how to solve physical problems.
     f. Child can classify and order.
     g. Child can place objects in a series (for example, small to large).
     h. Child begins to grasp geographical space.
     i. Child begins to grasp historical time.

  4. *Formal Operations* (12 to 14 years)

     a. Child does more of his thinking in abstract terms.
     b. Child can state propositions and he can perform operations upon these propositions either by combining them or transforming them.
     c. Child can arrive at principles underlying actual situations as a result of increased abstract thinking.[13]
     d. This is often called the *reflective thinking* stage because the child for the first time can think back over his thinking processes after having completed a problem.

What implications are there for teaching science from this knowledge of PERCEPTS → CONCEPTS → PRINCIPLES development and Piaget's stages of cognitive learning? They certainly effect *what* we teach as well as *how* we teach it!

Implications of How Children Learn for Teaching Science Content

What to Teach?

Science Curriculum. One of the curriculum approaches which attempts to prescribe science teaching consistent with the nature and structure of the disciplines of science, as well as with how children learn, is the *conceptual schemes* approach. Conceptual schemes are major principles or "big ideas" which summarize particular achievements in the sciences, around which a curriculum is structured. These advantages are given by advocates of the conceptual scheme curriculum:

  1. A "structure of science" is given to concepts. This structure helps children develop the stages of learning suggested by Piaget, for as Jerome S. Bruner has said, "To learn structure, in short, is to learn how things are related."[14]
  2. A relationship between concepts can be shown to children in a conceptual scheme curriculum. One concept reinforces the other.

---

[13] Frank G. Jennings, "Jean Piaget: Notes on Learning," *Saturday Review*, May 20, 1967, p. 82 *and* Celia B. Stendler, "The Development and Improvement of Logical Thinking in Children," *Intermediate Education: Changing Dimensions* (Washington, D.C.: Association for Childhood Educational International, 1965), pp. 27-38.

[14] Jerome S. Bruner, *The Process of Education* (Cambridge: Harvard University Press, 1960), p. 7.

What scientific and mathematical concepts might children develop from this activity?

3. Patterns in nature more readily are learned, which help children structure new concepts.
4. Concept development is furthered by the cumulative process over the years of different concept levels. Concepts are broadened each year as deeper and more complex relationships are perceived by the learner. (*See* Figure 7 for the increasing complexities of a conceptual scheme from Level I to Level VI.)
5. To aid teachers in meeting individual learning differences, no age or grade level need be assigned to conceptual scheme levels. Children in the same class could be investigating different rungs of a conceptual ladder at any given time.
6. Stability can be given to a science curriculum due to conceptual schemes that remain recognizable for many years selected by scientists. The learners are presented with the scientific past as a prologue for present and future explorations.
7. The *processes* of science are inherently a part of conceptual schemes, for the interaction in making new concepts from existing ones is constantly going on and modifying the present conceptual schemes. This gives a dynamic aspect to the conceptual schemes, so that children do not see them as static "truths."

There are many ways of stating conceptual schemes; however, these guiding principles—written jointly by a group of scientists, science teachers, and curriculum workers for the National Science Teachers Association—are valid criteria:

1. The "big ideas," or schemes, represent ideas in science that have been firmly established in the scientific community and are basic to the progress of research;

2. Each scheme represents a system of facts, principles, and concepts which hopefully can be organized into a sound learning sequence from simple (capable of being taught to very young children) to complex (the level at which "current problems" are researched).[15]

The National Science Teachers Association further suggests the following conceptual schemes as possible bases around which a curriculum could be organized. They are not intended to be irrefutable, dogmatic, authoritarian statements. They do, however, reflect the most commonly accepted and basic ideas of contemporary scientists.

CONCEPTUAL SCHEMES

I. All matter is composed of units called fundamental particles; under certain conditions these particles can be transformed into energy and vice versa.

II. Matter exists in the form of units which can be classified into hierarchies of organizational levels.

III. The behavior of matter in the universe can be described on a statistical basis.

IV. Units of matter interact. The bases of all ordinary interactions are electromagnetic, gravitational, and nuclear forces.

V. All interacting units of matter tend toward equilibrium states in which the energy content (enthalpy) is a minimum and the energy distribution (entropy) is most random. In the process of attaining equilibrium, energy transformations or matter transformations or matter-energy transformations occur. Nevertheless, the sum of energy and matter in the universe remains constant.

VI. One of the forms of energy is the motion of units of matter. Such motion is responsible for heat and temperature and for the states of matter: solid, liquid and gaseous.

VII. All matter exists in time and space and, since interactions occur among its units, matter is subject in some degree to changes with time. Such changes may occur at various rates and in various patterns.[16]

A more elaborate conceptual scheme plan is presented by Paul Brandwein in Figure 7, *A Structure for the Elementary School Science Curriculum*, to be found on pages 48-49.

From such conceptual schemes as found in the Brandwein chart, elementary school personnel are restructuring their science curriculums on a new foundation. Expansion of the implications of this for specific ideas in the planning and conducting of science experiences is presented in Chapter 6.

---

[15] *Theory Into Action . . . In Science Curriculum Development* (Washington, D.C.: National Science Teachers Association, 1964), p. 17.

[16] *Ibid.*, p. 20.

How Effective Are Conceptual Schemes Curriculums?   It is much too early to make any definitive evaluation of the conceptual schemes curriculums due to the newness of the programs and their limited exposure in schools. Research has been going on to investigate whether children learn science concepts and processes better through conceptual schemes curriculums, more conventional ways, or by a process-centered approach. The American Association for the Advancement of Science (AAAS), Commission on Science Education, has based a science program on the process-centered approach. This project is discussed in depth in Chapter 4.

J. Richard Suchman bases his Studies in Inquiry Training at the University of Illinois upon conceptual schemes. Suchman's results so far have been positive. Dr. Suchman found that the sixth graders in his inquiry groups (those constructing concepts around conceptual schemes) achieved physical concepts as well as, or better than conventionally taught groups in spite of the greater emphasis on conventional content.[17] Norval Scott, Jr. found in research parallel to Suchman's that among inquiry groups doing inductive reasoning in grade 5 as well as styles of categorization in grade 6, the results were related to science concept achievement.[18] It appears from these two studies, therefore, that not only do children learn science concepts better through conceptual schemes but they also learn skills in reasoning and categorization that aid in structuring their later concepts. This latter point is also related to *process* in methodology of teaching and will be explored later in this chapter.

Criticism of Conceptual Schemes.   David Ausubel has synthesized and brought together a summary of criticisms of the conceptual schemes approach to science curriculum for elementary schools. These criticisms break down into three areas:

I. On *philosophical* grounds, no set of conceptual schemes or principles of scientific method are applicable to *all* science. Each science has its own idiosyncratic undergirding themes and methods of inquiry. An all-encompassing set of conceptual themes is likely to be characterized (1) by a level of generality that is reminiscent of the philosophy of science, and hence beyond the cognitive maturity and scientific sophistication of elementary and high school students; and (2) by only farfetched relevance and applicability to many scientific disciplines. The seven Conceptual Schemes prepared by the NSTA Curriculum Committee are characterized by both of these features. They are both stated at a level of generality that has little applicability to the phenomenological and conceptual levels at which science is actually conducted and taught, and are applicable at this philosophical level to the physical science but not to the biological, behavioral, and social sciences.

II. *Psychologically*, little transfer, either in the understanding of scientific propositions or in problem solving, is possible across interdisciplinary fields. Hence, a science curriculum at the elementary-school level that stresses the "heuristics of discovery," and ignores substantive content as an end in itself, is psychologically and pedagogically unsound.

---

[17] J. Richard Suchman, "The Child and the Inquiry Process," *Intellectual Development: Another Look.* Papers and Reports from the ASCD Eighth Curriculum Research Institute (Washington, D.C.: Association for Supervision and Curriculum Development, 1964), p. 59-77.

[18] Norval C. Scott, Jr., "The Strategy of Inquiry and Styles of Categorization," *Journal of Research in Science Teaching*, Vol. 4, Issue 3 (1966), pp. 143-153.

	CONCEPTUAL SCHEME A	CONCEPTUAL SCHEME B	CONCEPTUAL SCHEME C
	Energy may be transformed; it is neither created nor destroyed. (Total sum of matter and energy is conserved: see *Conceptual Scheme B, Concept Level VI.*)	Matter may be transformed; in chemical change matter is neither created nor destroyed.	Living things interchange matter and energy with the environment (and with other living things).
CONCEPT LEVEL VI	Energy gotten out of a machine does not exceed the energy put into it.	In nuclear reactions, matter may be destroyed to release energy. (The total sum of matter and energy is conserved: see *Conceptual Scheme A, Concept Level VI.*)	Living things are adapted by structure and function to the environment.
CONCEPT LEVEL V	Once an object is in motion, it tends to remain in motion, unless energy is applied to produce an unbalanced force.	In a reaction, the totality of matter remains constant.	The capture of radiant energy by living things is basic to the maintenance and growth of all living things.
CONCEPT LEVEL IV	Molecular motion can be altered by the absorption or release of energy.	Matter consists of elements and compounds.	Living things capture matter from the environment and return it to the environment.
CONCEPT LEVEL III	Energy can be changed from one form to another.	Matter exists in small particles.	There are characteristic environments each with their characteristic life.
CONCEPT LEVEL II	There are different forms of energy.	Matter can change its state.	All living things depend on the environment for the conditions of life.
CONCEPT LEVEL I	Energy must be used to set an object in motion (i.e., when work is done).	Matter exists in various states.	All living things are affected by their environment.
	CONCEPTUAL SCHEME A	CONCEPTUAL SCHEME B	CONCEPTUAL SCHEME C
	Energy may be transformed; it is neither created nor destroyed. (Total sum of matter and energy; see *Conceptual Scheme B, Concept Level VI.*)	Matter may be transformed; in chemical change matter is neither created nor destroyed.	Living things interchange matter and energy with the environment (and with other living things).

FIGURE 7.   A Structure for the Elementary School Science Curriculum

III. From a *developmental standpoint* the seven Conceptual Schemes are not equally suitable for all age levels; some subject-matter principles cannot be transmitted to young children no matter how they are presented. Routine reliance on concrete empirical experience is unnecessary both for problem-solving purposes and for transmitting scientific subject-matter content to adolescent pupils. At the elementary-school level, on the other hand, the child's dependence on concrete-empirical experience makes unfeasible such suggestions as teaching him "first principles," basic abstract laws, or methodological canons of science either at the level of generality contemplated in this position paper or divorced from his everyday experience. Similarly unfeasible psycho-

CONCEPTUAL SCHEME D	CONCEPTUAL SCHEME E	CONCEPTUAL SCHEME F	
A living thing is the product of its heredity and environment.	Living things are in constant change.	The universe is in constant change.	
The characteristics of a living thing develops down in a genetic code.	Changes in the genetic code produce changes in living things.	Nuclear reactions produce the radiant energy of stars.	CONCEPT LEVEL VI
The cell is the unit of structure and function; a living thing develops from a single cell.	Living things have changed over the ages.	Universal gravitation and inertial motion govern the relations of celestial bodies.	CONCEPT LEVEL V
A living thing reproduces itself and develops in a given environment.	The earth is in constant change.	The motion and path of celestial bodies is predictable.	CONCEPT LEVEL IV
Plants and animals reproduce their own kind.	Organisms are related through structure.	There are seasonal and annual changes within the solar system.	CONCEPT LEVEL III
Related living things reproduce in similar ways.	Forms of living things have become extinct.	There are regular movements of the earth and moon.	CONCEPT LEVEL II
Living things reproduce.	There are different forms of living things.	There are daily changes on earth.	CONCEPT LEVEL I

CONCEPTUAL SCHEME D	CONCEPTUAL SCHEME E	CONCEPTUAL SCHEME F
A living thing is the product of its heredity and environment.	Living things are in constant change.	The universe is in constant change.

Source: Reprinted from *Substance, Structure, and Style in the Teaching of Science* by Paul F. Brandwein. © copyright, 1965, by Paul F. Brandwein. Reprinted by permission of Harcourt, Brace & World, Inc.

logically is the proposal to teach sciences in the "order of their phenomenological complexity."[19]

In spite of the controversy, there is one area of agreement for both advocates and critics of conceptual schemes. Both stress the need in science teaching not only for the transmission of structured bodies of knowledge but also for the development of *processes* of scientific inquiry.

[19] David P. Ausubel, "An Evaluation of the Conceptual Schemes Approach to Science Curriculum Development," *Journal of Research in Science Teaching*, Vol. 3, Issue 4 (1965), pp. 263-264.

Implications of How Children Learn for Teaching Science Processes

How to Teach?

To picture graphically the three dimensions of curriculum planning—intellectual *products* of science (major concepts), *processes* of science (methods of science), and *time*—observe Figure 8. Product and process are interrelated and each block represents a conceptual scheme with a base on both sides of the time axis. The total of the blocks would represent the "science" to which the learner would be exposed and hopefully perceive the science structure. Because the *process* is so directly influential upon the products, science teaching methods must utilize the best data available on both scientific processes and how children learn. This is accomplished by the *discovery approach* to science teaching-learning because it matches children's innate characteristics and maintains the integrity of the structure of science.

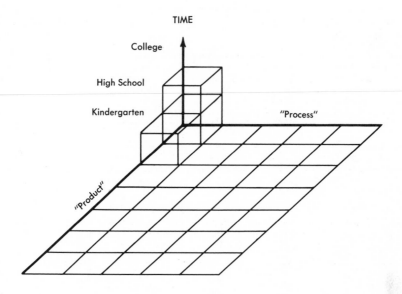

FIGURE 8. Three-dimensional Conceptual Schemes Curriculum[20]

What Is the Discovery Approach to Science Teaching?

Learning by discovery strives to teach the learner how to learn. It helps him acquire knowledge which is uniquely his own because he discovered it for him-

[20] Chart modified from "Theory Into Action . . . In Science Curriculum" (Washington, D.C.: National Science Teachers Association, 1964), p. 18.

What can a teacher do to make learning as exciting as the girl seems to find it?

self. Discovery is *not* restricted to finding something entirely new to the world, but encompasses all kinds of knowledge obtained by the use of one's own mind. Discovery is a matter of rearranging data internally so you can go beyond the data to form new concepts. It involves finding the meanings, the organization, the structure of the ideas.

The system of learning to learn is called *heuristics;* it has its roots in ancient Greece and it is said to have derived from Archimedis' cry of "*Eureka*" (meaning "I have found it!") when he discovered the percentage of gold in Heiro's crown. Discovery learning, or heuristics, is based upon Socratic method of asking questions to lead the learner to new "discoveries," and has been used by educators for a very long time.

Socrates (470-399 B.C.) distrusted the lecture method saying that the lecturer put ready-made ideas into the minds of the student. He believed that the student possessed the true ideas in his mind. The trick was to lead the pupil to discover his own wisdom. To Socrates, the *question* was a means of inducing thinking and not only a means of testing factual information. The Socratic method has two movements.

1. Ironic or destructive stage brings the student from "unconscious ignorance" to "conscious ignorance" by proper questions.

2. Constructive stage leads the student from "conscious ignorance" to "truth" by further questioning.

Learning by discovery is experiencing a sharply increased interest as a result of the research on learning spearheaded by Jean Piaget in Geneva, Switzerland, and Jerome Bruner in Cambridge, Massachusetts. Many educators have sought to define discovery learning. However, it is difficult if not impossible to precisely define discovery in learning. Robert B. Davis points this out and gives these examples of the essence of discovery as seen by a variety of educators:

> For some people, it lies in allowing the child freedom to explore. For others, it lies in *not* verbalizing the "patterns" that the child observes. For some, this verbalization is acceptable (or even desirable) provided it does not take place immediately. The child should be allowed to apprehend the newly perceived pattern for itself alone, unencumbered by descriptive words, for at least a few days, hours, or weeks. After that it is all right to talk about it.
> Other observers say it is all right for children to verbalize the pattern provided the *teacher* does not.
> Other observers reverse this: they say it is all right for the *teacher* to verbalize patterns, provided the *children* do not.
> Still other observers argue that the inexact language of the child has meaning for the child. It belongs to his world. By contrast, the "sophisticated" language of the adult is meaningless, and leads the child into rote repetition of what he hears.
> Others argue that *all* learning is necessarily "learning by discovery"—no matter whether the *experience* comes first, or the verbal discussion does, no real learning has occurred until the two are correctly paired together.[21]

Robert Karplus and Herbert D. Thier, co-directors of the Science Curriculum Improvement Study, have described a discovery as the *"recognition of a relationship between an idea and an observation, or between two ideas, or between two observations."*[22]

We ascribe to this definition of discovery in this book and present now some of the advantages of and necessary conditions for learning by discovery.

Advantages of Learning by Discovery.   Jerome Bruner compactly synthesized the advantages of learning by discovery under these four headings:

1. The Increase in Intellectual Potency.
2. The Shift from Extrinsic to Intrinsic Rewards.
3. Learning the Heuristics of Discovery.
4. The Aid to Memory Processing.

---

[21] Robert B. Davis, *The Changing Curriculum: Mathematics* (Washington, D.C.: Association for Supervision and Curriculum Development, NEA, 1967), pp. 54-55.

[22] Robert Karplus and Herbert D. Thier, *A New Look at Elementary School Science* (Chicago, Ill.: Rand McNally & Co., 1967), p. 40.

The following is a summary of Jerome Bruner's discussion of the four advantages of learning by discovery.

DISCOVERY
IS
LEARNING
TO
LEARN

1. *The Increase in Intellectual Potency.*
    Discovery in learning has precisely the effect upon the learner of leading him to be a constructionist, to organize what he is encountering in a manner not only designed to discover regularity and relatedness but also to avoid the kind of information drift that fails to keep account of the uses to which information might have to be put. It is a necessary condition for learning the variety of techniques of problem solving, of transforming information for better use, indeed for learning how to go about the very task of learning. Practice in discovering for oneself teaches one to acquire information in a way that makes information more readily viable in problem solving.

DISCOVERY
IS
SELF
REWARDING

2. *The Shift from Intrinsic to Extrinsic Motives.*
    Learning that starts in response to the rewards of parental or teacher approval or the avoidance of failure can too readily develop a pattern in which the child is seeking cues as to how to conform to what is expected of him. The child becomes self-motivated when he approaches learning by discovering something, rather than "learning about" it. Such a learner has the tendency to carry out his activities with the autonomy of self-reward, or more properly by reward that is discovery itself. The child comes to manipulate his environment more actively and achieves his gratification from coping with problems. To use the metaphor that David Reisman developed in a quite different context, mental life moves from a state of outer-directedness in which the fortuity of stimuli and reinforcement are crucial to a state of inner-directedness in which the growth and maintenance of mastery become central and dominant.

DISCOVERY
MEANS
ACTIVE
INVOLVEMENT
OF
LEARNER

3. *Learning the Heuristics of Discovery.*
    It is only through the exercise of problem solving and the effort of discovery that one learns the working heuristics of discovery, and the more one has practice the more likely one is to generalize what one has learned into a style of problem solving or inquiry that serves for any kind of task one encounters—or almost any kind of task.

DISCOVERY
LEARNING
IS MORE
USABLE
AND LONG
LASTING

4. *The Aid to Memory Processing.*
    The principal problem of human memory is not storage but retrieval. The key to retrieval is organization—or in simpler terms, knowing where to find information and how to get there. One can cite a myriad of findings to indicate that any organization of information that reduces the aggregate complexity of material by imbedding it into a cognitive structure a person has constructed will make that material more accessible for retrieval. Material that is organized in terms of a person's own interests and cognitive structures is material that has the best chance of being accessible in memory. In sum, the very attitudes and activities that character-

ize "figuring out" or "discovering" things for oneself also seem to have this effect of making material more readily accessible in memory.[23]

Discoveries may happen in two ways—a serendipity (an unexpected or indirect finding) or a direct finding as a result of a deliberate search for an answer to a well-defined problem. As teachers, we cannot afford the luxury of waiting only for serendipities. We must look for learning conditions that will also foster direct discoveries.

Conditions That Stimulate Discovery Teaching-Learning

Discrepant Event

In order for children to be guided toward making discoveries in science, they must have focus. There must be a stimulus that energizes the discovery processes, thus a problem or curiosity is needed. An excellent motivator is an observation of a phenomenon or event that is seen by children as a discrepancy with their conceptual framework or at variance with their expectancy. For instance, if children blow out trick birthday candles and the candles immediately relight without additional heat being added, they will want to know why. Their conceptual framework, built by numerous experiences with candles and heat, has led them to expect that the candles will remain extinguished until additional heat is added. The question "Why did the candles relight?" is triggered by the discrepant event. (*Note:* the candles relight because they have a very low kindling temperature and, although the flame is blown out, there is still sufficient heat to relight them.) As children investigate the conditions of the discrepant event, they will be encouraged to suggest theories and make inferences and hypotheses that may explain what happened. Their teacher will encourage testing of these theories and hypotheses, resulting perhaps in the abandoning, modifying, or strengthening of some as a result of the data collected.

Freedom to Discover

Another condition necessary for the discovery approach to teaching science is external and internal freedom. By external freedom is meant the freedom for the child to set forth his ideas without fear of being ridiculed or punished. It is a freedom to give wild possibilities, be wrong, or even at odds with what appears to be "right."

Internal freedom is somewhat affected by external freedom because it is the freedom a child feels inside to explore. As a result, he will develop autonomy and

---

[23] Jerome S. Bruner, "The Act of Discovery," *Harvard Educational Review*, Vol. 31, Issue 1 (1961), pp. 21-32.

may even question the teacher or other authority. At first a child is inhibited in the discovery approach because he generally is conditioned to follow the teacher's lead.

The teacher's attitudes toward authority and searching for scientific ways of solving problems may often be in conflict. An example of this can be seen in this episode from a second grade class:

> Danny, a precocious boy whose parents encouraged critical thinking and searching for information, visited the Hayden Planetarium in New York City. He had also read a great deal about planets and was one of the second grade "experts" on them. Danny discovered that the planet Uranus was pronounced *yoo' run us* at both the Hayden Planetarium and in his reference books, so he pronounced it that way in a discussion at school. His teacher immediately corrected him and said it was pronounced *u ra' nus*. After a brief argument, in which the child politely stated his sources for the pronunciation, the teacher said, "After all, Danny—I should know. I'm much older than you."

Need for Broad Knowledge

Helping a child in learning to discover solutions to problems is very dependent upon the knowledge that the child previously has acquired. This dependency of previous knowledge for discovery learning follows the pattern of learning: PER- CEPTS → CONCEPTS → PRINCIPLES. The child must call upon previous percepts, concepts, and principles to form new percepts, concepts, and principles. Robert Gagné makes these observations about the need for broad, generalized knowledge that are relevant to the discovery approach to science teaching:

What is the teacher's role in this individual learning situation?

1. Discovery learning can be undertaken only after the individual has acquired a store of broad and critical knowledge, and this in turn can be acquired only when he has learned some prerequisite but very fundamental capabilities.
2. At earliest levels of instruction, the individual needs to learn these prerequisites: how to observe, how to figure, how to measure, how to orient things in space, how to describe, how to classify objects and events, how to infer, and how to make conceptual models.
3. These prerequisites make possible the acquiring of broad knowledge of principles, the incisive knowledge which makes possible the self-criticism of new ideas.[24]

Practice in Discovery

A final condition vital for discovery learning is the provision by the teacher for children to *actively* engage in discovery approach activities. You don't learn to ski by reading a book about skiing. You have to get out on the slopes and try with skis on. Likewise you must engage in discovery approach activities in order to become a discoverer. This Chinese proverb crystallizes the need to actively engage children in such experiences:

> I hear, and I forget;
> I see, and I remember;
> I do, and I understand.

In summary, conditions that stimulate discovery learning are: exposure to discrepant events, freedom to postulate theories and hypotheses, need for broad knowledge and prerequisites, and much practice with the discovery approach.

The Teacher's Role in Discovery Learning

Discovery learning must be centered around a series of problem-solving situations *actively* involving children. This does not mean that the teacher says, "O.K. children—*discover*. I'll be in the teachers' room having coffee." The teacher must take a definite role in guiding the entire process. Listed here are some things the teacher must do if he is to help children "discover science":

1. The teacher must *allow* children to discover for themselves solutions for the problems in their work. At all times, he must resist *telling* where there is a chance for children to structure the learning in their own internalized way.
2. The teacher should select studies from the conceptual schemes suggested by scientists and science educators. These studies should be obtainable for his students.

---

[24] Robert M. Gagné, "The Learning Requirements for Enquiry," *Journal of Research in Science Teaching*, Vol. 1, Issue 2 (1963), pp. 144-153.

3. The teacher should be dedicated to the fact that learning by discovery takes a great deal of time but is vital for children to learn how to learn.
4. A general pattern for discovery learning should be class discussion (for topic identification), observations or experimentation, discussions and interpretation of data from observations and experiments, identification of new problems from interpretation, and new investigation starts again, etc.
5. The teacher should supply clues when students are bogged down in discovery learning to keep the process moving. This can best be done by supplying clues and cues when children are "stuck."
6. The teacher should have an overall plan to guide students in their studies.
7. Asking thought provoking questions is one of the best ways of stimulating discovery learning and keeping it moving along. Questions can provide clues and motivation if they are used in a manner which leads the learner to feel that he has a definite contribution to make to the investigation.
8. The teacher in discovery learning must have access to necessary supplies for his investigations with children.[25]

There is mounting evidence that children learn better through the discovery approach to teaching science. Robert Soar in *The American Biology Teacher* put it this way:

> . . . the more indirect the teaching (that is, the greater proportion of the teacher behaviors of asking questions, accepting, clarifying and using pupil ideas, praising and encouraging, and recognizing and accepting feelings), the greater the amount of subject matter achievement that takes place in the classroom, and the more favorable the attitudes of the student toward school and toward the teacher.[26]

Summary

The traditional method of teaching science relies upon memorization of "facts." Modern science teaching bases its methods on the processes of sciences and how children learn.

Children learn best by developing PERCEPTS → CONCEPTS → PRINCIPLES. Their learning has general patterns but is idiosyncratic for any individual. Jean Piaget identifies distinct stages of development, among which are sensory-motor, pre-operational or representations, concrete operations and formal operations.

---

[25] Many of the above points are raised in: John W. Renner, "A Case for Inquiry," *Science and Children* (March, 1967), pp. 30-33.

[26] Robert S. Soar, "New Developments in Effective Teaching," *The American Biology Teacher* (January, 1968), p. 44. Professor Soar cites the research in teacher behavior of the following to document his point: Amidon and Flanders (1961), Flanders (1965), Soar (1966), LaShier (1966), Furst (1967).

What role is this teacher playing in helping children discover concepts of sun and earth relationships?

One of the implications of the data on learning is to structure the content and methods of elementary science programs around the conceptual schemes or "big ideas" from science disciplines. Another implication is to actively engage children in processes similar to the way scientists work. This approach is teaching science through discovery. The conditions conducive to discovery learning as well as the teacher's role in this approach have been discussed.

SELF-EVALUATION AND FURTHER STUDY

1. Refer to Figure 3. Select several examples of stimuli, sensations, percepts, and concepts that could act upon individuals to produce two scientific generalizations or principles.
2. Explain this statement made by John M. Culkins in his discussion on effects of culture on perception: "Each culture as it were, provides its constituents with a custom-made set of goggles." Use examples from your own perception development and culture.
3. What are percepts, concepts, principles? Give examples of each and show their relationship.
4. Observe a child over a period of time during which you present some science activities or games new to him. How does he conform with some of the characteristics ascribed by Piaget to his developmental stage? Refer to the following for specific information:

    Bearley, Molly and Elizabeth Hitchfield, *A Guide to Reading Piaget*. New York: Shocken Books, Inc., 1967.
    Buell, Robert R., "Piagetian Theory Into Inquiry Action," *Science Education*, Vol. 51 (February, 1967), pp. 21-24.
    Piaget, Jean, *Psychology of Intelligence*. Totowa, N.J.: Littlefield, Adams & Company, 1963.

5. What do you see as advantages and disadvantages of the conceptual schemes structure for elementary school science?

6. Select a conceptual scheme from Figure 5, a Structure for Elementary School Science Curriculum, on a concept level appropriate for the children you are teaching. What percepts and concepts must your children have *before* they can develop the concepts on the level you chose? What activities might help them develop the needed percepts and concepts?

7. Do you agree or disagree with David Ausubel's criticism of the conceptual schemes approach to structuring elementary school science? Give reasons for your choice.

8. What is teaching science through discovery? Give some of the advantages and disadvantages. Refer to these:

> Butts, David P. and Howard L. Jones, "Inquiry Training and Problem Solving in Elementary School Children," *Journal of Research in Science Teaching*, Vol. 4, Issue 1 (1966), pp. 21-27.
>
> Crabtree, Charlotte A., "Inquiry Approaches: How New and How Valuable?" *Social Education*, Vol. 30 (November, 1966), pp. 523-525.
>
> Fish, Alphoretta S. and T. Frank Saunders, "Inquiry in the Elementary School Science Curriculum," *School Science and Mathematics*, Volume LXVI, No. 1, (January, 1966), pp. 13-22.
>
> Friedlander, Bernard Z., "A Psychologist's Second Thoughts on Concepts, Curiosity, and Discovery in Teaching and Learning," *Harvard Educational Review*, Vol. 35, No. 1 (Winter, 1965).

9. Describe the conditions necessary for stimulating and guiding children in the discovery approach to science teaching-learning.

10. How does the teacher's role differ from the traditional to the discovery approach in teaching science?

The key to the success of the lab program, of course, lies with the nation's teachers—in their openness and willingness to respond to innovations advanced by the institutions—and most importantly, in their willingness to take an active part in the venture, to offer their criticisms, and to make suggestions based on concrete experience.[1]

CHAPTER 4

INNOVATION, EXPERIMENTATION, AND REFORM IN ELEMENTARY SCHOOL SCIENCE

There have been many changes over the years in science education, especially since October 4, 1957, when the Russian Sputnik was launched. However, that date merely explosively focused our attention upon a need for improvement of science education that had quietly been going on for more than one hundred years. Education in general, not just science education, has reflected the unprecedented social, economic, scientific, and technological changes which have occurred over the past century. Elementary schools have always been most sensitive to these changes and have reflected the greatest educational changes of all the levels of education. It would be valuable to see how science in the elementary school has evolved over the past century as a perspective to viewing where it is now and where it may go in the future. The following summary gives some highlights of a century of progress in science education.[2]

Historical Perspective of Science in the Elementary School

BEFORE 1850	Children recited and memorized factual knowledge.
	Purpose: Support for theology.
THEOLOGY	*Criticism:* Dull, boring memorization and theological base.

1850's	Two distinct influences on American Science Education:
	1.) *British*—Instructional literature for private tutors or parents.
OBJECT	*Purpose:* Children's observations and study of nature.
TEACHING	*Criticism:* Obtainable only for upper economic classes.
	2.) *German*—Pestalozzian "object teaching." In America—the Oswego, N.Y., "Method."

[1] R. Louis Bright, Associate Commissioner, Bureau of Research, U. S. Office of Education.

[2] For a fuller account of the place and importance of the events summarized here, the reader is encouraged to see: Herbert A. Smith, "Historical Background of Elementary Science," *Journal of Research in Science Teaching*, Vol. 1, Issue 3 (1963), pp. 200-205.

Purpose: Observation, description, and memorization of animate and inanimate objects for preparation for studying science in upper grades.
Criticism:
a.) Emphasis upon description; interpretation and understanding of events and phenomena neglected.
b.) Extremely fragmented—lacked order.
c.) Capricious due to chance selection of "objects."

1870's FIRST ORGANIZED SCIENCE PROGRAM IN ELEMENTARY SCHOOL	Great influence of Herbert Spencer and rise of popular interest in science and technology in America; science pushed as a field of study in elementary schools. *Purpose:* Introduction of formalized science curriculum, William T. Harris, St. Louis, Mo., Public Schools—first organized curriculum in elementary school, based upon mastering scientific classification and terminology. *Criticism:* Old patterns of teaching-learning not suited to changing times and data beginning to appear on how children learn.
1890's NATURE STUDY MOVEMENT	Influenced by National Education Association, William F. Harris, G. Stanley Hall, Colonel Francis W. Parker, Henry H. Strait, Wilbur S. Jackman, Liberty Hyde Bailey. *Purpose:* a.) Emphasis upon laboratory and other direct experiences. b.) Need for special training for science teachers. c.) Nature study movement—helping children learn about and appreciate their environment. *Criticisms:* a.) Emphasis almost exclusively on biological sciences. b.) Fragmented—overemphasis upon identification and isolated bits of data. c.) Overemphasis on sentimental, emotional, and esthetic explanations. d.) Did not challenge thinking of younger children.
1920's METHODOLOGY AND UTILITARIAN ASPECT OF SCIENCE	Influence of Charles Saunders Peirce, William James, John Dewey, Gerald S. Craig. *Purpose:* a.) Emphasis upon pragmatism—meaning of concepts to be found in the working out process of experience. b.) Methods of science equal to, or greater than, actual information gathered. c.) Cognitive aspects also stressed attitudes, appreciations, interests. d.) Utilitarian aspect of science education as related to health, safety, economy, etc. *Criticism:* a.) Tendency to overemphasize attitudes, appreciations, interests. b.) Overemphasis upon methodology of science detracted from science content. c.) Overemphasis upon utilitarian view of science and technology.

1930's & 1940's	Influence of National Society for the Study of Education (31st Yearbook in 1932 and 46th Yearbook in 1947)
CURRICULUMS BASED ON SEQUENTIAL MAJOR SCIENCE PRINCIPLES AND THEIR APPLICATIONS	*Purpose:* a.) Sequence and articulation of science programs K-12. b.) Emphasis upon major generalizations or principles of science. c.) Selection of science content based upon personal and social criteria. d.) Emphasis upon understandings and applications of science. *Criticisms:* a.) Overemphasis upon practical application of principles. b.) Overemphasis upon personal and social aspects.

1950's-60's National Science Reformation Movements

Even before Sputnik, professional scientists were concerned with the type of science being taught in secondary schools. The scientists were concerned with the out-of-date material in science curriculums and texts as well as the inadequate view given of modern scientific methods and philosophies. Secondary school science was the first area for new course development because this is the place where individual science disciplines such as biology, physics, and chemistry first appear in the curriculum.

Physicists from the Boston area were the first to explore ways of organizing for the improvement of science teaching. Conferences were held with other scientists, learning specialists, and science teachers leading to the formation in 1956 of the Physical Sciences Study Committee (PSSC). With the financial support of governmental agencies and private foundations, the PSSC devised a new physics test, laboratory manuals, films and supplemental reading materials. The committee also published reports describing its purposes and progress.

What values do we find in this science specialist working with elementary materials?

The PSSC triggered what has been called a revolution in science curriculum modification for American education. It was revolutionary because:

1. It was the first time a large group of people (professional scientists) *outside* the public schools worked with classroom teachers to improve science teaching.

2. It was the first time science materials were produced by committees that underwent the following rigorous procedures, which became the pattern for succeeding science curriculum studies:

   A. Scientists, learning specialists, classroom teachers and professors were gathered to work during the summer to produce science curriculums, texts, inexpensive apparatus for the course, teaching manuals, etc.

How are these teachers improving themselves and how are they learning more about science?

   B. The materials produced were tested in selected schools throughout the country during the school year.

   C. Data from the test schools were sent to the project's headquarters for analysis.

   D. Materials were revised as an outgrowth of the data obtained.

   E. The revised materials were then tested on a larger sample of students the following school year.

   F. The data obtained from the second testing were followed by another revision and testing.

   G. The third revision was released to commercial publishers on a competitive bid for use by any school district.

3. PSSC set a precedent by being the first group in American history to receive huge financial grants from the federal government for curriculum revision. No group before PSSC ever received as much money for producing school materials.

Other groups followed PSSC to improve biology and chemistry teaching in secondary schools as well as science teaching generally in the elementary schools.

The die was cast by the PSSC, and curriculum studies that followed emulated the pattern set for operating, producing, and testing materials, and obtaining financial support.

These are the highlights of the 1950's-60's in science education:

1950's-1960's TEACHING SCIENCE AS PROCESS AND PRODUCTS— DISCOVERY APPROACH AND CONCEPTUAL SCHEMES CURRICULUMS	Influence of National Society for the Study of Education (59th Year-book in 1960), National Science Teachers Association, and many individual curriculum experiments, such as PSSC, wholely or partially supported by the American Association for the Advancement of Science, the National Science Foundation, and other public and private sources. *Purpose:* a.) Stress helping children learn science information, skills, attitudes to function as intelligent world citizens. b.) Stress characteristics of science process and products. c.) Use structure and content of scientific disciplines for shaping curriculum. d.) Greater use of data on how children learn for selection of activities for teaching science. e.) Stress teaching science through discovery approach. f.) Scientists, learning specialists, and classroom teachers must work together on preparation of science curriculums and instructional materials. *Criticisms:* a.) Process may be overemphasized to the exclusion of science content. b.) Structure of conceptual schemes may be too inflexible and rigid. c.) Work aimed at average and above-average students, not slow learner and "ghetto" children. d.) Teachers need in-service work to improve skills.

A summary of major science movements shows the direction science education has taken from 1850's to 1960's:

1850's	MEMORIZATION OF FACTS FOR THEOLOGICAL EXPLANATIONS
	DESCRIPTIONS AND MEMORIZATIONS IN OBJECT TEACHING
	STRUCTURED CURRICULUM BASED ON FORMAL SCIENTIFIC CLASSIFICATION AND TERMINOLOGY
	NATURE STUDY MOVEMENT
	METHODOLOGY AND UTILITARIANISM OF SCIENCE
	CURRICULUMS BASED UPON SEQUENCE OF MAJOR SCIENCE PRINCIPLES AND THEIR APPLICATIONS
	TEACHING SCIENCE AS PROCESS AND PRODUCTS—DISCOVERY APPROACH AND CONCEPTUAL SCHEMES
1960's	CURRICULUMS INFLUENCED BY FUNDED NATIONAL SCIENCE PROJECTS

This is the legacy we inherit in elementary school science. In what ways are our current elementary science programs influenced by and utilizing this legacy?

What is the current status of science in the elementary schools? What experimentation and innovation is there in elementary school science that influences the trends in this field?

Experimentation, Innovation, and Reform Projects in Elementary School Science

We are in an era marked by the financial support of science experimentation, innovation, and reform projects by governmental and private agencies. The outlay of money at first seems huge, such as the 1968 Congressional budget for the Elementary and Secondary Education Act (ESEA), Title III (Innovation), which was $208 million; however, when you compare it with the outlay of money expended in America for alcoholic beverages, cosmetics, and drugs for the same year, it is pitifully small. In addition to federal, state, and local governmental funding agencies, there are such private sources of funds as the Ford Foundation and others.

Presently there are over 125 funded projects designed to update elementary school science teaching and content. The reader is urged to secure the following publication if he is interested in detailed information on curriculum projects in science and mathematics:

> Lockard, J. David, ed., *Report of the International Clearinghouse on Science and Mathematics Curricular Developments.* College Park, Md.: University of Maryland, 1968.

Presented in Appendix A on page 590 is a Comparative Chart of Elementary Science Curriculum Projects developed by J. David Lockard.[3] The chart presents summary descriptions of fifteen elementary projects from Lockard's *Report of the International Clearinghouse on Science.* Appendix A contains this information about each project: address and telephone number, financial support, purpose of project, materials already produced, and present and/or future activities. This information can be augmented by writing to each project or by reference to Lockard's compilation mentioned here.

Samples of Innovative Science Programs

Although the purposes, procedures, and materials tend to overlap in different science projects, each has its unique approach to its content and structure. It is unfair and unproductive to compare one project with another. Each is based upon different theories of learning and areas of science investigation as well as the selection of activities for children to pursue their investigations. To visualize the

---

[3] Printed from *The Instructor* (January, 1968), pp. 52-53. Copyright © 1968, F. A. Owen Publishing Company. Reprinted by permission.

different approaches, we present briefly some of the characteristics of the following major science curriculum projects and a sample lesson from each:

1. Science—A Process Approach of the American Association for the Advancement of Science (AAAS)
2. Conceptually Oriented Program in Elementary Science (COPES)
3. Elementary Science Study (ESS)
4. Science Curriculum Improvement Study (SCIS)

These studies were selected because they represent the range of science projects in operation today.

In addition, although not technically science curriculum projects, the following will be discussed because of their potential impact upon innovation and change in science education:

5. State and Local Science Curriculums
6. Science Textbooks Revisions

AAAS process skills
behavior - stated

Science—A Process Approach (AAAS). By the very title of this project, the reader can see that the American Association for the Advancement of Science Commission on Science Education places its emphasis upon the basic *process* skills to further learning in science. The Commission chose these eight categories of processes used in science for their lessons for grades K-3:

Observing	Communicating
Classifying	Measuring
Using Space/Time Relations	Predicting
Using Numbers	Inferring

In grades 4-6, these categories of processes are introduced:

Formulating Hypotheses	Defining Operationally
Controlling Variables	Formulating Models
Experimenting	Interpreting Data

The materials and methods of this study have undergone the procedures of testing and revision mentioned previously.

Science content is not omitted, but it is introduced in each lesson for each grade while the child participates in the preceding processes. The content is not systematically related to particular scientific disciplines, but it is derived from familiar objects and phenomena in the child's world. The science lessons are arranged in an orderly, sequential progression. The objectives to be completed at the conclusion of each exercise are described very specifically in terms of expected student behaviors. To determine if these behavioral objectives have been attained, appraisal exercises are provided for each lesson. These will be discussed in Chapter 13 on Evaluation. The format followed in each AAAS exercise is:

1. *Statement of Objectives* (in behavioral skills expected by completion of exercise).
2. *Rationale* (for teacher's information of why the exercise is included plus other helpful background data).

3. *Vocabulary* (words not used in previous exercises).
4. *Materials* (may be obtained locally or from AAAS).
5. *Originating Problem* (for arousing student interest in topic to be discussed).
6. *Instructional Procedure* (to be done in sequence since each builds on skills developed in preceding ones).
7. *Appraisal* (to determine whether objectives have been attained).

Below is part of a sample exercise from Part Four of AAAS materials used in the third grade:[4]

PREDICTION 3

CASE OF THE SUFFOCATING CANDLE

Objectives: At the end of the exercise the child should be able to:
1. State predictions given a series of observations which contain a pattern of event repetition.
2. Recognize that prediction is not based upon a single observation (or careless observations) and demonstrate this recognition by an unwillingness to state any prediction.

Rationale: The present exercise will illustrate the use of the term prediction in the context of a simple experiment. After sufficient data have been collected in an experiment, it is frequently reasonable to predict what the results of a future trial will be. In making such a prediction, we are reasoning from our past or present experience. We are saying that if the conditions of the experiment are the same when we try it again, then the results will be the same as they were in the past. The outcome of the event about which we are making a prediction will itself either confirm or deny that prediction. In the activities of this exercise the class will first observe a series of demonstrations of the burning time of a candle covered by jars of several sizes. In the initial demonstrations they will observe that a candle will burn longer under a quart jar than under a half-pint jar. Prediction can occur when they are asked how long a candle will burn under a pint jar, a two-quart jar, or a gallon jar.

The idea of experimental error is introduced to the children in this exercise.

Vocabulary: No new vocabulary.

Materials:

Several small candles; food warmer type is preferred.

Wooden safety matches.

Five glass jars such as are commonly used in home canning, one each of the half-pint, pint, quart, two-quart and gallon sizes.

Measuring cup.

One tall narrow pickle jar—about one pint.

Clock with a second hand.

Originating the Problem: This lesson may begin with a discussion of fire and burning. Ask: What do you need to keep a fire going? (Wood, paper, or some other fuel will probably be suggested.) Do you need only fuel to get a fire started or to keep it burn-

---

[4] Arthur H. Livermore, "The Process Approach of the AAAS Commission on Science Education," *Journal of Research in Science Teaching*, Vol. 2, Issue 4 (1964), pp. 279-282.

ing? (Some class member may have experience that suggests the need for an adequate draft.) Do some fires burn faster than others? What makes a fire burn faster? Get the class to recognize that the rate of burning is in common experience related to wind or ventilation. Continue by asking how fires are put out. Remind them of their experience with jack-o-lanterns. The candle in a jack-o-lantern will often burn more or less brightly depending on the wind and the size of the holes.

Instructional Procedure: The operations of this exercise may be done by the teacher as demonstrations. Place the four glass jars and the candle on a table in the front of the room. Be sure that no flammable material is nearby. Take this opportunity to caution children in the use of fire. Discuss how to light a match safely and how to use a match to light a candle. This exercise may, if necessary, be done as a demonstration, but it would be preferable to have it done by groups of four or five children.

Activity 1

Fasten the candle to the desk with wax. Light the candle. Tell the class you are going to put a pint jar over the burning candle. Ask: What do you expect to happen? Someone will probably suggest that the candle will go out. Ask him why he expects this. Has he seen the experiment before? Or, has he reasoned from his experience with fire in other situations? Point out that this statement of expectation is a prediction. It is a statement based on observations that he has made or has heard about in the past.

Invert the quart jar over the candle and demonstrate the extinction of the flame to the class. Draw the attention of the class to the burning time by asking them to estimate how long the flame lasted under the jar. Get them to express this time estimate in seconds. Suggest that they measure the burning time with a clock.

Thoroughly ventilate the jar by stuffing a rag into it several times. Unless the air in the jars is renewed between repetitions of a demonstration, the burning time measurements will show too much variation. Ask the class to measure the burning time by watching the wall clock as you repeat the demonstration. Record the time on the chalkboard alongside the jar volume. Ask the class what they would expect the burning time to be if the experiment were repeated. Repeat the experiment. The burning time will probably be three or four seconds different from the first value. Record this. Repeat again and ask the class to determine the mean burning time for the candle under the quart jar.

Now use the half-pint jar. Relight the candle. Ask: Will the candle burn under this smaller jar for a longer or for a shorter time than under the quart jar? The class may be in some disagreement about this. Ask those children venturing predictions to give their reasons for making them. It is likely, but not necessary at this time, that some of the class will say that the burning time will be longer in the quart jar because there is more air in the quart jar than in the half-pint. Again, ask the class to measure the length of the burning time by the clock after you cover the candle. Record this time on the chalkboard with the previous observation. Again, as in the case of the quart jar, make two more determinations and calculate the mean of the results. Typical results might be as follows (Table 1):

Table 1

Jar Size	Mean Burning Time, Sec.
Half-pint	9
Quart	32

Discuss with the class the relationship of the half-pint to the quart—one quart is four half-pints. Ask them how long they would expect the candle would burn under one pint jar. Would it burn between 9 and 32 seconds? Would it be closer to 9 or to 32 seconds? Have them explain their predictions. Do they use the relationship of the volumes in making their predictions?

Perform the test with the pint jar, recording the burning time. Discuss the list of burning times and jar sizes as they stand now. The following data were obtained with wide-mouth canning jars and a food-warmer candle (Table 2). Your own data may be quite different due to variation in size of the flame and other factors.

Table 2

Jar Size	Mean Burning Time, Sec.
Half-pint	9
Pint	16
Quart	32

In reviewing these data, it will be helpful to prepare a graph on the chalkboard. This will bring out more clearly the increase in burning time associated with each doubling of jar size.

For further information about Science—A Process Approach (AAAS), the reader should send to the project offices listed in Appendix A or see:

Gagné, Robert M., "Elementary Science: A New Scheme of Instruction," *Science*, 151 (January, 1966), pp. 49-53.

Livermore, Arthur H., "The Process Approach of the AAAS Commission on Science Education," *Journal of Research in Science Teaching*, 2 (December, 1964), pp. 271-282.

Walbesser, Henry H., "Curriculum Evaluation by Means of Behavioral Objectives," *Journal of Research in Science Teaching*, 1 (December, 1963), pp. 296-301.

————, "Science Curriculum Evaluation: Observations on a Position." *The Science Teacher* (February, 1966), pp. 34-35.

Kits are available for use with the activities listed in the Student Manuals.

Conceptually Oriented Program in Elementary Science (COPES). COPES is a two-year pilot science project testing the feasibility of organizing a K-6 science curriculum around major conceptual schemes in science. A scope and sequence design has been developed for the teaching materials, leading to an ever-increasing awareness of the conceptual scheme: The Conservation of Energy. By referring to the scope and sequence chart in Figure 9, the reader can observe the hierarchy of concepts selected to guide the child through to the higher, more sophisticated concepts developed later in the sequence.

Written materials are prepared for *teachers* only. A teacher's guide is so designed that all teaching activities can be planned from it. The guides are very comprehensive and detailed including:

1. Twelve major parts, each representing one of the major concepts critical to the understanding of energy conservation.
2. Introductory materials and presequence learning; attempting to make clear how each major concept is related to antecedent concepts and how it leads to subsequent ones.
3. Suggested classroom activities that have been designed with regard to how the activity is intended to develop understanding of the particular concepts.
4. Questions that might be used to generate instructional discussion.
5. Supplementary activities that can be used for enrichment or clarification.
6. Background information for the teacher that explains the science concepts in greater detail and with more sophistication than the way they are presented in elementary classrooms.

A kit of materials is available that holds enough equipment for four students working in pairs. Kits are an integral part of this project as the COPES staff is firmly committed to the belief that children learn best by doing, manipulating, and experiencing the phenomena they are studying.

Figure 9 (page 72) shows a sample of the Teacher's Guide for the concept that forces might be acting without producing motion.[5]

PURPOSE OF ACTIVITIES 3-6

In the last two activities the children observed that a force can move an object from rest and can change its motion. They will now become aware that forces may be acting without producing motion. In this case the forces that we call "balanced" are acting in opposite directions and are of the same magnitude. Children can begin to analyze forces in some simple systems and see that they occur in pairs. They will find that motion occurs only when the opposing forces become unbalanced.

ACTIVITY D-3

STRETCHING RUBBER BANDS

Materials: 30 rubber bands, 3″

Preparation for Teaching: No special preparation is required.

Suggestions for Teaching: This activity is an introduction to the concept of opposing forces.

Distribute a rubber band to each child. Have him anchor one end of it to the desk top with a finger or thumb and stretch it with the other hand. Ask the children how many forces are acting on the band. If the response is one force ask them to identify its origin and the point at which it is being applied. Then ask them to grasp the anchored end and hold the rubber band above the desk with both hands as shown in Figure D-3. [COPES no. See unnumbered Figure , page 73.] The rubber band should be stretched the same amount as before. They will probably recognize two forces acting on the band in opposite directions.

---

[5] Conceptually Oriented Program in Elementary Science (COPES), *The Teacher's Guide for a Conservation of Energy Sequence* (New York: New York University), August, 1968, p. 130-131.

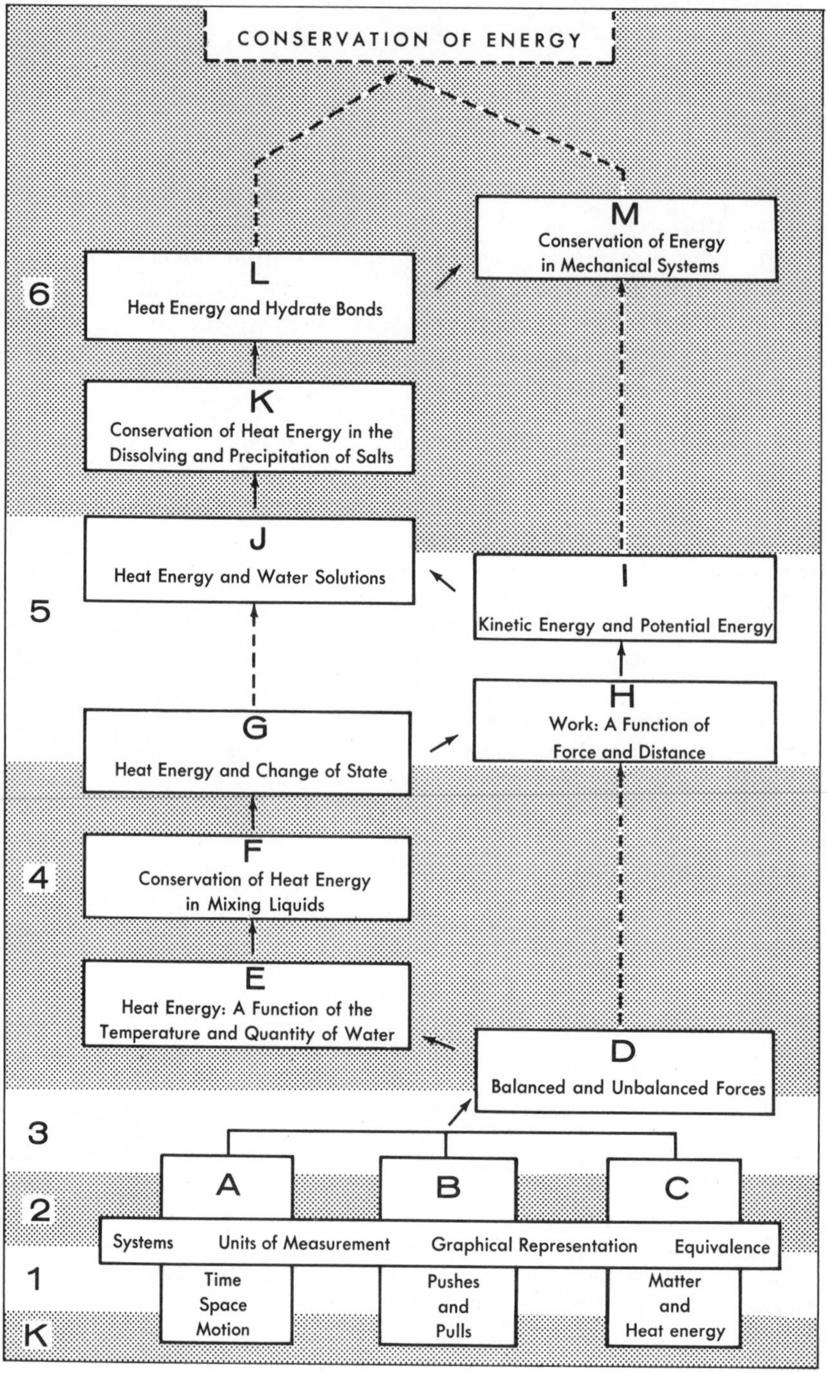

FIGURE 9. Conservation of Energy Scope & Sequence for Grades K-6 (COPES)[6]

[6] *Ibid.*, p. 6.

Focus attention on the stretch of the rubber band. Ask the children to describe the forces being exerted by the rubber band on their hands. By feeling the pull of the rubber band on each hand, they will probably understand that the force of the rubber band pulling on the right hand is just as great as the force of the rubber band pulling on the left hand. Furthermore, if the band is stretched to a greater degree, both forces exerted by the band on their hands will be greater.

It might be appropriate to use arrows to represent the forces acting on the rubber band and on the hands. The head of the arrow should indicate the direction of the force, and the length of the arrow will represent the magnitude, or amount of the force. The forces acting in the hands-rubber band system are shown in Figure D-3. The arrows show the magnitude and directions of the forces that are present when the band is stretched.

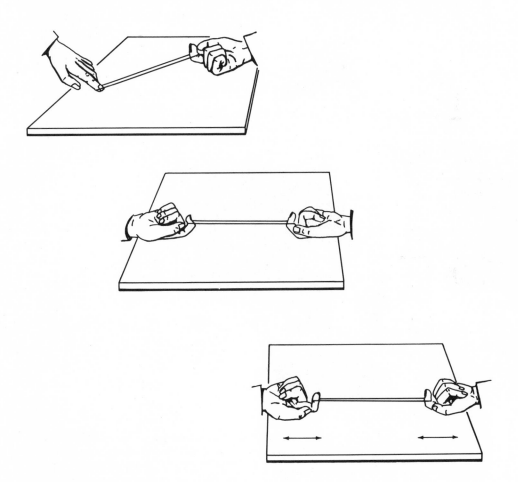

For additional information the reader can obtain brochures and newsletters free by writing:

COPES
New York University
4 Washington Place
New York, New York 10003

The Elementary Science Study (ESS). The ESS project is designed as *non-sequential* science units to be used anywhere in the elementary school years, when and how a teacher pleases. They can be integrated into an established school science curriculum or used independently. The units are flexible and have not been assigned definite grade levels, but most have a range of three or more grades with forty class lessons. The purpose of the thirty-three units is to present students with scientifically sound accounts of such areas as:

Behavior of Mealworms	Batteries and Bulbs	Kitchen Physics
Growing Seeds	Mystery Powders	Light and Shadows
Bones	Gases and Airs	Pendulums
		Eggs and Tadpoles

"I wonder if our plant is the biggest now?" How is the teacher utilizing these girls' high maturation for the inclusion of mathematics in the science program?

The program is a highly individual, experimental one in which children have access to the materials for open-ended rather than teacher or textbook directed investigations. All of the materials needed for each unit are supplied in kits. These kits utilize many items familiar to children from around their homes such as the kit on the opposite page.

In addition to kits, ESS has developed film loop cartridges and films to accompany and enrich the activities, student worksheets and booklets, as well as teacher's guides.

The teacher's guides attempt to provide teachers with as much help as possible while keeping the units free for children to discover things on their own. To accomplish this, all teacher's guides contain:

1. Microscope
2. Toothpicks
3. Tweezers
4. Optical lens
5. Euglena
6. Microscope slides
7. Test tube rack
8. Jar
9. Cover glass
10. Dropper
11. Iodine stain
12. Methylene blue
13. Rosin
14. Kosher salt
15. Brown sugar
16. Pond water culture
17. Paramecium caudatum
18. Soda straw balance
19. Amoeba proteus
20. Calcium chloride
21. Sugar
22. Calcium chloride
23. Straws
24. Empty bottle
25. Molasses
26. Vinegar
27. Coffee tin lid
28. Hotplate
29. Yeast
30. Measuring cup
31. Meas. spoons
32. Vegetables
33. Spoon
34. Knife
35. Weeds
36. Test tubes
37. Bottle brush

1. Summary of activities children can reasonably be expected to experience.
2. Materials needed in terms of teams of two students working together.
3. Suggested procedures which are intended to be models rather than directions.
4. Copies of student worksheets that accompany the unit.
5. Ideas for extending the unit further.
6. Notes on scheduling.

Below is part of Lesson Six of the *Teacher's Guide for Kitchen Physics* (A Look at Some Properties of Liquids).[7]

6. BLOTTERS AND TOWELS

SUMMARY OF ACTIVITIES

The children perform several experiments involving absorption and evaporation of different liquids in different materials to reveal still another aspect of grabbiness—cohesive

[7] Reprinted from *Teacher's Guide for Kitchen Physics* by Elementary Science Study. Copyright © 1967 by Educational Services Incorporated. Published by Webster Division, McGraw-Hill Book Company.

and adhesive forces at work. In the process, they become aware of the need to design experiments where they can study only one variable (changing factor) at a time, and they begin to develop an understanding of equilibria of systems.

Materials: For each team of two students you will need:

A balance.
Washers.
Blotter-paper sheets.
Blotter paper (cut in strips about 2 cm. wide).
Blotter paper (cut in strips ranging in size from 1/4 cm. to 4 or 5 cm.; we recommend that you cut the narrower strips yourself on a paper cutter since children find it difficult to cut strips of less than 1 cm.).
Polyethylene tubing (waxed paper, plastic wrap, or some such transparent material could be substituted).
Drilled plastic capillary block.

You will also need:

Paper towels (preferably light in color).
Paper clips.
Cloth (various types could be brought in by the children).
Plastic bags or glass jars.
Milk containers (cut the long way, or long plastic dishes; the milk containers may be lined with plastic bags or wrap for holding soapy water and oil).
Glass plates (optional).
Water.
Soapy water.
Rubber bands.
Cooking oil.
Food coloring.
Alcohol.
Microscopes (hand lenses or a microprojector may be used instead).
Thin pieces of wood.
Thin wire.
Rulers.
Paper cutter or shears.
Transparent mending tape.
A fan (optional).

Suggested Procedure:

1. How much water can a paper towel absorb? Throughout this unit (and many times in their daily lives), the children have used paper towels to soak up water they have spilled. You can lead into this experiment by asking, "How do you think a paper towel works?"

The usual response is, "It soaks up water." If you ask them, "What do you mean by soaks up?" they will probably substitute other words such as "takes up," "absorbs," and "picks up." That is, they can tell you what it does, but not how it does it. However, they can think of a way to find out how much a paper towel absorbs—and they usually do: "Weigh a dry towel; soak it in water; weigh it again."

To prepare the balance for weighing, bend a paper clip into a hook and hang it from the notch at one end of the balance beam. Then, hang a folded paper towel from the hook as shown in Worksheet II, "A Way to Find Out How Much Water a Paper Towel Can Absorb," . . . .

For additional information concerning ESS, the reader should write directly to their project offices listed in Appendix A or refer to:

Nichols, Benjamin, "Elementary Science Study—Two Years Later," *Journal of Research in Science Teaching*, 2: (December 1964), pp. 288-92.

Annual Report, 1968, obtainable free from:

Education Development Center
55 Chapel Street
Newton, Massachusetts 02160

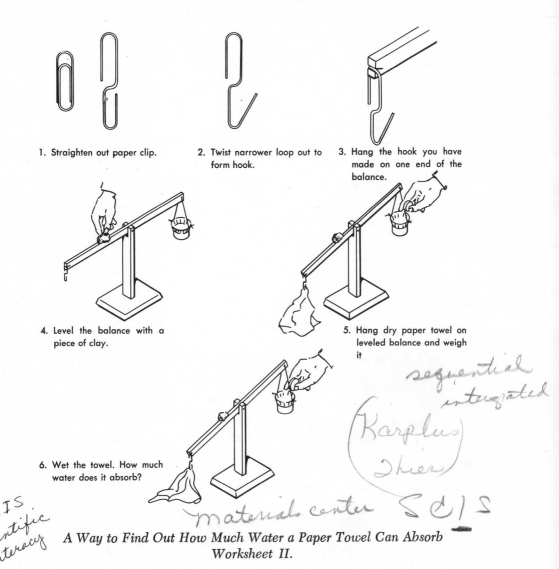

1. Straighten out paper clip.

2. Twist narrower loop out to form hook.

3. Hang the hook you have made on one end of the balance.

4. Level the balance with a piece of clay.

5. Hang dry paper towel on leveled balance and weigh it

6. Wet the towel. How much water does it absorb?

sequential
integrated
(Karplus)
(Thier)
material center   SCIS

SCIS
scientific
Literacy

A Way to Find Out How Much Water a Paper Towel Can Absorb
Worksheet II.

Science Curriculum Improvement Study, University of California (SCIS). SCIS attempts to develop a complete, integrated science curriculum in which its teaching units are conceptually interdependent. The program stresses concepts and phenomena with process learnings a by-product of direct experiences of children. It is a sequential rather than graded articulated elementary science program based upon the structure of science as seen by scientists today.

This project is based upon a hierarchy of levels of abstractions of science concepts. The first level of abstractions contains concepts from the area of matter, living things, conservation of matter, and variation in one property among similar objects. The second level of abstractions is concerned with concepts of interaction and relativity. The highest level of abstraction focuses upon concepts of energy, equilibrium, steady state, behavior, reproduction, and specialization of living matter. Figure 10 shows the hierarchy of subject areas of SCIS.

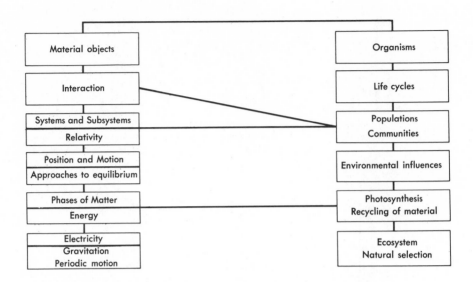

Figure 10. Subject Areas of the SCIS Program (1968)[8]

The main purpose of the project is to develop scientific literacy in children (functional understanding of science concepts) and an inquiring open mind. To achieve these aims, SCIS has developed a materials-centered approach in which the elementary classroom actually becomes a laboratory. Children manipulate specially designed equipment and observe, sometimes freely and sometimes under teacher guidance. Next, the teacher introduces scientific concepts that describe or explain what the children have observed. This is called the "invention lesson." Invention lessons are followed by other direct experiences that present further examples of the concept. These are called "discovery lessons" for the child is expected to recognize that the new concept has applications to situations other than the initial one.

Booklets are available for each unit accompanied by laboratory equipment and materials kits. Student activity booklets are available for recording observations, as well as teacher's guides. Each teacher's guide presents:

1. General background and introduction of the study and its philosophy and intent.
2. Overview of the science content included in the unit as well as general objectives for teaching-learning of the concepts involved.
3. Clues for the teacher on different approaches to teaching any given lesson.
4. Further teaching hints through use of the Student Activity Pages.
5. Within each lesson:
   a. Materials.
   b. Objectives of the Learning Experiences.

---

[8] Science Curriculum Improvement Study, *Relativity, Teacher's Guide* (Boston: D. C. Heath and Co. 1968), p. 3; copyright by the Regents of the University of California, Berkeley, California, 94720.

*How can the self-
contained classroom be
equipped adequately for
science?*

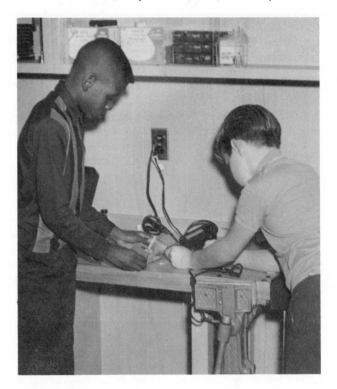

c. Teaching Suggestions.
d. Suggested Use of Student Activity Pages.
e. Replica of Student Activity Pages (for review lessons or recording).

Following is a sample of part of Lesson Eleven from the chapter on *"Interaction," Teacher's Guide Systems and Subsystems:*[9]

3. INVENTION OF THE SUBSYSTEMS CONCEPT

Teaching Materials: KEY: †(from Chapter 1)
*(provided by teacher)

For each child:
Student Manual pages 8, 9
For demonstration:

2 syringes.†	Vinegar.†
White plastic tube.†	Sodium Carbonate.†
Glass vial (Utility).	Bromothymol blue in squeeze bottle.†
Cork stopper with hole.	Plastic tumbler (Utility).
Translucent plastic capillary tube.	Small plastic bag and wire tie (Part Five).
Tumbler of very hot water (covered).	Teaspoon.*
Tumbler of cold water (Utility).	Paper towels.*
Calibrated thermometer (Part Five).	Tape.*
Food coloring (Part Five).	

---

[9] Science Curriculum Improvement Study, *Teacher's Guide Systems and Subsystems* (Pre-
liminary Edition) (Lexington, Mass.: Raytheon Education Co., 1968), pp. 44-47; copyright by
the Regents of the University of California, Berkeley, California, 94720.

Teaching Suggestions: When you introduce the subsystems concept in this chapter, you make use of some of the systems with which the children experimented in Chapter 1 and a thermometer model newly introduced in demonstrations here. The children will then be able to identify a system, subsystems within the system, and objects within the sub-systems, as they carry out investigations in this and later parts of the unit.

Advance preparation. Setting up all the materials before class will allow for a smooth-flowing demonstration. The only new apparatus you have to assemble is the thermometer model consisting of a vial with colored water and fitted with a cork stopper pierced by a thin-bore plastic tube. [(1)] When the water is heated, it expands into the plastic tube.

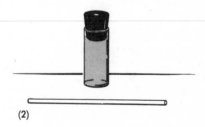

(1)

The assembly proceeds in four steps:
1. Put ten drops of food coloring into the vial, then fill it completely with water at room temperature.
2. Carefully insert the one-hole stopper into the vial, spilling some of the excess water and forcing some to come out the hole. Leave no air bubbles in the vial. [(2)]

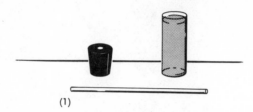

(2)

3. Push the plastic tube about three-quarters of the way into the stopper with a twisting motion. Some of the colored liquid will be forced up the plastic tube. [(3)]

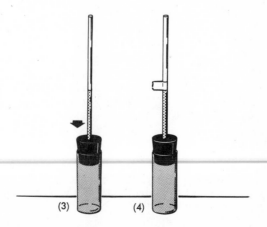

(3)   (4)

4. The colored liquid should reach about five to eight centimeters above the top of the stopper. If it stands lower, force the tube a little farther into the vial. Fasten a piece of opaque tape around the plastic tube to provide a reference mark for the liquid level, or mark the tube with a felt pen. [(4)]

For additional information send to project office listed in Appendix A for free copy of:

> Karplus, Robert and Herbert D. Thier, *Toward Scientific Literacy*, Reprinted from *Education Age*, Volume 2, Number 2, January-February, 1966.
> _____, "Science Teaching is Becoming Literate," plus other miscellaneous reprints, SCIS.

PROGRAM ELEMENTS	AAAS	COPES	ESS	·SCIS
I. ORGANIZATION OF CURRICULUM	COMPLETE, INTEGRATED, SEQUENTIAL	SCOPE AND SEQUENCE ENERGY UNIT	SELF-CONTAINED UNITS	COMPLETE, INTEGRATED, SEQUENTIAL
II. MAJOR EMPHASIS	PROCESSES (CONCEPTS-TOOLS, PHENOMENA-VEHICLES)	CONCEPTUAL SCHEMES	INVOLVEMENT WITH PHENOMENA (PROCESSES AND CONCEPTS BY-PRODUCTS)	CONCEPTS AND PHENOMENA (PROCESS A BY-PRODUCT)
III. MATERIAL PRODUCED	STUDENT/ TEACHER BOOKLETS, KITS, TESTS	TEACHER BOOKLETS, KITS	STUDENT/ TEACHER BOOKLETS, KITS, FILMS	STUDENT/ TEACHER BOOKLETS, KITS, FILMS

FIGURE 11. Summary—Elements of AAAS, COPES, ESS, SCIS

The chart in Appendix A will supply additional points of comparison between science curriculum projects.

State and Local Science Curriculums

Many elementary school districts have either developed or adopted a particular science curriculum, or are in the process of picking one. Most state departments of education have also produced science programs. Appendix B contains some of these state science courses compiled by the National Science Teachers Association.[10] National science projects are being examined by state and local curriculum groups to determine the applicability of all or part of the projects for local adaptation. The unique needs, goals, and aspirations of each community

---

[10] *Bibliography of Science Courses of Study and Textbooks Grades 1-9, 1966* (Washington, D.C.: National Science Teachers Association, 1966), pp. 1-7.

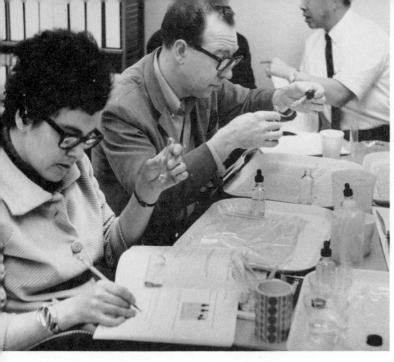

*How can you start
"retooling" for the newer
programs in science?
What roles do in-service
workshops perform for
helping teachers enrich
their classroom programs?*

are factors to be considered in their curriculum decisions. The place of national science projects will be further explored in the next chapter, titled "Selecting and Planning Discovery Science Studies."

Science Textbook Revisions

Textbook publishers have also kept pace with the movement toward greater involvement of scientists and the use of the latest knowledge about how children learn. The results can be seen in the great advancement in the quality of science textbooks for elementary grades.

1. The accuracy of scientific information is generally improved, with inaccuracies being kept to a minimum.
2. An approach which utilizes discovery is apparent in more recent textbooks through the greater use of a question-and-answer approach rather than the dialogue or telling techniques so popular in previous elementary science textbooks.
3. Authors are beginning to develop styles of writing that convey the fascination and intellectual excitement inherent in scientific disciplines.
4. Although rare in current textbooks, the process approach is appearing, even though its place is generally relegated to the teacher's edition under the "Enrichment Activities" section.
5. Limited opportunities are beginning to appear in texts for developing scientific attitudes as well as skills for creative and critical thinking.
6. The format of modern textbooks is much more inviting and inspiring than that of previous texts; more extensive use of visual aids is evident through excellent pictures and other illustrations and sequential photos of scientific phenomena.
7. Fewer or *broad* comprehensive science units are explored in greater depth than the numerous isolated lessons of the past; Chapter 5 discusses the specifics of this in relation to selecting and planning science programs.

Science textbooks, state and local curriculum guides, and national science projects are all influential in determining what and how science is and will be taught in classes. An extended discussion of the role of textbooks in science education is discussed in Chapter 8.

Similar Elements in Innovative Projects—Possible Trends

Although there is a wide range of experimental and innovative projects on the scene in elementary science, many similar elements can be observed. Some of these are listed here and form what probably will be the trends in science for the elementary schools.

1. Distinguished professional scientists have initiated science teaching innovations rather than professional science educators, state departments of education, or teacher-training institutions.
2. Scholars have gone into classrooms and in actual situations have created, tested, and revised materials and methods that succeed in schools.
3. Most of the projects claim to be geared to *all* children and not just to select groups.
4. Departure from the standard textbook is almost radical, blending development of skills with conceptual schemes. Movement is away from reliance upon a single text to a multi-text approach for finding information.
5. There is a definite trend away from teaching *many* science content areas to teaching relatively *few* content areas.
6. There is a trend toward open-ended, relatively unstructured methods of discovery rather than teaching *one* method of problem solving.
7. Knowledge is viewed as part of a creative process of finding out rather than the mere accumulation of knowledge being emphasized.
8. A definite trend toward greater utilization of quantitative techniques is apparent, such as measurement, graphing, recording.
9. Almost all projects use scientists to help structure the content and processes of the particular project.
10. The movement is away from emphasis upon technology and application of science to more concern with abstractions, theories, and basic ideas of science.
11. The projects generally wed the knowledge of good teaching-learning practices with the latest in science disciplines.
12. "Packaged programs," including hardware and software, are being constructed to give a whole program to teachers. These aid the teacher in attempting to adapt new programs to his particular situation. These packages also contain many new curricular innovations which provide the teacher with flexibility to handle a wide range of student abilities and varying teaching conditions.
13. Much stress is placed upon upgrading teacher skills in both science teaching and science content through the materials of the projects. A definite trend has developed in teacher training institutes and in-service work that reflects this dual concern.

14. Science is presented from the vantage point of what the scientist does and how he does it. The image presented of the scientist is very positive.
15. The science content selected presents general principles or generalizations recognized as basic by the scientists in that discipline.
16. Children are expected to take *active* parts in the learning process and to learn or structure their own concepts for themselves.

Ronald Gross presents the common elements shared by science projects in his article:

"Two-Year-Olds Are Very Smart," *New York Times Magazine* (September 6, 1964), p. 39.

Although there are the similarities noted here, much evaluative work remains to be done to sift out the more valuable from the less valuable. With new projects have come controversies and conflicting views among scientists and science educators as to the relative merits of aspects of these new projects.

Evaluation and Controversy of New Science Programs

Why are there such divergent views in new projects for science in the elementary schools? One of the reasons can be found in the divergent backgrounds and frames of reference of the scientists, educators, and psychologists involved in *curriculum* innovation. What each of these groups brings to its curriculum design results in curricula with very different bases. Basically, controversy is developing around these aspects of the new science projects: 1) relationship between science process and content structure, 2) extent of structure of project exercises, and 3) adequacy of project evaluation.[11]

Balance Between Process and Content Structure

As we pointed out in Chapter 3, it is generally accepted today in science for the elementary school that programs should involve both process and content. The educational pendulum has swung from almost complete stress by teachers upon science *content* to an almost complete stress (in some projects) upon the science *process*.

This reversal has caused much confusion among elementary teachers, administrators, and supervisors. Some projects highlight the structure of science content while others devote the majority of their activities and materials to skills of science processes. Eventually, scientists working on curriculum projects will first decide upon a structure of science concepts (conceptual schemes) and then design

---

[11] For a fuller account of these three controversial aspects of the new projects read: Edward Victor, "Controversial Aspects of the Elementary School Curriculum Projects," *Science and Children* (October, 1967), pp. 27-29.

exercises for children around those that would teach both process and content concurrently. COPES, one of the newer science projects for elementary schools, has attempted to combine a conceptual schemes structure *and* process activities.

Amount of Structure of Project Exercises

Controversy exists today on the amount of structure that is necessary and desirable in the new science projects. On the one hand, some structure is necessary and valuable, for most elementary school teachers are in need of very specific and detailed teaching suggestions and scientific information. Elementary teachers generally are hesitant to teach science as a result of their meager science backgrounds, inadequate curriculum guides, and the lack of sufficient science supplies and equipment in their schools. It is no wonder then that some projects with highly structured teaching directions and kits of materials are received so enthusiastically by teachers using them.

However, these same highly structured teaching materials have been attacked for their potential inflexibility that does not allow for individual differences of students and teachers. Criticism of too highly structured teaching materials centers on three aspects:

1. The lessons seem geared for the average and above average child while neglecting the below average or the "ghetto" or "inner-city" child.
2. The lessons tend to retard the creative teacher attempting to capitalize upon the unstructured or incidental happening in his teaching.
3. The lessons, especially the process-oriented ones, are narrowly designed and do not contain enough science background information to assist the teacher with "unexpected questions."

Attempts to offset these shortcomings are being planned into science projects in the form of in-service workshops and institutes for teachers using the materials. During these institutes, additional science background is presented to teachers along with activities and ideas for broadening and enriching the structured lessons. As teachers become more familiar with the projects, they will probably feel more comfortable experimenting with and deviating from the structured lessons.

Adequacy of Project Evaluation

With the exception of AAAS and several other studies, it appears that more real evaluation is needed in the new science projects. Too much reliance is being placed solely upon statements of enthusiasm by children, teachers, and scientists involved in the project. Evaluation of *complete* units of projects for accuracy and for effectiveness as learning guides have been done, using these criteria:[12]

1. Do the units cover the scope of science?
2. Do the units suggest many sources for obtaining information?

---

[12] Joseph Zaffroni. *New Developments in Elementary School Science* (Washington, D.C.: National Science Teachers Association, 1963), pp. 31-32.

3. Are the concepts appropriate for the educational level of the pupils?
4. Do the concepts challenge the learner?
5. Do the activities develop an understanding of the nature of science?
6. Is there provision for systematic development of a concept?
7. Is there orderly development of concepts?
8. Will the unit, as organized, promote growth in understanding of the objective?
9. Are sufficient and appropriate materials available for instruction?

Consistency of Evaluative Devices

One of the basic questions in all evaluation is: Are the methods of evaluating the project consistent with its goals? It is argued that a noticeable inconsistency in some new projects is the practice of using evaluative devices which are science content oriented to measure behavioral goals. Alphoretta S. Fish expresses it this way:

> For example, any new curriculum which purports to develop behavioral outcomes which in any way reflect inquiry should have an evaluative instrument designed *not to test subject matter and manipulative skill competences but* to answer such questions as:
>
> 1. As a result of the new curriculum design, do pupils who formerly asked questions only about subject matter now ask questions about the processes as well?
> 2. As a result of the new curriculum design, do pupils who formerly failed to question science meanings now build criteria for examining and judging meanings and demand precision in language, logic in argument, and responsibility in judgement making?[13]

Robert H. Carleton cautions us as to the difficulties of evaluation of behavioral objectives:

> Various approaches are being tried, among them observation of behavior based upon an observation schedule, tests using Richard Suchman "Predict-Control-Explain" tests as a model, and individual pupil interviews . . . . But we still have far to go. "Behavior" involves pupils both in and out of school (and who can follow a child 24 hours a day?). "Conceptualization" involves analysis of the thinking of an individual (and who can get inside another person's head?). We can list some very desirable attributes of the citizen literate in science, but can the goals of attitudes and appreciations be expressed in behavioral terms?[14]

If we strive for the behavioral changes in students in elementary school science programs, we must know the degree of change that has occurred as well as the direction of that change. What does this mean for the elementary school science teacher?

---

[13] Alphoretta S. Fish, "Evaluating New Programs in Elementary Science," *School Science and Mathematics*, Vol. 65, No. 6 (June, 1965), p. 532.

[14] Robert H. Carleton, "Science Education in the Middle or Junior High School Grades," *The Science Teacher* (December, 1967), pp. 28-70.

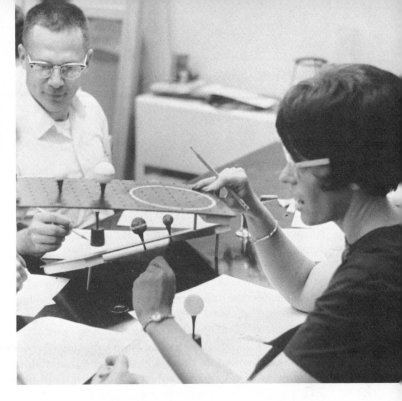

In what ways might these elementary teachers be contributing to the goals of science education?

Implications for Elementary Science Teachers

The typical elementary school teacher probably is saying to herself, "All this research innovation and experimentation is great, but what does it have to do with me? I'm only a classroom teacher not a science education researcher." It has a lot to do with her, for she's right in the midst of a great acceleration in the history of the production of educational ideas and materials. What used to take thirty years to accomplish from a new idea to actual classroom instruction is now occurring in months.

The implication of this for the elementary teacher is the fact that the task of testing the value of new science programs *with children* can only be accomplished by elementary school teachers. If they accept the challenge, they must improve their knowledge of the science discipline or system around which the new program is structured. They must develop the skills to make judgments whether "innovations (or the 'old ways' and materials for that matter) truly serve to advance *their* educational goals with *their* pupils in *their* particular setting or situation."[15]

Many decisions on new projects will eventually rest with classroom teachers. They must be informed and up-to-date on the current projects so that they can help select, conduct, and evaluate innovation in science education in the elementary school. This unique contribution and potential power of the elementary school teacher is summarized by this statement of Hubert H. Humphrey, when he was Vice-President of the United States:

> What you really need is a little teaching power. Who knows better what ought to go on in a classroom? Who knows better about the kind of teaching tools that work. Who knows better about young people than those who work with them and live with them? Who knows better what the purpose of education is than a trained teacher?

[15] *Ibid.*, p. 70.

Summary

Science in the elementary schools has changed radically in the past one hundred years, reflecting the century's unprecedented social, economic, scientific, and technological transformations. Each science program was born out of the needs and interests of its time. Our current programs show intense interest in viewing science as both process and products utilizing discovery approach and conceptual schemes curriculums.

Experimentation, innovation, and reform in elementary school science has been accelerated by massive grants of money from federal, state, and local governments, as well as private foundations such as the Ford Foundation and others.

Common elements are perceptible among the many science projects, such as a trend toward relatively unstructured methods of discovery rather than *one* method of problem solving, and viewing knowledge as part of a creative process of finding out rather than emphasizing the mere accumulation of knowledge.

Problems of adequate evaluation of these new projects center on three basic aspects: 1) What should the relationship be between science process and content? 2) To what extent should the project exercises be structured? and 3) How do we achieve consistency in our evaluation, so that we measure that which we hope to achieve?

The elementary school teacher is a pivotal person in the success or failure of these programs. It is difficult to see which, if any, current projects will survive and be the pattern for future science programs for the elementary school. It is likely that an eclectic pattern, taking the best part of many projects, will weld elements into a direction to follow.

SELF-EVALUATION AND FURTHER STUDY

1. Select a reading from among the following articles on the historical view of elementary school science. Point out the influence of the particular era discussed on modern science in the elementary school.

    Craig, Gerald S., "Elementary School Science in the Past Century," *Science Teacher*, 24, 4 (February, 1957), pp. 11-14.

    Lammers, Theresa J., "The Thirty-first Yearbook and 20 Years of Elementary Science," *Science Education*, 39 (February, 1955), pp. 39-40.

    National Society for the Study of Education, A Program for Teaching Science, Thirty-first Yearbook, Part I, Public School Publishing Company, Bloomington, Illinois, 1932.

    Underhill, Orra E., *The Origin and Development of Elementary School Science*. Chicago: Scott, Foresman & Company, 1941.

2. There have been some "giants" in the field of science for the elementary school. Find out their particular contributions and their effects upon science in the elementary schools today.

    Johann Pestalozzi, Herbert Spencer, William T. Harris, G. Stanley Hall, Colonel Francis W. Parker, Henry H. Strait, Wilbur S. Jackman, Liberty Hyde Bailey, Charles Saunders Peirce, William James, John Dewey, Gerald S. Craig.

3. Pick five of the projects on Lockard's chart in Appendix A. Write to these projects and ask for their latest report. Write a brief summary of each showing similarities and differences.

4. What advantages and disadvantages do you see of the above projects over your state or local school science guide? Which one would you prefer? Why? Send to several of the state curriculum guides listed in Appendix B if local guides are unavailable.

5. Do you see any ways in which the five science projects selected attempt to meet individual differences?

6. Try to predict what science for the elementary school will be ten years from now. What do you see as trends in classroom equipment, goals, objectives, science materials, tests, etc. The following is one source of assistance:

    Johnson, Philip G., "In the Future," Supervision for Quality Education in Science. Washington, D.C.: U. S. Office of Education; Document OI-29039, Bulletin 1963, No. 3., pp. 132-140.

7. It has been said that with the profusion of ideas being studied in new science programs a single national science program is needed. Give the pros and cons of this idea.

PART TWO

ORGANIZING AND PLANNING FOR TEACHING-LEARNING SCIENCE THROUGH DISCOVERY

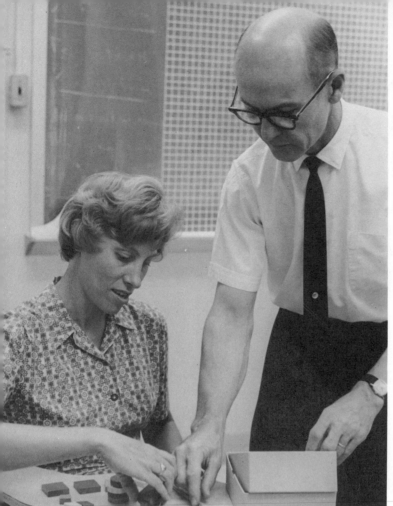

Qui Docet Discit
(*He who teaches, learns*)

CHAPTER 5

SELECTING AND PLANNING DISCOVERY SCIENCE STUDIES

The elementary school teacher is working in a period of national curriculum uncertainty and searching for direction for the content and methods of teaching science. In spite of the unprecedented number and variety of experimental programs, no single program is predominant for the sequence, structure, or methods of teaching elementary school science content and processes. No national science curriculum seems clearly superior to guide the science program. How then is the elementary school teacher to find answers for such practical problems in selecting and planning studies in science for his class as:

Which science content areas shall I select?
How do I make plans for these science studies?
Which activities are best for my class with its limited classroom space and equipment?
How do *I* learn and begin to feel adequate with science concepts, principles, and processes myself?

Katherine Hill poses these three questions as the *general* bases for deciding what to teach in a program of elementary school science:

1. How can we provide children with a continuously balanced exploration of their environment from year to year?
2. How can we provide children with opportunities to build the science skills needed for interpretation of phenomena in their environment?
3. How can we provide children with experiences which serve to strengthen understandings of fundamental concept systems which may be used in interpreting science phenomena?[1]

In pursuing answers to these general questions, the teacher will also find specific information applicable to the practical questions raised concerning planning for his particular class.

Selecting A Continuous, Balanced Science Program

It is currently accepted that there should be a planned and coordinated science program from kindergarten to twelfth grade. Basic science concepts, principles,

---

[1] Katherine E. Hill, "The Basis for Deciding What to Teach," *The Instructor* (January, 1964), pp. 41, 74-75.

and processes to be learned are arranged from the very simple to the abstract, depending upon children's maturation. This would meet the first general criterion for selecting what to teach.

Scope of Science Program

This arrangement of the science program is referred to as the *scope* and *sequence*—scope is the science content and sequence is the grade level assigned to the content. It is preferable that the areas of study be broad and limited to four to six science areas yearly. There is considerable agreement and similarity of topics for these broad areas, as exemplified in these samples from a science textbook series and a state curriculum guide:

State Curriculum Guide[2] *Broad Science Areas*	Science Textbook Series[3] *Broad Science Areas*
Living Things	Living Things
Our Growing Bodies	The Human Body
Air, Water, Weather	The Earth
The Earth and Its Composition...........	The Earth
The Solar System & Beyond	The Universe
Matter and Energy	Matter and Energy

The AAAS Science—A Process Approach is one of the science projects that organizes its scope and sequence on science processes rather than science content areas. These AAAS basic process skills have been identified in Chapter 4.

Sequence of Content

Similar agreement does *not* exist, however, in the area of *sequence* of content. Considerable variation exists in the grade placement of science concepts and principles. Research generally shows that children at all elementary grades can learn something about *all* science areas, if the concepts are presented simply and within the children's developmental level. In fact, science educators believe that it is almost impossible and certainly undesirable to try to develop *one* national science program with a rigid or static grade placement sequence. The variations are too wide in children's abilities, interests, and motivations—as much between schools in the same community as between schools in different communities, cities, and states. The exact grade placement of science concepts and principles can only be determined by the individuals *directly* in contact with the children in their own unique science programs. The *teacher*, weighing the curriculum guide against his knowledge of *his* children, is the person most competent to make the curricu-

---

[2] *Science for Children* (K-6), The University of the State of New York, The State Education Department, Bureau of Elementary Curriculum Development, Albany, New York, 1966, p. 6.

[3] *The Laidlaw Science Series* (Grades 1-6) (Palo Alto, Calif.: Laidlaw Brothers, A Division of Doubleday and Company, 1966).

lum decision of what specifics to teach his class. The wise teacher uses the information and suggestions found in the scope and sequence of his state or local science guide, science project teacher's guide, or his science textbook to make these decisions.

Variety of Activities

The second criterion cautions the teacher to select a variety of activities for children to participate *actively* in a science program. Figure 12 gives a graphic representation of this.

Dale

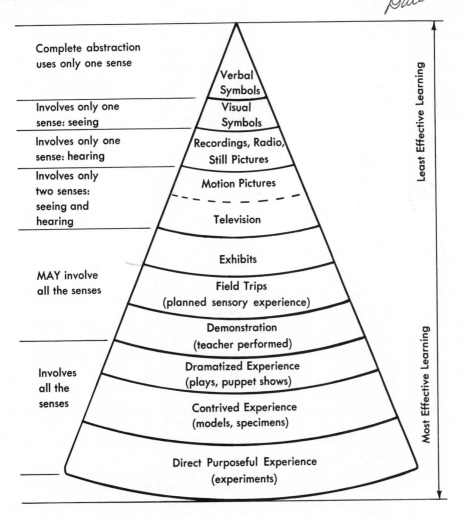

FIGURE 12. Cone of Experience[4] (Selecting Science Activities)

---

[4] Chart modified by the authors from *Audio-Visual Methods in Teaching*, Revised Edition, by Edgar Dale. Copyright © 1946, 1954 by Holt, Rinehart and Winston, Inc. Adapted and reprinted by permission of Holt, Rinehart and Winston, Inc.

The Cone of Experience shows us that:

1. Most effective and long lasting learning takes place from the concrete to the abstract.
2. Learning is longest lasting when as many senses as possible are involved.

Whenever possible, elementary school teachers should select activities as close to the bottom (concrete) of the cone as possible. Chapter 8 will deal with these teaching activities in depth.

Conceptual Schemes

If the teacher is to further avoid fragmentation and mere collection of isolated facts in his science program, he should note especially the third point—orient instruction around large conceptual schemes or ideas. Several of these conceptual schemes were presented in Chapter 3. Although science educators have not agreed upon one particular conceptual scheme, general acceptance has been reached and follows these seven ideas that Gerald Craig has for many years called "Large Patterns of the Universe":

1. The Universe is Very Large	—Space
2. Earth Is Very Old	—Time
3. The Universe Is Constantly Changing	—Change
4. Life Is Adapted to the Environment	—Adaptation
5. There Are Great Variations in the Universe	—Variety
6. The Interdependence of Living Things	—Interrelationships
7. The Equilibrium of Forces	—Equilibrium and Balance[5]

Similarities can be seen between these conceptual schemes and these postulated by the National Science Teachers Association:

I. All matter is composed of units called fundamental particles; under certain conditions these particles can be transformed into energy and vice versa.
II. Matter exists in the form of units which can be classified into hierarchies of organizational levels.
III. The behavior of matter in the universe can be described on a statistical basis.
IV. Units of matter interact. The bases of all ordinary interactions are electromagnetic, gravitational, and nuclear forces.
V. All interacting units of matter tend toward equilibrium states in which the energy content (enthalpy) is a minimum and the energy distribution (entropy) is most random. In the process of attaining equilibrium, energy transformations or matter transformations or matter-energy transformations occur. Nevertheless, the sum of energy and matter in the universe remains constant.

---

[5] Gerald S. Craig, *Science for the Elementary School Teacher*, Fifth Edition (Waltham, Mass.: Blaisdell Publishing Company, A Division of Ginn and Company, 1966), pp. 92-100.

How can this model aid the class in perceiving the relationships of our solar system?

VI. One of the forms of energy is the motion of units of matter. Such motion is responsible for heat and temperature and for the states of matter: solid, liquid, and gaseous.

VII. All matter exists in time and space and, since interactions occur among its units, matter is subject in some degree to changes with time. Such changes may occur at various rates and in various patterns.[6]

Teaching Tips—Picking Studies

The teacher then can find these specific helps for selecting studies:

1. Select only 4-6 broad science areas for your class each year.
2. Use state or local science curriculum guides, or science textbook series, for *suggestions* and possible scope and sequence of science content and processes. Reference should also be made to national science projects mentioned in Chapter 4 and listed in Appendix A. Send for information for total programs of science from such studies as AAAS, SCIS, or individual units from ESS, COPES, or University of Illinois Elementary-School Science Project.
3. Select a conceptual scheme from the above sources, this text, national science project, or other source for unifying your science study around large, basic science principles and processes.
4. Consider the following *before* attempting to choose a *specific* science study:
   a. Check on science areas to which your children have been exposed previously by talking to their former teachers, checking any written records kept, and especially *by asking the children themselves.*
   b. Make sure *all* broad areas of science are selected throughout the year, balancing studies in the physical and biological sciences. Avoid overemphasis or omission of one area.
   c. Is there a strong, current motivation or interest among your children as a result of a space flight, local air or water pollution problem, recent

---

[6] *Theory Into Action . . . In Science Curriculum Development* (Washington, D.C.: National Science Teachers Association, 1964), p. 20.

storm, or an assembly program? Use this whenever possible, but avoid dependence upon it.

d. Are there other teachers in your school or district teaching the same study at the same time? If yes, they may make getting supplies, equipment, books and films very difficult. (However, it could prove beneficial if several teachers team up for joint activities.)

e. Can this science study *naturally* (without forcing) be reinforced by correlation with other subject matter in your program?

f. Is this the best time of year for your study (certain plant and animal studies are difficult or impossible in winter) or is it irrelevant to the particular area?

g. Can you devote the amount of time from your entire program that is needed to adequately engage in this study?

h. Can you get the books and other supplies and materials needed to build up *your* science content and science activities background?

Planning Science Studies

After the teacher has selected broad science areas for study, he will find that it is valuable to develop a format for organizing and planning on a more detailed basis. Regardless of the source of study, one of the most widely used and efficient frameworks for planning science studies is the "unit."

Unit Approach in Science Teaching

A unit has been defined as a "single mass or quantity of subject matter (concepts, skills, symbols, and so forth) which for some logical reason appears to belong together or to form some reasonable single entity."[7] Units found in state, local, or textbook curriculum guides are usually referred to as *"resource units,"* for they generally contain much more than can be presented to any one particular class.

Resource units are extremely valuable because they supply many alternatives from which the teacher can selectively choose to tailor-make a science program to the unique needs, interests, and abilities of his class. The resource unit generally is not concerned with a chronological presentation. It has been likened to a well from which the teacher can draw a large amount of material at any needed time. An example of a resource unit is selected from the New York State Science Curriculum Handbook.[8] The format is very thorough and consistent throughout all the grades, and organized as follows:

---

[7] Walter E. McPhie, "The Teaching Unit: What Makes It Tick," *The Clearing House*, 38 (October, 1963), pp. 70-73.

[8] *Science for Children* (K-6), *op. cit.*, pp. 6-8.

General Format of Science Resource Units

Purpose of Unit	—Single large science principle around which unit is organized.
Apparatus and Materials	—Materials needed to perform activities in unit.
Introduction of the Unit	—Open-ended motivating activities. Open-ended motivating questions.
Experiences Relating to Unit	—Direct experiences on part of learner, some teacher demonstrations.
Enrichment	—Questions to stimulate further thought; topics for additional exploration.
Organization and Use of Information Gained	—Projects and questions to guide a summary of experiences.
Basic Understandings to Be Gained	—Statements summarize concepts which should be developed.
Vocabulary	—Words pertinent to unit.
Scientists	—List of people who have played major role in scientific work related to unit.

It should be pointed out that resource units are also developed in teacher's guides to science textbook series as well as the national science projects. Teachers will find valuable teaching suggestions in these unit guides.

Why do first-hand activities help children master science concepts more easily?

Following is part of a fourth grade unit on the broad science area of Air, Water, and Weather, following the general format for a resource unit.[9]

Fourth Grade: Air, Water, and Weather

Water——Purpose of the Unit: to determine the source of our water

Apparatus and materials

1. Bottle, large, wide-mouthed
2. Bottles, milk
3. Bottles, soda
4. Can, metal, fruit or vegetable
5. Cup, measuring, or graduated cylinder
6. Florence flask
7. Flowerpot
8. Geranium or coleus plant
9. Hand lens
10. Lift pump, demonstration
11. Pan, pie
12. Rain gauge
13. Sand
14. Scales, or balance
15. Sponge
16. Tube, glass, large bore
17. Tumbler, water

INTRODUCTION OF THE UNIT

Motivating Activities

1. Obtain a rain gauge from the high school earth science teacher or from an amateur weather observer. Set up a "What Is It?" display.
2. Display pictures of lakes, streams, rivers, and the ocean. Place a note on the bulletin board: "Where does this water come from?"
3. Fill a common clay flowerpot with well moistened soil; weigh it as carefully as possible. Record this weight. Place the pot of soil on a sunny window sill or in a warm place for the day, and weigh it again at the end of the school day. Can the children account for the loss of weight?
4. Make a sign, "What is precipitation?" and place it on the bulletin board. Let children supply pictures of examples.

Motivating Questions

1. Where does the rain come from?
2. Where do the clouds come from?
3. Which places on the earth receive very little rain?
4. Are there any deserts in the United States?
5. What is precipitation?
6. What is evaporation?

EXPERIENCES RELATING TO THE UNIT

Teacher-directed Activities

1. Rub a wet sponge over the surface of the chalkboard and watch the film of water evaporate. Where does this water go? Repeat with rubbing alcohol. Can the children smell it after it evaporates? What does this imply?
2. Dip a cloth in water, wring it out, and hang it over a clothes hanger. Hook the clothes hanger on a scale or on one end of a balance. As the water evaporates, its weight will change noticeably. Have the children discuss other examples of water entering the air by evaporation.

---

[9] *Ibid.*, pp. 31-36.

3. Cover a geranium or coleus plant with a large wide-mouthed bottle, or wrap the entire plant in a clear plastic bag. Place the covered plant in a sunny spot; notice the drops of water that form inside the container. Green plants give off great quantities of moisture into the atmosphere.
4. Using a graduated cylinder or a measuring cup, pour equal amounts of water into a pie pan, a tumbler, and a soda bottle. Have children speculate on the length of time it will require for this much water to evaporate. Set all three containers aside where they will not be disturbed. Observe them each morning and afternoon. When the pie pan is dry, measure the amount of water left in the tumbler and the bottle. Did any water evaporate from the tumbler and the bottle? Why were the evaporation rates different?

Questions to Guide a Summary of Experiences

1. What is precipitation?
2. Why are clouds usually high in the sky?
3. What is evaporation?
4. Why haven't all the oceans evaporated in the past years?
5. What is the water cycle?

BASIC UNDERSTANDINGS TO BE GAINED FROM THIS UNIT

1. Water evaporates into invisible vapor.
2. When water vapor cools, it condenses into liquid.
3. Condensed water vapor falling to the ground is called precipitation.
4. Rain, snow, sleet, and hail are all forms of precipitation.
5. Some precipitation soaks into the ground, while some runs off into streams, lakes, and oceans.
6. Excessive precipitation causes great damage by erosion and flood.
7. The process of continuous evaporation and condensation is called the water cycle.

VOCABULARY

altitude	erosion	flood	surface water
atmosphere	evaporate	groundwater	vapor
condense	extreme	precipitate	water cycle

desert

Making Resource Units into Teaching Units

When the teacher chooses selectively from the resource unit science concepts, principles, processes, and learning activities appropriate for his particular class, he is designing his *teaching unit*. One of the most important elements in a teaching unit is a realistic and flexible chronological arrangement of the content, to be presented to children. This assignment of time is very individualistic for there is a wide range of opinion concerning the exact allotment of time for the length of units as well as for weekly and daily science activities.

Scheduling Time for Science.   Science units require a considerable amount of time to contribute in their field the values and content that other units of instruction (social studies, for instance) have made in theirs. A survey completed by the United States Office of Education in 1962 showed that a wide range of time allotment for science exists in America's schools. In the lower grades only a small percent of schools taught science as much as 200 minutes a week, but in the fifth through eighth grades a substantial percent of schools taught science more than 200 minutes a week. Figure 13 shows the average number of minutes per week devoted to science teaching in elementary schools with 400-700 enrollment.

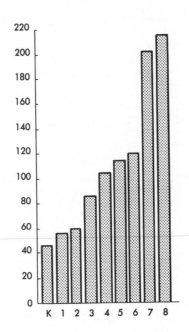

FIGURE 13. The Number of Minutes a Week Given to Science Teaching in Schools with 400-700 Enrollment.[10]

Different Patterns for Time Allotments.   The individual teacher's decision of large blocks of time allotted for science is influenced by these considerations:

1. How much time can I devote from my *total* elementary program for this science unit? (If only 4-6 broad science areas are selected annually, the teacher could devote 4-6 weeks to each unit. Attention span, maturation, interest of the class as well as other factors influence this decision.)
2. What, if any, are the *weekly* time requirements of your school for science? (If no specific requirements, many schools recommend a *minimum* of 120-180 minutes weekly, allocated as the teacher deems necessary and desirable. *DAILY EXPOSURE TO SCIENCE IS PREFERABLE FOR UNIT*

---

[10] Report of this survey appeared in: Paul E. Blackwood, "Science in the Elementary School," *School Life*, Vol. 47, No. 2 (November, 1964), pp. 13-15, 27-28.

STUDIES AS IT SUPPLIES REINFORCEMENT, CONTINUITY, IN-
TEREST, AND ACTIVE PARTICIPATION FOR CHILDREN'S
LEARNING.)

3. What, if any, are the *daily* time requirements of your school for science? (If no specific requirements, many schools recommend a *minimum* of 20-30 minutes for grades K-3 and 30-50 minutes for 4-6.)

The teacher's decision on *daily* science time allotment is *affected* by such things as:

1. His choice of science curriculum areas, content, and processes selected for teaching.
2. Whether science is taught as a separate subject or integrated with other curriculum areas.
3. The school policy and/or the interpretation of the teacher's immediate supervisor.
4. Whether the teacher is in a self-contained or departmental science program, or a combination using a science specialist.

How can you arrange time for your children to explore on their own?

In general, though, it appears more desirable for science to be taught daily and during large blocks of activity times. Science activities require more time than more sedentary activities like reading due to the time needed to set up and go over directions, have children actually work, and then clean up. Anyone who knows children realizes that it takes time to stimulate them to work on something; it is detrimental to the learning process, then, to stop in the middle of activities simply because the arbitrary allotment of time has run out. It would be unwise to arbitrarily set rigid periods of time to which *all* science lessons must adhere.

Following are three daily time schedules of the same fourth grade involved in the science unit of air, water, and weather included previously. Each day has its unique activities and the teacher has arranged his daily program in ways to best accomplish the daily goals.

1. *Single Large Block of Time for Science Lesson*

Time	Subject-matter Area	Minutes
9:00-10:00	*Science*—water evaporates into invisible vapor or gas (groups working on activities set up by teacher before school)	60
10:00-10:20	Clean-up	20
10:20-11:00	Reading (skill teaching)	40
11:00-11:30	Physical Education in gym	30
11:30-12:00	Music	30
12:00- 1:00	Lunch	60
1:00- 1:30	Arithmetic	30
1:30- 2:10	Language Arts (spelling and sentence structure).	40
2:10- 2:40	Art	30
2:40- 3:00	Clean-up and planning for next day	20

2. *Several Smaller Blocks of Time for Science Lesson*

Time	Subject-matter Area	Minutes
9:00- 9:20	*Science*—planning for walk around neighborhood for signs of weather and erosion damage	20
9:20-10:20	Reading skills	60
10:20-10:45	Recess	25
10:45-11:15	Arithmetic	30
11:15-12:00	Social Studies	45
12:00- 1:00	Lunch	60
1:10- 2:00	*Science*—neighborhood walk (taking pictures and noting weather and erosion damage)	50
2:00- 2:30	Spelling (vocabulary words from social studies and science)	30
2:30- 2:45	*Science*—brief evaluation of trip and suggestions for use of information gathered	15
2:45- 3:00	Clean-up and plans for next day	15

3. *Use of Whole Day for Science Lessons*

Time	Activity	Minutes
9:00- 9:30	*Science*—plan for the total day and give specific assignments to individuals and committees.	30
9:30-10:30	Reading skills-read books on weather obtained by teacher for different levels. Specific assignments are to find weather instruments and directions for building.	60
10:30-10:45	Recess	15
10:45-11:45	Work in committees for setting up a weather station—each group investigates different weather instruments from information found in books from reading time.	60

11:45-12:00	Read and correct each others letters of thank you to the weather station for the trip they took.	15
12:00- 1:00	Lunch	60
1:00- 1:30	See and discuss a motion picture about weather instruments, their use, construction, and weather forecasting.	30
1:30- 2:00	Music (not necessarily integrated)	30
2:00- 2:30	Total class plans together and makes rough draft of an outline for an original dramatization on weather to be presented in assembly for parents and other students.	30
2:30- 3:00	Make list of supplies that will be needed for constructing weather instruments. Make lists of new vocabulary words in science unit. Tomorrow put them into vocabulary books and find proper meaning and usage. Clean-up.	30

(*NOTE:* Although the whole day is devoted to science, other curricular areas are involved—reading, writing, spelling, discussion, etc. It should also be pointed out, that there will be times when science will *not* be included at all in this class' work.)

Now that the teacher has organized his resource unit into a teaching unit with weekly and daily assignments of concepts and learning activities, he must plan for each individual daily lesson.

Daily Lesson Plans

The specific way that a teacher prepares his lesson plans is as unique and personalized as the way he walks, dresses, and, of course, teaches. There are as many lesson plans as there are teachers. Why then should teachers bother to write plans?

Why Write Daily Lesson Plans?   The daily lesson plan is used to focus upon ways of achieving specific purposes within a given block of time utilizing specific, carefully chosen teaching-learning experiences and materials. Rarely, if ever, is teaching constantly at a level of excellence without some sort of planning by the teacher.

Plans force the teacher to crystallize her thinking into teachable activities. She is required to take her broad, general unit goals and objectives and write them down in daily, manageable specifics. Without daily plans, there is a tendency to ad-lib through the lessons; although some excellent, sporadic teaching may occur this way, little continuous, high quality teaching can be expected from this flighty approach.

Whether the teacher is new or experienced, she will derive considerable self-confidence when she goes into the classroom with a well planned lesson. By contemplating as many factors as she can *before* entering the classroom, she can minimize or eliminate potential discipline problems and learning difficulties.

Another value of written lesson planning is the building of a resource file from which to draw for future work in science. The teacher may not find these "used lesson plans" as fresh or applicable to each different class; however, the ideas and activities in the lesson plans would serve as a self-tested resource for the teacher.

What Goes into Daily Lesson Plans?   Regardless of the individual differences among lesson plans, these factors are usually considered by teachers before they write any science lesson plans:

1. What, if anything, do my children already know about the particular science content to be studied today?
2. What concepts and principles must they know *before* they can build these new concepts?
3. What are my children working on now that can lead into or enrich this lesson?
4. Where do I want my children to go next? What new concepts and principles will I include?
5. Have I selected the activities that are best suited for my goals or objectives?
6. Knowing my class, how much work can I realistically give them during this lesson?
7. What will I have ready to do for the children who finish before the others?
8. What will I do for those children who cannot function well enough to participate in this lesson?
9. Do I have all of the necessary materials available (in quantity needed and ready on time) for this particular lesson?
10. Do I understand the science principles involved and do I know how to perform all the activities in this lesson myself?
11. Have I included ways of checking and evaluating whether or not my children gained anything from this lesson?
12. What science and critical thinking processes will I stress in these lessons?

Writing Daily Lesson Plans.   The actual writing of plans and the amount of detail depend greatly upon the teacher's preference and experiences with planning, the administrative and supervisory requirements of his school, and other factors. Some teachers keep commercially prepared plan books covering all subject areas in brief outline form for each day; some teachers keep a running log; some devote a card or form for each daily curricular lesson. Regardless of the form selected, most carefully planned lessons contain these parts:

Suggested Format for Science Discovery-type Lesson Plan

Purposes: First find out how much of the material your children already know and then include a brief list of what you are hoping to have your class accomplish. Be specific and make your purposes realistic and attainable for your particular class.

Materials: Include all materials to be used by both teacher and children. The teacher should have used all materials, equipment, film, etc. before so that he will be thoroughly familiar with them and see the possible uses for each. Make certain that all materials and equipment are available and in good working condition before listing them for use in the lesson. Never count on anything being there ready for use unless you get it yourself and try it.

Procedures: List specific ways needed to arouse and maintain interest and include questions to be used for this purpose. Include specific activities to be done by the children themselves. Give somewhat of a sequential arrangement of the activities and make provisions for specific directions for individual and group activities. Provide opportunities for children who need special help. *Include thought-provoking questions to stimulate discovery-learning.*

Scheduling of Time: Include time estimates for the introduction and for the activities of the pupils including the evaluation and conclusions or generalizations. It is imperative that time be given to clean-up as this type of activity is more prevalent in science education studies. It can also develop responsibility in children.

Summary and Evaluation: Questions and activities for finding out if the children know what you have been teaching should be included in this section. Many of these items may appear under the other sections, especially procedures, because summarizing and evaluation are constantly going on during a lesson as a part of teaching.

Example of Daily Lesson Plan. Following is an example of the basic format for planning a daily lesson from this unit on weather for the fourth grade. Note that the plan is specific, practical, and very easy to follow. Attention is given throughout to concrete experiences to be done with and by the children. Stress is put on assisting the children in discovering concepts and relationships through careful, thought-provoking questions and direct sensory experiences. Because of its importance, the next chapter "Developing Discovery Questioning Techniques" is devoted to the role of thought-provoking questioning in the discovery approach.

The lesson plan presented here may be regarded as a traditional type of science lesson. The lessons described in Chapter 7 "Preparing and Guiding Discovery Laboratory Activities" and in Part Four "Discovery Laboratory Lessons" are more sophisticated. The laboratory lessons go beyond the conventional organization and are more detailed in the ways of stressing the processes and discovery techniques of teaching.

Daily Lesson Plan:
Air is Real and Occupies Space

Purposes

1. Acquaint children with these scientific phenomena:
    a. Air is real and occupies space.
    b. Air is colorless, tasteless, and odorless.
    c. Air is all around us.
    d. Living things need air.
2. Help children develop an understanding of living things and their dependence upon air.
3. Guide children's thinking through actual experimentation with simple materials and observation under the teacher's direction.
4. Provide supervised opportunities for children to have independent work which can teach self-responsibility and methods of working with people in groups.

Materials

One of each of the following for each child, except glass pans (six will be enough): polyethylene plastic bags (from shirts, food, etc.), water glasses, handkerchiefs, glass pans, safety matches, soda straws.

Procedures

1. For motivation and introduction, flatten an empty polyethylene plastic bag. Now fill the bag with apples and ask the children what is in it. How do you know there is

something in it? (Examples of answers: It bulges, you can feel it, etc.) Empty apples and fill bag with water. Again ask: Is anything in the bag now? How do you know? Empty water, open the bag wide, and move it through the air. Close the mouth of the bag by twisting after the bag has bulged. Now ask: What is in the bag? (Children of this age should answer *air*, but if not the teacher should suggest it.) Make it a point to establish what is real and how we can know if something is real. Although we cannot see, smell, or feel air, how are some other ways we might show that air is real and occupies space? If no suggestions come forth, the teacher can present the following experiments:

2. Turn a glass upside down and push the mouth as far as it will go in a pan of water. Why is the level of water in the glass lower than the water level in the pan? Why doesn't more water go into the glass? Tip the glass so one edge is above the water. Observe what happens. Why? [AIR OCCUPIES SPACE]

3. Have children put a clean, dry handkerchief in a drinking glass and invert into pan of water used in the preceding experiment. When the glass is removed, will the handkerchief be wet or dry? Why? (*Note:* The same experiment can be used by placing a safety match in the handkerchief before inverting it in the water and then striking the dry match after removing it from the glass. The teacher should strike the match. [AIR IS REAL AND OCCUPIES SPACE]

4. Capture air in the polyethylene bag and twist the mouth shut. Make sure air is staying in the bag. (*Hint:* If the air is coming out of small holes, just apply cellophane tape to the holes to seal immediately.) Place several heavy objects (such as books or pieces of wood) on the bag and be aware of what happens. Does the bag hold up the weight? Why? Ask if this knowledge has been put to any use for man's benefit (bicycle tires, inflatable rubber rafts, car tires, etc.) [AIR SUPPORTS OBJECTS]

5. Fill glass with water to overflowing and quickly place a piece of cardboard over it. Invert glass. What happens? Why? (*Caution:* Always perform this experiment over a pan or sink.)

6. Each child holds his finger over one end of a soda straw and immerses it in water. Water does not rise in straw. Why? Remove your finger and the water rises. Why? Put your finger back on the straw and move the straw out of the water. Why doesn't the water fall out? [AIR OCCUPIES SPACE AND EXERTS PRESSURE IN ALL DIRECTIONS]

7. After working the simple experiments and demonstrations himself with children taking part in the questioning and observing, the teacher will outline the procedure that will be used for children's participation. The teacher has set up six areas with materials at each for the performance of the experiments. The teacher has selected groups that will work together, and then he goes over the rules and regulations they all feel are necessary for conducting these experiments. When groups begin to work, a teacher should move about reassuring and helping his students. Directions given must be very clear and must be checked to see if they are understood.

8. Clean up quickly and quietly.

Evaluating

1. Discuss experiments and observations.
2. A report does not necessarily have to be devised so that children's observations can be shared and verified and checked, but there should be stress placed upon accuracy of observation.
3. Clues for future planning for the study can be obtained from the children either through direct questioning or as a result of the other evaluation techniques employed.
4. Teacher evaluation of the group activities should be done after the lesson is performed to ensure that the time was well spent. The teacher can obtain suggestions for improving the activities next time.

5. Teacher evaluation of the processes children actually performed should be noted.

Scheduling of Approximate Time (Total—75 minutes)
1. Introduction and motivation—5 minutes.
2. Teacher-conducted experiments and directions for group work—25 minutes.
3. Children-conducted experiments in groups at separate tables—25 minutes.
4. Cleaning up and replacing furniture—10 minutes.
5. Questioning and evaluation—10 minutes.

Note: Although the total lesson runs 75 minutes which is long for young children, the children engage in active physical participation after 30 minutes of relative passivity. The teacher sets up the six activity areas before children arrived at school.

Teacher's Guides in Textbooks

Elementary school science textbooks are another source of lesson planning for teachers. Each textbook comes with a Teacher's Guide which suggests lessons for teachers to accompany the textbook. If handled as suggestions instead of being used verbatim, these lessons can be useful, especially to inexperienced teachers or student teachers.

Teaching Tips—Lesson Planning

These tips will help the teacher in planning to teach science:

1. Selectively pick from resource unit those science concepts and activities, which will form your *teaching unit*.
2. Arrange your science concepts and activities into a sequence which is chronological and assign time spots for each day's work.
3. Write plans for each day's science lesson, using this general format:
   Objectives: Content and Processes (hypothesizing, comparing, inferring, controlling variables, etc.)
   Materials
   Procedures
   Time Schedule
   Summary
   Evaluation
4. Constantly assess during lesson what your children know and how well they are understanding the new concepts and processes being introduced.
5. Make provisions for children of all levels to participate in activities.
6. Have materials set up and ready to go *before* the lesson begins.
7. Always try activities yourself first before working with children.
8. Evaluate at end of lesson by asking yourself the questions raised by Paul Blackwood as follows:

How to Judge a Good Science Activity

1. Did the Activity involve the children in describing or explaining some phenomenon?

2. Did the children collect original data from which to draw conclusions?
3. Did the children organize and communicate about the data in useful ways?
4. Did the children have opportunities to speculate and predict?
5. Did the experiences relate clearly to development of major science concepts?
6. Were some questions raised that provided stimulation for further study?[11]

In addition to Blackwood's criteria for judging a good science lesson, you should consider these points:

1. Did the activity involve children in critical thinking and science processes?
2. Were sufficient opportunities provided for the creative potential of the children to be manifested?
3. Did the activities and the methods of presentation provide for the individual differences of the children?

How Do You Plan for Discovery Teaching?

Teaching science through discovery relies upon all of the elements of planning mentioned in this chapter. However, because this method stresses guiding the learner to learn for himself, it is vital that teachers develop specific skills in questioning techniques and preparing laboratory and demonstration activities. These skills in thought provoking questioning and laboratory activity preparation are relatively new for elementary school teachers. For that reason, these have been presented separately in Chapters 6 and 7 to give the reader extended discussion and examples. In Part Four, "Discovery Laboratory and Demonstration Lessons," the format and concepts of Chapters 6 and 7 for suggested use by teachers will be utilized.

Summary

Long range and daily lesson plans give the elementary school teacher flexible guides for selecting and planning science activities for his class. His selections of studies and activities should result in balanced science programs. This program should include a variety of activities based upon fundamental concept schemes and include the development of science processes. Content areas may be selected from state or local curriculum guides, experimental programs, or textbook series.

Teachers should limit themselves to only 6-8 broad science areas yearly, instead of many, small unrelated topics. This will allow children to study science areas in depth, making their learning more meaningful and retention of information better.

The unit structure of teaching science offers teachers an efficient and effective means of organizing science studies. Resource units are readily available and an

11 Paul E. Blackwood, "Science Teaching in the Elementary School," *Science and Children*, Vol. 2, No. 1 (September, 1964), p. 25.

aid to the teacher in building a teaching unit. Units can be gotten from state or local science guides (Appendix B), national science projects (see Appendix A), or from publishers of elementary science textbooks (see Appendix H).

After selecting appropriate science concepts and activities, the teacher should allocate time blocks for science each day. Daily written science plans will help the teacher in establishing well thought out activities for his class.

Teaching science through discovery generally requires some different emphases and techniques and will be discussed in depth in Chapter 6, "Developing Discovery Questioning Techniques," and Chapter 7, "Preparing and Guiding Discovery Laboratory Activities."

SELF-EVALUATION AND FURTHER STUDY

1. Select three current science curriculum guides from different states or school districts and concept charts from the publishers of three of the latest elementary school science textbooks. Compare curriculum guides and textbook charts to see similarities and differences in:
    a. Broad areas of science
    b. Concepts under each broad area
    c. Grade level of science concepts
    d. Science activities
    e. Process emphasis
2. Using Edgar Dale's "Cone of Experience" on page 95 select two science concepts and show examples for each of the activities on the cone for the particular science concept.
3. If you are teaching or student teaching in one class for an extended time, choose a resource unit selected from your state or local science curriculum guide, a national science project, the textbook series used in your school, or any other source. Plan a 4-6 week *teaching* unit for an elementary grade. Break your unit into approximately 20 teaching hours and include a variety of activities and different patterns of time usage.
4. If you are not teaching regularly, try to get permission from an elementary school teacher to teach one or two lessons in a science unit. Prepare plans for these lessons. What questions must you ask the teacher *before* planning for the lessons?
5. Select two national curriculum projects from Appendix A and compare them on criteria indicated in no. 1 above.
6. Select three units from those listed in Appendix A for the Elementary Science Study such as "Mealworms," "Gases and Airs," and "Kitchen Physics." Describe how you would use them in your science teaching.

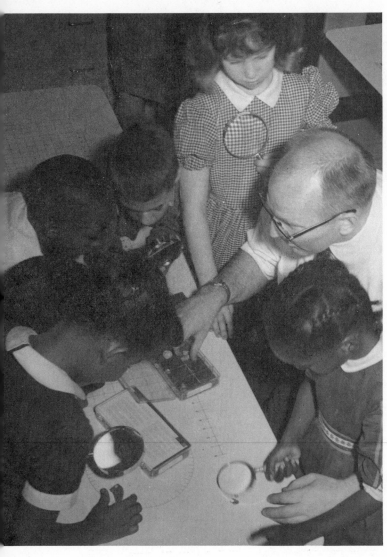

Most teachers rarely ask questions because they are curious to know what the pupil's think, believe, or have observed. And pupils adapt quickly to this situation; after a few years in school, answering questions is for them more a mind-reading proposition than a matter of reasoning about the substance of a problem.[1]

CHAPTER 6

DEVELOPING DISCOVERY QUESTIONING TECHNIQUES

The heart of teaching and learning science by discovery is in proper questioning which leads to the use of scientific processes for finding answers. Not only do teachers ask too many questions, more often than not they ask the *wrong* kinds of questions. Surveys indicate over 90 percent of all questions teachers ask require reproducing what has just been read, heard, or seen by children. These questions demand only the lowest level of thinking by children—memorization.

In Chapter 4, it was shown that one of the trends in new science programs is the stress on the *processes* of science along with the acquisition of scientific facts, concepts, and principles. It was pointed out that emphasis is placed on *finding answers* rather than merely on the answers themselves. The opening quotation by Karplus and Thier emphasizes that teachers' questions often do not stimulate children's problem-solving abilities.

Science Opportunities for Effective Questioning

In order to promote the development of science processes, stimulating teacher questions are a necessity!

Fortunately, the elementary school science programs abound with opportunities for the teacher to use exciting types of questions. All science activities should encompass areas of this nature:

1. Discussions
2. Laboratory experiences
3. Demonstrations
4. Student worksheets
5. Teacher-pupil evaluations
6. Films, filmstrips, and film loops
7. Field trips
8. Counter-intuitive Science Events
9. An Investigation to Discovery
10. Pictorial Science Riddles

Chapters 7 and 8 are devoted entirely to the selection, planning, and conduction of these activities with children, including the role of questioning. Because of this, only suggestions applicable to all broad science situations are included in this chapter.

---

[1] Robert Karplus and Herbert D. Thier, *A New Look at Elementary School Science* (Science Curriculum Improvement Study), New Trends in Curriculum and Instruction Series (Chicago: Rand McNally & Co., 1967), p. 86.

Planning Before Questioning

Before teachers begin their use of questioning with children, they should consider the following:

1. What is it I want to teach?
2. What do I expect to accomplish through questioning?
3. What types of questions could I ask?
4. How will I respond and use children's answers to questions?

Know What You Want to Teach

One of the most important considerations for planning effective questioning techniques is to know what it is you want your children to learn. The previous chapter on planning stressed identifying the specific science facts, concepts, principles, *and processes* before you begin to teach. Selection of questions will then follow from the goals and objectives you hope to guide children to achieve. There are levels of educational objectives in our science programs and these have been established in an extensive taxonomy by David Krathwahl and his associates:

Levels of Educational Objectives[2]

1. Knowledge	4. Analysis
2. Comprehension	5. Synthesis
3. Application	6. Evaluation

These levels indicate the depth of thinking needed, increasing in difficulty from 1. Knowledge to 6. Evaluation.

If teachers are to guide children toward the achievement of these objectives, teachers must develop corresponding levels of questioning:

Levels of Questioning[*]

1. *Knowledge*—Emphasizes memory, simple recall of:
   a. Classification
   b. Facts
   c. Definitions
   d. Generalizations—principles and concepts of science
   e. Values
   f. Processes—may know them but can't apply them
   g. Theories and structures
2. *Comprehension*—Knows what is being communicated and can:
   a. Explain in his own words meaning of what he has learned
   b. Translate information into different symbols
   c. Predict continuation of trends

---

[2] Levels of Educational Objectives and Levels of Questioning abstracted from material in David R. Krathwohl, Benjamin S. Bloom and Bertram B. Masia, *Taxonomy of Educational Objectives: The Classification of Educational Goals* (New York: David McKay Company, Inc., 1964), pp. 186-193. Reprinted by permission David McKay Company, Inc.

[*] *Ibid.*

3. *Application*—Uses abstractions to:
   a. Solve problem by applying concepts and principles previously learned
4. *Analysis*—Breakdown of a communication into its parts to:
   a. Investigate the parts and relationships
   b. Use inductive and deductive reasoning
   c. Compare and look for relevance
   d. Seek simple classification on elementary level
5. *Synthesis*—Putting together of elements and parts to form whole requires:
   a. Creative thinking
   b. Freedom to do divergent thinking
6. *Evaluation*—Quantitative and qualitative judgements using:
   a. Exactness of statements, observations, proof
   b. Comparison of theories, generalization
   c. Logical thinking

After establishing the levels of questioning, the question arises: Why do I ask children questions anyway?

Know Why You Ask Questions

Why do teachers ask children questions? One of the most important reasons is to find out what their pupils know and don't know. These questions are valid because they assist the teacher in planning and modifying his science program according to the needs, interests, and knowledge of his class. He can avoid going over what children already know or presenting material too difficult for their backgrounds.

In a similar vein, by knowing how his children are progressing on a lesson, the teacher can redirect or focus the questions he asks. Questions can then be utilized to keep the lesson relevant to the investigation at hand.

In addition to these points, teachers ask questions for the following reasons:

1. To arouse interest—motivating children to actively participate in lesson.

What questions might you ask to stimulate this child's interest about bones? How could you prepare for asking discovery questions?

2. To evaluate a pupil's preparation and to see if his homework or previous work has been mastered.
3. To review and summarize what is taught.
4. To develop insights by helping children see new relationships—discovery.
5. To stimulate critical thinking and development of questioning attitude.
6. To stimulate pupils to seek out additional knowledge and processes on their own.
7. To evaluate the achievement of goals and objectives of a lesson.

Types of Questions

Basically, questions in a science program may be included in two broad categories:

1. Evolutionary or serendipitous questions—*unplanned*.
2. Premeditated questions—*planned*.

Evolutionary or Serendipitous Questions—Unplanned

Evolutionary questions are of the kind that are asked spontaneously as the lesson evolves. They evolve moment by moment. Serendipitous questions refer to chance happenings that also pop up in a lesson as a result of some unforeseen and unplanned circumstance. For example, an experiment may "fail," a child may ask a question that leads in an entirely new direction, or the teacher may discover a new potentially productive path to pursue in the middle of this planned lesson. These unplanned questions may be more difficult to handle than planned ones. The teacher needs practice in dealing with these "on her feet."

How might an evolutionary question stimulate the growth of this display?

In science programs where active participation by children is encouraged, these unplanned questions appear more frequently. The teacher can establish a classroom environment that welcomes or squelches questions that go beyond his planned lessons. When things are happening or about to happen in science programs, many evolutionary and serendipitous types of questions arise.

Children's Questions—A Taxonomy

Nathan Washton has suggested it would be helpful for science teachers to develop a taxonomy of pupil's questions. A taxonomy is a set of classifications arranged and ordered on the basis of a single principle or set of principles. Figure 14 presents rudimentary classifications of pupil questions as an initial means of ultimately developing a taxonomy.

Classification of Question	Definition or Description	Example
1. Factual.	Low-level answered by reference book.	"What is speed of light?"
2. Related to scientific principles or laws.	Answered by statement of scientific law.	"Why does a rifle hit my shoulder as if going backwards as I pull the trigger and the bullet goes forward?"
3. Related to ability to transfer or make applications.	Transfer of knowledge.	"How does one explain the suggestion that on a very hot day and on a very long trip there should not be too much air in the automobile tires?"
4. Spontaneous.	Curiosity, chance happening, spur-of-the-moment.	"Can we speed up the amount of time it takes for a tadpole to become a frog?"
5. Problem solving.	Extension of transfer—identify, formulate plans, and solve problems.	A student on a camping trip has no cooking utensils, but would like to make hot chocolate. He has everything but something to heat the water in—except one paper cup.

FIGURE 14. Taxonomy of Pupil Questions[3]

Jean Piaget and Richard Suchman in different types of research designs have both pointed out the potentially creative aspects of children's questions and their utilization in elementary school science.

---

[3] Chart made from modified materials in Nathan S. Washton, "Teaching Science Creatively: A Taxonomy of Pupil Questions," *Science Education*, Vol. 51, No. 5 (December, 1967), pp. 428-431.

How has the teacher opened up channels of communication in this discovery demonstration?

Piaget and Children's Questions

Jean Piaget had advocated that much can be learned about how children think by asking careful, detailed questions. Questioning reveals how the child is thinking about a problem and what difficulty he is encountering in concept utilization. In one of Piaget's research designs he presented children with twenty-one pictures: three were ducks, four were birds but not ducks, four were animals that fly but not birds, seven were animals that do not fly, and three were inanimate objects. The children were asked to arrange the picture cards in piles so that the animals resembling each other were in the same pile. After performing this task, the children were asked the following specific questions:

> Suppose we were to put the cards into these three envelopes, each with its own label. This label says birds. Could we put this pile (ducks), and this pile (other birds) in the same envelope, and still keep this label?
>
> Now this label says animals. Could we put these (birds) in with these (animals that do not fly), and still keep the label, animals?
>
> Could we put these (animals that do not fly) in with these (birds other than ducks), and use the same label?

Next the children were asked:

> If all the ducks were killed, would there be any birds left?
> If all the birds were killed, would there be any ducks left?
> If all the animals were killed, would there be any birds left?[4]

The teacher asks the children to justify their responses after each question. For instance, if a child rejects the bird label for ducks, he is asked: "Aren't ducks birds?" If a child rejects the animal label for birds, the teacher asks: "Are not birds animals?"

---

[4] Jean Piaget and Babel Inhelder, *The Growth of Logical Thinking* (New York: Basic Books, Inc. 1958).

Each time the teacher probes with "Why not?" not only can the children benefit by being actively involved but the science teacher can learn much more about how the children are thinking about a problem and what specific difficulties they are having with the conceptualization process.

Two films are now available that will help the reader visualize these ideas. The films will also clarify the elements of Piaget's developmental theory hitherto difficult to grasp. Teachers will find these films useful in understanding the thought processes of children and the usefulness of proper questioning for diagnostic teaching purposes:

> *Classification,* 17 minutes, color
> *Conservation,* 28 minutes, color

For preview purposes, a five minute excerpt from *Conservation* may be obtained on request from the producer by writing to Davidson Films, 1757 Union Street, San Francisco, California 94123.

In *Conservation,* children between the ages of five and twelve are presented in individual interviews with tasks using Piaget's techniques. The tasks involve conservation of quantity, length, area, and volume. The four Piaget thought characteristics are identified from preoperational to formal operations. The tests are given and analyzed by Robert Karplus, Director of SCIS at Berkeley, California and Celia Stendler-Lavatelli of the University of Illinois at Urbana.

In *Classification,* further tasks are administered by Karplus and Stendler. Each task highlights a different mental operation essential to classification, such as multiple classification, class inclusion, and hierarchical classification.

Suchman—Children Question Teacher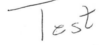

Richard Suchman's research is unique in that it is one of the few where *children* question the *teacher*, instead of the teacher questioning children. In this research, a set of 25 color films were made in 8 mm cartridges, each presenting puzzling events which students attempt to explain. The films are silent and do not contain any captions; for this reason, the films can be used by any grade although they have been suggested mainly for the upper elementary grades. The problem films are the endless-loop cartridge type and the titles are:

1. The Stalled Car	14. The Diving Bottle
2. The Cannon	15. The Knife
3. The Baseball Catcher	16. Drinking Boiling Coffee
4. The Man and the Dumbbell	17. The Spring
5. The Five Pendulums	18. The Amusement Park
6. The Ice Cubes	19. The Pendulum and the Peg
7. The Balloon in the Jar	20. The Man and the Wheel
8. The Restaurant	21. The Eight Pendulums
9. The Train and the Track	22. Boiling by Cooling
10. The Spring Carts	23. Puck on a String
11. Walking	24. The Long Pendulum
12. The Sailboat and the Fan	25. The Shrinking Balloon
13. The Wrenches	

One of the problem film loops is shown to children. This is a description of the Inquiry Session (Suchman's name for the thinking session that follows the film) ground roles:

> After seeing the problem event, the students attempt to construct a reasonable theory to account for it. They usually do this by making a guess at a theory and then gathering data to test it. The bulk of the inquiry session is normally devoted to data-gathering questions raised by the students and answered by the teacher.

Inquiry sessions are conducted under these simple rules:

1. The questions should be phrased in such a way that they can be answered *yes* or *no*.
2. Once called upon a student may ask as many questions as he or she wishes before yielding the floor.
3. The teacher does not answer *yes* or *no* to statements of theories, or to questions that attempt to obtain the teacher's approval of a theory.
4. Any student can test any theory at any time.
5. Any time the students feel a need to confer with one another without the teacher's presence, they should be free to call a conference.
6. Inquirers should be able to work with Experimental Kits, Idea Books or Resource Books at any time they feel the need.[5]

Following is a portion of an Inquiry Session reported by Suchman in his early research. The session dealt with the film "Ball and Ring Demonstration," in which

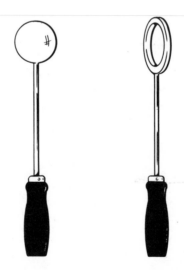

FIGURE 15. Ball and Ring Apparatus

a brass ball just fitting through a brass ring is heated. An unsuccessful attempt is then made to pass the ball through the ring. Figure 15 shows the ball and ring apparatus used in this inquiry session.

[5] J. Richard Suchman, *Putting Inquiry into Science: Learning-Inquiry Development Program* (Chicago: Science Research Associates, Inc., 1966), p. 4.

BALL AND RING INQUIRY SESSION

PUPIL: Were the ball and ring at room temperature to begin with?
TEACHER: Yes.
PUPIL: Would the ball go through the ring at first?
TEACHER: Yes.
PUPIL: After the ball was held over the fire, it did not go through the ring?
TEACHER: No.
PUPIL: If the ring had been heated instead of the ball, would the results have been the same?
TEACHER: No.
PUPIL: If both had been heated would the ball have gone through then?
TEACHER: That all depends.
PUPIL: If they both had been heated to the same temperature, would the ball have gone through?
TEACHER: Yes.
PUPIL: Would the ball be the same size after it was heated as it was before?
TEACHER: No.
PUPIL: Could the same experiment have been done if the ball and ring were made out of some other metal?
TEACHER: Yes.[6]

Premeditated Questions

Although the unplanned evolutionary and serendipitous questions are important in science education, little true, long range, creative teaching-learning is possible on such a hit-and-miss basis. Premeditated or planned questioning is essential for a starting point in a creative discovery science program.

Planned questions may be of two kinds—those developing science *facts, concepts, principles* and those developing science *processes*. The former questions have been termed *convergent* questions. The latter questions have been termed *divergent* questions.

Convergent Questions Move Toward Closure

Some questions cause children to move toward closure or to summarize and draw conclusions. They are called *convergent questions*. Guilford's definition of *convergent* is "Arriving at a recognized best or conventional answer from known and remembered information."[7] Recall questions fall into this category. There is only *one* answer. Although their importance is limited, convergent questions are nevertheless necessary. This was pointed out in Chapter 3 when Robert Gagné was quoted as cautioning that discovery could be undertaken only after the individual acquired a storehouse of broad and critical knowledge.

---

[6] Richard J. Suchman, "Inquiry Training in the Elementary School," *Science Teacher*, No. 27 (November, 1960), p. 42.

[7] J. P. Guilford, "Three Faces of Intellect," *American Psychologist*, 14 (1959).

What kinds of questions could the teacher have asked to get these children so involved and interested?

It has been said that convergent thinking processes help the person know what exists. When convergent questions are overused, however, more advanced and creative thinking is inhibited. An excess of convergent, stimulus-response questioning can be destructive to the development of process thinking in science. This is why these questions are referred to as unproductive. They rarely lead to further investigation, but only to closure, summary, or conclusions.

Divergent Questions Are Open-ended

Some questions, on the other hand, cause children to ask further questions, plan and carry out experiences with science equipment, and do library or other research. These are called *divergent* or *productive questions. Divergent* has been defined by Guilford as "Arriving at variety of unique responses not completely determined by known and remembered information."[8] Divergent questions go further than convergent questions. They stimulate the learner to find out what is to be. The learner is encouraged to broaden or deepen the area to be studied. He is required to gather facts, evaluate them, and to engage in higher creative thinking processes in order to answer divergent questions. Because of this broadening effect of divergent questions, they are referred to as open-ended or productive questions.

"Why do you suppose this is so?" is a divergent question. Children attempting to answer this type of an open-ended, divergent question will have to engage in these activities:

1. Collecting many more scientific facts, concepts, principles.
2. Engaging in discussions about the evidence gathered.
3. Giving ideas and opinions based on the evidence.
4. Evaluating the ideas and opinions given.
5. Coming up with answers to the question based upon the evidence and processes followed.

[8] *Ibid.*

There is a wide range of divergent questions. Some may be much narrower in scope and more concrete and pertain to an observation in an experiment or demonstration. The following classroom example is of that type.

Look At

Classroom Sample—Convergent and Divergent Questions

This is a record of a classroom using the Science Curriculum Improvement Study Program (SCIS). Questions marked with a "C" indicate convergency. Notice how they call for simple recall, definition, observation, and other simpler thinking processes. Questions marked with a "D" indicate divergency. Notice that they call for describing properties of bean pods ("How are the beans alike? different?"), checking on accuracy of observations ("How do you know?"). They are, however, focused upon the concrete, immediate experience.

> *Variation in Number of Beans in Bean Pods:* In a second grade classroom, the teacher introduced an activity on the variation of the number of beans in a collection of bean pods (those found in a can) by opening the can, removing the beans, and giving each child three beans. The following discussion takes place.

TEACHER:	*How are the beans alike?* (D)
PUPIL:	All sort of fat.
PUPIL:	Skinny.
PUPIL:	They have seeds in them.
TEACHER:	*How do you know?* (D)
PUPIL:	I can see in the little hole.
PUPIL:	They have lines (continuing with "how are they alike").
PUPIL:	None have holes.
PUPIL:	Have juice.
PUPIL:	Mine are squiggly.
PUPIL:	Smell good.
PUPIL:	All have points on end.
TEACHER:	*How are they different?* (D)
PUPIL:	One has a circle here and others have points on the ends.
TEACHER:	*What do you mean, "here?"* (C)
PUPIL:	On the end.
PUPIL:	One is light green, one is dark green, and one is very dark green.
TEACHER:	*There is a difference in color, then.*
PUPIL:	This one is bumpy and this is not.
PUPIL:	One has a seed at the end.
PUPIL:	Mine has a little part that is broken off.
PUPIL:	One is squishy.
PUPIL:	Some are dry and some are wet.
PUPIL:	Some are rough and some are smooth.
PUPIL:	They have different lengths.
TEACHER:	*How much different? How many found their beans to be different lengths.* (C) (About ⅓ did.) *Is there as much difference in length as with pea pods we used before?* (C)[9]

---

[9] Karplus and Thier, *op. cit.*, p. 87.

After the teacher has asked questions, how will he handle the answers? How he responds to children's answers is as important as the questions he asks.

Know How to Respond to Children's Answers

The way in which the teacher handles children's answers to questions helps to set the atmosphere and establishes the ground rules for his discovery science program. If the teacher fishes for only *one* right answer, he will effectively close down pupil participation considerably. A constant diet of this right-wrong, yes-no, stimulus-response questioning usually results in most children "tuning-out" completely in future guessing games. Few of us like to put our egos on the line or expose ourselves to public ridicule in front of our peers in such games as, "Let's try to guess what teacher is looking for." This handling of answers leads to dead ends; it defeats our intent of encouraging children to think creatively, enter into discussion, and probe deeper into the area being investigated.

Reward and Punishment

Teachers also use answers to questions as reward and punishment and for disciplinary purposes. All of us have observed the teacher who overuses the following potentially damaging responses to children's answers to their questions:

1. "You haven't studied, have you?"
2. "You weren't listening, were you?"
3. "That's wrong!"
4. "I knew you didn't know the answer when I called on you."
5. "You can bet Charlie never has the right answer."
6. "That's wrong. Write the correct answer five times tonight. Next time you'll listen."

The potential dangers of disciplinary use of answers to questions are well stated:

> The teacher that follows this procedure not only destroys the morale of the child he focuses upon, but also raises sincere doubts in the minds of the other children as to the sincerity of the teacher when he says he wants them to investigate, discover, and freely express their findings. Questions can be used productively in a disciplinary way only if they are intended to focus or redirect the attention of children upon the problem being considered.[10]

Implication for Planning Science Questioning

How can the elementary school science teacher weld together the ideas presented here into a usable teaching model? The chart in Figure 16 brings many of the ideas presented in this chapter into a graphic summary.

---

[10] John W. Renner and William B. Ragan, *Teaching Science in the Elementary School* (New York: Harper & Row, Publishers, 1968), p. 223.

CONCEPT FORMATION

OVERT ACTIVITY	COVERT MENTAL OPERATION	ELICITING QUESTION
1. Enumeration and listing.	Differentiation.	What did you see? Hear? Note?
2. Grouping.	Identifying common properties, abstracting.	What belongs together? On what criterion?
3. Labeling, categorizing.	Determining the hierarchical order of items; super- and sub-ordination.	How would you call these groups? What belongs under what?

INTERPRETATION OF DATA

1. Identifying points.	Differentiation.	What did you note? See? Find?
2. Explaining items of identified information.	Relating points to each other; Determining cause-and-effect relationships.	Why did so-and-so happen?
3. Making inferences.	Going beyond what is given; Finding implications, extrapolating.	What does this mean? What picture does it create in your mind? What would you conclude?

APPLICATION OF PRINCIPLES

1. Predicting consequences; Explaining unfamiliar phenomena; Hypothesizing.	Analyzing the nature of the problem or situation; Retrieving relevant knowledge.	What would happen if . . .?
2. Explaining, supporting the predictions and hypotheses.	Determining the causal links leading to prediction or hypothesis.	Why do you think this would happen?
3. Verifying the prediction or hypothesis.	Using logical principles or factual knowledge to determine necessary and sufficient conditions.	What would it take for so-and-so to be true or probably true?

FIGURE 16. Science Teaching-Learning and Questioning[11]

Hilda Taba in the chart in Figure 16 has three cognitive tasks—Concept Formation, Interpretation of Data, and Application of Principles. She has presented several levels of overt activity and covert mental operations for each cognitive task. By referring to the chart you can see that:

---

[11] Chart modified from one appearing in Hilda Taba, "Strategy for Learning," *Science and Children* (September 1965), pp. 21-24.

1. *Concept Formation* deals with organizing specific information into conceptual systems (involves grouping, categorizing, etc.).
2. *Interpretation of Data* deals with developing generalizations and inferences.
3. *Application of Principles* deals with explanation of unfamiliar phenomena, predicting, hypothesizing.
4. *Overt Activity* deals with specific observable behavioral actions of students.
5. *Covert Mental Operation* deals with specific thinking processes.
6. *Eliciting Question* deals with specific questions pertinent to each task and designed to trigger the overt activities and convert mental operations.

The presentation on this chart of *specific* overt activities, covert mental operations, and especially the eliciting of questions should aid elementary teachers in viewing the role of questioning in their science programs. The additional specific suggestions which follow can help improve questioning techniques.

Specific Techniques for Improving Your Questioning Skills

1. Write down specific wording of 6-8 questions in your lesson plan *before* coming into class.
2. Ask your question as simply, concisely, and directly as possible. Avoid such unnecessary introductions as, "What do you think about . . . ," "How many of you can tell me . . . ," etc.
3. Ask your question *before* designating which child should answer. Pause briefly after asking question so that all children have time to think about the question.
4. Ask an individual child to respond to your question. Total class shouting out of answers could result in classroom discipline problems for the teacher.
5. Ask questions of as many children as possible during the science lesson: volunteers and non-volunteers, slow and bright, etc. Suit the difficulty to each child's interest, science background, and abilities.
6. Ask a question about the most obvious part of the investigation for your first question. Such a question might be, "How much weight did the hamster gain since last week?"
7. Ask as many questions that stimulate creative thinking processes as possible using the following words in the question:

   a. Compare
   b. Summarize
   c. Observe
   d. Classify (group)
   e. Interpret
   f. Criticize
   g. Make assumption ⎫ involves analysis
   h. Collect and organize data
   i. Evaluate
   j. Apply

8. Ask questions that require children to use the thought processes involved in science:

a. Designing an investigation.	*Ask:* How would you find out?
b. Hypothesizing or predicting.	*Ask:* What do you think will happen?
c. Making operational definitions.	*Ask:* How would you define that?
d. Evaluating scientific procedure.	*Ask:* If you were to redo the experiment, how would *you* insure more accurate results?

9. Ask questions in a variety of ways in addition to "what," "how," "why," so that students are asked to:

a. Illustrate or show how	f. Interpret
b. Explain	g. Evaluate
c. Discuss	h. Contrast
d. Justify	i. Summarize
e. Trace	

10. Ask questions that lead to actual experimentation on children's part, because of the unique situation presented or the methods used to solve the problem. These questions contribute to open-endedness:
   a. (Present a discrepancy in an anticipated outcome to excite curiosity, then ask:) Why does the juice plop out of the can with only one hole, instead of running out?
   b. (Ask questions that suggest a possible test for solution, such as:) How are these metals affected by this magnet? Which metals are attracted by your magnet?
11. Ask questions that are specific rather than too broad or general.
   Poor Example: How do seeds sprout?
   Better: What conditions are necessary for seeds to sprout?
12. To avoid the possibility of frustration in "how" questions, ask questions that direct children to the variables and changing conditions of the experiment, such as:
   What do you think will happen if we . . .
   Will it work more or less quickly with . . .
   What might we do if we want this one to . . .
   Can anyone think of a way we might work to get the plant to . . .[12]
13. *Avoid* asking the following types of questions because they inhibit investigation and tend to be unscientific:
   a. Yes *and* No *types of questions*—use questions that ask children to engage in more creative and interesting thinking.
       Poor Example: How do seeds sprout?
       Better: How are these trees alike and different?
   b. *Teleological questions*—(this means use of design or purpose as an ex-

---

[12] For additional information on importance of questioning in science see Ben B. Strasser, "Posing Productive Questions," *Science and Children*, Vol. 4, No. 7 (April, 1967), p. 10.

planation of natural phenomena). This is the same as saying: Why does nature have the end in mind not to have a vacuum? The reason why this type of question is poor is that it tends to close possibilities for investigations and suggests that nature has a mind.

> *Poor Example:* Why does nature abhor a vacuum?
> *Better:* Why is it so difficult to maintain a vacuum?

c. *Anthropromorphic questions*—(this means giving human qualities to phenomena).

> *Poor Example:* Why do electrons *want to* leave the metal?
> *Better:* What causes the electrons to move? (After all, as far as we know, electrons are not capable of wanting.)

d. *Vague, indefinite questions.*

> *Poor Example:* Tell us about light.
> *Better:* What are some of the characteristics of light?

e. *"Tooth-pulling" questions.*

> *Poor Example:* Come on, you can think of a third kind of acid.
> *Better:* We seem to have difficulty thinking of a third acid. What kind of acid did we find in the orange juice we tested?

f. *Statements that suddenly turn into a question.*

> *Poor Example:* The growth of your plants with fertilizer since last month was what?
> *Better:* How much have your plants with fertilizer grown since last month?

g. *A battery of questions.*

> *Poor Example:* What is weather, how is it different from climate, and how can a weather map help predict it?
> *Better:* What are some of the elements that make up weather?

h. *Asking for information children cannot be expected to know.*

What might these children have learned about scientific method as they prepared their display?

> *Poor Example:* How does a Geiger counter work?
> *Better:* If charged particles like protons go into the Geiger counter tube, what happens in the Geiger counter to alert us to this?

    i. *The answer is obvious and a foregone conclusion.*

14. Avoid repeating children's answers to questions unless they could not be heard.

15. Avoid structuring your question too rigidly. This could lead to a type of stimulus-response situation, which stifles creative thinking.

16. Three teaching devices that can help you develop your skills in questioning are:

    a. An Invitation to an Investigation—A Discussion Technique

    b. Counter-intuitive Science Events

    c. Science Pictorial Riddles

How to Construct and Use an Invitation to Discovery—A Discussion Technique

Invitation to Discovery involves students in the processes of solving a problem worked on by scientists. A typical Invitation presents a problem to the student and through carefully designed questions invites him to devise an experiment, make hypotheses, draw conclusions from data, interpret data, or understand the factors involved in the problem. Invitations can be written for various levels of learning. They can be designed either in written form for children to read and write their answers or they can be performed orally as a discussion technique with small groups or the total class. Here is a sample of the discussion technique of an Invitation to Discovery:

How May the Wilting of Transplanted Plants Be Prevented?

The first part of an invitation states a problem and gives information about it.

Read this section aloud to the class.

A home gardener transplanted ten tomato plants, which were twelve inches high, from a propagating box to a vegetable garden in his back yard. He loosened the soil and pulled each plant out and then planted it in his garden. To do this he made a hole, put the plant roots in it, filled in around them with soil, and patted down the soil. He watered them all and repeated watering them each day. The first day the plants were transplanted, they began to wilt. The following day the leaves on all the plants were shriveled and collapsed. For five days after planting there was no sign of growth and the shriveled leaves dried up. On the sixth day after planting, small shoots appeared on the stems of seven of the tomato plants; the shoots developed into leaves. The seven plants continued to grow but the other three plants died.

Ask:

Why do you think some of the plants lived while the others died?

Ask:	How do you think the wilting of the tomato plants might have been prevented?
Ask:	What do you think was the main cause for the wilting of the tomato plants?
Ask:	How could you test your hypothesis?
Read to the Class: In this section further information is given to the students.	A week after the gardener planted the first tomatoes, he decided to plant ten more. This time, however, he pinched off all but three leaves from his young plants before transplanting them.
Ask:	Why do you think the gardener pinched off some of the leaves?
More information is given:	When he transplanted the tomato plants this time, nine of the plants wilted slightly but one lost its leaves and eventually died.
Ask:	Why do you think the plants still wilted?
Ask:	Why do you think one of the plants died?
Ask:	Was the gardener's idea of pinching off the leaves to prevent wilting verified by what happened in the second planting?
Ask:	In order for the gardener to be right, shouldn't he show that one of the plants wilted? Why?
Ask:	If you were to transplant plants, what would you do to attempt to avoid wilting? How would you go about proving your hypotheses?[13]

Practice writing one or two Invitations to Discovery using the science topics studied in your class. The steps to follow are:

1. Select your science content and process objectives.
2. Design a problem related to your objectives. Ideas for problems may come from current science magazines or may be modified to fit elementary school from Joseph J. Schwab, *et al., Biology Teachers' Handbook* (New York: John Wiley & Sons, Inc., 1963).
3. *Devise questions which provide opportunities for designing experiments; making hypotheses; analyzing, recording, and synthesizing data.*
4. Write each Invitation as a series of steps. Additional information should be inserted at different steps to aid student progress into higher processes.

How to Construct and Use Counter-intuitive Science Events

Counter-intuitive events in science are events which seem to go against your intuitions of how things really should happen. The most obvious counter-intuitive event would be dropping an object and seeing it rise in the air when all the clues indicate it should fall. These events may be presented to children in the form of a

---

[13] This Invitation was modified from one performed with children by Yolanda Clay while she was in teacher-training at the University of Hawaii.

What planning and preparation went on before this activity could be set up?

demonstration, laboratory activity, or a pictorial riddle. They generally will be followed by a discussion in which carefully designed questions can guide children to discover what happened in the event and why. Following are examples of counter-intuitive events which are rich in potential questions for developing thinking processes in children.

1. Fill a large graduate cylinder with water and three moth balls. A small amount of mossy zinc is placed on the bottom and some concentrated NCL is added. The moth balls continually go up and down.

2. Attach two pendulums on a single string. Set one in motion. Soon the other one will begin to swing and the first one will stop. The cycle is then repeated.

3. Fill two beakers with water, add a teaspoon of salt to one. Boil both and take the temperature of each. You will get a difference in boiling points.

4. A beaker of water, a beaker of alcohol, and a beaker with mixture of water and alcohol are placed side by side. An ice cube is placed in each of the three beakers. The ice cube floats, sinks, and is partially suspended—in that order—in the three beakers.

5. Obtain a large cork. Place a couple of drops of water on top of it. Then place a thin watch glass on top of the cork. Fill the watch glass with ether. The water will freeze.

6. Place a small beaker containing water on a small block of wood with a few drops of water in between the wood and beaker. Add ammonium nitrate and stir. The beaker will freeze to the block of wood.

7. Look through a crystal of calcite. See double images.

8. Stare at a picture for a while and then remove the picture. You still see the image or picture.

9. How does water get to the top of trees?

10. Crumple some paper into a ball. Drop it and a book from the same height onto a table or floor. They both hit the table or floor at the same time.

11. Tightly wrap the lower end of a thermometer with black cloth. Do the same to another thermometer using white cloth. Place both thermometers in the sun and observe the temperatures. There will be differences in the temperatures.

12. Insert a needle through the center of a small, thin, square of cardboard. Place a spool on the cardboard with the center hole over the needle. Holding the card in place with one hand, and the spool with the other, blow into the top of the spool. Release the hand holding the cardboard after you have started to blow. The cardboard will not fall.

13. Attach a piece of string to a paper clip. Hold one end of the string in your hand.

With the other hand, bring a magnet close to the paper clip so that it is suspended in air but not touching the magnet.

How to Construct and Use Pictorial Science Riddles

A pictorial riddle is a riddle presented to individual students or the class in picture form. The riddles generally illicit good student response if they depict some discrepant event. A *discrepant event* is one in which there is an inconsistency between what can reasonably be expected to happen in a given situation and what is depicted as happening. Pictorial riddles are pictorial counter-intuitive events. Riddles can be made by preparing diagrams or using pictures taken from magazine articles, photographs, or Polaroid pictures. The riddles may be drawn on the chalkboard, on transparency paper for use in overhead projectors, placed on poster board or on cardboard cards to be used in a file of riddles that students can go through on their own.

Riddles can illustrate an actual situation or a situation which has been altered and the students are to state what is wrong with what they see. In the first example here, the riddle shows an actual discrepant event. In the second example, the riddle presents a situation which is unrealistic or atypical and the pupils are supposed to tell what is wrong with it.

Pictorial riddles offer the teacher excellent opportunities for practicing questioning techniques. The teacher can focus upon *specific* aspects of the discrepant event for his questions that guide creative thinking in children. Suggested beginning questions are presented in each pictorial riddle here, but teachers can quickly add to these thought-provoking ones of their own. It is recommended that questions focus upon specific phenomena in the riddle and not general or broad ones.

PICTORIAL SCIENCE RIDDLES

WHY ARE THE RUBBER PLUNGERS DIFFICULT TO PULL APART?

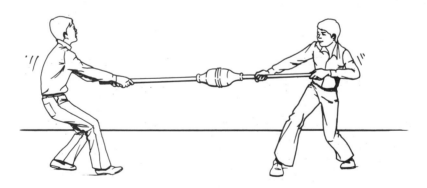

Ask: Why are the two young men having difficulty pulling the plungers apart?

Teacher's Note: The air pressure on the inside and outside of the rubber plungers is unequal. The air pressure (about 14.7 lbs. per square inch at sea level) on the outside is greater than the pressure inside because the cups have been partially evacuated. This unequal pressure causes the plungers to stay together. Since there are several square inches of surface on each of the plungers, each inch with about 14.7 pounds of pressure exerted on it, it takes a force greater than the two boys can exert to pull the plungers apart.

WHERE DOES SMOKE GO?

(3-5 Grade Level)

Ask: What is wrong with the picture?

What do you notice about the smoke? What are the properties of smoke?

Teacher's Note: Smoke consists of small particles, condensed water, and gases. Since the smoke is hot and is made of expanded gases, generally it is less dense than the air. It would, therefore, not fall but rise.

Ask: Where in our classroom is it the hottest, the coldest?

How would you find out?

Teacher's Note: The children could take a thermometer and place it in various parts of the room to collect readings. They should find out from this that the air (gas) may have different temperatures at different places and that it is hottest near the ceiling.

Ask: What conditions would have to exist for the smoke to fall?

Teacher's Note: Convection currents of cold air moving down over the smoke may cause it to alter its normal path.

WHAT HAPPENS TO A ROCK AND A CORK WHEN PLACED IN WATER?

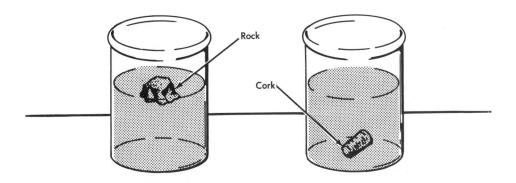

Ask: What is wrong with the diagram? Under what conditions could this happen?
What are the properties of things that float and of those things that sink?
Which of the following things would float in water: a board, nail, balloon, an
empty tin can, a filled tin can?
Why is a steel ship able to float?

Teacher's Note: The children should be able to point out that some things float
and other things sink: Rocks generally do not float (pumice is an exception since
it is filled with little air pockets), whereas a cork can float. A substance whose
density is less than that of water will float.

Summary

Proper questioning leads to using scientific processes for finding answers. This is
the heart of the discovery approach to science teaching. Science process as well
as science content questions should therefore be asked.

There are numerous opportunities in a science program to use stimulating
questions: discussions, laboratory experiences, demonstrations, student worksheets, etc.

Before entering the classroom, teachers should know specifically what they want
to teach, why they ask questions, what types of questions they want to ask, and
the responses they will accept. What they teach is influenced by levels of educational objectives, which in turn structure levels of questioning.

Teachers ask questions to find out what students do and don't know, to arouse
interest, to evaluate pupil progress, to review and summarize, etc. Children's
questions are potential sources for furthering creative thinking. Evolutionary or
serendipitous questions are unplanned and spontaneous.

Premeditated or planned questions are the basis for teaching science through
discovery. Convergent planned questions are non-productive because they lead to
summary or closure and consist primarily of recalled, memorized material. Divergent questions are open-ended and cause children to ask further questions, to
plan and carry out further investigations.

Teacher responses to children's answers are very important. The teacher sets the
atmosphere for questioning by the way he accepts and rejects answers. The elementary teacher can organize the questioning in his science program around three
cognitive tasks: concept formation, interpretation of data, and application of data.
A chart and specific tips on using questions in the science program are presented.

Teachers are especially cautioned *not* to use these types of questions:

1. "Yes" and "No"
2. Teleological
3. Anthropromorphic
4. Vague, indefinite
5. "Tooth-pulling"

Detailed activities are presented for teachers to practice questioning in *An Invitation to Discovery, Counter-intuitive Science Events,* and *Pictorial Science Riddles.* In a short while, teachers can improve their techniques of questioning.

SELF-EVALUATION AND FURTHER STUDY

1. Keep a running account of unplanned questions that arise in your classroom or in a class you are observing. Categorize them into two classifications—evolutionary and serendipitous.
2. Record and classify children's questions in six science lessons according to the Taxonomy of Pupil Questions on page 117.
3. Prepare a critical analysis of the studies of Piaget and Suchman, referred to in this chapter, in relation to the role of questioning in the discovery approach to science teaching.
4. Secure the needed materials and conduct an inquiry training session with children. See pages 119-20 for source of further information on this type of activity.
5. Conduct a questioning session with small groups of children using Piaget's twenty-one pictures. Tape record the session(s) if possible for further analysis of children's thinking. See footnote number 4 for further information on Piaget's research. If possible, view the films on *Classification* and *Conservation* mentioned on page 119 for additional information on how to conduct a Piaget task session with children.
6. Tape record your own teaching or take notes on another teacher's science lessons. Analyze the teacher's questions and mark "D" for each divergent question and "C" for each convergent question, as done in example on page 123.
7. Work with a group of children to improve their ability to ask productive questions. Have the children keep a record of questions asked and work out a set of criteria to evaluate these questions at the end of several lessons.
8. Devise an *Invitation to Discovery* for a class of children. Refer to sources mentioned in this chapter for a story situation and format that can be followed. If children are mature enough and have sufficient science background, have them write an Invitation individually or together with you.
9. After children have had some experience with them, ask children to write *Counter-intuitive Science Events* using their imaginations and scientific backgrounds. Have them write what can reasonably be expected to happen in their event so that you can see if they understand the scientific principles involved.
10. Present Pictorial Science Riddles to children on an overhead projector. After children develop some competency in seeing the discrepant events, have *them* draw or cut out pictures from magazines to design their own riddles.

... *In dividing the labor of scientific instruction, the laboratory typically carries the burden of conveying the method and spirit of science, whereas the textbook and teacher assume the burden of transmitting subject-matter content* ...[1]

CHAPTER 7

GUIDING DISCOVERY LABORATORY EXPERIENCES: EXPERIMENTS AND DEMONSTRATIONS

Laboratory experiences include science activities in which children *actively* participate in obtaining information and gathering data and evidence needed in solving a problem. These experiences for the elementary school are quite different from those typically associated with the term "laboratory" as used in high school or college. Elementary school laboratory experiences generally do not require expensive facilities such as special science rooms, costly materials, or complicated equipment. Regular classroom facilities often can be used as can be seen from this example of a first grade class participating in a laboratory experience.

> Each pupil has on his desk an assortment of objects, ten or twelve in number: bits of metal, paper, wood, plastic, and stone. He has collected these during a trip or object hunt around the school grounds. The problem is to manipulate the objects and discover different bases for grouping them. As the teacher looks over their shoulders, he finds that one pupil has divided his collection into three piles: bulky objects in one group, small ones in another, and medium-sized ones in a third. Another pupil has divided his objects into two piles, one of heavy objects, one of light objects. And one little girl has discovered that her objects can be classified according to color, light or dark, and according to surface texture, rough or smooth—and she's now separating them into piles of metal, paper, wood, plastic, glass, and stone.[2]

Laboratory experiences involve children in these fundamental objectives of science for the elementary school:

1. Development of scientific facts, concepts, principles, and skills.
2. Development of scientific processes and problem-solving activities.
3. Development of scientific attitudes and habits involving: accurate observation; record keeping and communication; care of apparatus; preparation, use, safe handling, proper cleaning and storing of materials.

As indicated in Chapter 3, Jean Piaget has found that *direct physical experience*, either through experimentation or demonstration, is essential for readiness for

---

[1] David P. Ausubel, "Some Psychological Considerations in the Objectives and Design of an Elementary-School Science Program," *Science Education*, Vol. 47, No. 3 (April, 1963), p. 284.

[2] Robert Karplus and Herbert D. Thier, *A New Look at Elementary School Science* (Chicago, Ill.: Rand McNally & Co., 1967), p. 71.

most concepts in the science curriculum. The importance of the role of experiments and demonstrations in supplying direct physical experience in elementary school science is clear.

Experiments and Demonstrations

Clarification of Terms

Two terms used frequently in relation to laboratory work in elementary school science are *demonstrations* and *experiments*. The following thumbnail comparison of demonstration and experiment is helpful:

> *Demonstration:* starts with exclamation point (!), to show something *science content-oriented*, reinforces previous learning, tends toward closure or summary of ideas.
>
> *Experiment:* starts with question mark (?), to find out something *science process-oriented*, problem solving, new learning, open-ended, can lead to further experimentation.

Put another way, the purposes of experiments and demonstrations as seen by Maxine Dunfee's study of the research in elementary science are:

> Demonstration methods are recommended when time and equipment are limited and the process complicated or difficult; laboratory work (experiment) is recommended when the important objective is the development of laboratory resourcefulness. *This last recommendation seems especially pertinent to today's emphasis upon pupil involvement in the processes of science investigation.*[3]

The Role of Demonstrations in Elementary School Science

There was a period when the only difference that was recognized by some science educators between experiments and demonstrations was that *students* carried on experiences involving concrete materials in *experiments* while *teachers* manipulated materials in *demonstrations*. The significant difference today is not *who* actually manipulates the materials—but *why*. Priscilla Eccles says:

> A teacher may carry out a true experiment as the agent of the class or a student may, by following directions, perform demonstrations for his individual instruction.[4]

---

[3] Maxine Dunfee, *Elementary School Science: A Guide to Current Research* (Washington, D.C.: Association for Supervision and Curriculum Development, 1967), p. 38. Italics added by authors.

[4] Priscilla J. Eccles, "Experiments, Demonstrations, and Other Types of First-Hand Experiences: A Classification and Definition of Terms," *Journal of Research in Science Teaching,* Vol. 1, No. 1 (1963), p. 86.

What then are the purposes or functions of demonstration in the science program? It has been said that demonstrations show what is already known of a scientific process, procedure, or phenomenon by a teacher or small group of students to a larger group, with the use of materials or equipment. *The prime purpose is to illustrate a process or method of doing something.* Demonstrations are also ways of reinforcing newly-learned science content and to make it more meaningful. Demonstrations, whether performed by teacher or student, may be used in elementary school science to:

1. *Introduce a lesson or topic.* Introducing a new lesson through a demonstration is an excellent method of motivating and arousing the interests of children.
2. *Raise questions or problems.* Questions or problems can arise from the observation in a demonstration and form the basis for further experimentation.
3. *Provide an understanding of a concept through visual means.* The multisensory experiences provided by a visual demonstration extend beyond the understandings obtained by children by mere reading or verbalizing.
4. *Verify observations made previously.* Demonstration can be performed either when controversy exists and they are used as the proof situations or when an individual repeats his work for the edification of the group.
5. *Help children learn how to think.* By encouraging children to apply what they see to new situations in a demonstration, they can be encouraged to think. By careful questioning, children can be stimulated to higher mental processes.
6. *Explain the proper use of science apparatus and equipment.*
7. *Illustrate special precautions and safety methods in handling science equipment.* The teacher should always perform or give specific directions for anything that can be potentially dangerous. This can include inserting tubing in stoppers, pouring chemicals, using sharp instruments, handling open flame, etc.[5]
8. *Use available equipment more effectively.* Demonstrations can be performed when there is insufficient equipment for all children to actively participate.
9. *Make difficult observations visible.* Demonstrations assist in making the results of difficult activities readily available, as those requiring unusually long periods of time (such as what happens to plants or animals over a month's time).

Experiments in Science Teaching

Experiments enable children to test their hypotheses, gather data under controlled conditions, evaluate the data, formulate tentative conclusions based upon

---

[5] Modified from *Tips and Techniques in Elementary Science*, The University of the State of New York, The State Education Department—Bureau of Elementary Curriculum Development, (1966), pp. 1-10.

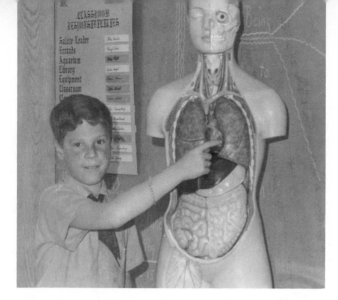

When this type of specialized equipment is not available, how can the teacher still deal with developing all concepts in a stimulating manner?

their data. In order for experimentation to be a valuable teaching method, some degree of student participation must be involved in the planning. John Renner and William Ragan, in emphasizing this point, say:

> In the most effective method of involving the child with science, he is given the objects and/or materials with which he needs experience. He performs all the manipulations himself, makes his own observations, records his own data, and makes his own interpretations. The findings he makes are his own property; he is not dependent upon information and data which has been gathered by others and in which he only vicariously participated in fathering. The frame of reference from which he views the problem confronting him is an extremely realistic one because "he was there" himself. To achieve the latter stage of involvement the child must be allowed to *do his own experimenting.*[6]

The greatest value of experiments lies in giving children opportunities to develop scientific *process* abilities as well as manipulative skills. As David Ausubel points out in the epigraph for this chapter, it is the *experiment* that ". . . carries the burden of conveying the method and spirit of science . . . ." Children learn the processes of science by engaging in experiments on their own level, paralleling real scientists' investigations. Experiments allow children to *do* rather than *see;* they are *participants* rather than *observers* in science processes.

Summary of Purposes of Demonstration and Experiment

To summarize, both the demonstration and experiment serve unique and useful purposes. One should not be discarded for the other, but rather used wisely and for the appropriate purposes. The use of both methods are recommended for variety, pupil interest, and for the part they can play in teaching-learning science by discovery. In using either experiments or demonstrations, stress should be put, however, upon those activities that are experimentation oriented. Experimentation-oriented activities are referred to in this book as *Discovery Laboratory Lessons.*

---

[6] John W. Renner and William B. Ragan, *Teaching Science in the Elementary School* (New York: Harper & Row, Publishers, 1968), p. 237.

Discovery Laboratory Lessons— Experimentation Oriented

Discovery laboratory lessons may be constructed to perform many functions. Basically there are three types of emphasis in discovery laboratory lessons. They are:

1. *Science Content Emphasis:* to teach facts, concepts, principles, subject-matter oriented (forms the basis for discovery demonstration lessons, and is also seen in many of the older elementary science texts).
2. *Science Process Emphasis:* to teach science processes; this is exemplified by (AAAS) the American Association for the Advancement of Science—Science, A Process Approach (see Chapter 4 for discussion and sample lesson).
3. *Integrated Science Processes and Content Emphasis:* this is exemplified by (COPES) the Conceptually Oriented Program in Elementary Schools and the types of lessons presented later in this chapter and in *detail* in Part Four in this text.

What concepts are these girls mastering in this shared activity?

Science Content Emphasis—Discovery Demonstration Lessons

The major stress in discovery demonstration lessons is upon the acquisition of science content by students. This does not mean, however, that science processes are completely overlooked in this type of activity. In fact, children are encouraged to engage in higher thinking processes than mere memorization by the very nature of the discovery questioning used.

Discovery demonstrations differ from a typical demonstration. When the teacher uses a typical demonstration, and there are legitimate uses for this in the classroom, he means to *show* how to do something or to *tell* how something works. However, a *discovery demonstration* does *not* tell the purpose of the demonstration at the beginning of the lesson. The objective is to have the students *discover* the scientific concepts and principles in the course of the demonstration. Generally, the teacher manipulates equipment and materials in front of his class. This may be necessary because of safety precautions, lack of sufficient equipment, or for other instructional reasons. Discovery demonstrations may, however, be carried out by students.

What technique is the teacher using to hold the attention of these children?

How to Prepare and Give Discovery Demonstrations. The teacher should select the concepts and principles to which he wants his students exposed. Before the teacher goes into the classroom to present a discovery demonstration, he should read his teaching plan thoroughly, go through the steps of the lesson, and actually perform the manipulative activities involved. Particular attention should be paid to the questions he is going to ask. Questions are really guides to the students in discovering the purpose of the demonstration and the science concepts involved. (Refer to Chapter 6 "Developing Discovery Questioning Techniques," for specific suggestions on ways to improve questioning.) Although a discovery demonstration may have been tested in a classroom situation before, no teacher can be certain a class will respond in the same step-by-step manner through the lesson. A teacher obviously should modify the delivery of his lessons as suggested by the responses he receives from his class while giving the lesson. No two classroom situations are identical. One lesson plan, regardless of how detailed, cannot meet the demands of *all* possible classroom situations.

A teacher who has never given a discovery demonstration may find it difficult at first. This is very understandable, because to ask questions and have children *discover* and *understand* the scientific concepts and principles of the demonstration is difficult. The teacher may be tempted, like a child bursting with a secret, to *tell* the children why something happened in the demonstration rather than have the children reason why from their observations and the guiding discovery questions. It may be difficult to present your first discovery demonstration for another reason. Students who are accustomed to *passive* participation, which requires that they look as though they are listening to the teacher or that they memorize certain facts, may be hesitant to participate in the more mentally active discovery demonstration. However, the teaching fun and challenge comes from overcoming these problems.

Following are some suggestions for using the discovery demonstration approach:

1. *Be enthusiastic!* Start a demonstration as though it were a riddle that is fun to solve. Ask such questions as, "Does anyone know what I am going to do with this equipment?" "Let's see who can be first to discover what is going to happen in this demonstration."

2. *Always encourage your pupils.* Use positive reinforcement. Don't criticize a student's poor efforts at thinking. If you think a student is off the track, don't say so. Say instead, "You have a point, and you seem to be really thinking," or "I am not quite sure what you mean, but I don't think it fits in with this problem; keep up that thinking." And when a child does come up with a good idea, compliment him. Tell him, "That is *good* . . . (wonderful . . . terrific)—we really have some thinking going on in the classroom!" Continually encourage and give recognition to your

How does working together help these boys develop skills they couldn't otherwise develop individually?

students for making good hypotheses, suggestions, and conclusions. This is one of the most important principles to follow in teaching science. Remember that positive recognition and reinforcement contribute to better learning. These are hard psychological principles to follow in teaching science. It is so easy to become irritated with what appears to be a stupid answer to a question and say, "That's wrong." "Where did you get that silly idea?" If you operate your classroom in this manner, you will obtain little response. Why should your pupils take a chance and reap your sarcasm? They will play it safe and in so doing learn less science.

3. What appears to be a silly answer to you might be due to the inability of a child to communicate. A silly answer on the surface, when investigated further by questioning, may be full of insight.
4. Deliberately encourage students to make hypotheses (guesses).
5. Write down the students' hypotheses about the demonstration on the board.
6. Have the class consider each guess before a demonstration is done. See if the children can eliminate some of them.
7. Always maintain an attitude that it is better to try to think and make mistakes than not to think.
8. Have fun yourself doing demonstrations. Don't worry if "it doesn't work."
9. If a demonstration doesn't come out the way it should, ask your class if any of them can help you figure out why. They may learn more from this experience than they would have if the demonstration had worked.
10. Above all, don't be afraid to do an elementary science demonstration if you don't know *all* about it. Your students don't expect you to know everything. They enjoy having their teacher learn with them, especially in science.
11. As much as possible, let students assemble the equipment for the demonstration and do it before the class. You can help them and even teach them to get the class to discover what they are going to do.
12. Wherever possible, have the students work alone on demonstrations. They learn much more about equipment and how to do demonstrations this way. See Part IV for sample discovery type demonstration lessons.

Science Process-Content Emphasis—Discovery Laboratory Lessons

In discovery laboratory lessons, children are involved in many of the same processes as in the AAAS—Science, A Process Approach materials. However, the discovery laboratory lessons may have children involved in *several* processes in one lesson, such as observing, hypothesizing, inferring, etc. The children use these processes in discovering, through laboratory investigations, an answer to a problem. They also discover the meaning of some specific concepts and principles at the same time. The AAAS materials on the other hand, have as the main emphasis children involved in *one* process. Science problems are introduced in AAAS to provide the bases for such involvement.

The outline for planning discovery laboratory lessons indicates how the processes are integrated with having children develop an understanding of scientific concepts and principles.

How to Plan a Discovery Laboratory Lesson

The elementary school science teacher will find the following general format helpful in planning a discovery laboratory lesson:

1. Statement of the Problem to be Investigated
2. Grade Level Range
3. Principle(s) and Concept(s) to Be Taught
4. Materials Needed
5. Discussion Questions
6. Pupil Discovery Activities
7. Critical Thinking and Scientific Processes
8. Open-ended (Divergent) Questions
9. Teacher's Notes or Teacher's Explanations

A study of the discovery laboratory lessons in Part Four will illustrate how the format is developed into a lesson.

Tips on Writing Your Own Discovery Laboratory Lessons

Outlined here are suggestions on how you can write your own discovery laboratory lessons:

1. *Problem* a. Decide what concepts and/or principles you want to teach.
   b. State the problem in the form of a question.
   Example: "What determines how long a candle will burn under a jar?"

2. *Grade Level* The grade level should probably indicate a *range* of grades. This is so because there usually is a wide range in mental age and achievement levels of children in any single class. Furthermore, the kinds of mental tasks required are not specific to any grade level but to a stage of mental development as outlined by Piaget and others in Chapter 3.

3. *Concepts* List the specific science content concepts and principles that are related to the problem and which you wish the children to learn.

4. *Materials*	Leave space for a list of materials but do not fill in this section until you have completed writing the activity section.
5. *Discussion*	a. Write questions which will set the stage of the lesson.
	b. In most cases the *problem* may be stated as one of the questions in this section.
	c. One general question you can almost always ask in this section is how they, the children, would go about solving the problem. This gives the children a chance to think of how they would design an investigation.
6. *Pupil Discovery Activities*	Consult science source books, science curriculums, or elementary science texts for ideas to use. The purpose of this activity section is to have children discover the principles and concepts you wish to teach as outlined under the concept section here. *The following part of the lesson is given to the children in writing if they are able to read, or orally if they can not.*
	a. Think of ways to design the activities you selected so that the children will be called upon to do process thinking.
	b. The processes that might be included are listed under the *process* section here.
	c. Write down a statement telling the children to collect the material needed in the activity. This may be followed by a question asking them how they would use the materials to solve the problem.
	d. Next write a question asking them what they think will happen if such and such procedure is used. *Example:* "How long do you think the candle will burn if you cover it with a quart jar?"
	e. Tell the children to perform the procedure and observe what happens in order to test their hypotheses. *Example:* "Cover the candle with a jar and record how long the candle burns."
	f. Ask the children to record what they observe. Strive to have the children use mathematics in measuring and graphing where possible.
	g. Ask them to interpret or make inferences about the data they collected.
7. *Critical Thinking and Scientific Processes*	a. After having written the *pupil discovery* activity section, re-read your statements in it and compare them with the following list of processes:
	1) *Cognitive-Critical Thinking Processes*
	Comparing
	Summarizing
	Criticizing
	Assuming
	Imagining
	Decision Making (evaluation of what to do)
	Applying

2) *Scientific Processes* (These are also Cognitive-Critical Thinking Processes but more related to carrying out scientific experimentation.)
   Observing
   Classifying
   Inferring or Making Interpretations
   Collecting and Organizing Data
   Measuring
   Hypothesizing or Predicting
   Designing an Investigation
   Operational Definition
   Formulating Models

b. List one of these appropriate processes in the left margin by each of the questions you asked in the *pupil discovery* activity section.

c. Once you have done this, compare your lesson with the list of processes and see if the lesson can be rewritten to include more of the processes. Modify the lesson to do this where appropriate. The comparing of your lessons with the process list is a way to evaluate how sophisticated your lessons are and what they require of students to do as far as cognitive abilities are concerned.

8. *Divergent or Open-ended Questions* (See also Chapter 6)   As pointed out in Chapter 6, divergent or open-ended questions are questions which suggest possibilities for further laboratory investigation. Questions which might be included in this section are:

a. If you were to repeat this activity how would you improve it?

b. What other possibilities for experimentation did this activity suggest to you?

Generally in the *pupil discovery* activities section the students have tested one variable or the influence of one factor on an object or organism. In this open-ended section, however, they might be asked questions involving the influence of other factors on the same object. Because of the importance of the relationship of factors and variables in questioning, a discussion of writing open-ended questions is presented.

9. *Teacher's Notes, Explanations, or Cautions*   Reread your lesson and in the vacant space you left under the materials section, list those materials and equipment needed in the lesson. *Be sure to be definite in writing the quantities used in the materials section. Example:* Don't write: "Some candles" but write "10 candles." Be sure to check the procedure section to see that you have listed accurately all the materials required.

Writing Open-ended Questions

Experimental Factors or Variables. In any experimental situation there are variables or factors being tested. Using the question "What effect does water have on the sprouting of seeds?" this is asking: What does the factor or variable—water—have to do with the sprouting of seeds? Look at the seed problem again stated in the question here. Think of three open-ended questions which suggest further investigation.

Probably you will have little difficulty in doing this. All you have to do is think for a minute what might influence the sprouting of seeds. You may think of such factors as: light, temperature, pH (acidity), seed population (the number of seeds present), etc. Some examples of factors or variables which may be involved in experimental conditions are listed here. You probably can think of many others. Use this list or prepare one yourself to help you in writing open-ended questions:

	Temperature
	Light
	Sound
	Water or Humidity
	Food or Presence of Minerals
EXPERIMENTAL	pH—Alkalinity or Acidity
FACTORS	Air or Other Gases or Lack of Them (Space Flight Conditioning)
OR	Pressure
VARIABLES	Type of Motion
	Fields—Gravitational, Magnetic, Electrical
	Friction
	Force
	Population Density
	Etc.

Qualitative Factors.   Several of the factors or variables listed here may vary in *qualitative* ways. For example, a child may have done an activity to find out whether light is needed for photosynthesis in leaves. He does not know, however, whether *all* wave lengths of light are necessary. The teacher may then ask the following *qualitative* questions about light in the open-ended questions section of the lesson:

"What colors of light do you think are necessary for photosynthesis to take place?" "Will different colors of light speed up or slow down photosynthesis?"

The children may then cover plants with different colored cellophane to find answers to these questions.

Quantitative Factors.   All of the factors in this list may also involve *quantitative* questions. For example: "How much light is necessary for photosynthesis to take place?" "How do different intensities of light affect photosynthesis?"

Look at the list of factors again and design qualitative and quantitative questions for the various factors that affect the sprouting of seeds. If you can accomplish this task, you will have little difficulty in writing open-ended questions to go with your own laboratory exercises.

Turn to the activity section of this text and look at many of the examples of discovery laboratory lessons. Go over the open-ended questions and see if you can determine which questions are quantitative and which are qualitative. Study these lessons and try to devise additional open-ended types of questions.

By perfecting your skill in how to prepare laboratory lessons as indicated by the suggestions here, you will become more creative yourself. In addition you will recognize more easily good, creative discovery laboratory lessons from the "cookbook" type. A "cookbook" lesson only requires children to fill in blanks and involves them to a minor degree in critical thinking or scientific processes.

Organizing and Conducting Discovery Laboratory Lessons

Converting a well-designed discovery plan into a successful discovery laboratory lesson depends greatly on how the teacher organizes and prepares the laboratory facilities and how well he guides the children while they are working.

Organizing and Planning Laboratory Activities

1. Decide what it is you *specifically* want your children to learn from being exposed to the laboratory activity—scientific processes, content, etc.
2. Select a *method* by which you will *introduce*, orient, and structure your laboratory activity. This may be done by a teacher demonstration or discussion. You should make certain that the purpose of the laboratory activity is understood by the children.
3. Decide whether or not you should prepare a *laboratory sheet* for children to use. With older children, this can form the basis for practice in record keeping. For younger children, you may decide to limit yourself to more oral directions.
4. Work out the details of *distribution* and *collection* of science equipment and materials. It is vital that you know the *specifics* and not just general ideas. Generally, it is more desirable and much safer if children stay at their laboratory stations (desks pushed together in a non-laboratory room) where the equipment is placed. Supplies and materials should be brought to the laboratory stations rather than having children come up for them. (*Note:* Chapter 9 presents detailed suggestions concerning science equipment and supplies for elementary schools, how to store them, and other specific related information.) The same holds true for collection of materials at the conclusion of the lab activity.
5. Will your children work *individually* or *in small groups?* If in groups, set them up so you have your "science leaders" in each group. Work out additional directions for children who finish before the rest of the class.
6. *You* should *perform* the lab activity before presenting it to your class. By doing so you will become familiar with the techniques and procedures in the activity. You will also be able to see any difficulties you have with the activity and find ways to overcome them. It is also possible for you to spot potential difficulties for your children with the lab activity.

Laboratory Preparation

1. Check to make certain that you have all necessary science equipment and supplies *in sufficient amounts* so that all your children may participate in the lab activity. Whenever possible have these at lab stations set up with equipment *before* children come into the room. This can be done in most elementary schools by setting up lab work for:
   a. First activity of the day.
   b. After lunch.
   c. After gym, music, etc., if children leave room to go to special activities.

How can preparation and advance planning assist the teacher in conducting smoothly moving lab sessions?

2. In order to further avoid wasting valuable time for the class, initial steps in setting up equipment should also be done prior to class. Some of these initial steps might include boiling water, heating or cooling of materials, double checking supplies, etc.
3. If any chemicals are used, even dilute vinegar, make provisions for children to have washing materials available.
4. Whenever possible, substitute plastics for glassware. Be careful when using heat, that the plastics are able to withstand the temperatures used.
5. Have a fire extinguisher available if open flame is to be used.
6. Avoid the use of electrical house current (110 volts) for children's lab activities. Use dry cells wherever possible when children are handling the equipment directly.
7. You should assemble glass tubing and stoppers *before* class. You will find it convenient to store these assembled arrangements of stoppers and tubing for later use, rather than disassembling them after each use. (See following discussion for further suggestions on tubing and stoppers.)

Conducting Lab Activities

Beautiful science laboratory lesson plans may end in chaos and frustration unless the lab activities are carefully conducted. It is impossible to plan beforehand for every eventuality that might occur during the lab activity. However, the following points are offered as minimal considerations you should make before attempting to put your lesson plans to work with the class. As you read the points, think of others that should be considered before you conduct lab activities. A few minutes of mental preplanning may spare you some grief during the activity.

1. Help children see the *purpose* of the lab activity.
2. Check to see if children understand the procedures to be followed. Either write the steps on the board or have the children refer to their lab sheets. Although structure is needed, allow for creativity and deviating from the established procedure within established limits.
3. Introduce *safety precautions* before beginning any work. These may be presented by the teacher or may be elicited by questions such as: "In the event that someone cuts himself, what should that person do?" Here are some general safety precautions to follow when conducting lab experiences with elementary school children:
   a. *All* accidents, regardless of how slight, should be reported to you.
   b. All directions should be followed exactly as they were given by you. If children are not certain about something, they should ask you.
   c. Instruct children to always cut materials *away* from them, being careful to stay far enough away from other students to avoid cutting them.
   d. Young children in grades K-6 should *not* be allowed to insert glass tubing into stoppers. Teachers should follow these safety precautions when inserting glass tubing into stoppers:
      1) Use only glass tubing that is fire polished at both ends.
      2) Liberally lubricate end of glass tubing *and* stopper hole with glycerine *before* inserting.
      3) After lubricating, start *twisting* tubing into stopper. *Hold tubing close to end being inserted* (reduces chances of snapping off tubing).
      4) Glass thermometers may be inserted in same way.
      5) Wrapped cloth on handles will give greater protection in case tubing should snap.[7]

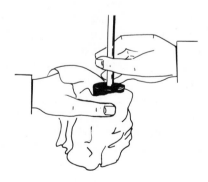

   e. Avoid use of strong acids with children. Whenever possible use substitutes such as vinegar. If acids spill or come in contact with skin, flush

---

[7] For specific information see *Lab Safety, A Guide to Safety Practices in the School Science Laboratory* (Trenton, N.J.: State of New Jersey Department of Education, 1963), 30 pages.

Manual dexterity becomes important in student projects. How and when could the teacher step in to avert failure when work becomes too difficult or should he allow children to see for themselves the ongoing science process of success and failure?

liberally with water and then use a baking soda solution to counteract acid or vinegar.

 f. Caution children *not* to smell or taste *anything* unless they specifically know what it is and that it's safe. Read all labels carefully.

 g. Make provision for all broken glass, excess chemicals, and other waste materials to be placed in proper containers. Avoid throwing things into sinks but give custodian such materials for him to dispose.

 h. Stress the serious nature of lab work. Do not permit *any* horseplay or levity during the science lab program.

 i. Check to see that there is adequate ventilation in room, especially when candles or other burning or fuming materials are used.

 j. When heating a solution in a test tube, always point the test tube away from any individuals.

 k. Tell children never to mix chemicals unless told to do so.

4. The names and functions of science equipment, supplies, and lab techniques should be presented to children as they perform lab activities.

5. The teacher should move about the room throughout the lab activity to help, redirect, answer questions, prevent or correct discipline problems, show or demonstrate, etc.

6. A *discussion* should be held at the conclusion of the lab activity to focus upon observations made by children during the activity. This can also be a way of reviewing what was learned and how to *apply findings toward tentative conclusions* or further study.

Summary

Laboratory lessons in elementary school science are different from those typically associated with "a laboratory" in high school or college. Regular classroom facilities can often be used. Laboratory lessons involve children *actively* participating in science activities where they gather data and evidence needed in solving a problem. These activities may be demonstrations or experiments.

Demonstrations start out to show something. They are primarily science content-oriented and generally tend toward a summary or closure of ideas. Discovery demonstrations differ, however, in that instead of being told the outcome of a demonstration, children are guided to discover the purposes of the demonstration. Demonstrations may be used to introduce a lesson, raise questions or problems, provide a visualization of a concept, explain the proper and safe use of science apparatus, as well as many other purposes.

Experiments start out to find out something. They are primarily science processes-oriented and generally are problem solving and open-ended. These activities generally lead to further experimentation and data gathering. Experiments enable children to test their hypotheses, gather data under controlled conditions, evaluate the data, and formulate tentative conclusions based upon their data.

Both the demonstration and experiment serve unique and useful purposes and both are recommended for use in elementary science. Stress should be placed upon inquiry in the use of either experiment or demonstration. These experimentation-oriented activities are referred to as discovery laboratory lessons.

Discovery laboratory lessons may be either demonstrations or experiments. Examples of both types of lessons may be found in Part Four.

Some of the suggestions for using discovery demonstration lessons are:

1. Be enthusiastic and start each lesson as a riddle.
2. Always encourage your students by using positive reinforcement.
3. Tolerate "silly" answers for they may turn out to be very insightful.
4. Encourage students to make hypotheses.
5. Don't feel you have to know everything about a topic before giving a discovery demonstration lesson.

The suggested format for the discovery laboratory lesson plan is:

1. Statement of the Problem
2. Grade Level Range
3. Concept(s) and Principle(s) to Be Taught
4. Materials Needed
5. Discussion Questions
6. Pupil Discovery Activities
7. Critical Thinking and Scientific Processes
8. Open-ended (Divergent) Questions
9. Teacher's Notes or Teacher's Explanation

Tips were presented for converting a discovery lesson plan into a discovery laboratory lesson. Some of these practical suggestions were: selecting a method for orienting children to lab procedures, working out the details for the distribution and collection of science equipment and materials, and ways of instructing children on safety.

Teachers should be cautious in discovery laboratory lessons that children do not arrive at conclusions prematurely.

SELF-EVALUATION AND FURTHER STUDY

1. Comment upon the ways in which the following approaches vary. Give examples of the science projects that are identified with each.

     Science Content Emphasis
     Integrated Science Content-Process Emphasis
     Science Process Emphasis

2. The following terms are used almost interchangably by some teachers. Define each in your own words and show any differences that may exist.

     Experiment
     Demonstration
     Exercises
     Laboratory Activities or Lessons
     Discovery Demonstration

3. Write a discovery laboratory lesson following the suggestions on pages 145-147.

4. Prepare and teach a discovery demonstration lesson to a group of children. Use the format and suggestions on pages 149-152.

5. Get sample lesson description from several of the innovative science programs listed in Chapter 4 and from sources in Appendix A. Compare them to see the types of laboratory activities presented.

6. Read the following article and explain why the author says that *an experiment never fails:*

     Plants, Robert W., "An Experiment Never Fails," *Science and Children,* National Science Teachers Association (May, 1966).

And a teacher who acts on the knowledge that children learn in different ways will have different materials of instruction available, in addition to texts. There are, after all, films, filmstrips, booklets, radio, TV, the daily newspaper, magazines. There are members of the community who would make a contribution: parents with special abilities, farmers, physicists, chemists, engineers, gardners—and a host of others.[1]

CHAPTER 8

OTHER INDOOR AND OUTDOOR SCIENCE DISCOVERY ACTIVITIES

The statement by Paul Brandwein captures the essence of teaching science through a multi-sensory approach. Discovery teaching-learning is more effective when approached from as many senses as possible. In addition to laboratory activities mentioned in the previous chapter, these teaching-learning activities stimulate, enrich, and supplement the science discovery program:

Indoor Science Discovery Activities

1. Reading and Other Language Activities
2. Audiovisual Activities

Outdoor Science Discovery Activities

1. Community Resource Activities
2. Outdoor Laboratory Activities
3. School Grounds Activities
4. Field Trip Activities

This chapter presents the function of each of these activities, practical tips on how to conduct the activity in a discovery science program, and a sample or picture of an appropriate part of the activity. Where applicable, the reader's attention will be brought to sections of the Appendix for further sources of information.

Indoor Science Discovery Activities

The effective teaching of science through discovery requires the effective teaching of science reading. The study of science enhances the learning of reading, and learning to read enhances the studying of science.

Purposes for Reading in Science Discovery Programs

Although children learn science best by participating in firsthand experiences, reading is an enriching and valuable activity. Studies by Esther Roossinck, J. Harlan Shores, and Paul Koester show the contribution of reading to attainment of

---

[1] Paul F. Brandwein, *Elements in a Strategy For Teaching Science in the Elementary School* (Cambridge, Mass.: Harvard University Press, 1962), p. 24.

the goals of the elementary school science program.[2] There are many ways that reading of science information contributes to the objectives of science in the elementary school. Some of these are:

1. In the primary grades, written symbols become more meaningful to children as a result of their firsthand science experiences. An outgrowth of these experiences is the construction of science vocabularies by the children. Understanding science words develops from firsthand experiences and is deepened and sophisticated by exposure to dictionaries, encyclopedias, textbooks, and other science books.
2. Experience charts can be used very effectively to summarize the discussions about the science problems studied, the procedures used in experiments, the observations and results of these experiments, and the analyses, interpretations, and applications of the results of these experiments.
3. In the upper grades, children might use reading to test, verify, and extend the information observed in their limited experiments.
4. In the event an experiment "does not work," reading might help give children clues as to what prevented the expected from happening and why.

What values do you see in children working together in science?

5. The development of reading skills enables students to critically analyze materials read to check for scientific accuracy. This scientific literacy is urgently needed in our scientific age so that citizens can read and interpret materials intelligently. The teacher's discovery questioning emphasizes the need for constant checking for accuracy and proper interpretation of data used in *all* reading material.

---

[2] Esther Pauline Roossinck, "Purposeful Reading of Science Materials by Scientists and Children" (Unpublished doctoral dissertation. Urbana, Ill.: University of Illinois, 1961); J. Harlan Shores, "Reading of Science for Two Separate Purposes as Perceived by Sixth Grade Students and Able Adult Readers," *Elementary English*, 37 (November, 1960), pp. 461-468; Paul William Koester, "Reading Science Materials for Two Specific Purposes at the Sixth Grade Level" (Doctor's Dissertation, University of Illinois, 1961), *Dissertation abstracts*, 22 (October, 1961), pp. 1097-1098.

6. Children's reading may also contribute to recreational enjoyment, for children may find simple experiments to perform in school or at home. They may also enjoy reading about scientific speculation (even science fiction) about space travel, other possible living organisms in space, etc.
7. Reading exposes children to the ideas of people other than themselves or their teachers, especially *scientists* who have conducted experiments impossible to perform in elementary schools.
8. Children can benefit by reading about the lives and works of famous scientists and the technology that has arisen from their contributions. Although we are *not* striving to recruit scientists in the elementary schools, there is occupational value in children reading about scientists.

Science Textbooks in Discovery Programs. Many elementary school teachers rely upon the textbook as the hub of their science programs. This reliance is due to the belief by teachers that a textbook has a structured organization of information, stresses important science concepts, directs student activities, and provides goals for the total science program. Although the textbooks can boast these contributions, they cannot by themselves achieve these goals. The textbook must be judged relative to the total science program.

Limitations of Science Textbooks. One of the most glaring limitations of science textbooks in the elementary schools is the problem of readability. George Mallinson found that science textbooks are too difficult for the children assigned to read them.[3] More recently Leroy Ottley found the same thing to be true.[4] Suggestions for overcoming this limitation are presented in the next sections of this chapter, "Overcoming Textbook Limitations" and "Individualizing Science Reading."

Another limitation in using the textbook as the *sole* source of scientific information is the fact that it may contain inaccuracies and misconceptions. This is especially true in the physical sciences as reported in a research conducted by Allen Weaver.[5]

A third limitation has to do with the grade placement of scientific principles and the way they are developed in science textbooks. This is an important consideration, especially since many schools frequently use the textbook as their sole curriculum guide in science. Robert Chinnis found there was little agreement in the textbook series as to the science principles developed.[6] Of the seventy-eight science principles identified, only *ten* were developed in *all* series.

In spite of these limitations, it seems likely some schools will continue to organize their science programs around the science textbook. The following suggestions are presented as possible ways of minimizing limitations and using elementary science textbooks properly and effectively in a discovery program.

---

[3] George G. Mallinson, "The Reading Difficulty of Unit-Type Textbooks for Elementary Science," *Science Education*, 39 (December, 1955), pp. 406-410.

[4] LeRoy Ottley, "Readability of Science Textbooks for Grades Four, Five, Six," *School Science and Mathematics*, 65 (April, 1965), pp. 363-366.

[5] Allen D. Weaver, "Misconceptions in Physics Prevalent in Science Textbook Series for Elementary Schools," *School Science and Mathematics*, 65 (March, 1965), pp. 231-240.

[6] Robert J. Chinnis, "Analysis of Elementary Science Textbooks," *The Science Teacher*, 30 (February, 1963), pp. 23-27.

Overcoming Textbook Limitations

1. *Careful Selection of Science Textbooks*

The teacher should use the following criteria in comparing science textbooks for purchase and possible adoption:

a. Factors which deal with the subject matter content and organization:
   1) Logical organization, sequence of difficulty, groupings of topics.
   2) Emphasis on principles and concepts.
   3) Accuracy of information.
   4) Usefulness of information, applications, and functional nature of the material.
   5) Recency of information, modern concepts, theories and applications.
b. Factors which deal with development of non-content objectives:
   1) Attention given to development of interests, appreciations, and attitudes.
   2) Attention given to problem-solving approach.
   3) Attention given to skills of science learning.
   4) Attention given to role of science in society, scientific literacy.
c. Factors which deal with experiments, demonstrations, and activities:
   1) Inquiry or verification approach.
   2) Student participation, activity, and investigation.
   3) Use of simple materials, degree of structure in laboratories.
   4) Emphasis on drawing conclusions on basis of observation and experimentation.
d. Factors which deal with mechanical features of the textbook:
   1) Binding, size, durability, attractiveness.
   2) Size of type, level of reading difficulty, summaries, glossaries, index.
   3) Illustrations, maps, charts, graphs, captions.
   4) General ease of use of the book for purpose intended.
e. Factors which deal with authors of the textbook:
   1) Qualifications (experience, level of preparation).
   2) Quality of writing, interest, and readability.
   3) References to purposes of the book and intended use.
f. Factors which deal with prospective useful life of the textbook:
   1) Copyright date, revisions, and reprintings.
   2) Nature of material, rate of obsolescence, years of usability.

It is suggested that the foregoing criteria be used with a rating scale for comparison of competing textbooks. A number scale like the one that follows might be used:

> 0—Book totally lacking in the characteristic.
> 1—Occasional evidence of the characteristic.
> 2—Greater evidence of the characteristic but below average.
> 3—Reasonably frequent evidence of the characteristic.
> 4—Excellent evidence of the characteristic.
> 5—Superior in all aspects of the characteristic.[7]

---

[7] Robert B. Sund and Leslie W. Trowbridge, *Teaching Science by Inquiry* (Columbus, Ohio: Charles E. Merrill Publishing Company, 1967), pp. 168-169.

2. *Proper Use of Adopted Textbooks*

The teacher should follow these general principles when using textbooks with children:

a. Because of the wide range of interests and abilities of children within any given class, a variety of textbook series should be used.

b. Because science involves children finding their own answers, small sets of different reading levels within a text series should be provided instead of one reading level.

c. Textbooks should be supplemented by a variety of such activities as discovery laboratory experiences, outdoor activities, audiovisuals, etc.

d. Textbook research skills should be taught to children so that they can become more effective data collectors. Some of these textbook research skills are: use of index, glossary, cross-reference, map reading, interpreting graphs, etc.

e. To avoid excessive reading *about* science, the teacher should follow these suggestions when using the textbook:

1) Science reading—unless recreational—should be done for a *specific* reason, such as to verify conclusions, answer questions, solve problems, find information, learn how to do experiments.

2) Science reading may be an activity from which other activities originate.

3) Science reading should be done from *several* sources so that sources may supplement one another and present varying points of view.

4) Science reading materials may be selected by teacher and pupils.

5) Science reading should provide experiences for such skills as the use of table of contents, index, and other reading references.

6) Science reading materials should be of *many* levels of reading difficulty if they are to be useful.

7) Science recreational reading and science information reading should be made clear to children; both should be stressed as serving a valid purpose, but children should develop a clear understanding and differentiation of them.

Individualizing Science Reading Materials and Activities. If the teacher allows and even encourages individuals to branch out from the main unit of study according to their interests and abilities, he must be ready to guide the students in a variety of materials and activities. The single science textbook will not suffice. By shifting the textbooks around from class to class and grade to grade, teachers have a range of reading levels from the easiest to the most difficult. In this way, the teacher will be better able to direct appropriate reading levels to individual students. This will enable all students to have a science book he can read. Another source of material for children who have difficulty in reading is the high-interest—low vocabulary science books produced today. Following are some of the low vocabulary—high interest science books:

What Is It Series (Chicago: Benefic Press)
All About Books (New York: Random House, Inc.)

Webster Classroom Science Series—Let's Read About (St. Louis: Webster Publishing)
About Book Series (Chicago: Melmont Publishers, Inc.)

Basic readers, social studies books, science trade books, pamphlets and magazines, weekly children's newspapers, and other commercially prepared science materials are becoming abundantly available and should be placed in the classroom. Some teachers have children bring in books from home for use in the class library, and many parents are very cooperative in supplying magazines with science content.

Local libraries generally loan books to teachers if they know sufficient time in advance the topic, age, reading levels of the children, and the length of time the material will be needed. Commercial companies and the federal and state governments prepare special materials in science for the classroom for both teachers and children. See the Appendix for sources of these materials.

Teacher-prepared materials are extremely valuable. During science studies, the teacher can rewrite difficult materials at a reading level useful for students having difficulty in reading. The teacher should consider the following guidelines set forth by R. Bradley and N. Earp, before undertaking the practice of modifying scientific articles for children:

1. *Use Care in Article Selection.*

    Select the articles to be modified with great care. The article selection varies according to the use you wish to make of it: (1) as a supplement to a lesson, (2) as a separate presentation for class work at a time other than the science period, or (3) as a self-contained lesson to be learned. In any case, specialized competencies (higher mathematics, knowledge of chemistry, technical vocabulary) on the part of the child, although desirable, should not be necessary for him to understand the meaning of the rewritten article.

2. *Keep Writing Style Simple.*

    Write clearly and simply, using words appropriate to the intended grade level. For children one writes to communicate, not to impress. Use short sentences.

3. *Relate Subject to Child's Environment and Development Level.*

    Use freely the techniques of comparing, contrasting, and developing examples and statements analogous to the child's experience and environment. Some knowledge of child growth and development is mandatory on the part of the editor. For this reason, it would be good if teachers of a given grade level provided their own rewrites of science articles for classroom use. They would be fully aware of vocabulary level, attention span, and the unique interests of their own group.

4. *Use Graphs and Charts.*

    If at all possible, organize some data into simple graph or table form. Children at the elementary level need to become familiar with graph and chart reading. Often, simple cutouts from construction paper of various colors will make a difficult idea easily comprehensible for the young child.

5. *Limit Details.*

    Avoid setting out to answer specific questions. Write in a style that lets the information unfold in such a way that it can be readily grasped by the pupil. Children generally get "bogged down" in any extraneous details.

6. *Be Consistent in Use of Grammar.*

    One should employ consistent uses and notations in rewriting an article. Italics can be used to show the use of technical terms or for emphasis. Parentheses might enclose the pronunciation of a strange scientific word, a definition, or an explanation. Abbreviations should be used with utmost care.

7. *Check Your Rewrite for Accuracy.*

Have another informed person read both the original and modified articles for accuracy in fact and interpretation. In all cases, give proper credit and concise bibliographical reference to any material that is rewritten.

8. *Use Testing to Determine Effectiveness.*

Prepare a brief but thorough test (preferably multiple choice) that calls for the child to reflect on what has been studied. On some occasions it would be well if a pre- and post-test evaluation were conducted to check on individual student achievement and improvement.[8]

Programmed Text and Teaching Machines

The programmed text or teaching machine is another attempt to individualize science instruction. Basically it works by presenting information in small written segments to the learner who responds to a question immediately following the printed information. This can be done by a cardboard slide in a printed textbook which covers up all but the part immediately being read. It can also be done by machines with levers and knobs which do the same thing. The learner then checks his answer with a correct answer. If correct he goes on to the next frame. If incorrect he may be corrected by being referred to earlier frames in the material that are easier and supply additional needed information. Many programmed texts do *not* give additional corrective frames, but rely upon giving the correct answer as the learning activity.

The evidence is inconclusive so far as to the effectiveness of such learning devices. John McNeil and Evan Keislar found that the first graders they tested were *not* able to generalize from their programmed experiences.[9] However, Sherman Dutton and William Hedges and Mary Ann MacDougall found fourth graders learned science concepts more efficiently by programmed materials than pupils being taught by conventional methods.[10]

Importance of Discussion in Discovery Science. Discussions in science programs are vital for the development of scientific attitudes, understandings of procedures and methods, and scientific vocabularies. Katherine Hill's study reports mental and verbal growth is perceptively apparent in children's abilities to question, speculate, recognize relationships, and draw conclusions when there is ample time for them to have science discussions.[11] When there is freedom in discussion pe-

---

[8] R. C. Bradley and N. Wesley Earp, "Rewriting Science Materials for Elementary Students," *Helping Children Learn Science*, National Science Teachers Association (1966), pp. 71-72.

[9] John D. McNeil and Evan R. Keislar, "An Experiment in Validating Objectives for the Curriculum in Elementary School Science," *Science Education*, 46 (March, 1962), pp. 152-156.

[10] Sherman S. Dutton, "An Experimental Study in the Programming of Science Instruction for the Fourth Grade" (Doctor's Dissertation, University of Virginia, 1963), *Dissertation Abstracts*, 24 (December, 1963), p. 2382; William D. Hedges and Mary Ann MacDougall, "Teaching Fourth Grade Science by Means Of Programmed Science Materials with Laboratory Experiences," *Science Education*, 48 (February, 1964), pp. 64-76.

[11] Katherine E. Hill, *Children's Contributions in Science Discussions* (New York: Bureau of Publications, Teachers College, Columbia University, 1947), p. 97.

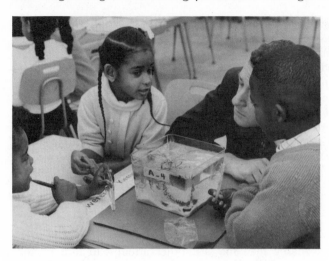

The ability to communicate ideas is essential in learning. How does the discovery approach to teaching science stimulate language development and thinking?

riods for children and teacher to openly express ideas, an excellent "discovery climate" exists for exploring answers to problems.

Oral discussions are especially necessary in the early years of the elementary school, for most children of that age are functionally illiterate in regard to the printed word. Robert Karplus and Herbert Thier say this about the importance and use of discussions in early childhood science:

> Although he is learning to read, the child has significant problems in following written instructions. He has a lack of understanding about how different state-ments fit together. Furthermore, his vocabulary and ability to express himself in writing are severely limited. Oral and even gestural language are a much more secure and powerful means of communication for the young child . . . . Child to child communication is also a most important aspect of the operation of a science classroom.[12]

There are times when children should share their newly-found information with others. Discussion periods allow for this type of activity. For instance, after investi-gating problems and sources of air and water pollution, children could discuss possible sources and solutions for pollution in their own communities.

Audiovisual Devices and Science Discovery

Audiovisual devices offer teachers excellent opportunities for the stimulating and enriching discussions mentioned here. The number and variety of audiovisual devices available to teachers today is staggering. Hardly a day goes by that a new teaching device, or an improvement over an older one, does not appear on the market. The modern teacher needs to be aware of these devices as possible aids in her teaching. She should understand how these devices can best be used for maxi-mum learning by her children. She should, however, avoid the naïve belief that *any* learning material possesses educative values. There are educative values in

---

[12] Robert Karplus and Herbert D. Thier, *A New Look at Elementary School Science* (Chi-cago, Ill.: Rand McNally Co., 1967), p. 81.

films, filmloops, multi-media kits, records, bulletin boards, etc. only when these devices are wisely used in teaching-learning processes.

Combination or Multi-sensory Equipment. Many pieces of equipment, as well as kits that use combinations of senses for learning are now appearing on the market. One device, Bell and Howell's Language Master, is worth noting for it uses the audio and visual approach in a rather unique way. This specially designed audiotape recorder has hand-fed cards that have lengths of magnetic tape adhered parallel to their bottom edges.

How does the Language Master combine audio and visual aspects of science learning?

The most common use of this equipment is for the child to push the "Student" lever and record what he sees on the card. He then runs the card through to hear the "Instructor" track to check his response. This procedure can be reversed or modified; the tape can be recorded and erased many times over. Below is a description of how the Language Master could be used in developing concepts using tactile, olfactory, and tasting experiences.

Beginners would start with the gross concept of "rough" and "smooth" whereas more advanced learners would deal with graduated distinctions and even make identifications of specific kinds of fabrics and materials.

Various metals are available as thin foils. Aluminum, brass, copper and even light-gauge sheets of iron can be utilized for mounting on the cards. Also, differentiated materials such as plastic, glass, porcelain, glazed and unglazed materials can be applied. . . . The accompanying recorded audio can include various simulations of the words "rough" and "smooth" to accompany the printed word for reinforcement. Also, it is possible to record, for example, the noise made by sandpaper being drawn across a piece of wood, etc. (See illustration marked "Tactile".)

Certainly, little has been done in this important learning area and it is important to explore the possibilities inherent in developing more effective techniques for bringing these experiences into the classroom. Some years ago an author produced a book dealing with spices obtained from various parts of the world. On each pair of pages, illustra-

TACTILE

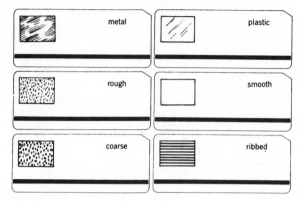

tions were provided to show the plant from which a particular spice was derived, and in addition, provide a close-up graphic of the spice itself. Most unique of all, however, was the fact that the ink used on that particular pair of pages was impregnated with the essence of the spice. The reader was able to master the printed information, then become familiar with the visuals involved and finally to hold the pages very close to his nose so that he could also identify by smell the particular odor of the spice involved. The imaginative teacher can use similar techniques in preparing Language Master cards to utilize not only spices but other materials which can be identified by odor. (See illustration marked "Olfactory".)

OLFACTORY

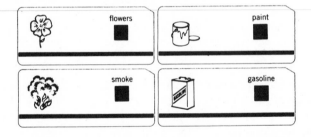

It is a standard technique for primary teachers to arrange "tasting parties." During these sessions children are systematically and progressively exposed to opportunities to taste different foods, candies, etc., to identify what is meant by sweet, sour, bitter, etc. It is possible to work out a plan to provide such tasting experiences in connection with Language Master. Of course, sanitary procedures in this connection must be observed.

One approach is to prepare a series of Language Master cards each of which refers to a particular edible product or spice such as sugar, salt, pepper, etc. Depending upon the level, these cards would have the word imprinted on the card and be accompanied by a visual that would be appropriate for the purpose. For example, a graphic of a sugar cube, salt shaker, pepper shaker, etc. Accompanying each set of cards would be a "taste sampler"–small glassine or cellophane bags attached to a card to be filled with a small amount of tasting material. The same graphic, reproduced on the card near the bag will coordinate the sample with the proper Language Master card.

In use, the learner would select the Language Master card with the sugar cube illustration and place it in the card slot. The audio track would comment, "sugar-sugar is sweet." The learner would also see the word sugar spelled out on the card and associate this with the sugar cube or the sugar container. He would then tear off the small glassine bag attached to the accompanying tasting card for this series, open it and taste some of the contents. Of course, the sampler card would be used only one time for each of the separate items and would have to be supplied anew for each learner. Perhaps the sampler card with the visuals could be used over and over merely by replacing the samples in fresh bags. (See illustration marked "Tasting".)[13]

TASTING

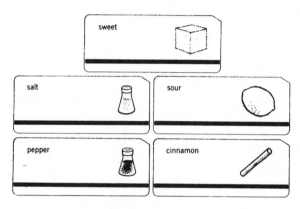

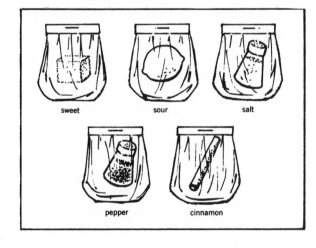

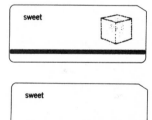

Bulletin Boards and Displays.   Attractively presented materials coupled with thought-provoking questions can stimulate children's interests in science. Bulletin boards and displays offer this aid to children's learning.

Following are suggestions for setting up a bulletin board or display. The most effective learning bulletin boards are jointly planned and arranged by children and teacher working together. The extent to which children participate is partially dictated by their maturation.

---

[13] Phillip Lewis, *The World of Language Master* (Chicago, Ill.: Bell & Howell Co., 7100 Mc-Cormick Rd., 1968), pp. 19-21.

How to Set Up a Bulletin Board Efficiently for Science Discovery

1. Decide the science concepts and principles you wish children to learn.
2. Teacher and children collect pictures from periodicals, newspapers, or prepare diagrams you think might help in teaching these concepts.
3. Teacher (and children if possible) plan how the pictures can be used effectively and attractively on a bulletin board display. Decide upon thought-provoking questions.
4. Make diagrams if needed to supplement the pictures.
5. See the example of a plan for a bulletin board drawn here.

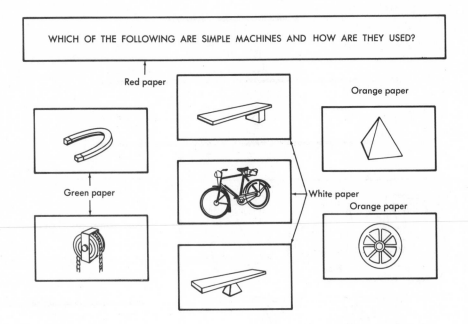

6. Prepare the lettering and materials needed for the display. This may entail pasting pictures on colored paper, etc.
7. The posting of the display may be done by children following the diagram plan agreed upon.
8. After the display has served its purpose, it may be taken down by some children and stored in a folder or envelope for possible use and modification next year.
9. Prepare a diagram plan of the bulletin board display and place it in the folder so students can follow it next year to put it up again. This will save you considerable time in the future since you won't have to give excessive directions of how to display the materials.

Displays generally have an advantage over certain bulletin boards because they allow the children to tinker with the materials that are set out. Tactile stimulation, or sense of feel, is very desirable for many children.

Microprojector. The microprojector is one of the most effective devices for showing microscope materials to elementary school children. Most elementary schools do not have individual microscopes for each child, nor can most elementary children use them properly. The teacher can do a better job of teaching when he can show the children what certain structures look like; this minimizes individuals developing misconceptions as a result of viewing an eyelash or dust in their own microscopes.

There are certain things that can be shown through a microscope or preferably a microprojector that can have quite a dramatic effect on children:

1. Blood circulation in the tail of a *live* goldfish (on a wet blotter).
2. Paramecia swimming in water droplets.
3. Epithelial cells from the inside of a child's cheek.

Overhead Projector. One of the most versatile aids to science teaching is the overhead projector. Following are some of the reasons the overhead projector is considered an indispensable piece of equipment by most science teachers:

1. The overhead projector is relatively low priced.
2. It is simple to operate and requires little or no maintenance.
3. The cost of the transparencies and materials to make them are also low priced.
4. Only modest darkening of a room is needed for adequate viewing.
5. The teacher faces the class when using the overhead projector.
6. It can be used with materials prepared before class and the materials are used from lesson to lesson without duplication each time.
7. The teacher can write on his materials with a grease pencil or washable ink for emphasis or to illustrate a point. These may be easily removed when finished.
8. Certain scientific demonstrations are possible on the transparency (magnetic lines of force, chemical reactions, sprouting seeds, etc.).

In what ways may the overhead projector contribute to the effective science program?

9. Overlay transparencies can be made to show succession of operations, steps in development, or other sequential presentations of ideas.
10. The projector is noiseless and the teacher can talk to the class without shouting.

Much commercially prepared material has appeared recently for use with the overhead projector. There are also attachments now for converting the overhead projector into laboratory demonstration devices.

Radio and Television. One of the prime uses made of radio and television as educational aids is the instantaneous coverage of scientific events such as space shots, scientific and medical occurrences, weather reporting, and natural disasters. The effect of instantaneous television coverage is great stimulation and interest in scientific things by the general populace. Katherine Hill's study shows that newly discovered scientific information quickly becomes a part of the thinking of elementary school children at every age level as a result of television viewing.[14] This is an excellent contribution to science learning, but it has limited value for sustained and continuing learning of scientific concepts and principles.

There has been some interest and experimentation in the direct teaching of science by means of radio and television. The success of educational television seems to depend upon how well it is integrated and coordinated with additional classroom activities. It was found in studies by Phyllis Busch and Ralph Garry that television viewing *alone* was not as effective as television combined with a teacher who encouraged, guided, and expected children to expand on and utilize the information received.[15]

An increasing number of national commercial programs and series are directly aimed at promoting scientific understanding. A few of these science series are:

Animal Secrets—National Broadcasting Company (NBC)
RCA Building, 30 Rockefeller Plaza
New York, New York 10020

(produced in cooperation with the National Education Association and the National Science Teachers Association)

Discovery   —The American Broadcasting Companies, Inc. (ABC)
1330 Avenue of the Americas
New York, New York 10019

21st Century —Columbia Broadcasting System, Inc. (CBS)
51 West 52nd Street
New York, New York 10019

Teacher guides are available from the networks for use with your classes. Copies are available upon request from your local affiliated television studio or from the

---

[14] Katherine E. Hill, "Varying Perceptions of Science Phenomena", *Science Education*, February 1961.

[15] Phyllis S. Busch, "An Urban Field Guide for the Enrichment of the New York City Course of Study in Science for the Elementary Schools: Grades K-6," Parts I and II (unpublished Doctor's dissertation, New York University, New York City, 1959); Ralph J. Garry, "Report of Research on the Integration of Science Teaching by Television into the Elementary School Program" (unpublished Doctor's dissertation, Boston University, Boston, October, 1960), 79 pp.; USOE Project No. 031, University Microfilm Pub. No. 61-3616.

*What should the teacher
do to make film loops
effective learning devices?*

New York City offices of the networks. See your local papers for days and times of telecasts.

Some geographic areas have developed extensive programming on non-commercial educational television. State and regional cooperative groups are presenting educational television programs available during school hours for use in conjunction with on-going science curriculums.

Cost and various technical problems have retarded the growth of closed-circuit television as a direct teaching tool in most elementary schools. Federal and state governments and private foundations are assisting school districts in experimenting with closed-circuit television. It will be some time before direct teaching by television is realized in most school districts, but the following advantages are recognized for television in the educative process:

1. Certain lectures and demonstrations by well prepared and adequately equipped scientists and master teachers lend themselves to presentation to large audiences of students. This is especially valuable in districts that cannot afford these advantages.
2. The close-up possibilities of the television camera can give outstanding visibility to all students, whereas present methods of demonstration are quite limited. This was shown in a study by John Schwarzwalder, where he found that visual continuity of camera shots and specially prepared visual materials added materially to student learning.[16]
3. Students can be involved in the television productions affording them experiences in science, television, teaching and learning techniques.
4. With a two way hookup, students can ask questions of the closed-circuit television teacher.

Television, or any of the previously mentioned audiovisual aids—no matter how desirable—cannot replace the live science teacher. Nor can they develop laboratory and thinking skills and scientific processes. They are tools to be used to enhance the learning by children.

Portable, relatively inexpensive (approximately $1000) video-tape recorders are now available and some school systems have purchased them. Teachers have used

[16] John C. Schwarzwalder, "An Investigation of the Relative Effectiveness of Certain Specific TV Techniques on Learning" (available from Research and Curriculum Office, St. Paul Public Schools, St. Paul, Minnesota, 1960).

these to tape special commercial programs, to record visiting science speakers, to make tapes of their own teaching for self-evaluation.

All of the science activities mentioned so far have been *indoor* discovery science activities. They offer some valuable aids to science teaching-learning, but they also have some drawbacks. They are at best vicarious or secondhand experiences. Our children must still be exposed to many direct or firsthand science experiences; *Outdoor* discovery science activities offer these.

Outdoor Discovery Science Activities

If you are to use the outdoors for an extension of learning activities, you must know what is there and how it might be used in your science program. The wise teacher makes a community survey as soon as possible to discover the community's resources and their potential educational uses.

How might a teacher use these locales as field trip experiences for children?

Community Resources—People

One of the most important educational resources in a community for use in a science program is its people. Engineers, florists, gardeners, bird watchers, rock collectors, high school and college students, 4-H club members are but a few of the people who can be of value to you and your children in your science program. School systems have found it valuable to establish files in which pertinent information is kept on potential community resource people. Such a file might be organized around broad areas of science such as:

Biological Sciences	*Chemistry*	*Earth Science*	*Physics*
Dentist	Chemical	Astronomer	Architect
Druggist	Engineer	Geologist	Builder
Farmer	Chemist	Mining	Automobile
Florist	Druggist	Engineer	Mechanic
Laboratory	Photographer	Pilot or	Electrician
Technician		Navigator	Electronics
Nurse		Weatherman	Engineer
Pet Shop Owner			
Physician			

Community resource people are invaluable to the teacher because they can:

1. Contribute specialized knowledge in their respective fields directly to children or to teachers who will modify the information for use with children.
2. Provide inspiration and occupational aspects of science to children, especially to economically deprived children.
3. Stimulate and enrich the teacher's science background and understanding.
4. Suggest potential community places, equipment, etc. for use in science programs.
5. Serve as guides and auxiliary personnel on trips taken in conjunction with studies in science.

From the help of these community resource people and through walking and motoring excursions throughout the school community, the teacher readily finds other valuable community resources.

Community Resources—Places

As the teacher becomes more oriented to the potential community resources, he begins to see potential educational experiences all around him. Before he leaves the *school building* he sees these potential aspects of science in the physical plant itself:

1. How is the school heated? (*Heat*)
2. Where does electricity come into school? How does it get from room to room? How is the school protected from short circuits? (*Electricity*)

3. How do the telephone and intercom systems work? (*Communications*)
4. How is food selected and prepared for school lunches? (*Health and Nutrition*)

Upon leaving the school building and entering the *school yard* and *grounds*, the teacher is now alert to these science possibilities:

1. Why does soil wear away in some places on the school grounds? How might it be stopped? (*Erosion and Conservation*)
2. What kinds of plants live on our school grounds? How do they change from season to season? (*Plants*)
3. What animals live in our school yard? How do you know? What do they eat? What are their homes like? (*Animals*)
4. What machines are there in our school yard? In our play equipment? (*Simple Machines*)

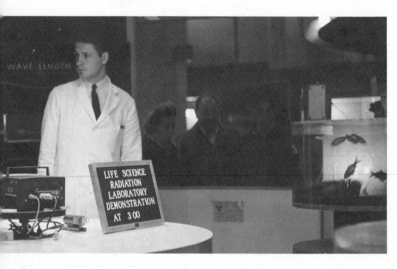

How should the teacher proceed with making arrangements to visit local demonstration facilities?

Moving off the school grounds into the community, these typical *community places* abound in interesting and useful opportunities for science teaching:

Biological Sciences	*Chemistry*	*Physics*	*Earth Science*
Biology Department (local college)	All Kinds of Factories	Airport	Abandoned Quarry
Farm	Chemistry Department (local college)	Astronomical Observatory	Field
Fish Hatchery		Electronics Factory	Geology Department (local college)
Food Processing Plant	Drugstore	Gas Station	
Greenhouse	Electroplating Shop	Physics Department (local college)	Museum
Hospital	Oil Refinery	Power Dam or Electricity Generator Plant	Seashore
House Excavation	Plastic Industry		Stream
Park	Water Purification Plant	Radio Station	Weather Station
Pharmaceutical Lab		Television Station	
Vacant Lot		Telephone Exchange	
		Newspaper Printing Plant	

A resource file kept up-to-date will serve the whole school system with these valuable potential resources for use in the science program. Figure 17 shows how a school organized trips in areas of distance from school.

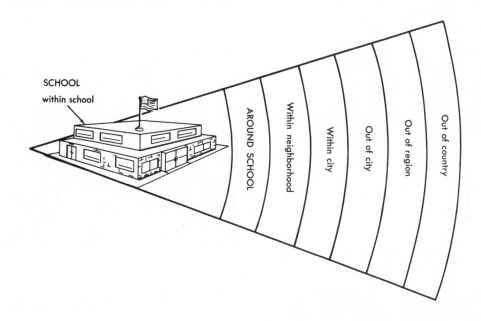

FIGURE 17. Trips Help to Broaden Concepts[17]

Types of trips available in each of the categories in Figure 17 were then filed on cards and periodically revised as teachers commented about the trips.

Educational Trips. All science program trips should have a definite purpose clearly understood by the participating children. When carefully planned and carried out, these educational trips bring scientific facts and nature together for the child, resulting in a broader and more inclusive science program. Ella Clark long ago showed that educational trips expand children's interests in the subjects being studied in the classroom.[18] Dwight Curtis also found evidence that development of scientific attitudes and methods of investigation are furthered through well planned and conducted educational trips.[19]

These educational trips are more than outings or relief from the classroom, although they frequently are seen by children as enjoyable breaks from the routine of the school day. Trips are catalytic agents. The effects of a trip have been com-

---

[17] Ideas and chart from *Trips for the Urban Child*, developed by Thelma Adair, Ruth Dale, Lucille Perryman, and Mildred Roberts, written by Ruth Dale of the School-University Teacher Education Center, P.S. 76, Queens, New York, p. 13.

[18] Ella C. Clark, "An Experimental Evaluation of the School Excursion," *Journal of Experimental Education*, 12 (September, 1943), pp. 10-19.

[19] Dwight K. Curtis, "The Contributions of the Excursions to Understanding," *Journal of Educational Research*, 38 (November, 1944), pp. 201-12.

To stimulate excitement in the long-range goals of science, how should the teacher make use of community displays as a supplement to mass media, "live" coverage of current science events?

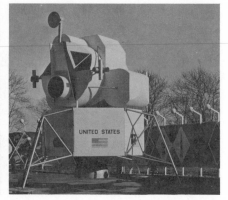

pared to the effects of pebbles thrown into a pond. Trips are the pebbles and the ripples moving out in the pond are:

1. Children's expanding science horizons
2. Clarified and illustrated ideas
3. Highlighted relationships
4. Questions raised for further study

This is particularly true for the disadvantaged child. The National Advisory Council on Education of Disadvantaged Children, in criticizing 116 Title I Elementary School Education Act projects (ESEA) in thirty-nine states, said that ". . . Most projects are ignoring field trips, which are especially profitable experiences for disadvantaged children when related to subjects being studied."[20] In

20 Anonymous, *Scholastic Teacher* (March 7, 1968), p. 4.

Figure 18 we see these roles and relations of home and community, school, and trips:

1. Home and community supply experiences that form the foundation for abstract ideas.
2. Schools provide experiences for developing and furthering abstract learning.
3. Trips provide opportunities for applying ideas learned in "life situations."

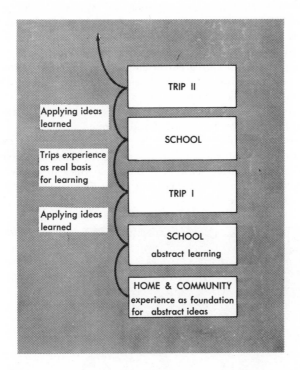

FIGURE 18. Trips and the Relationship Between Experience and Learning[21]

School Grounds Conservation Experiences

Trips need not be very extensive in either distance covered, time involved, or concepts developed. The school grounds and the immediate surrounding area offer countless possibilities for useful trips and outdoor experiences even in the largest and most industrialized cities. Erosion of soil from the bank of the playground, the planting of trees, shrubs, and grass on or around the school grounds, power lines carrying electricity to the school, the construction of buildings and roads, and the florist's greenhouse down the street all have possibilities for short, worthwhile trips.

---

[21] *Trips for the Urban Child, op. cit,* p. 13.

Children can also be helped to care for what is their heritage. Conservation programs on their own school grounds help children develop these basic attitudes and skills in their daily lives. They learn to be *active* citizens and do something about situations that need attention. Sally DeRoo, a sixth grade teacher in the Public Schools of Plymouth, Michigan, gave these examples of things in which children can actually participate to change their school ground environment:

1. Each grade can take a part in improving the school grounds, such as sixth grade planting grass on "dust bowl" ball field.
2. A general clean-up in Spring is an excellent beginning.
3. Ask children in all grades for suggestions for improving or correcting problems (worn-out bare spots where children cut across lawn, eroded spots, etc.).
4. Letters can be written to conservation officers for assistance.
5. Local gardeners or agricultural agents can be consulted.
6. A meeting or assembly program in auditorium with the custodian can be arranged so he can discuss his duties, responsibilities, and problems he has in maintaining the school grounds.
7. Other places where erosion has taken place on a large scale around the school and neighborhood can be recorded and mapped.
8. Shady trees can be planted as class project in corners of play areas.
9. Ivy vines can be planted along steel fencing for shade and color.
10. Children can help make sensible conservation rules to follow and feel better about following them as they feel a pride of "mine" whenever they see *their* trees, grass, vines, etc.[22]

What outdoor study could have these youngsters so involved in what they are doing?

School Outdoor Laboratory. The best kind of laboratory of this sort is a natural outdoor area set aside on the school grounds *before* construction of the school

---

[22] Ideas gathered from Sally DeRoo, "School Ground Conservation," *Helping Children Learn Science*, National Science Teachers Association, 1966, pp. 125-126.

begins. However, as this is not done when most schools are built, the next best thing is to set up an "outdoor classroom." This is best done by selecting an area protected on three sides by the school building (located between two wings of the school building) and a tall wire fence. Most schools can construct an outdoor classroom for $200-$500 depending upon fencing needed and items included.

The outdoor laboratory can be divided into sections to duplicate the varied conditions and habitats in your local area, region, or state. You can set up miniature meadows, swamps, pine barrens, upland areas, etc. Actual soil and vegetation can be brought in from their natural locations by children, parents, custodians, agricultural agents, and others interested in the project. This can be done before, during, and after school hours, including the weekends. Water can be supplied by downspouts, and outdoor faucets and plastic liners can make ponds and meadows leakproof.

Animals and insects can also be brought in along with the soil and vegetation to set up an ecological environment. Water and land insects, fish, frogs, rabbits, and turtles can be gathered easiest. Birds can be attracted by placing feeders and houses in the protected area. The school can constantly add to its animal and plant life and need not start "full bloom."

The maximum value is derived from the outdoor laboratory only if it is available at all times to students and teachers. They must be able to go into the area whenever it is needed to answer a question, or observe an action or relationship that cannot be obtained from a textbook or any other source. The outdoor laboratory serves the same functions *outdoors* as the indoor laboratory serves in the classroom. Erling Clausen, Superintendent of Schools, Freehold, New Jersey, lists these values of an outdoor laboratory installed in his school:

> In our outdoor laboratory, science classes learn about the relationship of plants and animals to their invironment. The conservation of natural resources is an important part of the general study. Specifics include the study of plants, such as identification of flowers, shrubs, and trees. The pupils study the actual damage inflicted on plants by insects. They use the outdoor laboratory as a source of living things, both plant and animals, for class room use. Long-range projects are another continuing interest, such as the study or erosion and the rate of growth.[23]

Having the outdoor laboratory in your school backyard saves time, cost, and effort. Other trips outside the immediate school area require more effort and planning, but offer great values also.

How to Conduct Field Trips

If you believe giving children opportunities to use more of their senses in science education is necessary, you will include field trips in your program. These trips provide experiences for making the written and spoken words of the classroom more meaningful. The following tips are offered for planning, motivating, conducting, and using the results of field trips in the science program:

---

[23] Erling W. Clausen, "A Nature Area," *Helping Children Learn Science*, National Science Teachers Association, 1966, p. 65.

Serious sample gathering isn't for the timid. To what extent should the teacher encourage active participation within the limits of safety?

1. *Why Are You Taking the Trip?*

    The field trip should be tied to the overall objectives of your science program. You may use the trip as a motivating device to arouse curiosity or raise questions in children's minds. The trip may be to collect data for questions previously raised. Pulling together many fragmentary bits of information may be still another reason for the trip. The question you should answer is: Does this trip help children learn better than any other way?

    Tips: In early fall, take those trips that require the *least* background, planning, and preparation. Use the trip to raise questions. Later in the year use trips to gather information for on-going classroom research and study. Avoid seasonal selection of trips but tie it to science program. An "off-season" trip to the zoo, museum, or factory can be an outstanding one if related to science programs.

2. *How Will You Prepare for the Trip?*

    Maximum learning will occur on trips if children have questions in mind related to the place they will visit. The teacher can be best prepared to stimulate her class *before* the trip if she follows these tips:

    Tips: Whenever possible take the trip yourself before taking the class. Study every aspect of the place to be visited and write down as many thought-provoking questions concerning it as possible. Take photos or slides to use in class to orient children. Send for any printed material available so you and your children can become familiar with the physical layouts, the overall operations, scope, and procedures of the place you will visit. Bring in resource books on the subject for the children along with related films, filmstrips, slides, etc. *You* should become as knowledgeable about the trip as possible to clarify trip purpose, procedures, rules, and regulations. *Make certain that permissions are secured from the school administration, place to be visited, and parents.*

3. *How Will You Conduct the Trip?*

    Two aspects of the trip should be given thought before beginning the trip: going to and coming from the destination and at the destination itself.

    Tips: Arrange games for developing observational skills. Point out interesting features along the route that you noted on your pre-tour. Have a list of questions handy to ask about them such as:

a. Does anyone know the name of that big factory at 11 o'clock and what is manufactured there? (Front of bus 12 o'clock, back 6 o'clock)
b. How are the trees on this street different from those at our school?
c. Why are those telephone wires sagging now when they didn't back in December when we went to the museum?

At the destination, help children observe—don't lecture or give lessons. Direct attention to items by questions. Answer any questions asked you either directly and briefly or by redirecting through a question. Relate classroom work to trip. If a guide is supplied, occasionally ask questions to direct his presentation. Ask him for clarification and simpler language if necessary. Be sure all children can hear by moving around group. Judge the pace according to the group's interest; move on to the next point *before* children get restless. Prepare them for the next point with questions requiring observation and answers. Plan stops for rest, toilet, snack, and discussions, increasing frequency with younger children.

4. *How Will You Follow Up After the Trip?*

The ways in which you conduct the follow-up of a trip are almost as important as the trip itself. Your attitudes about the trip are quickly sensed by your class. They know by your enthusiasm and interest if you feel the trip was poor or excellent. These tips are offered for making the follow-up of a trip as meaningful as possible:

Tips: A summary session at the site of the trip should be arranged when possible at the conclusion of the trip. Questions fresh in children's minds can be raised. These can possibly be answered by guides, or recorded on miniature tape recorder or written by teacher to be answered with further study back in school. When class gets back to school, children should be encouraged to record their experiences in a variety of ways:

a. Oral and written reports encompassing experiments, demonstrations, charts, graphs, etc. for classmates and other invited classes.
b. Both narrative and creative stories.

The rapport of mutual discovery. What can the teacher do to make the field trip truly enriching?

   c. Poems.

   d. Dramatic plays.

   e. Discussions based upon answering initial questions raised and information gathered.

   f. Debates on controversial issues raised as result of trip.

   g. Class newspaper for distribution to other classes and parents.

Teacher and children can devise creative evaluative devices. (See Chapter 13, "Evaluation as a Discovery Teaching Technique.") New problems and questions that arose from the trip can be considered for further action. This may lead to individual or group study and reporting, planning laboratory experiences related to the trip, or teacher presentations to the class. Teacher should relate all the results of the trip back to the purposes for taking the trip and the concepts in the area of science being studied.

When wisely used, educational trips are among the most valuable teaching tools in the science program.

Summary

If a teacher is to expose his children to learning science by discovery, he must enrich his program with as many discovery type activities as possible.

There are many *indoor* science discovery activities. The wise use of reading can contribute to a science program by relating direct, science experiences to written symbols. Children can use reading to find, extend, and verify the data they collect in their own limited experiments. Reading aids in developing skills for reading, interpreting, and evaluating science information. Students are aided in developing scientific literacy through instruction in reading in the science program; they read about the scientific ideas of others, collect additional factual material, and learn to use references effectively for further research. Suggestions were presented for using science textbooks in a discovery science program as well as for individualizing science reading materials and activities. Programmed text material and teaching machines were ways of presenting reading materials in an individualized approach.

Discussion is another language skill vital for the discovery approach in science. The teacher can use discussion to learn much about his class and the science concepts and misconceptions. The verbal skills necessary to communicate children's newly acquired information with their peers are developed. Through open discussion an excellent discovery environment is encouraged for finding answers to questions; scientific attitudes as well as skills are fostered through discussion.

Audiovisual devices are essential to a discovery teaching-learning program. Description of and discovery techniques for the following audiovisual devices were explored: films, filmloops, filmstrips, tape recordings, multi-media kits, bulletin boards and displays, microprojectors, overhead projectors, radios, and television.

Outdoor activities can also contribute to science discovery programs. Community resource people and places offer almost unlimited educational opportunities for enrichment of science programs. Suggested places and their wise use were presented. Suggestions were included for use of school grounds for teaching conservation skills, information, and attitudes. The construction and use of a school outdoor laboratory were detailed for inclusion in any science program.

Taking trips further away from school involves a great deal of teacher preparation. These questions were explored in depth for teachers anxious to develop their skills in conducting field trips:

1. Why are you taking the trip?
2. How will you prepare for the trip?
3. How will you conduct the trip?
4. How will you follow up after the trip?

The next chapter will offer practical suggestions for science facilities, equipment, and material.

SELF-EVALUATION AND FURTHER STUDY

1. How would you plan activities for overcoming the limitations of a single textbook series? Include activities for individualizing science reading.
2. Investigate programmed science materials for possible use in a science program.
3. Tape record several sessions of discussion in a science program.
4. Select a science film, filmloop, and filmstrip for use in an on-going science study. Preview the films and prepare a film guide and student worksheet for each as outlined in this chapter. Include thought-provoking discovery-type questions.
5. Evaluate multi-media packages either commercially-made or teacher-made. See Appendix for sources.
6. Design a bulletin board to illustrate some scientific concepts or principles. Include discovery-type questions.
7. Show how you would incorporate a television program in a science unit. Use either a commercial show as discussed in this chapter or an educational television show in your area. Preview it first if possible, or use guides developed by the television network.
8. Establish a card file on community people and places as discussed in this chapter. Start with your neighborhood. You may wish to expand into a grade-level or school-wide project. Involve children whenever possible.
9. Plan a trip. Follow the procedures indicated in this chapter. If possible, take children on the trip and then evaluate the results.
10. Prepare a 10 minute science tape to use with children.
11. Prepare a set of 35 mm. slides you have taken to go with a tape you prepare that students could use on an individual basis in a science study.
12. Prepare your own filmstrip. You will need a special camera for this purpose. Often one may be obtained from the Instructional Media Center of your college or university or school system.
13. Prepare a multi-media approach to a lesson in cooperation with several other individuals in your class and try it out on some children.

*It is easy to fill up a
school with things until it
becomes a showplace,
but the really important
thing is what is being
done with it; how do they
use it and do they use it
successfully.*[1]

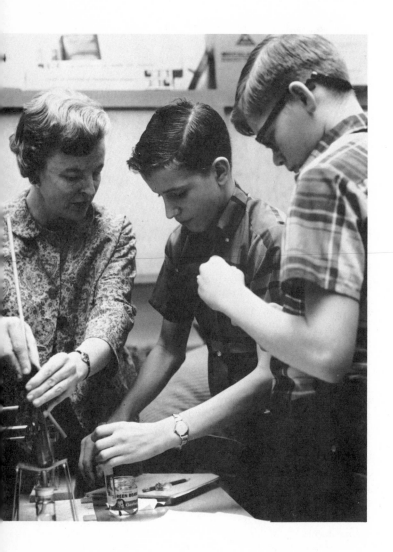

CHAPTER 9

SCIENCE FACILITIES AND MATERIALS FOR DISCOVERY TEACHING-LEARNING

Dr. Gilliand's statement says to science teachers: The goals of science programs should determine the facilities and materials needed, rather than the reverse. In this connection, teachers should ask themselves this question: What science facilities and materials will I need to present my children with optimum discovery learning conditions? The question has even more importance as schools attempt to *actively* involve children in *doing* science, rather than *passively* reading *about* science.

If science programs are to progress beyond the planning stages, elementary schools must provide adequate facilities and materials. Science teaching (especially the discovery, doing, kind) requires its own unique facilities and materials. Teachers would not think of teaching art, music, or map-making without the facilities and materials unique to each of these fields. It has been expected for too long that elementary school teachers would scavenge for necessary science materials and teach in inadequate facilities. It is true many science items can be improvised, obtained from home or from local stores. However, substitutions for some items are impossible or undesirable and at best lead to fragmentary, patchwork science programs. In addition, elementary teachers are usually too busy to improvise everything they need for science. When children are expected to engaged in laboratory activities, there must be adequate facilities, equipment, and apparatus for this purpose. If SCIS, ESS, COPES, AAAS or other science programs are to be followed, still other innovations in science equipment will be needed. Studies have shown many elementary school teachers are not familiar with science equipment and how it can effectively be used in an activity-type program.[2]

For these reasons it is recommended that the planning, purchasing, construction, and distribution of science facilities and materials be done on a total school or school district basis. In this way, greater efficiency and coordination of materials can be accomplished. Some items can be shared, some stored in a central school facility, while others can be placed in each individual classroom. This raises a question: Which is better for science teaching—self-contained or classroom science laboratories?

---

[1] John W. Gilliand, "The Educational Edifice," *Educational Equipment and Materials*, No. 1, 1968.

[2] John F. Newport, "It's Time for a Change," *School Science and Mathematics*, 65 (November, 1965) pp. 725-28; Kenneth Scott Ricker, "Guidelines for Effectiveness of Selection of Science Equipment for Elementary Schools and a Survey of the Utilization of Science Equipment in Elementary Schools in the State of Maryland" (Doctor's Dissertation, University of Maryland, 1963), *Dissertation Abstracts*, 24 (June, 1964), p. 5252.

How do the facilities of this science room influence the learning that takes place?

Self-contained or Specialized Rooms

There are advantages and disadvantages of teaching science in self-contained or specialized rooms designed especially for science teaching. Actually, the room itself is not the only issue involved. A more pertinent issue is whether regular or special teachers teach science in either self-contained or specialized rooms. In some schools, regular teachers teach science either in self-contained or special science rooms. Two of the major arguments concerning which kind of teacher-room arrangements are best are summarized as:

Self-contained Room, Regular Teacher. It is difficult for any teacher to really get to know 150-200 students a day. A teacher who has the same children all day, however, can better apply her knowledge concerning human growth, development, and learning. The room is secondary to good learning relationship between teacher and students. This view seems to be more prevalent and accepted for the primary grades than for grades 4-8.

Special Room, Special Science Teacher. It is difficult, if not impossible, for elementary school teachers to become competent in all curriculum areas. Therefore, teachers should specialize and have rooms fully equipped to stress their teaching strength.

The arguments continue and all shades of opinions exist today as to the relative merits of each teaching procedure. Joseph Zaffroni and Edith Selberg have edited a book that presents a wide range of examples of instructional practices of science teaching, should the reader wish to read further on the subject.[3]

---

[3] Joseph Zaffroni and Edith Selberg, eds., *New Developments in Elementary School Science* (Washington: D.C.: National Science Teachers Association, 1963).

In spite of a trend toward specialization, the predominant pattern in American elementary schools today is still the regular classroom teacher presenting science in a self-contained classroom. Consequently, this chapter will emphasize science facilities and materials useful in such a pattern, while also presenting total school items where pertinent for other patterns as well. It should be said, however, that some schools have provided specialized, individualized science instruction in special elementary science laboratories with promising results. School systems have also recognized the values and shortcomings of self-contained and specialized science teaching for elementary schools. Rather than look at the either/or decision, school districts have recognized the need to minimize the negative features of either way of organizing their elementary school science programs. It should be noted that although a large section of this chapter is devoted to self-contained classroom teaching of science, it does not indicate that the authors are not cognizant of the values of other patterns of organizing for the teaching of science.

Science Facilities and Materials in Self-contained Classrooms

In many cases, the self-contained elementary classroom must encompass the total elementary curriculum. Therefore, the physical arrangement of facilities, equip-

How do adequate facilities and materials affect the discussion of these children as they share a science experience?

ment, and materials must be flexibly used in the classroom. The nature of the discovery approach to science teaching necessitates provisions be made for the following science areas in the regular classroom:

1. Activity area
2. Research and library area
3. Conference area
4. Discovery area
5. Storage areas

Figure 19 presents a drawing of a self-contained classroom containing the science areas listed as recommended by the National Science Teachers Association.

Science Activity Area

Most elementary classrooms today contain movable furniture. The center of the room usually houses the movable desks or tables and chairs. The wall space areas provide opportunities for more stationary equipment and facilities. Science facilities should be grouped as much as possible in one general area of the room. The needed equipment, supplies, and other materials should be readily and easily available for making, assembling, experimenting, and demonstrating.

The National Science Teachers Association recommends the following provisions be made in order to make this a dynamic working area:

1. A work counter with one or more sinks with hot and cold water.
2. A convenient electric outlet (110-120 volt AC) for a hotplate at the work counter.
3. Safe sources of heat for experiments, such as the small liquid petroleum burners.
4. Dry cells or a low-voltage direct and alternating powerpack for electrical experiments. (These electric substations may either be portable or permanently installed in the work counter; for safety, they should be installed beyond reaching distance of the sink and its hardware.)[4]

In active pupil participation in the discovery science program, there must be adequate space for all children to work. Even in small and crowded classrooms experiments, demonstrations, construction, and other activity parts of the science program can be performed. Space next to and beneath window sills can be used for work areas, as can counter tops. Flat top desks can be moved together for larger work areas. The teacher will find at least one large table in a classroom is a great help in doing science experiments and other activities. The tables used should be water and acid resistant. This can be accomplished by using Masonite or laminated plastic such as Formica to cover desks and tables. Where burners are going to be used, the best tops are stone or composition stone.

Temporary work areas, preferable in most self-contained elementary classrooms, can be improvised by putting boards or plywood across two wooden boxes or sawhorses. A workbench and hand tools are desirable in this area for constructing simple equipment. Schools can purchase standard workbenches in any size to fit the age and size of the children who will use them. These work benches are generally used for preparing materials in other areas of the curriculum besides science. Handsaws, hammers, pliers, screwdrivers, shears, and other hand tools can be hung on plywood in back of the workbench.

---

[4] "Science Facilities for Our Schools K-12," *Science Teacher*, Vol. 30, No. 8 (December, 1963), p. 58.

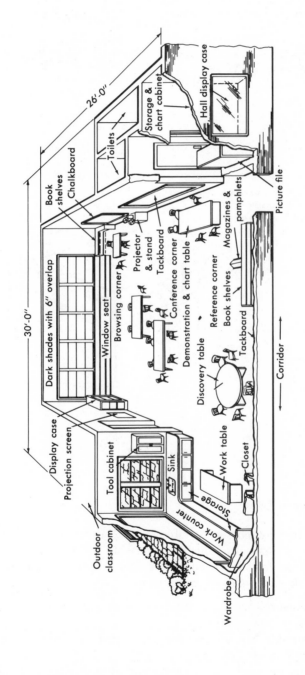

FIGURE 19. The Boys and Girls in This Self-contained Classroom Will Find Many Opportunities to Study Science.[5]

[5] John S. Richardson, ed., *School Facilities for Science Instruction*, (Washington, D.C.: National Science Teachers Association, 1961), p. 56.

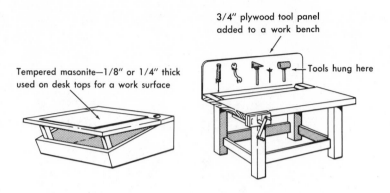

3/4" plywood tool panel added to a work bench

Tempered masonite—1/8" or 1/4" thick used on desk tops for a work surface

Tools hung here

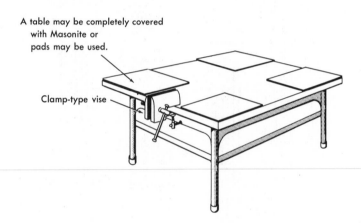

A table may be completely covered with Masonite or pads may be used.

Clamp-type vise

FIGURE 20.

Portable Science Labs

Some schools have purchased portable science labs for use in their activity programs. These are especially valuable in very old buildings lacking flexibility and conditions needed for such science programs. Although rather expensive, these portable labs offer the following advantages:

1. All needed science apparatus, equipment, and supplies are included, even water and sources of heat.
2. The portable labs are compact (no larger than the size of a table) and contain their own storage.
3. They are extremely easy to move and even children can wheel them from room to room.
4. Construction is good and the portable labs are very durable.

5. Cost per class is cut down by the proper scheduling of the portable lab for many classes.

Suggestions are presented later in this chapter for constructing your own mobile science lab-work area.

Figure 21 is a picture of a commercial portable science lab. A discussion of practical consideration in purchasing these will be presented later in this chapter under "Total Science Facilities and Equipment." Commercial suppliers of these labs are listed in the Appendix.

FIGURE 21.

Science Research and Library Area

An area should be set aside in the classroom for science research from textbooks, encyclopedias, and other reference books, pamphlets, charts, maps, and graphs. The research area should be well lighted and should contain adequate furniture such as tables, chairs, and bookshelves. There should also be supplementary audio-visual equipment such as 8 mm cartridge filmloops, filmstrips, tape recorders and tapes, phonograph records, and programmed materials.

Every effort should be made to include a wide range of reading level materials covering various science fields and interests. This should be a quiet place where children go to find answers to their questions. Encouragement should be given by the teacher to stimulate the use of this area by the students. The teacher should point out to children that scientists spend considerable time researching the work of other scientists. The rules and regulations for the use of the research area should be cooperatively worked out by teacher and children. Teaching of reference skills should stress the use of multiple references and not just one source of information. Children should be encouraged to bring in science research materials.

Science Conference Area

There is very often need for the teacher and children to hold small conferences or carry on group planning in the science program. An area can be set aside for such a purpose. Often a table and six chairs is satisfactory if it is placed away from distracting influences. Occasionally the classroom research area serves as the conference area. Other times it merely means moving six chairs to the back of the room. Regardless of how it is done, the conference area should allow small groups to confer and plan quietly without disturbing others in the room.

It is helpful to have a chalkboard in conference areas for illustrating a point. Refer to the drawing of the self-contained classroom in Figure 19 for ideas, and think how you would modify the room to make it a more effective learning center.

Science Discovery Corner

In a discovery science program, a science corner is necessary in which an assortment of materials is available during *free time* for exploring, discovering, experimenting, and just plain tinkering. This corner should contain a workbench as mentioned previously and materials for constructing such things as animal cages, models, and apparatus for demonstration and experiments. A work area of this

What are the values to a science program of a science discovery center in a classroom?

kind can be simply two desks pushed together, or it can be a commercially made furniture unit with all necessary materials and workbench built in. Storage space should be provided so tools, equipment, and other materials can be put away when not in use. A list of equipment, supplies, and materials that are useful in a discovery area are presented in the Appendix.

It is vital that free time be provided for *each* child to spend some time in the science discovery corner. This can be done by assigning time for individuals or small groups to work there as part of their current work in science or other curricular areas. Children can also select this area when they complete their regular assignments. This area may be used as incentive for children to finish their work quickly and correctly.

Storage Areas in Classroom

Planning for work and storage space should be done concurrently. Teachers should decide what equipment they need for activities in science and at the same time how they will store their equipment. Adequate storage is one of the chief concerns of science teachers in new as well as older schools. Science teachers must store science supplies, apparatus, equipment, consumable items, chemicals, charts, models, audiovisual supplies, hand tools, etc. If possible, schools should purchase science cabinets, shelving, and other laboratory storage furniture from any of the scientific supply houses listed in the Appendix. For example, see Figure 26 in the discussion "Elementary Science Laboratories" later in this chapter. The excellent quality and flexibility in today's laboratory storage furniture are well worth the money in durability and protection of students and teachers. This investment also reduces loss of equipment and supplies due to improper and unprotected storage.

How could these drawers be organized for the storage of science *supplies? How might the children do this?*

Later in this chapter the use of a central storage room for some items will be discussed. Although the central storage room may alleviate the teacher's burden of storing seldom-used or bulky materials in each classroom, storage *within* the classroom must be provided for frequently used items.

Activity Area Storage. Excellent storage space can be obtained by using space beneath window ledges, counter tops, and sinks. Commercially-made cabinets that fit any of these spaces plus others around or above heating units in the classroom can be purchased.

If funds are unavailable for purchasing storage furniture, or if the teacher feels it is a valuable learning experience for his children, storage cabinets for these areas can be easily improvised. Temporary storage cabinets can be easily constructed by children, teachers, and/or school custodians using wooden crates or boxes as in Figure 22. The only tools needed are handsaws, hammers, and screwdrivers and children of almost any age can do much of the work required.

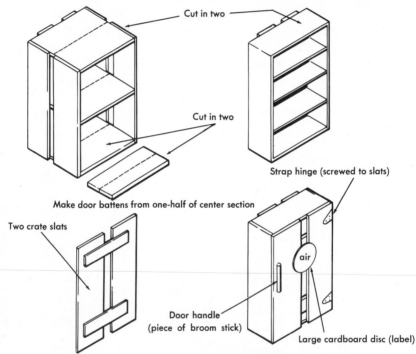

FIGURE 22. Storage Cabinets from Crates or Boxes

These storage cabinets can be attractively painted and arranged in a variety of ways. They can be placed side by side under window sills, sinks, or along walls of the science activity area. Casters can be attached to the bottom of these cabinets so they can be moved around the classroom or from one classroom to another. Additional space, possibly for displays, can be achieved by attaching a piece of plywood across the back of one or more cabinets and extending over the top. Cabinets can be stacked several high and bolted or screwed together where they join. The possibilities for a variety of uses for these converted crates are limited only by the ingenuity of the children and the teacher.

Work Area Storage.   Another storage need arises in the area where children engage in construction activities. Considerable storage space can be obtained by simply enclosing the bottom of a workbench, as illustrated in Figure 23.

Casters can be attached to the legs of these workbenches; this alleviates storage problems and provides easily movable work space. These benches may be moved from room to room as needed. Actually, any table (preferably at least six feet long) around the school can be mounted on casters. The area under the table can be

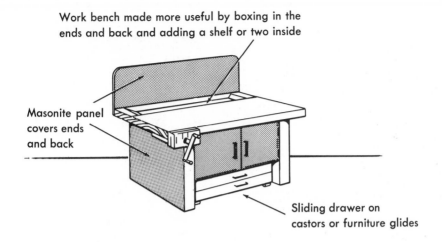

Work bench made more useful by boxing in the
ends and back and adding a shelf or two inside

Masonite panel
covers ends
and back

Sliding drawer on
castors or furniture glides

FIGURE 23. Storage Space Under Workbench

used for storage in the same way as the workbench. Having one of these for each two or more rooms provides flexibility in the science program. School custodians can make portable workbenches or tables in a couple of hours. The cost of converting a table into a portable work-storage area is minimal. Occasionally parents can be asked to contribute their time for doing this conversion.

Small Item Storage—Shoe Box Collections. There is constant need for storing the numerous small items used in discovery science activities. Shoe boxes, wooden cheese or cigar boxes, or other small boxes provide space for collecting, organizing, and storing the small, readily available materials for particular science areas. For instance, let us assume that the fifth grade has just completed a study and activities in the area of magnetism and electricity. During the activity part of the study the children collected and used bits of wire, bells, light sockets and bulbs, dry cells, and iron filings; they also made switches and telegraph sets. The teacher decided after all the effort required to collect these items, he would save them for next year's work. The collected magnetic and electrical materials were put in the shoebox along with a note indicating the contents (for replacement of lost or consumed items) and directions on how to use the materials. Discovery questions were put on cards to guide children's explorations in this science area. The idea caught on so well that the teacher and his children did the same for other science lessons. Eventually there were many shoe box collections of science materials organized in the manner shown in Figure 24.

One of the advantages of using shoe boxes, cigar boxes, or cheese boxes is their size limits the amount of stored materials; this forces the teacher to be more discriminating in selecting and keeping only essential materials. Plastic shoe boxes and trays are available commercially and are easily stored in the cabinets previously described.

Larger cardboard boxes may be used for storage and placed in steel shelving especially designed for the purpose. Teachers have found cardboard cartons can be obtained free from moving and storage companies, shipping departments of most commercial businesses, and stores, as well as the school's own cafeteria and

SHOE BOX COLLECTION　　　　　CHEESE BOX COLLECTION

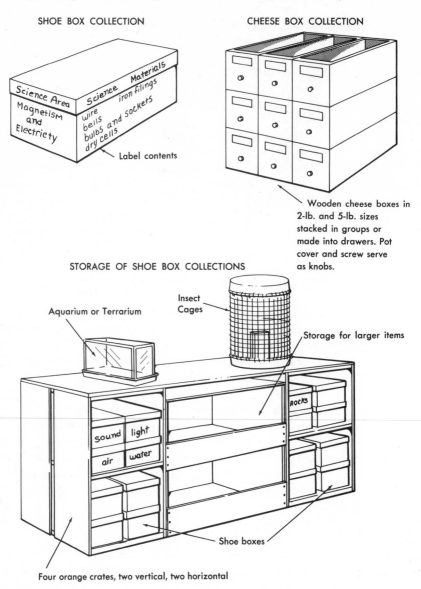

FIGURE 24. Construction and Storage of Shoebox Collections

school supply shipments. The carton faces can be gaily painted or covered with decorative adhesive paper.

Additional information for constructing science shoe box kits can be found in concise, practical articles by Gantert, Lange and Payne, and Sabolewski and Fung.[6]

---

[6] Robert L. Gantert, "Science Kits As Classroom Aids," Laboratories in the Classroom (New York: Science Materials Center, 220 East 23rd Street, 1960), pp. 87-88; Erwin F. Lange and K. E. Payne, "Science Kits in Elementary Science Teaching," *The Science Teacher*, Vol. 25, No. 6 (October, 1958), pp. 321-23; Chester A. Sabolewski and Lynette B. Fung, "Science in a Shoe Box," *The Grade Teacher* (September, 1965), pp. 148-49.

Materials and Storage—Living Things

Provisions must be made for caring for all types of living things in the classroom. In order to encourage children to bring in animals and plants, the classroom must have a variety of suitable containers for housing them. The wise teacher will always have the following containers available in his classroom: insect cages, small animal cages, aquariums, and terrariums.

Insect Cages. Use small cake pans, coffee cans, or covers from ice cream cartons for the cover and base. Roll wire screening into cylinder to fit the base and lace the screening together with a strand of wire.

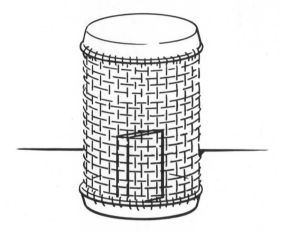

Cut windows in a paper coffee container, oatmeal box, or shoe box. Glue plastic wrap, cellophane, silk, or nylon stocking over the windows.

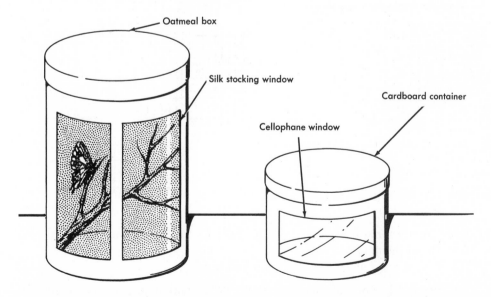

Fill a wide-mouthed quart or gallon pickle jar with soil to within two inches of top of jar. Cover the jar with a nylon stocking and place the jar in a pan of water.

This type of a container can be used for ants, termites, worms, etc. Cover the jar with black construction paper after putting in the insects.

Animal Cages. Some of the insect containers can also be used for small animals. Larger animals can be housed in easily constructed cages.

A cage for a larger animal can be made from wire screening. Cut the wire screening as shown here. Fold where dotted lines are indicated. Tack or staple three sides of the screening to a wooden base; hook one side to enable easy cleaning.

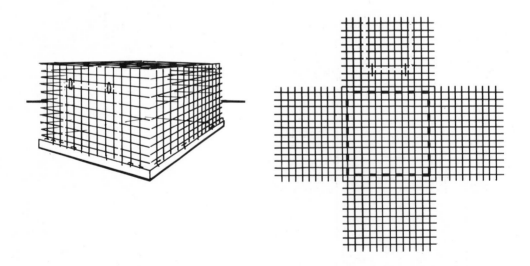

Listed here are some things you need for housing the more commonly used animals in the elementary school.

For housing *non-gnawing animals* you will need:

1. Wooden box or crate about 24″ × 16″ × 12″ with door that can be securely closed.

2. Wood shavings, sawdust, or strips of newspaper on floor of cage making soft sleeping and hiding materials.
3. A bottle with a one-hole stopper and tubing hung on the side of the cage to supply water.
4. Some animals, like snakes, require a wooden branch for support of body; snakes also need a tight fitting cover as they squeeze out of the smallest opening.

For housing *gnawing animals* you will need:

1. Metal or wire mesh cages as animals gnaw through wood; a removable solid metal bottom is preferable for cleaning purposes.
2. Rabbits require a great deal of ventilation; use wire cage shown here but enlarge it to about 3′ × 3′ × 2′.
3. Floor covering and water supply as for non-gnawing animals.

Terrariums. Terrarium means "little world." In setting one up for any animal or insect, try to duplicate in miniature the conditions similar to those in which the animal or insect originally lived. Plants, soil, water, temperature, etc. should be

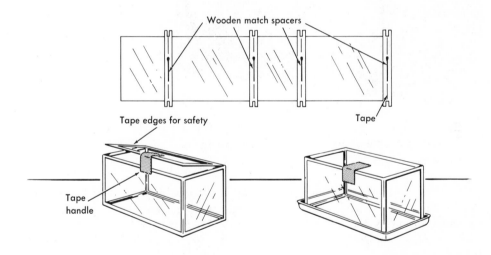

matched as closely as possible to the natural conditions. To make a terrarium, obtain six pieces of glass (custodian can be of assistance here) and place as follows: arrange the glass according to the drawing using wooden matches for proper spacing. This spacing is important to allow for making corners. Use tape one inch wide (plastic or adhesive) on joints and rub very hard to insure good adhesion. *Remove the matches.* Turn the glass over and put tape on the other side in the same manner. Place tape on the lid according to the drawing and another piece for a handle. Place the finished glass terrarium in a large cookie or cake pan. A terrarium also can be set up from commercially made equipment as shown on page 200.

Suggestions for plants, animals, and conditions for setting up different kinds of terrariums can be obtained from:

Biological Supply House, Inc. 8200 South Hoyne Avenue, Chicago, Illinois 60620. *Free* by writing on school stationery for Turtox Service Leaflets, especially: No. 10—The School Terrarium; No. 25—Feeding Aquarium and Terrarium Animals.

National Science Teachers Association, 1201 Sixteenth St., N. W., Washington, D. C. 20036. Send 25¢ for How to Do It Phamplets, especially: "How to Care for Living Things in the Classroom" by Grace K. Pratt (Stock No. 471-14288).

Why do you think a terrarium is valuable in a science classroom?

Food and other requirements for a variety of water and land animals are presented in the Appendix for your use in setting up and caring for terrariums and aquariums.

Aquariums. An aquarium should be set up in the classroom. Any glass container that could house water plants and animals will do; such as commercial-size mayonnaise jars usually available from the school cafeteria. Directions for construction of an aquarium are available free by writing to the Biological Supply House and asking for the following Turtox Service Leaflets:

No. 5—Starting and Maintaining a Fresh-Water Aquarium
No. 11—Plants for the Fresh-Water Aquarium
No. 48—Aquarium Troubles: Their Prevention and Cure

A photo of a commercially made aquarium is presented on the next page.

Science Facilities and Materials for Total School Use

Several kinds of facilities and activities are more suitable for total school involvement than for self-contained classrooms. These are:

How does an aquarium enrich a scientific program? Is it necessary for it to be absolutely clean? Can it still contribute to science learning if it is murky?

1. Elementary science laboratories
2. Elementary school science center
3. Central apparatus and supply storage
4. Science study carrels
5. School science club room
6. School science museums

Considerations will be given to the kinds of facilities and equipment suggested for each area as well as the best utilization of these rooms in science discovery programs.

What advantages (and disadvantages) do you see for a discovery science program in this "school-in-the-round," in which all rooms open into a carpeted teaching area?

Elementary Science Laboratories

The elementary science laboratory is gaining prominence in schools utilizing departmentalized science for grades four, five, six; and those schools organized as "middle schools" with grades five, six, seven, and eight. The laboratories should *not* be miniature replicas of the traditional high school science laboratories with their huge stone tables and uncomfortable stools. They should be flexibly set up so that rearrangement of furniture and apparatus can be done quickly and quietly. The labs should have movable and adjustable chairs and tables for maximum use by children of many ages and sizes. The perimeter of the room should have as much counter space and storage as possible. Whenever possible, an adjoining preparation and storage area should be provided. There should be several sinks with hot and cold water; these should be on the periphery of the room in what is known as island or peninsula fashion. Several children at one time can work around these types of sink areas instead of just one child at a traditional-style sink. At least one sink should be large enough to accommodate a large aquarium for cleaning.

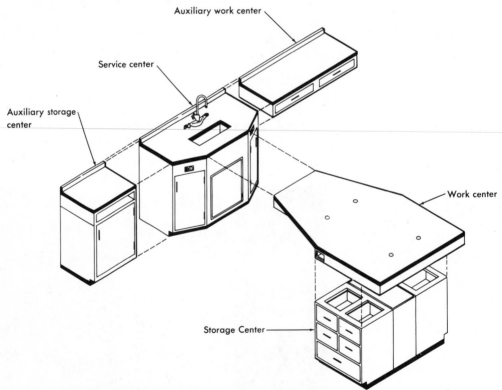

FIGURE 25. Flexible Arrangement of Science Lab Work and Storage Areas

Figure 25 shows this work-sink area, as well as the storage space available.[7] The Uni-Lab in the exploded diagram gives an idea of how many different assemblies are possible from the basic pieces of modular lab units. A minimum of seven children can use the area at one time.

---

7 Uni-Lab—courtesy Kewaunee Technical Furniture Co., Statesville, N.C.

Converting Older Classrooms Into Science Laboratories. Flexible science labs are possible not only in modern, up-to-date structures but may be added in older, existing buildings. The National Science Teachers Association recommends that consideration b₂ given to these factors when renovating or converting rooms for use as elementary science laboratories:

1. Adequate lighting, through adding windows and providing more artificial illumination.
2. Enlargement of rooms by removing partitions.
3. Installation of adequate heating and ventilating systems.
4. Renovation of old floors by sanding and sealing, or covering with prepared flooring materials of light color.
5. Provision for running water in classroom.
6. Acoustical treatment of ceilings and walls.
7. Resurfacing of chalkboards and conversion of chalkboard space to tackboard and chart rack.
8. Installation of electrical outlets.[8]

Labs should have sufficient electrical outlets at each work area. Equipment, supplies, and apparatus should be extensive and in sufficient quantities for active child participation. Suggestions are given in the Appendix for such equipment.

In a departmental arrangement, classes would be scheduled for their science work in the laboratories. With a self-contained classroom arrangement, teachers could use this room for activities that are not possible in their regular rooms due to shortage of space or equipment. In addition, this classroom could also function as an Elementary School Science Center.

Elementary School Science Center

An elementary school science center can be a versatile adjunct facility for any science program. Among its many possible functions are:

---

[8] John S. Richardson, *op. cit.*, p. 63.

1. Storage of equipment and supplies.
2. Place for the teacher preparation of science materials for use in the classroom.
3. The teacher can send a student or small groups of children to the center for the preparation of science materials for a project.
4. The teacher can bring his class to present a demonstration or experiment.
5. In-service science workshops and demonstration lessons can be conducted here.

Any room may serve as a science center—from a classroom to an over-sized storage room. Essential in a center are very large amounts of storage, working counters and tables, a sink with running hot and cold water, electric outlets, and cages and houses for living plants and animals. It is very useful to have a rolling cart so equipment can be moved easily from the center to classrooms.

One school set up a schedule of center orientation sessions for the *students*, beginning with older children who then helped orient the younger children. During the orientation, the purpose of the center was discussed along with equipment and kinds of activities that could be done. In their classes, children worked out rules and regulations and activities for use in the center.

Once work started, children contributed equipment and supplies. Each teacher was assigned several hours a week of duty in the center to assist children and catalog equipment and supplies. As the center developed, older children assumed these responsibilities along with conducting tours for younger children. The centers also can serve as central storage for a school as well as science club rooms and museums. It is strongly urged that one be started in every elementary school.

Some school districts, such as De Kalb County in Georgia, have set up science centers for kindergarten through college. The Firbank center in De Kalb County operates, and its plant looks something like, a modern science museum. It differs, however, from a museum in that its total function and staff are devote to education. Firbanks has many student laboratory work areas and all of its facilities and staff serve as an adjunct to the science programs given in the various schools.

Separate Science Building.   Other school districts, such as the Nashville Metropolitan Public Schools in Tennessee, have established experimental science experience centers in separate buildings. Figure 26 shows an interior floor plan for one such unit, the Science Experience Center housed in a portable metal building next to the Carter Lawrence Elementary School in Nashville, Davidson County, Tennessee.[9] The facilities in this 30′ × 40′ building were designed by the E. H. Sheldon Equipment Company of Muskegon, Michigan, and contain such items as:

1. Temperature and light controls.
2. Portable interior walls for flexible room division.
3. Portable tables and other equipment.
4. Mathematical designs and scales fabricated into the floor covering, with washable surfaces.
5. Diamond-shaped tables for individual or team work, each with its own

---

[9] Interior floor plan, as well as photo and interesting description of the Science Experience Center are found in: Neil W. Carter, "Science Experience Center," *Science and Children*, Vol. 4, No. 5 (February, 1967), p. 14.

storage cabinet, tote trays, waste container, supply of most frequently used materials; 110 volt AC outlets and portable AC/DC power supplies 0-12 volts, etc.

6. Growing carts and animal cases with light controls.
7. Movable demonstration desks.
8. Roll-up projector screens.

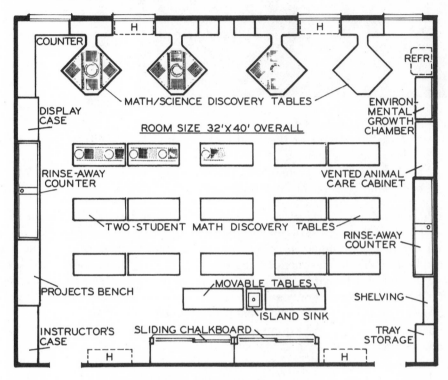

FIGURE 26. Science Experience Center

The facilities of a science experience center are designed to offer pupils an opportunity to participate in firsthand science experiences in a laboratory environment not possible in many elementary schools.

Central Apparatus and Supply Storage

Many schools cannot afford, nor is there space in classroom, to provide each teacher with all the science equipment he needs for the entire year. Storage becomes more difficult as more teachers move toward student-conducted laboratory activities. The solution to this problem is that each teacher be provided with such basic equipment as dry cells, wire, heat source, assorted glassware, some simple tools, etc. in his classroom. Other less frequently used or bulky apparatus, equipment, and materials are stored in a convenient, centrally located storage area. This area could be set up in any of the following places:

1. Corner of properly outfitted furnace room.
2. Part of science center with adequate number of locked cabinets.

In what ways can children help set up tools and work areas for science?

3. Large supply closet.
4. Boxed-in corners or the dead ends of blind halls with plywood or wallboard and shelving.
5. Part of teachers' lounge or lunchroom.
6. Behind the stage of an auditorium.

Pieces of the more expensive, unusual, delicate, or "exotic" equipment should be stored in this area. Microscopes and microprojectors, demonstration models and exhibits, galvanometers, telescopes, and other apparatus could be made readily available to classroom teachers from this area. Items should be checked out through a cataloging system so each piece of equipment can be accounted for at all times. This not only assures security of equipment but allows all teachers to know where an item is in the event it is needed quickly.

Some pieces of special equipment such as Geiger counters may be borrowed for a short time from the high school physics department, a local hospital, lab, or from industries nearby. These pieces of equipment can be kept locked in the central supply area until needed. Other items not to be handled except by the teacher, such as acids, sharp dissecting tools, hypodermic needles, or combustible materials, can be stored safely in the same way.

Supplies. This area also could serve as a supply depot for items necessary for the science program. Responsibility for ordering, replenishing, delivering, maintaining, and housekeeping should be carefully worked out. This can be the work of a science consultant or specialist, the librarian, an audiovisual coordinator, a classroom teacher, the school secretary or clerk, the principal, a competent custodian, or a committee of trained and responsible older children. Periodical replacements should be made of worn, damaged, or consumed items; unless this is carefully done, supplies become depleted and unavailable for classroom use. All teachers should be supplied with an up-to-date list of supplies and equipment in the science room. Supplies and equipment can be scheduled by teachers and used in the special science areas or delivered to the classrooms. Schools have found cafeteria or supermarket carts valuable for delivery purposes.

Ordering and Inventorying Science Materials. There has been a sharp increase in the purchase of science apparatus and supplies partly as a result of the National Defense Education Act of 1958 and the Elementary and Secondary Edu-

Where can the teacher most easily find simple science equipment for use with young children?

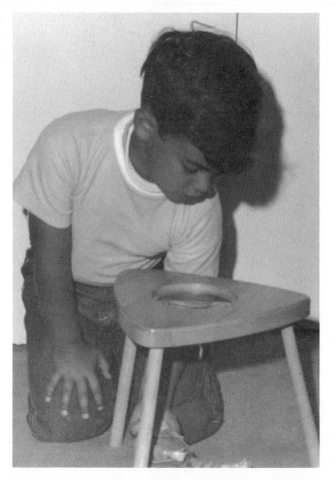

cation Act of 1965. Both of these acts made large sums of money available to elementary schools for purchasing science equipment as well as for constructing new science facilities. Too often elementary school teachers have not been asked, nor have they felt competent, to participate in ordering science equipment and supplies. Elementary school science teachers *must* help decide what shall be purchased because they are the ones who directly use the equipment. Presented here are some guidelines for teachers as they take part in ordering science equipment and supplies.

Tips for Inventorying, Ordering, and Cataloging Science Materials

1. Review your specific science goals and objectives for the year from your curriculum guide or other source; especially list activities and the equipment and quantity needed for children to participate.

2. Send for the following to obtain suggested items for each science area and its relative importance—audiovisual aids, annotated lists of furniture and equipment, etc.:

    Purchase Guide for Programs in Science and Mathematics, Boston: Ginn and Company, 1965. Outstanding for annotated descriptions of science hardware,

What kinds of activities do these science supplies suggest?

professional and trade books, curriculum studies, and ways to use science materials.

3. Secure catalogs and brochures from suppliers listed in the Appendix. Scan to familiarize yourself with kinds of equipment that are available. Wherever possible, have representatives of companies demonstrate their equipment for the elementary teachers.

4. Teachers, science consultants, and/or responsible older children should make *two* inventory lists of items anywhere in school building: non-expendable and expendable science materials. These inventories will help to avoid unnecessary duplication. They can be used for cataloging new items as they are received (see item 8. in this list) or for quickly observing which materials must be replenished. Examples of index card forms to be kept on file are presented here.

	EXPENDABLE SCIENCE MATERIALS INVENTORY				
Date	*Description of Item*	*Condition*	*Quantity on Hand*	*Quantity Needed*	*Needed Expenditure*
11/68	Balloons—rubber 8″	good	24	none	none
11/68	Dry cells, 6 volt	weak	12	12	$1.25 ea.
11/68	Flasks, Florence 1000 ml glass	excellent	12	24 (purchase plastic ones)	$2.00 ea.
11/68	Glass Tubing 10mm	broken lengths	50 ft.	5 lbs.	$ .40 per lb.

NON-EXPENDABLE SCIENCE MATERIAL INVENTORY			
Description of Item	*Condition*	*Quantity*	*Where Located*
Magnifying glass—4″ lens	good	6	Room 16
Aquariums—5 gal. with cover	good	2	Room 8

5. Find out from science consultant, supervisor, or principal, amount of money allocated for purchasing science materials. *Reminder:* Have school investigate possible funds available from federal or state governments for this purpose.

6. Make a *priority list* of items, quantities, and prices for your total expenditure. This will aid you if budget is cut or certain items are unavailable or higher priced than originally allocated.

7. Submit your list to science consultant, supervisor, principal, high school science teacher, or other teachers for their advice and guidance. These people can also see if you have a balance of science aids covered as well as the wisdom of your selections.

8. It is efficient to have one person responsible for coordinating and submitting the inventory and science material orders, cataloging items as they come in, and distributing the material. The science consultant, principal, or designated teacher can serve in this capacity. A squad of older, responsible children can assist in these functions.

9. Items can be grouped by science areas and stored as suggested previously in this chapter.

10. Whenever possible, a petty cash account should be established in each school. This is valuable for quickly picking up small items from local stores, rather than through cumbersome purchasing procedures.

Reminder: Don't overlook community sources and mail order houses such as Sears, Roebuck and Co. for free and inexpensive science materials. A list of some of these available community supplies, equipment, and materials are listed in the Appendix. Children are also a source of materials for the science program.

Kits and Other "Packaged" Science Materials. A trend in science today is the purchase of ready-made science kits and other "packaged" science materials. Although expensive, these kits are gaining in popularity due to:

1. Proliferation of science equipment and supplies available for use in elementary school science.
2. Administrators and teachers too busy to select and order separate items from the numerous science catalogs.
3. Inexperienced science teachers might prefer a ready-made program and all available materials right at hand.
4. Kits are easy to store as the manufacturers package all needed items in compact boxes.

Due to the profusion of science material "packages" on the market today, extreme care should be used in selecting, buying, and using kits. The following are highly recommended for authoritative information concerning the practical considerations in selecting, buying, and using kits in elementary school science:

Piltz, Albert, "Science Equipment and Materials for Elementary Schools." Washington, D. C.; Office of Education Bulletin 1961, No. 28, U. S. Dept. of Health, Education, and Welfare.

——————, "Getting the Most from the Equipment Dollar," *The Instructor* (January, 1964), pp. 49-79.

—————— and William J. Gruver, "Science Equipment and Materials: Science Kits." Washington, D. C.; Office of Education Bulletin 1963, No. 332, U. S. Department of Health, Education, and Welfare.

The EPIE Forum. EPIE, Box 2379, Grand Central Station, New York 10017. Subscription: $25 annually. A monthly publication of the Educational Products Information Exchange Institute created by and for professionals in education. This non-profit organization has as its two central objectives:

(1) Building an easily accessible, nationwide system for exchanging descriptive and evaluative product data among all sectors of the educational community on a cooperative cost-sharing basis, and,

(2) Stimulating educational professionals in schools and in industry to contribute and to use regularly this base of data as a part of their professional responsibilities.

On its advisory board, EPIE has representatives from the National Science Teachers Association, Department of Classroom Teachers of NEA, National Council of Teachers of Mathematics, etc.

A list of commercial suppliers of kits is in the Appendix of this book.

By keeping kits in the central storage area and signing them out to teachers when needed, reduced costs per class can be realized. By careful scheduling, one kit can service many classes. Kits can easily be stacked and moved on mobile frames such as illustrated here. Generally speaking, cardboard kits do not hold up as well as plastic or metallic containers.

Science Study Carrels

There is growing interest in schools for setting up places where children can approach the learning of science on an individual basis. Two research projects that have tried this auto-tutorial approach to learning science were conducted by Joseph Lipson and Joseph Novak. Each used special rooms where children worked at their own individual learning stations called *carrels*.

In Joseph Lipson's work at the Learning Research and Development Center of the University of Pittsburgh, children worked on thirty individualized laboratory lessons concerning light and its properties.[10] The children worked at their own pace on kits of materials, tapes, records, worksheets. They then took special tests of performance to measure their achievement (examples of which will be presented in the next chapter, "Evaluation"). The results so far show the auto-

---

[10] Joseph J. Lipson, "Evaluating Light Lessons Designed for the Elementary School Laboratory" (a paper presented at the Fortieth Annual Meeting of the National Association for Research in Science Teaching, Chicago, Illinois, February 24, 1967).

What advantages and disadvantages are there in using kits for discovery teaching?

tutorial approach to be effective in developing science concepts in young children. Because of this original success, the Learning Research and Development Center has expanded the project to prepare totally individualized science curriculum for grades K-6.

Joseph Novak also found the auto-tutorial approach to be effective.[11] He made audiotape recordings of science lessons on plant growth which were combined with filmloops and kits of materials. These learning aids were used by children in individual study carrels. The children not only learned science concepts but were successful in the use of the study carrels, the use of learning equipment, and developing self-learning skills.

A study carrel can be arranged in the back of an elementary school lab, science club or museum, or even in a self-contained classroom. Self-learning materials and equipment such as audio tapes, records, filmloops, and science kits are required for this approach. See Chapter 8 for the use of such devices.

Science Club Room

Science clubs and museums are becoming more commonplace in elementary schools, especially in those with departmentalized fifth and sixth grades. Times are

---

[11] Joseph D. Novak, "Development and Use of Audio-Taped Programmed Instruction for Elementary Science" (a paper presented at the Fortieth Annual Meeting of the National Association for Research in Science Teaching, Chicago, Illinois, February 24, 1967).

designated in such schools when children can participate in clubs organized in such areas as science, music, art, literature, etc. A teacher volunteers to work with each club in guiding and directing his particular area of interest. Because of the self-selection basis for the clubs, motivation and interest of the children are high. Teachers may present science ideas through demonstrations, experiments, films, etc., but usually the bulk of the time is devoted to student activities.

The elementary school laboratories or school science centers (mentioned earlier in this chapter) are most appropriate for science clubs because of the activity facilities. However, any classroom can be arranged for activities by following the suggestions made earlier in the chapter. It is recommended that the science club period of time be in blocks of at least two hours each due to the time needed for preparing and conducting activities and cleaning up. Clubs are another avenue for enriching the science programs for highly stimulated children. It must be pointed out, however, these children are not necessarily the "best" students.

Science Museum

A science museum may be set up anywhere in the school, such as in the special science lab, science center, or back of a gym or lunchroom. A museum may start with collections of shells, rocks, or plants, etc. by children, teachers, parents, or commercial firms. The science club can add works to the museum and can also help maintain, inventory, and do the necessary housekeeping. As the museum increases its offering, the science club members or other responsible children can be trained to serve as "tour guides" for other classes in the school. If the room can be locked, animals and plants could be kept here also; children can be helped to care for these living things. They can also use the outdoor science facilities mentioned in this chapter when weather conditions are suitable.

Mobile Science Laboratory

Many school districts recognize that their science programs cannot be limited to the school building if the entire spectrum of science is to be explored. For this reason, outdoor facilities are needed and some were introduced in Chapter 8. An additional outdoor facility gaining in popularity is the mobile science laboratory.

This scene is from a mobile science lab. How might this laboratory be used effectively in your school district?

These mobile science labs may be buses or large semitrailer trucks converted into fully equipped portable laboratories.

The public schools of Albert Lea, Minnesota, have set up a mobile unit with the necessary materials and equipment for in-depth study of biological materials while specimens are fresh and can be studied in relation to their total environment.[12] A tour of the mobile laboratory from front to rear shows the library, instructors' areas, and the fourteen student stations. A double row of continuous fluorescent ceiling lights illuminate the interior and an appropriate ventilation system provides eleven changes of fresh outdoor air per hour. Examination of a student station shows wall cabinets, undercabinet fluorescent lighting, electrical, gas, and water outlets. Formica wall backing and counter tops are provided along with drawers for equipment storage.

As shown in the photo, the mobile science laboratory is used by elementary and junior high students from both the public and parochial schools in the district during the regular school year as well as during the summer for extensive, traveling science programs. Mobile science laboratories and programs may be as simple or as complex as the science needs and financial resources of a school district.

Summary

Adequate science facilities, equipment, and materials are vital if teachers are to engage in discovery activity programs in science. Regardless of whether science teaching is done in a self-contained or special science room, provisions must be made for an activity area where children can actively participate in laboratory experiences. There should also be a research and library area for children to go beyond their immediate activities with reference materials. The science room should have provisions for a conference area for teacher and children to use for planning and conferring. A discovery corner should be provided so children can explore and tinker with an assortment of science materials during their free time. Of utmost importance to any science room is adequate storage for keeping science equipment and supplies organized and secure. Practical suggestions were provided for easily making storage facilities.

It is desirable for elementary schools to have certain central science facilities regardless of where the science instruction takes place. Total school science facilities and materials should be coordinated to service the self-contained and/or special science room. The elementary school should have a science laboratory, science center, central apparatus and supply storage, and school science club room and museum. Wherever possible, individual science study carrels, or self-learning stations, should be set up in the self-contained classroom, science lab, science center, club, or museum. A mobile science laboratory extends the science classroom to fields and streams.

---

[12] *The 1966 Mobile Science Laboratory Program* (Albert Lea School District 241), Lea, Minnesota, 56007, p. 5, 6.

Suggestions were made for ordering science supplies and equipment, their sources, and practical suggestions for cataloging, inventorying, storing, and distributing science materials.

SELF-EVALUATION AND FURTHER STUDY

1. You have been selected as coordinator for materials and equipment for five teachers of your grade level. Assuming that very few science materials or equipment are now available in your school, make a list of essential items you would recommend for purchase or construction with a $300 budget. Indicate the name of the equipment, quantity, price, and source of supply. Some sources of such materials are listed in the Appendix.

2. Draw a floor plan on graph paper for your classroom and arrange the room for these science areas: activity, research and library, storage, conference, discovery, display, and bulletin boards.

3. Devise innovations of your present room which would allow you to provide for the areas in 2. above. Indicate which items would be made in school and which items would have to be purchased. On purchased items give specific description of item, source, price, and quantity needed.

4. Devise a list of criteria for selecting scientific apparatus and equipment using the references mentioned in this chapter. See also:

    Molyneaux, Marjorie B., "Choosing Elementary Science Equipment," *Science and Children*, Vol. 4, No. 5 (February, 1967), pp. 20-21.

    Apply this criteria to 1. above.

5. Select a commercially prepared science kit and write a critical analysis of it. Refer to section on kits in this chapter for sources of information upon which to develop standards for this critique. See also:

    Gantert, Robert L., "Science Kits as Classroom Aids," *Laboratories in the Classroom* (New York: Science Materials Center, 220 East 23rd Street, 1960), pp. 87-88.

    Lange, Erwin F., and K. E. Payne, "Science Kits in Elementary Science Teaching," *The Science Teacher*, 25, No. 6 (October, 1958), pp. 321-323.

    Sabolewski, Chester A., and Lynette F. Fung, "Science in a Shoe Box," *The Grade Teacher* (September, 1965), pp. 148-149.

    "New Line of Classroom Kits to Aid Teachers Without Science Training," *Teacher Topics*, I, No. 1 (Spring, 1962), pp. 1-3.

6. Select a science area, preferably one in which you work directly with children. After identifying concepts and activities for this science study, organize and collect materials for a shoe box science kit. Include as much science material as possible in the kit along with sufficient information for conducting the experiences.

7. Set up and maintain an aquarium or terrarium. Once established, add a small animal or animals.

8. Construct several small cages for insects or animals, using the information in this chapter.

9. Pick a textbook and a science kit for the same science unit. Compare the costs of the science materials needed to teach both. In addition, comment upon the quality, durability, and teaching value of each.

10. Find a room in your school to be used as a school science museum. If possible, involve interested children in the planning, inventory and necessary housekeeping for the museum. In addition, plan to train these children as "Museum tour guides."

PART THREE

ENRICHMENT ACTIVITIES FOR DISCOVERY SCIENCE TEACHING-LEARNING

We must redouble our
efforts to create an
educational system that
will provide the maximum
individual fulfillment for
each American.[1]

CHAPTER 10

INDIVIDUALIZING SCIENCE DISCOVERY

Teacher education traditionally has emphasized the importance of individual differences and the existence of wide variations among the individuals. Each student learns at a different rate and in a different way. Teachers often profess they adjust their teaching to meet the individual differences, but this can mean they occasionally give an exceptional student some extra reading. Good teachers of science endeavor to motivate their students to achieve in accordance with their potential; this, however, requires that teachers be well prepared and sophisticated in their teaching techniques. Although teachers are usually aware of the desirability of organizing their class according to individual differences, they seldom adjust their instruction enough to accomplish complete motivation of all students.

There are exceptions; there are teachers and classes that typify the new emphasis on individualized instruction—an emphasis likely to accelerate in the decades ahead. John Goodlad, Dean of the School of Education at the University of California at Los Angeles, stated in an address that the main endeavor of education in the 1970's will be to individualize instruction so each child may advance at his own rate.[2] It is his view that this will be accomplished by 1980 because of team teaching, upgraded schools, and flexible class scheduling. The American Association of School Administrators School Building Commission has expressed similar views:

> In response to these and other challenges appearing on the horizon, educators today are turning to nongraded grouping, independent study, self-starting techniques, and programs in which each pupil progresses at his own pace. They are slowly but surely becoming aware that lock-step, grade-by-grade education simply will no longer do the job which must be done.[3]

What do educators mean by the term *individualization?* Dwight W. Allen of the School of Education, Stanford University, has defined it as follows:

> Individualization is a type of instruction in which the student engages in activities uniquely appropriate to his learning. This type of instruction promotes independence, provides opportunities for study beyond the regular curriculum, and permits maximum use of instructional resources. . . . The goal of individualization is not a tutorial situation, but an appropriate instructional content for each student.[4]

---

[1] John W. Gardner, "The Ten Commitments," *Saturday Review,* July 1967, p. 39.

[2] Anonymous. "Futuristic View." *Scholastic Teacher,* September 28, 1967, p. 5.

[3] *School for America,* American Association of School Administrators (Washington, D.C.: 1967), p. 4.

[4] Dwight W. Allen, "Individualized Instruction," *CTA Journal* (October, 1965), p. 27.

How is this boy participating in processes similar to those used by scientists? Which processes?

Research on Individual Differences

Research in psychology has revealed individuals vary in several ways: by intelligence, aptitude, type of occupations they choose, availability of educational materials in their environments, type of communities from which they come, social and economic status, parental attitudes and cultural backgrounds, personal and avocational interests, mental health, emotional stability, and physical well being. Because of these differences, it is obvious that treating all children as if they were exactly alike is entirely unwarranted.

Studies done by Burk and Washburne, Jones, Peters, Suppes, Schindler, Grant, and Possien indicate that when provisions are made for individual differences the effectiveness of the classroom teaching is enhanced and the spread in achievement levels becomes greater.[5] The gifted students move out in front of their classmates

[5] Carleton Washburne, "Burk's Individual System as Developed at Winnetka," Adapting Schools to Individual Differences, Twenty-fourth Yearbook, NSSE, Part I (Bloomington, Illinois, Public School Publishing Company, 1925), pp. 77-82; Daisy M. Jones, "An Experiment in Adaptation to Individual Differences," *Journal of Educational Psychology*, 39 (1948), pp. 257-72; C. C. Peters, "An Example of Replication of an Experiment for Increased Reliability," *Journal of Educational Research* 32 (1938), p. 39; Patrick Suppes, "Modern Learning Theory and the Elementary-School Curriculum," *American Educational Research Journal* (March, 1964), pp. 79-94; Arlene K. Shindler, "A Study of the Attitudes of Fifth Grade Children Toward Group and Individual Work" (unpublished Ph.D. Dissertation, University of Michigan, 1964); Jettye F.

and achieve to a greater extent. In a study of individualized science instruction with fifth graders, Raymond O'Toole found these pupils did more collateral reading and preferred the individualized approach to teacher-centered instruction.[6] Other findings indicate that some students when allowed to progress at their own rate finish the equivalent of a year's work in a few months and have less discipline trouble.[7]

Numerous other studies done on the high school and college level report similar results.[8] In fact, some of the most interesting and advanced individualized science projects have been established at Purdue University, Colorado State College, and Pennsylvania State University.

In summary, research indicates the following:

1. Students achieve well in individualized classes.
2. Gifted students achieve to a greater extent than with the traditional group instruction.
3. Discipline problems are likely to decrease.
4. Children do more collateral reading.
5. Children prefer the individualized over the traditional approach.

The Techniques of Individualizing

Individualizing instruction is not new to the American school system. When a parent, scoutmaster, or some other individual teaches one child, he uses essentially an individualized approach. The one-room schools that dotted our landscape until the early part of this century were to a large degree individualized. Preston Search introduced an individualized work and progress plan in Pueblo, Colorado, in 1888 and Frederick Burk, an educator at San Francisco State College Training School, between 1913-24, helped develop what came to be known as the Winnetka Plan. The plan divided the curriculum into academic subjects to be taught individually and creative activities to be taught in large and small groups. These early efforts at individualizing were followed by others.

Historically, individualized instruction has taken many forms. Theodore Munch in a National Science Teachers Association pamphlet entitled *How to Individualize Science Instruction* suggests the following techniques:

> Students can be grouped according to ability. Class size may be restricted.
> Team teaching can permit more thorough development of lesson plans and

Grant, "A Longitudinal Program of Individualized Instruction in Grades Four, Five and Six" (unpublished Ed.D. Dissertation, University of California, Berkeley, 1964); Wilma M. Possien, "A Comparison of the Effects of Three Teaching-Methodologies on the Problem Solving Skills of Sixth Grade Children" (unpublished Ed.D. Dissertation, University of Alabama, 1964).

[6] Raymond O'Toole, "A Study to Determine Whether Fifth Grade Children Can Learn Certain Selected Problem Solving Abilities Through Individualized Instruction" (unpublished Ed.D. Dissertation, Colorado State College, 1966).

[7] Allen, *op. cit.*

[8] Theodore W. Munch, "How to Individualize Science Instruction," *National Science Teachers Association* (Washington, D.C., 1966).

How would you enrich this learning situation and still retain its individualization?

laboratory situations. A wide diversity of audiovisual aids and printed resources can be utilized to help teachers tailor their lessons to fit their classes.[9]

As Munch's statement indicates, the advent of technology has stimulated the production of educational aids with great significance for individualizing instruction. These include: films, and very recently the sound film cartridge, filmstrips, filmloops, computers and computer consoles, tape recorders, television, and programmed materials including an array of teaching machines to use with the programs. It is availability of this hardware with the concurrent development of materials to be used with these machines that have suddenly made it possible to individualize with greater effectiveness.

Before the advent of such technological educational aids, individualized instruction was mainly text-centered. Educational research has long revealed that all individuals do not learn equally well under the same method of instruction. For example, some students just don't learn well by reading, but might learn very well through laboratory activities or listening to a tape recorder. The advent of modern educational instructional machines has made it possible for education to make a breakthrough in escaping from text-dominated instruction. Recently, a study was conducted by Harvard Project Physics (HPP), a curriculum group founded to produce an innovative physics course for the secondary schools. This group has produced physics laboratory manuals, texts, supplementary reading materials, kits, films, filmloops, and other aids. In one of the classes that HPP worked with to test the effectiveness of these materials, they allowed students to study physics by using any of their learning aids. This study revealed that some

[9] Munch, *Ibid.*

students concentrated mainly on reading, others on laboratory work, and others on observing films. At the end of the experimental period, HPP tested all of the students according to the objectives of the unit. Taking into account the different capabilities of the students, which they determined prior to the study, they found no significant differences in the achievements of students, regardless of what materials they selected. This suggests that when students are given a choice, they will learn the way most effective for them. Further investigation of this influence needs to be tested, especially on the elementary level. However, the advantages of having a multi-media approach to instruction can hardly be argued.

Individualized and Continuous Progress Plans

There have been two main approaches used in individualizing the elementary school—the continuous progress or nongraded plan, and the individualized instruction plan.

What are the advantages for these girls learning to work with science equipment before they reach higher grades?

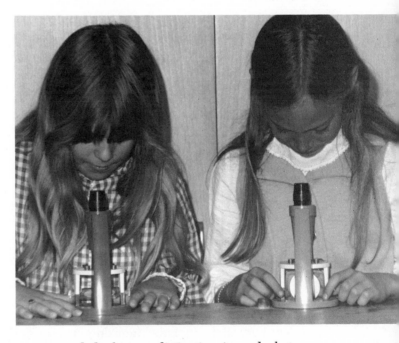

In the continuous progress, nongraded plan no distinction is made between grades; all of the instruction is individualized. A child progresses individually through a series of units. If he completes all the units equivalent to his grade level, he continues on to a set of units used for the next grade level. Under this plan a child might finish the equivalent of two years of work in one year. When he has completed all of the work required for the elementary school, he passes on to junior high school. This approach has been implemented in the Nova Schools in Florida, Aspen Schools in Colorado, and is being developed in numerous other districts throughout the United States.

The individualized and continuous progress plans are similar except that in the individualized approach the child remains within his grade level and is not accelerated. There are still units and levels of competency outlined for him. When a child completes a unit with an accepted level of performance, he progresses to more advanced work. A gifted student under this approach often studies an area in considerable depth. The study in depth is used to replace the idea of accelerating the student through the grades even though his work may warrant it. The individualized noncontinuous progress method is used in schools where all grades have not been individualized. Obviously, if the continuous progress plan were used, the entire school would have to be individualized and students accelerated from one grade level to another or moved up to junior high school when their work warranted it.

Advantages of Individualized Instruction

The advantages of individualized instruction have been outlined by Sidney Rollins of the Middletown Project in Rhode Island:

1. Pupil progress ranges from a year or more ahead of where pupils would be if they attended a graded school to half a year behind the usual achievement of a given grade level.
2. Dropout rate (less than one per cent at Middletown) is drastically lower than the national rate of 30 per cent.
3. Pupils recover from extended absences from ungraded school more quickly and easily than from graded schools.
4. Pupils stimulate themselves to greater effort—even in April, May or June when they normally begin to ease up on studies.
5. Pupils seem to appreciate the opportunities for avoiding the boredom and frustration that the ungraded structure can offer.[10]

Because individualized approaches are less teacher-centered and more pupil-centered, students become more self directive and responsible for their learning, a behavior which should continue after formalized schooling. Students taught by these approaches are also less likely to experience anxiety since they can learn at their own rate. The bright ones are not held back and the slower ones are not frustrated by achievement levels out of their grasp.

The Teacher's Role in Individualizing

Robert Glaser, University of Pittsburgh, has outlined six requirements for redesigning a school for individual instruction. These are:

1. Redesigning grade levels
2. Establishing sequences of objectives in subject areas
3. Developing assessment methods
4. Providing performance standards for student self-evaluation

---

[10] Sidney P. Rollins, "Ungraded High Schools: Why Those Who Like Them Love Them," *Nation Schools,* LXXII (April, 1964), p. 110.

5. Providing special training for teachers, and
6. Providing data on schools.[11]

In addition to these suggestions, three factors must be considered in individualizing. They are: *facilities*, *materials*, and *procedures*.

Generally speaking, facility modification need not be great. Provision should be made for children who will be taking tests, reading, watching filmstrips, films, film-loops, slides, listening to tape recorders, studying programs using teaching machines, or discussing in small groups. Nevertheless, an individualized program can be started even though such provisions are not complete; modifications and improvements can be made as the economics allow. The greater the resources, however, the better the individualizing can be. The best way a teacher can convince the administration, PTA, school board, or other authorities of the need for instructional media in individualizing a class is to show what can be done and what you could do if you only had adequate provisions. In schools where there has been a small budget, the facilities problems have not been unsurmountable.

How does working through a science problem enhance the child's understanding of a concept?

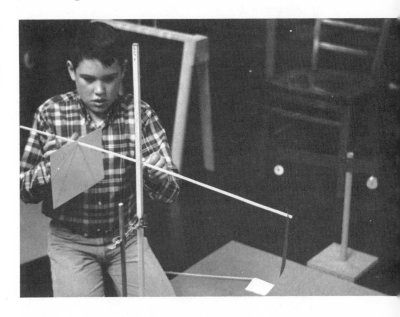

Until recently a main problem in organizing classes for individualized instruction has been an insufficient supply of educational materials adapted for various ability levels. Since the introduction of programmed instruction, teaching machines, and the wealth of materials produced by national science curriculum projects, this problem has been largely overcome. The Elementary Science Study, for example, has numerous units complete with kits that can be adapted for individualized instruction. As discussed in Chapter 4, the materials of the American Association for the Advancement of Science, the Science Curriculum Improvement Study, and many of the other curriculum projects can be utilized in individualized instruction with little reorganization. Essentially what a teacher has to do in using these materials is write a series of student syllabi for the pupil to fol-

---

[11] Robert Glaser, quoted in "Individualizing," *Scholastic Teacher* (November 30, 1967), p. 4.

low like a map in progressing through his tasks. A syllabus may tell the pupil to read a portion of an elementary science text, do certain laboratory activities, observe a filmloop, filmstrip, film, or listen to a tape recording. The syllabus should give the child all the directions he needs to progress from one learning activity to another. The syllabus plus worksheets and other materials may be placed in packets for children to use when ready. It is the preparation of these unit syllabi or packets which require the most time by the teacher. Once these are complete, however, much of the time teachers require for planning is lessened allowing him to use his time for other educational purposes.

An example of how the format of a syllabus may be constructed is indicated here.

STUDENT SYLLABUS

Required Activities

B. _____ | 1. |
C. _____ | |

B. _____ | 2. |
C. _____ | |

Suggested Additional Activities

B. _____ | 1. |
C. _____ | |

The "B" on the left hand margin is where the student should mark the date he *began* the activity and the "C" where he should mark the date he *completed* the activity. In this way the teacher can quickly consult with the children to see how rapidly they are progressing through the course work. The teacher would include in the "required activities" block the things he wished all students to do. For example, he might have them read pages 10 to 15 of the text under number 1, do a laboratory investigation under number 2, etc. Under the "suggested additional activities" section, he might include any of the following things:

Write a summary of what you have learned from reading a newspaper article, science book, magazine article, viewing a filmstrip, filmloop, slides, film, taking a field trip, doing additional laboratory investigations, answering pictorial riddle questions, listening to a tape recording, and preparing a collection.

The procedures used in individualizing may vary from teacher to teacher. One instructor may have the science equipment stored in cupboards with labels on the outside so the children may go to the storage area, look at the labels, and select the equipment they need for the activity. Another approach is to produce kits, about shoe box size, filled with all of the equipment needed for a certain laboratory activity. The kits are numbered. The child's syllabus will indicate the number of

Why do you think the teacher of this class would have little trouble with discipline?

the kit he is to use. He then proceeds to the storage area for these and collects his kit. Needless to say, each method has advantages and disadvantages. The first approach has the advantage of requiring less equipment since many pieces of apparatus may be used for several science activities. The kit approach, however, has the advantage of reducing confusion, saving time, and making it possible to keep the class more orderly since the child returns the equipment to the kit container when he is not using it. The kits, however, require more laboratory apparatus and because of the number of kits needed for a year's work, a large storage area.

If the teacher has had training in programmed instruction, he may spend a considerable amount of his time preparing science programs to be used in individualized classes. These may be supplemented by commercial science programs which are now available.

Although the preparation of a student syllabus, kits, and programs may require time, once they are produced, the additional preparation required by the teacher during the year is minimal. Essentially what he has done is planned and organized his instruction before school started. This allows him time during the school year to give special attention to those children who require it and to produce teaching aids and packets to improve the instructional program.

General Techniques to Use for Individualized Instruction

Good teachers have always tried to adjust their teaching to individual differences even though their preparation may have been teacher-centered and large-group oriented. Some of the ways teachers have allowed for such human variations in science classes are outlined here. The list is by no means exhaustive. A wise teacher

What is meant by the saying "Some children learn through their fingers"?

aware of teaching for maximum learning and not afraid to try new approaches to teaching science will undoubtedly discover many more. The students may:

1. In the upper grades 4-8 act as cadet teachers for the lower grades. It has been said there is no better way to learn something than to teach it. Students in these upper grades because of their closeness in age to the lower grade children sometimes can teach certain things better to peers than can adult teachers, while at the same time learning themselves. Overland Park, a suburb of Kansas City, has over 350 children—more than a tenth of the total enrollment of its elementary schools—involved in this type of program. These cadet teachers have lessons with their pupils twice a week for thirty minutes. This often is supplemented by extra, voluntary non-class time sessions the cadet and pupil work out on their own. Often the cadets even make their own teaching aids.
2. Complete a commercially- or teacher-prepared programmed science lesson.
3. Outline and carry out a science investigation to find out what factors influence the growth of plants or chicken eggs.
4. Read materials adjusted to the individual's reading level.
5. Prepare a report on some scientific phenomenon such as the cause of the tides, northern lights, bird or salmon migrations.
6. Record and observe evidence of a natural event such as an eclipse.
7. Prepare science notebooks which may vary considerably in length and depth depending on the capability of the child.
8. Complete a collection, for example, of rocks, leaves, or insects.
9. Complete some especially assigned elementary science unit; for example, those producd by the Elementary Science Study.
10. Make reports on trips to museums, planetariums, observatories, and parks. Parents should be encouraged to accompany and help develop learnings in these places.
11. Carry out an assigned task such as caring for a rock garden, bird house, bird bath, aquarium or terrarium, raising animals or plants.
12. Participate in science nights or science fairs.
13. Prepare a science display for the class or school.
14. Give an oral report about some original scientific investigation done by the student.
15. Study and give a report on the lives of great scientists.
16. Prepare, write up, and give a science demonstration to the class or some other group.
17. Participate in a panel discussion related to solving problems of a scientific exploration such as: What provisions would be needed to take a trip to the moon, Mars, Antartica, and what types of research should be done once there?

18. Collect material and prepare a bulletin board about a scientific topic.
19. Do a study or help maintain a nature area near a school. The children should find out what types of rocks, plants, and animals are present. The environment of the community might provide a pond, forest, seashore, or desert for further study of organisms and their relationship to the community.
20. Make book reports on science books.
21. Listen to recorded science tapes or observe a filmloop, filmstrip or cartridge sound film. If the child wishes to listen or view the films several times he should be encouraged to do so. He should have some discovery-oriented questions to answer about these materials before, during, or after he has used them.
22. In the upper elementary grades, make reports for the personal progress file. Each pupil should have a file in which he places summaries of all types of science activities he performs. This is one way to keep records on the progress and interest of the pupil. For each project the student should place a note in the folder about what he learned. Any of the activities suggested here could be included in the folder.
23. Attempt to answer what is in the *science surprise box*. The science surprise box is an activity which is popular with students, especially with slow learners. Periodically the teacher displays a labeled box. On the front of the box is a statement of its contents. An example is:

I am hard.
I can push something without you seeing me push it.
I can pull something without you seeing me pull it.
I am iron and nickel.
What is my name?

The opening of the surprise box is a wonderful way to introduce an area of study to the class. In this particular box, of course, there would be a magnet.
24. Contribute to the *science discovery chart*. The science discovery chart is a chart or bulletin board which has lines or pieces of string going to the objects on the board. A student prints what he thinks the object is, along with his name, on a small card. He pins the card to the end of the string. After several children have had a chance to pin their cards on the board, the teacher then discusses their answers. A typical chart might show some simple machines: inclined plane, pulley, lever, wedge, screw, wheel and axle. A chart showing the different heavenly bodies in the solar system creates interest. The discovery chart also can be used to review or introduce an area of study.

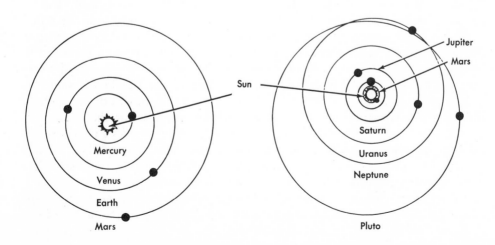

How are these activities contributing to the over-all goals of the school?

25. Show a collection. The *collection of the month* is a display of a pupil's collection such as: rocks, leaves, insects, shells, twigs, types of wood, or seeds. It is desirable to give every child an opportunity some time during the year to show and explain his collection.

26. Answer the questions on a *riddle card*. A riddle card has a science riddle written on it. Some teachers have been successful in having students write riddles which are placed in a box until the instructor is ready to use them. An example of a riddle card is:

> Something in this room has stored sunshine in it.
> We can see this sunlight again by changing how it is stored.
> What will we have to do?

After several days, if there is no answer to the riddle, the teacher may light a wood splint with a match. He would then ask if the children see any of the sun's light coming off the burned splint. These riddle cards may also contain examples with *pictorial riddles* (see Chapter 5 for examples of these).

Gifted Students

Teachers often have difficulty helping gifted students, This is especially true in science because the elementary teacher has not majored in science and the gifted child may know considerably more about some area of science than the teacher. However, if encouraged properly, gifted science students can be a great aid to the teacher. They love to do experiments and work on science projects. If an instructor does not feel totally competent with science, this should not stop him from having gifted students do science projects; he can learn with them. Children like to have their teacher learn with them, and they enjoy seeing the teacher get excited about the results from some experiment. This method motivates gifted children and often makes the learning process come alive. In addition, this approach tends to break down the traditional view of teacher as giver of knowledge. The important point to remember in working with these children is that individual attention must be a rule rather than an exception. Most of the general techniques previously mentioned will work with and stimulate gifted students. Some additional suggestions are outlined as follows:

1. Let children prepare science kits. They may suggest what should be included in a kit to show some scientific principles. A science kit contains the directions, all the materials, and apparatus necessary to conduct a demonstration or experiment. Shoe boxes serve for the container. The name of the experiment can be labeled on the outside of the kit. When a pupil has time, he can obtain a kit, take it to his desk or the science work area, and perform the activities without disturbing the teacher. The gifted have fun assembling kits and others enjoy doing the experiments. Some teachers call the kits "surprise boxes" because of the discoveries made in science when the children do the experiments. There are commercially prepared kits that do the same job. An excellent one is called *Things of Science* produced by Friends of Science, 1719 N. St. N.W., Washington, D.C. 20036.
2. Assign gifted children to do research problems. They could consult with a scientist or engineer in the community on a problem. Local museums, zoos, botanical gardens, and hospitals have resource people who will often help.
3. Encourage them to enter the school or district science fair.
4. Obtain special equipment for them to use. The federal government has supported through the National Defense Education Act (NDEA) extensive purchase of such equipment. These expenditures are likely to continue in the future. Local laboratories such as those in hospitals, high schools, or industries will often give or loan equipment and chemicals to elementary teachers for special project work.
5. Encourage the parents to obtain books and toy science kits for their children and to discuss science with them. Often desirable science-learning situations arise when the family takes a vacation. In your talks with parents at PTA and other activities emphasize how they can utilize their opportunities to reinforce the school science program. Stress the importance of the parent buying supplemental booklets such as the "How and Why Wonder Books" and the "Golden Books." Explain the desirability of motivating the gifted, and clarify any misconception the parents might have about gifted children. They may think that gifted children are abnormal and as adults lead unsuccessful lives. Assure them that this is not true.
6. Ask gifted students to be science assistants to help with the preparation of materials, dispensing of equipment, and collecting of information about investigations.
7. Encourage them to take a leading part in school or community conservation projects.
8. Suggest that they create models related to science units being studied. The models might include weather instruments, simple electrical devices, atomic and solar system models.
9. The school might sponsor a club for the highly motivated students, encouraging them to join and participate in such activities.

With perhaps several different activities being carried out at once, how can the teacher structure and guide the science lesson in meaningful ways?

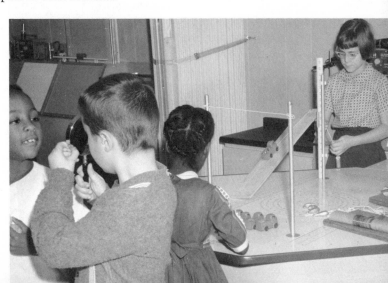

10. The teacher should produce some laboratory investigations with minimum of information so that these children can outline and carry through an investigative procedure on their own.

11. William Shockley has suggested a technique for developing the thinking processes of children, particularly on the junior high and high school level.[12] The activity, however, can also be used with gifted students in the upper elementary grades. Shockley proposes that a scientific principle be given to the children to be followed by the statements: "is always true," "no matter what," "provided that." The children are then asked to respond. For example, he suggested the following: *What goes up must come down.* This is "always true," "no matter what," provided that the body doesn't acquire enough speed to overcome the earth's pull of gravity. Another example might be: *Water boils at 100° C* "is always true," "no matter what," "provided that" the conditions are standardized at sea level.

Think of some other principles you could use with gifted students.

Try out your idea on some children if possible; you might also have children suggest principles to be stated in this format.

Slow Learners

Recess was just ending when Jerry came running across the playground with a jar covered with a piece of cardboard. He yelled, "Miss Bedreau, look what I have found buzzing around some bushes. What kind of bug is it?" Miss Bedreau looked at it closely and replied, "I am not sure, Jerry, but let's take it into class." In the classroom, the teacher carried the jar to the front of the room for all to see. Some children expressed concern that the bug might be lonely. Others thought it needed water to drink. "Buzzy," the name the class eventually gave their bug, presented Miss Bedreau with what she needed to teach her slow learners about insects. She asked, "How many legs and body parts does Buzzy have? What kind of food does he need to eat? How could we collect some other insects for study?" With interest aroused, the children agreed they should collect other insects for study; several children offered to bring some the next day. The teacher cautioned them that they should only bring in insects and suggested that Jerry look in an encyclopedia to see if he could find how to tell an insect from other animals. Jerry found the information and with Miss Bedreau's help read the section to the class. An insect home was then prepared out of an old commercial mayonnaise jar. It was labeled "Home of Buzzy and Other Insects."

A student teacher watching Miss Bedreau said, "You know, this class is so enthusiastic about science that I was not even aware it was a group of slow learners." The student teacher did not realize it was Miss Bedreau who made science exciting for her class. Miss Bedreau knew firsthand experience was extremely important in teaching slow learners. Reading difficulties often cause a child to fall

---

[12] William Shockley, Press Release: "Proposed Important Mental Tools for Scientific Thinking at the High School Level," 100th Annual Meeting of the National Academy of Sciences in Washington, D.C.

behind in school and may be the main reason for him being placed in a slow group. Miss Bedreau's instruction centered around activities, experiments, observations, and oral reports. She used text material only to supplement. She did not talk about science; she had children live science. As a result, her slow learners appeared far from slow in their interest and understanding of the subject. The following list gives some general suggestions and activities for teaching science to slow learners. Many of the suggestions outlined previously under the heading "general techniques" also work:

1. Rely as much as possible on all of the senses. Base your science instruction on firsthand experiences in which a child can see, feel, hear, touch, smell, and taste the things being studied. The Biological Sciences Curriculum Study in investigating how slow learners learned science came to the conclusion that laboratory activities were the most meaningful to them.[13] The implications for the elementary level are obvious.
2. Tests and reading assignments should be used in order to help clarify some experiment or science activity but not as the main approach to learning science.
3. Use below average high school students to tutor underachievers in your elementary school class. The Manhattan Lower East Side Project in New York has tried this with considerable success. The Manhattan project has been in operation since 1963 and was started to combat the trend in scholastic retardation of Negro and Puerto Rican children. The program has helped both the elementary and high school students involved.
4. Children with limited ability need more precise directions and examples to follow in making out laboratory or research reports. If left on their own, they might be completely lost. So as not to stifle creativity, permission may be granted to students to deviate from these reports once they have the general idea of how to report their experimental information.
5. Teacher-prepared study questions can be particularly helpful to this group of children.
6. Above all, use praise and not censure as much as possible with low ability children. They need continual assurance and feelings of success. Think of them being able to do better work than the average student and they may surprise you. Robert Rosenthal and Lenore Jacobsen, who is principal of Spruse School in South San Francisco, California have found that if teachers are falsely told their children have relatively high I.Q.'s, the children achieve much better than if the teachers are told the students are slow. It's how the teacher looks at the children that makes the difference. If he looks at them as slow, then they are going to be slow.[14]

Project Head Start Children

Science activities may play a major role in achieving the objectives of Project Head Start programs. Because children selected for the Head Start group come mainly

---

[13] John R. Schaefer, "Special Materials (SM) Program for the Slow Learner" (unpublished report, BSCS, February, 1964), p. 1.

[14] Robert Rosenthal and Lenore Jacobsen, "Self-Fulfilling Prophecies in the Classroom: Teacher's Expectations as Unintended Determinants of Pupils Intellectual Competence" (unpublished paper: reproduced by the South San Francisco Unified School District, November 1967).

from deprived environments, it is important they be surrounded with as many scientific materials as possible to challenge their curiosity. An aquarium filled with fish and plants; a terrarium filled with plants, toads, and turtles; pulleys, thermometers, kits to develop abilities of discriminating color, texture, and form; blocks, various plants, seeds, a cross-cut of a tree showing its annual rings, and many toys similar to those produced by Creative Play Things (The Learning Center, Inc., P.O. Box 330, Princeton, N.J.) should be standard in these classes. In fact, the more the room looks like an organized mess, probably the better it is for the children's learning. Head Start children above all need to have sensory-motor experiences with objects. They need to touch, feel, smell, see, and manipulate. Remember, as Piaget has emphasized, there is no learning without experience, and "to know an object is to act on it." These children suffer from a lack of experience and therefore they require active involvement with objects and processes. Above all, their science should be activity-centered. Because science involves children with things and performing mental operations, it serves as a means of developing desirable attitudes, skills, and cognitive abilities.

Many of the activities outlined under the general techniques list can be adapted for the Head Start group. Several of the activities outlined in elementary science texts and curriculum projects for kindergarten and first grade can also be used according to the interests and abilities of the children. The main point to remember is keep the instruction activity-centered.

With science learning as the objective, how can a teacher best learn to cope with "creative confusion?"

The Mentally Retarded Child

There are about 4.5 million mentally retarded individuals in the United States but only about 250,000 of these are enrolled in any kind of formalized instruction. Far greater efforts than have been made thus far are needed to improve the educational opportunities of these children. An issue of *Look* magazine pointed out that in some states "snakepit" conditions exist for a large segment of these children. Mentally retarded children certainly *can* learn and should have opportunities to learn according to their abilities. Over the last two years several studies have been made at Colorado State College and Florida State University in teaching science to mentally retarded children. These studies indicate *trainables*, the lowest intelligence group of the mentally retarded, can learn some basic science concepts. The *educables*, the higher level of mentally retarded, are able to learn science concepts and principles and demonstrate such cognitive abilities as predicting, comparing, grouping or classifying, controlling a variable, outlining a simple investigation, measuring, observing, communicating, and interpreting simple data.[15]

For motivation and interest, science teaching with the mentally retarded must be activity-centered where the children have opportunities to touch, feel, smell, and generally interact with phenomena. These children often have difficulty centering on one aspect of an activity at a time. For this reason, it is best to limit your objectives for each lesson period. For example, a unit on magnets might let them find out by testing that a magnetic field goes through glass, wood, paper, etc. The next lesson might involve the idea that both ends of the magnet produce magnetism but the poles are different. The teacher shouldn't try to develop both of these concepts in one lesson. At the conclusion of the lesson when he wants the children to discuss their findings, he should collect all of the materials from the children before the discussion begins. This should be done because the children are easily distracted by the materials before them and will not be able to pay attention to the discussion.

Presently at Colorado State College a study is underway to determine the use of science audiovisual media with these children. Although the findings are not conclusive at this point, indications are that science film media do have a positive influence on the learning of mentally retarded children, provided there are proper discussions related to the film. These investigations indicate it is better to show part of a science film and discuss it before another portion is shown. If one part is played one day, and the next part another day, the first part should be replayed with the new section and additional concepts discussed. This process of successive replays and discussion of one section involving one concept at a time seems to insure better achievement. With this approach, the retention over short periods of time has been found to be better. However, retention over longer periods of time and the showing of the whole film and then parts of the film with discussions needs further investigation.

---

[15] William Sweeters, "A Study to Determine if Educable Mentally Retarded Children Can Learn Selected Teaching Objectives Through Individualized Discovery Oriented Instruction" (unpublished Ed.D. Dissertation, Colorado State College, Greeley, Colorado, 1968).

The amount of work with science curriculums for the mentally retarded has been limited. The state of Illinois has produced a publication called the *Illinois Plan for Special Education of Exceptional Children* published by the Interstate Printers and Publishers, Inc., Danville, Illinois. The publication contains a section on a subject-matter centered curriculum approach. Its methods and resources do not indicate there has been any systematic evaluation of the program and the attention given to the development of cognitive processes is lacking.

Investigators at Colorado State College, and Bill Tillery of the Science Education Department of University of Wyoming, have been working on the development of a cognitive process discovery-oriented science curriculum for the mentally retarded. The success of the approach thus far has warranted further investigation and the work continues.

The Blind

There has not been much investigation of the teaching of science through discovery with blind children. A limited study at the Special Education Center, Colorado State College, however, has indicated blind children can learn science through discovery techniques. One study, for example, involved the adaptation of the Mealworms unit of the Elementary Science Study for these children. Al-

How can a city street be used for the observation and collection of scientific data?

though the blind children could not see the mealworms as suggested by the unit, they did learn much about the characteristics and behavior of this organism.

There is no evidence to indicate that most science activities if adapted for the blind child will not work. A number of investigations are needed to find out more about how these children learn through involvement with science activities. An effort worthy of endeavor would be to try to integrate a science-mathematics curriculum for the blind.

Specific suggestions for how to have blind children experience phenomena through their senses of feeling, hearing, smelling and tasting are outlined here:

1. Listen to tapes or records of animals, birds, machines, insects, etc. The blind child could also learn about pitch, loudness, and softness of sounds by listening to tapes or testing a stringed instrument.
2. Discriminate and distinguish one material from another by feeling texture, roughness, smoothness, softness, hardness, dryness, wetness, lightness, taste, and degrees of heat and cold.
3. Feel the structure and texture of leaves, flowers, and other parts of plants.
4. Determine distances in terms of time, or sound.
5. Assemble and experiment with apparatus such as pulleys.
6. Perform one of the units from the new curriculum projects adapted for the use of blind children.

Examples of School Systems Which Have Individualized Science

There are several schools in the United States which have individualized science programs. Listed here are but a few of these; no effort has been made to prepare a complete list. The purpose is to show that school systems are involved in this activity and to give some idea of their geographical distribution.

The Oakleaf Individualized Elementary School Science Project. The Oakleaf project has been produced in cooperation with the University of Pittsburgh Learning and Research Development Center, Pittsburgh, Pennsylvania. In the project, each child has been pre-tested to note his performances in each of the instructional areas of the curriculum. These test results are analyzed and specific exercises are assigned to help the child acquire the desired behaviors. On an average there are 7–15 content behavioral objectives for each unit. The objectives are similar to those of the AAAS Process Approach and the SCIS content objectives. The Oakleaf science Individually Prescribed Instruction (IPI) staff eventually hopes to have about 5000 activities, each of which will involve manipulative experience requiring twenty minutes of student time.

The Skokie, Illinois, Individualizing Instruction in Elementary Science Program. Skokie, Illinois, elementary schools have developed a discovery-oriented individualized science program. The purpose of this plan is to guide each child through a sequence of levels based on mastery of the inquiry skills. The science specialists have been involved in the teaching of classes and have centered their instruction on firsthand experiences and direct contact with science laboratory activities. The directors of the project state there is no effort to force the children to make a "timed race over facts" and that this approach has allowed for greater attention for the slow learner.

The Nova School System.   The Nova School System, Ft. Lauderdale, Florida, has in operation a continuous progress plan operating from kindergarten through high school, with plans to continue on into college. The K–6 part of the program was started in one nongraded elementary school in September, 1965, and was followed by another in the school district in 1966. The elementary science curriculum emphasizes both concept development and process goals, including learning how to learn, using reference tools, and scientific methods. Students progress through the curriculum at their own rate. The Nova system has also been set up in Carbondale, Illinois.

The Aspen School System.   The Aspen School System, Aspen, Colorado, a district with a relatively small student population, introduced the continuous progress plan for its school system in 1962. In succeeding years a number of grade levels were added to the program until now the entire system from elementary through high school is individualized. The progress of each individual in the schools is determined by the teachers. They rate the individual against himself and not against some externally determined norm. In this system there are no failures. The child moves through the work according to his ability and when he has completed the number of units required for elementary school, he moves on to the high school.

Recognition Stimulates Individual Achievement

Everyone, teachers and students, likes to receive recognition for his work. In some schools a great amount of recognition traditionally has been given for athletic endeavors. Seldom, however, does academic excellence receive equal recognition. There is no substitute for praise from teachers, parents, and other interested individuals. A scientist visiting a classroom to see the students' achievements in science can do much to encourage students to continue their scientific endeavors. Much can be learned from the coaches in our school districts about how they motivate students. Coaches are usually masters in the techniques of giving and getting recognition for their students' abilities. Many of their methods can be adopted to stimulate science achievement as well. Awards, whether they be stars on a chart, a pin, a certificate, ribbons, or an emblem have their influence. Elementary science fairs or science nights do as much for the science contributor as a football game does for the football player or a band concert for a band player. Displaying student science projects gives recognition and develops interest among children. Regardless of how the learning is reinforced, it is mandatory that teachers

How can a teacher learn to "read" a child's face as she strives to plan lessons which stimulate his responses?

be constantly aware that students need to receive reinforcement and positive recognition. The method by which teachers do this can take many paths; all will contribute to better science learning and better achievement.

Summary

Most teachers state they teach for individual differences. This usually means giving special assignments to the better students. To organize an elementary class so each pupil progresses on a science assignment at his own rate requires a dynamic teacher who is well prepared. Teachers, however, often do not adequately regulate their teaching toward individual differences because it is easier to give all children the same material at the same rate.

Research indicates when provisions are made for individual differences, the effectiveness of the classroom teaching is enhanced and the spread in achievement levels becomes greater—pupils do more collateral reading and prefer individualized approaches to instruction. Some children when allowed to progress at their own rate finish the equivalent of a year's work in a few months, and individualized classes have fewer discipline problems.

There are several techniques for individualizing. They include the preparation of individualized units or packets, use of the continuous progress nongraded approach, and giving special assignments to meet individual differences. Individualized classes generally utilize more resources than traditional classes. Some of these resources are: filmloops, films, filmstrips, audio tapes, programs, teaching machines, science kits, etc. The advantages of individualizing instruction are that pupils progress to a greater extent, have a lower dropout rate, can recover quickly in their work from absences, stimulate themselves to a greater extent, and appreciate opportunities of avoiding boredom.

The teacher's role in individualizing is mainly one of preparing and organizing the instructional pattern, making educational aids, selecting the proper material according to the child's competence, and giving assistance when required. Most of the new science curriculum materials can be adapted for individualized instructional approaches. In addition to these there are numerous general techniques that may be used for individual differences. There are also special considerations that should be made for the gifted student, slow learner, Project Head Start child, the mentally retarded, and the blind.

Not only the classroom but the school as a whole can present enrichment activities for varied capabilities. Giving recognition for academic excellence insures higher achievement, better individual attention, and greater student growth. An individualized instruction revolution is presently underway in the American schools and, as Dr. Goodlad has suggested, its dynamism is likely to become the pattern over the next decade.

SELF-EVALUATION AND FURTHER STUDY

1. Describe how students in an individualized classroom compared with students in a traditional classroom would look while at work.
2. Why do individual variations make teaching more difficult?
3. How would you give attention to individual variations in science in a traditional class?
4. What is the difference between individualized instruction and the continuous progress plan?
5. If you were told by your principal that next year you would have to organize your grade level for the continuous progress plan, how would you organize it?
6. A leading science educator has said that generally large group instruction is antithetical to the teaching of science and giving attention to individual variation. Explain what you think he meant by this.
7. Indicate what research says about individualized instruction as it pertains to achievement, discipline, and attitudes.
8. What are the advantages of individualizing?
9. Review the list of general techniques for individualizing. Choose three you think are best and explain why you chose them.
10. Describe some special ways you would give individualized attention to the following:
    a. The gifted
    b. The slow learner
    c. The mentally retarded
    d. The blind

11. You have just been appointed Project Head Start Director in a ghetto area of a large metropolitan city. You suggest to the other members of your staff that science teaching should be a part of your program. You receive considerable resistance to this suggestion. What would you say to convince the staff?
12. You have just been employed as a VISTA volunteer teacher and given the assignment of developing a science program for a certain grade level. What would you do and why?
13. How would you go about developing recognition for science achievement in the school you teach?
14. How would you use a filmloop, a tape recorder, and science kits in individualized instruction?
15. Read "Development and Educational Achievement: Academic Growth" in D. C. Dinkmeyer, *Child Development: The Emerging Self* (Englewood Cliffs, N.J.: Prentice-Hall, 1965), and write a short paper on what you learned from the chapter.

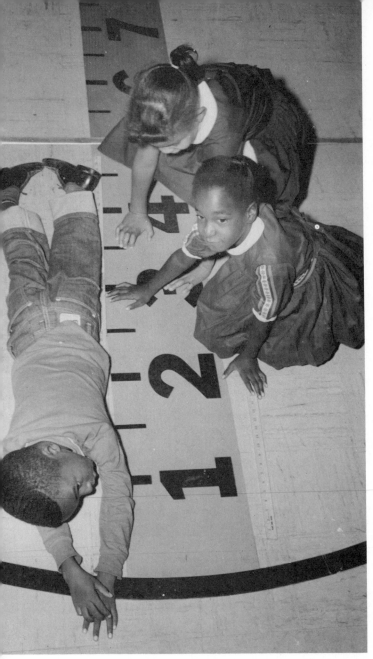

Tomorrow's grade school child may think of mathematics and science as being a single subject—not because they are identical (they are not), but because his school will probably present them in an integrated form.[1]

CHAPTER 11

THE ROLE OF
MATHEMATICS IN
SCIENCE DISCOVERY

Throughout the ages mathematics has been integrally involved in the development and advancement of science. The history of the growth of the scientific enterprise, from its beginnings in the valleys of Mesopotamia and Egypt, has been characterized by periods of rapid growth followed by others of relative inactivity. The uneven development of science through the millenniums of time can be explained to a large degree by the lack of sophistication in mathematics. Often in history there have not been sufficient mathematical tools to analyze natural phenomena.

Mathematics has changed science and science has influenced mathematical endeavors. These two disciplines have been joined in man's efforts to fathom the universe. The advent of non-euclidean geometry, for example, made it possible to widen man's view of spheres and better understand the vistas of outer space. The unification of calculus by Liebnetz and Newton facilitated the analysis of rates of change, necessary when studying objects in motion, whether they be marbles moving on a floor, the moon falling through space, or satellites whirling around a relatively insignificant planet, the earth.

Interrelationship of Science and Mathematics in Schools

Because science and mathematics are so integrally involved, almost every science activity on the elementary school level has mathematical implications and many of the mathematical problems have *scientific* ramifications. The National Science Teachers Association in their publication *Theory Into Action in Science Curriculum Development* has emphasized in the following statement the importance of the role of mathematics in teaching science:

> One cannot speak realistically of a sound science curriculum without considering the important role played by mathematics. Just as science itself could not have developed to its present stage without mathematics, so it is unrealistic to think the true character of science can be portrayed without mathematical reasoning. Mathematics is the language by which one describes the order in nature and which in turn leads to a clearer understanding of that order.[2]

---

[1] Andrew M. Gleason, "Science, Mathematics and Tomorrow's Child," *The Instructor* (January, 1968), p. 54.

[2] Curriculum Committee, National Science Teachers Association, *Theory Into Action in Science Curriculum Development* (Washington, D.C.: National Science Teachers Association, 1964), Appendix, p. 3.

The interrelation of mathematics and science in the modern elementary school program is keenly evident in the similarities of the objectives of these two disciplines, of which there is considerable overlapping. The Colorado State Department of Education has attempted to summarize objectives common to most elementary mathematics programs as follows:[3]

> Social aims of the mathematics program: *to develop proficiency with certain skills and the application of these skills in solving problems* that students will encounter in real life situations (a common expectancy); to develop reading ability, a precision of expression, and accuracy; to develop desirable attitudes in pupils towards understanding mathematics and mechanical procedures.
>
> These objectives are reflected in evaluation procedures which measured primarily only the proficiency of skills and application of these skills.
>
> With the reform movement in mathematics came other general objectives. Among the most important of these were: A thorough understanding of numeration systems, axioms, properties of operations on numbers—emphasis of proofs and language of sets received a great deal of attention; early introduction of pupils to the real number system; understanding of *induction*, as well as *deduction*, concerning mathematical proofs; some instruction in geometry from an intuitive and non-metric viewpoint in the primary grades.
>
> The content of the elementary school mathematics program at present certainly reflects these objectives, as well as those of the mathematics curriculum prior to the reform movement.
>
> It is the purpose of this publication to look carefully at these topics and to write sample objectives in terms of pupil behavior for each grade level.
>
> *Grade Level Strands:* The following strands are those usually taught at the kindergarten level and spiraled throughout the six-grade mathematics program.

The Concept of Sets	Properties and Techniques
Numbers and Numerals	of Operations on Numbers
Systems of Numeration	Inequalities
Geometry	Measurement
	Probability and Statistics

> Although these topics are not all-inclusive, they are felt to be representative of what is usually taught in the mathematics classrooms of today. This listing may seem at first to indicate a so-called *"new arithmetic curriculum."* However, recent revisions in almost every major publishing company's offering for elementary arithmetic certainly reflect these topics to some degree of treatment.

The School Mathematics Study Group has outlined 11 basic content areas and seven levels of intellectual activity that students up to the 12th grade should experience.

The content areas include: Structure of Numbers, Measurement, Informal Geometry, Deductive Geometry, Coordinate Systems, and Graphs, Algebraic Sentences and Their Solutions, Relations and Functions, Algebraic Expressions, Probability and Statistics, Logic, and Applications.

---

[3] Glyn H. Sharpe, *Some Behavioral Objectives for Elementary School Mathematics Programs* (Denver, Colo.: Colorado State Department of Education, 1966).

The intellectual behaviors associated with these subject areas have been outlined by Thomas A. Romberg as follows:[4]

UNITS OF SUBJECT MATTER IN MATHEMATICS

1. Systems of Numbers
   a) Real, Rationals, etc. and their Structure
   b) Complex Numbers
   c) Vectors
   d) Finite Number Systems
   e) Sets as Basis of Numbers and Structure
   f) Algorithms
   g) Linguistics
   h) Ordering Relationships
2. Measurement
   a) Notion of Measure
   b) Line Length, Circle Length, etc.
   c) Area of Plane Figures
   d) Volume
   e) Angle Measurement
   f) Rate and Time
   g) Indirect Measurement
   h) Error, Approximation, and Estimation
3. Informal Geometry
   a) Sets of Points, Lines, and Planes and their Configurations in the Plane and 3-Space
   b) Properties of these Sets and their Configuration
   c) Constructions
4. Deductive Geometry
   a) Theorems for Content
   b) Organization of a Deductive System
   c) Constructability
5. Coordinate Systems and Graphs
   a) Units and Direction
   b) Representation of Geometric Ideas Algebraically
   c) Choice of Coordinates and Representation

   d) Types—Bar, Line, etc.
   e) Transformation of Coordinates
   f) Conics
   g) Vectors
6. Algebraic Sentences and their Solutions
   a) Linear
   b) Quadratic
   c) Simultaneous
   d) Polynomial
   e) Logarithmic and Exponential
   f) Inequations
7. Relations and Functions
   a) Functions on Discrete Sets
   b) Functions on Continuous Sets— Trig., Exponential, Logarithmic, Polynomial, and Rational
   c) Special Functions—Absolute Value, etc.
8. Algebraic Expressions
   a) Informal Structure of Polynomials
   b) Algebraic Algorithms—Identities, Polynomials, Factoring, Simplification, Exponents, Radicals, etc.
   c) Linguistics of Algebra
9. Probability and Statistics
   a) Concept of Chance Events
   b) Descriptions of Data
10. Logic
    a) Simple Algebraic Proofs
    b) Intuitive Ideas about Implications, Equivalences, etc.
    c) Intuitive Ideas about Undefined Terms, Postulates, etc.
    d) Direct Proofs
    e) Indirect Proofs
11. Applications
    a) Modeling "Real Life"
    b) Recognition of Patterns

Review this list! Each time you read these general and subject matter objectives ask yourself whether or not the objectives overlap with those of the sciences.

---

[4] Thomas A. Romberg, "The Development of Mathematics Achievement Tests for the National Longitudinal Study of Mathematical Abilities" (unpublished paper, Wisconsin Research and Development Center for Cognitive Learning). The paper was read at the California Advisory Council on Educational Research (CACER) held in San Francisco, California, March, 1965.

Obviously there is considerable duplication of objectives. This will probably appear most apparent to you in activities involving children in the use of numbers, sets, measurement, probability, statistics, and vectors.

Dichotomous and Metrical Data

Scientists collect data. The data they collect can be of two types, dichotomous or metrical. The word *dichotomy* comes from the Greek word "dichotomia" which means to divide into two parts. The word *meter* comes from the Greek word "metron" which means to measure. If a scientist looks at an experimental situation in a dichotomous way, he looks at it in an all (one group) or none (the other group) way.

For example: If a scientist wants to determine whether light is necessary for seeds to sprout, he may perform an all or none type of experiment. He establishes two groups. One group of seeds receives light; the other group, the control, receives no light. From the experiment, he will be able to determine whether light is necessary for the seeds he is using to sprout. However, he will not be able to know how much light is necessary.

In setting up an experiment to determine how much light is necessary, the scientist would have to design it so that he could obtain metrical, measurable, data. He would have to establish an experimental situation to determine how intense the light would have to be over varied periods of time to get seeds to sprout. Obviously this metrical experimental situation would be far more sophisticated than the simple dichotomous experiment and mathematics would be required in determining the intensity of light and the periods of time. However, the scientist's knowledge of the relationship of sprouting seeds to light would be far more sophisticated.

Because mathematics aids in delving more deeply into understanding of natural phenomena, the metrical aspects should be encouraged as much as possible in elementary science activities. Dichotomous types of experiments may be done in the primary grades or as an introductory experiment but should be followed by open-ended questions leading to metrical experimental situations.

Mathematics Reveals Relationships

Mathematics, in addition to its measurement uses in scientific investigation, is also used to reveal relationships. Mathematics is often used by the scientist to organize data so that meaning may be evolved from it. Look at Newton's formula for the law of gravity:

$$F = \frac{GM_1M_2}{d^2}$$

where F = force

M_1 = mass of one object

M_2 = mass of another object

d^2 = distance between the two masses (objects), squared

G = a constant, its value is 6.67×10^{-11}

Review the formula. What relationships can you see between the force, the mass of the objects, and the distance between objects? What will happen if the distance (d) is increased between the two objects? Substitute some simple number for (d) in the formula and you will see. What will happen if the mass of one of the objects is increased? Substitute simple numbers for the masses in the formula. The formula enables you to see and retain in your mind the relationships of gravitational force to the masses of any two objects and the distance between them. Newton's formula for the law of gravity is a fantastic intellectual tool which enables you to determine the gravitational relationships of any object to any other object in the entire universe.

Extrapolation and Interpolation

Mathematics is also used by scientists to interpolate and extrapolate. *Interpolate* means to estimate values and functions between two knowns. For example, if elementary children measure the height of bean plants one day and find them to be five inches high and then measure them again four days later and find them to be seven inches high, they can interpolate that the plants were six inches high two days after their first measurement. They were able to estimate the unknown datum from the two known data.

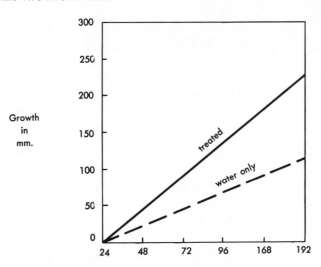

FIGURE 27. Little Marvel Peas

Extrapolate means to project or expand into an area not known or experienced. Often graphing is used as an aid in extrapolation with elementary children. For example, some children in the 8th grade were to determine how dipping pea seeds in a plant hormone solution affected their growth. The children obtained seeds, dipped some in plant hormone solution and others in water. They measured their growth every 24 hours and then plotted the graph in Figure 27.

Several days after the children started the activity, the teacher asked if they could hypothesize how high the hormone treated peas would be when they were 216 hours old. The children were asked to extrapolate, go beyond, what the graph indicated. They could, by referring to their graph, make some statements which were better than wild guesses about the growth of their plants. The teacher then went on to discuss how a graph, such as the one they made, aids in revealing information not actually determined. He explained that they were extrapolating and how this process aids scientific investigation. This instruction helped to make the children aware of the utility of mathematics in scientific investigation.

What study and activities may have led to these graphs? Do the graphs display extrapolation or interpolation?

Mathematics and Science Are Both Concerned with Problem Solving

Since mathematics and science are both involved with problem solving, they require children to perform similar mental functions. Both disciplines use inductive and deductive reasoning. Often these two disciplines and the reasoning processes they involve are joined in the discovery process. George Polya has illustrated how the marriage of these disciplines might occur in learning by discovery in a seventh grade class. He says: "The teacher might ask the following:

"What is the time at noon in San Francisco?"
"But, teacher, everybody knows that," may say a lively youngster, or even "But, teacher, you are silly: twelve o'clock."
"And what is the time at noon in Sacramento?"

"Twelve o'clock—of course, not twelve o'clock midnight."

"And what is the time at noon in New York?"

"Twelve o'clock."

"But I thought that San Francisco and New York do not have noon at the same time, and you say that both have noon at twelve o'clock!"

"Well, San Francisco has noon at twelve o'clock Western Standard Time and New York at twelve o'clock Eastern Standard Time."

"And on what kind of standard time is Sacramento, Eastern or Western?"

"Western, of course."

"Have the people in San Francisco and Sacramento noon at the same moment?"

"You do not know the answer? Well, try to guess it: does noon come sooner in San Francisco, or to Sacramento, or does it arrive exactly at the same instant at both places?"[5]

From these questions children might obtain globes, make measurements, reason, and make conclusions.

Mathematics Aids Scientific Objectivity

Mathematics plays a large role in insuring objectivity and accurate communication in scientific work. If a scientist were to determine, for example, the growth affects of hormones on peas as previously outlined and made no measurements, he might say the affect is great. When he makes a statement of this type, the person reviewing the scientist's research is uncertain as to what is meant by the vague word "great." What may be "great" to one individual may be "small" to another individual. However, if the scientist reports the information as indicated in the graph, the person reviewing the scientist's findings knows just how the growth was affected and its magnitude. There is greater accuracy and communication insured as a result of reporting data in mathematical terms.

Mathematics also makes it possible to insure replication of an experiment. Say, for example, you doubt the findings of the student scientists who did the experiment on the growth affects of hormones on pea seeds. You decide to check their work by repeating the experiment. It would be impossible for you to replicate the experiment unless you knew exactly what concentration of hormone was used, how long the seeds were left in the solution, the number of days they were grown, and the growth rate each day. The fact that a scientific experiment may be replicated or checked by another investigator insures that a scientist is cautious and truthful about his work. If this were not the case, there probably would be individuals reporting frequently they found a cure for cancer or the common cold. If such a report is made, you can be certain other scientists will check this work. If their results vary from those reporting the cure, the original investigators' work and their stature in the profession will be questioned.

---

[5] George Polya, "On Learning, Teaching, and Learning Teaching," *Mathematical Monthly* (June-July, 1963), p. 611.

These boys are comparing the reactions of different liquids. How can their findings be used by them to predict what will happen under similar circumstances?

The nature of scientific investigation is objectivity. Therefore, one purpose of elementary school education should be to have children learn how mathematics insures accuracy, communication, and replication of scientific experiments. In this way, children will see the relevance of mathematics for science and should become better investigators as a result.

Science and Mathematics Instructional Approaches Overlap

As with science, there are numerous nationally supported mathematics curriculum revision projects. Many of these are innovative and attempt to apply the principles of child development revealed by the work of Brüner, Piaget, Vygotsky, and others. Essentially these projects operate under the following points of view in constructing their materials:

1. Children learn concepts by actual manipulation of physical materials. This is the secret of teaching "meaning." A child must interact with objects first in developing concepts and out of many experiences he develops a meaningful understanding of them.
2. Students are motivated best when they are actively involved with objects.
3. The sole use of verbal techniques with young children leads to what Piaget refers to as "pseudo-learning," learning without meaningful understanding. The manipulation of physical objects often leads to scientific

What part does sensory experience play in concept development?

types of problem-solving behaviors. In this respect all of the new mathematics and science curriculum projects overlap. Although most of the mathematics projects do not have as their fundamental purpose the development of scientific problem-solving skills, some projects have specifically set out to attempt to better integrate mathematics and science.

The Integration of Science and Mathematics in Curriculum Reform

The importance of integrating science and mathematics instruction is receiving greater attention by curriculum reformers. The National Science Teachers Association in one of their publications states:

> Those sciences which rely heavily on mathematical demonstration have been most successful in structuring man's experience. Efforts in science curriculum development should be accompanied by corresponding development in mathematics, and the two must be closely correlated at all levels.[6]

Melvin Tumin in a *Saturday Review* article, looking at the American schools from a sociological and anthropological viewpoint, has criticized the overemphasis on subject matter organization rather than integrative experiences to help children. He says:

---

[6] National Science Teachers Association, *op. cit.*

The idea that the "curriculum" should consist of experiences that help children acquire certain basic understandings, values, and skills also is hardly a new idea. In the name of this idea, but out of the misplaced awe for "subject matters" certified by centuries of use, the schools have endowed these "subject matters" with a sacred *persona*. One need only ask the mildly herectical question to divest these subject matters of their awesome hold on the educational imagination. We have done that already with such subjects as Greek and Latin. Now it is time to ask the same mildly herectical question about the notion of subject matter itself. Can we really not rise to the idea that all kinds of different experiences can help children learn to become what we desire them to become.[7]

What processes are these children engaging in?

There has been for many years a group of American educators who have been of the same opinion as Dr. Tumin. Through their efforts several newly designed curriculum projects have been originated with the fundamental purpose of teaching children basic skills in the sciences and mathematics. These are integrated curriculums. Their effect on the American educational scene is causing considerable questioning and analysis of the relationships of these two disciplines and the desirability of teaching them in the same behaviorally integrated context. It was the opinion of the designers of science and mathematics curriculum projects attending the Cambridge Conference on School Mathematics that greater efforts should be made to interlock these two disciplines. Andrew Gleason, summarizing the views of those attending the Cambridge Conference, states:

> No one at the Conference felt that mathematics should be taught entirely as a tool of science or that science teaching must go all out for quantitative experimentation. Commutative, associative, and distributive laws are pure mathe-

---

[7] Melvin Tumin, "Teaching in America," *Saturday Review* (October 21, 1967), pp. 77-84. This article is an edited and expanded version of a talk given to the 1967 Annual Convention of the National Committee for the support of the Public Schools.

matics, and indispensable for understanding arithmetic and algebra. Similarly, the egg-caterpillar-cocoon-butterfly cycle is important science even if kept nonquantitative.

In the integrated curriculum of the future, there will be units that are science, others that are purely mathematical in their outlook. There will be scientific experiments designed primarily to motivate mathematical development, and there will be mathematical topics introduced because of their applicability to science. Finally, there will be units in which the interlocking of scientific ideas with mathematical applications is so close that they cannot be described as either science or mathematics. It is in this interlocking area that some of the greatest challenge to science and technology lies, and designing these units will present the greatest challenge to educators.[8]

The New Science-Mathematics Curriculum Projects

Minnesota Mathematics and Science Teaching Project

Minnesota Mathematics and Science Teaching Project, or MINNEMAST as it is called, was originated in 1961 at the University of Minnesota. The objective of this project is to produce a coordinated mathematics and science curriculum for grades K–6 and materials to help teachers learn how to use and teach these courses.

The experimental testing of the efficacy of these materials has involved 200 teachers associated with ten college centers. These teachers tested the materials in actual classroom situations and made suggestions for revision before the materials were released for national use. To date they have produced ten integrated science-mathematics units for K and first grade and are in the process of producing and testing others for grades 2–6. The project materials are being evaluated by testing children on achievement tests, changes in subject matter performance, and attitudes towards mathematics and science. The work of the project continues.

Study of Quantitative Approach in Elementary School Science

The Study of Quantitative Approach in Elementary School Science originated at the Physics Department, State University of New York, Stony Brook, New York, in 1964. The purposes of this project are to show:

1. The average grade teacher should be able to teach the science program with a minimum of special extra training.
2. Science in the grades should not be confused with technology, nor should it involve the study of complex mechanisms, physical or biological.
3. The science program in the grades should be designed as a base for future science studies in the junior and senior high schools.
4. From the very beginning, science should be presented as a discipline usu-

---

[8] Gleason, *op. cit.*

2 Your Heart as a Clock

Most of the basic units of measure are "human size." You can easily lift a kilogram or a pound of something. A foot is just about the size of a foot. And a second is very close to a heartbeat. It is probably because of our hearts that we measure time in seconds.

To see why this is so, measure how long it takes for each of your heartbeats. You can hear your heart beat with a stethoscope, or you can feel your pulse. There are many places on your body where the pulse can be felt. Usually, a doctor feels your pulse by placing his fingertips on your inside wrist. ● A main artery just under the wrist tendons can be felt as the blood pulses through it. The pulse can also be felt on either side of the windpipe in the throat. ■

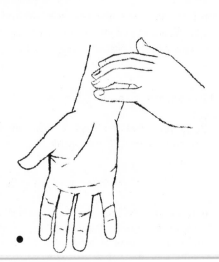

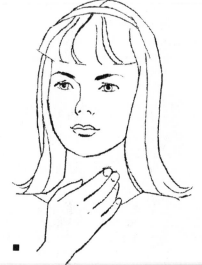

Copyright © 1968 by Scott, Foresman and Company

If you try to time just one pulse, your measurement will not be very accurate, even if you use a stopwatch. Do as your doctor does and count the number of pulses in 60 seconds. *If you count 60 pulses in 60 seconds, how long is each pulse?* _____second. *If you count 70 pulses in 60 seconds, how long is each pulse?* _____ second.

Your heart is not a very trusty clock. You can test it at three different times: 1. when you are sitting quietly; 2. after walking normally for a couple of minutes; and 3. after exercising vigorously for a couple of minutes. For *vigorous* exercise you could hop up and down on one foot, do pushups, or touch your toes rapidly without bending your knees. To make these measurements you will need a clock with a second hand, or a stopwatch. *When you have heartbeat measurements for yourself, write them in the spaces below.*

Number of heartbeats
    in 60 seconds   Time of each pulse

Resting _____   _____

Walking_____   _____

Vigorous exercise _____   _____

    Does everyone have the same rate of heartbeat?

_____

Copyright © 1968 by Scott, Foresman and Company

ally requiring quantitative treatment. Grade by grade the science program should be tied to mathematical studies.

5. The grade school science program should not deal with any generalizing model that cannot be examined directly by the students.
6. The science program should have specific grade by grade goals which can be tested.
7. The science program must not entail large expenditures of money for equipment or consume unwieldy blocks of time.[9]

The materials produced are units containing several lessons. No attempt has been made to produce a spiral curriculum. Over three hundred lessons are in various stages of development for use by teachers. A sample of one of these lessons is shown on pages 254-55.[10]

These materials, like other curriculum projects, have been field tested for their efficacy in elementary classrooms.

School Mathematics Study Group (SMSG)

The School Mathematics Study Group was formed at Yale University in March 1958. It has been, by and large, one of the most prolific producers of mathematical materials to be used on the elementary and secondary school levels. Although its fundamental objective has been to foster research and development in the teaching of school mathematics, the group has produced several integrative units such as the following:

> Mathematics Through Science—Part I: Student's Text
> Part   I: Teacher's Commentary
> Part   II: Student's Text, Measurement and Graphing
> Part   II: Teacher's Commentary
> Part   II: Student's Text, Graphing, Equations, and Linear Functions
> Part III: Teacher's Commentary
> Part III: Student's Text, An Experimental Approach to Functions
> Mathematics and Living Things—Student's Text
> Teacher's Commentary—Mathematical Methods in Science

SMSG also produces without charge a series of newsletters which explain the purposes and sources through which these materials may be obtained. The work of the group continues in producing similar types of materials.

The Elementary Science Study

Although, as the name indicates, the Elementary Science Study has been mainly concerned with science, many of the units produced actually deal to a great extent with the development of mathematical concepts as well. Some of the many

---

[9] Clifford Swartz, "Elementary School Science by a Quantitative Approach," *Journal of Research in Science Teaching*, Vol. 2 (1964), pp. 349-351.

[10] Clifford Swartz, *Quantitative Science for the Middle Grades* (Scott, Foresman and Company, 1969). Reprinted by permission of Scott, Foresman and Company.

units which deal with this are: Mirror Cards (Grades 1–7), Light and Shadows (Grades K–3), Attributive Games and Problems (Grades K–8), Peas and Particles (Grades 4–6), Primary Balancing (no grade listed), Changes (Grade 1–4), Optics (Grades 6–8), Pattern Blocks (Grades K–5), Balloons and Gases (Grades 6–8), Tangram (Grades K–8), Mapping (Grades 6–7), Musical Sound (Grade 6), Matrix Blocks (Grades K–8), Measuring (Grades K–3), Checkerboard (Grade 4), Thermometry (Grades 4–6), Time and Clocks (Grades 3–5), Counting the Slide Rule (Grades 7–8).

International Curriculum Revisions

Throughout the world there is extensive curriculum revision being made in both mathematics and science. In many instances the United States is assisting countries by providing consultants and examples of United States materials through the activities of the Agency of Internal Development or the Peace Corps. A complete list of these projects, and a short synopsis about each of them, is available in the Report of the *International Clearinghouse on Science and Mathematics Curricular Developments* compiled under the direction of J. David Lockard, Science Teaching Center, University of Maryland, College Park, Maryland.

One of the projects of particular interest listed in this publication is the Nuffield Mathematics Teaching Project in England.

What are these youngsters learning about sorting, classifying, and counting in this activity?

The Nuffield Mathematics Teaching Project. The Nuffield Project is involved both in mathematics and science revisions. It was established through a grant from the English Nuffield Foundation in 1964. As with the United States mathematics projects, Jean Piaget's work has had a considerable influence on the Nuffield curriculum design. For example, teaching addition before the children have a good understanding of numbers, one of Piaget's main points, is argued against. In the following statement, the project illustrates why this should be the case:

For example, it is easy to drill children into writing a statement like "3 + 2 = 5" before they can really appreciate the meaning of the symbols. Does this mean "take 3, add 2 and you get 5" or "3 plus 2 gives 5" (what is "plus"?) or "3 added to 2 makes 5" or "whenever I have 3 things and then get 2 more, I end up with 5 things" or none of these things?[11]

The Nuffield Project bases its learning on having children manipulate physical materials. Some of the activities children do are sorting of physical objects (classifying) in various ways, measuring distances on a map, using stopwatches to measure the speed of an electric train as it moves around a track, measuring the angle of elevation of a flagpole, working with balances, and studying volume by pouring water into containers of different sizes or shapes.

School Science Curriculum Project—University of Illinois

The School Science Curriculum Project has become concerned with the importance of mathematics and science. The project committee has published a very interesting booklet by Richard Salinger and Ira Glasser entitled *A Little Math with Your Science*. The booklet explains to the teacher the need for reproducibility and quantifiable data in scientific investigations and uses the study of the relationship between the weight applied to a spring and the length of the spring as indicated in the diagram here.

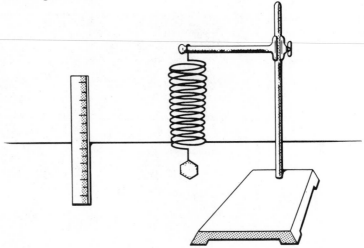

Explanations of how to graph data, the horizontal axis, dependent variables, plotting, preparing a table of data, interpolation, extrapolation, plus other concepts are also contained in the booklet. The booklet concludes with the statement:

> Don't be afraid to use mathematics. Remember, while mathematics is not a means of establishing facts about nature independent of observation, it is a tool for education and "the language of science."[12]

---

[11] Nuffield Foundation, Mathematics Teaching Project, "Beginning" (unpublished paper, London, S.W. 1, England, 1965), p. 1.

[12] Richard Salinger and Ira Glasser, *A Little Math with Your Science*, School Science Curriculum Project, Trial Edition (University of Illinois, 1967), p. 20.

How Do Teachers Stimulate the Use of Mathematics in Science?

The fundamental objective of this chapter has been to show that mathematics and science cannot be divorced. The new curriculum projects in mathematics as well as in science include many activities in which these two disciplines are entwined. Although there have been major efforts to combine mathematics and science, many teachers will be faced with materials which fail in this respect. When confronted with the more traditional type of instructional material, a teacher should endeavor as much as possible to interrelate mathematics with science activities. This can be done by bringing the use of measurement into science as much as possible, by controlling variables metrically, and by organizing and reporting data mathematically—especially by the use of graphs. Children should also be given numerous opportunities to interpret graphs, to learn how to set up experiments involving measuring variables, and to develop the concept of how experimental error can be lessened by averaging. By having children perform in this manner, the teacher not only teaches a more sophisticated level of science but mathematical concepts as well. This framework is more likely to have greater meaning and therefore be retained better by the children.

Summary

Mathematics and science have been integrally involved and have contributed to each other's advancement through the ages. It is difficult to think of certain science disciplines, such as physics and chemistry, existing to any degree of sophistication without mathematical tools. Because mathematics and science are wedded in the investigation of natural phenomena, many of the educational objectives of these two disciplines overlap. It is the opinion of mathematics and science curriculum specialists that science curriculums should be constructed utilizing mathematical concepts to show the role of mathematics in scientific problem solving. When a scientist collects data, he often does so in a quantitative manner. Mathematics aids the scientist in collecting objective data, revealing relationships, interpolating and extrapolating, suggesting problem-solving techniques, and in the replicating of experiments. As a scientist works, mathematics and science are often both involved in the inquiry process requiring many mental operations which are fundamentally inductive or deductive.

Educators more recently have increased their efforts to better integrate science and mathematics in curriculum design. Although as yet there is no completely integrated mathematics and science curriculum for all grades, many modern curriculum projects have made special efforts to develop units or courses for some of the grade levels. Science curriculum projects and the more recently published elementary science texts have also included more investigations utilizing quantitative approaches. Some of those curriculum projects which have integrated mathematics and science materials are: the Minnesota Mathematics and Science Teaching Project, the Study of Quantitative Approach in Elementary School Science, the Elementary Science Study, the School Science Curriculum Project—University of Illinois. It is the opinion of Dr. Gleason, chairman of Harvard University Mathematics Department, that a more integrated mathematics and science curriculum will become the typical pattern of elementary education in the not too distant future.

SELF-EVALUATION AND FURTHER STUDY

1. How has the history of science been influenced by developments in mathematics?
2. What are the arguments for/against the separation of mathematics and science into individual subject matter disciplines for teaching elementary children?
3. Describe how you would set up a dichotomous experiment and a metrical experiment. Which is considered to be more sophisticated and why?
4. How does mathematics reveal relationships?
5. What is the difference between interpolation and extrapolation and how do these mathematical concepts contribute to an understanding of natural phenomena and scientific reasoning?
6. It has been said that mathematics and science objectives overlap. In what ways is this true?
7. How does mathematics contribute to the objectivity of scientific investigation?
8. What are some of the movements presently going on in the elementary school indicating a curriculum reorientation as far as mathematics and science are concerned?
9. Why wouldn't it be wise to teach children addition before they have developed some concept of numbers?
10. What is meant by the term "meaning" relative to children learning mathematical concepts?
11. If you were going to develop a better understanding of what space means for children, what would you do in your class and why?
12. How would you go about encouraging the use of mathematics in your science teaching?

Should school attempt to create individuals who are capable of understanding everything that has been done in the history of ideas, and capable of repeating all this history, or should they focus on forming individuals who are capable of inventing, of finding new things in all areas: in modest technical inventions—that is, people who are capable of going beyond the present and previous generations? This gives us the alternative between two types of pedagogy, one in which the child is receptive, the other in which he is active— education which stimulates the activities of the child in the area of his inventiveness.[1]

CHAPTER 12

ENCOURAGEMENT OF CREATIVITY IN DISCOVERY SCIENCE

J. W. Osburn defines a creative person as ". . . one who perceives and imagines hidden relations and has the impulse to incorporate them in material form so that others may perceive them. Such people can and do frame in their constructive imagination poems, paintings, sonatas, and symphonies that have never before been perceived. It is they who can see angels in a block of marble, 'sermons in stones,' and 'theories in deep sea ooze'."[2]

Paul Torrance, a leader in research in the field of creativity says: "I have chosen to define creative thinking as the process of sensing gaps or disturbing missing elements; forming ideas or hypotheses concerning them; testing these hypotheses and communicating the results, possibly modifying and retesting the hypotheses."[3]

Brewster Ghiselin suggests "the measure of creative product be the extent to which it restructures our universe of understanding."[4] Morris I. Stein says of creativity: "It is a process of hypothesis formation, hypothesis testing, and the communication of results. Creativity may be manifest in any one or all of the aspects of this process."[5]

Creativity is generally thought of in two ways. Some think true creativity involves the production of an idea never before known to man. Obviously, this view does not have much relevance for elementary teaching. A more inclusive view holds that whenever an individual produces something original or makes some innovation new to him, creativity is involved. This latter view has the more relevance for elementary teachers and is the one held by the authors of this text.

What Constitutes a Creative Classroom?

A prospective teacher from a college observation class observed a third grade elementary classroom in a rural school where the children were involved in excit-

---

[1] Frank G. Jennings, "Jean Piaget: Notes on Learning." *Saturday Review* (May 20, 1967). Copyright © 1967 Saturday Review, Inc.

[2] J. W. Osburn, *Enriching the Curriculum for Gifted Children* (New York: The Macmillan Company, 1931), p. 37.

[3] Paul Torrance, *Guiding Creative Talent* (Englewood Cliffs, N.J.: Prentice Hall, Inc., 1962), p. 16.

[4] B. Ghiselin in C. W. Taylor, *Creativity: Progress and Potential* (New York: McGraw Hill Book Co., 1964), p. 86.

[5] Morris I. Stein, "Creativity and the Scientist," Bernard Barber and Walter Hirsch, eds., *The Sociology of Science* (New York: The Free Press of Glencoe), p. 331.

ing tasks. The classroom was a workshop for pupils doing a variety of activities. One child, who was enthralled with the mystery of a cocoon asked, "When will my moth hatch?" One girl was reading to try to find out what to feed her pollywogs. Two boys were busy watching the movement of their snails. A group of students were planting seeds in milk cartons and arguing about how deep they should plant them. Another group watched a turtle eating his meal. The amateur weathermen recorded on the board temperature and barometric pressure changes they detected from their homemade instruments. There was diverse activity; and yet, there was order and purposeful work. Some children worked in groups, others by themselves on their individual projects.

Some children were working on projects for the coming science night sponsored by the PTA. The tasks being performed for this purpose were: the preparation of different environments such as a desert, an aquarium, and a bog terrarium; the

A good teacher allows time for introspection. How can she develop her "sixth sense" in determining which situations of this type should break into her planned program?

creation of murals illustrating prehistoric animals and sea life; the preparation of various displays illustrating some scientific principle. Several children were involved with data from their experiments with plants and animals and were preparing them for display with cards explaining their results. The college student discovered this was one of those periods set aside as a science interest period.

The children in this classroom were involved in many experiences requiring some degree of creativity. Contrast this class with one in which the teacher stands in front of his fifth grade class and reads and talks about science. He says "Science is important, and we must learn it. Today I want to talk about a special field of science, blood. Now the body has blood. It is red and is pumped by the heart. The heart has valves which stop the blood from going backwards. Blood carries food and oxygen to all parts of our body. All parts of the body need oxygen. We get oxygen from the air and the blood absorbs it. The heart beats several times a minute." He stops talking for a minute to ask two boys to pay attention. He then goes on with his lecture for another fifteen minutes.

Some children listen attentively, but most squirm in their seats. Others look out of the window. One boy is obviously dreaming of happier times. It is evident that most of the children have forgotten the teacher. They are bored, the teacher is tiring himself wastefully, and the level of learning is low. Finally, the children receive a needed respite, recess. What chance is there for creativity to manifest itself in this uninspiring classroom? How much does the lecture-oriented teacher rob his children of a chance to discover their creative potential? The discovery and development of the creative genius of youth is of prime importance in the educational process. It is precisely this ability we most want to develop. Teachers have a great responsibility to children and society to see this ability manifested to the maximum of the individual's potential.

What Are the Characteristics of Individuals with Pronounced Creative Ability?

Although Dr. Ghiselin points out that every individual is creative to an extent, some children have outstanding creative ability. These individuals can be recognized by the following characteristics:

1. Curiosity
2. Like to discover
3. Self-sufficient and independent
4. Prefer difficult tasks
5. Resourceful and self-assertive
6. Enjoy problem solving
7. Flexible thinkers
8. Dedicated to work and may work for long periods on unsolved problems
9. Likely to give rapid and unexpected responses to questions
10. Likely to show ability to synthesize and see implications
11. Usually well read [6]

[6] Ghiselin, *op. cit.*

In science activities, creative children may be particularly recognized by their enthusiasm and persistence in solving problems.

Research on Creativity

Research indicates science instruction in the schools has not rewarded the creative individual. Calvin Taylor, in a study done on creative scientists, found little correlation between academic achievement and high creative production in industry.[7] Donald McKennon, in studying outstanding creative individuals, found the majority received C's and B's in school rather than A's.[8] Teachers have probably failed to reward creative children with high marks because they have judged them mainly on academic achievement. They think being academically gifted is correlated with all types of human behavior. Numerous studies, however, indicate there is *not* a high correlation between I.Q. and creative potential. In other words, the student defined as gifted may not be creative and the creative individual usually is not gifted as determined by the I.Q. tests. Dr. Torrance says of this:

> Traditional tests of intelligence are heavily loaded with tasks requiring recognition, memory, and convergent thinking. . . . In fact, if we were to identify children on the basis of intelligence tests, we would eliminate from consideration approximately seventy per cent of the most creative. This percentage seems to hold fairly well, no matter what educational level we study, from kindergarten through graduate school.[9]

The National Merit Scholarship Corporation, which has given thousands of scholarships to high school graduates, became concerned about using intellectual criteria as the sole means of making their awards. As a result, in 1961 they started giving scholarships to students who demonstrated creative ability but had not scored sufficiently high on tests to receive an award. Intelligence tests and scholastic aptitude tests, because of their emphasis on convergent thinking, fail to identify the person with creative ability. Other tests are now being perfected to supplement the traditionally intellectual testing instruments to reveal creative ability in children.

Although intelligence and creativity are not the same, Ann Roe found the minimum intelligence required for creative production in science is decidedly higher than the average I.Q.[10] The fact that traditionally the individuals with the highest

---

[7] Calvin Taylor (ed.), *Creativity: Progress and Potential* (New York: McGraw-Hill, 1964).

[8] Donald McKennon, "The Creative Individual," Broadcast #50250 V.E. Columbia Broadcasting System, University of California, Explorer (unpublished, January 28), 1962.

[9] Torrance, *op. cit.*

[10] Ann Roe, "The Psychology of the Scientist," *Science* (August 18, 1961), p. 134.

How might this device be used to stimulate interest and further creative thinking?

grades are not the most creative ones indicates quite clearly that schools have not fully recognized nor rewarded creativity.

The Critical Years for Developing Creative Talent

Dr. Torrance has stated there is general agreement among psychologists that the elementary school years are critical ones in developing creative ability.[11] Robert

---

[11] Torrance, *op. cit.*

Hess has generalized a similar view from his research.[12] In one research study he took two groups of rats and blindfolded one group from infancy. Both groups were allowed to develop for three months. He then blindfolded the other group. At the end of five months he tested both groups on maze problems. He found those raised in the unblindfolded group up to three months of age did significantly better in solving maze problems.

He followed this study by raising two groups of rats from the same litter. One group was taken home and raised as pets. The rats in the other group were allowed to remain in laboratory cages. After several weeks both groups were tested on maze problems. The rats raised as pets did significantly better than those kept in the laboratory. Hess concludes from this research that stimulation should occur early for children; the type and variety of experience a child has affects his ability to learn later and deprivation during the early years may affect a loss of mental ability.

Can Creativity Be Enhanced and Nurtured in the Elementary School?

Torrance reports there have been outstanding examples of creative activity by individuals at an early age.[13] In summarizing many research projects, he found variations of creative ability at different ages, but *all* age groups in the elementary school demonstrated some creative abilities. The development of creative attitudes and modes of thought probably is most critical during the elementary school years. Children tend to be naturally creative, but creativity may be dampened before they leave school if elementary teachers have not sought and kindled creative potential. Calvin Taylor, reporting on the implications of research findings on creativity, has stated that there may be an above average dropout rate of creative individuals in schools with traditional form of instruction. He goes on to say that evidence indicates both teacher and fellow students may actually disfavor the creative person.[14] Torrance has indicated that freedom to be creative may affect a person's mental health because the stifling of creative ability may inhibit a person's feelings of satisfaction.[15] If an individual does not gain feelings of satisfaction in the school environment, he is therefore more likely to be a dropout prospect.

How can schools enhance an individual's creative potential? There is empirical evidence to show schools can play a major role in encouraging creative development. Irving Maltzman and his associates found that when subjects were instructed to be original and were given instruction requiring originality, they were

---

[12] Robert D. Hess, "The Latent Resources of the Child's Mind," *Journal of Research In Science Teaching*, Issue 1 (1963).

[13] Torrance, *op. cit.*

[14] Calvin Taylor, "Some Implications of Research Findings on Creativity" (unpublished paper, University of Utah, 1961).

[15] Taylor, *Creativity: Progress and Potential, op. cit.*

With the wonder of it showing on her face, what science concepts do you think this child may be developing?

better able to solve problems later requiring original responses.[16] R. H. Van Deren divided 215 seventh grade students into matched control and experimental groups. He pretested both groups for creativity. The experimental group teachers were then given instruction in the nature and development of creative thinking. After this instruction, these teachers produced students who did significantly better on post-test creative results. On the basis of this study, Van Deren has suggested that all teachers be given training to improve creativity in the classroom.[17]

Richard E. Ripple and John Dacey have found problem solving and verbal creativity can be facilitated through programmed instruction which has these aims as objectives.[18]

Although an individual cannot be taught to be creative because being creative is an active mental process a person undergoes, the teacher clearly can structure the educational environment and through his own attitudes and desires engender the creative ability of children.

---

[16] I. Maltzman, "On the Training of Originality," *Psychological Review* (1960), p. 67.

[17] R. H. Van Deren, "The Development of Selected Creative Thinking Abilities Through Creative Discussion in the Seventh Grade Curriculum" (unpublished Ed.D. Dissertation, University of Southern California, 1967).

[18] Richard E. Ripple, and John Dacey, "The Facilitation of Problem Solving and Verbal Creativity by Exposure to Programmed Instruction (unpublished paper, Cornell University, 1966).

What techniques should a teacher try to avoid mere copying of data by children?

Why Have Teachers Neglected the Development of Creative Potential?

Why have so few teachers really contributed to the development of creative abilities? In the past, one of the main reasons was a lack of research in the field of creativity. Over the last decade, however, considerable research has been accumulated with implications for the schools. Unfortunately most teachers are unaware of it and, as a consequence, hold many unsubstantiated ideas about creative learning. One such idea has been that the accumulation of knowledge will lead to an intelligent and creative person. Taylor has pointed out, however, that individuals who possess nearly the same information may differ considerably in creativeness.[19]

The general pattern of the school and traditional forms of instruction leave much to be desired in establishing an environment for creative activity. Creative ability is inhibited by requiring children to sit cemented to their classroom desks, soaking up like sponges the knowledge the teacher pours out, and dropping one subject area to rush to another in the effort to cover all subject disciplines. If schools were designed solely with the idea of producing the maximum creative abilities of the children, very likely the school plant, class schedules, teaching patterns, and classroom environment would be uniquely different from most of the schools today.

Another problem in developing creative innovation in schools has been the lack of leadership on the part of administrators. Too often the elementary school administrators have been status quo caretakers of the school. Today, however, because of the advent of federal financial aid, which has made research possible, there is a new breed of innovative administrators who are in many communities becoming true leaders in education, particularly in curriculum reform and encouraging instructional modification.

To teach children so they can develop their creative abilities is hard work, because the creative child often is more difficult to teach. He usually does not want to follow the crowd, and his ways of thinking may be quite divergent. More often

---

[19] Taylor, *Creativity: Progress and Potential, op. cit.*

than not he refuses to accept a superficial statement about science or the environment. A teacher who accepts the objective of trying to develop creative potential of these children must, therefore, work harder. There is no room for lazy teachers.

Covering Versus Learning the Material

Curriculum pressures may prevent teachers from developing creative scientific abilities. Teachers feel obligated to hurry through units of study in an effort to cover the material. These teachers present the material, but they fail to teach it. There is never any assurance that because a teacher "covers" lessons the students have learned them. An intelligent beginning teacher soon learns this fact.

There is no more rewarding and efficient way to learn than creatively. It may appear that creative teachers do not cover as much science, but their children remember what they have taken part in creatively. Proof of this comes to any teacher who ponders his own experience as an elementary pupil. The things truly learned almost always have some actively creative enterprise involved. What value is it to have "covered" everything but to have learned little?

Science Curricula—Texts and Creativity

There has been no science curriculum constructed nor elementary science series written with the specific objective of developing creativity. Calvin Taylor,[20] a leader in research on creativity, has studied new science curriculum materials. He is of the opinion that it is unlikely neglected areas of education will automatically receive attention with the emergence of new instructional programs. He emphasizes, therefore, the need for deliberate techniques to develop creative ability and to determine how instructional media might be effective for this purpose. To reiterate, what is needed today in science education, is a curriculum project which develops conceptual schemes, processes, and creative ability.

There is no reason to think because a school district has adopted a new curriculum there will automatically be an increased development of creative ability, especially since teachers may use these materials in very uncreative ways. However, the new curriculum projects and science text series published over the last two years give far greater attention to discovery activities. These activities should, where possible, be modified to allow for further experimentation and opportunities for children to suggest other investigations. The open-ended laboratory activities which appear in Part Four endeavor to do this. This section contains questions which in most cases evolve out of the laboratory experiments the children performed in the lesson. The questions provide opportunities for children to make hypotheses and suggest further investigations, many of which may be experimental in design.

---

[20] Taylor, *Some Implications of Research Findings on Creativity, op. cit.*

One of the best ways a teacher can help develop creative science ability in children is to provide them with opportunities to suggest, outline, and carry out their own experiments. The ideas for these investigations may arise out of student interests, class discussions, and other experiments they have performed. By allowing children to set up their own investigations, teachers can break away from formalized texts and curriculums. The more structure there is in a lesson the fewer opportunities there are for children to be creative in devising the structure themselves.

What can youngsters learn about temperature by observing the melting of ice?

In the primary grades obviously the degree of structure needs to be greater than in the upper elementary grades. A teacher should guide his pupils to predict, or hypothesize, control and manipulate variables, and encourage them to investigate, giving guidance only when needed. He must be the judge of how much structure is required. Too much structure kills creativity, too little results in chaos. Instructors should break away from commercially prepared materials when the situation warrants it and supplement these with what they have devised themselves. In other words, the teacher should become creative himself in building the science program. A creative teacher, because of his own involvement, is more likely to nurture creative ability and in the process come to enjoy, understand, and convey what it means *to have fun with science.*

What has been said about the value of science curriculums and texts in developing creative ability is even more true for materials produced more than five years ago. Outdated materials must be replaced by newer, up-to-date instructional aids. The newer texts and curriculum guides can often be adapted to allow for better creative opportunities.

Techniques for Developing Creativity

Creativity cannot be taught as a process, but by developing situations that demand imagination, originality, and problem solving, the children are more likely to be creative. The following list provides suggestions to assist the teacher in encouraging creative science potential:

1. *Invitations:* Prepare and give an "Invitation to Inquiry" to your class. In the upper grades if you have some children with a keen interest in science, help and encourage them to write some simple invitations. Refer to the Chapter 5 for suggestions on how to write these.
2. *Pictorial Riddles:* After the children have seen some examples of pictorial riddles similar to those given in this text, have them prepare their own pictorial riddles. Refer to the Chapter 6 for help in constructing riddles.
3. *Inventions:* Give the children some common material and ask them to invent what they can with it. This is what Dr. Torrance calls putting things to new use. For example, you might give them a tin can, clothes hangers, buttons, and let them arrange these into whatever they wish.
4. *Diminishing Structure:* Provide some activities with little structure. For example, give the children some putty, three long, thin sticks (chopsticks or popsicle sticks will do), a pin, paper clips, and ask them to devise a balance.
5. *Silent Demonstration:* Have the class watch a silent demonstration.
6. *Films:* Use a film or filmloop in an inquiring manner as outlined in Chapter 8.
7. *Positive Reinforcement:* Give positive reinforcement for creative work. Never laugh at a student's ideas or conclusions. Compliment children for sincere guesses even

How can a teacher encourage an open sharing of responses and reactions? What does this child's picture tell you about him?

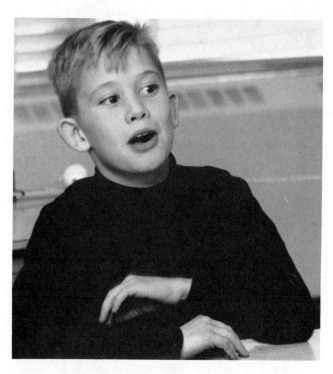

when the guesses may be bizarre. Do not criticize answers to questions. If a child's answer seems wrong to you, ask other children to comment about it. The members of the class often will point out the flaws in the answer. The expression of conflicting viewpoints will help to reduce in the individual what Piaget has called the "egocentric view" of the world. When a child sees that other children may look at natural phenomena in a manner different from his own, he begins to build in his mind the idea that there may be several ways of looking at a problem. He tends to become less egocentric as a result. Conflict of opinions might also lead to possibilities for investigating and determining which child's ideas are true. Try not to use the phrase, "that is wrong." Instead, respond positively by saying, "You are thinking and that is good, but you haven't quite discovered something else." Try to eliminate negative statements from your criticism. Use instead, "That is good." "We are on the right track now." "That is an idea." "Wonderful." "Good thinking." Nothing pays like praise. Above all, respond to the child's answer; no reply may be interpreted by the child as a negative response.

8. *Encourage New Ideas:* Welcome and encourage new ideas. Demonstrate how pleased you are when a child comes up with a new idea. When this occurs, interrupt the class and say, "Did you hear what John said?" Explain his suggestion or idea and then say, "Isn't that a good idea? We have good thinkers in this class."

9. *Accept Deviation from Norm:* Accept and encourage students who deviate from the norm in the ways they think about science and do their science experiments.

10. *Seek Out Inquisitiveness:* Endeavor to differentiate between a child being impudent and one being inquisitive. Remember, children usually are not impudent. They have problems communicating and often fail to say what they really mean. This does not mean that a child should be lax. If you think a child is being impudent, try to get him to explain his ideas. Otherwise, you may be fooled. Avoid head-on collisions before the class; use private conferences when necessary.

11. *Use Activities that Fail to Advantage:* Do not be afraid to do demonstrations you have not done. If you make a mistake or your demonstration does not work, turn the incident into a learning situation. Ask the class to see if they can discover what you did wrong. An example of a demonstration that did not work the first time was done by a second grade teacher: She took a fruit jar and filled it with water. She slid a three by five card over the top of the jar and inverted it. The water was supposed to stay in the jar. The teacher, however, had a flimsy card which bent and soon let air into the jar. The air forced the water out, causing the demonstration to fail, but the teacher did not look at it that way. She asked the class why the water stayed in the jar just a few seconds. What should be done to get the water to stay in the jar longer without securing anything to the jar. Why didn't it work? One bright boy suggested using a round cap from a Mason jar instead of a card. Other pupils suggested using heavier cardboard. All of these suggestions were tried. The pupils had fun doing this demonstration, had opportunities to think, profited from the teacher's mistake, and learned much more about science.

12. *Learn Science with Your Children:* Children like to have their teacher learn with them, to be able to give the teacher advice, and to do experiments the teacher has done. Give your children a chance to show you how they would solve problems. Have fun teaching science!

13. *Give Possibilities for Ingenuity:* Encourage ingenuity. Ask your pupils how they would prove some specific problem scientifically. Give them problems and ask how they would find the answer. Tell them you want to prove some scientific idea or principle. Ask how they would go about showing it. For example, ask them how they would prove what amounts of fertilizer are beneficial to plants. If they need some help, ask the following questions to guide them: How many plants will we

need? Should we put fertilizer on all the plants? How much should we put on each plant? Do we need to think of anything else about our experiment before we try it?

14. *Do Not Rush Pupils:* Do not hurry pupils on their projects. Give them time to think how best to do a science project or solve a problem.

15. *Encourage Pupil Involvement:* Give children opportunities to participate. Let them do experiments or demonstrations in front of the class, or have them tell the class something they have seen or studied in science. Ask questions but seldom tell them the answers. Let them discover the answer through the types of questions you ask, their background knowledge, and experimentation.

16. *Encourage Student Questioning:* Make your class feel student questions are important. Ask questions to stimulate creative responses. You should ask questions such as: How could the experiment have been done better? What is wrong with our apparatus? How could you be more certain about your answers? Why do you think you got these results? (See Chapter 6 on questioning)

17. *Encourage the Attitude "It's Good to Try":* Develop the attitude that it is better to try and fail than not to try at all. Remember what was said about Ehrlich and Land's positive approach to failure. How many thousands of experiments have "failed" in the history of science? Often more can be learned from our failures if we study the results carefully. A fourth grader had been trying to raise brine shrimp. He had raised several batches, but none of them grew very large. He failed in a sense, but he enjoyed his "failures" because he had more experiments to do. In the process, this student learned to analyze problems and their results while having fun with science.

18. *Be a Creative Teacher:* Be creative yourself in the methods you use to teach science. Vary your approaches and think of things children of different abilities may choose to do in studying science. Make some of your own science lessons rather than those commercially prepared. Remember, creativity is infectious. You inspire your children, and they in turn will inspire you. A teacher who is not creative is probably a boring teacher because he is not inspired with teaching. Nothing is more boring than routine, but a creative teacher does more than a routine job. Furthermore, varied activities insure more attention to individual differences. Be experimental in your approach to teaching science and you are on your way to being creative.

19. *Encourage Pupil Initiative:* Let the children take some initiative and responsibility for developing science lessons and for doing demonstrations and experiments. The more they do the more opportunity there is for them to grow.

What could have stimulated this activity?

20. *Don't Overemphasize Group Work:* Never overemphasize group work. Let students work as individuals on science tasks if they choose. Introduce more individual study when the situation allows. Creative individuals often work best alone rather than in groups. An example was a gifted fifth grade student who was fascinated with butter-flies. Her teacher discovered this and encouraged her to study them on her own. The girl spent many hours reading about them and making and arranging her collection. A professor from the local college heard of this student's interest and volunteered to assist her with some larvae experiments. In the spring the girl entered the elementary science fair and won a first place.

21. *Encourage Problem Solving:* Encourage students to solve problems or construct and perfect some science equipment. For example, one teacher teaching in Hawaii had the children working with a balance made of blocks of wood and a straw for the balance arm. She asked her children in the fifth grade if they could construct a better balance. Two boys took up this challenge and made a balance using blocks and chopsticks.

22. *Encourage Hypothesizing:* Stimulate, encourage, assist, recognize, and reward children for formulating hypotheses. Ask: Can anyone guess what will happen in this experiment if it is done in this way? What do you think is the best way the answer to our questions can be found? An example of getting the children to think creatively might be: How would you make a miniature greenhouse? What materials should you get? How could you determine whether your miniature greenhouse is better than another one? After looking over several children's greenhouses (cans, shoe boxes, cigar boxes, etc.), what is your hypothesis as to which greenhouse would serve best to raise radishes?

23. *Display Creative Work:* Show your children creative work done by other students in your class or other classes. Also have creative work in your class shown to other classes. Have a class fair and invite others in to see your science creative work, etc.

24. *Encourage Artistic Ability:* The creative arts can be a valuable aid in teaching sci-

What applications to conservation will these boys make as a result of creating this micro erosion problem?

ence. For example, have students write a play describing some scientific event or a science fiction story. Children enjoy writing. Have them draw a home, car, or city of tomorrow. Use these drawings for class discussions to illustrate science concepts and principles.

25. *Improve your Sophistication in Writing Creative Questions:* Use the following words suggested by Paul Blackwood in constructing creative questions.

Hypothesize	Reflect	Incubate	
Induce	Propose	Predict	Formulate
Deduce	Criticize	Estimate	Interrelate
Speculate	Conceive	Explain	Generalize
Analyze	Invent	Appreciate	Forecast
Select Data	Guess	Infer	Extrapolate
Designs Experiments	Comprehend	Abstract	Interpolate
	Doubt	Synthesize	

26. *ABOVE ALL, LET CHILDREN DISCOVER AND INVESTIGATE!*

Summary

Creativity has been defined as the process of forming ideas, hypothesizing and testing, modifying, and communicating these ideas. Individuals with obvious creative potential can be identified by their curiosity, desire to discover and do difficult tasks, resourcefulness, problem-solving abilities, dedication to work, flexible thinking, ability to synthesize and see implications, well-read backgrounds, and their rapid responses to questions. Research in the field of creativity has shown creative ability is widely distributed. It can be nurtured or stifled, and the elementary school years are critical ones in its development. If creative potential is not stimulated during these formative years, it probably will not manifest itself fully in adulthood. Creativity does not necessarily correlate with intelligence, although creative scientists generally have above average intelligence.

Creative individuals have a tendency to deviate from the norm, are divergent thinkers, and are reluctant to accept superficial and dogmatic authority. Schools traditionally have not rewarded creative children. Teachers generally have not encouraged creative ability because of a belief that gifted individuals are also creative, a lack of knowledge about creativity, curriculum pressures, attempts to cover prescribed material, an emphasis on group instruction, and a lack of support or encouragement from administrators.

There presently are no science curriculums or individual texts that have creativity as a fundamental objective. However, several recently developed texts and materials can be adapted to contribute to this objective.

Although creativity cannot be taught since it is an innovative attitude for approaching tasks, the classroom environment and teaching techniques can be organized to stimulate creative enterprise. Twenty-six suggestions for how teachers may accomplish this were given in the chapter.

What would you do to involve more children in science activities?

Science teaching, because of the nature of science itself, is concerned with problem solving, which can do much to foster creative abilities. Students must be "actively" involved in learning to make discoveries and to come to know science as a process as well as a body of knowledge. Science investigations designed to utilize the imagination, originality, and curiosity of children will most likely foster the development of creative thought and will build toward the attainment of better science teaching.

SELF-EVALUATION AND FURTHER STUDY

1. Refer to the list of words given in number 25 of the techniques for developing creativity in this chapter. Use ten of these words to formulate ten questions that will require creative responses from children.
2. How would you define *creativity* to give you direction in your teaching?
3. How would you run a classroom to kill creative ability?
4. What evidence is there that the schools have inhibited the development of creative scientists?
5. How would you identify individuals who are above average in creative ability?

6. What does research indicate about how creative ability is distributed and the importance of opportunities to be creative?
7. Why have teachers often failed to develop creative potential in their pupils?
8. What are the critical years for developing creative potential and what evidence shows that this is so?
9. How may a creative person's mental health be affected by the school?
10. What is the present status of science texts and curriculum materials relative to the development of creative abilities?
11. How can the classroom environment contribute to creative production?
12. How can teachers nurture creative ability in science?
13. What can you do to develop your own creative ability in science teaching?
14. What would you do in class to stimulate creative activity?
15. If you were going to build a school with the idea of encouraging the maximum creative abilities of children, how would you plan the curriculum, organize the class, and design the facility?
16. Read: Calvin W. Taylor, "Creativity and Productive Thinking in Science Education," in *Learning and Creativity*, National Science Teachers Association, Washington, D.C., 1967. After reading this part of the pamphlet, write a paper describing how you would apply the information you read to your teaching.

Evaluation should be considered an integral part of the total teaching-learning process, and it should be continuous. The assessment of the effectiveness of teaching is a day-by-day, perhaps even an hour-by-hour, procedure. The results of evaluation supply the impetus for the redirection of the teaching-learning with all that this implies. The evaluation process will lead to the examination of previously accepted goals, and of the merits of the very evaluation procedures themselves.[1]

CHAPTER 13

EVALUATION: ANOTHER DISCOVERY TEACHING-LEARNING EXPERIENCE

The Roles of Evaluation

In teaching science, teachers first determine *what* they will teach—science content and processes. They are next concerned with *how* they will teach—teaching methods. Finally they need to know *how well* they taught and how well children learned—*evaluation*.

New roles and procedures for evaluation are evolving as emphases in science programs evolve. Teachers now look for newer techniques of assessing pupil progress in acquiring both science content and skills in scientific processes. Teachers also have become interested in self-evaluation for assessing the effectiveness of their role in the teaching-learning process.

Evaluation Is Continuous and Cumulative

Evaluation is not merely a device to be used at the *end* of a science lesson or unit of study; instead, evaluation goes on minute-by-minute throughout each lesson. This can be accomplished by careful teacher questioning. Evaluation helps teachers quickly spot which science areas his children have been exposed to previously. He can then determine what other diagnostic information is needed.

Evaluation Is Diagnostic

Evaluation procedures can supply the teacher with considerable diagnostic data about individual children in his class. Such procedures could help the teacher identify a child's science strengths, weaknesses, and interests. This information would indicate how well the child works alone or in groups. By pre-testing the child *before* instruction begins, the teacher can determine what experiences would be most effective in encouraging the child's science progress.

The Individually Prescribed Instruction in Science (IPIS) program at the University of Pittsburgh shows how diagnostic testing may be used. Following is an

---

[1] *Rethinking Science Education*, 59th Yearbook of the National Society for the Study of Education, Part I (Chicago: University of Chicago Press, 1960), p. 144.

excerpt from a description of the role of diagnostic testing and "prescription writing" in the IPIS program. Prescription writing as used in this study refers to the daily process of designating a task for the student to complete. The specific task prescribed for him depends heavily upon valid diagnostic information, which is secured by this process:

One of the most important elements of a program of individualized instruction is diagnosis. There must be a reliable system for continually assessing the competencies and instructional needs of each student. Effective diagnostic techniques are necessary for the initial placement of an individual in the instructional program and guiding his subsequent progress through the program.

In order to initiate the diagnosis, a PLACEMENT TEST is given to each student before he begins instruction in the science program. The placement test enables the teacher to identify the *general* areas of the curriculum in which the student lacks competency and those in which he exhibits mastery. The placement test is given to 15 to 20 children by the teacher. The teacher asks a series of oral questions that relate to a materials demonstration and/or to some drawings in the students booklet. The students respond to the oral questions by marking their answers in their booklet.

The placement test is scored in terms of individual "test units." Each "test unit" is a small cluster of related objectives which is a subset of all the objectives found within a unit of study. By examining the individual placement scores for each "test unit" the teacher can determine which "test units" the student has "placed out of" (demonstrated mastery and no need for instruction), and which "test units" require extensive diagnosis to determine his exact instructional needs. To pinpoint the child's *exact* needs, a PRE-TEST is given prior to any instruction.

Each pre-test is a short comprehensive examination concerning a specific sequence of behavioral objectives. Most pre-tests can be completed in one science period of 25 minutes. The pre-test consists of items related to *each* objective in the "test unit," and is scored with individual totals for each objective. The results of the pre-test will enable the teacher to diagnose precisely which objectives the student should receive instruction in.

The pre-tests are administered to the students individually. Presently (with the non-readers) this is accomplished by use of a tape cartridge which contains all the necessary instructions and the test questions. Each pre-test has a designated set of materials which the student may manipulate to his liking in order to arrive at his answers. Generally, the student records his answers by marking a booklet. At times oral responses are required. In these situations the pupil raises his hand as a signal for teacher aid. The teacher comes to the student and asks a specific pre-designated question and the notes the student's response in his answer booklet. No evaluation of the response is made at this time. It is important to mention that when a student is assigned a pre-test he works independently and takes as much time as he feels is necessary to complete the test to his satisfaction.

The last element of diagnosis is the POST-TEST. Each pre-test has a corresponding post-test. After the student completes the prescribed instructional sequence in a "test unit," he must take a post-test. The post-test is also comprehensive and consists of items related to each objective in the "test unit." The student is thus tested on both the objectives he has received instruction in and the objectives he has "placed out of."

The post-test and pre-test are identical in format. Both are administered to the students individually by means of a tape. A designated set of materials is available to the student, and he marks his answers in a booklet. The student works independently and at his own rate. The distinguishable features between the pre- and post-test are that the individual items on the tests vary and the materials are different.

If the student demonstrates mastery on the post-test, he then begins the next unit sequence as prescribed by his teacher. Failure to exhibit mastery of specific objectives or the unit as a whole indicates that the student needs further instruction. At the present time, he may be prescribed the same lesson(s) again and/or assigned whatever related worksheets and supplementary materials are available. In the future we plan to have alternate lessons which will be available for the student who does not acquire mastery after the first instructional sequence.

The information gained from the above-mentioned diagnostic techniques (placement test, pre-test, post-test) is used extensively in prescription writing. Prescription writing is the daily process of designating a task for the student to complete. The task prescribed for the student may be a test (pre or post) to continue the diagnostic aspect of the program, or it may be a prescribed lesson designed to fulfill the diagnosed learning needs of the student. The required process of prescription writing provides for a daily evaluation of each student's progress and his individual instructional needs.[2]

Evaluation Appraises Achievement and Provides Motivation

Evaluation gives the teacher insights into how well the children are learning science content and processes. By skillfully using this achievement data with children, interest and motivation can be provided by:

1. Setting realistic goals and providing data concerning progress toward them.
2. Making the child an *active* partner in the teaching-learning act, rather than a passive absorber of information.
3. Showing the child that progress has been made (no matter how small) can help him attain satisfaction and a desire to continue learning.
4. Guiding him to become increasingly self-directed as he puts into perspective where he was, is, and should be in the future.
5. Showing him that an adult really cares about his progress.

The ways teachers interpret evaluation results to children affect their future achievement. Joseph Gehrman found this to be true in his study showing that teacher interpretation definitely affected pupil self-ratings and estimates of self-perception.[3] The adage in this case is valid: success breeds success. Show a child he can do something, convince him he can, and he *will* do well on the next try.

[2] J. Cohen and W. Shepler, *Individually Prescribed Instruction in Science* (The Oakleaf Project)—*A Status Report*, Research Report of the Learning Research and Development Center, University of Pittsburgh (December, 1967), pp. 9-12.

[3] Joseph Leo Gehrman, "A Study of the Impact of Authoritative Communication of Expected Achievement upon Actual Achievement in Elementary School Science," *Doctor's Dissertation Abstracts*, 26 (November, 1965), pp. 2559-60.

What does this teacher do to encourage student participation in this demonstration?

Evaluation Affords Pupil Differentiation

Evaluation supplies sound evidence upon which differentiation among students can be made. This differentiation could be identifying similar needs, strengths, or weaknesses of children as the basis for skills, individualizing instruction, and enriching experiences. Although still controversial, evaluative devices could form the basis upon which classes are homogeneously arranged for instruction. Such tests can also identify gifted elementary school children with outstanding science talents. A test of this type has been developed and validated by Lesser, Davis, and Nakemow at Hunter College in New York City.[4]

Evaluation as Communication of Information

Evaluation can provide the raw data upon which reports to parents and the community are based. This directs home and school cooperation toward the best possible learning experiences for all children. By having good evaluative procedures and solid information upon which to make interpretations to the community, teachers are better able to handle questions and criticisms of their science programs intelligently. They will also be better equipped to communicate the objectives, achievements, and shortcomings of their science program with such information. Through adequate evaluation procedures in our science education programs, administrators also will be provided with valid information upon which to make their judgments and recommendations to superintendents of schools and boards of education. With the millions of dollars and countless hours of effort being spent on science programs, communities deserve to know the effectiveness of the programs they support. This communication of science program evaluation

---

[4] Gerald Lesser, Frederick B. Davis, and Lucille Nakemow, "The Identification of Gifted Elementary School Children with Exceptional Scientific Talent," *Educational and Psychological Measurements*, 22 (Summer, 1962), pp. 349-64.

Why is this a good way to teach science?

to the public must be in *specific*, concrete terms devoid of fuzziness and ambiguity. This requires specificity of objectives and evaluation.

Behavioral Science Objectives and Evaluation

It was pointed out in Chapter 3 that science objectives must be phrased in specific *behavioral terms* if they are to be of any practical help to teachers. That is, objectives must be stated in terms of some behavior a student will be able to perform after having completed a learning period. Earl Montague and David Butts state:

> Behavioral objectives offer a format for a statement of goals in terms of observable behavior. Such objectives provide direction to both the learning experience and the appraisal of the effectiveness of a specific experience—*the evaluation.*[5]

---

[5] Earl J. Montague and David P. Butts, "Behavioral Objectives," *The Science Teacher* (March, 1968), p. 33.

By stating science goals in terms that convey *observable behavior*, Martin Haberman says the teacher receives the following benefits:

1. Teacher and students get clear purposes.
2. Broad content is broken down into manageable, meaningful pieces.
3. Organizing content into sequences and hierarchies is facilitated.
4. Evaluation is simplified and becomes self-evident. (Could he do it, or couldn't he? Grades and global subjective judgments are replaced by checklists next to specific behaviors.)
5. Selecting of materials is clarified. (The result of knowing precisely what youngsters are to do leads to control in the selection of materials, equipment, and the management of resources generally.)[6]

On what criteria can children be grouped in school science programs?

Limitations of Behavioral Objectives

Although there are overwhelmingly useful purposes served by trying to identify educational goals in terms of observable behavior, J. Myron Atkin, speaking for many science educators, raises these reservations:

NOT ALL GOALS ARE EASILY IDENTIFIED

1. There is an assumption that we either know or can readily identify the educational objectives for which we strive and therefore the educational outcomes that result from our programs. One contention basic to my argument is that we presently are making progress towards thousands of goals in any existing

---

educational program, progress of which we are perhaps dimly aware, can articulate only with great difficulty, and that contribute toward goals which are incompletely stated (or unrecognized), but which are worthy.

BEHAVIORAL OBJECTIVES
MAY LIMIT THE RANGE
OF EXPLORATION

2. Certain types of innovation, highly desirable ones, are hampered and frustrated by early demands for behavioral statements of objectives. Early articulation of behavioral objectives by the curriculum developer inevitably tends to limit the range of his exploration.

INSTRUCTIONAL PRIORITIES
MUST BE FLEXIBLE

3. It is detrimental to learning not to capitalize on the opportune moments for effectively teaching one idea or another. Riveting the teacher's attention to a few behavioral goals provides him with blinders that may limit his range. Directing him to hundreds of goals leads to confusing, mechanical, pedagogic style and loss of spontaneity.

GOALS SHOULD COME FIRST
—THEY ARE NOT WAYS OF
MEASURING BEHAVIOR

4. It is difficult to resist the assumption that those attributes which we can measure are the elements which we consider most important. The behavioral analyst seems to assume that for an objective to be worthwhile, we must have methods of observing progress.[7]

Martin Haberman, in his previously mentioned article in which he gives the advantages of using behavioral objectives, cautions against these additional limitations:

1. The most powerful element in the process of schooling is *social* interaction, not content.
2. The interrelations of content are *internal* as well as external. Pupils organize content psychologically as well as logically.
3. Skills become overemphasized—generalizations are undervalued.
4. All content does not fit the behavioral approach.[8]

In spite of their limitations, behavioral objectives cannot be ignored and must be contended with, since they offer potentially valuable assistance to curriculum development. The behavioral objective approach promises to be one of the major vehicles for revising curriculum in the future. For these reasons, we will focus upon observable behavioral objectives and *evaluation*.

Taxonomy of Educational Objectives

There are many ways of classifying the educational objectives in science education. Benjamin Bloom has arranged all educational objectives into three large

---

[7] The ideas presented here appear in this outstanding brief article which explores the much-discussed topic of behavioral objectives in science education: J. Myron Atkin, "Behavioral Objectives in Curriculum Design: A Cautionary Note," *The Science Teacher*, 35 (May, 1968), pp. 27-30.

[8] Haberman, *op. cit.*, pp. 92-93.

categories: cognitive, affective, and psychomotor domains.[9] These domains are defined as:

> *Cognitive Domain*—remembering knowledge previously learned.
>
> *Affective Domain*—interests, appreciations, attitudes, values.
>
> *Psychomotor Domain*—motor and manipulative skills.

The rest of this chapter is devoted to looking at ways of implementing Bloom's three domains; the relationship between the three domains and the purposes and procedures of elementary school science is explored. Reference is made to pertinent science curriculum projects and their evaluation devices, as well as illustrations of other specific tests and measuring instruments.

Cognitive Domain

The cognitive domain contains the behaviors associated with scientific products and processes in the elementary school. This area receives major emphasis in science education. Emphasis today is on knowing and applying knowledge. This is not to say schools are disinterested in attitudes, values, and skills. Studies have shown, however, the bulk of tests given by teachers require only the lowest form of the cognitive domain—recall.[10] The area of cognitive learning has received much attention by educators while the affective and psychomotor have received little. This is probably due to the difficulty of writing objectives for these latter domains.

In Figure 28, the reader can visualize:

1. Bloom's cognitive domain arranged into six divisions.
2. The ascending order of complexity of the thinking processes involved in the six divisions of the cognitive domain.
3. The relationships between Bloom's cognitive domain divisions and science education objectives.

Each of the cognitive divisions in Figure 28 builds upon and is dependent upon each preceding division. This means the learner must have certain *knowledge* (1.00) and *comprehend* (2.00) the interrelationships of this knowledge before he can make any intelligent *application* (3.00) of it. You will also note that 1.00 *Knowledge* is primarily concerned with the building of scientific *products*—facts, concepts, principles, laws, etc. Although a lower or base thinking process, knowledge is nonetheless vital for performing the higher mental acts associated with the thinking process found in 2.00 *Comprehension*, 3.00 *Appreciation*, 4.00 *Analysis*,

---

[9] Benjamin S. Bloom and David R. Krathwohl, eds., *Taxonomy of Educational Objectives* (New York: David McKay Company, 1956).

[10] Edwin B. Kurtz, Jr. "Help Stamp out Non-Behavioral Objectives," *The Science Teacher* (January, 1965), pp. 31-32; David E. Newton, "The Problem Solving Approach—Fact or Fancy?" *School Science and Mathematics*, 61 (November, 1961), pp. 619-22; William B. Reiner, "Meeting the Challenge of Recent Developments in Science in Assessing the Objectives of Modern Instruction," *School Science and Mathematics*, 66 (April, 1966), pp. 335-41.

5.00 *Synthesis*, and 6.00 *Evaluation*. The latter processes are the ones associated with scientific *processes*.

The headings in Bloom's cognitive domains may be viewed as objectives; however, because they are so general they are not behavioral objectives. When illustrations of evaluative devices for Bloom's cognitive objectives are presented in this chapter, each one will be stated in specific *behavioral form*.

| | SCIENCE EDUCATION |
| BLOOM'S COGNITIVE DOMAIN[11] | OBJECTIVES |

1.00 *Knowledge*
    1.10 Knowledge of Specifics
        1.11 Knowledge of Terminology
        1.12 Knowledge of Specific Facts
    1.20 Knowledge of Ways and Means of Dealing with
        Specifics   *Scientific*
        1.21 Knowledge of Conventions   *Products*
        1.22 Knowledge of Trends and Sequences   (Facts, Concepts,
        1.23 Knowledge of Classifications and Categories   Principles, etc.)
        1.24 Knowledge of Criteria
        1.25 Knowledge of Methodology
    1.30 Knowledge of the Universals and Abstractions
        1.31 Knowledge of Principles and Generalizations
        1.32 Knowledge of Theories and Structures

2.00 *Comprehension*
    2.10 Translation
    2.20 Interpretation
    2.30 Extrapolation

3.00 *Application*

4.00 *Analysis*
    4.10 Analysis of Elements   *Scientific*
    4.20 Analysis of Relationships   *Processes*
    4.30 Analysis of Organizational Principles   (Problem-solving

5.00 *Synthesis*   and Critical
    5.10 Production of a Unique Communication   Thinking Skills)
    5.20 Production of a Plan, or Proposed Set of Operations
    5.30 Derivation of a Set of Abstract Relations

6.00 *Evaluation*
    6.10 Judgments in Terms of Internal Evidence
    6.20 Judgments in Terms of External Criteria

FIGURE 28. Relationships between Bloom's Cognitive Domain and Science Education Objectives

Testing Scientific Knowledge—Products

It is not unexpected that the area of knowledge is the one most stressed by teachers in their evaluation of teaching-learning. Historically the schools have emphasized

---

[11] Bloom and Krathwohl, *op. cit.*, pp. 186-93.

the elements of knowledge that Bloom calls 1.10 Knowledge of Specifics, 1.20 Knowledge of Ways and Means of Dealing with Specifics, and 1.30 Knowledge of the Universals and Abstractions of a field. Because of this emphasis upon the teaching of knowledge, many techniques for evaluation of knowledge have been tried. The following techniques have been used and found to be very valuable and potentially rich in information:

1. Tape recordings of discussions and questions and answer sessions
2. Teacher observation
3. Anecdotal record keeping
4. Teacher-pupil interviews

Unfortunately these techniques are laborious and time-consuming to use. Elementary school teachers are busy, overworked professionals. Most teachers, although highly motivated, have difficulty fitting such techniques into an already overcrowded day. Most elementary teachers find themselves relying to a greater extent on written tests. For that reason, we will concentrate primarily upon techniques for improving written tests. However, for those teachers who would like to improve their uses of tape recordings, teacher observation, anecdotal record keeping, etc., the following references are recommended:

Fleming, Robert S., ed., *Curriculum for Today's Boys and Girls* (Columbus, Ohio: Charles E. Merrill Publishing Company, 1963), Chapter 15.

Hill, Katherine E., "How Well Have We Taught," *Science for the Eight-to-Twelves* (Washington, D.C.: Association for Childhood Educational International, 1964).

Landsdown, Brenda, "How Good Was My Science Lesson?" *The Packet*, 16, No. 1 (Boston, D.C. Heath, Spring 1961), pp. 18-29.

Tape Recorded Evaluation Device.   An excellent, easy use of the tape recorder is the simplest test devised to assess children's accuracy of observation of objects and events. This device can even be used by nursery, preschool, and kindergarten children by themselves. Situations and questions are tape recorded, children listen to the tape, and they perform with materials whatever operations are required. The teacher can learn much about the child's ability to identify objects and events as well as many other behavioral traits of the child.

The following is an excerpt from a typical science script from an audio tape lesson of the previously mentioned Individually Prescribed Instruction in Science Project.[12] The bells are cues to the student to stop the tape recorder and carry out some operation with the materials provided.

Behavioral Objective: Identify by testing with a magnet objects that a magnet picks up and objects that a magnet does not pick up.

1. Hi! Today we are going to do some things with a magnet. A magnet can pick up some things but there are some things a magnet won't pick up. (*Slight pause*) Find the red magnet. (**BELL**)

2. Touch the bottle caps with the magnet. (**BELL**)

---

[12] Cohen and Shepler, *op. cit.*, pp. 14-15.

3. Does the magnet pick up the bottle caps? (*Long pause*) Yes, the bottle caps stuck to the magnet. (*Pause*) Take the bottle caps off the magnet and put all of them back into their part of the plastic box. (**BELL**)

4. Now let's see what else the magnet can pick up. Touch the pennies with the magnet. (**BELL**)

5. Does the magnet pick up the pennies? (*Pause*) The magnet did not pick up the pennies. (*Pause*) Touch the magnet to the paper clips. (**BELL**)

6. Did the paper clips stick to the magnet? (*Pause*) Yes, the paper clips stuck to the magnet. Take all the paper clips off the magnet and put them in their part of the box. (**BELL**)

7. Touch the magnet to the nails. (**BELL**) . . .

Another simple way of informally assessing children's accuracy of objects and events is the use of record keeping. Records are notations about events or observations which children put into some form for future use in their science studies. By referring to the record made by the child, the teacher is able to check the accuracy of the child's observations. For instance, the simple drawing of a sun by the kindergartener on a calendar indicates his observation of the weather for the day.

Figure 29 presents a list compiled by Mary Clare Petty showing types of records children can make for the purpose of checking their observational accuracy.[13]

The simplest type of tests can be devised to find out children's knowledge of terminology and specific facts. The teacher determines the specific observable behavioral objective and then prepares a test. Two examples are:

Behavioral Objective: To observe whether student can define technical terms by giving their properties, relations, or attributes.

Circle the letter that best describes the scientific term: A volt is a unit of:
A. Weight
B. Force
C. Distance
D. Work
E. Volume

Behavioral Objective: To observe whether student can recall terms, events, discoveries, reactions:

Which of the following types of waves can travel through a vacuum?
A. Sound
B. Light
C. Electromagnetic
D. A. and B.
E. B. and C.
F. All of the above

These devices are termed *recall tests.* As the term implies, recall questions ask the student to bring back to consciousness, information he explored in the past. Psychologists have found people associate items with other items and rarely, if

---

[13] Mary Clare Petty, *How To Record and Use Data in Elementary School Science* (Washington, D.C.: National Science Teachers Association, 1965), p. 4.

Labels and Lists	of collections, specimens, parts of plants, parts of diagrams . . . of birds, plants, shrubs in community or on school grounds, materials needed for experiment, characteristics of insects, objectives, or purposes . . . . Lists may be very simple or relatively highly organized, showing classifications and/or relationships . . . .
Pictures and Symbols	of smiling suns, rotund snowmen on weather records, pictures of parts of plants we eat, drawing of "signs" of winter or spring . . . .
Diagrams	of parts of a simple machine, location of trees in park, plans for a spring garden, relative size of planets, set-up of apparatus for an experiment . . . . Diagrams may be copies or original drawings.
Graphs	of numerically expressed data: rainfall, temperature, relationship of height and weight, proportion of different gases in air, a balanced diet . . . . Use of line graphs, bar graphs, circle graphs, and pictographs should be developed.
Tables and Charts	of information about geologic eras, or the force needed to lift a weight with three different arrangements of pulleys, or the description of temperature zones.
Records of Sequence	of care and development of small animals, or development of eggs in incubator, growth of plants used in experiment, observations of changes in moon over period of weeks, water level in dishes during evaporation studies . . . .
Simple Memoranda	of details about care of pets or plants in the classroom, plans about future activities, responsibilities accepted, ideas and theories to be checked later. The memoranda may be incorporated later into more complex forms of records; they insure accuracy of recall and minimize oversight of significant information at a later date.

FIGURE 29. Types of Science Records

ever, completely isolate them. The ways in which individuals associate isolated items is still a mystery. Even tests of isolation, such as the inkblot designs used in the Rorschach tests, evoke widely divergent responses. This is due to the unique backgrounds, perceptions, and formed associations of individuals. The testing of recall with children thus becomes a problem of framing questions in such ways as to stimulate the remembrance of the situations in which the intended information occurred. One of the best ways is the use of pictures, especially for younger children.

Picture Tests for Knowledge of Classification. Picture tests can be used for the more complex aspects of knowledge such as classification, methodology, principles, abstractions, generalizations, and theories. An example of *Knowledge of Classification* (1.23) follows on page 293.

Records of Raw Data of Observations	of elements of time, selection of appropriate units of measure, approximate nature of all measurements, weights pulled by pulleys, length of time candles burn in containers of different sizes, measurements of the same surface obtained by different children, temperature at which they find water boils . . . . *Children must be encouraged to record raw data they obtain and not what they believe these data should be.*
Narrative and Descriptive Records	of accounts by the class, with teacher serving as "secretary," following a trip to a zoo, visit to a resource person, a discussion stimulated by an article in the newspaper . . . . These reports are not "unscientific" and can stimulate interest, raise questions, and help in identification of valuable scientific problems for study.
Tape Recordings	of use for narrative and descriptive records. Tape recordings allow more freedom to the children, who can concentrate better on *what* they have to say. Playback may be followed by discussions and lead to questions such as: "Why did we say that?" "What is wrong with this conclusion?" "Is this a reasonable statement?" Recordings may be used to explain diagrams or models, supplement pictures and drawings . . . .
Reports in Three Dimensions	of models of cross section of earth's crust, of an oil well, the solar system, collections of leaves and bark, displays of seeds in different stages of germination . . . . These are best used when children have a major interest in sharing information with others. Three-dimensional reports make concepts more vivid, accurate, and meaningful.
Formal Reports of Experiments	of actual results obtained by the children in their experiments. Experience with formal reporting makes for "scientific literacy" and prepares the students for the type of records expected of high school students.

Behavioral Objective: To observe whether student can classify things on the basis of whether they are alive, are animals, and are mammals.[14]

Children: 1) Put an X on the card for the pictures of things that are *alive.*

2) Put an X on the card for the pictures of each thing that is an *animal.*

3) Put an X on the picture of each thing that is a *mammal.*

[14] Modified from Clarence H. Nelson, *Improving Objective Tests in Science* (Washington, D.C.: National Science Teachers Association, 1967), p. 18.

Matching Test—Principles. Another way of testing for children's knowledge is the matching test. By giving the student two columns of items and asking him to watch the related items, the teacher can quickly and easily see if the student perceives relationships existing between the columns of items. There is less stress on sheer memory or recall of fragmentary information because the necessary information is supplied to him; he must put the items together so that they form their relationships.

Examples of *Knowledge of Principles, Generalizations, Theories* (1.30) follow:

Behavioral Objective: To observe whether the student is familiar with the principles of gas laws of Boyle, Charles, and Avogadro.

Below are two columns of words that apply to our science study of gases. Draw a line from the gas law to the man who advanced it. Some laws are purposefully inaccurate, so please omit them.

Gas Law	*Scientist*
When a gas is compressed into a smaller space, internal pressure increases.	Boyle
When a gas is heated, molecules move more rapidly.	
Pressure is in direct proportion to the density of the gas.	
Gas expands when cooled and contracts when heated.	Avogadro
Equal volumes of different gases at same temperature and pressure have an equal number of molecules.	
The smaller the space confining a gas, the greater the pressure exerted on the gas.	Charles

Because matching tests focus primarily upon putting items into pigeonholes, they are not always indicative of the students' ability to perceive deeper meanings or relationships. The following multiple choice test probably involves evaluating a child's understanding of a principle in a better way than the matching one.

Behavioral Objective: To determine whether the student understands the principle of why sap goes up the trunk of a tree.

Which one of these theories explains why sap rises up the trunk of a tree?
  A. Heat
  B. Atmospheric Pressure
  C. Root Pressure
  D. Capillary Action
  E. Cohesion of Water Molecules

Crossword Puzzles. Another technique for evaluating children's knowledge of specifics and terminology is the crossword puzzle. Generally children in the primary grades are limited in the range of words in their reading vocabularies, and primary grade teachers have made simple crossword puzzles using words from primary reading lists. Intermediate and upper grade teachers find children respond favorably to science crossword puzzles. In fact, children like to create their own puzzles at the conclusion of a science study. A student teacher wrote this puzzle for her fourth grade:

		^{3}E					
			^{1}E			D^2	
			A		S T A R		
^{5}P	L	A	N E T	S	U	Y	
		S		H	M		
		T			^{6}M O O ^{7}N		
		W I	N T E R			I	
		O		R		G	
		O				H	
	S U N		W E S T				

DOWN	ACROSS
1. The planet on which we live.	4. Twinkle, twinkle little _____.
2. When the sun shines.	5. The earth is a _____.
3. The sun rises in the _____.	6. The man in the _____.
4. The hot time of the year.	8. The time of the year when it snows.
7. When we see the stars.	10. The yellow ball that shines in the daytime
9. When the sun is straight over your head.	11. The sun sets in the _____.

All of these illustrations of testing devices are limited to Bloom's simplest level of thinking—knowledge. This level is equated with scientific *products*. Let us examine now the higher levels of thinking.

Testing Scientific Understandings—Processes

Bloom's next five levels of thinking enter the realm of testing children's understanding of thinking processes—*Comprehension, Application, Analysis, Synthesis,* and *Evaluation.* The scientific processes we are really trying to evaluate are the child's abilities to:

1. *Translate* major ideas into his own words.
2. *Interpret* the relationships between major ideas.
3. *Extrapolate* or go beyond data to implications of major ideas.
4. *Apply* his knowledge and understanding to the solution of new problems in new situations.
5. *Analyze* or break an idea into its parts and show that he understands their relationships.
6. *Synthesize* or put elements together to form a new pattern and produce a unique communication, plan, or set of abstract relations.
7. *Evaluate* or make judgments based upon evidence.

Many possible testing devices are available to assess children's levels of process thinking.

Essay Tests—Translation.   The use of essays in science is a two-headed proposition. Like all testing devices, the essay presents many serious disadvantages along with many positive evaluative advantages. This brief summary gives some of the more obvious advantages and disadvantages of the essay test:

1. Shows how well the student is able to organize and present ideas, *but* scoring is very subjective due to a lack of set answers.
2. Varying degrees of correctness since there is not just a right or wrong answer, *but* scoring requires excessive time.
3. Tests ability to analyze problems using pertinent information and to arrive at generalizations or conclusions, *but* scoring is influenced by spelling, handwriting, sentence structure, and other extraneous items.
4. Gets to deeper meanings and interrelationships rather than isolated bits of factual materials, *but* questions usually are either ambiguous or too obvious.

In an effort to offset the disadvantages, the teacher must carefully consider the construction of each essay question. The teacher should word the question in such a way that the pupil will be limited to a certain degree to the concepts being tested. For instance, it is better to use:

> If you moved to Greenland, how would the days and nights differ from where you live now? How would the seasons differ?
>
> *than*
>
> Discuss the differences between the places in the world in relation to their days and nights throughout the seasons.

The second question is much too broad and does not give the pupil direction to know what is expected.

The teacher will be able to successfully overcome or minimize the shortcomings of excessive subjectivity in scoring essay-type questions by preparing a scoring guide beforehand and by scoring each question separately. If a list of the important ideas that are expected is made before scoring, there is less chance for indecision while scoring.

Teachers should be flexible and open-minded in setting up the important ideas they will accept as answers for essays. There may be valid student ideas that the teacher has not considered. The teacher should also give the student an explanation of his scoring so he can benefit from the test and use it for a further learning experience.

An example of an essay to test the student's ability to translate scientific concepts into his own words might be:

> *Behavioral Objective: To determine whether the student is able to state a scientific principle in his own words.*
>
> In one or two paragraphs in your own words, explain the role of chloroplast in photosynthesis.

Testing Interpretation.   Cause and effect interpretations are difficult for students to grasp. Interpretation of this kind requires understanding of the ideas presented and the relationship that exists between them. The following test from the *Forty-fifth Yearbook of the National Society for the Study of Education* was designed to evaluate the students' understanding of cause-effect relationship.[15]

Tell whether each of the statements following the fact is:
  A. A cause of the fact
  B. A result of the fact
  C. Not related to the fact

Fact: A flash of lightning occurs.

   Statements

   3. A roar of thunder can be heard.   3. _____
   4. Electricity passed between clouds and the earth.   4. _____
   5. It is dangerous to stand under a tree
      during a rainstorm.   5. _____

Fact: Metals expand when heated.

   Statements

   12. The molecules of metal become
       farther apart when heated.   12. _____
   13. When the temperature increases, the mercury
       in the thermometer rises.   13. _____
   14. Telephone wires are slack in summer
       and tighter in winter.   14. _____

Testing Analysis Skills.   The Nelson-Mason Test of Comprehension can be used to test children's abilities to analyze science situations and identify their elements and their relationships.[16] This test presents eight situations in brief story form—

---

[15] Nelson B. Henry, ed., "The Measurement of Understanding," *The Forty-fifth Yearbook of the National Society for the Study of Education*, Part I (Chicago: University of Chicago Press, 1946), p. 135.

[16] Clarence Nelson and John Mason, "A Test of Science Comprehension for Upper Elementary Grades," *Science Education*, 47 (October, 1963), pp. 319-322.

three from biology, three from physical science, and two from the earth sciences. Each situation is followed by questions designed to test the students' abilities to make distinctions between:

1. What is given and what is to be learned by further observations
2. Problems and hypotheses
3. Facts and assumptions
4. Inductive and deductive generalizations

The questions in the selected story situation are designed to probe the students' abilities to identify observations, assumptions, and deductions stemming from the science principle in the story.[17]

> Numbers 36 through 45 refer to the following situation:
>
> > One hot July morning the center span of a low steel bridge across a river was swung open to allow a long string of barges to pass through. While the bridge was open the temperature rose many degrees. When the bridge tender tried to close the bridge again, the center span would not fit. It was too long!
>
> > *Problems:*
> > 1. What had happened to the bridge to prevent it from closing?
> > 2. What could be done to get the bridge closed?
>
> Numbers 36 through 45 are statements that have some bearing on the solution of these two problems. Classify each one into one of these three groups:
>
> > 1. Something that could be seen (observation)
> > 2. Something taken for granted that has to do with scientific theory (assumption)
> > 3. Something that can be figured out from scientific theory (deduction)
>
> 36. The center span of the bridge had increased in length. (1)
> 37. The center span was composed of rapidly moving molecules. (2)
> 38. An increase in temperature causes an increase in speed of movement of molecules. (2)
> 39. When the molecules of which a steel structure is composed move faster, the steel structure becomes slightly larger. (2)
> 40. If the steel bridge span was made of moving molecules, then increased speed of movement due to increased temperature caused the bridge span to become longer. (3)
> 41. Molecules move faster when the temperature goes up; molecules will slow down when the temperature goes down. (2)
> 42. If a hot piece of steel is cooled, its molecules should slow down, and the piece of steel should shrink in size. (3)
> 43. After the fire department had squirted cold water on the bridge span for about 15 minutes, the bridge swung shut without any difficulty. (1)
> 44. Cooling the bridge span caused it to become shorter. (1)
> 45. Cooling the bridge span caused the molecules in it to move more slowly. (2)

Testing Application of Knowledge.   The Sequential Tests of Educational Progress (STEP) focus upon children's abilities to apply previously learned knowledge to solving new problems. The science STEP tests measure the students abilities to:

---

[17] *Ibid.*, p. 329.

1. Identify and define scientific problems
2. Suggest or illuminate hypotheses
3. Interpret data and draw conclusions
4. Select procedures for testing their hypotheses
5. Critically evaluate other people's statements
6. Reason symbolically and quantitatively [18]

Each science test presents sets of problem situations followed by multi-choice objective questions. The tests range from fourth, fifth, and sixth grade level to freshmen college level. The situations are of everyday life familiar to most children.

The selected sample of the STEP science test given here shows how it attempts to discover children's abilities to select procedures, experiments, and data to solve the problem presented.[19]

The Jackson Garden

Tom and Alice Jackson help to plant a garden every spring.

18. They have many kinds of garden tools. What is the main job of the tools which are wedge-shaped like the drawing?

E. Breaking up soil
F. Flattening soil
G. Moving soil
H. Packing down soil

19. After they bought seeds and prepared the soil, they got some string and stakes to mark out the rows. How should they decide the distance to leave between the rows of seeds?
A. Leave room to walk between the rows
B. Follow the instructions on the seed package
C. Leave 12 inches between the rows of plants
D. Find out how tall a plant grows.

20. Tom and Alice decided to plant carrots in their garden. Tom read from the back of the package of carrot seeds these planting instructions: "Make sowings every two weeks up to early July; the last sowing will make full-sized roots for winter storing." Why do you think the package said to plant several times instead of only once?
E. Because the temperature changes throughout the summer
F. Because the amount of rainfall changes from week to week
G. So that all the carrots would be full grown at one time
H. So that the gardener could have fresh carrots all summer long

21. Then Tom read, "When the plants come up, thin them so that they are 2 to 3 inches apart in the row." Tom asked his father, "Why must I pull out

---

[18] *Manual for Interpreting Scores, Cooperative Sequential Tests of Educational Progress* (Princeton, N.J.: Cooperative Test Division, Educational Testing Service, 1957), p. 5.

[19] *Sequential Tests of Educational Progress, Science,* Form 4A (Princeton, N.J.: Cooperative Test Division, Educational Testing Service, 1957), pp. 4-5.

some of my good carrot plants?" Which of these answers do you think his father gave?

A. The soil has too little plant food in it
B. Many carrots grow in different shapes
C. Carrots need the additional room underground to grow and store food
D. Some carrots are dwarf and some are giant carrots

22. Which method would be best for Mother to use to keep several carrots when she brings them in from the garden?

E. Wrap them tightly in a plastic bag
F. Place them in the home freezer
G. Store them in a dry part of the kitchen
H. Put them in a plastic bag in the refrigerator

23. Tom wanted to learn which of three types of soil—clay, sand, or loam—would be best for growing lima beans. He found three flowerpots, put a different type of soil in each pot, and planted the same number of lima beans in each. He placed them side by side on the window sill and gave each pot the same amount of water.

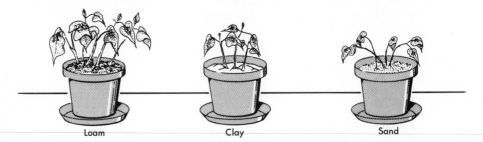

Loam   Clay   Sand

The lima beans grew best in the loam. Why did Mr. Jackson say Tom's experiment was *not* a good experiment and did *not* prove that loam was the best soil for plant growth?

A. The plants in one pot got more sunlight than the plants in the other pots
B. The amount of soil in each pot was not the same
C. One pot should have been placed in the dark
D. Tom should have used three kinds of seeds

24. Tom saw that moist clay stuck together tightly and dry clay was almost as hard as rock. The clay held the water so that the water did not run through. Why didn't the plants in the clay soil grow as well as the plants in the loam?

E. The roots lacked air and rotted
F. The clay was dark in color
G. The clay dried and cracks were formed
H. There were no earthworms in the clay

25. Tom and Alice watched the birds in their garden. Some of the birds they saw in the summertime were not in the garden in winter. They wondered what happened to them. Which of their friends gave the best answer?

A. Jack said, "The birds die because in winter there are no insects to eat."
B. Bill said, "Birds only live one summer."
C. Jane said, "The birds sleep all winter in a winter nest."
D. Ruth said, "The birds fly to a winter home in the warmer South."

Testing Evaluation of Evidence. In Chapter 4—"Innovation, Experimentation, and Reform"—is a description of Science—A Process Approach. This science project of the commission on Science Education of the American Association for the Advancement of Science (AAAS) is built upon observable behavioral objectives. To assess the students' mastery of these behaviors, AAAS developed competency measures to accompany each of their science units. The stress in each of these Competency measures is upon finding out if the *specific* desired behavior of the student has been altered as a result of the completion of the exercises in each science unit. The competency measure for each exercise is intended to see if children can demonstrate what they have learned in new situations.

Competency measures may be administered to individuals or groups of children. Each child has a book with competency exercises as well as any needed material, such as pencils, rules, protractors, or graph paper.

Each task described in the competency measure is related to a behavioral objective for that exercise. The competency measures use situations and materials different from those used in guided science lesson exercises. The purpose is to see if the desired behavior can be applied to the new situation and not just to test recall.

All of the observable behavioral objectives are tested in the competency measures. Each competency task on every competency measure is a direct assessment of one of the objectives of an exercise. Examples of these tests can be secured by contacting the American Association for the Advancement of Science, Washington, D.C.

The types of evaluation mentioned, especially science competency measures, can be of great value to teachers, even though they do not follow any or all of the AAAS Science—A Process Approach. Competency Measures are not standardized with norms, reliabilities, and established validities. Therefore, these competency measures allow a teacher to view his children's responses as individuals, rather than comparing them with other classes. The teacher does have, however, excellent tests of scientific accuracy to determine how well his students master the cognitive skills described by Benjamin Bloom.

Standardized Tests

There are several commercially-available tests in science that have been standardized for elementary school children. If judiciously used, standardized tests of these kinds can be valuable to the teacher. Standardized tests are carefully constructed and refined as a result of having been given to thousands of children on several grade levels. This refining process eliminates items that have little value, as well as picking up inaccuracies in science concepts, grammatical structure, and wording. The results of the standardized tests can be used for diagnostically for a general view of a teacher's purposes and for a general view of a given class to other groups.

The major disadvantages or shortcomings of standardized tests are:

1. Low scores on tests do not necessarily show little learning. The test may not be measuring the science ideas to which the child was exposed.

2. Many of the tests measure recall with only little if any emphasis upon scientific methodology or the higher cognitive skills of analysis or interpretation.

Some of the newer science projects are beginning to develop semi-standardized testing materials. The three most active projects in this area are: Elementary Science Study, Science Curriculum Improvement Study, and the American Association for the Advancement of Science. Information about the projects can be secured from their headquarters listed in the Appendix.

Following is a list of standardized science tests for elementary schools with the publisher and address. Buro's *Mental Measurement Yearbooks* should be consulted for critiques of these and other standardized science tests.

Standardized Science Tests for Elementary Schools

Coordinated Scales of Attainment: Science—Grades 4-8
Victor C. Smith. Educational Test Bureau, 1946-1954
720 Washington Avenue, S.E., Minneapolis, Minnesota

Elementary Science and Health: Every Pupil Test
First and second semesters in grades 4-6
Ohio Scholarship Tests, 1935-1961
State of Ohio, 751 Northwest Boulevard, Columbus, Ohio 43215

Elementary Science: Every Pupil Scholarship Test—Grades 5-8
Bureau of Educational Measurements, 1926-1961
Kansas State Teachers College, Emporia, Kansas

Elementary Science Test: National Achievement Tests—Grades 4-6
Lester D. Crow and W. L. Shuman. Acorn Publishing Co. 1948-1958
Rockville Centre, Long Island, New York

Metropolitan Achievement Tests: (Science, 1960 Edition)—Grades 5-6, 7-9
Walter N. Durost, Harold H. Bixler, Gertrude H. Hildreth, Kenneth W. Lund, and
J. Wayne Wrightstone, Harcourt, Brace and World, 1932-1960
757 Third Avenue, New York, New York 10017

New Cooperative Science Tests: General Science—Grades 7-9
Educational Testing Service, Cooperative Test Division, 1963
Princeton, New Jersey

Testing Affective Domain

Bloom's taxonomy of behavioral objectives lists affective objectives as those which emphasize a sense of feeling, an emotion, or a degree of acceptance or rejection of ideas. They include interests, attitudes, appreciations, values, and emotional sets or biases. Historically, science education has done relatively little to include these objectives in its instruction and evaluation. Indeed many science educators either feel the affective domain does not belong in science education or that it is too hard to define and evaluate to be useful. Others have argued, however, that it is just as important for children to build positive social value systems with their acquired science knowledge.

Scientists[20]

1. Good	: ____ : ____ : ____ : ____ : ____ : ____ : ____ :	Bad
2. Small	: ____ : ____ : ____ : ____ : ____ : ____ : ____ :	Large
3. Fast	: ____ : ____ : ____ : ____ : ____ : ____ : ____ :	Slow
4. Unpleasant	: ____ : ____ : ____ : ____ : ____ : ____ : ____ :	Pleasant
5. Strong	: ____ : ____ : ____ : ____ : ____ : ____ : ____ :	Weak
6. Quiet	: ____ : ____ : ____ : ____ : ____ : ____ : ____ :	Active
7. Clean	: ____ : ____ : ____ : ____ : ____ : ____ : ____ :	Dirty
8. Light	: ____ : ____ : ____ : ____ : ____ : ____ : ____ :	Heavy
9. Hot	: ____ : ____ : ____ : ____ : ____ : ____ : ____ :	Cold
10. Worthless	: ____ : ____ : ____ : ____ : ____ : ____ : ____ :	Valuable
11. Soft	: ____ : ____ : ____ : ____ : ____ : ____ : ____ :	Hard
12. Dull	: ____ : ____ : ____ : ____ : ____ : ____ : ____ :	Sharp

Checklist for Scientific Attitudes. The following checklist and description by Paul Blackwood and T. R. Porter are valuable for use in the affective domain:[21]

	Names of Children					
A child						
Shows willingness to have his ideas questioned.						
Modifies his views in the face of new evidence.						
Shows a disposition not to jump to conclusions.						
Looks upon guesses and hypotheses as ideas to be tested.						

---

[20] Semantic Differential Scale adapted by The American Association for the Advancement of Science from Charles E. Osgood, George J. Suci, and Percy H. Tannenbaum, *The Measurement of Meaning* (Urbana, Ill.: University of Illinois Press, 1957).

[21] Paul E. Blackwood and T. R. Porter, *Evaluating Science Learning in the Elementary School* (Washington, D.C.: National Science Teachers Association, 1968), p. 7.

	Names of Children							
A child								
Shows respect for ideas of others.								
Seeks data and information to validate observations or explanations.								
Exhibits a healthy skepticism for generalizations not based on verifiable (repeatable) observations.								
Questions conclusions based on incomplete data.								

Evaluating Development of Scientific Attitudes

The evaluation of attitudes can best be made by observing children directly as they work and play with other children, not only during the time science is being studied but at other times as well. As suggested earlier, defining attitudes as behavioral objectives is not easy. Attitudes generally predispose children to behave in certain ways. These ways can be observed in the children's conversations, their approach to the solution of problems, how they react to opinions of others. The items on this check list . . . provide a beginning for evaluating each child in selected behaviors related to scientific attitudes.

Much remains to be done in evaluation of the affective domain. Teachers find they they learn much about their children's attitudes and interests by structuring their own tests like the checklist here.

Psychomotor Domain

Behavioral objectives which emphasize muscular or motor skills or manipulation of materials are being used increasingly in science education. Until very recently, these skills were limited to writing, drawing, or other paper and pencil activities. With the advent of science activity programs, interest has grown in assessing children's abilities to use materials and equipment. In an effort to make this assessment more objective and specific in terms of behavioral goals, teachers are turning more to observation checklists and rating scales of performance.

Following is a sample of a structured teacher observation checklist for assessing the student's ability to use a microscope properly.[22] Notice the specific behavioral objectives listed in place of broad, nebulous goals as "can use microscope."

Teacher Observational Checklist

Behavioral Objectives:

1. Handle the instrument with great care. Clean the lenses only with "lens tissue" or with a soft, clean cloth.
2. Never focus the microscope downward toward the slide. Always move the objective downward while the eye is away from the eyepiece and then focus the microscope upward with the eye looking through the microscope.

What are these children learning about the variation in samples and methods of testing?

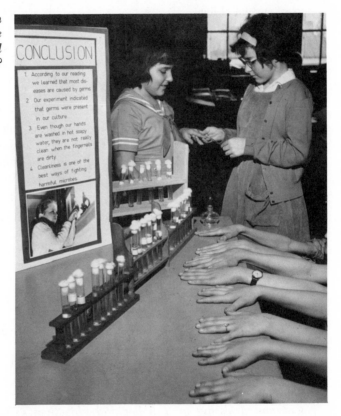

3. Arrange the mirror for optimum amount of light. Too much light is quite as unsatisfactory as too little light.
4. Prepare materials for observation using the techniques most appropriate to the things being examined; comparatively large materials (minute crustacia, for example) require either depression slides or bridge arrangements so that they are not crushed; smaller items can simply be covered with a cover slip.

---

22 Harold E. Tannenbaum, Nathan Stillman, and Albert Piltz, *Science Education for Elementary School Teachers,* 2nd ed., p. 270. Copyright © 1965, by Allyn and Bacon, Inc., Boston. Reprinted by permission of the publisher.

Checklist or Rating Scale—Use of Microscope

Behavioral Objectives	Always	Sometimes	Never
Is careful in handling microscope.			
Cleans lenses properly.			
Focuses instrument properly.			
Prepares slides correctly.			
Arranges mirror for correct amount of light.			

Evaluation Tips for Teachers

1. *Identify your objectives clearly.* Avoid vague, nebulous, or global objectives.
2. *Whenever possible, write objectives in specific, observable terms.* Emphasize objectives that are phrased in observable human behavior. The following objectives are:

   1. Specific
   2. Capable of being observed and therefore evaluated
   3. Varied
      a) First one tests a skill
      b) Second one tests recall
      c) Third one tests reasoning

   Behavioral Objective: To determine if student can read an alcohol thermometer.

   Behavioral Objective: To determine if student can identify the parts of a flower.

   Behavioral Objective: To determine if student can analyze experiment and suggest alternate plans for solution of problem.

3. *Determine content, methods and materials, and type of evaluation for achievement and assessing your behavioral objectives.* The following is a format teachers have found useful in organizing their planning for teaching and evaluating science:[23]

Objective	Methods and Materials	Type of Evaluation
The ability to record and interpret temperature data from information gathered using outdoor thermometers.	Make simple bar graphs of the daily temperature as found at noon in the shade next to the building.	Examine the charts prepared by each child. Does the chart show that the child can make an accurate and under-

---

[23] *Ibid.*

Objective	*Methods and Materials*	*Type of Evaluation*
	Use the graphs to find significant temperature information; make comparisons among the days studied and also among reading made by different children.	standable table of data? Written questions to be answered by individual children, each using his own chart: Which day was hottest? Which day was coldest? On which two days was the temperature about the same at noon?
	Have sufficient supply of outdoor thermometers so that variations in readings can be observed.	
	Have necessary graph grids prepared so that each child has appropriate equipment.	

4. *Select a variety of evaluation devices.* Avoid overdependence upon one type of testing device. Include a wide range of tests such as:

a. Essay   e. Multiple-choice   i. Situational
b. Short Answer   f. Matching   j. Performance or Motor
c. Fill In   g. Crossword Puzzles   k. Others
d. True-False   h. Picture Tests

5. *Make your test sample what was taught.* Test only for those things to which your children were exposed or can reasonably be expected to project into relatively similar situations.
6. *Test often and have children participate in the results.* Children should be exposed to frequent testing. This can assist them in lessening their anxiety and fears of tests, especially if the results of the tests are used for instrumentation instead of punishment. Stress testing as one step along the path to learning and not the end of the journey.
7. *Your tests should show what you value in teaching-learning.* Students will follow your lead. If you stress memorization or recall in your selection of tests, they will memorize. If process and higher cognitive levels of thinking are important to you, make certain that your tests reflect these criteria.
8. *Continually evaluate your evaluation.* Scrutinize your testing and revise tests as a result of children's responses to them. Invite children's comments on tests and have them try writing tests.
9. *Continue teacher self-evaluation.* Teachers today are professionally committed to improving the learning of *all* children. Individually and collectively, teachers subscribe to the belief that: "Children do not fail to learn—schools fail to teach them." Teachers are looking more introspectively at their own teaching to examine the impact of their goals, methods, and techniques. This self-evaluation will not permit the luxury of excusing children's lack of learning because of "culturally deprived home environments" or shortage of science facilities and equipment. Teachers and student teachers along with their science supervisors and principals are looking at the evidence of strengths and weaknesses in their science teaching for improving children's learning.

Microteaching Evaluation.   One technique used for teacher evaluation is micro-teaching evaluation. A microteaching evaluation session is a short, observed teaching lesson or part of a lesson, usually lasting no more than 5 to 15 minutes. It is the same as regular, observed teaching sessions only shorter and more structured. A checklist or other form presents items to be observed during the microteaching session. For instance, the *Cognitive Microteaching Evaluation Form* here focuses the observer upon the kinds of cognitive skills (knowledge, intellectual abilities, and application of knowledge) the *teacher* uses. This form may be used by teacher, science consultant or supervisor, principal, or student teacher to evaluate a lab, science discussion or lesson, test, or other teaching technique. By checking the appropriate items during the microteaching session, the observer can provide the teacher with feedback concerning his teaching. Some schools also make use of video tape as a means by which the teacher is able to evaluate his own work in a microteaching session.

COGNITIVE MICROTEACHING EVALUATION FORM

Cognitive—Critical Thinking Processes

Applying				
Comparing				
Criticizing (Analysis)				
Decision-making (Analysis of What to Do)				

Scientific Processes

Classifying				
Collecting and Organizing Data				
Designing and Investigation				
Formulating Models				
Hypothesizing or Predicting				
Inferring or Making Interpretations				
Measuring				
Observing				
Operational Definition				

General Remarks

Teacher Self-evaluation Checklist. Although extremely valuable, microteaching observational skills require considerable training for developing the desired accuracy of observed teaching. Paul Blackwood has compiled the following simple checklist teachers can use with relative ease for self-evaluation of past teaching and as suggestion for direction in the future.[24]

I. *In my teaching is there opportunity or provision for children to:*

	None	Some	Much
(a) Raise questions and problems of importance or interest to them?			
(b) Study these questions and problems?			
(c) Help plan "things to do" in studying science problems?			
(d) State clearly the problems on which they are working?			
(e) Make hypotheses to be tested?			
(f) Gather accurate data (information) in a variety of ways:			
Through reading on the subject?			
Through taking field trips?			
Through watching demonstrations?			
Through doing experiments?			
Through talking to resource persons?			
(g) Analyze the data (information) to see how it relates to the problem?			
(h) Think about the applications of their science learnings to everyday living?			
(i) Think about science relationships and processes instead of merely naming things and learning isolated facts?			
(j) Bring science materials of different kinds to school for observation and study?			
(k) Engage in individual science interests?			

II. *In my teaching do I periodically and systematically check on the children's growth in:*

	None	Some	Much
(a) Ability to locate and define problems right around them?			
(b) Acquiring information on the problem being studied?			
(c) Ability to observe more accurately?			
(d) Ability to make reports on or record their observations?			
(e) Ability to solve problems?			
(f) Ability to think critically?			
(g) Ability to explain natural phenomena?			
(h) Ability to distinguish between facts and fancies?			

[24] Paul Blackwood, *Evaluating Teaching Practices in Elementary Science*, Education Briefs, No. 21 (July, 1959), OE-20009-21 (Washington, D.C.: Department of Health, Education, Welfare, Office of Education), p. 8.

	None	*Some*	*Much*
(i) Suspending judgment until evidence is collected?	_____	_____	_____
(j) Being open-minded, or willing to change belief?	_____	_____	_____
(k) Cooperating with others?	_____	_____	_____

Summary

Evaluation is a continuous and all encompassing part of the science program. With greater emphasis upon scientific processes in the science program, evaluation must shift from stress on recall to an application of knowledge.

Evaluation is vital for the proper diagnosis of children's knowledge and for prescribing learning experiences for further growth. Proper evaluation aids in determining pupil achievement, provides for pupil differentiation, and forms a basis for communicating with parents and the community.

In spite of some limitations noted, behavioral objectives should be the basis for teaching-learning-evaluating activities wherever feasible. Bloom's categories of behavioral objectives are cognitive, affective, and psychomotor. Cognitive behavioral objectives refer to remembering knowledge previously learned and being able to apply it to the solving of problems; affective refers to interests, attitudes, and values; psychomotor refers to muscular and manipulative skills.

Suggestions were given for techniques that teachers can use for testing scientific knowledge. Among these are: tape recordings of discussions and multiple-choice tests, picture tests, matching tests, and crossword puzzles.

To assess children's higher levels of process thinking, these evaluative devices can be used: essays, interpretation tests, story situation analysis tests, application of knowledge tests, evaluation of evidence tests. The affective domain behavioral objectives are more difficult to test. Several ways to test attitudes are: science story tests, and the AAAS Semantic Differential Scale, and checklists. The psychomotor behavioral objectives can be evaluated by: teacher observational checklists, rating scales, and performance tests.

If judiciously used by teachers, standardized tests can be valuable in the science program. Sources of standardized tests are presented in the chapter along with advantages and disadvantages of standardized science tests.

You can improve your science evaluation techniques. To do this you should identify your objectives specifically and in observable behavioral terms whenever feasible. Have your science content, methods, and materials of teaching, and your evaluative devices geared to accomplishing your behavioral objectives. Select a variety of evaluation devices and make your tests samples of what was taught. Test often and include the children in evaluating the results of the tests. Remember: your tests show what you value in science teaching-learning. If you want to stress process along with content, your tests must reflect this.

Continual teacher self-evaluation is vital for creative thinking. Scrutinize your testing and revise as a result of children's responses to the tests. Use microteaching evaluations, self-evaluation checklists, and other techniques for self-evaluation of your past teaching as a means of directing your future teaching.

SELF-EVALUATION AND FURTHER STUDY

1. Describe the roles of evaluation in the modern elementary school science program. The following sources contain information in addition to those in the footnotes of this chapter:

Anderson, Ronald D., "Evaluation in Elementary School Science," Part I, *Science and Children*, Volume 5, No. 1. (September, 1967), pp. 20-23.

Anderson, Ronald D., "Evaluation in Elementary School Science," Part II, *Science and Children*, Volume 5, No. 2. (October, 1967), pp. 33-36.

Balch, John, "The Influence of the Evaluating Instrument on Students' Learning," *American Educational Research Journal I* (May, 1964), pp. 69-182.

Cronbach, Lee J., "Course Improvement through Evaluation," *Teachers College Record* (May, 1963), p. 680.

Fleming, Robert S., ed., *Curriculum for Today's Boys and Girls.* Columbus, Ohio: Charles E. Merrill Publishing Company, 1963, Chapter 15.

Sears, Pauline S., and Ernest R. Hilgard, "The Teacher's Role in the Motivation of the Learner," Chapter 8, *Theories of Learning and Instruction*, Ernest R. Hilgard, ed., *63rd Yearbook of the National Society for the Study of Education*, Part I. Chicago: University of Chicago Press, 1964.

"Special Feature on Testing," *NEA Journal*, 52 (October, 1963), pp. 16-25.

2. Construct an evaluative device or technique for each of Bloom's three domains: cognitive, affective, and psychomotor. Enumerate the specific behavioral objective(s) in each. For additional help on test construction see:

Adkins, Dorothy, *Test Construction.* Columbus, Ohio: Charles E. Merrill Publishing Company, 1961.

Dunfee, Maxine, *Elementary School Science: A Guide to Current Research.* Washington, D.C.: Association for Supervision and Curriculum Development, National Education Association, 1962.

Ebel, Robert L., *Measuring Educational Achievements.* Englewood Cliffs, N.J.: Prentice-Hall, Inc., 1965.

Hedges, William D., *Testing and Evaluation in the Sciences for the Secondary Schools.* Belmont, Calif.: Wadsworth Publishing Co., Inc., 1966. *Note:* Although this book is written for secondary school science teachers, elementary school teachers will find it excellent for ideas on implementing Bloom's taxonomy.

Tannenbaum, Harold E., Nathan Stillman, and Albert Piltz, *Evaluation in Elementary School Science.* Circular 757, Washington, D.C.: U.S. Office of Education, 1964.

3. Use Paul Blackwood's checklist on page 309 to assess the effectiveness of your science teaching.

4. Select a standardized science test from those listed on page 302. Try to pick a test that assesses higher cognitive skills, not just recall of knowledge. Administer this test to a small group of children or an entire class.

5. Make arrangements to observe a science lesson. Using the *Cognitive Microteaching Evaluation Form* on page 308, analyze the interactions of that lesson. If it is possible, have your own lesson videotaped and apply the checklist to a microteaching session of your own.

6. Evaluation of the affective and psychomotor domains has had little attention. Construct devices similar to the *Microscope Skills* in this chapter.

7. Construct picture tests for primary grade children for science content areas.

8. Arrange a table or tables on which some very simple equipment is present. Structure a problem situation that students have not seen before and have them seek solutions. Keep a record or tape recording of the responses children make in trying to solve the problem. For further help in structuring the situation see:

> Jacobson, Willard J., and Harold E. Tannenbaum, *Modern Elementary School Science*, Science Manpower Project Monographs. New York: Bureau for Publications, Teachers College, Columbia University, 1961.
>
> Mills, Lester C., and Peter M. Dean, *Problem Solving Methods of Science Teaching*, Science Manpower Project Monographs. New York: Bureau for Publications, Teachers College, Columbia University, 1960.

9. Using the setup in 8. above and the checklist on page 306, assess a group of children's abilities to manipulate materials for the solution of problems.

10. Secure lesson scripts and student workbooks from the Individually Prescribed Instruction in Science (Oakleaf Project) by writing to Dr. Warren D. Shepler, Learning Research and Development Center, University of Pittsburgh, Pittsburgh, Pennsylvania 15213. Tape record these lesson-evaluations and have children record their responses in their workbooks. Try to devise some taped lesson-evaluations of your own.

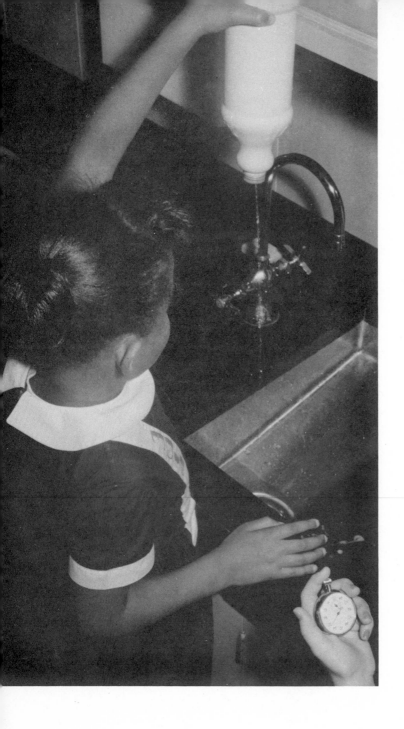

PART FOUR

DISCOVERY LESSON PLANS

*The most significant gain to be expected from increasing the range and quality of teaching in the elementary school curricula is the effect on the cognitive faculties of the child and upon his image of the purposes and possibilities of education.**

RESOURCE LESSONS FOR SCIENCE UNITS

The following portion of this book contains tested elementary science lessons. Included are discovery lesson plans, organized under conceptual schemes, in biology, physical science, and earth science. A teacher may use several of these lessons, listed under one scheme, in constructing part of a unit. She undoubtedly would supplement the lessons with additional activities taken from other sources. In Chapter 3, it was pointed out that the discovery approach has many advantages. For example, there is greater involvement of the learner when the discovery approach is used. Also, student and teacher interest in science is greater when the subject is approached through discovery lessons because the learner has a chance to participate in mental activities similar to the creative mental processes of a scientist.

All of the following lessons have been tested by elementary teachers in four rural elementary schools and in the seventh and eighth grades of one junior high school. The teachers testing them had no special preparation in science. In fact, science had not been a part of the elementary teachers' curricula until the year these lessons were introduced. All of the lessons have been evaluated by several teachers, rewritten, and changed to meet their suggestions. Although the lessons were originally written to be given mainly as demonstrations, in most cases they have been modified to be used as student experiments.

The topic areas of the lessons are those suggested by the recent national Feasibility Conference on elementary science education sponsored by the American Association for the Advancement of Science.** The concepts for each lesson are taken from the list of principles of science thought by scientists to be important for any person having a general education. The complete list of these principles is available from the United States Office of Education.† No effort has been made, however, to cover all concepts and principles embodied in an elementary curriculum since such a project would require an entire book. The lessons are organized in departmental areas such as physical science and biological science. This is done only to help teachers locate them. They need not be taught in the order found in this book. These lessons are only sample lessons. In order to be of value in the elementary classroom, they would have to be supplemented and integrated with

---

* Robert D. Hess, *Journal of Research in Science Teaching*, Vol. 1, Issue 1 (1963), p. 23.

** "Science Teaching in Elementary and Junior High School," *Science*, 133 (June 23, 1961), pp. 2019-2022.

† E. W. Martin, "Major Principles of the Biological Sciences of Importance for General Education," Selected Science Services, Circular No. 308-IV, Division of Secondary Schools, U.S. Office of Education, Government Printing Office, Washington, D.C.

H. E. Wise, "Major Principles of Physics, Chemistry, and Geology of Importance for General Education," Department of Health, Education, and Welfare, U.S. Government Printing Office, Washington, D.C.

In what ways might the pooling of observations bring about new, unexpected discoveries?

many other activities and similar lessons, preferably in units. After a teacher has had experience in teaching several of these sample lessons, she will easily gain competence in designing others for her own curriculum.

The instructor should not tell the class the purpose of the lesson before beginning it. The objective is to have the students discover the concepts in the course of the lesson. Before the teacher goes into the classroom and presents a lesson, she should read it thoroughly and go through the steps of the lesson. Particular attention should be paid to the questions asked. These are guide questions which are aids to the students. Although these lessons have been tested in actual class situations, no teacher can be certain a class will respond in a step-by-step manner through a lesson. A teacher obviously should modify the delivery of these lessons for her particular class.

Suggestions for Using the Discovery Approach

1. Be enthusiastic; start a demonstration or an experiment as though it were a riddle that is fun to solve. Ask such questions as, "Does anyone know what I am going to do with this equipment?" "Let's see who can be first to discover what is going to happen in this demonstration."

2. Always encourage your pupils. Use positive reinforcement. Don't criticize a student's poor efforts at thinking. If you think a student is off the track, don't say so. Say instead, "You have a point, and you seem to be really thinking," or "I am not quite sure what you mean, but I don't think it fits in with this problem; keep up that thinking." And when a child does come up with a good idea, compliment him. Tell him, "That is good . . . wonderful . . . terrific—we really have some thinking going on in the classroom!" Continually encourage and give recognition to your students for making good hypotheses, suggestions, and conclusions. Re-

member that positive recognition and reinforcement is a hard psychological principle to follow. It is so easy to become irritated with what appears to be a stupid answer to a question and say, "That's wrong." "Where did you get that silly idea?" If you operate your classroom in this manner, you will obtain little response.

3. What appears to be a silly answer to you might be due to the inability of a child to communicate. A silly answer on the surface, when investigated further by questioning, may be full of insight.

4. Deliberately encourage students to make hypotheses (guesses).

5. Write down the students' hypotheses about the experiment or demonstration on the board.

6. Have the class consider each guess before an experiment is done. See if the children can eliminate some of them.

7. Always maintain an attitude that it is better to try to think and make mistakes than not to think.

8. Have fun yourself doing demonstrations or experiments.

9. If an experiment doesn't come out the way it should, ask your class if any of them can help you figure out why. They may learn more from this experience than they would have if the demonstration had worked.

10. Above all, don't be afraid to do an elementary science experiment if you don't know all about it. Your students don't expect you to know everything. They enjoy having their teacher learn with them, especially in science.

11. When doing demonstrations, let students assemble the equipment before the class. You can help them and even teach them to get the class to discover what they are going to do.

12. Wherever possible, have the students work alone on experiments. They learn much more about equipment and how to do experiments this way. Many of the activities that follow have been written for this purpose.

How can the alert teacher develop skills in asking questions that stimulate children's thinking?

How to Use the Discovery Laboratory Lessons

Each discovery laboratory lesson in this section of the book includes the following parts:

1. Statement of the Problem
2. Grade Level Range
3. Concepts
4. Materials
5. Discussion Questions (not used in all lessons)
6. Pupil Discovery Activities
7. Processes
8. Open-ended Questions
9. Teacher's Notes or Teacher's Explanation

These are teaching lessons. This means much of the information of the lesson is to be used by the teacher and other parts by the students. The Statement of the Problem, the Pupil Discovery Activities, and the Open-ended Questions sections should be duplicated for the children in the upper grades. The rest of the above format is for the teacher. In the primary grades where the children do not read, the teacher must read the Pupil Discovery section to them or put the directions on tape for them to listen to. The children should discover the concepts through actually doing the activities. The pupil activities are designed for this purpose and may be performed by individuals or small groups of students.

Explanation of the Lesson Format

The *Problem* of each lesson is stated as a question.

The *Grade Level* is usually written as a range because many of the activities have been tested in several grades and found to work reasonably well in all of them.

The *Concepts* include scientific principles and concepts the children are to discover in doing the activities outlined in each lesson.

The *Discussion Questions* are to be asked by the teacher before the children start the discovery activities. It is the purpose of this section to set the stage for the activities that follow.

The *Pupil Discovery Activities* are the investigations the children do leading to their discovery of the concepts listed in the teacher section of the lesson.

The *Processes* are listed to show the teacher the types of mental operations the children are required to perform in each part of the lesson.

The *Open-ended Questions* are questions that should suggest to the children additional investigations they might do. The teacher should encourage students who are interested to attempt to answer these questions through further investi-

What preparation and instruction must the teacher anticipate in order to make the activity successful?

gation. Many of the activities suggested by these questions could be done at home and need not take additional classtime.

Teacher's Notes are suggestions made to the instructor involving how the lesson may be given.

Teacher's Explanations are given in the more complicated lessons to explain the activities of the lessons or give some background information.

Discovery Lesson Plans

PHYSICAL SCIENCE

Geology

How Does Erosion Affect the Soil?   458
What Is a Fault?   461
How Are Rocks Alike?   465
How Do Limestone, Marble, and Granite Differ?   466
How Does a Geyser Work?   467
How Are Crystals Formed?   470

Meteorology

How Can Solar Energy Be Used?   474
What Is a Barometer?   476
How Can You Make a Cloud?   478
How Big Should You Make a Parachute?   480
How Much Water Will Snow Make?   482

BIOLOGICAL SCIENCES

Anatomy and Physiology

What Is a Cell?   485
What Do Your Bones Do?   487
What Enables Our Bodies to Move?   490
How Do Our Muscles Work?   492
By What Process Do Humans Breathe?   496
How Does Blood Circulate?   501
What Does the Heart Do?   503
What Happens to Starch in the Food You Eat?   507
How Does Our Skin Protect Us?   510

Animals

How Many Different Types of Animals Do You Know?   513
What Is the Difference between a Frog and a Lizard?   516
How Do Ants Live?   518
What Do You Know about the Birds around You?   519
How Do Birds Differ from Mammals?   521
How Does the Lack of Oxygen Affect Animals?   523

Plants

What Are the Parts of a Plant?   526
What Is a Seed?   528
How Do Roots Grow?   530
How Does Water Get into a Plant?   532
What Is the Purpose of a Stem?   533
Why Do Some Parts of Plants Grow Upward?   535

Physical Science

AIR PRESSURE

What Is Air? (K-3)

CONCEPTS

Air is real.
Air is around us all the time.
Air is found inside solids and liquids.
Air takes up space and has weight.

MATERIALS

Piece of cardboard
A commercial sized mayonnaise jar or aquarium
A drinking jar

DISCUSSION

How do you know something is real?
What could you do to find out whether or not air is real?

Processes	Pupil Discovery Activity
	1. Swing your hands back and forth.
Observing	What can you feel?
	2. Swing a piece of cardboard.
Observing	What do you feel now?
Inferring	What is the cardboard pushing against?
Observing	What do you feel pushing against you when you ride your bicycle down a hill?
Hypothesizing	What do you think will happen to a jar if it is turned upside down and placed under water?
	3. Obtain a drinking glass. Turn the glass upside down and hold it in a large jar of water or aquarium.

Observing

4. Turn the glass sideways.
What happens to the inside of the glass?
What are the bubbles that escape from the glass?

OPEN-ENDED QUESTIONS

1. How can you keep water in a straw by holding it?
2. If you fill a paper bag with air and then crush it, what happens and why?

What Shapes and Volumes May Air Occupy?   (1-6)

CONCEPTS

A gas has no fixed shape.
A gas has no distinct surface of its own.
A change in shape or state is a physical change.
Air or gas is elastic in that it can expand or contract to fill a space.
Air can exert a force.

MATERIALS

Plastic bag (quart size)   Beach ball
Balloon (oblong shape)   Tire pump

Teacher's Note: These materials are for a group of two or three children.

DISCUSSION

What helps a kite to fly?
Why does your hair blow in the wind?
What do you breathe?

Where do you find air?
How do you know air is around you?
What form or shape does air have?
How can you find out?

Processes   **Pupil Discovery Activity**

PART I

                1. Obtain a balloon, a plastic bag, a beach ball, and
                   a tire pump.
                2. Inflate the balloon by blowing into it.

Observing   What is the shape of the balloon?
Inferring or interpreting   What made it that shape?

                3. Squeeze the balloon.

Observing   What shape is it?
Inferring   Why does it take on different shapes when you
                   squeeze it?

                4. Open the balloon.

Observing   What happened to the air?
Inferring   What is the shape of the air now?

PART II

                1. Obtain a plastic bag and blow into it.

Comparing   2. Is the shape of it the same or different from the
                   shape of the balloon?

                3. Release the bag.

Inferring   What happened to the shape of the air?
Inferring   Why was the shape of the balloon similar to the
                   shape of the plastic bag even though they are dif-
                   ferent?

PART III

                1. Obtain and inflate a beach ball.
Comparing   Is the shape of it the same or different from the
                   way it was before inflating?

Inferring   Why do you think the ball changed its shape?
Summarizing   What can you say about the shape of the air in all
                   these things?

Designing an   How do you think you could use a tire pump to
  investigation   show that air will fill any container?
                2. Obtain a tire pump. Have your partner put his
                   finger over the end of the pump.
                3. Push the plunger of the pump down.
Observing   Was it easy or hard to push it down?
                4. Keep the finger over the end, push the plunger
                   down, and then let go of the plunger.
Observing   What happened to it?
Inferring   What caused it to bounce back?

5. Now remove the finger and push the plunger down again.

Comparing — Was it easy or hard to push?

Inferring — Why does it push differently now?

Comparing — How does this compare with the stretching of a rubber band or a balloon?

Inferring — How was it possible for the air to cause a balloon to become larger?

Teacher's Note: Explain that a force is a push or pull, and then ask the children to determine if air can exert a force and to explain how they know that it can or cannot.

OPEN-ENDED QUESTIONS

1. How can you use an inflated ball and an uninflated ball to show that air can fill a big space?

How Can Air Pressure Move Objects?   (K-8)

CONCEPTS

Air pressure may be strong enough to crush a strong can.

A partial vacuum is a space in which the atmospheric pressure has been lessened; in other words, the space contains fewer molecules of air than the air surrounding it.

MATERIALS

Empty ditto fluid can   Bunsen or alcohol burner   Marking ink
Water   Cork

DISCUSSION

What are some things you know about air?
What ways can you think of to crush a can?
What would happen to the can if you took out some air?
How could you remove some of the air from a can?

Processes

Pupil Discovery Activity

Teacher's Note: This activity should be done as a demonstration in the lower grades and may be done in groups in the upper grades. Caution: If children do the activity, it is best to use an alcohol burner instead of the bunsen burner.

1. Obtain an empty ditto fluid can.
2. Add some water to it.
3. Place it on a Bunsen or alcohol burner for several minutes.
4. When the steam starts to rise from the can, cork it and *take it off the burner immediately.*
5. Mark the cork where it enters the can.

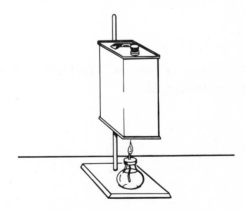

Inferring   Why did you put water in the can before heating it?

Inferring   What is happening to the air inside the can as it cools?

Hypothesizing   Now that the can is cooling, what do you think will happen to it?

Observing   What changes do you observe taking place beside the can?

Inferring	What is causing the sides of the can to be changed?
Observing	What happened to the cork?
Hypothesizing	How can you prove your answer?
Inferring	Why did this happen to the cork?
Inferring	What is now inside the can?
Hypothesizing	Why didn't the can cave in immediately?
Inferring	Why did you put the cork in the can?
Hypothesizing	What would have happened to the can if you had not put the cork in it?

OPEN-ENDED QUESTIONS

1. How could you have made the can cave in faster?
2. How do some women use the ideas involved in this activity when they can fruit?
3. Why should you open a can of food before heating it?

Teacher's Note: When the can is heated, the water in the can changes from water to water vapor. This warm water vapor expands into the can exerting a pressure causing some of the air in the can to escape. This process is fairly complete by the time the water has boiled for a few minutes. When the burner is removed and the can corked, the air inside the can begins to cool. As the air cools, some of the water vapor condenses back into water resulting in reduced pressure. The remaining air also contracts. Actually a partial vacuum is formed by this process inside the can. Since there is less pressure pushing outward than there is pushing inward, the can is caved in.

How Does Moving Air Differ from Non-moving Air? (5-8)

CONCEPTS

The pressure of liquids or gases will be low if they are moving fast and will be high if they are moving slowly.
This principle is called Bernoulli's principle.

MATERIALS

Three pieces of notebook paper	One thread spool	One ping pong ball
One Coca Cola bottle	One small card (3" × 3")	One thistle tube
	One needle	

Teacher's Note: **Before** this pupil inquiry activity, "potential" and "kinetic" energy should be explained.

Processes

PART I

                              Pupil Discovery Activity

1. Obtain a piece of notebook paper.
2. Make a fold 1 inch high from the long end of the paper.
   Make another fold at the other end as indicated in the diagram.
3. Place the paper on a flat surface.

Hypothesizing

    What do you think will happen if you blow under this folded paper?

4. Blow a stream of air under the paper.

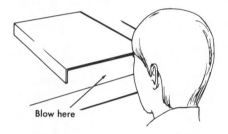

Blow here

Observing

    What do you notice about the way the paper moves? Describe how the air was circulating under the paper before you blew under it.

Comparing

    What do you know about the air pressure under the paper (when you blew under the paper) as compared with the air pressure exerted on the paper in the room.

PART II

Hypothesizing

    What do you think will happen to a wad of paper placed in the opening of a Coca Cola bottle if you blew across the bottle opening?

1. Obtain a small piece of paper and a Coca Cola bottle.
2. Wad the paper so it is about the size of a pea. (¼″ diameter)
3. Lay the Coca Cola bottle on its side.
4. Place a small wad of paper in the opening of the bottle, next to the edge of the opening. (See diagram.)
5. Blow across the opening in front of the bottle.

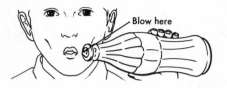

Observing	What happened to the wad of paper?
Inferring	Why did the wad of paper do this?
Comparing	What do you know about the air pressure in the bottle and the air pressure at the opening of the bottle when you blew across it?
Hypothesizing	What do you think will happen if you place a wad of paper in the opening of a Coca Cola bottle (as before) and blow directly into the bottle?
	6. Blow directly into the bottle.
Observing	7. Record your observations.
Inferring	8. What do you conclude from your observations?

PART III

Hypothesizing	What will happen to a card with a needle thrust through its center if it is placed into a hole of a spool and a person blows into the hole of the spool as indicated in the diagram?

1. Obtain a spool, a small card (3″ × 3″), and a needle.
2. Place a needle in the center of the card.
3. Stick the needle into the center of the hole of the spool. (See diagram.)
4. Hold the card, with your hand, against the bottom of the spool.
5. Blow into the hole of the spool from the top of the spool.
6. While blowing, let go of the card.

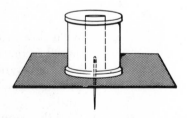

Observing	What did you see the card do?
Inferring	Why does the card do this?
Inferring	What is holding the card?
Inferring	Why doesn't the air you blow through the hole make the card fall?

Inferring

Why do you need the pin in the middle of the paper?

PART IV

Hypothesizing

What will happen to a ping pong ball if it is placed in a large end of a thistle tube, and you blow through the small end of the thistle tube?
1. Obtain a ping pong ball and a thistle tube.
2. Place the ping pong ball in the wide, larger opening of the thistle tube and blow through the other end.

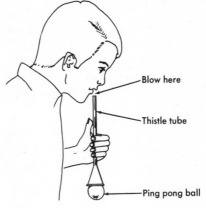

Blow here

Thistle tube

Ping pong ball

Observing
Inferring

Record your observations.
Why did the ball do what it did?

PART V

Hypothesizing

If you were to hold a piece of paper by each corner and blow across the top of the paper, what would happen to the paper?
1. Obtain a piece of paper.

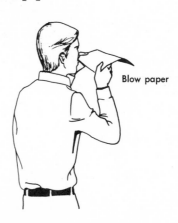

Blow paper

2. Hold the lower left corner with your left hand and the lower right corner with your right hand. (See diagram.)
3. Blow across the top of the paper.

Observing

Inferring

Applying

What happened to the paper?

Why did the paper move in this direction?

Why wouldn't it be wise to stand close to a moving train?

OPEN-ENDED QUESTIONS

1. When you rapidly pass by another pupil's desk with a sheet of paper on it, what happens to the paper?
2. How would this principle of air pressure work when you fly a kite?
3. What happens to a girl's full skirt if a car speeds closely by her?
4. What would happen if the plane stopped moving in the air?
5. Why would this happen?

Teacher's Note: If a plane is moving fast enough, the upward pressure on the wings is enough to overcome gravity. It must keep moving to stay aloft. If it stopped in midair, it would glide down immediately.

6. In the drawing of the airplane wing below, is the air moving faster at A or B?
7. How do wing slopes vary and why?

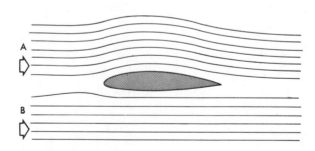

HEAT

What Is Heat?   (K-8)

CONCEPTS

When an object is heated, its molecules move faster or vibrate more.
When an object is cooled, its molecules move more slowly.
Heat is the total energy an object has because of the motion of its molecules.

MATERIALS

1 hammer   2 boards (suggested size: $1'' \times 5'' \times 12''$)
2 nails   1 sheet of sandpaper

Processes   **Pupil Discovery Activity**

Teacher's Note: This activity may be done in groups of 2 or more.

PART I

The children should know what molecules are before doing this activity.

Hypothesizing   What do you think a nail head will feel like after it has been hit several times with a hammer?

1. Obtain a board, a hammer, and two nails.
2. Lay one nail next to where you are working.
3. Drive the other nail partially into the board, hitting the nail several times with the hammer. *Immediately* feel the nail you pounded into the board.

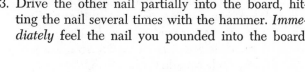

Observing   How does the nail feel?
                              4. Feel the other nail.
Observing   How does it feel?
Comparing   Did you notice any difference in the two nails?
Inferring   Why do you think the nail hit by the hammer felt
                                    the way it did?
Inferring   What do you think happened to the molecules of
                                    the nail when you hit them with the hammer?

    PART II

Hypothesizing   What do you think a board will feel like after you
                                    rub it very rapidly with sandpaper?
                              1. Obtain a board and a sheet of sandpaper.
                              2. Feel the board.
                              3. Using the sandpaper, sand the board very rapidly.
Observing   *Immediately* feel the sanded board.
Inferring   Why does the board feel the way it does?
Comparing   What do you notice about how the board feels be-
                                    fore it was sanded compared to after it was sanded?
Inferring   What did you do to the molecules in the board
                                    when you rubbed it quickly with sandpaper?

                              Teacher's Note: When the board was rubbed, its mole-
                                    cules were agitated and therefore vibrated more,
                                    producing heat. The board, when touched, produced
                                    the sensation of being warmer.

OPEN-ENDED QUESTIONS

1. Why do you rub a match against the side of a match box?
2. Why don't matches catch fire sitting in a match box?
3. When you bend a wire back and forth several times, why does it get warm?
4. When you put two pencils together and rub them back and forth several
   times, what happens to your hands?
5. A man tried to strike a match against a piece of glass in order to light it.
   The match wouldn't light. Why?
6. If you feel the tires of your car before you take a trip and then just after
   you get out of the car, they will not feel the same.
   How do you think they will differ?
   How would you explain the difference?
7. A man was chopping wood with an axe. After chopping very hard for
   about 10 minutes, he felt the axe.
   How do you think the axe felt and why?

What Causes the Molecules of a Liquid to Move?   (3-4)

CONCEPTS

The molecules in liquids are constantly moving in a random pattern or Brownian movement.
This motion is caused by heat.

MATERIALS

Glass	Microscope	Microscope slide
Water	Pen	India ink
Food coloring bottles		

DISCUSSION

1. What would happen if you added a drop of food coloring to a glass of water?
2. What would you do to find out?

Processes	**Pupil Discovery Activity**
PART I	*Molecular Motion of Liquids*
	This activity may be done in groups.
	1. Obtain a glass filled with water and food coloring. Share the bottle of food coloring placed on your table with the other children.
	2. Add a drop of food coloring to the glass of water.
Observing	3. What do you think will happen to this mixture if you do not move it?
Observing	4. What is happening to the water and food coloring?
Inferring	What do you think is happening to the molecules of food coloring and water?
Inferring	How do you think water molecules move?
Designing an investigation	How could you find out?
PART II	*The Movement of Water Molecules*
Applying	1. Obtain a microscope, a microscope slide, a pen, water, and India ink.
	2. Place a drop of water on the microscope slide. Dip only the tip of your pen into the India ink. Place the tip of the pen into the drop of water on the

microscope slide. Place as little ink in the water as possible.

Hypothesizing

What do you think is happening to the ink and the water?

Teacher's Note: Caution the children about being careful when focusing and handling the microscope. Check to make sure the children are seeing what is expected.

3. Carefully place the slide, with the drop of water and the ink, on the microscope stand. Focus the microscope on the drop. Caution: do not crash the microscope lens into your slide.

Observing
Observing
Observing
Inferring
Inferring

4. Observe the ink in the water.
   What are the particles of ink doing?
   How are they moving?
   How is this motion caused?
   What evidence is there that the molecules of water may also be moving?

Teacher's Note: The motion the children see is Brownian movement, which means there is random movement of molecules.

OPEN-ENDED QUESTIONS

1. How would the temperature of the liquid affect the movement of the liquid molecules?
   How would you find out?
2. What other factors in addition to temperature affect the movement of liquid molecules?
3. How do other liquid molecules move?

What Happens to Molecules of Liquids and Gases When They Are Heated?   (6-8)

CONCEPTS

Convection is the process whereby warm liquids or gases rise and cooler gases fall.

Warmed liquids and gases expand and occupy more space. As a result they have fewer molecules per volume than when they were cold. They are therefore less dense.

Warm liquids and gases rise because they are less dense than they would be if they were cold.

MATERIALS

Newspaper

4 matches

Metal waste basket

Smoke paper or string that has been dipped in benzene or kerosene and dried

Plate glass (6″ by 6″)

Ink or small paste bottle

Cork to fit small bottle

2 glass tubes or medicine droppers

Food coloring

Glass container (quart size)

Hot water

Cold water

Beaker

Coloring crystals—potassium permagenate crystals or food coloring are suggested

Paper towel

Processes

Pupil Discovery Activity

Teacher's Note: Step two below probably can best be done as a demonstration.

Hypothesizing

1. What do you think might happen when a newspaper is lighted and held by an open window?
2. Obtain a newspaper, a jar of water, and matches. Roll a newspaper tightly. Light one end of it and hold it near a window opened at the top. Observe carefully what happens for a few seconds; then smother the flame in a jar of water. Place the wet newspaper in a wastebasket.

Inferring

What did you notice about the movement of the smoke?

What did you notice when the burning paper was placed near the window?

Why do you think the smoke moved the way it did?

Teacher's Note: If the room is warmer than the air outside the room, the warm air in the room will pass out of the top window. The smoke then will move out of the room. The reverse is the case for the lower window. The cold air will move into the room through the lower window. This shows warm air rises and cold air falls.

3. Set up apparatus. (See diagram.) Obtain some twine, or purchase from a scientific supply house some special smoke paper. Place it in the bottom of the chimney. Light the twine or paper so that it gives off smoke.

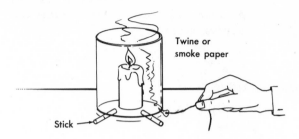

Twine or
smoke paper

Stick

Observing	What happens to the smoke?
Inferring	Why is it rising?
Interpreting	Is the smoke warmer or colder than the air around it?
Summarizing	What can you say from this activity about the movement of warm air?
Inferring	Which do you think is more dense, warm or cold air? Why?

Teacher's Note: Students should understand that before the smoke paper was lit, all air in the chimney was the same temperature. Through discussion lead the students to realize that warm air expands, occupies more space, and is lighter than cooler air around it. Cold air on the other hand falls because it is heavier than warm air.

Hypothesizing

Knowing what you do about warm and cold gases in air, how do you think warm compared to cold bodies of water might behave?

4. Obtain a small ink bottle, two glass tubes, a cork that will fit the bottle, food coloring and a large glass container in which to put the bottle. Insert the glass tubes in the cork so that one is higher than the other one as indicated in the diagram. *Caution:* Wet the cork and glass tubes before you try to insert them. Hold a paper towel folded several times around the glass tubes as you insert them. This is done to protect your hand in case the glass tubes

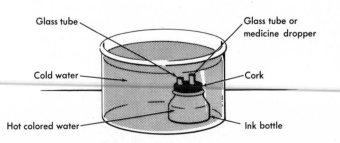

Glass tube

Glass tube or medicine dropper

Cold water

Cork

Hot colored water

Ink bottle

break. Twist the glass tubes into the cork. *Do not use excessive* force inserting them. (See diagram.)

5. Put a few drops of food coloring in the small bottle. Fill it with hot water and insert the cork. Fill the larger glass container with cold water.

Hypothesizing

What do you think will happen if you drop the small bottle into the container of cold water?

6. Drop the small bottle into the cold water container.

Observing

What happened when the small bottle was dropped into the larger container?

Inferring

Why did it happen?

The process of water and gases moving in this way is called convection.

Inferring

Why would it be possible for such currents to occur in the ocean?

7. Obtain a beaker and some colored crystals and fill the beaker with water. Place some of the colored crystals in the beaker. Place the beaker on the stand over a burner. Heat the water.

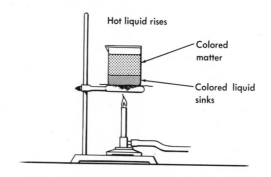

Hot liquid rises
Colored matter
Colored liquid sinks

Hypothesizing
Observing
Inferring

What do you think will happen to the crystals?
Describe what happens as the water is heated.
Why does this happen?

8. Convection is defined as the transfer of heat by means of currents in the liquid or gas that is heated.

Summarizing

Explain what this definition means to you in your own words.

OPEN-ENDED QUESTIONS

1. What happens to the air in a room when the cold air becomes the same temperature as the rest of the air in the room?
2. Why does smoke rise?
3. To stay as cool as possible, what part of a room should you occupy?
4. Explain the best arrangement of windows in a room for good circulation?

How Is Heat Transmitted by Conduction and Radiation? (5-8)

CONCEPTS

A candle gives off radiant heat.

Heat can be transmitted from one body to another by conduction and radiation.

Light objects reflect radiant energy more than dark objects.

Some surfaces conduct heat better than others.

MATERIALS

Quart size tin can
Small can of black paint
2 match sticks
Candle
4 × 4-inch square of aluminum foil
Silver or stainless steel knife
4-inch length of copper tubing
Bunsen or alcohol burner
4 × 4-inch square of asbestos

Penny
Candle
9 thumb tacks
Small paint brush
Piece of black paper
2 patches
Tripod stand
Wood splint

Processes	Pupil Discovery Activity
PART I:	*Radiation*

Teacher's Note: This activity may be done in groups.

Hypothesizing

What do you think will happen to two sticks attached with wax to the outside of a tin can when one-half of the inside of the can has been painted black, and a burning candle is placed inside the can? (See diagram.)

1. Obtain a large one-quart tin can, two match sticks, a candle, a small can of black paint, and a small paint brush.
2. Paint one-half of the inside of the can with black paint; *leave* the outside natural metal.
3. Light a candle and let some of its wax drip on each side of the can as indicated in the diagram. Place the sticks in the wax while it is soft and hold them until the wax cools.
4. Place the candle inside the tin can as close as possible to the center of the can.
5. Light the candle with a wood splint.

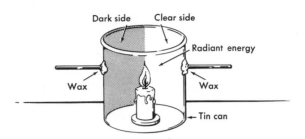

Hypothesizing	What do you think will happen to the sticks on the side of the can?
Observing	6. Observe and record what happens to the sticks.
Observing	Did this happen to each stick at the same time?
Inferring	Why do you think this happened?
Hypothesizing	What do you suspect about the inside surfaces of the can?
Hypothesizing	What happens to your eyes when you look at aluminum foil in sunlight?
Hypothesizing	What happens to your eyes when you look at a sheet of black paper in the sunlight?
	7. Obtain a piece of black paper and a piece of aluminum foil.
	8. Look at them in the sunlight.
Observing	How did the black paper and foil make your eyes feel as you looked at them in the sunlight?
Inferring	Why did each make your eyes feel differently?

Teachers' Note: Aluminum foil reflects radiant energy whereas black paper absorbs most of the radiant energy.

Inferring	Knowing what you do about how light (radiant) energy reacts on different surfaces, how would you explain why the sticks fell at different times from the can?
PART II:	*Conduction*
Hypothesizing	What do you think will happen to tacks which have been attached with wax to a strip of aluminum foil, a silver knife, and a copper tube, when the tips of these metals are heated? (See diagram.)
	1. Obtain a 4 × 4-inch square of aluminum foil, a candle, a match, and 9 tacks.
	2. Roll the aluminum foil tightly.

3. Drip some wax from a candle on to three tacks and the aluminum foil rod so that the tacks stick to the foil.
4. Obtain a Bunsen or alcohol burner, tripod stand, silver knife, and a 4-inch length of copper tubing.
5. Stick three tacks each to the knife and the tube as you did with the foil.
6. Light the burner.
7. Place foil, knife, and copper tubing on a tripod stand as indicated in the diagram. Heat the tips of each of these with a flame from a burner.

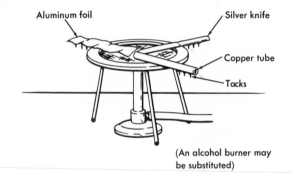

Aluminum foil   Silver knife

Copper tube

Tacks

(An alcohol burner may be substituted)

Observing	Observe and record what happens.
Inferring	Why didn't the tacks all fall at the same time?
Inferring	From observing this activity, how do you think the heat affected the three metals?

PART III

Hypothesizing

If you were to place a penny on top of a piece of asbestos, on a ring or tripod stand, and place a flame below the asbestos, would the penny or asbestos feel warmer?

1. Obtain a ring stand, a piece of asbestos, a Bunsen or alcohol burner or candle, a match, and a penny.
2. Place the piece of asbestos on the ring of the ring stand.
3. Place the penny in the center of the piece of asbestos.
4. Light the burner or candle.
5. Place the burner or candle below the asbestos for a few minutes.

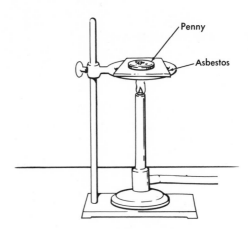

6. Carefully touch the penny, then the asbestos.
7. Remove the burner and turn it off.

Observing   Which of these, the penny or the asbestos, feels
                   warmer?

Inferring   Why does one feel warmer than the other?

Interpreting   Since you know what happens to molecules when
                   they are heated, what can you tell about the mole-
                   cules in the penny compared to the asbestos?

OPEN-ENDED QUESTIONS

1. When you stand in front of a fireplace and the front of you is warmed by
   the fire, how is the heat transferred?
2. How does heat energy come from the sun?
3. What colors are more likely to absorb heat?
4. Why do people generally wear lighter colored clothes in the summer?
5. In the can experiment, what kind of energy did the black surface absorb?
6. How was the heat transferred from the black surface to the wax?
7. Why is it desirable to have a copper-bottomed tea kettle?
8. Why wouldn't you want a copper handle on a frying pan?
9. What metals conduct heat well?
10. Why would asbestos be a good insulator against heat loss?
11. What advantage would there be in ordering a car with a white rather than
    a black top?
12. Why do many people in warmer climates paint their houses white?
13. Why would you prefer to put a hot dog on a stick rather than a wire to
    hold the hot dog above a camp fire?
14. Why do cooks sometimes use asbestos hot pads?

What Is an Insulator?

CONCEPTS

Water is a poor conductor of heat.
Wood, cork, glass, asbestos, and air are poor conductors of heat.
Heat from a burner rises.

MATERIALS

Clamp	Wood
Steel wool	Glass
Test tube	Glass rod
Ice	Metal rod (a brass curtain rod or aluminum foil rolled
Candle	to make a rod can serve for this purpose)
Matches	Wax
Ring stand	Aluminum foil (4″ × 4″)
Ring clamp	Alcohol or Bunsen burner
Asbestos (4″ × 4″)	

DISCUSSION

Is water a good conductor of heat?
What could you do to find out?

Processes

Pupil Discovery Activity

PART I

1. Obtain a test tube, clamp, steel wool, ice, candle, candle holder, and matches. Set up the equipment as shown in the diagram below.

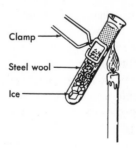

Clamp

Steel wool

Ice

2. Heat the water above the ice cubes for several minutes until the water boils.

Inferring

Inferring

What happens to the ice in the test tube?
From this, what can you conclude about water as a conductor of heat?
Why did you put steel wool in the lower part of the tube?

Teacher's Note: Steel wool was placed in the tubes to hold the ice cubes down.

PART II

1. Obtain the following items: aluminum foil, a Bunsen or alcohol burner, a ring stand, ring clamp, asbestos, and matches.
2. Set up the apparatus as indicated in the diagram. Place three matches on the asbestos.

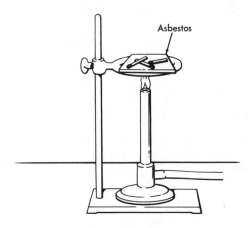

Measuring

Comparing

3. Heat the lower surface of the asbestos.
4. Time how long it takes for the matches to burst into flames.
5. Repeat the above procedure substituting aluminum foil for the asbestos.
What can you conclude about the ability of aluminum foil to conduct heat compared to asbestos?
Which of these would you call an insulator?

PART III

Hypothesizing

1. Obtain a glass rod, a metal rod, a candle, a candle holder, wax, and matches. Place wax on each of the rods as shown in the diagram below.
What do you think will happen when you heat these rods as indicated in the diagram?

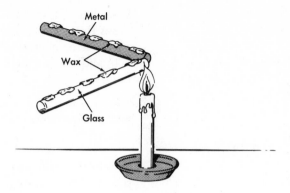

2. Heat the rods gently over the candle.

Observing   On which rod did the wax melt first?

Comparing   Which is the better conductor of heat: metal or glass?

Defining   Define in your own words what a conductor and an insulator of heat are.

OPEN-ENDED QUESTIONS

1. What are some materials you would use if you wanted to conduct heat from its source to another place?
2. Why can you safely hold your hand below a burning candle but not above its flame?
3. What materials would be good for making cups to hold hot drinks?
4. Where are insulators of heat used in your home?

STRUCTURE OF MATTER

What Are Atoms?   (5-8)

CONCEPTS

Changing the size of an object does not change its physical characteristics. All elements are composed of atoms.

An atom is very small.
Atoms are grouped in various ways to make molecules.
An atom is made up of electrons, protons, and neutrons.
Negatively charged bodies have more electrons than protons.
Electrons are negatively charged particles.
Protons are positively charged particles.
Neutrons have neither a positive nor a negative charge.

MATERIALS

Piece of coal
Wool cloth
Wax paper
3 plastic rulers
Wooden block
2 clothes hangers of wire
Picture of a solar system

Plasticine or styrofoam ball about the size of a
    ping-pong ball
6 rubber jack balls
Paper towel
String
Wire cutters

DISCUSSION

What do you know about atoms?
What do you think an element is?
What do you think an electron is?
What do you think protons and neutrons are?
How big do you think an atom is?
What do you know about molecules?

Teacher's Note: Atoms are very small. The thickness of a human hair probably
   contains at least 500,000 atoms. An atom consists of fundamental particles
   called electrons, protons, and neutrons. Protons and neutrons are found in
   the center (or nucleus) of the atom while electrons revolve around the
   nucleus. The revolving electrons are grouped together in shells or orbits
   around the nucleus. The neutron has nearly the same mass as the proton
   and, as could be guessed from its name, is electrically neutral and carries no
   charge. The nucleus contains most of the weight or matter and is the most
   important part of the atom. Therefore, the nucleus is also the heaviest part
   of an atom. When an atom is neutral, it has an equal number of electrons
   and protons. If there are more electrons, the atom is negatively charged. All
   atoms have a tendency to balance the number of electrons and protons by
   drawing electrons or giving off extra ones and in the process become
   neutral.

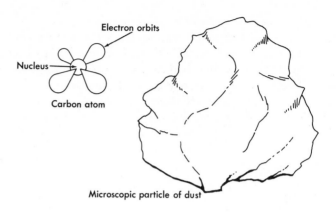

Electron orbits

Nucleus

Carbon atom

Microscopic particle of dust

Processes

Pupil Discovery Activity

PART I

1. Obtain a piece of coal (mostly carbon), a hammer, and a paper towel.

   Place the coal on the paper towel and pound the coal with the hammer until you see some fine coal dust.

Observing   How does the pounding change the coal?

Hypothesizing   Do you think you have made a new substance? Why?

Hypothesizing   2. What would you have to do to change the coal to a new material?

Hypothesizing   If you kept pounding the dust into smaller and smaller pieces, what would you ultimately end up with?

Teacher's Note: Explain that all elements are composed of tiny particles. These tiny particles are called atoms. Be sure that you do not convey to the children the idea that the dust from the coal is single atoms. Atoms are too small to be seen even through a powerful microscope. The dust particles are aggregations of molecules which in turn are made of atoms. (See the above diagram.) However, if the dust were pounded excessively, ultimately some free carbon atoms might be produced. These atoms, however, could not be broken down by further pounding.

PART II

1. Obtain a wire clothes hanger, a block of wood, some plasticine or styrofoam balls, and 6 rubber jack balls.

   Assemble the materials as shown in the diagram.

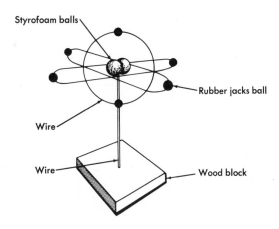

Inferring

2. In what ways is your model different from a real atom?

Teacher's Note: All the particles in the atom would be in motion. The orbits the electrons follow would not be so definite as those formed by the wire in the student model.

Hypothesizing

3. How could you improve the model shown in the diagram?
4. Look at a picture of our solar system.

Comparing

What do you notice about the solar system that can be said about an atom?

Comparing

5. In what ways is the solar system different from an atom?

Comparing

How is it similar?

What Are Water Molecules and How Do They Affect Each Other? (3-8)

CONCEPTS

The deeper the water, the greater the pressure.

Water has cohesive force.

A force is defined as push or pull on an object.

Molecules of the same substance tend to stick to each other because they are attracted by an invisible force.

Each molecule of the substance pulls other atoms to it.

The force of attraction between molecules of the same kind is called *cohesive force.*

MATERIALS

A quart milk carton
Water (enough to fill containers as desired)
A pencil or nail
Ruler
Hammer

Processes   **Pupil Discovery Activity**

PART I

If the side of a milk carton were punctured with
holes (one above another) and the can filled with
water, what do you think would happen to the
water in it? How would the water pour out of the
holes?

1. Obtain a clean milk carton which has the top cut
   out of it.
2. Puncture a hole with a pencil or nail from the bottom, about 1-1½ inches. Puncture three additional
   holes ½ inch apart above the preceding one.

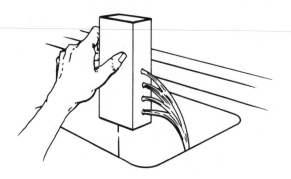

3. Fill the container over a sink with water to within
   an inch of the top.

Observing   What do you notice about the way the water comes
                     out of the holes of the carton?

Inferring   Why do you think the water comes out of the holes
                     like this?

Hypothesizing   If the carton were filled closer to the top with water,
                     do you think there would be a difference in the way
                     the water comes out?

4. Fill the carton until the water is closer to the top.

Observing   What do you notice about the way the water comes
                     out of the holes?

Comparing

Inferring

Did you notice any difference in the water coming from the holes of the carton when there was less and when there was more water in it?

What can you say about how water pressure varies with depth?

PART II

1. Puncture holes in the bottom of the carton about 1 centimeter apart as shown in the diagram.

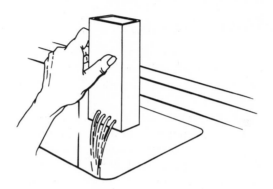

Hypothesizing

Hypothesizing

Observing
Designing an
   investigation

What do you think will happen when water is poured into this carton?

How many jets of water will you get coming out of the holes in the bottom of the carton?

2. Pour water into the carton.

How many jets of water came out?

What should you do to the water pouring out of the carton at the bottom so that you could only get one jet of water without plugging any holes?

3. Test your hypotheses.

Teacher's Note: The children should pour water into the carton and pinch the jets of water together with their fingers just as though they were going to pinch someone. The jets will form one stream. If the water comes out in one jet, there must be some kind of force holding the water together. The force that holds similar molecules to each other is called cohesive force. Each molecule of water has cohesive force which pulls and holds other molecules of water to it. See the diagram (p. 356) which represents how molecules of water are held together to form a water droplet due to cohesive force. The pinching of the water brings the jets of water in contact, allowing cohesive force to hold together. This is true because the cohesive force between two substances increases as the distance between them decreases.

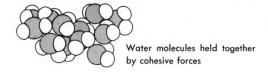

Water molecules held together by cohesive forces

OPEN-ENDED QUESTIONS

1. Why do you think a dam must be built with very thick walls at the bottom and thinner walls at the top?
2. Why do your ears sometimes hurt when you dive deep in a swimming pool?
   What pushes in on your ears as you go deeper?
3. Why are the walls of a submarine so thick and strong?
4. What would happen to the water escaping from two of the holes of a can if you stopped one hole?
5. What will happen to the water coming out of the bottom hole as the water gets lower in the can?
6. Why do many towns have water storage tanks towering high above the city or built on a hill?

CHANGES OF STATES OF MATTER

How May Matter Be Changed? (K-6)

CONCEPTS

Matter may be changed chemically or physically.
If matter is changed chemically, its chemical makeup will have to be altered.
Matter changed physically may be altered in its form but its chemical makeup remains the same.

MATERIALS

Sugar cubes	Butter	Candle
Small dish	Water	Matches
Tablespoon	Hot plate	Quart container (pan)
Prepared jello	Measuring cup	Glass

Teacher's Note: Assemble the above items in the classroom. *Caution:* In the interest of safety, only you should handle the hot plate. Place all these materials on your demonstration area.

DISCUSSION

What kinds of things are there on the desk?
How do they vary?
In what ways could you cause these things to change?
What changes do you think would occur in these items?
What would change other than the form?
How can you find out?

Teacher's Note: The terms for matter should have been introduced in previous lessons.

Processes	Pupil Discovery Activity
	1. Obtain a sugar cube, a candle, some prepared jello, and a match.
Observing	Is the sugar cube solid, liquid, or gas?
Hypothesizing	What ways would you use to change the form of the sugar?
	2. Change the form and describe how you did it.

Teacher's Note: The children should suggest crushing, dissolving, melting, or changing cubes to carbon.

	3. Light a candle.
Observing	Observe and record the changes you see.
	4. Observe the jello.
Observing	What is its form?
Hypothesizing and designing an investigation	How could you change its form?
	5. Try to change the jello's form.
	6. Obtain some butter.
Observing	What is the form of the butter?
Hypothesizing	How can you change its form?
	7. Try to change its form.

Teacher's Note: Set butter in a warm place or in a pan over the candle. Students should suggest that, after melting, the butter's form can be restored by cooling it.

Summarizing

What have you learned about how matter can be changed in this activity?

OPEN-ENDED QUESTIONS

1. Which of the things above could easily be restored to the form they were originally in?
2. What is the difference between a physical and a chemical change?

What Happens to Gases When They Are Heated or Cooled?   (3-6)

CONCEPTS

Gases expand when heated.
Gases contract when cooled.
When gases are heated, the molecules move farther apart and exert greater pressure on the walls of the container.

MATERIALS

3 balloons (same size)
String (5 ft. long)
Measuring tape
Gallon container filled with ice water

DISCUSSION

How could you use a balloon to determine if gas will expand or contract when filled with air and heated?
What happens to the molecules in an object when it is heated?
With a given rise in temperature, will gases or liquids expand the most?

Processes   **Pupil Discovery Activity**

1. Obtain 3 balloons, a 5-foot piece of string, and a measuring tape. Blow up the balloons so they are about the same size and tie them closed.

Hypothesizing

What do you think will happen to the air in a filled balloon if it is heated?

2. Measure with the measuring tape one of the balloons. Tie this balloon to the upper arm of a chair and place the chair about two feet from a heater.

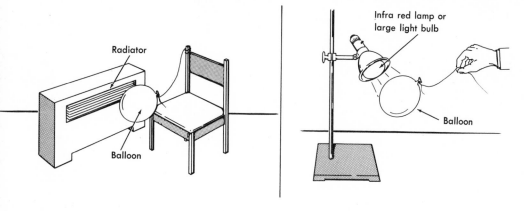

Observing

3. Observe the size and shape of the balloon as it is being heated.

Measuring

4. At the end of 4 minutes, measure and record the balloon's diameter again.

Hypothesizing

What do you think will happen to the shape of a balloon if it is cooled?

Designing an investigation

What should you do to find out?

5. Measure a second balloon. Place it in ice cold water.

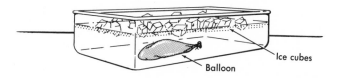

Observing

6. Observe the size and shape of this balloon as it is being cooled.

7. Leave the third balloon at room temperature.

Inferring

What is the purpose of leaving this balloon at room temperature?

Observing
Applying

Which of the three balloons expanded?

What do you think happened to the speed of the molecules inside the expanding balloons?

Observing
Applying

Which balloons contracted?

What do you think happened to the speed of the molecules in the cooled balloon?

Inferring	In which of the three balloons do you think the molecules are moving faster and hitting the sides with greater force?
Summarizing	What evidence do you have that gases expand when heated?
Summarizing	What evidence do you have that gases contract when cooled?

OPEN-ENDED QUESTIONS

1. What would happen to a balloon if the air inside was overheated?
2. What might happen to a tire if the car was driven very fast down the highway on a hot summer day?
3. What might happen to a partly filled bottle brought into a warm room from the refrigerator?

What Happens to Metals When They Are Heated or Cooled? (6)

CONCEPTS

Heat is a form of energy.

Heat energy can be transferred.

Matter changes if heat energy is gained or lost:

When heat energy is increased, the molecules move faster and further apart (expansion).

When heat energy is decreased, the molecules move slower and are closer together (contraction).

MATERIALS

Candle	Nail
Metal pan	Eye-screw (the eye of this should be
Matches	just slightly larger than the nail)
Test tube holder	Forceps

DISCUSSION

What is heat?

What is energy?

What are molecules?

What do you think heat does to molecules?

What is a nail made of?

How does heat affect metal? What could you do to find out?

Processes	**Pupil Discovery Activity**

Teacher's Note: This activity should be done in groups of two students.

PART I

1. With the aid of your partner, obtain a candle, matches, a metal pan, forceps, nail, and eye-screw.
2. Fix the candle so it stands in the center of the pan. To do this, light the candle wick and permit enough wax to drip onto the center of the pan (about the size of a quarter). Then blow out the candle and place it, wick end up, in the puddle of wax. Hold the candle steadily in the puddle until the wax hardens.
3. Try to fit the nail into the hole of the eye-screw.

Observing Does the nail fit the eye-screw?

Observing How easily does the nail go into the eye-screw?
Hypothesizing What do you think will happen if you heat the nail and try to put it through the eye-screw again?

Teacher's Note: The nail will have expanded so that it will not enter the eye of the eye-screw because the heat has caused the molecules to move faster and further apart (expansion).

4. Light the candle.
5. With the forceps, pick up the nail. Hold the head of the nail over the hottest part of the flame. If you do not know where this is, ask the teacher.
   Heat the nail for two minutes.

Teacher's Note: The candle flame is composed of two parts: a lower dark section and an upper bright part. The tip of the darker part is the hottest point of the flame. Always have your children hold the object they are heating over the dark tip. Also, be prepared to explain the products of combustion if the children question the black deposit of carbon on the nail and later on the test tube.

6. Pick up the eye-screw and try to put the nail head through it. After you have done this, put the nail and eye-screw in the metal pan—remember they are still hot.

Observing What happened when you tried to put the nail head through the eye-screw?

Inferring	Why do you think this happened?
Inferring	What happened to the molecules in the nail when you heated them?
Inferring	What did the heat do to them?
Inferring	Did the molecules move faster or slower?
Inferring	Did they gain or lose energy?
Inferring	Are the molecules in the heated nail closer together or farther apart than before heat was applied?
Inferring	How can you tell?
Explaining	Using the words *molecules, energy,* and *space between molecules,* try to explain what happens to a metal when it is heated.

What Effect Does Heat Have on the States of Matter? Part I—Solids   (3-6)

CONCEPTS

There are many forms of sugar.
It is possible to obtain carbon from burning sugar.
Sugar may be broken down chemically.

MATERIALS

Bunsen or alcohol burner	1 teaspoon sugar
Aluminum pie pan	1 cube of sugar
Ring stand and ring or electric hot plate	Empty glass cup (tall)
	Pot holder

DISCUSSION

Hold up a piece of sugar and ask, "What are some of the characteristics of this piece of sugar?"

Teacher's Note: They might say it is white, cubical in shape, small, made up of crystalline material, sweet, etc. In its present form, sugar is a white solid. There are, however, ways of changing its appearance. One of the easiest ways is simply to crush the cube, producing sugar in smaller crystal form. These crystals can be crushed further to make a powdered sugar. Another way to change this cube's appearance is to dissolve it in a cup of water. No sugar can be seen, yet the solution will taste sweet. It is nevertheless sugar because some of its characteristics are identifiable.

In what way can sugar be changed so that it cannot be identified?

Processes   **Pupil Discovery Activity**

1. Obtain an aluminum pie pan and place it on top of an electric hot plate or ring stand. Regulate the burner so the pan is heated slowly.
2. Obtain 1 teaspoon sugar and place it in the middle of the pan.

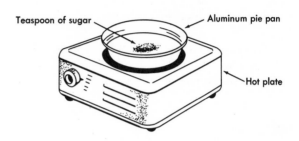

Teaspoon of sugar   Aluminum pie pan

Hot plate

Hypothesizing   What do you think will happen when the sugar is heated?

Observing   3. Watch what happens to the sugar.

Observing   What happens as the sugar begins to melt?

4. Obtain a tall empty glass cup and hold it upside down over the bubbling sugar. Use a pot holder to do this.

Hypothesizing   What do you think will appear on the inside of the glass?

Observing   5. Observe the inside of the glass.

6. Touch the inside of the glass with your fingers.

Observing   What do you feel?

Inferring   What do you think it is?

Teacher's Note: It is probably carbon. Sugar has carbon combined in its molecular structure. When it does not burn completely, it may produce carbon called soot which would collect on the cup.

7. After the sugar stops bubbling, describe what you see in the pan.

Inferring   What do you think this material could be?

Comparing   What does it look like?

Taste this material.

Observing   How does it taste?

Does it have the properties of sugar?

OPEN-ENDED QUESTIONS

1. From what you have learned about sugar, can you explain why a marshmallow turns black when roasted over a fire?

What Effect Does Heat Have on the
States of Matter? Part II—Liquids   (6-8)

CONCEPTS

The temperature of water rises to the boiling point proportional to the amount of heat it absorbs.

At the boiling point the temperature of water remains constant.

The heat added to water at the boiling point works to change the state of water to water vapor.

Whenever a state of matter is changed, for example, a liquid to a gas or a gas to a liquid, a considerable amount of energy must be added or given off in the process.

MATERIALS

Beaker (500 ml.)	Bunsen or alcohol burner	Wire gauze
Thermometer (centigrade)	Graduated cylinder	Stop- or
Stirring rod	Ring stand	wristwatch
Crushed ice	Ring clamp	

Processes   **Pupil Discovery Activity**

1. Obtain a 500-ml. beaker, ring stand, ring clamp, wire gauze, thermometer, stirring rod, crushed ice to fill the beaker, a watch, and a Bunsen or alcohol burner.

2. Arrange the ringstand, ring, and wire gauze according to the diagram. Using the graduated cylinder, measure out 50 ml. of water and pour it in the beaker.

3. Fill the rest of the beaker to the top with crushed ice. Place the wire gauze on the ring.

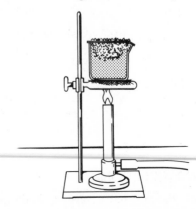

4. Light and adjust the burner.
5. Adjust the height of the ring on the ring stand so the tip of the flame will just touch the wire gauze.
6. Place the burner under the beaker and time it with the stopwatch for 30 seconds.

Measuring

7. At the end of the 30-second interval remove the burner. This will constitute one unit of heat. Stir continuously while heating, and as soon as the burner is removed, take the temperature as quickly as possible. The data should be recorded in a manner similar to the example below.

Sample Data Table

No. of Heat Units	Temperature
0	(initial)
1	
2	
3	
etc.	

8. As soon as the temperature has been read and recorded, replace the burner and add another unit of heat, quickly taking the temperature again. Continue doing this, working as rapidly as possible, until all of the ice has melted and the temperature seems to have risen as far as it will go (until it becomes constant). Make a line graph of the data from the table. Use the following coordinates. (Make the graph on graph paper.)

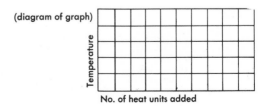

(diagram of graph)

Temperature

No. of heat units added

Inferring	How many units of heat were added before the temperature began to rise?
Inferring	What is the significance of the point at which the temperature begins to rise?
Inferring	What is the significance of the point at which the temperature seems to reach a maximum?
Inferring	What happens to the heat supplied when no temperature change takes place?

OPEN-ENDED QUESTIONS

1. How do you think your results would have varied if you had used sugar or salt water?

SOUND

What Is Sound and
How Is It Produced and Conducted?   (1-3)

CONCEPTS

When an object vibrates, sound may be produced.
Sound may be produced by vibrating a number of different objects.
Sound may be conducted by a number of different objects.

MATERIALS

Teacher's Note: As many of the following things as possible should be placed on the desks of groups of 4 or more children.

Rubber band	4 feet of string	Toothpicks
Alarm clock	Aluminum foil pie pan	Cotton
Bell	6 empty pop bottles	Piece of thick glass
Fork and spoon	Aluminum foil	

DISCUSSION

How could you make a sound with a rubber band?

| Processes | **Pupil Discovery Activity** |

Designing an
investigation

1. How could you make a rubber band produce a sound?
   How was the sound produced?

   Teacher's Note: The children should stretch the rubber band and vibrate it. They should get the idea that the vibration causes the sound.

Rubber band

Hypothesizing

How many ways can you hear sound by placing your ear to the objects you have and causing a sound to occur?

2. Try these different ways.

Hypothesizing

What can you do to stop the noise once the sound is started?

3. Test your ideas.

Observing

4. Determine what materials are better than others to produce sound.

Comparing

In what ways are these materials the same or different?

OPEN-ENDED QUESTIONS

1. How would you produce a loud sound?
2. What would you do to make a room less noisy?

How Does the Length of the
Vibrating Body Affect Sound?   (2-6)

CONCEPTS

Bodies in vibration make a sound.
The longer the vibrating body, the lower the tone.

MATERIALS

Balsa wood strip 12″ long   3 tacks or nails
10 straight pins   Rubber band
Piece of wood approximately 6″ × 6″ × 1″   Hammer

DISCUSSION

What do you think would happen if you vibrated pins set to different depths
in a strip of balsa wood?
Would you get the same sound from each of the pins?
If you think that different pins will give off different tones, which one would
give off the highest tone?

Processes   **Pupil Discovery Activity**

PART I

1. Obtain a balsa strip and set pins in it to varying
depths. (See the diagram below.)

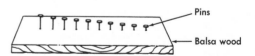

| | Observing | 2. Determine if each vibrating pin gives off the same tone. |

Observing   2. Determine if each vibrating pin gives off the same tone.

Inferring   What relationship is there between pin length and tone?

Hypothesizing   What can you do to make the vibrating pins sound louder?

Hypothesizing   Would nails stuck in balsa wood give the same results as the pins?

PART II

Hypothesizing

Hypothesizing

1. Look at the diagram below.
   Where would you pluck the rubber band to get the highest note?
   Where would you pluck the rubber band to get the lowest note?

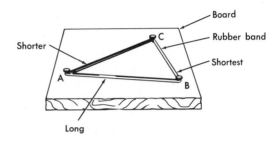

2. Obtain three tacks or nails, a rubber band, and a piece of wood. Pound the tacks or nails into the wood block as shown in the diagram above. Place the rubber band around the tacks or nails.
3. Pluck the rubber band to see if your hypothesis was correct.

Comparing

4. How do the results of Part I compare with the results of Part II?

OPEN-ENDED QUESTIONS

1. What would happen if you plucked rubber bands having the same length but different thicknesses?
2. What would happen to a tone if the vibrating length of the rubber band were kept the same, but different amounts of tension were applied?
3. How does sound travel from the rubber band to your ears?

How Does the Length of an Air Column Affect Sound?   (2-6)

CONCEPTS

The higher the pitch of a note, the more rapid the vibrations of the producing body.

Pitch can be varied by adjusting the depth of an air column.

The higher the water level, the shorter the air column, and the higher the pitch.

MATERIALS

8 identical pop bottles   Medium-sized beaker

DISCUSSION

What would happen if you blew across pop bottles filled with varying amounts of water?

Would a sound be produced?

If sounds were produced, would they all be the same? If not, which would be the highest? the lowest?

Processes   **Pupil Discovery Activity**

1. Fill eight pop bottles with varying amounts of water.

Hypothesizing   What will happen if you blow across the lips of the bottles?

2. Blow across the bottles.

Observing   Do all bottles give off the same sound?

Observing   Which bottle gives off the highest note? the lowest note?

Hypothesizing   How could you make a musical scale out of the pop bottles?

3. Arrange the bottles to make a musical scale.

4. After you have made the musical scale, try to make a harmonizing chord. If you number the lowest note "1" and the highest note "8," what are the numbers of chords?

Inferring   5. What conclusions can you draw concerning the length of an air column and the sound produced?

Hypothesizing   What is the relationship between the length of an air column and a note produced in an open tube?

OPEN-ENDED QUESTIONS

1. How would the results vary if you put the same amount of water in bottles of varying sizes?
2. Does the thickness of the glass in the pop bottle affect the tone produced?
3. Could you produce the same results using test tubes?

How Does a Violin or Cello Work?   (5-6)

CONCEPTS

Tension of string determines pitch.
If the tension is increased, the pitch is raised.
The length of the string determines the pitch.
A thick string will give a lower tone than a thin string if both are the same length.
The longer the string, the lower the tone.

MATERIALS

Cigar box
Strings of equal and varying thicknesses—about 18 inches long (nylon fishing line may be used)
3 thumb tacks
Weights of equal and varying weight—small metal film containers filled with sand can serve this purpose
A small board to serve as a bridge—8 inches long

DISCUSSION

What are some things you know about sound?
If you were to stretch three strings of varying thicknesses across a cigar box and vibrate them by plucking, how would the pitch and tone of the sound vary?

Processes   **Pupil Discovery Activity**

1. Obtain a cigar box, thumb tacks, weights, and strings of varying thickness. Insert the thumb tacks at one end of the box. Tie strings around these tacks.

Tie the weight to the other end of the strings. Place the strings over the box.

Hypothesizing

What do you think will happen when you vibrate each string by plucking it?

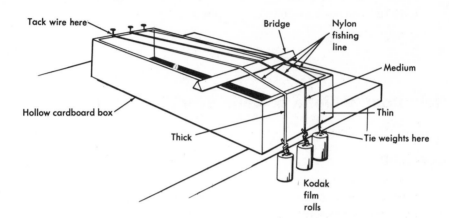

Comparing and Inferring   2. Record which string gave the highest tone. Why?

Comparing and Inferring   3. Which string gave the lowest tone? Why?

Hypothesizing   What do you think would happen to the tone of the string if you were to take a weight off one of the thin strings and add a heavier weight to it?

4. Replace one of the weights with a heavier one.

Inferring   What does increased tension on the string do to the sound?

Hypothesizing   What other ways do you think you could arrange the strings to get different sounds?

5. Place a small triangular ruler under the strings and move it back and forth as you pluck them.

Classifying   What happened to the sound made by the strings?

OPEN-ENDED QUESTIONS

1. What other things could you do to show how sounds can be changed from lower to higher pitch?

2. List some of the different sounds you hear every day and classify them from high to low.
   Why do you think they are high or low?

3. When you listen to a violin or cello, what can you say about how the sounds are produced in these instruments?

What Causes Sound to Be Louder? (K-6)

CONCEPTS

Sound is made when an object vibrates.
Loudness of a sound is caused by an object's vibrating with increased energy,
   but not an increased number of times per second.
The pitch is not changed by increased vibration.

MATERIALS

Tin can   Stick
Piece of rubber large enough   Cork
   to fit over the can

DISCUSSION

What is pitch?
Is pitch affected by the loudness of sound?

Processes   **Pupil Discovery Activity**

1. Make a drum by fitting a piece of rubber over the
   opening of the can. Place the cork on top of the
   drum.

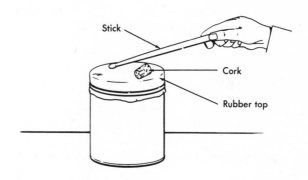

Hypothesizing   What will happen to the cork if you hit the drum
                           lightly?
Observing   2. Hit the drum hard. What happened to the cork?

Hypothesizing

3. What do you think will happen if the drum is hit much harder?

Inferring

4. How did the pitch of the drum change by hitting it harder? Did a change in loudness occur? Why?

OPEN-ENDED QUESTIONS

1. How would you use a piano to show what was demonstrated on the drum about pitch and loudness.
2. How can musicians play loud and soft music and still retain the pitch?

How Do Solids and Liquids Conduct Sounds? (4-6)

CONCEPTS

Sound can travel through solid substances.
Sound can travel through liquid substances.

MATERIALS

2 paper cups	Wooden ruler
12 feet of strong cord	1 bucket
12 feet of steel wire	Water
12 feet of copper wire	2 rocks
1 thick board about 12″ × 4″ × 1″	

DISCUSSION

Have you ever heard people talking when you were in one room and they were in the room next to yours?

How do you suppose you could hear them through the wall?

You know that sound travels, but what substances will sound travel through?

Processes

Pupil Discovery Activity

PART I

1. Obtain two paper cups and 12 feet of string.
2. With a pencil punch a small hole in the bottom of the paper cups just large enough to stick the string through.

3. Stick the ends of the string through each one of the paper cups. Make a knot in the ends of the string so that the string will not be easily pulled from the cups.

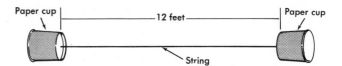

| Hypothesizing | When you talk into one end of the cups, what will happen to the other cup? Why? |

4. Talk into one cup while a student holds the other cup to his ear and listens.

| Designing an investigation | Determine how sound can best be transferred from one cup to the other. |
| Observing | Record what you did to transmit the sound the best. |

| Hypothesizing | 5. How will the sound be conducted if you use copper or steel wire? Try it. |

| Observing | What happened when you used copper wire? |
| Inferring and Comparing | Was the sound carried better through copper wire than through string? Why or why not? |

PART II

1. Obtain a small board and a pencil.
2. Hold a board to your ear. Scratch the other end with a pencil.

| Observing | What happened? |

3. Hold the board away from your ear and repeat the activity.

| Applying | Does sound travel better through a solid or through air? |

PART III

1. Obtain a wooden ruler. Hold it firmly with one hand against a desk. With the other hand pluck the overhanging part of the ruler, causing it to vibrate.

| Hypothesizing | 2. What causes the sound to be produced? |
| Designing an investigation | Produce a high-pitched sound by vibrating the stick. Produce a low-pitched sound by vibrating the stick. |

PART IV

| Hypothesizing | How is sound carried in liquids? |

Designing an
  investigation

How would you find out?

1. Obtain a large bucket full of water. Obtain two pieces of metal or two rocks and hit them together under water.

Inferring

2. Did you hear a sound when you hit them together? Why?

   What is your conclusion about the ability of a liquid to carry sound?

OPEN-ENDED QUESTIONS

1. How far do you think sounds would travel between phones using copper wire, string, and steel wire.

   Design an experiment to see which conducts sound farther.

2. How would you use eight rulers to make a musical scale?

   Think about what you did to get a low pitch and a high pitch.

3. What is the purpose of making musical instruments out of wood?

4. How do you think liquids other than water conduct sounds?

How Can the Reflection of Sound Be Changed?   (3-6)

CONCEPTS

When sound waves hit a hard surface, they may be thrown back.

Sound waves may be taken in and held in much the way a sponge holds water.

Some things absorb sound waves better than others.

MATERIALS

Two large tin cans (about the size of a two-pound coffee can)

Nail

Hammer

About one square foot of cotton cloth

About one square foot of wool cloth

About one square foot of silk

About one square foot of paper

Aluminum foil

Sheet of newspaper

Shoebox with its lid

Alarm clock or small transistor radio

Coat

Sweater

DISCUSSION

What would happen to the sound of your voice if you yelled into a large can?

What would happen to the sound of your voice if you put holes in the end of the can and yelled into it?

What do you think would happen if you put something into the can before yelling into it, for example, a wool cloth?

What would you do to find answers to these questions?

Processes

Pupil Discovery Activity

PART I

1. Obtain two large tin cans about the size of a two-pound coffee can (the larger cans are better), a nail, hammer, several pieces of cloth, newspaper, an alarm clock or small transistor radio, and aluminum foil.

Hypothesizing
What do you think will happen if you yell into one of these cans?

Observing
2. Yell into one can and note what happens.
Inferring
What did you hear?
Inferring
What do you think happened to the sound waves when they hit the end of the can?

3. Take the other can and make six nail holes in the end of it.
Hypothesizing
What do you think will happen to the sound now if you yell into it?

Comparing
4. Yell into the unpunctured can and then into the punctured can and note any differences.

Inferring
Why do you think the sounds coming from each can were not the same?

Hypothesizing
What happened to some of the sound waves in the punctured can?

PART II

1. Take a piece of cotton cloth and put it into the can without holes.
Hypothesizing
What do you think will happen to the sound when you yell into this can?

2. Yell into the can and note what happens.
Inferring
Why did the sound seem different?
Hypothesizing
What do you think will happen to the sound when you use other substances such as newspaper, wool, or aluminum foil?

3. Repeat Steps 1 and 2 in Part II using a different substance each time such as newspaper or wool and note any differences in the sounds produced.
Comparing
What did you notice about the sound produced when you used each of these substances?

4. Obtain an alarm clock or transistor radio and some wool cloth.
Hypothesizing
What do you think will happen to the sound of the alarm clock if it is wrapped in the wool cloth?

5. Turn the alarm clock on with the alarm ringing and wrap it in the wool cloth.

Observing
What happened to the sound of the alarm when the cloth was wrapped around the clock?

6. Repeat Steps 4 and 5 in Part II using a different material each time to wrap the clock in, such as cotton, silk, newspaper, a coat, and a sweater.
Record your observations.

Inferring
Why were the sounds different for each of the articles?

7. Turn on the alarm and place the clock in the shoebox and cover the box with its top.

Inferring
Why doesn't the sound seem as loud?

Hypothesizing
What happens to the sound?

OPEN-ENDED QUESTIONS

1. What kind of surface do you need for sound to reflect well?
2. What suggestions would you make for building an auditorium so that there would be no reflected sound or echoes?
3. What things do you have in your classroom to help reduce noise or reflection of sound?

LIGHT

How Does Light Travel?   (3-6)

CONCEPTS

Light appears to travel in a straight line.

MATERIALS

Round box such as oats come in   Rubber band   Matches
Waxed paper   Candle

DISCUSSION

Teacher's Note: You may help pupils by demonstrating this simple activity and by raising the following questions.

What do you know about light?
How does it seem to travel?
How does a camera work?
In what direction does light travel?

Processes

Pupil Discovery Activity

Teacher's Note: This activity should be done in groups of two. One child will perform the activity for the other pupil and vice-versa.

1. Obtain an oats box, waxed paper, rubber band, candle, and matches. Puncture a small hole in the end of the box with your pencil. Cover the other end of the box with waxed paper and secure the paper with a rubber band. Place the candle in front of the box and light the candle. Darken the room. One student should move the small-holed end back and forth in front of the candle while the other student watches the waxed papered end.

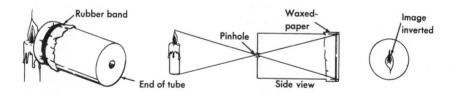

Observing	What appears on the waxed paper?
Observing	What does the image look like on the waxed paper?
Inferring	Why does the image appear this way?
Hypothesizing	Why did the student move the punctured end back and forth?
Inferring	From this activity, what would you conclude about how light travels?
Inferring	How do you think a picture of an object appears on the film in the back of a camera?

OPEN-ENDED QUESTIONS

1. What would happen to the image on the waxed paper if you moved the box two or three feet from the candle?

2. What would happen to the image if you blew the candle flame out? Why?

Teacher's Note: After the children have completed the above activity, place the diagrams below on the board and have the children draw the image of the candle. They should draw something like the first diagram. Discuss how the light travels through the hole as indicated by the second diagram.

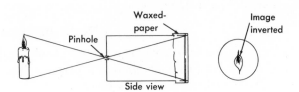

How Is Light Reflected?   (4-8)

CONCEPTS

When light is reflected from a mirror, it is reflected at the same angle as the angle of light hitting the mirror. A physicist would say that the angle of incidence equals the angle of reflection.

MATERIALS

Rubber ball
Mirror

DISCUSSION

How is light refracted?
How is light reflected?
What are some ways that light is reflected?

Processes	**Pupil Discovery Activity**
	1. Obtain a rubber ball and bounce it at an angle against the wall.
Observing	How did the ball bounce away from the wall?
	2. Continue to bounce the ball against the wall, hitting the wall at various angles.
Observing	At what angles does the ball bounce back from the wall?

Hypothesizing	What do you think will happen to light if you shine it onto a reflecting surface in a manner similar to the way you threw the ball?
Comparing	How does the way light reflects off a wall resemble the way a ball bounces off a wall?

3. Hold a mirror so that you can see yourself.
   Where did you have to hold the mirror?
4. How did the light coming from your face reflect so you could see your face?
   Hint: Remember how a ball bounces when you throw it straight against a wall?

Hypothesizing

What will happen if you hold the mirror at an angle?

5. Hold the mirror in front of yourself.
   Move the mirror so that you can see another person or another part of the room.
6. Diagram on a piece of paper your location compared to the mirror. Indicate with arrows how the light comes from the mirror to you.
7. Now hold the mirror at different angles.

Observing and inferring

How is light reflected when you hold the mirror at different angles?

OPEN-ENDED QUESTIONS

1. What things besides mirrors may be used to change the direction of light?
2. How would you make a periscope from mirrors? Tell how it would work.

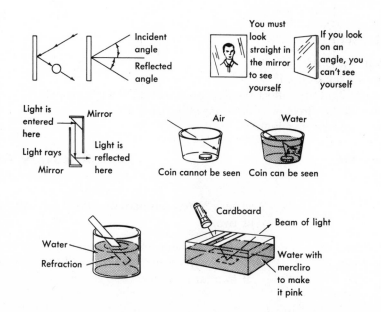

Teacher's Note: To summarize what the children have discovered about light, draw the diagram on page 381 on posterboard by using a felt pen. Hold the charts up and ask the children to explain what is taking place.

How Is Light Changed When It Passes from Air to Water? (3-6)

CONCEPTS

A substance that is curved and transparent can be used as a lens.
Light may be refracted (bent) when it passes through water or glass.

MATERIALS

1 quart jar filled with 16 ounces of water and 8 ounces of cooking oil	Flashlight
	Straw
Pint jar or small aquarium (only one of these is needed for a class)	Black paper
	One-half teaspoon powdered milk
Water	Milk
Ruler	Flashlight
Coin	Sheet of black paper or piece of card-
Shallow pan	board

DISCUSSION

What is a lens?
How are lenses used?
How do light rays affect the appearance of an object in water?
How can the direction of light rays be changed?
How can light rays be bent?

Processes	**Pupil Discovery Activity**
PART I	

Teacher's Note: This activity should be done in groups of two.

| Hypothesizing | How may water serve as a lens? |
| Hypothesizing | How do you think a ruler would look if you placed it in a jar of water? |

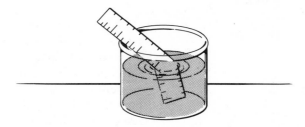

1. Obtain a jar of water and a ruler.
2. Place the ruler in the jar.

Observing

3. Observe the ruler.
   How has the ruler changed in appearance?

PART II

1. Obtain a pan, a small coin, and a jar of water.
   Put the coin in the bottom of a pan. Have a student back away from the pan until the coin just disappears out of his line of sight.

Hypothesizing

How could it be possible for the student to see the coin again without moving?

Designing an experiment

2. Another pupil should gradually fill the pan with water until the pupil observing the pan sees the coin.

Hypothesizing

Why was it easier to see the coin after water was added than it was before?

Applying

What must the water have done to the light rays coming from the coin to your eyes?

Inferring

How was the light bent?

Inferring

What conclusions may be drawn from the activity with the coin and ruler?

Teacher's Note: After the activity you might insert the following diagram and discuss it.

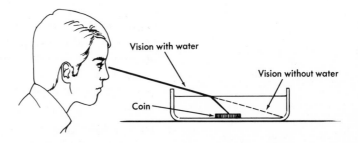

PART III

1. Obtain a glass jar or square aquarium filled with water, a flashlight, a piece of black paper, and a teaspoon of milk.
2. Add just enough milk to the jar or aquarium so that a light beam from a flashlight is visible when passing through the milk.
3. Make a small hole in a piece of black paper.
4. Turn the flashlight on and shine a beam of light through the hole in the black paper into the milky water as shown in the diagram below.

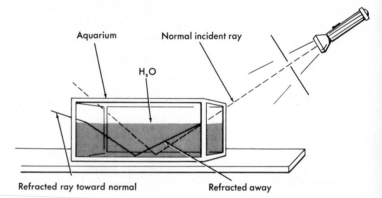

Aquarium   Normal incident ray

H_2O

Refracted ray toward normal   Refracted away

Observing

How is the beam of light refracted (bent) when it enters the water?

5. Have another pupil hold the jar or aquarium off the desk and shine the light through the hole in the paper onto the solution from above as before.

Observing

How does the light beam leaving the bottom of the aquarium or jar look?

Comparing

How does this differ from the way the light behaved when entering the solution?

Teacher's Note: Air is said to be less optically dense than water. This means that when a light beam goes from some less optically dense medium into something more optically dense, it will bend. Oil is optically more dense than water. Do not confuse optical density with the density of a substance. Remember oil is really less physically dense than water because it will float on water.

Hypothesizing

Draw how you think light rays would look when passed through a jar of water containing a layer of oil.

6. Obtain from your teacher a jar of water with oil and determine whether your ideas were correct.

Teacher's Note: When the activity is complete, ask the class to draw on the chalkboard what happened as the light passed through plain water with milk. They should make a diagram something like the following:

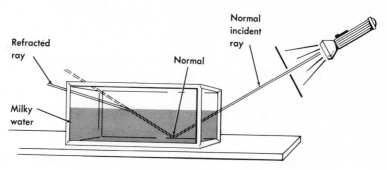

Observing

Discuss how light bends.
How is the light refracted when it leaves the solution?

Teacher's Note: Draw the last two diagrams above on the board after the lesson and explain that when a light ray passes obliquely from one medium into another of greater optical density, it is refracted toward the normal. The normal is defined as a perpendicular line to the plane at a given point.

OPEN-ENDED QUESTIONS

1. Would colored water change the way light rays are reflected from the ruler? What would you do to find out?
2. What other substances could you use to show that light rays may be altered?
3. What would happen if you used a clear plastic glass and rubbing alcohol or vinegar instead of water?

What Does a Prism Do to Light?   (4-6)

CONCEPTS

White light, when passed through a prism, disperses to form a continuous spectrum similar to a rainbow.

White light is a mixture of many colors of light.
Each color in the spectrum has a different wave length.

MATERIALS

A prism

DISCUSSION

What is a prism?
What does a prism do?

| Processes | **Pupil Discovery Activity** |

PART I

Teacher's Note: This activity should be done in groups of two or more children.

1. Obtain a prism.

Hypothesizing
What do you think will happen to the light rays after they pass through the prism?

2. Place the prism in the path of a strong beam of light as indicated in the diagram.

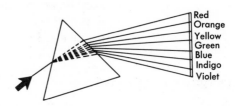

Observing
What does the prism do to the light rays when they pass through it?

Observing
What colors do you see?

Observing
What color seems to have been bent the most?

Observing
Which color has been bent the least?

Inferring
What do you know about the way the different colors of light are refracted (bent) by the prism?

Inferring
What is white light made of?

Teacher's Note: The children should see that white light is produced by the combination of several wave lengths of light. Draw a prism on the board and have the children show how the spectrum is formed.

Their drawing should be something like the previous diagram.

Hypothesizing

What do you think will happen if you look through the prism at your partner?

Experimenting

1. Look through the AB side of the prism at your partner.

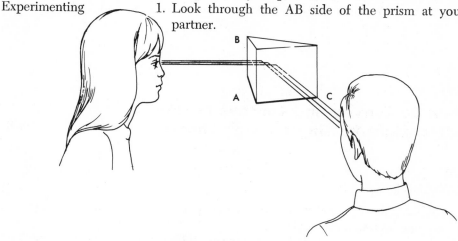

2. Record your observations.

Inferring

Why was it possible to see what your partner was doing without looking directly at him?

Inferring

What happened to the light entering the prism that made it possible for you to see your partner?

Inferring

What did the prism do to the light rays?

Comparing

What is the difference between a prism and a mirror in the way that each affects light?

Teacher's Note: A prism is used in expensive optical equipment instead of mirrors because prisms absorb less light. At the conclusion of the activity, place a diagram of a prism on the board and have the children draw how light passes through it. If they do not understand how a prism can be used in a periscope, draw and discuss the diagram below.

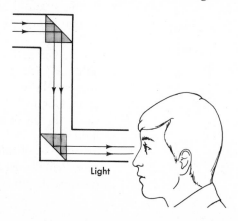

Light

OPEN-ENDED QUESTIONS

1. What happens to X-rays when they pass through a prism?
2. What would happen if you passed light through two prisms?
3. Why are prisms used in expensive optical equipment instead of mirrors?

How Do Convex and Concave Lenses Affect Light Passing through Them? (6-8)

CONCEPTS

When light is passed from a dense to a less dense medium or vice-versa, it may be refracted (bent).
A convex lens may magnify close objects and invert objects far from the lens.
The thicker the lens, the more the light rays will be bent.
Convex lenses converge light rays.
Concave lenses diverge light rays.
Concave lenses make objects look smaller.

MATERIALS

1 convex lens	Paper and pencil
1 concave lens	Cardboard box and a pair of scissors
1 piece of plain glass	Flashlight (or slide projector)

Processes

Hypothesizing

Pupil Discovery Activity

In what ways could you find out if a lens can change the direction of light?

1. Obtain a convex lens, a concave lens, a piece of plain glass, a cardboard box, a pair of scissors, paper and pencil, and a strong light source such as a flashlight or slide projector. Take the cardboard box and cut the top and one end as shown in the diagram. Cut a slit for the light to pass through as indicated in the diagram. Place a projector or strong light source in front of the slit. (A good flashlight may be substituted for the projector.) This apparatus will be used with the lenses and glass to find out how they work.

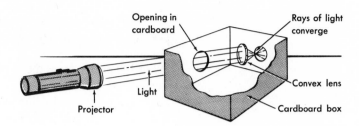

Observing

2. Before using the cardboard box, examine the two lenses and the piece of glass very carefully. Hold them to your eye. Look at the class through them. Have someone look through the other side.

3. Compare what you saw through each of the three lenses.

Comparing

How did the objects differ?

4. Take the convex lens and move it slowly away from your eye.

Observing
Inferring
Hypothesizing

What happens as you move the lens away?

Why do you think this happens?

What could you do to find out the reason for what happens?

Teacher's Note: The image becomes inverted. This happens because as the lens is moved away from the eye, it reaches a point where the distance is greater than the focal length of the lens, and the image becomes inverted as a result. (The focal length is the distance from a lens or a mirror to the point where rays of light are brought together to form an image.) When a student first looks at another student through a convex lens, the student appears right-side up. As the student moves the lens away from his eye so that it is at a greater distance than the focal length of the lens, the student he is looking at becomes inverted as shown in the diagram.

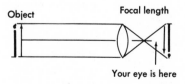

5. Take the concave lens now and place it near your eye and move it slowly away like you did the convex lens.

Observing
What happens as you move the lens back and forth in front of your eye?

Comparing
What did you see in the two lenses that differed from what you saw with the plain glass?

Hypothesizing
What do you think will happen when you shine light through the lenses and flat piece of glass onto a surface?

6. Hold the plain piece of glass inside your box as indicated by the diagram.

Observing
What happened to the light?

Observing
What effect, if any, did the box have on the lens?

Collecting data
7. Draw a side view of the lens light when it passes through the glass onto the cardboard.

8. Repeat this step but substitute the concave and convex lenses for the plain glass.

Teacher's Note: In a convex lens the edges are always thinner than the center. When light passes through a convex lens, it converges as shown in the diagram.

Convex converges light

The edges of a concave lens are always thicker than the center, and light is diverged by this type of lens as shown in the diagram.

Concave diverges light

9. Observe your lenses again.

Comparing
How does the shape of the concave lens differ from that of the convex lens?

Comparing
In what ways does the shape of the plain lens differ from the convex and concave lenses?

Comparing
In what way does the light passing through the convex lens differ from the light passing through the concave lens?

Inferring
What evidence do you have to support the statement that a converging lens may cause light to approach a single point?

Teacher's Note: Draw the diagrams from the previous
page on the board and discuss them.

OPEN-ENDED QUESTIONS

1. What proof is there that light can be refracted (bent) by lenses?
2. If you wanted to start a fire and had no matches, which lens could you use and why?
3. How might fires be started by old bottles lying in dry grass?
4. What kind of lenses do you have in your eyes?
5. Why do some people have to wear glasses?

Why Do You Need Two Eyes?   (2-6)

CONCEPTS

To judge the third dimension adequately (depth and distance), you need two
eyes.

Two eyes are needed to see well, especially to see how far away things are
and how high or low they are.

MATERIALS

Table or desk lower than waist high
Pop bottle
Nickel or object similar in size and thickness

Processes	**Pupil Discovery Activity**
Hypothesizing	What do you suppose will happen if you try to flip a coin standing on end out of a bottle using only one eye? (See diagram.)

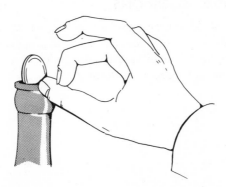

Organizing	1. Obtain the following materials: a pop bottle, a nickel from the teacher (or your own). Be sure to work on a table or desk that you have to look down upon. This is below your eye level.
Observing	2. Place the coin in the pop bottle on the desk; walk 10 to 15 feet away from the table in any direction. Facing the table, cover one eye with your right hand. With the left hand held waist high, walk toward the table at a normal pace. When you reach the bottle, flip the coin without hesitation with your free hand. Do not just push the coin off the pop bottle, but flip it with your finger. (See diagram.)
Observing	What happened to the coin?

Teacher's Note: Most people will not flip the coin out of the bottle because they cannot locate it easily. One cannot judge depth and distance well with only one eye.

	3. Repeat the activity again. Follow Step 3 very carefully, only this time cover your eye with your left hand and use your right hand to flip the coin.
Observing	What happened to the coin this time?
Inferring	Did changing hands make any difference?
Comparing	How did this differ from the first time?
Hypothesizing	What would happen if you repeated the activity again, only this time using both eyes?
	4. Repeat it and use both eyes.
Observing	What happened to the coin this time?
Inferring	Why do you think using both eyes is better? Explain your answer.
Inferring	5. What effect does repeating this activity have on how accurately you can flip the coin?

OPEN-ENDED QUESTIONS

1. What do you suppose would happen if the room were darkened a little while doing this activity? Explain your answer.
2. Why does a man usually aim a rifle with one eye closed?
3. What are optical illusions?

MECHANICS

Why Use a Single Fixed Pulley?   (4-8)

CONCEPTS

A single fixed pulley has no positive mechanical advantage, but it can be used to move an object in one direction while pulling in the opposite direction.

If a pulley is attached to a beam and does not move, it is called a fixed pulley. The mechanical advantage (M.A.) of a pulley is computed by using the formula

$$\text{M.A.} = \frac{\text{Resistance}}{\text{Effort}} \quad \text{or} \quad \text{M.A.} = \frac{\text{Number of strands holding up the resistance}}{\text{Number of strands holding up the effort}}$$

MATERIALS

Single fixed pulley   One 50-gram weight
Pull-type scale   One 100-gram weight

DISCUSSION

What do you think will happen if you attach a weight and a scale to the ends of a pulley and attempt to move the weight?

How will the scale be affected when you raise the weight?

Processes   **Pupil Discovery Activity**

1. Obtain a single fixed pulley, a pull-type scale, and a 50-gram weight. When assembled, your equipment should be similar to the diagram at the top of p. 394.

2. Pull the scale, lift the weight, and record your observations.

Inferring

Why did the scale measure more force than the weight being lifted?

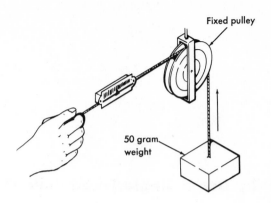

Fixed pulley

50 gram weight

Hypothesizing Inferring Measuring	What do you think happened to the extra force? Why should the activity be done more than once? 3. Complete the activity several times and record each measurement. 4. Compute the average measurement. The formula listed below is used to compute mechanical advantage:

$$\text{Mechanical Advantage (M.A.)} = \frac{\text{Resistance weight}}{\text{Effort weight}}$$

Inferring	Where in the formula will you use the measurement recorded from the scale?
Applying	Where in the formula will you use the gram weight used in the activity? 5. Compute the mechanical advantage of a single fixed pulley as used in your activity.
Applying	What can you tell about the M.A. of the pulley in the following diagram?

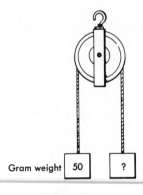

Gram weight   50   ?

Hypothesizing	What would you have to do in the situation shown in the next diagram to keep the weight in place?

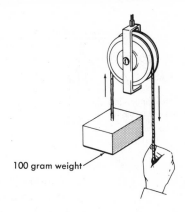

100 gram weight

Summarizing   What are the advantages in using the single fixed
                           pulley?

OPEN-ENDED QUESTIONS

1. How would you make a single fixed pulley so that it produced very little
   friction?

Why Use a Movable Pulley?   (6-8)

CONCEPTS

Pulleys that move with the resistance are called movable pulleys.
Movable pulley systems have a mechanical advantage greater than one.
The mechanical advantage of a movable pulley system is equal to the num-
   ber of strands holding up the resistance.

MATERIALS

A ring stand for attaching pulleys   One 100-gram weight
Two single pulleys   One 50-gram weight
Pull-type scale   Yard or metric stick

Processes   **Pupil Discovery Activity**

1. Obtain a ring stand and a clamp for attaching a
   pulley, a single pulley, a pull-type scale, and a 100-
   gram weight. Assemble your equipment as shown
   in the diagram at the top of p. 395.

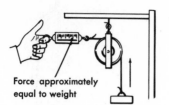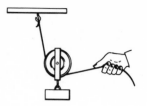

Force approximately
equal to weight

Hypothesizing	How much do you think you will have to pull on the scale to raise the 100-gram weight?
	2. Pull on the scale and raise the weight.
Observing	How was the scale affected when you raised the weight?
Measuring	3. Repeat this activity several times and record each measurement.
Hypothesizing	What do you think will happen when you use two pulleys to raise the 100-gram weight as shown in the diagram below?
	4. In addition to the equipment you have, obtain a single fixed pulley and a 50-gram weight. Assemble your equipment as shown in the diagram.
Observing	5. Pull the 50-gram weight and record your observations.

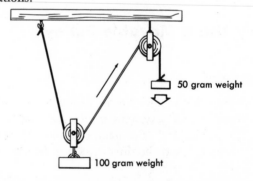

50 gram weight

100 gram weight

	6. Remove the 50-gram weight and attach the scale. Your equipment should be constructed as shown in the diagram on p. 397.
Hypothesizing	How will the scale be affected when you raise the 100-gram weight?
	7. Raise the weight by pulling on the scale.
Observing	What happened to the scale when you raised the weight?
Measuring	8. Repeat the activity several times and record each measurement.
Inferring	Why is there an advantage in using this type of pulley system?

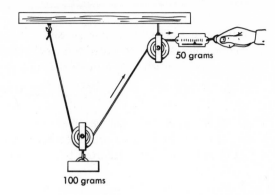

50 grams

100 grams

9. Remove the scale and once again attach the 50-gram weight.

Hypothesizing   How far do you think the 50-gram weight will move when it raises the 100-gram weight?

Hypothesizing   How far do you think the 100-gram weight moves when it is raised by the 50-gram weight?

10. Obtain a yard or metric stick.

Observing   11. Move the 50-gram weight and measure how far both the weights moved.

Measuring   12. Repeat this part of the activity several times and record your measurements.

Summarizing   What can you say about pulleys from the measurements you just recorded?

13. Look at the measurements you recorded when 1 pulley was used and those you recorded when 2 pulleys were used.

What does the information tell you about pulleys?

OPEN-ENDED QUESTIONS

1. What kind of pulley system would be needed to raise a piano weighing 300 pounds?

Draw a sketch of that pulley system.

Why Use a Lever?   (6-8)

CONCEPTS

A lever is a simple machine.

A lever cannot work alone.

A lever consists of a bar which is free to turn on a pivot called the fulcrum.

By using a first-class lever, it is possible to increase a person's ability to lift heavier objects. This is called the mechanical advantage.

The mechanical advantage of a lever is determined by the formula:

$$\text{M.A.} = \frac{\text{Effort Arm}}{\text{Resistance Arm}}$$

The weight times the distance on one side of the fulcrum must equal the weight times the distance on the other side if the lever is balanced.

A first-class lever has the fulcrum between the resistance and the effort.

MATERIALS

Roll of heavy string   20-gram weight
One ruler   Assorted weights of various sizes
100-gram weight   Platform with an arm for suspending objects

Teacher's Note: Define *resistance, force,* and *fulcrum* before beginning the activity.

Processes   **Pupil Discovery Activity**

1. Obtain some heavy string, a ruler, a 100-gram weight, a 20-gram weight, a ring stand, and a ring clamp.

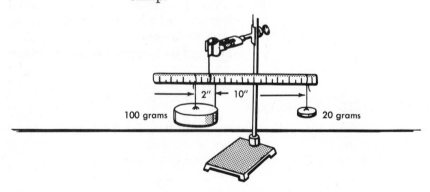

2. Assemble the apparatus as shown in the diagram. Where do you think you should attach the 100-gram weight and the 20-gram weight so the ruler will balance?

Hypothesizing

3. Attach the weights so that the ruler is balanced. How far is the 100-gram weight from the end of the ruler?

Observing

How far is the 20-gram weight from the end of the ruler?

Observing

4. Look at these 3 things: the string, which is suspending the ruler, the 20-gram weight, and the 100-gram
   weight.

Inferring   What is the relationship between the weight and
                   distance on each side of the fulcrum?

Inferring   What are the advantages of using a first-class lever
                   of this type?

5. Use the formula listed below to calculate the mechanical advantage (M.A.) of the lever.

$$\text{M.A.} = \frac{\text{Effort Arm}}{\text{Resistance Arm}}$$

Teacher's Note: At the completion of the activity, explain to the class that a first-class lever consists of a
bar which is free to turn on a pivot point called the
fulcrum. The weight moved is called the resistance.
The force exerted on the other end of the lever is
called the effort. Draw the diagram below on the
board to illustrate this point. State that in a first-class
lever, the fulcrum is always between the resistance
and the effort. Have the children do some different problems as suggested by the formula:
$\text{M.A.} = \dfrac{\text{Effort Arm}}{\text{Resistance Arm}}$. Use metric measurements,
if possible.

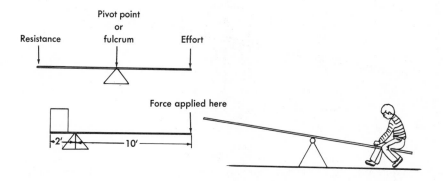

OPEN-ENDED QUESTIONS

1. How is the M.A. affected when different weights are used?
2. What does a M.A. of 4 mean?
3. Where are first-class levers used?

How Does a Second-Class Lever Work? (4-6)

CONCEPTS

In a second-class lever, the weight is located between the effort and the fulcrum.

The closer the resistance is to the fulcrum, the less the effort required to move the lever.

Teacher's Note: This lesson should follow the first-class lever activity.

MATERIALS

Board for a lever—a ruler will do
Triangular block of wood
Rock
Pull-type scale
Yard or metric stick

DISCUSSION

How is the lever in the diagram below different from a first-class lever?

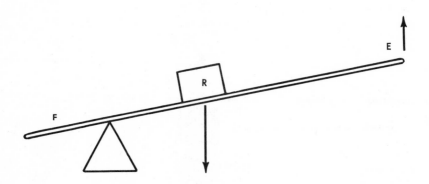

Where do you think the effort and the resistance are in the diagram?

You used a formula when working with the first-class lever in the last activity. What do you think the mechanical advantage will be with this type of lever?

Processes

Pupil Discovery Activity

1. Obtain a lever, a block of wood, and a rock. Assemble your equipment as indicated in the diagram on p. 401.

Hypothesizing   What would you do to determine the effort needed
                       to move the rock?
                    2. Obtain a pull-type scale and attach it to the end
                       of the lever farthest from the fulcrum and raise the
                       rock by lifting the scale.

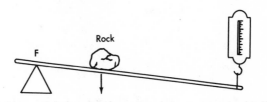

Observing   How was the scale affected when you raised the
                       rock?
Hypothesizing   What do you think the distance of the rock from
                       the fulcrum has to do with how much effort is
                       needed to raise the rock?
Designing an   What should you do to find out?
  investigation
                    3. Test your ideas.
Hypothesizing   What do you think would happen if a lighter rock
                       were used?
                       How would the amount of effort needed change?

OPEN-ENDED QUESTIONS

1. How could a yard stick be used to obtain additional information in the
   above activity?
2. What are some examples of second-class levers?
3. How are second-class levers useful?
4. Which of the following are second-class levers and why?

   a. crowbar
   b. nutcracker
   c. ice tongs
   d. bottle opener
   e. balance
   f. teeter-totter

5. What advantage is there to having long rather than short handles on a
   wheelbarrow?
6. Where is it easiest to crack a nut with a nutcracker and why?

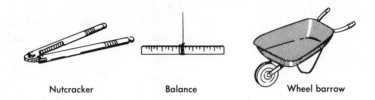

Nutcracker   Balance   Wheel barrow

How Does a Third-Class Lever Work?   (4-8)

CONCEPTS

In a third-class lever the effort is always between the resistance and the fulcrum.

Third-class levers make it possible to multiply distance at the expense of force.

The mechanical advantage of a third-class lever is always less than one.

MATERIALS

Ring stand	Spring scale	Scissors
Ring clamp	String	Ice tongs
Meter stick	200-gram weight	Ice cubes

DISCUSSION

How many types of levers have you learned about?

What are some examples of each type?

How many types of levers are there?

Teacher's Note: This activity should be done in groups of two.

Processes

Pupil Discovery Activity

1. Obtain a ring stand, ring clamp, meter stick, spring scale, 2 feet of string, 200-gram weight, and a pair of scissors.
2. Assemble the equipment as shown in the next diagram by fastening the end of the meter stick to the ring clamp. With the string at 10 cm., tie a loop of

string around the meter stick at the 95-cm. mark. Slip the hook of the 200-gram weight over the bottom of the loop. Slip the hook of the spring scale under the meter stick at the 50-cm. mark.

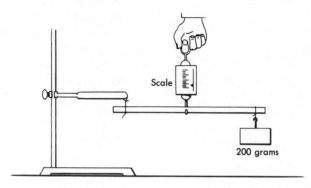

Inferring

What kind of a machine do you have?
How do you know?

Comparing

What is different about this machine compared to others you have studied? Refer to the diagram below for help.

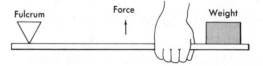

Hypothesizing

What effect will the arrangement have on the force necessary to lift a weight?

3. Using this arrangement and the scale, determine the effort necessary to support the weight as shown in the diagram.

4. Do this two or three times by moving the position of the 200-gram weight. Note the lengths of the effort resistance arms in each case. (Be sure the spring balance remains between the fulcrum and the load.)

Inferring

What do you conclude about the effort required to lift a load with a lever of this type?

Inferring

What can you say about the mechanical advantage of this kind of lever?

5. Calculate the force that should be necessary to support the weight in each case you tested by using the

lengths of resistance and the effort arms. In order to do this, use the following formula:

$$\text{Resistance} \times \text{Resistance Arm} = \text{Effort} \times \text{Effort Arm}$$

Inferring

Do these figures agree closely with those obtained experimentally in Part I? If not, what are the reasons for the difference?

6. Obtain some ice tongs and a piece of ice.
7. Pick up the piece of ice.

Observing and Inferring   8. What type of lever are the ice tongs, and why?

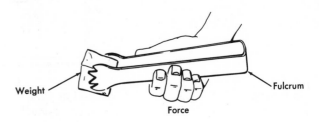

Weight   Fulcrum

Force

OPEN-ENDED QUESTIONS

1. For what purpose is a third-class lever used?
2. Mark in front of each of the following what class lever each represents:

    a. _____ sugar tongs
    b. _____ tweezers
    c. _____ scissors
    d. _____ human forearm
    e. _____ crowbar
    f. _____ nutcracker
    g. _____ wheelbarrow

3. What examples of first-class levers do you find in school yards?
4. What machines may consist of two levers?
5. What advantage is there in using pliers?
6. What advantage is there in using a rake?
7. What kind of a lever would you have had if, in your experimental procedure, you had placed the spring scale beyond the weight?
8. A shovel is often used in two different ways: to dig and to throw material. What class lever does the shovel represent when used to dig?
9. What class lever is represented in the action of throwing with your arm?
10. How could you change the experimental procedure in Part I and find the answers to the same questions? (Remember not to change it in such a way that you would no longer have a third-class lever.)

Why Use an Inclined Plane?   (6-8)

CONCEPTS

Inclined planes are used for moving objects which are too heavy to lift directly.

The work done by moving an object up an inclined plane is equal to the weight of the object times the height of the plane.

Resistance × the Height of the plane = Effort × the Length of the plane

An inclined plane is one example of a simple machine.

MATERIALS

Smooth board 4' long by 6" wide   Block with screw eye in one end or a
Support block 4" by 8"   rubber band wrapped around it to be
Spring scale   pulled by a scale

DISCUSSION

What is an inclined plane?
Why use an inclined plane?
Where are there inclined planes on the school grounds?

Processes

Pupil Discovery Activity

1. Obtain a smooth 4' long by 6" wide board, support block 4" by 8", spring balance, and a block with a screw eye.

2. Take the 4' long board and place the 4" by 8" block under one end so that the end of the board is raised 4". Place the block with the screw eye in it on the inclined board as shown in the diagram. Slip the hook of the spring scale through the eye of the block.

Hypothesizing

What force do you think will be required to pull the block? Will it be greater or less than the weight of the block? Why?

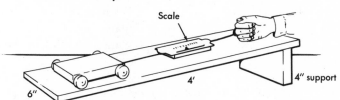

Scale   4" support

4'

6"

Measuring

3. Slowly and evenly, pull the scale and block up the board.
4. Record the amount of force needed to pull the weight up the board. Do this several times, and record your observations.
   Using the data obtained, determine the average force required to pull the weight.
5. Repeat the activity, but this time make the inclined plane steeper by changing the support block so that its 8″ dimension is under the end of the board.

Measuring

6. Again find the average force needed to pull the weight up the board.

Comparing

How do the two forces compare?

Applying

7. Lift the weight straight up, as shown in the diagram. Repeat this several times and find the average of the readings.

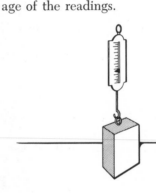

8. The following formula is used to calculate the force needed to move a weight up an inclined plane:

Resistance × Resistance distance =
Effort × Effort distance

Inferring

Use this formula to calculate the force that should have been necessary to move the weight up the inclined plane.

Inferring

Why don't the experimental results and the calculated results agree exactly?

Hypothesizing

What can you say about the amount of force required as an inclined plane becomes steeper?

Hypothesizing

What is the advantage of having a long inclined plane rather than a short inclined plane if both planes are the same height?

OPEN-ENDED QUESTIONS

1. Why don't roads go straight up and down mountains?
2. Which of the following examples is an inclined plane?

a. _____ ramp
b. _____ hill
c. _____ gangplank
d. _____ stairway
e. _____ wedge
f. _____ head of an axe

3. A man moved a 100-pound safe up an inclined plane 20′ long and 2′ high. How much effort did he have to use to move the safe?

Why Use a Jack?   (4-6)

CONCEPTS

A screw is an inclined plane wrapped around a rod.
As with an inclined plane, force is gained at the expense of distance.
A large weight can be moved by a small force if the smaller force is applied over a greater distance.

MATERIALS

Triangular pieces of paper	Screwdriver	Nail
Pencil	Tape measure	Several screws
Ring clamp	Model of a hill	Colored pencil or crayon
Hammer	Board	

DISCUSSION

Teacher's Note: Show the class several examples of screws and ask the following questions:

What are these called?
What purpose do they serve?
Where are they in the classroom?
What advantage do they have over nails?
What type of machine studied thus far resembles a screw?

Teacher's Note: A screw is a circular inclined plane.

Processes   **Pupil Discovery Activity**

1. Obtain a small piece of paper and cut it in the shape of a triangle as shown in the next diagram. The paper will wind around the pencil. Color the edge of the paper so you can see it.

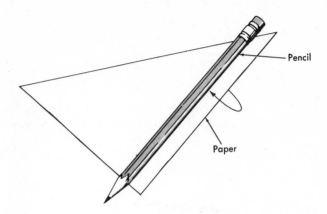

Observing	What kind of machine did the paper represent before you rolled it around the pencil?
Observing	What kind of machine did the paper represent after you rolled it around the pencil?
Comparing	How are the screw and the inclined plane related?

2. Obtain a ring stand clamp and insert a pencil as shown in the diagram below.

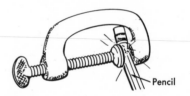

Hypothesizing	What do you think will happen to the pencil when you move the screw inward?
Hypothesizing	How much effort will have to be applied to break the pencil?

Jack

3. Look at the diagram of the jack.

Communicating	Describe how the jack works.
Comparing	How is the jack similar to a screw?
Inferring	What is the purpose of using a jack on a car?

Inferring   How is it possible for a man who weighs 150 pounds
                             to lift a car weighing 3000 pounds with a jack?

OPEN-ENDED QUESTIONS

1. When are jacks used in a barber shop?
2. Where else are jacks used?
3. How many seconds would a man have to exert a force to raise a car a small distance?
4. What machine is involved in a spiral notebook?
5. If you were asked to push a heavy rock to the top of a hill, how would you move it up the hill?

What Is the Advantage of Using a Wheel and Axle?   (5-8)

CONCEPTS

A wheel is a simple machine that aids in moving an object.

Every wheel has an axle. The wheel is used to turn the axle or the axle is used to turn the wheel.

The work obtained from a simple machine is equal to the work put into it less the work used in overcoming friction.

A small effort applied to a large wheel can be used to overcome a large resistance on a small wheel.

A wheel and an axle usually consist of a large wheel to which a small axle is firmly attached.

The mechanical advantage is equal to the radius of the wheel divided by the radius of the axle.

MATERIALS

1 bicycle per class	1 nail	5 or 6 round pencils
1 board	Rubber bands	One of the following: can opener, egg
1 hammer	Balance weight	beater, or meat grinder
1 screw hook	4 spools	

Processes   **Pupil Discovery Activity**

PART I

Hypothesizing   1. In what way does the wheel help to move objects?
                             2. Obtain a screw hook. Turn the hook into the end

of a block of wood. Attach a rubber band to the
hook (spring balance can be used) and measure the
stretch of the rubber band as you drag the block
on the floor. Use a wooden ruler and make a measurement just before and after the block begins to
move.

Measuring   Record all your measurements.
Observing   3. With the rubber band on your finger, lift the block
                 into the air and measure the stretch.
Observing   4. What change was made in the stretch of the rub-
                 ber band?
              5. Now place two round pencils underneath the block
                 and measure the stretch of the rubber band just
                 before and after the block begins to move.

Observing   6. What happened to the stretch of the rubber band
                 this time?
Comparing   7. What difference did the pencils make underneath
                 the wood when you were moving it?
Comparing   8. How did your measurement change?
Inferring   9. What do you suppose is the purpose of measuring
                 the movement of the block of wood?
Observing   10. Try the experiment again, only this time use four
                 spools for the wheels and round pencils for the

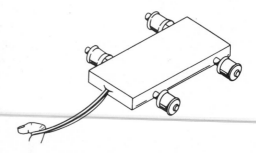

axles. Place the wood on the axle. Observe what happens as you push the block of wood very gently.

Measuring

Measure the stretch of the rubber band as you pull the block of wood.

Comparing

11. What difference was there in the stretch of the rubber band this time compared to moving the board without wheels?

PART II

1. Obtain a small wheel and axle or use a pencil sharpener, meat grinder, or can opener.

Hypothesizing

What is the advantage of using a wheel and an axle?

2. Hook a weight to the axle as shown in the following diagram.

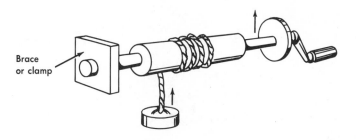

Brace or clamp

Hypothesizing

What do you think will be gained if a large wheel is turned to move a small axle?

3. Turn the large wheel.
4. Count the number of turns you make to raise the weight two inches.

Teacher's Note: A small force applied to a large wheel can be used to move a large resistance attached to the axle. This is done, however, at the expense of distance, since the large wheel has to be moved a great distance to raise the resistance a short way.

PART III

1. Observe a bicycle.

Inferring

Where on a bicycle is friction used to advantage? How is the bicycle wheel constructed to help reduce friction?

Teacher's Note: The wheel produces less friction because there is less of its surface coming in contact with pavement than if a weight such as a person were pulled along a surface.

Observing

2. Where are the wheels and axles on a bicycle?
   When you ride a bicycle where do you apply the force?

Inferring

Why do you apply the force to the small wheel?

Teacher's Note: The effort is applied to the small wheel in order to gain speed. You move the small sprocket with a great force a short distance, and it, in turn, moves the large wheel a greater distance but with less force. Look at the diagrams of the following objects. Write below each of the diagrams whether they increase the ability to move heavier objects or increase the speed.

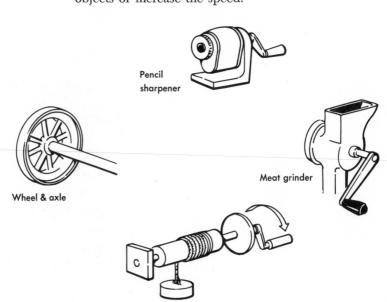

Pencil sharpener

Wheel & axle

Meat grinder

OPEN-ENDED QUESTIONS

1. Pulling an object across the table produced a force.
   How can you tell whether or not you applied a greater amount of force by pulling the board without pencils under it or by using the pencils as axles?

Teacher's Note: A spring scale can be substituted for the rubber band. If you have a balance, you can determine how many pounds of force you need to pull the board across the table. If you use a rubber band you must calculate how far the rubber band stretches. The rubber band will not stretch as much the first time.

2. How are roller bearings and ball bearings used?
3. A boy wants to move a heavy desk drawer across his room to another shelf. How will he go about doing this with the least amount of effort and the greatest amount of speed?

MAGNETISM AND ELECTRICITY

What Is a Magnet?   (K-6)

CONCEPTS

A magnet has two poles. One end is called the north, and the other is called the south.

Like poles repel.

Unlike poles attract.

Around every magnet is an area called the magnetic field made up of magnetic lines of force.

MATERIALS

2 round bar magnets	Cork	Water
String	Glass or plastic pan	2 rectangular bar magnets
Steel needle		

Teacher's Note: Materials listed are for a group of two or three children. Set up stations and equip each as indicated above.

DISCUSSION

Teacher's Note: Display a round bar magnet to the class.

What is this called?
What is it made of?
How can it be used?

What are the properties or characteristics of a magnet?
What things can a magnet do?
What do you think will happen if two magnets are placed side by side?
How could you find out?

Processes

Pupil Discovery Activity

PART I

1. Obtain 2 round magnets. Place one magnet on the
   table. Place the second magnet near it.

Observing
   Observe what happens.

2. Reverse one of the magnets.

Observing
   Observe what happens.
   What happened when you put the second magnet
   beside the first one?
   What happened when you turned one magnet
   around?
   Why do you think one magnet rolled when the
   other came near it?
   What did you notice when the magnets pulled
   together?
   What did you notice when the magnets pushed
   apart?

Inferring
   How do you know from this that both ends of the
   magnet are not the same?

Inferring
   What did you do to make the magnets push apart?

Inferring
   What did you do to make the magnets pull together?

PART II

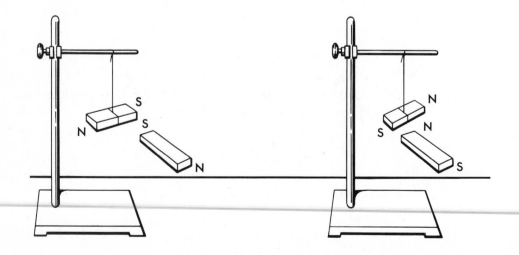

1. Obtain two rectangular or round bar magnets.
2. Tie a string around the middle of one of the magnets.
3. By holding the string, suspend the magnet in air.

Hypothesizing What do you think will happen when another magnet is brought near the suspended one?

4. Bring another magnet near the suspended one.

Inferring Why do you think the magnet moves?

Hypothesizing What do you think will happen when you reverse the magnet in your hand?

Observing 5. Reverse the magnet and bring it near the suspended magnet.

Inferring Why did the suspended magnet react differently when you approached it with the other end of the magnet in your hand?

Inferring What causes the magnet to react in different ways?

Inferring How do you know there is a force present when it cannot be seen?

Explaining What is a force?

Teacher's Note: Point out to the class that a force is a push or a pull. This can be demonstrated by pushing or pulling a child in a chair.

PART III

1. Obtain a steel needle, a magnet, and a pan with an inch or two of water in it.

Hypothesizing What can you find out about the needle and the magnet?

2. Magnetize a needle by holding a magnet in one hand and stroking a needle downward several times. Insert the needle in the cork so the needle is in a vertical position. Float it in the water you have placed in a pan.

3. Bring a magnet near the cork and needle.

Inferring Why do the cork and needle move when you bring a magnet near them?

Inferring What happened to the needle when it was stroked with the magnet?

Summarizing What caused the cork and needle to move?

OPEN-ENDED QUESTIONS

1. How does a compass work?
2. How could you use a magnet to make a compass?

What Is a Magnetic Field?   (K-3)

CONCEPTS

Around every magnet there is an area where the magnet can change the direction of iron filings. This is called the magnetic field.

Not every part of the magnetic field around a magnet is the same.

MATERIALS

A bar magnet   Some string
A paper clip   3 books

DISCUSSION

What happens when a magnet is brought near a steel object?
Why doesn't the magnet have to touch the object to move it?
What causes the object to move when a magnet comes near?
What part of the magnet has the most pull?
How can you show there is a force around a magnet?

Processes   **Pupil Discovery Activity**

1. Obtain a paper clip, some string, heavy books, and a magnet.
2. Tie the string around one end of the paper clip.
3. Put the other end of the string on the table and put a heavy book or two on it.
4. Hold up the string and paper clip. Place the magnet just above the paper clip and place another book on it. Be sure the clip and magnet do not touch as indicated in the diagram.

Magnetic field
Paper clip
String

Observing   5. What happens to the clip when you let go of it?
Inferring   Why does the paper clip stay suspended?
Inferring   Why doesn't gravity pull the clip down again?
Inferring   What force overcame gravity?

6. Bring another magnet close to the clip.

Observing — What happened to the clip?

Inferring — Why do you think this happened?

Inferring — How did the second magnet affect the pull of the first magnet?

Teacher's Note: The children should discover that around every magnet there is an area capable of attracting or repelling objects. This area is called the magnetic field.

OPEN-ENDED QUESTIONS

1. Where is the field of force of a magnet?
2. How could you find out where the field is?

How Does a Magnetic Field Look? (3-6)

CONCEPTS

Around every magnet there is an area where the magnet can change the direction of iron filings. This is called the magnetic field.

In a magnetic field there are magnetic lines of force.

The earth has a magnetic field.

The concentration of the lines of force around any part of the magnet determines the strength of the field at that point.

Magnetism will pass through solid objects.

MATERIALS

Bar magnet

Piece of cardboard or thick paper

Iron filings

Colored pencil or crayon

DISCUSSION

What do you call the area of force around a magnet?

What parts of the magnet attract objects with the greatest pull?

Why doesn't a magnet need to touch a magnetic object to attract it?
What part of a magnet do you think has the greatest field of force around it?
What can you do to show where most of the force is located around a magnet?

Teacher's Note: Make a study sheet for the children to use in showing lines of force and the magnetic field similar to the diagram above. Have them label the poles, magnetic lines of force, and magnetic field.

Processes	**Pupil Discovery Activity**
PART I	

1. Obtain some cardboard or thick paper, some iron filings, a colored pencil or crayon, and a bar magnet.
2. Place the magnet on the table and put the paper or cardboard over it.
3. Sprinkle some iron filings on the cardboard.

Observing — How are the filings scattered around the cardboard?

Inferring — How far out are the filings affected by the magnet? What do you notice about the way the filings arranged themselves?

Observing — Are the filings in lines or are they solidly grouped?

Observing — Where is the greatest concentration of filings?

These lines are called magnetic lines of force.

Comparing — In what way is the pattern that these lines make similar to a map?

Inferring — Where is the greatest force located around a magnet and why?

Teacher's Note: The iron filings have become magnetized by induction. They organize themselves into little magnets which point north and south and which are arranged in lines. These are called magnetic lines of force. They run from the north to the south pole without crossing. The more lines of force there are in an area, the stronger the magnetic field. Since the ends of the magnet have the most lines, they have the greatest force.

How is the earth's magnetic field distributed?
What similarities can you think of concerning a magnet and the earth?

Teacher's Note: Make mimeographed lab sheets showing lines of earth's field of force and magnetic field similar to the diagram below and hand it out to the children to discuss.

In what direction does a compass point?

Inferring — Why does a compass point north?

Designing an investigation How can you show the lines of force of the earth's field?

Hypothesizing How do you think the lines should be placed around the earth?

Assuming How do you know that the earth has a magnetic pole?

Hypothesizing Where should the magnetic poles be placed? How can you show this?

PART II

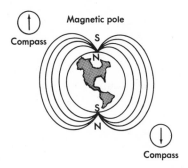

1. Obtain a lab sheet showing the earth.
2. Label the poles of the earth.
3. Color the magnetic field.
4. Label the magnetic lines of force.
5. Show the direction a compass will point on the lab sheet.

Summarizing What pole of the magnet of a compass will really point north?

Inferring or interpreting Why does that end of the compass needle point north?

Summarizing What can you say will always happen to the needle of a compass in reference to the poles of the earth?

Summarizing What other things can you say about the magnetic field?

Inferring How do you know that magnetism can pass through solid substances?

Summarizing 6. Draw on a piece of paper the lines of force and the magnetic field of a bar or round magnet.

OPEN-ENDED QUESTIONS

1. How does the magnetism of other planets vary from the earth's?
2. What else do you know of that has a north and a south pole?

What Is Static Electricity?   (4-6)

CONCEPTS

All bodies are capable of producing electrical charges.
Conductors allow electrons to move, but insulators do not allow electrons to
  move easily.
Like charges repel; unlike charges attract.

MATERIALS

Lucite or resin rod or   Glass rod   Tap water
  a hard rubber comb   Small pieces of paper Piece of silk about the size
Wool   Large piece of paper   of a small handkerchief
Flour   Balloon

DISCUSSION

What can you state about the reactions of poles of magnets toward one
  another?
What is the energy that we use to produce light and to operate many machines
  and household equipment?
What things can produce electricity?
How can you find out if all charges of electricity are the same?

Processes   **Pupil Discovery Activity**

PART I

1. Obtain the following materials: a lucite or resin
   rod or a hard rubber comb, wool, flour, a glass rod,
   small pieces of paper, a large piece of paper, a
   balloon, tap water, and a piece of silk.
2. Take the resin rod (or hard rubber comb) and rub
   it with the wool cloth.

Hypothesizing   What do you think will happen when the rod is
                       touched to the flour?
                    3. Touch the rod to some flour.
Observing   What happened to the flour?
Hypothesizing   Why do you think the flour is affected by the rod?
                    4. Clean the rod, rub it again, and touch it to small
                       pieces of paper.
Observing   What did the rod do to the paper?

PART II

                    5. Rub the rod briskly with the wool cloth.
                    6. Turn on a water tap so a very slow stream of water
                       comes out.
Hypothesizing   What do you think will happen to the stream when
                       the rod is moved close to it?
                    7. Move the rod close to the stream.
Observing   What happened as the rod came near?
Inferring   Why did the water react as it did?
Inferring   Why do you think it reacted as it did without be-
                       ing touched?

                    Teacher's Note: The students should note how close
                       they have to bring the rod before it affects the stream
                       of water. Develop the concept that there is an in-
                       visible field of electrical force around the rod which
                       either pushes or attracts the water. This force cannot
                       be seen, but it must be there because it affects the
                       stream of water. Define force as a push or pull. In
                       this case, the water is pushed or pulled without be-
                       ing touched by moving the rod toward and away
                       from the water.

Designing an   How can you find out if the rubbing of the cloth
  investigation   on the rod caused the electrical force?

Electric field

                    8. Rub the rod again with the cloth.
                    9. Now rub your hand over the rod.
Hypothesizing   What do you think will happen to the stream of
                       water?

10. Repeat the procedure by approaching the slow stream of water with the rod.

Observing

What effect did the rod have on the water this time?

Inferring

Why did the rod not have the same effect?

Inferring

What happened to the charge that the wool cloth induced in the rod?

Inferring

Why do you think the charged failed to last?

Teacher's Note: When the resin rod is rubbed with wool or fur, electrons are rubbed off these materials onto the rod. The rod, however, is an insulator, so the electron movement is slight. The rod becomes negatively charged since each electron produces a small amount of negative charge. When a hand is rubbed over the rod, the rod becomes discharged because the electrons leave the rod and enter the hand. The rod is then neutral.

Explain the difference between a conductor and an insulator.

PART III

Summarizing

1. After your discussion concerning conductors and insulators would you say the rod is a conductor or an insulator?

Inferring

Why do you think so?

2. Obtain two balloons.
3. Inflate the balloons.
4. Tie a string to each balloon and suspend it from a bar as shown in the following diagram.

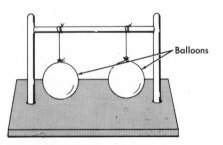

5. Rub each balloon with the wool cloth.

Observing

What did the balloons do?

Inferring

Why did they repel each other?

Summarizing

Do you think the balloons are conductors or insulators?

Hypothesizing

What do you think will happen if a charged resin rod is brought near the balloons?

6. Rub the resin rod with wool and place it near the balloons.

Observing
Inferring
Assuming

Hypothesizing

In which direction did the balloons move?

Why do you think they were repelled by the rod?

Do you think the balloons have a like or unlike charge? Why?

What do you think will happen to the balloons if you touch them with a glass rod?

Teacher's Note: These balloons were charged in the same way; therefore, each must have the same charge. When they do have the same charge they repel each other because like charges repel.

7. Rub the glass rod with the piece of silk.
8. Place it near the balloons.

Observing
Comparing

Comparing

What happened as it came near the balloons?

How did the glass rod affect the balloons in comparison to the resin rod?

What can you say about the charge on the resin rod compared to the glass rod?

PART IV

1. Rub one of the inflated balloons against the piece of wool.
2. Place it next to a wall. (See diagram.)

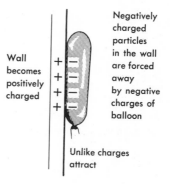

Hypothesizing

What do you think will happen to the balloon?

Teacher's Note: The glass rod will have a positive charge since electrons were rubbed off the rod onto the silk. It will attract the balloon because the balloon was negatively charged by the resin rod, and unlike charges attract.

Inferring

Why does the balloon not fall?

Inferring   Is the force that pulls the balloon to the wall greater or less than the gravitational force pulling the balloon down to earth?

Inferring   What happened to the negatively charged particles in the wall when the balloon came near?

Summarizing   What can you say about charging matter after following the above steps?

Summarizing   What is a conductor?

Summarizing   What is an insulator?

> *Teacher's Note:* When you rub the balloon, it becomes negatively charged. When it is placed next to the wall, its negative charge forces the electrons in the wall away from the surface, leaving the surface positively charged. The balloon sticks because the unlike charges attract. The balloon is negative and the wall surface is positive, as was indicated in the diagram.

OPEN-ENDED QUESTIONS

1. What is electricity?
2. How can you use a magnet to make electricity?

How Can You Make Electricity by Magnetism?   (4-6)

CONCEPTS

Around a magnet there are magnetic lines of force.
If you break the magnetic lines of force, you can make electricity.
A force is defined as a push or a pull.

MATERIALS

Copper wire (about 3 yards)   Compass   Bar magnet

DISCUSSION

How is electricity used?
How does electricity get to your home for you to use?
What happens when you slide your feet across a wool rug?

What can you produce when you rub a glass rod with wool?
What is the area of force around a magnet called?
What is a force?
How can you use a magnet to produce electricity?

Processes   **Pupil Discovery Activity**

1. Obtain a length of wire (about 3 yards), a bar magnet, and a compass.
2. Take the wire and wrap it 20 to 30 turns around the
   compass as indicated in the diagram.

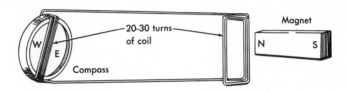

3. Loop the other end of the wire several times as
   as shown in the diagram.

Inferring   What happens when electricity goes through a wire?
Inferring   What do you think the area around the wire could
                   be called?
Inferring   What has the electricity produced?
Designing an   How do you think magnetism could be used to
   investigation   produce electricity?
Observing   4. Take the bar magnet and plunge it back and forth
                   inside the loops of wire. Instruct your partner to
                   watch what happens to the compass.
Observing   What happened to the compass?
Inferring   Why do you think the compass needle did what it
                   did?
Applying   What attracts a compass needle?
Hypothesizing   What do you think caused the needle to be de-
                   flected?
Hypothesizing   Where do you think the magnetism was produced
                   to cause the compass needle to move?
Inferring or   If there is magnetism produced in the wire around
   interpreting   the compass, what do you think the plunging of the
                   magnet through the loops of wire had to do with it?
Inferring or   When was electricity produced in the wire?
   interpreting
Summarizing   What is the force of a magnet called?
Summarizing   What does a magnet do to a magnetizable object?

Summarizing   What does a magnet do to a non-magnetizable ob-
                                   ject?
Summarizing   Explain how magnetism can be used to produce an
                                   electrical current.

Teacher's Note: Around every magnet there is an area
which can push or pull objects such as iron filings.
This area is thought to consist of lines of force.
When these lines of force are broken by plunging the
magnet back and forth through a coil of wire, electricity is made in the wire. Electricity is defined as a
flow of electrons along the wire, making an electrical
current. Whenever there is an electrical current produced, there will be a magnetic field around the
wire. This magnetic field causes the magnet (compass) in this activity to move. Using magnets to produce electricity is the principle involved in making
electricity in a dynamo.

OPEN-ENDED QUESTIONS

1. How can you use electricity to make a magnet?

How Can You Make an Electromagnet?   (4-8)

CONCEPTS

When electricity passes along a wire, it produces a magnetic field around the
wire which acts like a magnet.
A magnetic field can make iron temporarily magnetic.
The more current flows through a wire in a unit of time, the more magnetism
is generated around the wire.
If a circuit is broken, electricity will not flow.

MATERIALS

Teacher's Note: These following supplies are for two or three students.

| Insulated copper wire | Dry cell battery | Paper clips |
| Steel nail | Teaspoon of iron filings | |

DISCUSSION

How is magnetism made by electricity?

By using a wire that is carrying a current, how could you make a large magnetic field?

If you wanted to magnetize a nail, how would you do it?

Processes

Pupil Discovery Activity

1. Obtain a dry cell battery, a steel nail, a piece of copper insulated wire, some iron filings, and a paper clip.
2. Wrap the wire around the nail several times as shown in the diagram.

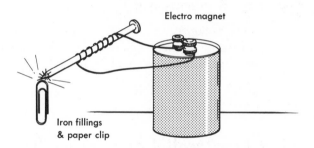

Electro magnet

Iron fillings & paper clip

3. Scrape the insulation off two ends of the wire. Connect one end of it to one terminal of the dry cell and the other end to the other terminal of the dry cell.

Hypothesizing — What do you think will happen to some iron filings if you place them near the nail?

4. Place them near the nail.
5. Place a paper clip on the nail.

Observing — What happened to the filings and paper clip?

Inferring — Why do the iron filings stay on the nail?

Inferring — What has been produced around the wire?

Inferring — What has the nail become?

Hypothesizing — What do you think will happen if you disconnect one of the terminals?

6. Disconnect one of the terminals.

Observing — What happened to the iron filings?

Inferring — Why did they fall when you disconnected the wire?

Applying — What must you do with the circuit to produce electricity?

Summarizing — What can you say about the production of mag-

	netism around a wire when electricity goes through it?
Summarizing	What would you call the magnet you made by passing electricity through a conductor?
Designing an investigation	How do you think you could increase the magnetism in the nail?
Hypothesizing	What do you think would happen if you wrapped more wire around the nail?
Hypothesizing	Will the magnetism increase or decrease? Why?
Assuming	Is the magnet you produced a temporary or a permanent magnet? Why?
Inferring	How do you know?

OPEN-ENDED QUESTIONS

1. In what other ways can you use a battery and wire to make a circuit?
2. How could you make a parallel or series circuit?
3. By what other means could the magnetic field around the nail be increased?

What Are Parallel and Series Circuits? (4-6)

CONCEPTS

In order for the electrons to move in a circuit, there must be a path that is unbroken to and from the source of electrical energy.

If one lamp burns out in a series circuit, the circuit is broken.

In a parallel circuit one lamp can burn out, but the rest of the circuit will still function.

MATERIALS

2 batteries	4 sockets	2 switches
4 small lamps	Connecting wires	

DISCUSSION

What would happen if one light on a string of Christmas tree lights were unscrewed?

What would you do to find out?

Why don't all strings of Christmas tree lights behave the same?

Processes

Pupil Discovery Activity

1. Obtain a battery, 2 small lamps, a switch, 2 sockets, and connecting wires.
2. Connect these things so that the lights work.

Hypothesizing
What do you need to make the lights work?

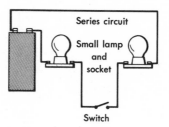

Series circuit

Small lamp and socket

Switch

Teacher's Note: The above diagram of the series circuit is for your information. It should not be shown to the children until they have done the activity.

Hypothesizing
What purpose does the switch serve?

Hypothesizing
What do you think will happen when you unscrew one of the lights?

3. Unscrew one of the lights.

Inferring
Why did the other light go out?

Hypothesizing
What can you do to make the lights go on again?

4. Using the same equipment, rearrange it so that if one light goes out, the other will burn.

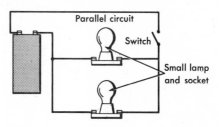

Parallel circuit

Switch

Small lamp and socket

Teacher's Note: The above diagram of a parallel circuit is available for your information. It should not be shown to the children until after they finish this activity.

5. Unscrew one of the lights. If you wired it differently than the first time, one of the lights should

Inferring
Comparing

still burn even though you unscrewed the other. Why?

What is the difference between the two types of circuits you have constructed?

Teacher's Note: In a parallel circuit there may be more than two paths for the current to take to complete its circuit. If one of the circuits is broken, the current can still use the other circuit as indicated in the preceding diagram.

OPEN-ENDED QUESTIONS

1. What kind of circuits do you have in your home?
2. How could you find out what kind of Christmas tree lights you have?
3. Examine a flashlight, what kind of a circuit does it have?

Earth Science

ASTRONOMY

What Is the Shape of the Earth? (K-3)

CONCEPTS

The earth is round like a globe.
The earth is very large.

MATERIALS

Globe of the earth
Several rubber balls of various sizes
Pictures taken of the earth's surface from outer space

Teacher's Note: This activity is to be done as a demonstration.

DISCUSSION

What shape do you think the earth is?
How do you think you could find out?

Processes	**Pupil Discovery Activity**
	1. Obtain a world globe and several rubber balls of different sizes.
Observing	What do you notice about each of the balls?
Comparing	If the earth is round, what is there about the earth that is like the balls?
	Teacher's Note: Each ball has a different curve according to the size of the ball. A large ball would have a very slight curve.

431

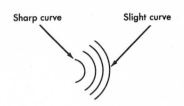

Sharp curve   Slight curve

Observing   2. Look out the window and observe the place where
                          the sky and the earth meet.
Inferring   What do you think the horizon is?
Hypothesizing   What could you do to see more of the earth's sur-
                          face?
Hypothesizing   If you were to see a ship sail into the distance, what
                          part of it would you see last? Why?

                       Teacher's Note: They would see the top of the mast
                          last since the earth is curved and the ship would be
                          moving over the earth's curvature.

Classifying   Would you see more or less of the earth's surface if
                          you were flying in a plane?
Hypothesizing   Why can a man in a space capsule take a picture
                          of so much more of the earth than a man on a
                          mountain?

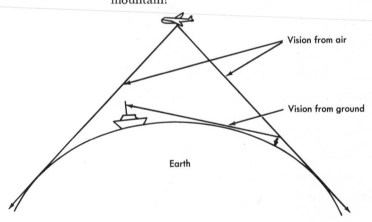

Vision from air

Vision from ground

Earth

                       3. Look at some pictures taken by rockets of the earth's
                          surface.
Observing   What shape is the earth's horizon?
                       4. Go to the second story of a building.
                          Observe the different things you did not see on the
                          ground floor.
Inferring   What did you see that might prove the earth is
                          round?

OPEN-ENDED QUESTIONS

1. If you were observing an eclipse of the moon, what could you find out about the shape of the earth?

Why Is There Day and Night?   (K-3)

CONCEPTS

The earth rotates.
It turns from west to east.
It takes 24 hours for the earth to make one complete turn.
The rotation of the earth explains why part of the 24-hour period is night and part is day.
The sun is always shining.

MATERIALS

Strong flashlight
Knitting needle
Clay

DISCUSSION

It is daytime here. Where would it be night?
When it is night here, where would it be day?
What could you do to find out about daytime and nighttime on the earth?

Processes	Pupil Discovery Activity
	1. Obtain a strong flashlight, a knitting needle, and some clay. Make a clay ball as large as a baseball; use it as a model of the earth.
Comparing	In what way do you think the clay ball is like the earth?
	2. Push the knitting needle through the clay globe. Darken the room. Let the flashlight shine on the ball. The flashlight represents the sun.
Inferring	What side of the globe do you think is having night?
Inferring	What side of the globe do you think is having day?

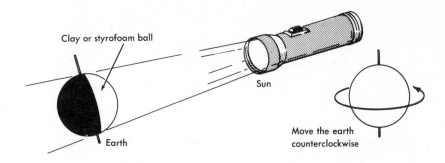

Inferring	What tells you that the sun is always shining some-where on the earth?
	3. Stick a pin in the globe to represent the place where you live. Turn the globe slowly to the sun-light side.
Hypothesizing	Using the globe, how could you make night come to the place where you live?

Teacher's Note: The globe is turned slowly to show where night would begin to fall and where it would be midnight and sunrise. In order to show this, the globe must be turned counter-clockwise.

Inferring	What time of day is it when your pin is on the same side as the sun?
Inferring	When your pin is away from the sun, what time of day would it be?

OPEN-ENDED QUESTIONS

1. What would happen if the earth did not turn?
2. If the earth did not turn, which side would you rather be on? Why?

Why Does the Moon Shine? (2-4)

CONCEPTS

Objects are seen when they give off their own light or when they reflect light from another source.

The moon does not give off its own light. Its light is reflected light from the sun.

MATERIALS

Flashlight   Small foil ball, about 1″ in diameter, with attached string
Globe   Larger styrofoam ball, about 3″ in diameter, with attached
Masking tape   string
Large ball   Box with tight fitting lid

DISCUSSION

Teacher's Note: Place a ball on the table. Darken the room.

What is on the table?

What do you need to be able to see the object?

Turn on the lights.

Why do you see the ball now?

Do you see it because it is giving off its own light or because it is reflecting light?

Look at the ceiling lights.

Why is it possible for you to see the lights?

How is this light different from the light you see when you look at the ball?

Darken the room.

What are two reasons why you may not see any lights in the room?

Processes

Hypothesizing
Inferring

Pupil Discovery Activity

How do you think the moon shines?
What is reflected light?

1. Obtain the following materials: box with tight fitting lid, foil made into a ball with attached string, flashlight, and masking tape.

2. Suspend the small ball on a string 1″ long from inside the lid of the box as shown in the diagram. Insert flashlight in the end of the box and seal any space around it with masking tape. Make a small eyehole at the end of the box under the flashlight.

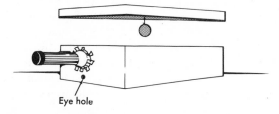

Eye hole

Put on the lid with the ball suspended inside the box. Seal the edges around the lid.

Observing and Inferring

What do you see when you look through the eyehole? Why?

3. Turn on the flashlight.

Observing and Inferring   What do you see when you look through the eyehole? Why?

Inferring   Did you see the ball because it reflected light or because it gave off light of its own?

Classifying   What two kinds of light did you see?

Inferring   What was the source of each kind of light?

4. Look out the window.

Inferring   Why are you able to see some objects?

Inferring   What is the source of the light on the objects?

Inferring   Do the objects seen outside the window give off reflected light or light of their own?

Inferring   What does the sun give off?

Inferring   Why does the moon shine?

5. Obtain a styrofoam ball, 3″ in diameter, with attached string. Use your box, flashlight, suspended foil ball, but add the larger styrofoam ball suspended 2″ down, as shown in the diagram. Seal the edges again. Seal the old eyehole and make a new eyehole as indicated in the drawing.

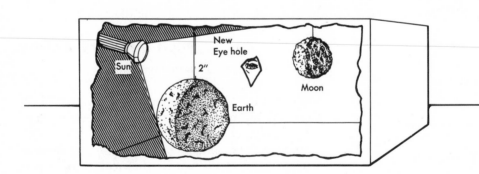

Formulating a model   If the small ball is the moon, what does the flashlight represent?

6. Turn on the flashlight and look through the new eyehole.

Inferring   What does the large ball represent?

7. Look at the ball representing the earth and tell which side is day and which side is night.

Inferring   On which side would you be if you could see the moon?

Inferring   How is it possible for you to see the moon if you are on the dark side of the earth?

Summarizing   Why does the moon shine?

OPEN-ENDED QUESTIONS

1. If you lived on another planet, would you be able to see earth?
2. What are the positions of the sun, moon, and earth (a) when it is night for you, (b) when it is day for you?

Why Are There Phases of the Moon?   (3-6)

CONCEPTS

Sometimes the moon appears fully round.
The moon seems to change shape.
Sometimes the moon seems to get smaller and smaller.
Sometimes the moon seems to get larger and larger.

MATERIALS

Black construction paper	Small ball
Soft white chalk	Basketball
Globe	Flashlight

Teacher's Note: Prior to the experiment consult the local paper to see when the moon's last quarter will be visible during the day.

Processes   **Pupil Discovery Activity**

1. Obtain a large piece of black construction paper and some white chalk.
2. Take this home and observe the moon for the next five days. Draw the shape of the moon as you see it each night.

Observing
    In what way did the moon's shape seem to change?
3. Obtain a globe, small ball, and a flashlight from the science cabinet.

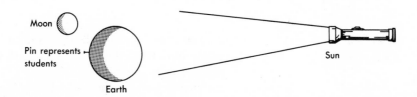

Moon
Pin represents students
Earth
Sun

Inferring

Inferring

Inferring

4. Using this equipment, make the following arrangement.
5. Place a pin on the night side of the earth as indicated in the diagram on p. 437. The pin represents you.

Draw below how much of the moon you would see if you were where the pin is?
6. Move the moon around the earth.

On which side of the earth is the moon when you cannot see it?

Where is the moon when it is full?
7. Make diagrams to help you explain the last three questions.
8. Look at the following diagram showing some phases of the moon.

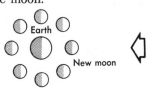

9. Prepare 8 drawings showing how the moon would appear to you during the 8 phases as indicated in the diagram.
10. Obtain a basketball and flashlight.
11. Choose two partners to help you. Have one partner hold the flashlight and shine it on the basketball being held by your second partner as he walks in a circle around you.

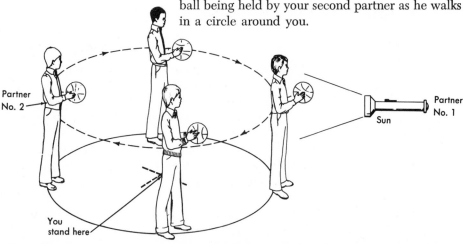

Inferring

Inferring

12. As you observe the ball, diagram on a piece of paper how the light on the ball is similar to the phases of the moon.

In what position is the ball when it is covered by the shadow?

Inferring	Where would the moon have to be when it is covered by a shadow?
Inferring	When a ball showed no shadow, what phase of the moon would this represent?
Summarizing	13. Draw how the full moon looks from earth.
Summarizing	What causes the phases of the moon?

OPEN-ENDED QUESTIONS

1. If the moon is not out at night, on what side of the earth must it be located?
2. If the moon could remain still in the sky, how would it look every night?

What Causes the Tides?   (5-8)

CONCEPTS

Gravitational attractions of the moon and sun on the earth cause tides.

The moon is smaller than the sun, but because it is closer to the earth, its tidal pull is greater than that of the sun.

Tides are highest when the moon and sun are pulling on the earth in a straight line. This occurs twice a month.

Low tides occur when the moon and sun are pulling at right angles to each other.

Gravity decreases with the increase of distance between two objects.

MATERIALS

Horseshoe magnet	Paper clip
Ring stand	Styrofoam ball, 9″ in diameter
String	Styrofoam ball, 2″ in diameter
Book	Small round shaped balloon

Teacher's Note: This activity should be done by groups of three or more students.

Processes   **Pupil Discovery Activity**

	1. Obtain a ring stand, horseshoe magnet, some string, a paper clip, and a book.
	2. Set up the equipment as shown in the next diagram.
Inferring	What holds up the paper clip?
Observing	Are you able to see this force?
Assuming	How do you know it is there if you cannot see it?

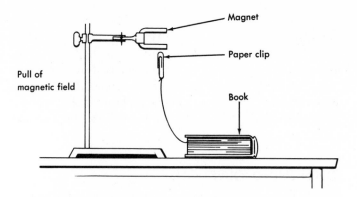

Teacher's Note: This force is magnetic force. It is shown here to illustrate what a force is and that a force may be invisible. Tides are not caused by magnetic force but gravitational force. The children should have done some activities involving gravity before they do this lesson.

Hypothesizing   Knowing this, what effect do you think the moon's gravitational force has on the water of the earth?

Hypothesizing   How will it pull the water?

3. Obtain two styrofoam balls, 9″ and 2″ in diameter, and a small balloon from the science table.

4. Ask two partners to help you.

5. Blow up the balloon and tie the end closed. Have the two partners each hold one of the styrofoam balls. You should hold the balloon in the positions of the diagram below.

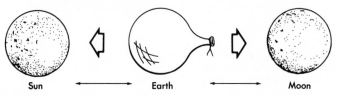

Sun ⟷ Earth ⟷ Moon

6. Pull the balloon with one hand toward the sun. Pull with the other hand toward the moon.

Inferring   What would the pull being exerted on the balloon represent?

Hypothesizing   What do you think will happen if the sun and moon are placed at right angles to the earth?

Hypothesizing   How will the gravitational forces vary?

7. Pull the balloon mostly toward the moon and exert much less force in the sun's direction.

Comparing   From the way the balloon is being pulled, which has greater gravitational pull on the earth, the moon or the sun?

Hypothesizing   Why do you think the moon has greater pull on the earth when it is so much smaller than the sun?

Teacher's Note: The moon has greater effect because it is much closer to the earth than the sun is.

For summarization, draw these two diagrams on the board and discuss them with the class.

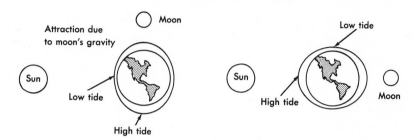

At the conclusion of the activity, discuss with the class the following concepts to be sure the students understand them:

Force is either a push or a pull exerted on an object. Gravity is a force you cannot see.

The greater the mass of an object, the heavier it is, and the more gravitational force it has.

The closer an object is to another, the greater the gravitational attraction there will be between them.

Mass is defined as the amount of matter a body contains.

OPEN-ENDED QUESTIONS

1. Draw the positions of the moon, earth, and sun when there is a very high tide on part of the earth. How does the water around that part of the earth look?
2. When there is low tide at a place on the earth, how does the water look?
3. Why does the moon have a greater effect on the tide than the sun does?
4. What holds you down in your chair?
5. What effect do the gravitational forces of the moon and sun have on the world's continents?

What Is an Eclipse? (4-6)

CONCEPTS

The shadow of the moon on the earth causes a solar eclipse.
The shadow of the earth on the moon causes a lunar eclipse.

To see a solar eclipse, one has to be on the sunny side of the earth.
To see a lunar eclipse, one has to be on the night side of the earth.

MATERIALS (For Each 3-5 Students)

Flashlight, slide projector, or similar light source
Styrene (or similar) ball approximately 8″ in diameter
Styrofoam (or similar) ball approximately 2″ in diameter

DISCUSSION

What does the word eclipse mean?
If something is eclipsed, what does it mean?
What would it mean to say the sun is eclipsed?

Processes

Pupil Discovery Activity

1. Investigate the following questions, letting the flashlight represent the sun; the large ball, the earth; and the small ball, the moon.

Hypothesizing

2. How must the sun, earth, and moon be arranged for a solar eclipse to occur?

Teacher's Note: The moon must be between the earth and the sun.

Observing
Inferring

3. Describe the shadow which falls upon the earth. When a solar eclipse occurs, would everyone on earth be able to see it? Explain your answer.

Teacher's Note: No, because the moon's shadow only touches a small part of the earth.

Inferring

Can a solar eclipse be seen at night? Explain.

Teacher's Note: No, it can only happen in the daytime when the moon can block out the sun's light.

Hypothesizing

How must the sun, moon, and earth be arranged for a lunar eclipse to occur?

Teacher's Note: The earth must be between the sun and moon for a shadow to fall upon the moon.

Hypothesizing

When is it possible to see a lunar eclipse?

Teacher's Note: Only at night.

OPEN-ENDED QUESTIONS

1. The almanac indicates solar and lunar eclipses do not occur regularly each month as it seems they should. Use your equipment to see if you can discover an explanation to determine why this is so.

Teacher's Note: The children's activity should show that if the moon passes above or below the plane of the earth's orbit, the earth's shadow could miss the moon entirely, or the moon's shadow could miss the earth. In either case, the eclipse might be visible only from some point in space. The formulated hypothesis should be similar to the following:

> The plane of the moon's orbit is tilted away from the plane of the earth's orbit; eclipses can only occur when the earth, sun, and moon are in a straight line, and this does not happen each month.

What Size Is the Sun Compared to the Earth?   (K-2)

CONCEPTS

The sun is many times larger than the earth.

Objects of similar size appear smaller when they are far away and larger when they are near.

Stars are very big in size, bright, and far away.

MATERIALS

Basketball

Several radish seeds

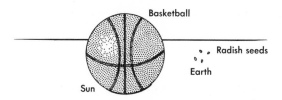

Processes

Comparing

Pupil Discovery Activity

1. Look at the basketball and the seeds. Which would you have represent the earth and which the sun? Why?

2. As you look at the stars on a clear night, how do they differ from each other?

   Teacher's Note: Some are brighter than others, some are different colors.

3. Darken your classroom. If this is not possible, go with your teacher into a darkened gymnasium, auditorium, or hallway, and have one of your classmates hold a flashlight at the opposite end of the room. He should walk slowly toward you.

Observing

How does the light change as it gets closer to you?

Teacher's Note: They should notice that the light gets brighter and bigger.

Inferring

Knowing this, why do you think some stars look different?

Teacher's Note: Some stars look closer to us than other stars because they are brighter or they are bigger.

OPEN-ENDED QUESTIONS

1. If you had two flashlights giving off the same amount of light, what would you do to one to make it look dimmer than the other in a large, dark room?

What Does the Sun Do for Us? (1-3)

CONCEPTS

The sun gives off energy in the form of heat and light.
The light of the sun can be brought to a point by using a lens.

MATERIALS

Hand magnifying glass (one for every two students)
Sheet of paper

Processes

Pupil Discovery Activity

1. Obtain a magnifying glass and a piece of paper.
2. Hold the magnifying glass over a piece of paper outside in the sunlight. Move the magnifying glass up and down above the piece of paper until the light comes to a point. Hold it there for a few seconds.

Observing

What happens to the paper?

Teacher's Note: The paper will begin to smoke and burn.

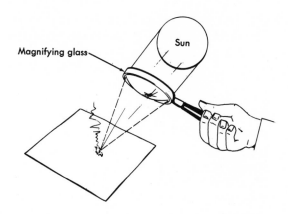

Hypothesizing

Why did the paper react as it did?

Teacher's Note: The paper burned because the magnifying glass concentrated the sun's heat rays into a small point.

3. Try the same experiment with the light from a light bulb.

Observing

What happens to the paper?

Teacher's Note: Nothing happens to the paper because the light is not intense enough.

Hypothesizing
Inferring

Why did the paper react as it did this time?
What do these activities tell you about the sun?

Teacher's Note: This shows that the sun gives off a great deal of heat and light.

OPEN-ENDED QUESTIONS

1. If you wanted to melt some wax and did not have any matches, how would you do it?
2. On a cold day, why do you feel warm in sunlight but very cold when in a shadow?

How Long Is a Year? (3-6)

Teacher's Note: This should be a demonstration activity.

CONCEPTS

The earth moves around the sun (revolves).
It takes one year for the earth to make one trip around the sun.

An earth year is 365¼ days.
The earth rotates as it revolves around the sun.
The earth moves around the sun in an elliptical path.

MATERIALS

Globe   Masking tape
Lamp   Chalk
Cardboard for each child   Overhead projector
Paper for each child   Mirror
Two pins for each child   Transparency of the planets in orbit
String—9″ for each child   Opaque circles to represent the sun and
String—24′   earth
                                         Planetarium if available

DISCUSSION

Teacher's Note: Have a pupil use a globe and lamp to review how rotation
causes day and night.

If the rotating of the earth explains the length of day, how can a globe and a
lamp be used to show the length of a year?

What kind of path does the earth make when it revolves around the sun?

Processes

Pupil Discovery Activity

1. Obtain a piece of paper, cardboard, 2 pins, string
and a pencil.
2. Try to draw a circle by sticking two pins 7 inches
apart in the middle of the paper, which is resting
on the cardboard. Form a loop from a piece of
string nine inches long. Slip the loop over the pins.
Pull the loop tight with a pencil and, using the
string as a guide, draw a line around the pins.

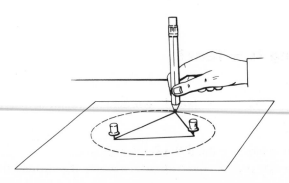

Comparing

How does the shape you made differ from a perfect circle?

What might you call this shape?

Teacher's Note: If none of the children know, tell them that it is called an ellipse.

3. Use a longer string loop, masking tape, and chalk to make an ellipse on the floor.
4. Place a lamp in the center of the ellipse.

Inferring

What does the lamp represent?

Inferring

What does the ellipse you drew around the sun represent?

Hypothesizing

What could you use to represent the earth?

Teacher's Note: A child should walk on a line around the sun (the light) and should rotate as he follows the line.

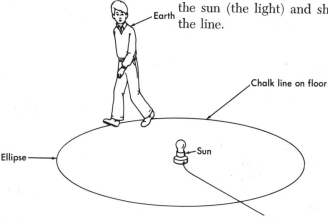

Earth

Chalk line on floor

Ellipse

Sun

Applying

In what way should the earth move around the sun?

5. Demonstrate rotation as you move around the sun.

Teacher's Note: Children should take turns rotating as they revolve around the sun. You might tell them that rotation is like spinning, while in revolving, one object must go around another object.

Hypothesizing

What is the process of the earth moving around the sun called?

When something revolves, what is it doing?

Teacher's Note: One trip around the sun is called a revolution.

How many days make a year?

Inferring

How can you find out?

Teacher's Note: After they have checked the number of days in a year, the children might investigate why some of the statements say there are 365 days and others say 365¼ days.

Summarizing

6. Rotate like the earth.
   How long does it take the earth to rotate on its axis to make a day?
7. Demonstrate how the earth revolves around the sun.
   How long does it take for the earth to make one complete orbit around the sun?
   What is the name of the imaginary line on which the earth travels around the sun?
   How long is an earth year?

Teacher's Note: "Convert" the overhead projector into a planetarium by placing on the stage of the projector an opaque circle to represent the sun and a smaller opaque circle to represent the earth. Have a child show how the earth revolves around the sun by moving the earth correctly.

OPEN-ENDED QUESTIONS

1. What else revolves around the sun?
2. How could you determine if other planets have the same length of year as the earth?
3. Which planet has the longest year? Why?
4. Which planet would have the shortest year?
   How could you demonstrate the revolution of the planets?
   What effect would the various lengths of years have on birthdays of people if all planets were inhabited?

Teacher's Note: If a planetarium is available, use it as a visual aid. The overhead projector also may be used. Focus a transparency of the planets in orbit onto the ceiling and discuss their solar system.

What Causes the Seasons?   (6-8)

CONCEPTS

The sun gives off light and heat.
The more sun rays that hit a section of the earth, the warmer that section will get.
When it is light on one side of the earth, it is dark on the other side of the earth.
The rotating of the earth causes night and day.
The earth makes one revolution around the sun in one year.

MATERIALS

Flashlight   2 plastic or rubber balls
2 thermometers   A globe

Teacher's Note: This investigation should not be crowded into a single period.

DISCUSSION

How do the four seasons differ?

Why does the continental United States have different seasons?

How could you use simple apparatus such as used in this activity to demonstrate night and day and to show the cause of the seasons?

Processes   **Pupil Discovery Activity**

PART I

1. Shine a flashlight as shown in Diagram 1.

Thermometer

(1)   (2)

Observing	What do you notice about the way the light shines on the paper?
Observing	What kind of area is covered by the light as it shines on the paper?
Hypothesizing	If you shine the light as shown in Diagram 2, what do you think will happen to the area covered?
Hypothesizing	In which way, direct or slanted, do you think the temperature would be greater?
Designing an investigation	How could you determine whether or not your answer is correct?

2. Take two flashlights and two thermometers and shine them as in Diagrams 1 and 2. Place a thermometer in the path of each of these rays to see if you can detect a difference in the temperature.

Comparing	How did the temperatures differ?
Inferring	What do you think caused the variation?
Comparing	How does the temperature vary with the seasons?

PART II

Hypothesizing	How could you use a globe to show the cause of the seasons?

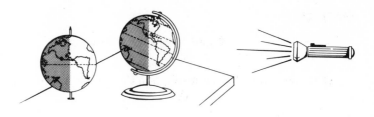

Observing

Hypothesizing

Hypothesizing

1. Obtain two plastic or rubber balls. Place each ball on a nail as shown in the diagram. A globe of the earth may be substituted for the second ball. Shine a flashlight beam directly on each globe.

What do you notice about the way the light hits the two globes?

What would you have to do to the globes to show what causes day and night?

If the earth were not inclined as in the second globe, how could you determine if there would be any seasons?

2. Point the flashlight at the second globe, and move the globe around the flashlight.

Observing

What do you notice about the way the light strikes the globe as you move the globe, stopping at several places?

Inferring

What do you think the season would be at each point that you stop?

Hypothesizing

Why does the United States get more sunlight in summer than in winter?

Hypothesizing

Why does the sun not shine on the earth the same way every month of the year?

Observing

Which covers a larger portion of the earth, the slanted rays or the direct rays?

Applying

How can you determine which rays are cooler on the earth's surface—direct or slanting?

Summarizing

How long does it take for the earth to make one trip around the sun?

Observing

When it is winter in New York, what season is it in Argentina?

Inferring

How does the angle of the earth affect the seasons?

Teacher's Note: Parts of the earth receive more heat from the sun at one time of the year than at another time because of the tilt of the axis. Place the following diagram on the board after the lesson and have the children point out the various seasons and explain them.

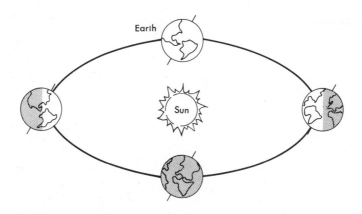

OPEN-ENDED QUESTIONS

1. What other investigations can show why the earth has seasons?
2. In what way would a knowledge of seasonal variations help you to better understand the peoples of the world?

Why Do Stars Appear Close or Far Apart? (K-4)

CONCEPTS

There are millions of stars, and they are tremendous distances from each other.

The earth's great distances from the stars make the stars appear closer together.

MATERIALS

50 bottle caps or 50 marbles

DISCUSSION

How do the stars appear to you as you look into the sky?
Explain why they look near to each other or far apart?
Why do they look small?
What can you do to show how things look at a distance?

Processes   **Pupil Discovery Activity**

1. Obtain and place 50 bottle caps in a cluster so that no bottle cap is less than one inch from its nearest neighbor. Stand in front of the bottle caps, facing them.

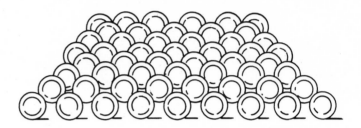

Hypothesizing   What do you think will happen as you move away from these objects?

2. Move away from the caps.

Observing   How do the bottle caps appear as you move 5 steps away from them?

Observing   3. How do the bottle caps appear as you move 10 steps away from them?

Observing   4. How do the bottle caps appear as you move 15 steps away from them?

Summarizing   How did the bottle caps look as you moved away from them?

Observing   5. Draw how the marbles looked when you saw them in front of you and then how they looked when you took 15 steps away from them.

Designing an   In what way could you go about finding how the
    investigation   stars look in the sky?

                                Teacher's Note: The more immature pupils will need more guidance. They may be asked to observe the night sky. The next day you and the pupils could discuss the result of their observation and investigation.

Inferring   How could you use this investigation with bottle caps and observation of the sky to explain why the stars look so close together?

Inferring   Why do you think stars look close together yet are so far apart?

Summarizing   What do you know now about how far away the stars are?

OPEN-ENDED QUESTIONS

1. If you were to fill a Chinese checker board with marbles, would it make the shape of a star, or would it represent many "little" stars? Why?
2. If you were to look at cars at different distances, which would appear smaller, the near ones or those far away?

How Do the Planets Move? (5-8)

CONCEPTS

Planets move around the sun.
There are nine planets that move around the sun.
Planets vary in size and distance from the sun.
The planets farthest from the sun have the longest years and the longest paths to follow.

MATERIALS

Lamp
Ruler
Clay or styrofoam balls

Teacher's Note: Some things cannot be seen, felt, or measured. Therefore, a scientific model must be formed. The pupils may select styrofoam balls, purchased at the local dime store, to make the planet models. They can hang these from the inside of a cardboard box.

DISCUSSION

On what planet do you live?
How does the earth move?
How do you think the movement of the earth corresponds to the orbit of the other planets?
How can you show the planets and how they move?

Processes

PART I

Pupil Discovery Activity

1. Obtain some clay and shape it into balls so that they vary in sizes as indicated on the following scales:

Planet	Small Scale Size in Diameter	Large Scale Size in Diameter
Mercury	1/16	1/4
Venus	2/16	5/8
Earth	2/16	5/8
Mars	3/32	3/8
Jupiter	1 5/16	6 3/4
Saturn	1 1/16	5 1/2
Uranus	1/2	2 1/4
Neptune	9/16	2 1/4
Pluto	7/16	1/4
Sun		5 feet

The scales of 1/16 or 1/4 inch are equal to about
4,000 miles. Make a ring of paper to place around
Saturn.

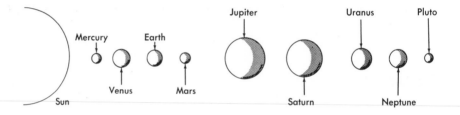

Inferring	Where does the earth get its light?
Inferring	Where do the other plants get their light?
Applying	How can you show that planets reflect their light from the sun?
Hypothesizing	Where should the sun be placed?
Hypothesizing	What planet should be placed next to the sun?
	2. Attach the clay balls to paper clips and hang them from a tackboard. Write the names of planets on small paper and fasten the names below the planets.
Observing	How many planets are there?
Comparing	How do the planets differ in size?
Comparing	Which is the largest planet?
Comparing	Which two planets are the smallest?
Inferring	Why can you not have an accurate comparison of the planets with the sun?
	What is the name given to the sun and the planets?
Applying	Why is it called the Solar System?

Teacher's Note: Pupils may use a reference book, or you
may need to explain to some pupils that the word
"solar" comes from the Latin word meaning sun.

PART II

1. Work with your planet models and refer to resource materials to determine answers to the following questions:

Observing — Which planet has rings?

Observing — Which planet is closest to the sun?

Observing — Which planet is farthest from the sun?

Inferring — Which planet takes the longest to go around the sun?

Inferring — Which planet would have the longest year?

Inferring — Why would that planet have the longest year?

Applying — Which planet do you think would be the warmest?

Designing an investigation — How can you determine if all the planets move in the same direction?

OPEN-ENDED QUESTIONS

1. What else could you do with your planet models to show how they move around the sun?
2. How could you construct an apparatus which would show all nine planets revolving around the sun?

Teacher's Note: The planets which children made could be fastened onto a wire which is attached between spools on dowel rods as shown in the diagram below.

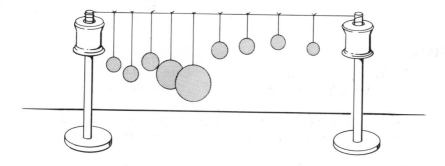

What Causes Some Stars to Be Different Colors? (5-8)

CONCEPTS

When objects are heated, they may change color.

White-hot objects are hotter than red-hot objects.

Stars which are white are believed to be hotter than yellow stars, and yellow
   stars are hotter than red stars.
A star is a giant-size mass of tremendously hot glowing gases.
White stars have temperatures of 40,000°F at their surfaces, yellow stars,
   10,000°F, and red stars, 3,000°F.
Color is related to the age of a star.
Young stars are white.
Old stars are red.

MATERIALS

   Pliers
   Copper wire
   Bunsen or alcohol burner

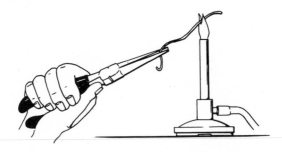

DISCUSSION

   Teacher's Note: Because of the equipment used—the possible danger of a
      child being burned—this activity should probably be done as a demonstra-
      tion.
   If you saw two pieces of iron, both of which had been in a furnace, and one
      piece was red and the other was white, which one would you think was
      the hottest?
   Why would one be hotter than the other?

Processes	**Pupil Discovery Activity**
	1. With a pair of pliers hold a wire above a Bunsen burner.
Hypothesizing	What do you think will happen to the wire as you heat it?

   Teacher's Note: The wire will change color, becoming
      red, then yellow, and finally white as the tempera-
      ture increases.

Inferring	What did you notice about the way the wire changed color?
Inferring	What made it change color?
Summarizing	What were the different colors that the wire gave off in the process of being heated?
Inferring	What color do you think was the hottest? The coldest?
Hypothesizing	If you saw a red and a yellow star through a telescope, which of these do you think would be the hottest? Why?

Teacher's Note: Red stars are cooler than yellow stars, and white stars are hotter than either red or yellow stars.

Explain from this demonstration how it is possible for an astronomer, a scientist who studies the stars, to tell how hot a star is without ever going to it?

Teacher's Note: Explain that the color of the stars cannot be detected with the naked eye. The astronomer must use astronomical instruments in order to do this.

OPEN-ENDED QUESTIONS

1. If you were going to heat some charcoal, which of the following types of light do you think it would give off first: red, yellow or white?
2. What color is radiated from the hottest source in your home?
3. What other things might an astronomer study in the laboratory to help him better understand the stars?

GEOLOGY

How Does Erosion Affect the Soil?   (3-6)

CONCEPTS

Soil consists of several different layers.
Soil is made from rock.
There are many kinds of soil.
Erosion is the wasting away of soil.
Soil has organic material (material which is living or had been living) that enriches it.

MATERIALS

Hammer
Rock, about the size of a tennis ball, which can be easily chipped.
Quart jar, three-fourths filled with soil; lid
2 cans (preferably the size of Campbell's soup cans): one three-fourths filled with soil; the other three-fourths filled with soil, dead grass, leaves, and peat moss

2 milk cartons, quart-size
Soil, approximately eight cups
2 aluminum pie pans
Grass seed, one teaspoon
Scissors
Damp cloth large enough to cover a quart-size milk carton
Tap water, one-half gallon
2 blocks of wood, each $1\frac{1}{2}'' \times 3''$
Measuring cup

DISCUSSION

You have all played with dirt (soil) or at least handled it in some way, such as washing it off your feet or hands.
Where does soil come from?
How could you make soil here in the classroom?

Processes   **Pupil Discovery Activity**

This activity may be done in groups of two or more pupils.

1. Obtain a rock about the size of a tennis ball and two sheets of newspaper.

Teacher's Note: For safety reasons, have the children wrap a rock in newspaper before hitting it so that the chips do not fly.

2. Place the covered rock on the table. Hold it in place with one hand and with the other hit it gently 5 or 6 times with the hammer. Unwrap the newspaper.

Observing   What do you observe?

Observing   Does the rock appear the same?

Observing   What do you see that looks like soil?

Inferring   Soil varies from one place to another. Can you suggest from this activity any reasons why?

Comparing   How does the soil on the desert or beach differ from the soil in the mountain?

Teacher's Note: Soil varies because it is made from different types of rocks, and its particle sizes may also vary. Some soils are made of coarse grains while others are composed of fine grains.

3. Obtain a quart jar three-fourths filled with soil and decayed plant material, a half gallon of water, and a lid for the jar.

Hypothesizing   If you add water to this jar and cover it and shake it, how do you think the soil will settle?

4. Add water (about three cupfuls) to the jar until it is about two inches from the top. Shake the jar for about a minute. Then place the jar on the table and allow the soil to settle. Do not disturb the bottle.

Observing   What do you notice about the way the soil is settling?

Inferring   Why do certain particles of the soil settle to the bottom first?

Observing   In which layer is the organic material (material which is living or had been living) mainly found?

Inferring   What can you say about layers of soil?

5. Obtain two soup cans filled with soil, about a half gallon of water and a measuring cup.

6. Pour about one cup of water into each can.

Hypothesizing   What do you think will happen to the water in the soil of both cans?

Comparing, Observing   Which can seems to be able to hold moisture best?

Comparing, Observing   What difference do you notice in the soil in the two cans?

Comparing, Observing
Interpreting

Which has more organic material?

Why is organic material good for the soil?

7. Obtain two quart-size milk cartons, eight cups of soil, half gallon of water, measuring cup, a package of grass seed, two aluminum pie pans, two blocks of wood, damp cloth and a pair of scissors.

8. Using the scissors, cut out one of the long sides of both milk cartons (see diagram).

9. Fill the milk cartons with soil, leaving about one-half inch from the top, and label the cartons X and Y.

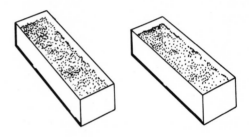

10. In carton X, plant the grass seeds just under the surface of the soil.

11. Water carton X and place the damp cloth over it to keep the moisture in. Continue to water the seeds until they have sprouted and are one inch high.

12. When carton X is ready, place one block of wood under one end of each carton. Carefully make 5 holes in each of the bottoms of the lower ends of carton X and Y, and place these ends into the aluminum pie pans (see diagram).

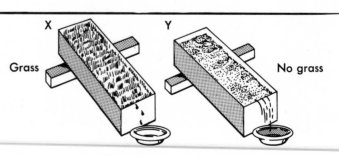

Aluminum pan

13. Place these cartons in an area out of direct sunlight and wind.

Measuring, Observing

14. Measure one cup of water and gently sprinkle this water over carton X. Do the same to carton Y.

Collecting and
Organizing data

Repeat this each day for three days and write what you see.

Inferring

Why are the cartons set up in such a position?

Hypothesizing

Which carton do you think will lose the most soil?

After three days:

Observing

Which carton has lost the most soil?

Interpreting

Why does one carton lose less soil than the other?

Interpreting

How can you prevent erosion (washing or wearing away) in soils?

Applying

What, other than grass, can be planted to prevent erosion?

15. Draw a diagram to show what you would do to control erosion.

OPEN-ENDED QUESTIONS

1. Make a "mountain" of pebbles, soil, and sand.
   What do you think will happen if you pour water down on it?
   Pour water over the mountain and observe what happens.
   What erodes first?
   What conclusions can you draw from this activity?
2. Take a walk around the schoolyard. What signs of erosion are there?
   What could be done to prevent this erosion?
3. How do you know there are many kinds of soil?
4. What are some of the ways by which erosion can be controlled?
5. Where is organic material mainly found in the soil?
6. In the experiment you did with the milk cartons, why did you not plant seeds in both cartons?
7. Why is erosion control important to farmers?
8. What are terraced rice fields? Why are they necessary and important?

What Is a Fault?   (5-8)

CONCEPTS

Some land has been formed by sedimentation, causing layering.
When too much force is applied to the earth's layers, they crack.

The point where the earth's crust cracks and moves is called a fault.

A normal fault is where the earth's crust drops.

A thrust fault is where the earth's crust rises over an adjacent part of the earth.

Earthquakes may be caused by the earth's crust sliding along a fault.

MATERIALS

One-quart jar	Balance
One quart of water	Two cigar box molds filled with layers
Sand	of colored plaster
Several different types of soil—	A knife to cut the plaster mold
light, dark, etc.	3 food colors
Two paper cups	

Teacher's Note: This activity should be done in groups of two or more students. The molds should be made by mixing two or three pints of plaster of paris with different food coloring. The wet plaster of paris should be layered in the cigar boxes and allowed to dry partially before cutting as indicated below. Do not let the plaster of paris become too dry or it will be too hard to cut.

DISCUSSION

If great force is applied to a rock or parts of the earth's structure, what will happen to the rock or the structure?

What is an earthquake?

What causes an earthquake?

Processes   **Pupil Discovery Activity**

PART I

1. Obtain a quart jar, some sand, and several types of soil. Half fill the quart jar with water. Add sand to the jar until it is an inch thick in the bottom of the jar.

Observing   What happened to the sand?

Hypothesizing   What will happen if you pour soil onto part of the sand?

2. Add several other types of soil to the jar and observe.

Comparing   How do the materials in the jar resemble parts of our earth?

Inferring   Explain how you think parts of our earth have become layered.

3. Obtain a balance, a paper cup half-filled with water and another cup half-filled with sand.
Place the cup of sand on one side of the balance and the cup of water on the other side.

Hypothesizing

What ways can you balance the sand and water?

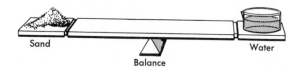

Sand   Water

Balance

4. Use one of your methods to balance the sand and water.

Hypothesizing

Now that these are balanced, what will happen if you take some sand from one side of the balance and place it on the other side by the cup of water?

5. Do this and observe.

Inferring

How is what you did with the balance similar to some of the things that happen in the earth's crust?

Teacher's Note: The land surface of the continents is always being worn away. The particles formed from this wear often flow into streams and are carried to the sea. When the material gets to the ocean floor, it causes that part of the floor to become heavier and may cause the crust of the earth and the layers to bend. If they bend far enough, faults may appear. This is an explanation for one type of fault, though it is a rare type.

PART II

1. Obtain a cigar box mold from your teacher and remove the plaster block. Using the knife, cut the block in two. Raise one of these blocks above the other as indicated in the diagram.

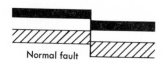

Normal fault

A place where the earth's crust and layers have broken similar to your cut is called a fault.

Comparing

How is the appearance of the block similar to the appearance of the earth in some places you have seen?

Summarizing

Explain how you think a rock structure could reach the condition similar to the one you have arranged in your model.

Teacher's Note: The rock structure could have formed a fault owing to stresses within the earth which drew the sections of rock apart. This stress could then have caused one section to fall. This kind of fault is called a normal fault.

2. Obtain a 2″ × 4″ piece of wood which has been cut in two along a sloping line.

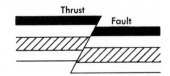

Comparing

How is this fault different from the normal fault? What would you call this type of fault?

Teacher's Note: Explain that this type of fault is called a *thrust fault.* The fault occurs when compression pushes sections of rock closer together, forcing one section of rock to move or slide up.

Inferring

How could this structure have been formed in nature?

Summarizing

How would you define a thrust fault?

Teacher's Note: Other faults, such as the one which caused the San Francisco earthquake of 1906, may be caused mainly by horizontal movement of the earth. The San Andreas fault in California is of this type.

Hypothesizing

What connection is there between an earthquake and a fault?

Teacher's Note: Explain earthquakes may be caused by the earth's crust sliding along a fault or by the forming of a fault.

OPEN-ENDED QUESTIONS

1. What effect do faults have on our earth?
2. Could faults be prevented? How?

How Are Rocks Alike?   (K-6)

CONCEPTS

Some rocks are heavy and some are light.
Different rocks have different colors.
Some rocks are smooth and some are rough.
Some rocks are hard and some are soft.

MATERIALS

Knife	Magnifying glass
Penny	Sedimentary rocks
Glass	Conglomerates
Newspaper	Igneous rocks
Hammer	Metamorphic rocks
Cloth	

DISCUSSION

Where could you find different kinds of rocks?
When you feel rocks, how do they differ?

Processes

Pupil Discovery Activity

Teacher's Note: This activity should be done in groups of two or more children.

1. Obtain the following materials: knife, penny, glass, newspaper, hammer, cloth, magnifying glass, and several types of rocks the teacher has available for you.
2. Place these materials on your newspaper.

Observing
Comparing
Comparing
Comparing

3. Observe the rocks closely.
   In what ways are the rocks alike?
   In what ways are the rocks different?
   When you feel the rocks, how do they differ?
   Compare two rocks of the same size.

Comparing
Inferring
Inferring

   How does their weight compare?
   Why do you think some rocks are rough and jagged?
   What do you think has happened to the rocks that are smooth and rounded?

Classifying

4. Place your rocks in groups.
   In what other ways could you group the rocks?

Designing an investigation	How do you think you could tell the hardness or softness of a rock?
	5. Try some of your ideas on the rocks.
Hypothesizing	If two rocks were the same size, how could you find out which rock was heavier?
Designing an investigation	How could you tell whether a rock looked the same on the inside as it did on the outside?
Designing an investigation	How would you find out how rocks become smooth and rounded?
Inferring	Why are some of the rocks made of many smaller rocks or pieces?
Observing	Are the pieces of the rock rounded or jagged?
Observing	Are the pieces dull or shiny in the rock?

OPEN-ENDED QUESTIONS

1. In what ways are soft rocks used?
2. In what ways are hard rocks used?

How Do Limestone, Marble, and Granite Differ?   (3-6)

CONCEPTS

A sedimentary rock can be changed by compression and compaction.
This change may cause lower rocks in a sedimentary bed to become harder.
Limestone and marble are chemically the same.

MATERIALS

Piece of granite	Vinegar
Piece of limestone	Knife
Piece of marble	

DISCUSSION

How are limestone and marble alike?
How are limestone and marble different?
Why do you think these rocks could be different colors?

Processes   **Pupil Discovery Activity**

1. Obtain 3 or 4 pieces each of limestone, marble, and granite, 20 cc. of vinegar, and a knife.
2. Look at the rocks closely.

Designing an   How can you tell which is limestone and which is
  investigation   marble?
Comparing   How does the granite compare with the others?
Hypothesizing   In what way could you tell that the rocks are
                    related?
Hypothesizing   Which of these would scratch the other rocks?

3. Scratch the different pieces across each other.

Classifying   Which are harder?
Hypothesizing   What do you think will happen if you place a few
                    drops of acid or of vinegar, on your rocks?

Observing   4. Place a few drops on the pieces and record what
                    happens.

Teacher's Note: Explain to the class that geologists determine the similarity of substances by scratching them and by using chemical tests such as dropping acid on the rocks to see if they react chemically. They also have many other tests. Explain that limestone through heat and pressure in the earth is compacted into a harder substance called marble. Although its physical properties have changed, its chemical composition has remained the same. Marble may vary in color because of the various types of minerals that may be mixed with it.

OPEN-ENDED QUESTIONS

1. How does man use limestone, marble, and granite?
2. Which substances are the most common?
3. If you saw a substance you thought was salt, how would you prove it was salt?
4. What other ways do you think geologists identify substances? How could you find out?

How Does a Geyser Work?   (2-6)

CONCEPTS

Geysers are hot springs which throw up hot water and gases with explosive force from time to time.

Geysers are formed when ground water, heated by hot rocks or gases, gets so hot that it expands and releases dissolved gases in the water which exert pressure.

The expansion of water forces the water to the surface through partially obstructed cracks in the earth.

Geysers are found in volcanic regions or areas where there used to be volcanoes.

MATERIALS

Saucepan   2 bottle caps
Water   Hot plate
Pyrex funnel

Teacher's Note: This activity should involve one or two students.

DISCUSSION

What is a geyser?
How does a geyser work?
Where are geysers found?

Processes   **Pupil Discovery Activity**

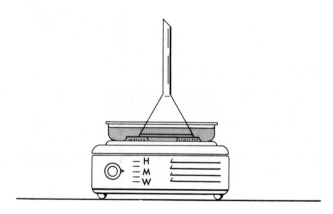

1. Obtain a saucepan, water, a funnel, two bottle caps, and a hot plate. Fill the saucepan half-full with water. Place the funnel in the saucepan, resting it on the two bottle caps. Set the saucepan on the hot plate and heat the water.

Hypothesizing   What will happen to the water?
Observing   2. As you observe the water, record what you see.

Observing   What happened to the water when it was heated?
Inferring   Why do you think this happened?
Hypothesizing   How did the funnel affect this experiment?

Teacher's Note: Water expands when heated. When
the water at the bottom of the pan boiled, it was
forced by pressure out through the top of the funnel.

3. Remove the saucepan from the hot plate.

Hypothesizing   What will happen to your experiment if the source
of heat is removed?

Teacher's Note: When the water is allowed to cool,
pressure will be reduced, thus causing the water to
remain in the saucepan.

Hypothesizing   How does water inside the earth become heated?

Teacher's Note: Ground water beneath the earth's surface is heated by hot rocks or gases.

Hypothesizing   What happens to the water inside the earth when
it becomes heated?

Applying   Why does hot water inside the earth escape?
Hypothesizing   How does the water inside the earth escape?
What is this type of geological feature called?

Teacher's Note: A geyser is an underground spring
which releases hot water with explosive force from
time to time. When ground water heats, it expands
and releases dissolved gases in the water which exert pressure. This forces the water to the surface
through cracks in the earth, thereby forming a geyser.

Summarizing   Explain how your experiment demonstrates what
happens in nature when a geyser occurs.

Hypothesizing   How could you cause your geyser to erupt again?
Applying   How do geysers in our earth erupt again and again?
Hypothesizing   In what regions of the world are geysers found?
Where are the most famous geysers located?

Designing an   How would you find out?
 investigation

Teacher's Note: Geysers in the earth erupt periodically
as the ground water is heated and expands under
pressure. Geysers are found only in volcanic regions
or in areas where there used to be volcanoes. The
most spectacular geysers are found in Yellowstone
National Park. "Old Faithful," the best known geyser, erupts at fairly regular intervals of about one
hour.

OPEN-ENDED QUESTIONS

1. What other experiments could you devise that would demonstrate how a geyser works?
2. What would you do to make your geyser shoot higher? Why might it not be a good idea to do this?
3. Why are geysers not found everywhere?
4. In what ways are geysers helpful to man?
5. In what ways are geysers a problem?

How Are Crystals Formed?   (1-6)

CONCEPTS

Crystals are non-living substances which grow into bodies of various shapes.
Crystals grow by adding on more layers of the same substance, keeping the same shape at all times.
Crystal size is determined by differences in the rate of crystallization.
If crystals are disturbed in the growing process, they will break apart into hundreds of microscopic pieces.
True solids are crystalline in form.
Crystalline form is important in determining some of the properties of substances.

MATERIALS

Tablespoon	Sugar
2 jars	2 pieces of clear silk thread
2 jar lids	Copper sulfate
Salt	2 pencils
Water	Plastic wrap
2 small glasses	

Teacher's Note: This activity will involve one or two students.

DISCUSSION

What are crystals?
How could you grow a crystal?
What happens when a crystal is growing?
Why is a study of crystals important?

Processes   **Pupil Discovery Activity**

PART I

1. Obtain a tablespoon of salt, a jar lid, and a small glass. Mix a tablespoon of salt in the glass of water. Stir the water well. Let the solution stand for a few minutes until it becomes clear.

Observing   What happened to the salt?

2. Very gently pour some of the salt solution into the jar lid and let it stand for several days where the lid will not be disturbed.

Hypothesizing   What do you think will happen to the salt solution?

3. After several days have passed, look at the materials in the lid.

Communicating   4. Describe what you see.
Comparing   5. How are the materials in the lid different from your original salt solution?

Inferring   Why do you now have a solid when you started out with a liquid?

Hypothesizing   What name could you give to the formations in the lid?

Teacher's Note: The salt dissolved in the water and when the salt water stood for several days, the water evaporated leaving salt crystals. Crystals are non-living substances which are found in various geometrical shapes.

PART II

1. Obtain a tablespoon of sugar, a jar lid, and a small glass of water. Be sure the tablespoon is clean. Mix a tablespoon of sugar in the glass of water. Stir the water well. Let the solution stand for a few minutes until it becomes clear.

Observing   What happened to the sugar?
Comparing   How is the sugar solution similar in appearance to the salt solution?

2. Obtain a lid and very gently pour some of the sugar solution into the lid and let it stand for several days.

Hypothesizing   What do you think will happen to the sugar solution?

3. After several days have passed, look at the materials in your lid.

Communicating   4. Describe what you see.
Comparing   How are the materials in this lid different from the materials in the lid containing the salt crystals?

Inferring   What happened to the sugar solution?

Teacher's Note: When the sugar water stood for several days, the water evaporated leaving sugar crystals.

PART III

1. Wash your hands carefully. Obtain two pieces of clear silk thread, two jars, copper sulfate, two pencils, plastic wrap, and water.
2. Fill the two jars three-fourths full of hot water and add copper sulfate until the water is saturated with it.
3. Obtain two seed crystals of copper sulfate, and tie each one to one end of separate pieces of silk thread. (Seed crystals, which should be ⅛″ to ¼″ in length, can be prepared in the same way that you just prepared sugar crystals.) Tie the free end of each piece of thread to separate pencils. Rest each pencil on a separate jar, allowing the crystals to fall into the copper sulfate solution. Place the jar where it will not be disturbed.

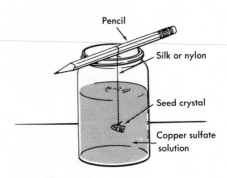

Pencil

Silk or nylon

Seed crystal

Copper sulfate solution

Hypothesizing
Hypothesizing

Why was it necessary for you to wash your hands?
What do you think the copper sulfate solution will do to the crystals?

4. Watch your crystals carefully for several days.

Observing

Record what happens to your crystals.

Teacher's Note: The copper sulfate solution causes the seed crystals to grow. Crystals grow by adding on more layers of the same substance, keeping the same shape at all times.

Hypothesizing

How could you grow larger crystals?

Teacher's Note: The slower crystals grow, the larger they become.

Hypothesizing

How could you slow down the growing process of the crystals?

Teacher's Note: Reducing the rate of evaporation causes the crystals to grow at a slower rate.

Hypothesizing

How could you slow down the rate of evaporation of the copper sulfate solution?

5. Remove one of the pencils. Obtain some plastic wrap, and cover the top of the jar from which you removed the pencil. Be sure to pierce a hole in the plastic wrap large enough for the suspended crystals to pass through when the pencil is returned to the top of the jar.

Comparing
Observing
Inferring

6. Compare both jars closely over several days.
   How do the crystals formed in the two jars differ? Explain why the crystals are different.

Teacher's Note: The crystal in the closed jar will be larger since the plastic wrap slowed down the rate of evaporation, therefore causing the crystal to grow at a slower rate. The open jar will have a smaller crystal since the faster rate of evaporation causes the crystal to grow at a faster rate.

Hypothesizing

After the third day, what do you think would happen if you disturbed the crystals during their periods of crystallization?

Observing

7. Gently shake the jar without the plastic wrap and explain what happens.

Teacher's Note: If crystals are disturbed in the growing process, they will break apart into hundreds of microscopic pieces.

Inferring
Summarizing
Classifying

Where are crystals found in nature?
How are crystals grown?
Explain how crystalline form is important in determining the properties of substances.

Hypothesizing

Why do some rocks have large crystals and some have small crystals?

Teacher's Note: True solids are crystalline in form. Crystals grow by adding on more layers of the same substance, keeping the same crystalline form at all times. Crystalline form is important in determining some of the properties of substances. Differences in the rate of crystallization determine differences in crystal size.

OPEN-ENDED QUESTIONS

1. What other experiments could you devise that would involve growing crystals?
2. How are crystals used in industry?
3. If there were no crystals on earth, how would man's way of living be affected?
4. How would you grow large crystals?

METEOROLOGY

How Can Solar Energy Be Used?   (2-4)

CONCEPTS

Water in a salt solution absorbs the sun's energy and evaporates, leaving the salt behind.

Water vapor when cooled is condensed and changed into water.

MATERIALS

Salt	Ring stand (see diagram)
2 dishes	Ring clamps
Water	Spoon
Plastic bag	

DISCUSSION

What ways can you make the sun do work for you?

Processes   **Pupil Discovery Activity**

PART I

> *Teacher's Note:* This activity should be done in groups of five.

1. Obtain 2 small dishes and some salt.
2. Pour a spoonful of salt into one dish, add water, and stir with a spoon until all the salt is dissolved.
3. Cover both dishes with a plastic bag, setting up the equipment as shown in the diagram below.

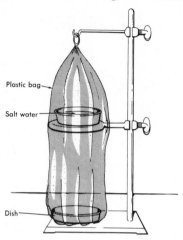

Plastic bag

Salt water

Dish

Hypothesizing
Hypothesizing

Observing

4. Place your equipment in the sunlight.
   What do you think will happen to the salt water?
   Why do you think you were told to cover the salt water with a plastic bag?
5. Record your observations every day.

Teacher's Note: When there is only salt remaining in the top dish and the water is in the bottom dish, the following steps should be done by the group:

PART II

Comparing
Inferring

Inferring
Inferring
Inferring
Applying

Applying

1. Taste the water in the bottom dish.
   How does the water taste?
   Where did the water in the bottom of the dish come from?
   What happened to your salt solution?
   Where did the water go?
   Why did the water disappear?
   How does the sun's energy (solar energy) benefit man?
   How could this method be helpful to people who live near the ocean but do not have enough drinking water?

OPEN-ENDED QUESTIONS

1. What are some other uses for this method *of obtaining drinking water?*

2. What are some other ways in which the sun's energy (solar energy) can be used to help man?

What Is a Barometer?   (K-6)

CONCEPTS

Air exerts pressure.
Air pressure changes.
Air pressure may indicate the type of weather.
Low air pressure usually indicates rainy or cloudy weather.
High air pressure usually indicates fair weather.

MATERIALS

Coffee can	Straight pin
Large balloon or a rubber drum	Card
Straw	Large rubber band
Glue	

DISCUSSION

Teacher's Note: Have each child blow up a balloon.

What is in the balloon?
How do you know there is pressure exerted in the balloon?
How can you discover whether or not air has the same pressure at all times and at all places?
What is a barometer?
What is it used for?
How might location affect the readings of the barometer?

Teacher's Note: The room temperature will affect the barometer the children will make in this activity. It does not, therefore, only measure air pressure differences. It might be desirable to have some students keep their barometers outside class and compare their readings with those in class.

Processes   **Pupil Discovery Activity**

1. Obtain a coffee can, large rubber balloon, rubber band, straw, glue, straight pin, and a card.
2. Cover the coffee can with a piece of rubber to make a drum. (Cut the balloon to make a drum head.)

Slip a rubber band around the rubber of the balloon
to keep it on the can.

3. Place a small amount of glue in the center of the
   drum and attach a straw as shown in the diagram.
   Place another drop of glue on the end of the straw
   and attach the pin.

4. Mark a card with some lines which are the same
   distance apart. Tack it on the wall as shown in the
   diagram.

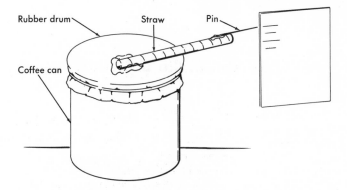

Hypothesizing

What will happen to the rubber drum if the air
pressure on it increases?

Hypothesizing

What will happen to the rubber drum if the air
pressure decreases?

Teacher's Note: When air pressure increases, it pushes
down on the rubber drum, causing the straw to give
a high reading. When the air pressure is low, the
opposite will happen. A falling barometer may indicate that a storm is approaching.

5. Record the readings of the barometer three times a
   day for a week.

Comparing

How do the readings of the barometer differ during
the day?

Comparing
Inferring

How do the readings differ from day to day?
What causes the readings to vary?

6. Record the type of weather existing at the time the
   barometer readings are made.

Inferring

What kind of air pressure generally exists during
fair weather?

Inferring

What kind of air pressure exists during stormy
weather?

7. Compare the readings of barometers in different
   locations.

Inferring   What reasons can you give for the readings?
Applying   By using the readings of the barometer, predict
                            what the weather will be.

OPEN-ENDED QUESTIONS

1. Does air travel from an area of high pressure to an area of low pressure, or
   from an area of low pressure to an area of high pressure? Why?
2. What would you do to improve the barometer?
3. What other materials could you use to make a barometer?

How Can You Make a Cloud?   (3-6)

CONCEPTS

Water needs to have dust or other small particles in order for it to condense
   easily.
The decreased air pressure causes the temperature of air to drop.
The higher you go in the lower atmosphere, the more the temperature drops.
There is more rain and snow in mountain regions than in the lowland regions.
When the air is cooled, the water condenses.
Many fluids vaporize.

MATERIALS

Gallon jug   Two flasks
Matches   One burner
Ice cubes

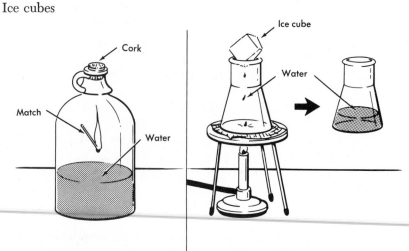

Activity 1   Activity 2

DISCUSSION

Teacher's Note: This activity should have been preceded by those on air pressure and molecules.

What is the name scientists give to the smallest particle of a substance?
What are the three states of matter?
What are the characteristics of each state?
How do you change a liquid to a gas?
How do you change a gas to a liquid?
What state of matter is rain?
What does rain come from?
What is a cloud made of?
What causes a cloud to form?
What types of air pressure do you know about?

Processes

PART I

Pupil Discovery Activity

1. Obtain a gallon jug with about an inch of water in it, and a match. Light the match, and drop it in the jug. Try to let it burn for a few seconds.
   As soon as it goes out, blow hard into the jug and then pull it away from your mouth quickly.

Assuming
Inferring   What did the jug contain?
Inferring   What happened in the jug?
             Where did the water come from that made the cloud in the jug?

2. Try this activity again, but this time don't use the match.

Observing   3. Record your results.
Inferring   Why did you use the match?
Applying   What kind of air pressure existed in the jug while you were blowing into it?
Inferring   What happened to the air pressure in the jug when you pulled the jug away from your mouth?
Inferring   Why did the water condense?
Summarizing   What must happen for a cloud to form?

Teacher's Note: In the jug activity the match was necessary because it gave off tiny smoke particles which the water uses as a nucleus on which to condense. The sudden release of pressure in the moist air in the jug causes the temperature in the jug to drop, and the water then condenses.

PART II

Teacher's Note: Caution students about the dangers of boiling water.

1. Obtain two flasks. Fill them about one-quarter full with water. Heat one of the flasks. After it is fairly warm, remove it from the burner and place an ice cube on the top of it.
2. Record what happens.

Comparing
Inferring

3. Compare this flask with the other one.
   Why did a cloud form in one flask and not in the other?

Inferring

What did the ice do to the water in the air?

Applying

When air rises it cools. From what you have learned in this experiment, can you explain why there is more rain and snow in the mountains?

Imagining

What has to be done to air to see water in it?

Applying

Why does the air over heated water have more moisture?

Inferring

What happens to the moisture in the air when it cools?

Summarizing

How are clouds made?

Teacher's Note: In this activity, the water in the flask is saturated with moisture. The ice cube cools the air and causes the water to condense. Emphasize to the class that the higher you go in the lower atmosphere, the more the temperature drops. This causes condensation and helps to explain why there is more rain and snow in mountain regions.

Clouds can also be made with alcohol and an air pump. This can be done to show that many fluids vaporize.

OPEN-ENDED QUESTIONS

1. What substances other than water can you use to make a cloud?
2. How could you make a cloud quickly?
3. What other factors could be involved in the formation of a cloud?

How Big Should You Make a Parachute?   (K-4)

CONCEPTS

Air has pressure.
A larger surface will collect more air beneath it.

The more air beneath the surface of a parachute, the slower it will fall to the earth.

Large weights need larger parachutes.

MATERIALS

3 pieces of cloth—square in shape and various sizes.
3 objects which weigh the same (nuts and bolts will do).

DISCUSSION

Fan your hand from one side of your body to the other in front of you.
What can you feel?
How does fanning affect the movement of air?
Cup your hands together and fan them from one side of your body to the other in front of you.
How does this affect the movement of air?

Processes   **Pupil Discovery Activity**

1. Obtain 3 pieces of cloth and a weight for each.
2. Make three parachutes of different sizes but attach equal weights to each parachute as shown in the diagram.

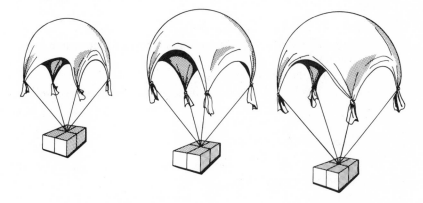

	3. Throw the parachutes into the air and let them fall.
Observing	4. Record what happened.
Comparing	Which parachute fell the fastest?
Inferring	Why do you think one parachute falls faster than another?
Applying	What are the parachutes catching as they fall?
Inferring	From this activity, what can you tell about the air?

Hypothesizing   What do you think would happen if you used lighter
                             weights on your parachutes?
                         5. Obtain some lighter weights and repeat the activity.
                         6. Record your observations.
Summarizing   What general rule could you make about the size
                             of a parachute?
Applying   Could anything besides the size of the parachutes
                             be a factor?

OPEN-ENDED QUESTIONS

1. Do the activity again and change other factors.
2. How would you improve the observations and data you recorded to make
   them more accurate?

How Much Water Will Snow Make?   (2-6)

Teacher's Note: If snow is not available, substitute crushed ice, but tell the
class that snow varies from ice in the amount of water it contains.

CONCEPTS

When snow falls lightly on the earth, the crystals leave air spaces between
them.
When snow melts, it becomes water.
When a substance changes from a solid state of matter to a liquid state, it ab-
sorbs heat.
Heat affects the rate of melting.
Water molecules occupy less volume as a liquid than as a solid.

MATERIALS

Glass jar   Candle
Meter or centimeter stick   Matches
Crayon or pencil   Clock (with second hand)
Cup full of snow or crushed ice Ring stand and ring

Teacher's Note: Show the picture on p. 483 to start the discussion.

DISCUSSION

What can you tell about this picture?
Why is the man in the picture measuring the depth of the snow?

What will the snow change to?

When it melts and changes to water, how much water will this snow make?

Why does a soil conservationist want to know how much water snow will make?

What is he measuring that will help tell him how much water he is going to get from the snow?

What could you do to find out how much water the snow would make?

Processes

Pupil Discovery Activity

Teacher's Note: This activity should be done in groups of two.

1. Obtain a jar and fill it with snow.
2. Mark the level of the snow with a crayon.

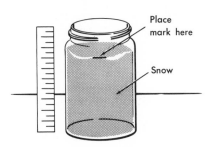

Place mark here

Snow

3. Let the snow melt.
4. Time the rate of melting in minutes and seconds, using the clock on the wall or your wrist watch.

Observing — As the snow melts, what do you see collecting in the bottom of the jar?

Inferring — What causes the snow to melt and change to water?

Hypothesizing — How might you make the snow melt faster?

5. Fill another jar with snow.
6. Mark the level of the snow.
7. Obtain a ring stand and ring.
8. Set the jar on the ring.
9. Obtain a candle and light it. Place it under the jar so the flame is about 5-8 cm. from the bottom of the jar.
10. Time the rate of melting in minutes and seconds as you did with the first jar.
11. When the snow in each jar finishes melting, record the time it took.
12. For each jar mark the level with a crayon.
13. Measure the water level in centimeters and record your findings.

Inferring

Observing and inferring

What can you conclude about snow when it melts? Did heating the snow affect the amount of water produced? Why?

OPEN-ENDED QUESTIONS

1. What happens to water when it freezes?
2. What do you think would happen if other substances such as dry ice were heated?

Biological Sciences

ANATOMY & PHYSIOLOGY

What Is a Cell? (5-8)

CONCEPTS

The smallest unit of life capable of existing independently is the cell.
The cell consists of many different parts.
Each part functions in a special way.
There are many types of cells.
All living things are made of cells.

MATERIALS

Onion	Iodine, ink, or methylene blue stain
Eye dropper	Glass cover slip
Water	Knife
Small paper cup	Toothpick
Glass slide	Microscope

DISCUSSION

How does a rock differ from a plant?
What do you think living things are made of?
How would you find out?

Processes

Observing

Pupil Discovery Activity

1. Obtain an onion and a knife. Cut the onion in half. What do you notice about its structure?
2. Obtain an eye dropper, a cup of water, a glass slide, iodine, and a glass cover slip. Peel off an inside ring of the onion. From this ring, pull off the outer layer of tissue. This layer should be as thin as tissue paper. Place this tissue in a drop of water on a glass slide.

Hypothesizing

What do you think will happen if you place a drop of iodine on the tissue?

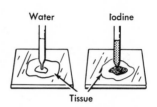

Water   Iodine

Tissue

3. Place a drop of iodine on the tissue.

Observing   What effect does iodine have on the onion tissue?
Inferring   How will this help you to see the tissue?
Observing   4. Observe the tissue through the microscope.
Record your observations.
The small things you see are called cells.
Observing   How are these cells arranged?

Teacher's Note: The children should see the following:

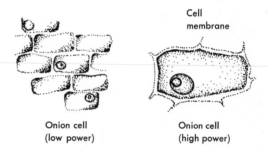

Cell
membrane

Onion cell   Onion cell
(low power)   (high power)

Hypothesizing   What do you think you will see if you look through the high power?

5. Try the high power.
Observing   What do you see?
Designing an   How could you find out what the parts of cells are
   investigation   called?
Designing an   How could you find out about the functions of these
   investigation   parts?
Inferring   How do you think human tissue is similar to plant tissue?

Designing an   How would you find out?
   investigation

6. Obtain a toothpick, a knife, a glass slide, and a coverslip. Gently scrape the inside of your cheek or lip with the toothpick. With a knife, scrape some of the white material on the toothpick into a drop of water on a glass slide. Then add a drop of iodine.

7. Spread the material out in the water and place a glass cover slip over it. Examine the material with your microscope under high power.

Observing — What do you see?

Comparing — How are the cells similar to those you saw in the onion tissue?

Inferring — From what you have observed, what could you say about living matter?

OPEN-ENDED QUESTIONS

1. What are some similarities and some differences of all living tissue?
2. How long can living tissues exist without water?
   How would you go about finding out?
3. How could you find out what effect prolonged darkness will have on living tissue?

What Do Your Bones Do? (4-6)

CONCEPTS

Bones are the framework of the body.
Bones are composed of calcium and phosphate salts.
Bones of an adult are different from the bones of a child.
Bones are classified as round, flat, long, and short.
The function of a bone is limited by its size and shape.
Bones may have defects.
Bones are made of organic and inorganic substances.
Calcium is necessary for the development of bones.
X-rays pass through tissue and can be used to tell where a bone is broken.

MATERIALS

Human skeleton (small model), skeletal chart, or good picture of a skeleton
5 chicken bones (legs or thighs are best)
Small tree twig
Small saw
2 X-ray pictures, one of a good bone and one of a broken bone
Vinegar or weak hydrochloric acid
Medium-sized beaker or sauce pan
½ pint of milk

DISCUSSION

How are the structure of a skyscraper and the structure of your body similar?
What is the framework of your body called?
What makes up the skeleton?
If you wanted to determine how bones function, what could you do to find out?

Processes	**Pupil Discovery Activity**
PART I	
	1. Obtain a model of a skeleton.
Observing	What are some functions of the skeleton or skeletal system?
Inferring	How do bones protect the softer parts of your body? Name some places in your body where bones cover or protect important organs? Point to some of these places on your body.
Observing	Where are some places that bones are joined together to allow you to move? Point to some of these places on your body.
Observing	Which bones help you to stand up? Point to some of these places on your body.
Observing	Feel the top of your head. Your head is really made up of several bones.
Inferring	How are they joined to each other? Feel the jawbone. Open and close your mouth.
Observing	Does the bottom jawbone or the upper part of the jaw move? Feel your spine.
Inferring	From feeling it, what can you say about the spine?
Observing	How many bones are in the spine?
Designing an investigation	How could you find out?
	What is a fracture?
Classifying	What are the different types of fractures?

Teacher's Note: There are two types of fractures, simple and compound. A simple fracture occurs when the bone but not the skin is broken. A compound fracture is a bone fracture which produces a wound by puncturing soft tissues.

PART II	
	1. Obtain two chicken bones.
Hypothesizing	How could you fracture a chicken bone?
	2. Fracture one of the chicken bones.
Describing	Describe the appearance of the fracture you made.

Teacher's Note: You might have the children compare the fractured bones. Some of them will probably be simple and others compound. Give them the names for the appropriate fractures. (To properly observe a compound fracture, you will need a chicken leg or thigh with the skin and flesh still intact.)

3. Obtain a set of X-rays and look at them.

Describing
Inferring
Hypothesizing

Describe what you see.
How do X-rays help a doctor treat a broken bone?
What does a doctor do to correct or treat a broken bone?

4. Obtain a twig and the fractured bone.

Hypothesizing

How would you use the twig to support the bone and keep it from moving?

Hypothesizing

What do you think a doctor does to keep the bone from moving?

Inferring

Older people fracture their bones more easily than do children.

Designing an
  investigation
  PART III

What can you do to find out why?

1. Obtain a bone, vinegar or hydrochloric acid, and a beaker. Fill the beaker with one of the above solutions.

Hypothesizing

What do you think will happen to the bone if placed in the solution?

2. Take the bone out of the solution after a minimum of two days.

Observing
Inferring
Hypothesizing

What effect did the solution have on the bone?
How has the strength of the bone changed?
What could you do to find out?
Compare an untreated bone to the treated bone.

Comparing
Inferring

How do they differ?
Which of these two types of bones do you think are similar to those of older people?

Teacher's Note: Older peoples' bones are more calcified than those of young people. As a result they are more brittle.

PART IV

Hypothesizing	What do you think bones are made of?
Designing an investigation	How could you find out?

Teacher's Note: Bones contain organic material and calcium and phosphate salts.

1. Obtain a ½ pint of milk. Open the carton. Examine the milk.

Observing
What do you notice about it?

Teacher's Note: The white material in the milk contains calcium minerals necessary for bones to grow.

2. Obtain a bone and a saw.
   Cut the bone in half.

Observing
What do you notice about the inside of the bone and the dust material produced from sawing?
What is the center of a bone called?

Teacher's Note: The center of the bone is called the marrow. It is important for making blood and for keeping the bone in good health.

Name some foods you need to eat in order to keep your bones growing and in good health.

OPEN-ENDED QUESTIONS

1. What effect would the lack of milk over an extended period of time have on a person?
2. What are the steps a doctor goes through in setting a bone?
3. Why do some people need to have plates or rods attached or fitted to broken bones?

What Enables Our Bodies to Move? (6-8)

CONCEPTS

Nerves are sensitive to touch, to chemicals, and to electrical shock.
Man is not sensitive to charges below 6 volts.
A person should not handle electrical equipment with wet hands.
In order for current to flow, there must be a complete circuit.
Dry paper is a nonconductor of electricity.

MATERIALS

1 or 2 earthworms
Blunt metal object (tweezers)
2 ounces of vinegar (acid)
Dry cell—1½ volt with wires connected to the electrodes
2 copper wires, each 8 inches
Waxed paper (enough to wrap a worm in)

DISCUSSION

What happens when you touch a hot stove?
Why do you jerk your hand away?
How does this reaction help protect you?

Processes   **Pupil Discovery Activity**

Teacher's Note: This activity should be done in groups
of two.

1. Obtain a worm and place it on your desk and observe it without touching it.

Hypothesizing   What do you think the worm will do if you touch
                  it?

2. Touch the worm with a blunt metal object.

Observing   What did it do?
                  What do you think caused it to react?

3. Soak the tip of some paper in the vinegar.

Hypothesizing   What do you think will happen if you touch the
                  worm with this paper?

4. Touch the worm with the paper.

Observing   How did the worm react?

5. Hook the copper wire to each terminal on the dry
   cell. Be sure the ends of the wire have the insulation
   around them scraped off.

6. Touch both wires of the dry cell yourself.

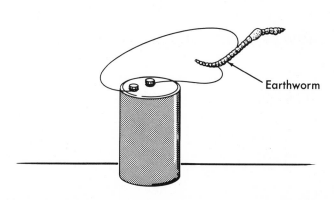

Earthworm

Observing	What did you feel?
Hypothesizing	What do you think will happen when you touch the worm with both wires?
Observing	7. Touch the worm first with one wire and note the reaction. Then, touch it with both wires and see how it reacts.
Comparing	Which caused the most reaction, one wire or two? Why?
Comparing	Which caused the most reaction: the metal, acid, or electricity?
Hypothesizing	What do you think will happen if you wrap the worm in waxed paper and repeat the above tests?
	8. Wrap the worm in waxed paper and repeat step 7.
Observing	What was the reaction?

Teacher's Note: If possible, dissect a frog to show to the class by taking out all of its organs and exposing its backbone. The silvery strings you see entering and leaving the spine are the nerves. If these nerves are touched with metal tweezers, some of the frog's muscles will respond. All of the activities above can be performed on toads and frogs as well as on earthworms.

OPEN-ENDED QUESTIONS

1. Why do you think too much electricity might kill you?
2. Why should you never pick up an electrical appliance or unscrew a light bulb when your hands are wet?
3. Why should you never touch an electrical piece of apparatus unless you know how it works?
4. Why is it a bad idea to have a radio plugged in near a bathtub or even in the bathroom?

How Do Our Muscles Work?   (6-8)

CONCEPTS

Muscle cells make it possible to move parts of your body.
There are two different types of muscles: voluntary and involuntary.
Voluntary muscles are arranged in pairs and work on opposite sides of a bone.

There are three types of levers operated by voluntary muscles, causing the movement of various parts of the body.

MATERIALS

Uncooked chicken leg and wing, or frog leg, preferably with the feet attached to the legs

Forceps (to pull the skin off the leg)

Processes

Pupil Discovery Activity

1. Where have you seen a muscle?
   Hold up an uncooked chicken leg and wing (a frog leg may be used).

Inferring
Observing

How is the chicken able to move its legs or wings? What kind of tissue do you mainly see around the bones of the wing and leg?

Teacher's Note: Most of the tissue seen and most of the meat you eat is muscle. The chicken has several hundred different muscles to move various parts of its body. Muscle tissue covers the body in sheets and bands that lie between the skin and skeleton.

What are the names of some of the voluntary muscles in the upper arm?

Teacher's Note: You may have to explain that muscles which move bones are called voluntary muscles. The body also has involuntary muscles such as those that are in the wall of the intestines. The involuntary muscles move without a person having to think about them. Some common voluntary muscles are biceps (located in the front of the upper arm), triceps (the large muscle at the back of the upper arm), deltoid (large, triangular muscle of the shoulder which raises the arm away from the side).

2. Obtain some forceps and pull the skin off the chicken leg. Point out several of the different bundles of muscles.

Applying

Can anyone show me one of his muscles?

Teacher's Note: The most common reaction to this is for someone to double up his fist and bring it up close to his shoulder. Have the class take a good grasp of the triceps (underside of the upper arm; see diagram below) and hold it while they raise their lower arms.

Observing   What happens to the triceps when you raise your
                              arm?
                              Have the class lower their arms.
Observing   What happened to the arm the second time?
Hypothesizing   Why did the upper part of the arm get thicker when
                              the arm was raised?

> *Teacher's Note:* To raise your arm, the muscle has to
> contract. As it contracts, it becomes shorter and
> thicker, forming a "bump." Have all the class flex
> their arms to show their biceps. Teach them the
> names of these upper arm muscles. The biceps are
> composed of two muscles connected to the bone by
> a tendon. The triceps consist of three muscles con-
> nected to the bone by one tendon. The triceps lie
> on the opposite side of the arm from the biceps. The
> chief characteristic of all muscles is that they can
> contract. This is because of the special function of
> the cells which form muscles. When one muscle con-
> tracts, the opposing muscle relaxes.

Hypothesizing   3. If a muscle can only contract how is it possible to
                                 return your arm to its original position?

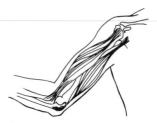

> *Teacher's Note:* Muscles work in pairs. Biceps contract
> to raise the arms. To lower the arms, the triceps
> contract and the biceps relax. All bones are moved
> this way. Example: When you show someone how
> strong you are, you "make a muscle" by contracting
> your biceps, and your forearm is pulled up toward
> your shoulder. If you want to lower your arm, you
> relax your biceps and contract your triceps. As you
> bend your arm back and forth at the elbow, each of
> these muscles relaxes and contracts over and over.
> Draw the above diagram on the board to show how
> skeletal muscles work.

                              4. Show the lower part of the chicken bone to the class.
Observing   Where can you see part of a tendon on the chicken
                                 leg?

Teacher's Note: If the foot of the bird has been cut off, only part of the shiny white tendon will be seen.

Inferring

5. How is a muscle fastened to the bone?

Teacher's Note: Some muscles are connected directly to the bone, whereas others are connected to a tough, nonstretchable cord, or tendon, which is connected to the bone. (Write "tendon" on the board.)

Where can you feel a strong tendon in your own body?

Teacher's Note: If you reach down and grasp the back of your foot just above the heel, you can feel the strong tendon called the Achilles tendon that connects the muscle of your leg to your heel bone. (Write "Achilles" on the board.) Raise yourself on the ball of your foot. You can feel the calf muscles tighten and bulge as they contract and pull upward on your heel.

Hypothesizing

6. What is the correct way to lift an object so you do not strain your muscles?

Have a child demonstrate by picking up two small objects as shown in the following diagram.

Incorrect   Correct (use legs)

Hypothesizing

Why do you think one method of lifting objects is better than the other?

Teacher's Note: With the correct method you use more of your skeleton and many more muscles than in the other, so there is less likelihood of straining any one muscle. Have all the members of the class practice the correct way to lift heavy objects.

Inferring

7. What kinds of machines make it possible for the body to lift more weight?

Teacher's Note: A lever is often used. A lever is a device consisting of a bar turning about a fixed point, the fulcrum, using power or force applied at a second point to lift or sustain a weight at a third point. Our body contains many levers. The joints act as the fulcrum, our muscles as the force, and the weight is that part which we lift.

OPEN-ENDED QUESTIONS

1. What are some examples of levers?
2. Where are some levers in the human body?

By What Process Do Humans Breathe?   (5-8)

CONCEPTS

When a person exercises, breathing increases.
Breathing increases because more carbon dioxide is produced.
Carbon dioxide causes the diaphragm to work more rapidly.
When the diaphragm moves up in the rib cage, it forces air out of the lungs.
When the diaphragm moves down, air is pulled into the lungs.
Gases and water vapor are exhaled from the lungs.

MATERIALS

Large rubber band	Balloon
Stop watch	Model of the chest cavity
Tape measure	Mirror

Glass tube or jar 6″ in diameter and 10″ tall with a hole in the bottom

Cork or rubber stopper with a hole in the center

Piece of pliable rubber or a part of a balloon (preferably 8″ × 8″)

Paper cups or glasses

Straw or glass tube

½ cup or 100 cc. of limewater or calcium hydroxide

Water

Sealing wax

String

DISCUSSION

How many times a minute do you breathe?

How would you go about finding out?

Processes   **Pupil Discovery Activity**

Teacher's Note: This activity should be done in groups of two or three children. For exercise the children may jump up and down. Put the boys and girls in separate groups.

PART I

1. Do the following with another student. Record the number of times he breathes. Let him also record the number of times you breathe.

	At Rest	After Exercise
One minute	_____	_____
Two minutes	_____	_____
Three minutes	_____	_____

Comparing — What is the average number of times a person breathes per minute at rest?

Comparing — What is the average number of times per minute a person breathes after exercise?

Hypothesizing — What makes a person breathe faster?

Inferring — Why did you count the number of times a person breathes for several rather than for just one minute?

Hypothesizing — What gas do you need from the air?

Hypothesizing — What do you exhale?

Designing an investigation — How can you prove that you exhale water?

Designing an investigation — How can you prove that you exhale carbon dioxide?

What gas do you breathe from the air that your body does not use?

Teacher's Note: Explain that air contains about 80% nitrogen, 20% oxygen, 0.03% carbon dioxide, and small percentages of other gases. But the body does not use the nitrogen.

How does the size of your chest vary when you breathe?

Designing an
investigation

How would you find out?

2. With the tape measure, check and record these measurements.

	Top of Chest	Lower Diaphragm
Inhale	————	————
Exhale	————	————

Interpreting data

3. Construct a graph to illustrate these variations.

PART II

1. Obtain a glass jar, glass tube, cork or rubber stopper, balloon, rubber sheet, string, and some sealing wax.
2. Fit the stopper into one end of the jar, and insert the glass tube with the balloon tied on it through the hole in the stopper. Seal any holes around the tube with the sealing wax.
3. Fix the rubber sheet onto the opened end of the jar with a large rubber band.

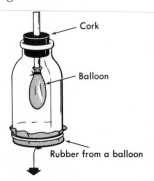

Cork

Balloon

Rubber from a balloon

Hypothesizing

What do you think will happen to the balloon if you pull down on the rubber cover at the bottom of the jar?

4. Pull down on the rubber balloon.
   Record your observation.

Hypothesizing

What do you think will happen if you push up on the rubber cover?

5. Push up on the balloon.
   Record your observation.

Inferring

Why do you see these changes?

Inferring

Where in your body do you have something that works like this?

Teacher's Note: Introduce the word "diaphragm."

Use a model or a chart of the chest cavity for reference.

Observing

How do the diaphragm, lungs, and chest lie in relation to one another in the chest cavity?

6. Diagram and label the parts of the body used in breathing.

PART III

What do you exhale?

1. Obtain a mirror.

Hypothesizing

When you breathe, what leaves your mouth?

2. Take a mirror and exhale on it. Hold the mirror near your nose.

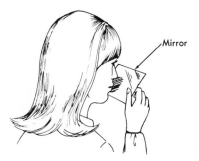

Person exhales on mirror

Observing
Inferring
Assuming
Hypothesizing

What do you see on the mirror?
Why does moisture collect on the mirror?
Where does the moisture come from?
What kinds of gases do you think you exhale?

Teacher's Note: Explain that exhaled air contains about 80% nitrogen, 16% oxygen, 3.0% carbon dioxide, and small percentages of other gases.

Inferring
Inferring
Inferring

What happens to the nitrogen you inhale?
What gas in air do you need?
What gas do you exhale more of than you inhale?

PART IV

1. Obtain a straw and 100 cc. of limewater (or some calcium hydroxide). Mix the limewater with water. Let it settle.

2. Blow through a straw or glass tube into the limewater.

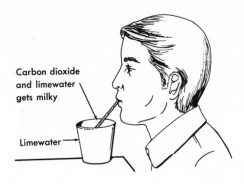

Carbon dioxide
and limewater
gets milky

Limewater

Observing

What happened as you blew (exhaled) into the limewater?

Inferring

Why did it change color?

Teacher's Explanation: When carbon dioxide is added to limewater, it changes to a milky color because the carbon dioxide combines with calcium hydroxide to form a white precipitate.

PART V

Teacher's Note: This part of the activity should be done in groups of two.

1. Obtain a mirror.

Observing

How does the rate of your breathing vary over several minutes?

Designing an investigation

What would you have to do in order to make your breathing increase?

Measuring

2. One member of the team should close his mouth and hold a mirror near his nose. The other member should count the number of times the first one breathes during a three-minute period.

3. Record your findings.

Inferring

Why should you determine the rate over three minutes rather than over one minute?

4. Have one member of the team jump up and down 10 times or more. Determine the rate of breathing in the same way you did for the person at rest.

Measuring

5. Record your findings.

Observing

How did the rate of breathing change?

Comparing

How does the pumping action of your heart at rest compare to the pumping action after you have exercised?

Hypothesizing

What does your blood carry through your lungs?

Inferring

If your heart pumps faster, how will the amount pumped per minute vary?

Inferring Why must the blood pass through your lungs when you exercise?

OPEN-ENDED QUESTIONS

1. How does exercise cause the heart to beat faster?
2. Why does an increase in carbon dioxide in the blood cause the heart to beat faster?
3. Explain the hypothesis "A person needing oxygen naturally breathes faster."

How Does Blood Circulate? (6-8)

CONCEPTS

The heart beats and pumps blood through the body.
Other animals have hearts.
Blood moves rapidly through the blood vessels.
Blood vessels are not all the same size.
Blood circulates.
All animals have individual variations.
Some animals are warm-blooded; some are cold-blooded.

MATERIALS

Several live earthworms	Paper cup
Paper towels	Ice water

DISCUSSION

What is a warm-blooded animal?
Snakes and turtles are cold-blooded animals. Would they be more active on a cold day or a warm day? Why?
What advantages are there in being a warm-blooded animal?
What evidence is there that an earthworm has blood vessels?
How can you find out if blood moves in the worm's blood vessels?
What evidence is there that the worm has a heart?
How many times per minute does the earthworm's heart beat?
How could you find out?

Processes	Pupil Discovery Activity

PART I

Teacher's Note: This activity should be done in groups of two or three.

1. Obtain an earthworm and a paper towel.
2. Place the worm on the paper towel.
3. Observe the worm to see if you can find any blood vessels.

Teacher's Note: There is an obvious blood vessel on the back of the worm.

Observing — Where did you find the blood vessel on the worm?

Observing — How does the vessel seem to vary in color?

Inferring — What is going through the blood vessel to give it that color?

Inferring — What makes you think the earthworm has a heart?

Observing —
4. Observe and record how many times the heart beats a minute.

Collecting data —
5. Determine the average heartbeat by using your figures and those of your classmates.
   What does *"average"* mean?

Inferring — Why did you average these figures in order to get the number of times the heart beats for a worm?

Teacher's Note: Each worm is a little different. The individuals counting the heartbeat might also have made a mistake. By taking the average, the mistakes are evened out.

Designing an investigation — What would you do to find out whether the earthworm is a warm-blooded animal or a cold-blooded animal?

PART II

1. Obtain a paper cup with ice water in it and an earthworm.
2. Place the worm in the ice water.

Observing —
3. Observe and record the actions of the worm.
4. After the worm has been in the water 5 minutes, remove it.

Observing —
5. Count and record how many times the heart beats.

Collecting data —
6. Determine the average.

Inferring — How does the heartbeat of the worm vary after it has been placed in cold water?

Teacher's Note: A worm is a cold-blooded animal. This means its body temperature is the same as the temperature of the environment. The colder the conditions, the slower the worm's body functions. The heart, therefore, beats slowly in a cold environment.

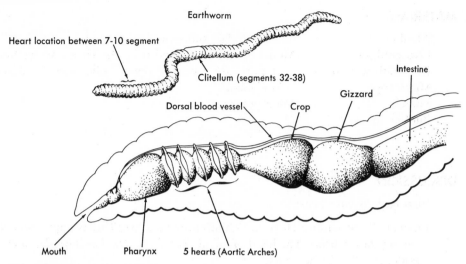

Earthworm

Heart location between 7-10 segment

Clitellum (segments 32-38)

Intestine

Dorsal blood vessel

Crop

Gizzard

Mouth   Pharynx   5 hearts (Aortic Arches)

OPEN-ENDED QUESTIONS

1. How many hearts does the earthworm have?
2. How do the hearts function?
3. How does the earthworm ingest and digest?

What Does the Heart Do?   (7-8)

CONCEPTS

The heart pumps the blood through the body.
The heart beats many times per minute.
When you exercise, the heart beats faster.
The heart has four chambers.
Blood moves in an orderly fashion through the body.

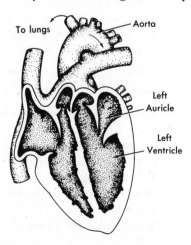

To lungs   Aorta

Left
Auricle

Left
Ventricle

MATERIALS

2 balloons	Y-shaped glass tubes or a small funnel
Live goldfish	Model of heart obtained from the Heart Association,
Dish with wet cotton	or purchase a calf or sheep heart (may be stored
Microscope	in alcohol)
Funnel	Microprojector
Rubber tubes	

DISCUSSION

How large is your heart?

Teacher's Explanation: Have the children make a fist. This is approximately the size of the heart. The heart of an adult is about 5 inches long, 3½ inches wide, and 2½ inches thick.

What does a heart look like?

Teacher's Note: This activity should be done in groups of four children.

Processes	**Pupil Discovery Activity**
PART I	
	1. Obtain a model of the heart, Y-shaped tube, a funnel, and 2 rubber tubes.
Observing	How many compartments do you see in the model of the heart?
Observing	2. Observe how these compartments are arranged and their similarities and differences.
Observing	Where is the heart located in your body?
	3. Place your hand at the center of the rib cage, near the lower edge.
Observing	What do you feel?
Designing an investigation	4. Make a stethoscope by attaching rubber tubes to the three ends of a Y-shaped glass tube. Attach a funnel to the tail of the "Y" tube.
	Teacher's Note: A small funnel with one rubber tube can be substituted if a "Y" tube is not available.
	5. Place the funnel on the chest of a friend.
	6. Place the other two ends in your ears. Caution: Use extreme care when placing the tubes in your ears so you do not harm the eardrums.
Observing	What do you hear?
Hypothesizing	Why do you think the heart sounds something like a drum?
Inferring	What makes the drum noise?

Teacher's Note: At this point, display a large chart or model. Identify the various parts of the heart and their functions. Trace the route of blood through the heart.

PART II

1. Obtain and observe a calf or sheep heart prepared by your teacher.

Comparing
In what ways are the real heart and the model alike?

Comparing
In what ways are they different?

Teacher's Note: This part of the activity should be done in groups of two.

PART III

1. Obtain a balloon. Have your partner fill the balloon half full of water.

Designing an
investigation
How can the balloon be used to demonstrate how the heart pumps blood?

Inferring
What does the water in the balloon represent?

Hypothesizing
What do you think would happen if you released the end of the balloon and pushed on the side of the balloon a little?

2. Gently push some of the liquid out of the balloon.

Inferring
How do you think the heart moves blood out of its chambers?

Teacher's Note: The heart is similar to the balloon in that it has liquid in it, but the heart actually has two pumps, one on the left side and one on the right side. The sound the students hear is due to the pumping of the heart.

3. Feel your pulse as shown in the diagram.

Observing
What do you feel?

Inferring
What causes the beats you feel?

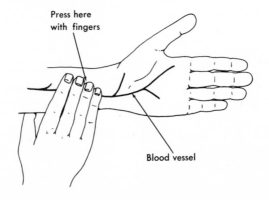

Press here with fingers

Blood vessel

Teacher's Note: The pulse is caused by the surge of blood that passes through the blood vessels each time the heart pumps.

4. Listen to your partner's heart and record the number of its beats per minute. Then have your partner jump up and down 15 times. Record the number of heartbeats after the exercise.

Observing

What happens to the rate of the heartbeat after the exercise?

Inferring

Why does the heart beat faster?

Teacher's Note: When you exercise, your muscles use more oxygen and food energy. Your heart is stimulated because of this activity, and it pumps faster, sending more blood to all parts of the body.

Describing

How does the blood move through the body?

Designing an investigation

What could you do with a goldfish to see how the blood moves through its body?

PART IV

Teacher's Note: This part of the activity may have to be done as a demonstration because of the complexity of the equipment.

1. Obtain a goldfish on a dish with wet cotton. Be sure to keep the cotton well soaked and in contact with the gills.
2. Place the fish under a microscope or microprojector.
3. Observe the blood circulating through the blood vessels in the tail or the fin of the fish.
4. Record your observation.

Summarizing

What can you conclude about the flow of blood?

Inferring

How does the beat of the heart influence this flow?

5. Quickly shake your fish by the tail fin and return it to the aquarium.

OPEN-ENDED QUESTIONS

1. Why is it necessary for the blood to continue moving through the body?
2. What does the blood do with waste materials picked up from the cells in the muscles?
3. What causes the heart to beat faster after exercise?
4. What effect would the temperature of the water have on the flow of blood in a goldfish?

What Happens to Starch in the Food You Eat?   (6-8)

CONCEPTS

Large food particles must be broken down into smaller molecules before they can be absorbed.

The breaking down of food by chemical means is called digestion.

Food must be dissolved before it can be used by the body.

Starch is a food.

Starch must be changed to dissolved sugar in order for it to pass through the lining of the small intestine.

MATERIALS

Cornstarch (one teaspoon)	3 paper towels
Sugar (one teaspoon)	3 test tubes
Iodine (a small bottle with an eye dropper)	Scale
Spoon	Beaker
3 glasses	Rubber band
Cracker	Flour (one gram)
2 jars with covers	4 cubes of sugar
Funnel	Hundred-cc. graduate

DISCUSSION

Look at the cracker.

How is the cracker going to help my body when I eat it?

What is going to happen to the cracker?

When will the cracker be ready to be used by the cells?

How is the body going to prepare this cracker for use?

If the body does not use every bit of the cracker, what is going to happen to that which is not used?

Where is the body going to digest this cracker?

What substances does the body contain to break down the cracker into usable substances?

Processes   **Pupil Discovery Activity**

1. Obtain a teaspoon of cornstarch, 2 glasses of water, and a teaspoon of sugar. Put the cornstarch into one glass of water and the sugar into the other. Stir each glass with a spoon.

Observing   How does the starchy water appear?

Observing   How does the sugar water appear?

Inferring	Which has dissolved?
Hypothesizing	What do you think would happen if you let the glasses stand for a day?
Inferring	How would this experiment help to explain why starch has to be changed so your body can use it?
	2. Stir the starch and water again until the starch is mixed with the water. Take a teaspoon of the starch and water mixture and put a drop of iodine into it.
Observing	What color does the mixture turn?
	3. Repeat the above step, substituting sugar water for the starch and water mixture.
Comparing	How does the result differ?
	Put a drop of iodine on your cracker.
Observing	What is the result?

Teacher's Note: Iodine is used to test for starch. Starch in the presence of iodine turns blue-black.

Summarizing	How would you summarize this test in terms of the results you have observed?
	4. Obtain a funnel, line it with a piece of paper towel, and set it in an empty glass. Stir the starch in the glass of water again. Slowly pour some of the starch water into the funnel.
	After the water has run through, look at the inside of the paper.
Observing	Is there any starch left inside the funnel?
Hypothesizing	How could you test the water to find out if any starch went through with the water?
	5. Perform this test for starch.
Observing	What color did the mixture turn?
Inferring	Is there starch present?
Hypothesizing	What do you think will happen if sugar water is poured through filter paper?
Hypothesizing	How can you tell if there is sugar in the water *before* and *after* you pour it into the funnel?
Inferring	Which do you think could go through the wall of your intestine better—starch or sugar? Why?
	6. Make a one per cent starch solution by taking one gram of flour and adding it to 100 cc. of water. (The 100-cc. measurement can be determined by using a graduate.) Stir the solution thoroughly in a beaker.
Measuring	Obtain three test tubes. Collect 20 cc. of saliva from your mouth in one test tube. Pour ½ of the saliva into the second test tube so that there are 10 cc. in each tube. Label one of the saliva test tubes the CONTROL. (Put a rubber band around it.) Add

10 cc. of starch solution to the other saliva test tube and 10 cc. of starch solution to the empty third test tube. Now put equal amounts of iodine (1 to 2 drops) into each of the three test tubes. Label the test tubes as shown below:

I: 10 cc. saliva   II: 10 cc. saliva
   control + iodine   10 cc. starch
                           solution + iodine

III: 10 cc. starch
     solution + iodine

Observing
Observing
Inferring
Observing
Inferring
Inferring
Observing

Inferring
Inferring

Applying

7. Allow the test tubes to stand for several hours. Observe and record your results.
Which test tubes turned blue?
Why?
Which test tube did not turn blue?
Why?
Why do you think you added saliva to test tube II?
After the tubes have stood for an hour, what tube changed color?
Why?
What effect does saliva produce on the starch in your mouth?
Why do you think you should chew your food well?

8. Obtain two jars with covers. Pour equal amounts of water into each of the two jars. Place two cubes of sugar into each jar and screw the covers on tightly. Place one jar aside and let it stand still. Shake the other jar vigorously.

Comparing
Inferring
Applying

Compare the results occurring in the two jars.
Why did the sugar dissolve faster in one jar?
What does this activity tell us about chewing your food before swallowing it?

Teacher's Note: The more the children chew their food, the more enzymes will mix with the food to break it down chemically. Chewing also helps to break the food down into smaller particles so more of it comes in contact with the enzymes.

OPEN-ENDED QUESTIONS

1. How does saliva affect other foods such as poultry, fruits, and vegetables?
2. Why should diabetics not eat starchy foods?
3. Test other foods for starch content.

How Does Our Skin Protect Us?   (2-6)

CONCEPTS

The skin protects us from microorganisms that cause disease.
A cut or wound in the skin can let microorganisms enter the body.
Microorganisms sometimes cause infection and disease.
A cut or wound in the skin should be properly treated immediately to prevent microorganisms from causing infection.
Antiseptics kill microorganisms, thus they can be used for the treatment of cuts or wounds.
Heat can kill microorganisms.

MATERIALS

4 unblemished apples   Book of matches
Rotten apple   5 small pieces of cardboard for labels
3 sewing needles   Candle
Small sample of soil

DISCUSSION

How is the covering of an apple or an orange like your skin?
What advantages are there for apples, oranges, and other types of fruit in having a covering?
How does the covering of your body, the skin, protect you?
What does a person mean when he says he wants to sterilize something?
In what ways might you sterilize something?

Processes   **Pupil Discovery Activity**

Teacher's Note: This activity should be done in groups of 2 to 5 children.

1. Obtain 5 pieces of cardboard for labels, a candle, a match, 3 needles, 1 rotten and 4 unblemished apples.
2. Put labels A, B, C, and D with the four unblemished apples.
3. Sterilize three needles by heating them in the flame of a candle.
4. Puncture apple A with a sterile needle in three different places. Apply iodine over two of these punctures.

5. Push the second sterilized needle into the soil and then into apple B in three places.

6. Puncture apple C with the third sterile needle but do not apply any iodine to the three punctures.

Iodine

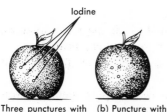

(a) Three punctures with sterile needle; and iodine applied on two punctures

(b) Puncture with needle stuck in soil

(c) Puncture with needle but no iodine

(d) Control

Rotten

7. Do nothing to apple D and the rotten apple.

8. Place all four labeled apples in a warm place for several days.

   Why was apple D not punctured?

Teacher's Note: If necessary, point out that this is the control in the experiment. Be sure children understand the term "control."

Hypothesizing — What do you think will happen if the apples stand for a few days?

Comparing — In what ways do you think they will look alike?

Comparing — How will they be different? Why?

Observing —
9. Observe the apples daily. Every other day make a diagram or illustration of the changes taking place. Discuss these with your lab group.

Observing — What has happened to some of the apples?

Comparing — How are the apples alike?

Comparing — How are they different?

Inferring — What do you think might have caused some of these changes?

Comparing — Which spots on the apples seem to be the most prominent? Why?

Comparing — Which other apple does apple C resemble most?

Observing — What has happened to apple D?

Inferring — What was apple D in your experiment?

10. Cut all five apples in half.

    Caution: Do not eat the apples because the iodine is poisonous.

Comparing — Which apples seem to look most like a rotten apple?

Inferring

Why did you apply iodine over two punctures on apple A?

Observing

What effect did the iodine have?

Teacher's Note: Iodine is an antiseptic. The iodine probably destroyed any microorganisms present in the wound.

Inferring

What happened to all the microorganisms on the needles after they had been heated?

Comparing

The skin of an apple is similar to what part of your body?

Inferring

Why did the rotten spots seem to grow a little larger each day?

Teacher's Note: Microorganisms have a fantastic growth rate. As long as there is a substantial amount of food present and space enough for growth, they will continue to reproduce.

Inferring

What do you think would happen if our skin were punctured?

Hypothesizing

What might a person do to a wound or puncture if he did not want to get an infection.

Teacher's Note: The wound should be cleaned, an antiseptic applied, and the wound covered with a sterile bandage.

OPEN-ENDED QUESTIONS

1. How might you set up the above experiment using oranges instead of apples?
   What do you think would happen?
2. Conduct the same experiment, but this time place the apples in a cool place.
   What effect does temperature have on decay?
3. In what other ways does your skin protect you?

ANIMALS

How Many Different Types of
Animals Do You Know?   (4-6)

CONCEPTS

Each animal lives in a place (environment) that best suits it.
The way the animal is built depends on where and how it lives.
Animals that live on dry land breathe through lungs.
Animals that usually live in water breathe through gills.
Land animals usually move by legs and may run, hop, or crawl.
Many land animals have claws and sharp teeth.
Animals live in water, on land, in the air, and on both land and water.
Animals that fly have wings and light bones.

MATERIALS

Fish to be dissected (this may be obtained from the local fish market)

Aquarium with large goldfish

Frog or chicken leg to be dissected

Aquarium with a frog (live)

Cut-away model of a human chest cavity showing the lungs

Animal's lung in alcohol

Dry bones from a chicken, cow, and any others that may be available

Claws, beaks, and teeth from as many animals as possible

As many models of stuffed animals as can be obtained

Live animals that take a minimal amount of care (such as salamanders, goldfish, crayfish, and white mice)

Set of scales for weighing the bones

Dissecting kit

Pictures (Set I): common animals, birds, fish, and reptiles

Pictures (Set II): rare or unusual animals, birds, fish and reptiles

Paper towels

Pencil and paper

DISCUSSION

How can animals be classified?
How do animals breathe?
What does a gill look like, and how does it function?
What kinds of animals use gills for breathing?

What does a lung look like, and how does it function?
What kinds of animals use lungs for breathing?
How does an animal's body structure affect its locomotion?
How does its body structure affect its diet?

Processes	**Pupil Discovery Activity**

PART I

Observing

1. Observe the fish in the aquarium. Note its breathing, locomotion, and feeding.
2. Obtain a dead fish, dissecting kit, and paper towels. Carefully dissect a fish. Your teacher will demonstrate the proper method for you to follow.

Observing
Inferring

3. Describe what you see in the area of the gills. What function do you think the various sections serve?

Gill filaments

Teacher's Note: You may want to demonstrate the proper method for dissecting a fish. Have the children work in groups of four. Cut the fish along the ventral side from just below the anus to the throat. Cut up from this incision to the dorsal side (top) of the fish at both ends of the incision. Using the scissors in the dissection kit, cut the ribs and expose the air bladder. Also remove the operculum or gill cover on one side. This will expose the gill filaments. (See diagram below.)

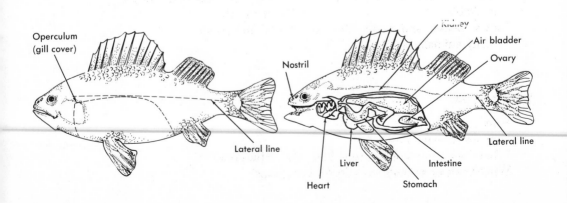

Operculum (gill cover)

Nostril

Kidney

Air bladder

Ovary

Lateral line

Lateral line

Heart

Liver

Stomach

Intestine

Inferring	In what ways does a fish use its fins and tail?
Inferring	How does their structure affect their use?
Inferring	In what manner does a fish ingest its food?
	Describe the bones of the fish.
Inferring	How do you think they affect its ability to swim?

PART II

1. Obtain a frog or chicken leg, two bones from a bird and a cow, and a scale.
   Carefully dissect and record your findings about the frog or chicken leg and how the leg affects the animal's locomotion.

Measuring

2. Measure and weigh two bones of equal length; one of a fowl and one of a cow.

Observing and inferring

3. Obtain and examine at least two sets of claws, beaks, and teeth and describe what you think the diet of each animal might be.

4. Obtain a cut-away model of a human chest cavity showing the lungs.

Observing

Describe the lungs.

Hypothesizing

What is their function?

Name some animals that breathe with the use of lungs.

Comparing

How do human lungs differ from those of other animals?

Hypothesizing

Why do land animals have lungs rather than gills?

Chicken bone   Beef bone

PART III

1. Obtain a collection of pictures of animals and a pencil and piece of paper.

Classifying

2. Sort the pictures of animals into categories on the basis of the data you obtained from your previous investigations.

3. List the animals down the left-hand side of a sheet of paper by the categories you have determined. Leave two spaces between each entry. Rule your paper into three lengthwise columns. Title the columns as follows:

   a. How does the animal breathe?

b. How does the animal move?

c. What physical characteristics influence its diet? diet?

4. Complete the columns for each entry as indicated.

OPEN-ENDED QUESTIONS

1. How would you use balloons to show how a lung operates?
2. Using the data gathered in your experiments, how would you construct, illustrate, or give a written description of an imaginary animal that can live in water or on land, fly, crawl, and walk.

What Is the Difference between a
Frog and a Lizard?   (4-6)

CONCEPTS

A frog is an amphibian.

Amphibians are animals that spend part of their life in water and part on land.

As tadpoles, amphibians live in water. They have a slippery skin, and late in their development they have toes without claws.

A lizard is a reptile.

Reptiles have skin covered with scales; there is no tadpole stage; toes, if present, have claws.

Reptiles produce eggs with shells because they must lay their eggs on land and depend on the sun for hatching them.

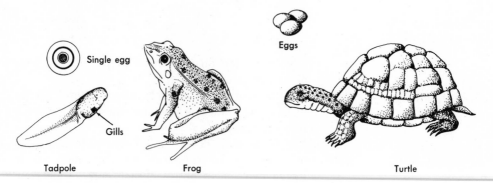

Teacher's Note: This activity should be done in groups of 5 or more students. Commercial-sized mayonnaise jars may be used for terrariums.

MATERIALS

2 terrariums—one equipped with water and aquatic plants for the frog; one equipped with sand and a rock for the lizard

Containers of water for the frogs

Frog for each group

Lizard for each group

Variety of insects for feeding both frog and lizard

Eggs or young of both the frog and the lizard

Teacher's Note: If it is not possible to obtain the developmental stages of the frog and lizard, get some pictures of the different stages.

DISCUSSION

To which group of animals do lizards belong?

To which group of animals do frogs belong?

What are the general characteristics of each of these groups?

How are these animals like or unlike each other?

How does a given environment affect each animal?

Processes	Pupil Discovery Activity
Observing	1. Observe the frog and lizard in the 2 terrariums.
Observing	How do they breathe?
Observing	How do they move?
	Describe their physical characteristics.
	Do they have any young?
Observing	How do they react to their environment?
Observing	What are the characteristics of the environment?
Comparing	2. Compare your observations with those in the classroom reference books.
	3. Note any additional differences as indicated in your reading.
Classifying	4. Using the data gathered in steps 1 and 2, list the characteristics of an amphibian in one column and the characteristics of a reptile in another column.
Inferring	5. List the names of some other amphibians and reptiles.

OPEN-ENDED QUESTIONS

1. Obtain other amphibians and reptiles. Use the same procedure as in the previous activity to compare them.

2. How would you prepare an environment to grow salamanders?

How Do Ants Live?   (1-6)

CONCEPTS

Ants are social insects.
All insects have three parts to their bodies.
All insects have six legs.
Ants are beneficial because they help keep the forests and fields clean.
There are different kinds of ants in a colony.
These different ants do different kinds of work in the colony.

MATERIALS

Large glass jar (commercial mayon-
naise or pickle jar)
Soil to fill the jar two-thirds full
Sponge
Large pan

Sheet of black construction paper
Crumbs and bits of food: bread, cake,
sugar, seeds, etc.
Colony of ants

DISCUSSION

What do the different kinds of ants look like?
In what ways are the ants different?
How does the body of a worker ant compare to that of a queen ant?
How many pairs of legs do ants have?
What are the antennae on the head used for?
What does the egg of an ant look like?
Where do ants make their homes?
How do ants move?
How could you keep ants from leaving a jar?

Ant eggs

Mature ant

Processes	**Pupil Discovery Activity**
	Teacher's Note: This activity should be done as a large group activity.

1. Obtain a large glass jar, soil to fill the jar two-thirds full, sponge, large pan, sheet of black construction paper, crumbs and bits of food: bread, cake, sugar, and seeds, a colony of ants, and water.

Designing an investigation
> How could you arrange these materials to make a home for ants?

Hypothesizing
> What effect will a sheet of black paper placed around the jar have on the ants?

Observing
2. Observe and record what the ants do.

Observing
> How do the ants connect their homes in the jar?

Hypothesizing
> What would happen to the ants if they did not carry soil to the surface?

Hypothesizing
> What do you think would happen if there were no queen in the ant colony?

Comparing
> What changes have been made by the ants since they were first placed in the jar?

OPEN-ENDED QUESTIONS

1. In what ways are ants useful to man?
2. What are some other insects that live and work together?
3. What are some living things that are sometimes mistaken for insects?
4. What would happen if the ant colony were placed in a light, warm place?
5. How are ants different from spiders?
6. What would be a good description of social insects?

What Do You Know about the Birds around You?   (K-3)

CONCEPTS

Birds vary in color and size.
Birds sing different songs.
Birds make different kinds of nests.
Birds eat many different kinds of food.
The male may have a more colorful plumage than the female.

Some birds migrate.
Some birds change color with the season.
Birds care for their young.
Some birds prey on birds.

MATERIALS

No special materials are necessary, however, the following may be helpful:
   Bird book (showing local birds)
   Pictures of birds—if birds cannot be observed in nature

DISCUSSION

Teacher's Note: Carefully record the responses of the pupils on the board to
   the following questions:

What are the names of some birds?
What do these birds look like?
How do chickens and ducks differ?
What are the main differences between a turkey and a robin?
Where do some birds go in the winter?
Where do baby birds come from?
Where do birds lay their eggs?
What kinds of food do birds eat?

Processes   **Pupil Discovery Activity**

Teacher's Note: If the natural environment lends itself
   to observation of birds, have the children observe
   birds on the way to and from school or take a field
   trip in the local area, park, or zoo. If this is not possible, you may provide pictures of different birds,
   nests, and eggs for the pupils to observe. The pupils
   should report to the class the things they have observed about birds. After the children have made
   their observations, record their findings by asking
   and writing on the board their answers to the following questions:

Comparing   In what ways are birds alike?
Comparing   In what ways are birds different from each other?

OPEN-ENDED QUESTIONS

   1. What advantage is there of laying eggs in nests?
   2. What could you do to find out more about birds?
   3. On the bulletin board are the lists of the important things you have learned

about birds. In the next few days try to find out as many new things as you
can to add to the lists.

4. What are the different ways birds build their nests?
5. How could you find out if there are more birds in the city or in the country?

Teacher's Note: The following types of questions can be asked about any of
the local birds. These questions will have to be modified depending on the
kinds of birds that are found in your region.

Redheaded Woodpecker   (1) Where does the woodpecker build his nest? (2) How
does he build his nest? (3) What kind of food does the woodpecker eat?

Hummingbird   (1) How does the male hummingbird differ in color from the
female? (2) Where do hummingbirds get their food? (3) Are hummingbirds as
big as the cardinal or sparrow? (4) Why do you have difficulty finding their
nests?

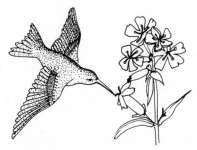

Starling   (1) Why do many other birds prefer not to live near starlings? (2) What
color is the starling? (3) How does the starling vary in color compared to the
hummingbird and woodpecker?

How Do Birds Differ from Mammals?   (6-8)

CONCEPTS

Birds are the only animals that have feathers.
Both mammals and birds are warm-blooded.

Birds have two legs and two wings.

The female mammal has glands for nourishing her young with milk.

Mammals are more or less covered with hair.

Birds do not vary as much in structure as mammals.

The bones of birds are somewhat hollow and light in weight. Mammal bones are not hollow and are proportionately heavier in weight.

Birds tend to eat approximately the amount of their weight in food each day.

Mammals do not eat much per body weight as do birds.

Birds use considerable energy in flying and therefore need a great amount of food.

Female birds lay eggs.

Almost all female mammals give birth to live babies.

Only a few mammals, such as the platypus, lay eggs.

Teacher's Note: This activity should be done in groups of two or more students.

MATERIALS

Live or stuffed specimens of birds and mammals, or pictures of them

Beef and chicken bones (one of each for every two students) If possible, these should be cut in half

Wing bones of chickens (or any other bird)

DISCUSSION

Give as many characteristics as you can that *birds* have in common.

Give as many characteristics as you can that *mammals* have in common.

In what ways do birds differ from mammals?

What could you do to compare more closely the differences between birds and mammals?

Teacher's Note: The teacher should record on the board the students' ideas on these questions. Or allow the students to divide into groups and discuss the questions. Each group could report their ideas to the class.

Children should be encouraged to bring pictures of animals to class, and these can be placed on a bulletin board (similar to that on page 523).

Processes   **Pupil Discovery Activity**

Teacher's Note: Encourage children to bring specimens, alive or stuffed, to school. Perhaps a pet day or animal show might be arranged to make the most of this activity. The children should be allowed to help in furnishing any of the other supplies such as beef and chicken bones.

1. Obtain a cut chicken bone, a cut beef bone, and a wing bone of a chicken.

Birds   Mammals

Lay eggs

Have feathers   Have hair

Are born alive

Woodpecker   Duck   Hawk   Are warm-blooded

Other mammals: man, whales, bears, deer, etc.

Classifying	How did you know which bone was from a chicken and which was from a steer?
Observing and comparing	Examine the centers of the two bones and record how the structure of the beef bone differs from that of the chicken bone.
	2. Look at the chicken wing bone.
Comparing	How does its structure compare with the arm bones of man?
Summarizing	3. Make a list of all the characteristics in which birds and mammals differ.
Comparing	4. Compare your list with those made by other members in your class and make any corrections or additions to your list that you think should be made.

OPEN-ENDED QUESTIONS

1. What are the main structural differences between birds and mammals?
2. How does the structure of the feather help a bird to fly?

How Does the Lack of Oxygen Affect Animals?   (4-6)

CONCEPTS

Animals need oxygen in order to live.
Oxygen dissolves in water. Some animals need dissolved oxygen in water.

A gas will dissolve better in a cool liquid than in a hot liquid.
Fish breathe through gills.

MATERIALS

2 one-pint bottles with caps
2 goldfish or any small fresh-water fish in a small bottle
Burner and a stand or electric hot plate on which to boil water
Matches
Pan large enough to boil a pint of water

DISCUSSION

What happens to the air dissolved in water when you boil it?
What do you think would happen to fish if they were placed in water that
    had been boiled and then cooled?
What would you do to find out?

Processes

Pupil Discovery Activity

Teacher's Note: This activity may be done in groups of two or more pupils.

1. Obtain the following materials:
   A jar with a fish, two pint-sized jars with caps, a burner or electric hot plate, and a large pan.

Designing an
investigation

    How would you boil water?

2. Heat the water to boiling and let it boil for several minutes.
3. While the water is being heated, label one jar "Boiled Water."
4. After the water has boiled, turn the burner off.
5. Pour the boiled water into the jar labeled "Boiled Water," cap it, and allow it to cool to room temperature.

Hypothesizing

    What will happen if you place a fish in tap water?
    Place a fish in a jar filled with tap water and cap it.

Observing

6. Observe its movements.

Hypothesizing

    What would happen if you placed a fish in the cooled boiled water and capped the jar?

7. Place a fish in the jar of boiled water and cap the jar.

Observing

    Observe its movements. (Caution: If the fish turns on its side, take it out of the jar quickly, shake it in the air by the tail for a second, and place it into a jar of regular unheated water.)

Comparing   How did the movements of the two fish vary?
Inferring   Why did the fish in the cooled boiled water seem
                       to vary in its movements compared to the other
                       fish?

                       Teacher's Note: When water is boiled, the air mole-
                       cules dissolved in it move more rapidly and escape
                       into the air. The water lacks air as a result. Fish get
                       the oxygen they need from air dissolved in water.
                       When the air passes over the gills, the oxygen is ab-
                       sorbed by the blood passing through the gills. Fish
                       are not able to survive in the boiled water because
                       it contains little oxygen for the gills to absorb.

Inferring   Why did you first heat the water and then cool it?
                    8. If you have not already done so, take the fish out
                       of the jar of boiled water, shake it for a second or
                       two by the tail, and place it in a jar of plain water.
Inferring   Why is it necessary to shake the fish in the air for
                       a few seconds?

                       Teacher's Note: The shaking of the fish causes the air
                       to pass over the gills so the fish gets oxygen from
                       the air, the shaking also stimulates the circulation of
                       the blood in the fish.

Inferring   What do animals in the sea need in order to live?
Inferring   How do they get the oxygen they need?

                       Teacher's Note: Explain to the class that air is com-
                       posed of a mixture of gases and that it is the oxygen
                       in the air that animals need to breathe.

OPEN-ENDED QUESTIONS

   1. What experiment would you do to determine whether other animals re-
      quire air (oxygen) in order to live?

PLANTS

What Are the Parts of a Plant? (K-3)

CONCEPTS

Plants have leaves, roots, stems, and flowers.
Not all plants have the above four parts.
Leaves are able to make food.
The stems carry minerals and water from the roots to the leaves and flowers.
Flowers make seeds which can produce more of the same type of plant.
Some roots store food.

MATERIALS

A complete plant such as daisies, geraniums, or petunias for entire class

Carrot, radish, turnip, parsnip, and/or sugar beet

Stems from assorted plants

Flowers from assorted plants

Milk cartons

Soil

Several small potted geranium or coleus plants

A measuring stick—preferably metric

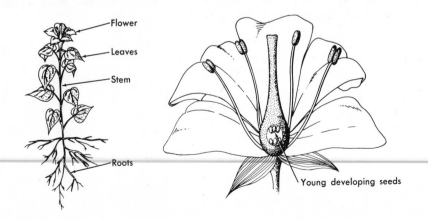

Teacher's Note: Pull up a complete plant for all the children to see. How do you think roots are useful to this plant? Expect and accept various ideas. Allow the children opportunities to propose and examine their ideas.

Processes	**Pupil Discovery Activity**
PART I	*How Are Roots Useful?*
	1. Obtain a petunia and remove all the roots. Obtain some soil and fill the bottom half of a milk carton. Place the plant, with its stem down, on top of the soil.
Observing	What do you notice about the plant when you let go?
Inferring	How do you think roots might have helped this plant?
	2. Turn the stem right side up and push it to a depth of almost two inches into the soil. Water the plant daily. Allow it to set for 4 or 5 days.
Hypothesizing	What do you think will happen to the plant?
Observing	3. After 4 or 5 days, record what happens.
Summarizing	How do you think roots might have helped the plant?
	Teacher's Note: Some plants develop roots in this situation. If they do, remove the plant and develop the lesson around the function of the newly developed roots.
PART II	*Why Are Stems Important to Plants?*
	1. Obtain three stems different from those provided by your teacher.
Comparing	In what ways are they different?
Observing	Which parts of the plant are attached to the stem?
Hypothesizing	How do you think water and minerals get from the roots to the leaves and flowers?
	2. Break open several of your stems.
	3. Feel the inside of the stem.
Observing	What evidence do you have that stems contain water?
Inferring	Why do you think stems contain water?
PART III	*How Do Roots from Different Types of Plants Vary?*
	1. Obtain and compare a carrot, beet, turnip, or parsnip.
Comparing	How do their roots vary?
Comparing	How are they alike?
Applying	Why do you think you eat these roots?

PART IV   *Why Are Leaves Important?*

Hypothesizing   What do you think would happen to a plant if you removed all the leaves from it?

1. Obtain two potted plants and remove the leaves from one. Do not remove the leaves from the other. Water both plants regularly for 4 days.
2. Place the plants where they can obtain sunlight.
3. Measure the growth of these plants for a week, and record your results.

Inferring   Why do you think your results vary?
Inferring   In what ways do you think leaves are important to plants?

OPEN-ENDED QUESTIONS

1. How do plants vary in the number of leaves they have?
2. What plants do not have roots?
3. How are some plants able to survive without roots?

What Is a Seed?   (K-3)

CONCEPTS

Seeds store food.
A seed has a young undeveloped baby plant in it called an embryo.

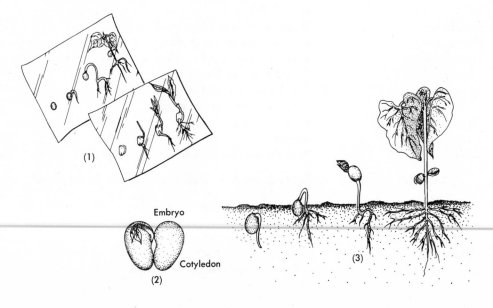

(1)

Embryo

Cotyledon

(2)

(3)

Seeds usually sprout faster when it is warm.

The embryo obtains the food it needs to grow from the storage area of the seed.

MATERIALS

Bean seeds and corn	Small dish or jar lid
Paper towels	Magnifying glass
Plastic wrap	

DISCUSSION

Sometimes farmers have to replant their crops. Why?

What would you do to prepare the best conditions for seeds to sprout?

Teacher's Note: There are many variables, therefore, many suggestions can result. Evaluate and discuss the ideas and then allow pupils to perform acceptable experiments in addition to the substitute activities that follow:

Processes   **Pupil Discovery Activity**

PART I

How Does Temperature Affect the Sprouting of Seeds?

1. Obtain 4 bean seeds, 4 corn seeds, and some plastic wrap. Place the seeds on well-soaked paper towels.
2. Wrap the seeds and towel material in plastic wrap.
3. Repeat the above procedure and place one plastic wrap near a heater and another in a cool place.

Hypothesizing

How do you think the difference in temperatures will affect the sprouting seeds?

Collecting data

4. Observe your wrapped seeds each day for one week and record your observations.
5. At the end of the week compare the seeds in each plastic wrap.

Comparing

What differences do you note?

Inferring

Why do you think these differences occurred?

PART II

What Are the Parts of a Seed?

1. Obtain several bean seeds and plastic wrap. Place them on wet paper towels in a dish or jar lid.
   Cover with plastic wrap. After several days the seeds should be swollen. Break them open and look carefully at the parts using one of the magnifying glasses.

Observing

2. Describe what you see.
   The baby plant you see is called the embryo.

Inferring

Where do you think it got its food while it was growing?

Hypothesizing   What do you think would happen to the embryo if
                                 you removed it from the seed and planted it?
Designing an   How could you find out?
  investigation

OPEN-ENDED QUESTIONS

1. Why do seeds die after they have sprouted if they are not planted in the
   ground?
2. How long will sprouts live if not planted?
3. Do some kinds of sprouts live longer than others?
4. What happens to seeds if they remain wet for a long period of time?

How Do Roots Grow?   (1-6)

Teacher's Note: In the primary grades, this activity will have to be done as a
   demonstration because of the difficulty children have in manipulating the
   equipment. This activity should be done in groups of four students.

CONCEPTS

Roots move around objects in the soil.
Seeds need water in order to grow.
Roots grow downward.

MATERIALS

Sprouted bean plant   Plastic wrap
Bean seeds   2 pieces of glass or thick plastic to place
Small milk carton cut in half   seeds between
  lengthwise   2 tongue depressors or applicator sticks
4 paper towels

DISCUSSION

What do you think would happen to roots if they were placed so that they
   were growing up instead of down?

Processes   **Pupil Discovery Activity**

1. Obtain 4 bean seeds, plastic wrap, a paper towel,
   a milk carton cut in half, and a cup of water.

Place the paper towel in the bottom of a milk carton, and press it down. Soak the towel with water from your paper cup. Place 4 bean seeds on the paper towel. Cover the top of the milk carton with plastic wrap.

Hypothesizing

What are the reasons for preparing the seeds this way?

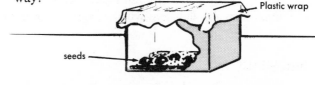

2. When the seeds sprout, place them on several layers of paper towels, between two pieces of glass so that the roots point up. Put applicator sticks or tongue depressors between the pieces of glass.

Hypothesizing

What is the reason for putting the tongue depressors between the pieces of glass?

3. Stand the glass so that the roots point up and the stems down.

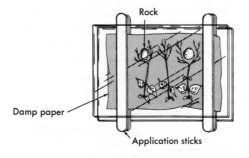

Hypothesizing

What do you think will happen to the growth of stem and roots?

4. Observe the plant growth for several days and record your observations.

Inferring

Was your hypothesis true or false, or does it need to be modified?

Designing an investigation

If you were going to do this activity again, how would you change it to make it better or more interesting?

OPEN-ENDED QUESTIONS

1. How would the roots react if objects like cotton, a piece of wood, or a rock were placed in their way?

How Does Water Get into a Plant? (4-6)

CONCEPTS

Roots absorb water through small root hairs.
Root hairs are damaged when a plant is transplanted or pulled.

MATERIALS

Radish seeds   Plastic wrap
Pan or dish   Water
Paper towels

DISCUSSION

What could you do to determine what a root does (its function) for a plant?

Processes   **Pupil Discovery Activity**

1. Obtain a paper towel, several radish seeds, and some plastic wrap. Soak the towel so that it drips with water. Place the towel in a dish or pan. Place several radish seeds on the towel and cover the pan with plastic wrap.

Radish seeds   Plastic wrap

2. Observe for several days and record your observations.

Observing
What do you notice about the roots?
What are the small fuzzy-like projections from each root called?

Inferring
Why do you think the root has root hairs?

Hypothesizing
What happens to the roots of a plant when it is transplanted?

Hypothesizing
Why is some transplanting unsuccessful?

Designing an investigation
What would you do to determine the function of the root and root hairs?

Hypothesizing   What do you think will happen if you remove the
                       root hairs from the root?

Hypothesizing   What do you think will happen if you expose the
                       root hairs to air and sun?

OPEN-ENDED QUESTIONS

1. Why are roots different shapes?
2. Why are some roots comparatively shallow and others deep?
3. How does man utilize roots of plants?
4. What are the functions of the root other than absorption of food materials?

What Is the Purpose of a Stem?   (4-8)

CONCEPTS

Water must move from the roots to the leaves if a plant is to make food and
    live.
One of the main purposes of the stem of a plant is to carry water from the
    roots to the leaves.
There are small tubes inside the stem that carry water to the leaves.
Water moves up the stem.

MATERIALS

Geranium or coleus stem   Blotter paper
Red food coloring or ink   Water
Drinking glass

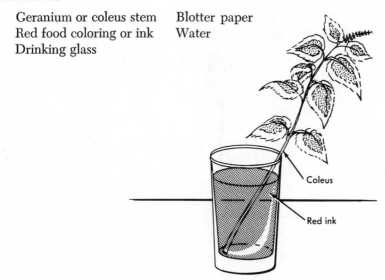

Coleus

Red ink

DISCUSSION

How does the water get from the roots to the leaves?

How do you think a florist obtains a blue carnation?

If you wanted to change a white carnation into a blue carnation, what would you do?

How could you find out if your idea was correct?

Processes	Pupil Discovery Activity
	1. Obtain a geranium or coleus stem with leaves on it, food coloring or red ink, water, and a drinking glass. Put some water in the drinking glass and color it with the food coloring or ink.
Hypothesizing	Why do you think you have added coloring to the water?
	2. Cut a small slice from the bottom of the stalk of your stem and set it into the glass of colored water. Allow it to sit in a sunny area for two hours.
	3. At the end of this period, cut open the stem.
Observing	What has happened to some of the colored water?
Observing	What parts of the stem appear to contain the colored water?
	Describe these parts.
Inferring	What can you conclude about how a stem functions from this activity?

OPEN-ENDED QUESTIONS

1. What effects might different temperatures have on how rapidly a solution moves up a stem?

2. What do you think will happen if you put half of a split stem in one color of water and the other in another color of water?

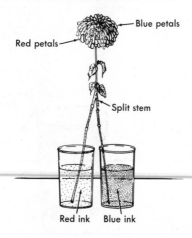

Blue petals

Red petals

Split stem

Red ink   Blue ink

3. What happens to the upward movement of water in a stem when it is dark?

How could you find out?

Why Do Some Parts of Plants Grow Upward?   (4-8)

CONCEPTS

Light and gravity play a role in determining how plants grow.
Roots respond to gravity.
Stems are affected by light.

MATERIALS

Flat glass or plastic wrap about   Tape
    4 inches square   Light source
2 glasses   Paper towels
Geranium or coleus plant   Cup of dirt
3 or 4 bean seeds   Ruler

DISCUSSION

What do you think will happen to a plant if its roots are placed in a glass of water?

What do you think will happen if the plant is inverted and the stem is placed in the water?

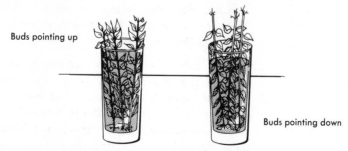

Buds pointing up

Buds pointing down

What affect does light have on the way a plant grows?
What would happen to the way a plant grows if it were placed near a window?
What affect does gravity have on the parts of sprouting seeds?
What could you do to find out?

Teacher's Note: The children should suggest the arranging of the sprouting seeds and apparatus as shown below.

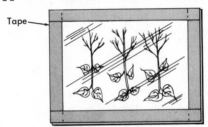

Seeds on soaked paper covered by glass
or plastic wrap

What do you think would happen to the growth of seeds if they were left on the top of some moist dirt for a few days?

Processes

Pupil Discovery Activity

1. Obtain a geranium or coleus plant, 2 glasses, flat piece of glass, 4 bean seeds, tape, paper towel, cup of dirt, and a ruler.

2. Carefully outline the procedure you will follow for investigating the above questions. After your teacher has checked your outline, proceed with the investigations.

Teacher's Note: The children could make several cuttings of geraniums or coleus or other plants that will root easily in water. Several of these should be placed right side up and others should be inverted. The inverted ones will not grow roots. To check for the effect of light on plants, the children could take a potted plant and place it on its side near a window. The plant will turn toward the light source.

Observing

2. On a sheet of paper, carefully record any important changes in plant growth during your day to day observations.

Inferring	Hint: How could you use your ruler in your observations?
Inferring	What can you conclude from your data?
Hypothesizing	What would you expect other plants and seeds to do under similar conditions?
Hypothesizing	What results would you expect if you used different light sources?
Applying	Of what value is this experiment to you?

OPEN-ENDED QUESTIONS

1. What other living things are affected by light and gravity?
2. What are some other factors that affect the growth of plants?
3. Design an experiment to test some of these factors?
4. If you were to do this activity again, how would you change it to make it better?
5. What do you think would happen if you were to scatter mixed parakeet seed on a wet plastic sponge kept in a pan with a little water?
6. What do you think would happen if you obtained two milk cartons filled with soil and planted a handful of seed in one and only 4 seeds in the other.
   Which plants would grow better? Why?

How Can You Tell the Age of a Tree? (1-5)

CONCEPTS

The age of a tree may be determined by counting the number of growth rings.
A tree grows from the outer edge of the wood to the inner bark.
Trees will have thicker growth rings during wet years.

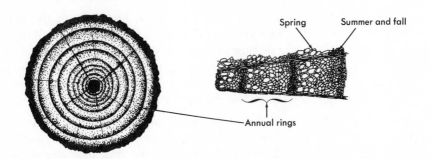

MATERIALS

Limb cross sections of various sizes
Tree cross sections of various sizes

Teacher's Note: Each child should have access to a cross section. You should have, preferably, several sections from trees grown under different conditions, such as low or high rainfall regions. Sometime before the conclusion of this activity an arrangement might be made with resource people such as forest rangers to speak on core sampling and other growth ring studies.

DISCUSSION

Teacher's Note: In grades 1-3, it is suggested the children learn only that there are annual rings and that these rings vary from year to year.

How can you tell the age of a tree?
Why are some rings thick and others thin?
Where does growth take place in a tree?
How can you tell the climate of an area from the growth rings of trees.
How can you tell the age of a living tree without cutting it down?

Processes	**Pupil Discovery Activity**
	1. Obtain some cut pieces (cross sections) of a limb and a trunk of a tree.
	Teacher's Note: If possible, have samples of cross sections of trees grown in areas with ample rainfall and in areas deficient of rainfall.
Observing	What do you notice about each section?
Comparing	How are the limb and trunk sections alike or different?
	2. Compare your sections with those your teacher has.
Comparing	What do you notice about the rings of the trees grown in different areas?
Inferring	Why are some rings thick and others thin?
Inferring	How old do you think your cross section is?
	Teacher's Note: Each year, just beneath the bark, a new ring is added on to the thickness of the tree. If the ring is thick, this indicates that the cells had ample water, grew larger, and produced more cells during the year. The thicker the ring, the more rain there was during the growing season.
Inferring	Why did you count the rings?
Inferring	Why do you think there is a ring for each year? Describe the area of the ring that you think developed during the summer.

Describe the area of the ring you think developed during spring.

Summarizing

3. Draw a diagram of your cross section and label the areas of spring and summer growth.

Teacher's Note: The inner part of each ring was produced in the spring.

OPEN-ENDED QUESTIONS

1. What affect do you think fertilizer would have on the size of the rings?
2. What do you think the amount of sunlight would do to the size of the annual rings?
3. How do you think it is possible to make a mistake in the counting of the number of rings in the cross section of the tree?
4. If a tree were grown under the same conditions all the time, how would the annual rings appear?
5. What do you think disease in a tree would do to the appearance of its cross section?

How Do Leaves Breathe? (3-6)

CONCEPTS

Leaves have air in them.

Gas will expand when heated.

Because gases are lighter than water, they will go up through the water and escape.

Leaves have little openings (called stoma) through which air enters or leaves the leaf.

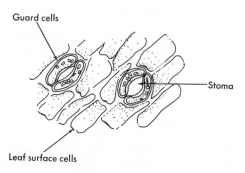

Guard cells

Stoma

Leaf surface cells

MATERIALS

Elm, coleus, or geranium leaf   Lamp or sunlight
Beaker, dish, or sauce pan   Cold and warm water

DISCUSSION

What happens when your head is under water and you let some air out of
your mouth? What do you see?

What do you think might happen to a leaf if it were placed under water?
How would you find out?

Processes	**Pupil Discovery Activity**
	1. Obtain a leaf, a lamp, and a beaker or pan filled with cold water.
	2. Place the leaf in the water with the under side up.
	3. Place a lamp so its light shines on the leaf.
	4. Observe the surface of the leaf for 5 minutes.
Observing	What appears on the under side?
Comparing	How does the appearance of the top and bottom of the leaf vary?
Inferring	Why?

Teacher's Note: Leaves generally have more pores on
the lower than on the upper surface.

Hypothesizing	What do you think would happen to the leaf if you used warmer water in the above activity?
Inferring	What does this indicate about the surface of the leaf?
Inferring	If these bubbles are escaping from inside the leaf, how are they able to move to the surface?

Teacher's Note: Leaves have small pores called stoma
through which air enters and gases escape.

OPEN-ENDED QUESTIONS

1. What could you do to improve this investigation?
2. What could you do in addition to the above activity to prove that the
surface of a leaf contains holes?

What Is Variation?   (1-6)

CONCEPTS

There is tremendous variation in nature.

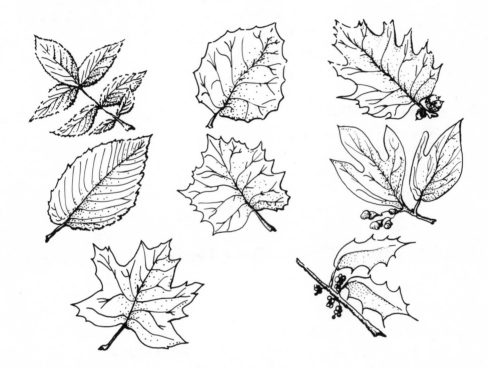

MATERIALS

Fallen leaves collected from your yard at home or at school to show variation
Twigs, stones, and shells to show variation also

DISCUSSION

How do leaves vary?
How could you find out?

Processes   **Pupil Discovery Activity**

1. Collect different kinds of leaves and obtain a ruler.
2. Place them on your desk and compare them.

Inferring   What can you say about the shapes of the leaves?

Comparing   How do they differ in size?
Classifying   3. Place the leaves in groups according to color.
                                 How many groups did you get?
Inferring   Why do you think leaves vary?

Teacher's Note: They may vary because of inheritance, or because of the environment in which they live. For example, the leaves of a particular species may be large if the environment in which the plant grew richly supplied the needs of the plant.

Summarizing   Summarize how leaves vary.

OPEN-ENDED QUESTIONS

1. What other things in nature vary?
2. How do humans vary?
3. How do dogs vary?

How Do Bacteria Change Some Foods?   (4-6)

CONCEPTS

Milk may be soured by the action of bacteria.
Apple juice can be turned to vinegar by the action of bacteria.
Bacteria multiply slowly in a cold environment.

MATERIALS

¼ cup of milk
¼ cup of apple juice
2 pint-sized jars
Red and blue litmus paper

Teacher's Note: This activity can be done in groups.

DISCUSSION

What happens to apple juice or milk if it is kept at room temperature for several days?
What could you do to find out?

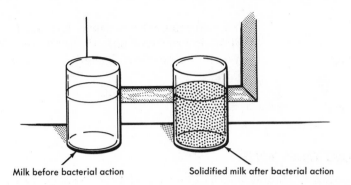

Milk before bacterial action   Solidified milk after bacterial action

Processes   **Pupil Discovery Activity**

1. Obtain ¼ cup of milk, ¼ cup of apple juice, and two pint-sized jars.
2. Pour the milk and apple juice into two separate jars.
3. Place your jars where directed by your teacher.
4. After two days, look at the milk and juice.

Observing   What changes do you notice?
Observing   What do you notice about the smell?
Observing   How has the milk changed in appearance?
Hypothesizing   What do you think the milk will taste like?

5. Taste the milk.

Inferring   Why do you think the milk soured?
Designing an   How could you find out?
  investigation
Applying data   How could you test the sour milk to see if it is acid or base?

Teacher's Note: Use red and blue litmus paper. This can be obtained from a scientific supply company, high school science teacher, or the local pharmacy. Red litmus paper turns blue in the presence of a base. Blue litmus paper turns pink in the presence of an acid.

Designing an   How could you find out if the fresh milk was an
  investigation acid or a base?

6. Test fresh milk and your milk sample to see if they are acid or base.

Inferring   What caused the milk to change?
Hypothesizing   How do you think you could have prevented the milk from souring so fast?

Teacher's Note: Explain to the children that there are bacteria in the air which cause the change in the milk.

Inferring	Why do you think you cannot see bacteria?
Inferring	How do you know bacteria are present in the air?
Hypothesizing	What do you think bacteria would do to apple juice?
Designing an investigation	How could you find out?

OPEN-ENDED QUESTIONS

1. If you were a farmer and had to keep milk for two days before the milk truck could come for it, what would you do?
2. What would you do to milk to make it sour faster?
3. How does man use sour milk in his daily life?

How Does a Fungus Grow?   (4-8)

CONCEPTS

Fungi are plants.
Fungi are sometimes parasites.
Fungi reproduce by spores.
Mildew is one type of fungus.
Mold is another type of fungus.
Fungi need warmth, moisture, and usually darkness in order to grow well.

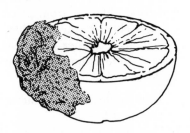

MATERIALS

Orange	String
Bread (at least four pieces)	Tripod lens
2 dishes or plates	Microscope
Small pieces of various kinds of cloth (such as wool, rayon, and cotton)	Plastic bags

DISCUSSION

What would happen to a piece of moist orange peeling if it were put in a dark place and left there for several days? Why?

How could you find out?

| **Processes** | **Pupil Discovery Activity** |

PART I

1. Obtain an orange and a plastic bag.

Designing an
investigation
Hypothesizing

What can you do with the orange peeling to make sure it remains moist?

Where should you store the orange peeling for several days?

Why?

Teacher's Note: If the children do not suggest anything, have them peel the orange, wet the peeling, place the peeling in a plastic bag, and put it in a dark place.

Observing
Inferring

2. After several days, look at the peeling.

What do you think the green material on the peeling is?

Teacher's Note: This will probably be one of the green penicillin molds which grows well on orange peelings.

PART II

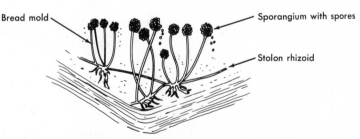

Bread mold — Sporangium with spores — Stolon rhizoid

Hypothesizing
Hypothesizing

What effect does light have on mold?

What effect does the lack of moisture have on mold?

1. Obtain four pieces of bread, two plastic bags, and two plates or dishes.

Designing an
investigation

What can you do with the bread to see if light and lack of moisture have any effect on mold?

Teacher's Note: The children might do any of the following: wet one piece of bread and place it in a sealed plastic bag in the dark. Wet another piece and place it in a sealed bag where it will receive a considerable amount of light. Wet another and place it on a dish where it will dry out. Place a fourth piece on a plate. (Do not wet it.)

Collecting data

2. Keep a record of what happens to the bread over a four-day period.

Inferring

Did all of your bread tests change in the same way? Why?

Observing

What is on some of the bread?

Inferring

Do you think it is growing? Why?

Designing an
investigation

How could you find out if the mold is growing?

Teacher's Note: The children should leave the bread in the bag for two more days to see if the mold growth increases in size. If it does become larger, it is logical to conclude that it is growing. The idea of measuring the size of the colonies accurately might also be introduced.

Inferring

Why did the bread placed in the sunlight not become very moldy?

Summarizing

What conclusions could you make about mold and its need for light?

Inferring

Why did the mold not grow well on the dry plate?

Summarizing

What conclusions can you make about mold and its need for water?

PART III

Mildew

Hypothesizing

What would happen to damp clothing left in a dark place? Why?

1. Obtain a small piece of cloth, a string, and a plastic bag from your teacher.

Designing an
investigation

With these things how could you prove moisture and lack of light affect cloth?

Teacher's Note: Each student should have a small plastic bag and a small piece of cloth such as wool, cotton, or rayon. All but two of the students should dampen the cloth. Place the dampened cloth in a plastic bag, and tie the bag closed. Two students should put a piece of dry cloth in bags and prepare the bags in the same manner. Two or three students should place their bags containing dampened cloth in sunlight. One student should place a bag containing cloth which has not been dampened in sunlight. The rest of the class should place their bags in the dark.

Hypothesizing

What do you think will happen to the cloth in each bag? Why?

Hypothesizing

Which pieces of cloth will change the most? Why?

2. Observe the cloth in the bags each day for several days.

Observing

What do you observe?

Inferring

Why do some of the pieces of cloth appear the way they do?

Observing

In which bags did the spots appear first? Why?

Inferring

Why do some of the pieces of cloth have black spots on them?

Inferring

What evidence is there that something is growing on the cloth?

Designing an investigation

How could you prove whether or not something is growing on the cloth?

Teacher's Note: Allow the bags to remain in the room and have the students compare the size and number of spots.

What is this type of fungus called?

Teacher's Note: This type of fungus is called a mildew.

Inferring

Why is it a good idea to hang your clothes up to dry when they are wet rather than waiting several hours before you hang them?

Hypothesizing

In what way does mildew affect cloth besides discoloring it?

Designing an investigation

How could you find out?

Teacher's Note: Take some of the cloth out of the bag and test its strength by tearing it. How easily does it rip compared to cloth which has not been infected with mildew.

Summarizing

What does mildew do to clothing?

Teacher's Note: Mildew is a fungus which weakens cloth by producing substances that change the chemicals in the fiber of the cloth.

OPEN-ENDED QUESTIONS

1. How does the amount of moisture present affect the growth of fungus?
2. At which temperature does mildew grow the fastest?

How Can Food Be Preserved? (3-8)

CONCEPTS

Spoiling of food is caused by bacteria and molds.
Food can be preserved by canning, salting, drying, refrigeration, and chemical means.
Bacteria do not live well in an acid solution.
Bacteria do not reproduce rapidly in a cold environment.
Bacteria will not multiply without moisture.
Sterilization and immediate sealing will prevent spoilage.

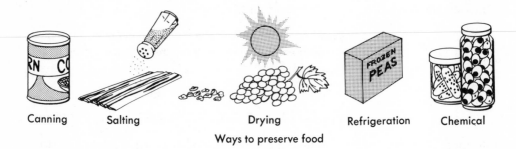

| Canning | Salting | Drying | Refrigeration | Chemical |

Ways to preserve food

MATERIALS

Teacher's Note: This activity should be done in groups.

1 package frozen peas

6 small jars, ½ pt. or smaller (milk carton can be substituted for all but one of these jars)

Hot plate

A small sauce pan

Enough vinegar to cover the peas in the bottle

A tablespoon of salt

1 paper towel

DISCUSSION

What causes food to spoil?
How can you prevent food from spoiling?
How could you find out the best way to preserve food?

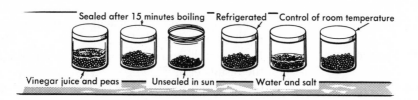

Sealed after 15 minutes boiling ⌐Refrigerated ⌐Control of room temperature

Vinegar juice and peas ═══ Unsealed in sun ═══ Water and salt ═══

Processes   **Pupil Discovery Activity**

PART I

1. Obtain 6 small jars, enough frozen peas to fill all the jars one-fourth full.
2. After numbering the 6 jars, 1 through 6, fill them one-fourth full with defrosted peas.

Teacher's Note: In the following activity, the children are encouraged to devise tests. After the class has written down their tests, discuss their proposals and have them carry them out. Refer to the diagram above for suggestions.

Hypothesizing
What are some possible ways to keep the peas from spoiling?

Hypothesizing
What are the best ways to preserve the peas using the materials you have?

Designing an investigation
How could you test vinegar, a weak acid, to see if it will prevent the peas from spoiling?

Designing an investigation
How could you test to see what effect sunlight has on the peas?

Teacher's Note: The children would have the best results if they spread the peas out on paper to dry.

Hypothesizing
What effect would boiling the peas for 10 minutes have? Caution: Do not boil a sealed jar with peas. Why?

Designing an investigation
What could you do with peas to test the effect of a low temperature on them?

Designing an investigation
What could you do with peas to determine what effect salt and water would have on them?

Hypothesizing
What would happen to peas if nothing were added to them?

Designing an investigation
How could you find out?

PART II

Hypothesizing	How long do you think it will take for bacteria and mold to spoil the peas?
Collecting data	How should you record your data so others can see the results easily?
Observing	3. Observe and record what happened to the peas in the jar with the acid (vinegar).
Hypothesizing	Why was the acid added to the peas?
Inferring	How do bacteria and fungi grow in acid?
Hypothesizing	Why did you boil the jar and lid before sealing it?
Hypothesizing	Why did you seal the jar after boiling it?
Observing	What happened to the peas you placed in the sunlight?
Inferring	Why do they look this way?
Inferring	Why haven't the mold or bacteria grown well?
Observing	What effect did a cold temperature have on the peas?
Inferring	Why haven't the mold or bacteria grown well in the refrigerator?
Observing	What has happened to the peas in the jar with salt water?
Inferring	How can salt water help preserve the peas?
Observing	What has happened to the jar to which you added only the peas?
Inferring	What conditions contributed to the growth of bacteria and mold in this jar?

OPEN-ENDED QUESTIONS

1. What could you do to preserve peaches?
2. How are foods preserved?

REPRODUCTION AND DEVELOPMENT—ANIMALS

How Do Some Insects Develop from Egg to Adult?

(4-6)

CONCEPTS

Insects develop from eggs.
Insects change in body form until they become adults.
Some insects pass through stages (metamorphosis) at different rates.
Flies lay their eggs on filth or decaying food.

MATERIALS

1 quart jar	Dissecting needle
1 pint jar	Caterpillars
Small hamburger patties	Green leaves and twigs
Flies	Grasshoppers
Plastic wrap	Small box with moist soil
Paper towel	

Eggs	Larva	Pupa	Adult

Processes

Pupil Discovery Activity

Teacher's Note: This activity should be done in groups of five.

PART I   *Flies*

1. Make a small pattie of hamburger (about the size of a quarter). Place it in a pint jar.

2. Catch a fly and put it in the jar. Put a small piece of soaked paper in the jar. Keep the jar covered with plastic wrap and place it outside the room.

Hypothesizing

What effect will the moist paper towel have on the meat and air?

Observing
Inferring

3. Observe the meat for several days.

What causes the meat to change in appearance?

4. Obtain a dissecting needle and move the hamburger meat.

Teacher's Note: By this time, the meat should start to decay due to the action of bacteria from the air and in the meat. The children should also be able to see the eggs the flies have laid.

Observing

What do you see in the meat?

Cover the jar again with plastic wrap.

5. Observe the meat for several more days.

Observing

What do you see?

Inferring

Where did the white "things" come from?

6. Leave your jar undisturbed for several more days.

7. Record your observations each day.

Observing

What developed in the jars?

Observing

What effect does temperature have on the white things?

Teacher's Note: A common name for the white thing is maggot. This is really the larva stage of fly metamorphosis.

Observing

What happened to the maggots that were in the meat?

Summarizing

8. Tell in your own words what happened from the time you put meat in the jar to the time the flies developed.

Teacher's Note: Flies pass from eggs to larvae to pupae and finally to adults.

PART II

Moths

| Eggs | Caterpillar | Cocoon | Adult |

Developmental stages of moth

Hypothesizing

1. Obtain a quart jar with several fresh green leaves, a couple of twigs, and two caterpillars. Place a moist piece of cloth in the jar.
   Where do caterpillars come from?
2. Cover the jar with plastic wrap.
3. Observe the caterpillars over several days.

Observing

   What do they do?
4. Leave the caterpillars in the jar until they change.

Teacher's Note: Be sure the paper in the bottom of the jar is kept moist. Make sure the children loosen the plastic wrap every two or three days to allow fresh air to enter the jar.

Inferring

What would happen if you did not keep the air moist?
What is the last stage that you see called?

Summarizing

Describe in your own words the four stages of a moth.

PART III

Grasshoppers

1. Obtain some grasshoppers.
2. Place the grasshoppers in a small box with moist soil and cover the box with plastic wrap.

Hypothesizing

   What might the female grasshopper do while in the box?

Observing
Inferring

3. Observe them over several days.
   What evidence do you have that some of the female grasshoppers did something?
4. Leave the box in the classroom, keeping the soil fairly moist but not soaking.
   Observe the box for several months.

Observing
Observing

   What happens to the grasshoppers?
5. After several months, try to find some nymphs in the top of the soil.

Inferring

   What are these nymphs?

Teacher's Note: The nymphs are young, developing grasshoppers.

Applying data

Where did these nymphs come from?

Teacher's Note: The nymphs came from the eggs which the female grasshopper laid. If you do not want to take time for the children to observe the development of the grasshopper, you might show them some pictures of grasshopper development and ask the children to put them in their proper order of development.

OPEN-ENDED QUESTIONS

1. What effect would the cutting of the outer layer of a cocoon have on what is inside the cocoon?
2. What effect would dry, rather than moist, air have on the fly eggs?
3. What would happen if you put shredded paper in the jar with the flies instead of meat?
4. After the flies have layed their eggs in the hamburger, what would happen to them if you placed the jars in a refrigerator?

Why Do You Look Similar to Your Parents?   (4-6)

CONCEPTS

Every living thing comes from another living thing of the same kind.
Heredity is the passing on of traits and characteristics from parents to offspring.
Food is necessary for growth.
At every stage of development, the individual is an integrated organism.
All cells, tissues, and organs are correlated and act together as a unit.

MATERIALS

Day-old chick (or picture of one)   Food
Hen (or picture of one)   40-watt light bulb
Box or cage   Growth chart (one per child)
Water   Piece of cardboard for lid

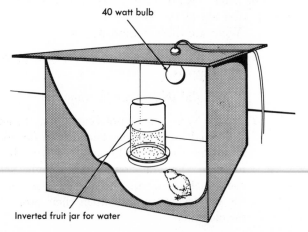

40 watt bulb

Inverted fruit jar for water

Teacher's Note: If you cannot get a hen, you can make a brooder to keep the chick warm by obtaining a small cardboard box about 18 × 18 inches and suspending an extension cord with a 40-watt bulb in it. (See the above diagram.)

Processes

Pupil Discovery Activity

Teacher's Note: This activity is to be done by groups of eight or more children.

1. Obtain an extension cord with a 40-watt bulb, cardboard box, and a piece of cardboard to cover the box.
2. Insert a light socket with a 40-watt bulb into a piece of cardboard. This will be used to cover the top of a cardboard box about 18 × 18 inches.
3. Put the chick into the box. Place the hen in also if you have one.

Teacher's Note: If a hen is not available, have the children refer to a picture of one.

Comparing | How is the chick like the hen?
Comparing | What are some other examples of living things that are like their parents?
Comparing | In what ways are these animals alike?
Inferring | Where did the chick come from?
Hypothesizing | What would happen if you tried to get something living from something non-living?
Imagining | What would be the result of trying to get a chick from a horse or a cow?

Teacher's Note: The children should decide that living things come only from living things which are alike.

Summarizing | What can you say about the way living things look when they are born?
Comparing | In what ways does the chick look different from the hen?
Observing | 4. Keep a record of the growth of the chick for the next two weeks. Record everything you notice about the changes in growth of the chick.
Comparing | In what ways do you resemble your parents?

Teacher's Note: The children should decide that all organisms inherit traits and characteristics from their parents. They should see that the growth of the parts of the organism is balanced.

Designing an investigation | What could you do to find out if you look anything like your parents when they were your age?

OPEN-ENDED QUESTIONS

1. If some goose eggs were placed under a hen and side by side with the chicken eggs, what would be the result?
2. What evidence is there that a chicken egg needs or gets air?
3. What will happen if you take a needle and puncture a fertilized egg and place the egg in a warm box and wait for it to hatch?

How Does a Chicken Develop?   (5-8)

Teacher's Note: The pupils should have done some work using microscopes before doing this lesson.

CONCEPTS

When an animal grows, its cells divide.

When a chicken develops in the egg, it passes through different stages.

A chick embryo needs a constant temperature and moisture level in order to grow and develop.

A large part of the egg contains stored food for the young embryo to use in its growth.

MATERIALS

Commercial incubator or gallon jar with lid

6-8 fertile eggs from a feed store

40-watt bulb and cord

Baby food jar or water dish

Binocular scope

Slides and cover slips

Stains for slides

Thermometer

Binocular microscope (If one is not available, a high power magnifying lens may be used.)

Teacher's Note: This activity is to be done in groups of 5 pupils.

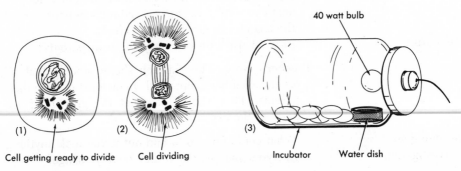

(1) Cell getting ready to divide   (2) Cell dividing   (3) Incubator   Water dish   40 watt bulb

Processes

Pupil Discovery Activity

1. Obtain a gallon jar and a 40-watt bulb; make an incubator for the fertile chicken eggs as shown in the lesson: Why Do You Look Similar to Your Parents? The incubator should have a temperature of 37°C in order for the eggs to develop properly. Make sure the temperature can be kept constant over a period of days before placing the eggs in the incubator. A dish of water should be placed in the incubator. After the eggs have been placed in the incubator, they should be turned every other day.

2. After 3 days, carefully crack open one egg. Place the embryo under the binocular scope and focus under low power.

Observing — Describe what you see.

Inferring — What evidence is there that the developing chick embryo has a heart?

3. After 12 days of incubation, take another egg and crack it open. Place the embryo under the scope.

Observing — Make a drawing of the chick embryo.

4. After 18 days, take another egg and compare its development with a 12-day embryo.

Comparing — How does the 18-day chick differ?

Observing — How is the chick able to escape from the egg?

OPEN-ENDED QUESTIONS

1. How would you find out if the mother hen actually provides a temperature of 37°C when she sits on her eggs?

2. How do changes in the cell make-up of the chick explain how the chick grows in size?

REPRODUCTION AND DEVELOPMENT—PLANTS

How Can You Get Two Plants from One?   (1-6)

CONCEPTS

Some plants can be grown from stems by using a method called slipping.

MATERIALS

Freshly cut stems 2 to 4 inches long from any of   Pint jar or 250-ml.
the following plants: coleus, geranium, begonia,   beaker
philodendron, wandering jew (trades-cantia), or   Pint of soil (optional)
ivy   Water
                                                    6″ ruler

DISCUSSION

If you had a geranium plant and wanted to produce another one like it, what would you do?

Teacher's Note: You will probably have to provide the stems for the children.

Processes   **Pupil Discovery Activity**

1. Obtain some stems provided by your teacher.
2. Make a slip by cutting or breaking about 5 inches off the tip. Cut this slip at a point on the stem just below where leaves or other stems are attached. The point where leaves or branches arise from a stem is called a node.
   Remove some of the leaves (not all) from the lower part of the slip and place the slip in the jar filled with water.

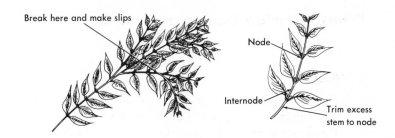

Break here and make slips

Node

Internode

Trim excess
stem to node

Teacher's Note: The slip may be planted in soil provided the soil is kept moist.

3. Place the jar containing the slip in a place where
it can be kept for several weeks and will receive
light from the sun.

4. Add water to the jar as necessary to keep it nearly
full at all times.

Hypothesizing — What changes do you think will take place on the
slip?

Hypothesizing — Where do you think the water in the jar goes?

Observing — 5. Make daily observations of your plant. Record what
changes you see each day. Measure how much the
plant grows each week.

Observing — What happened to the rate of growth after roots
appeared?

6. Compare your observations with those of others in
the class to see if you can find answers to the following questions:

Inferring — How does the number of leaves affect the growth of
the new plant?

Inferring — How do you think the amount of sunlight affects
the growth of the new plant?

Hypothesizing — What do you think would happen if the slip had no
leaves?

Designing an
investigation — What are other factors that might affect the growth
of the new plant? How could you find out?

OPEN-ENDED QUESTIONS

1. What would happen if you grew slips in soil instead of water?
2. What do you think would happen if you tried to grow willow or apple
trees by slipping?
3. What types of plants might be difficult to slip?

What Function Does a Flower Serve?   (4-8)

CONCEPTS

The chief parts of most plants are the stem, leaves, flowers, and roots.
All seed-producing plants form either flowers or cones.
The flower contains the reproductive parts of the plant.
The flower is the seed-making structure of the plant.
Animals help pollinate plants.
Pollination is the process of pollen falling on the pistil of a flower.
Fertilization occurs when part of the pollen enters the ovule or egg of the plant.

MATERIALS

2 flowers or male cones	7 microscope slides
3 microscopes or magnifying lenses	Sheets of white paper
	Single-edged razor blades

DISCUSSION

How many of you have ever taken a flower apart?
What, if any, purpose does the flower serve for the plant?

Teacher's Note: Explain to the class that flowers serve as a reproductive part of the plant and that reproduction is a process of making more of something. Every flower has a material called pollen. The pollen is found on the part of the flower called a stamen.

Processes   **Pupil Discovery Activity**

1. Obtain a flower, a sheet of paper, a single-edged razor blade, a glass slide, and a magnifying glass or microscope.
2. Shake the flower over the sheet of paper.

Observing   3. Observe the material on the paper.
Analyzing   What is the material which you see?
Inferring   Where did it come from?
Inferring   What purpose or function does this material have in the flower?
Hypothesizing   Why is it necessary for a plant to produce flowers?
4. Place some pollen on the microscope slide.

Observing   5. Observe the slide under the microscope or magnifying glass.

Observing   6. Describe and draw a diagram of what you see.

7. Separate your flower into its different parts.

8. Place each part into a separate pile.

9. How many piles do you have?

Comparing   Refer to the diagram below and try to find similar parts on your flower.

Observing   Name as many parts of the flower as you can.

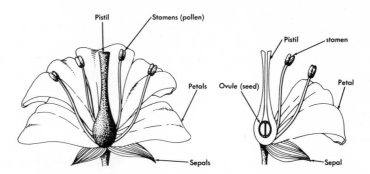

10. Place one of each of these parts on the piece of white paper and write the name of it next to the part.

Observing   11. From what part of the flower did the pollen come?

Teacher's Note: Be sure to inform the class that each flower may have more than one stamen.

Observing   How many stamens does your flower have?

Inferring   What is the function of the stamen?

Teacher's Note: Explain that the stamen is the male part of the flower and that the pollen is found there.

Observing   12. Find the pistil.

13. Feel the tip of the pistil.

Describing   How does it feel?

Inferring   What purpose do you think it serves?

Teacher's Note: The pistil is the female part of the flower. The tip of the pistil is sticky. When pollen lands on it, it therefore sticks to it.

Inferring   How do you think pollen gets from one flower to another?

Teacher's Note: Certain animals such as the bee can help spread pollen from plant to plant so that it comes in contact with the pistil. Wind may also help the spreading of pollen. Brightly colored flowers are pollinated by insects and birds. Flowers, such as grains, which are not brightly colored usually are pollinated by the wind.

Hypothesizing

What do you think the process of pollen landing on the pistil is called?

Teacher's Note: Explain that pollination is a process whereby the pollen from the stamen falls on the pistil.

Inferring

What parts of a flower are necessary for the process of pollination?

Inferring

What do you think happens during the process of pollination? (Refer to the diagram below.)

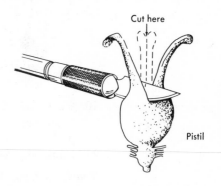

14. Carefully cut the pistil of your flower lengthwise, as shown in the diagram.

Observing

What do you see at the bottom of the pistil?

Observing

Draw a picture of what you see in the pistil and label it.

Hypothesizing

What do you think the ovules will become?

Teacher's Note: At the bottom of the pistil, tiny ovules are located. When a pollen grain and an ovule join together, a seed eventually is formed. This is fertilization. Explain that fertilization is the process of the male pollen joining with the female ovule to form a seed. Every seed that results contains a baby plant with a food supply to nourish it until it is able to make its own food when planted in the ground.

Summarizing

Why is pollen necessary for the formation of a seed?

Summarizing

Why are ovules necessary for the formation of a seed?

Summarizing

Where do you think the seed is formed?

Inferring

Teacher's Note: Re-emphasize that each part of the flower serves a purpose in the reproductive cycle. When the various parts have fulfilled their purposes they are no longer necessary and therefore will fall from the flower.

What do you think is the purpose of the sepal?

Teacher's Note: The sepals help to protect the flower before it opens. Look at the diagram and your flowers and also think of the flower before it opens.

Inferring

Inferring

What do you think is the purpose of the petals?

What do you think will happen to the petal and stamen once the seed is formed?

Teacher's Note: Petals and stamens usually drop off after fertilization, and the seeds develop inside the lower part of the pistil.

Inferring

Why do you think this occurs?

OPEN-ENDED QUESTIONS

1. What would happen if there were no flowers?
2. What animals can help pollinate flowers?
3. What do you think would happen if the process of pollination did not occur?
4. How does a plant reproduce without flowers?

Why Is There Plant and Animal Breeding? (6-8)

CONCEPTS

The offspring produced by plants or animals tend to inherit characteristics from their parents.

Some characteristics may be good, and some may be undesirable.

MATERIALS

One small potato (type does not matter)
One large potato
Tape measure

Processes

Pupil Discovery Activity

Teacher's Note: This activity may be done in groups of two or more pupils.

1. Obtain two potatoes and place them side by side on the table.

Comparing
Comparing

     How are they alike?
     How do they differ?
     Mark one potato "A" and the other "B" and complete the information below.

	Size (roughly in inches)	Color	Type of skin (texture)
Potato A			
Potato B			

Teacher's Note: When a potato or any part of a potato containing an "eye" is planted in soil, it will grow and produce a potato plant, which will in turn produce potatoes.

2. A farmer wants to grow potatoes on his farm. His neighbor who has two potato patches has offered to let him choose some potatoes in order to start his own patch. Every day the neighbor's wife tends the two potato patches which she started from two different potato types. The two "starter" potatoes were different in size. Potato patch #1 was started with a small potato and potato patch #2 was started with a much larger potato.

3. Suppose the larger potato on the table in front of you came from patch #1.

Inferring
     What factor(s) do you suppose influenced its size?

Inferring
4. If the neighbor's wife had taken equal care of both patches and the larger potato had come from patch #2, what factor(s) do you suppose would influence its size?

Hypothesizing
5. What would you expect to happen if the larger potatoes were used in your potato patch?

Inferring
     If larger potatoes were desired, from which potato patch would it be best to select the starter potatoes?

Inferring
     If the potatoes planted came out large, and the soil, water, and temperature conditions were the same, from which patch do you suppose the potatoes came?

Inferring
6. What do you think "heredity" is?

	Look the word up in the dictionary.
Comparing	How did your definition differ from the meaning given in the dictionary?
Inferring	7. What characteristics do you think potatoes "A" and "B" inherited from their parents?

OPEN-ENDED QUESTIONS

1. Look at two other working partners in your class.
   How do they differ and how are they alike in the following ways: a. height; b. skin color; c. hair; d. eye color?
2. From whom do you inherit your characteristics?
   From whom did your parents inherit their characteristics?
3. From the potato example above, what are some factors influencing plant breeding?
4. How can these factors be applied to animal breeding?
5. Given two red hibiscus or carnation plants (one large and one small), which flower would you select to obtain seeds if you wanted a large red hibiscus or carnation?
   How would you test to see which flower produces large offspring?

ECOLOGY

What Types of Life
Can You Find in a Pond?   (1-6)

CONCEPTS

The color in animals or plants usually helps to conceal, disguise, or advertise their presence.

Every living organism has some body parts which are adapted for the life it leads.

Each species is adapted to live where it does.

A pond is a small body of water containing many forms of life.
Some forms of life are very small and can be seen only under a microscope.
If a pond is not disturbed, its life forms will remain in balance.

MATERIALS

A pond which the pupils may observe
2 quart jars with lids
Thermometer
Microscope and slides

Dip net (may use nylon stocking and hanger)
Magnifying glass
Pencil and notebook

Processes	Pupil Discovery Activity

Teacher's Note: This activity should be done in groups of 3 or 4 children. When the class collects materials, it would be desirable to have one or two other teachers as chaperones. Since this lesson is designed as a field trip, you may want to collect other specimens for later study. Instruct the children to be on the lookout for cocoons, old bird nests, leaves, etc.

1. Obtain the following materials: 2 quart jars with lids, magnifying lens, thermometer, dip net, pencil, and notebook.

Observing
2. As you approach the pond, notice the different kinds of plant life in the area.

Inferring
How were you able to tell you were approaching a pond?

Observing
Classifying
Inferring
Summarizing
Observing
3. Look carefully for living things.
Count the different kinds of organisms you see.
Why was it hard to see some of these things?
How many different kinds of insects did you see?
What kinds of things did you find under the water?

Measuring
4. Determine the temperature of the water at different depths.

Observing	How does the temperature change with the depth of the water?
Hypothesizing	How is the temperature of the water important to the life in a pond?
Hypothesizing	What might be living in the water that is so small you cannot see it?

Teacher's Note: There probably are microscopic plants and animals in the water.

5. Fill a jar with pond water and take it back to school.

Inferring

6. Find an insect (or other animal) that you think could live only near a pond.

Observing

What is there about this animal that helps him to live where he does?

Designing an
investigation

How could you find out if this animal could live only near a pond?

7. Take this specimen back to school to find out whether or not he can live in a classroom. Some animals eat both plants and animals, and other animals eat only animals.

Hypothesizing

What do you think would happen if a farmer killed all the plants around a pond?

8. Collect any other specimens to study at home or in school.

Teacher's Note: If the children have had no experience with a microscope, it might be necessary to demonstrate the proper technique before doing the following part of the lesson.

Applying

9. When back in school, have your teacher help you set up a microscope, and look at the water you obtained from the pond.
What looks like it might be alive in the water under the microscope?
What makes you think it is alive?

OPEN-ENDED QUESTIONS

1. How many different kinds of insects can you name that live near a pond?
2. You may have been lucky enough to have seen some single-celled animals called protozoa under the microscope. You may want to read about them. How many different kinds can you find in the pond you studied?
3. How do different temperatures affect protozoa?
4. How could you kill protozoa?

5. Could the plants that live under water in a pond live above water?
6. How do animals that do not live near ponds adapt to their environments?

How Does the Environment Affect Life?   (4-6)

CONCEPTS

Certain environmental factors determine community types.

Some types of communities are on land and some are in water.

Land communities can be subdivided into forests, bogs, swamps, deserts, and others.

A community is a collection of living organisms having mutual relationships among themselves and with their environment.

All living things have certain requirements that must be met by their surroundings.

Habitat is a place where an animal or plant naturally lives or grows.

Different environments are needed to sustain different types of life.

MATERIALS

3 large commercial-sized mayonnaise jars; two of them with lids in good condition

Cup of coarse-grained gravel

4 cups of beach sand

5 small aquatic plants (approximately 3 to 4 inches in height)

Freshwater fantailed guppy

2 water snails

5-inch square of fine-mesh screening material

Coca Cola bottle cap

2 small cactus plants (approximately three to four inches in height)

Chamelion, lizard, skink, horned toad, or colored lizard

2 small dried twigs (no longer than three-fourths of the length of the mayonnaise jars)

Small water turtle or frog

Several small ferns, mosses, lichens, liverworts

DISCUSSION

What does environment mean to you?

What are some things that live around you?

Name some environments that you know about.

Processes	Pupil Discovery Activity
PART I	*Aquarium*
	Teacher's Note: This activity is to be done in groups of

4 or 5 children. Each group might be responsible for only one of the habitats.

1. Obtain the materials listed in the Materials section.
2. Clean the mayonnaise jar thoroughly with soap and water and rinse it well.
3. Wash 2 cups of sand to be placed in the jar. Spread this over the bottom of the jar.
4. Fill the jar with water and let it stand for several days before adding plants and fish.
5. Place the aquatic plants as suggested by the pet shop owner.
6. Place the guppy and snails in the jar.
7. Now cover the jar with the screening material.

Inferring — Why do you think it is necessary to clean the jar before using it?

Inferring — Why should the sand and gravel be washed before putting them in the jar?

Inferring — What would dirty water do to the gills of the fish?

Inferring — Why must the gills of the fish be kept clean?

Inferring — How do fish breathe?

Inferring — Why do you think the water was allowed to stand for several days before the fish were placed in the aquarium?

Inferring — What does our health department add to water that might be injurious to fish?

Inferring — Why were the snails added to the water?

Teacher's Note: The snails will eat the small green algae (the slimy plants that collect on the side of the tank).

Hypothesizing — Will the snails always be able to keep the tank clear?

Inferring — What does this imply that you as a group have as a responsibility?

Teacher's Note: The children from time to time will probably have to clean the aquarium.

Inferring — Why were plants added to the aquarium?

Inferring — What would the fish eat in nature?

Inferring — Would your guppy live if it did not feed on anything? Why?

Inferring — What do plants make that the fish can use?

Inferring — What does the fish make that the plant can use?

Teacher's Note: Plants make oxygen and food, and the fish produce carbon dioxide and waste products. The aquarium probably is not balanced so food must be added from time to time for the fish.

PART II   *Terrarium (desert)*

1. Obtain one of the large commercial-sized mayon-naise jars.
2. Clean the mayonnaise jar with soap and water and rinse it well. Wash and rinse the lid also.
3. Dry off the jar, and screw the lid on.
4. With the jar on the floor, pound holes into the lid by hitting a nail with a hammer through the lid.
5. Place the jar on its side.
6. Spread the remaining two cups of sand onto the bottom of the jar.
7. Place the small bottle cap filled with water, the cactus, and one twig into the jar.
8. Place a lizard, skink, chamelion, or horned toad into the jar.
9. Cover the jar with the punctured lid.
10. Water the terrarium once every two weeks. Place the jar in a sunny area.
11. Feed the animals live meal worms. These can be obtained from a local pet shop.
12. Keep the bottle cap filled with water.

PART III   *Terrarium (bog)*

1. Clean one of the mayonnaise jars with soap and water and rinse it well. Wash and rinse the lid.
2. Dry off the jar and screw the lid on.
3. With the jar on the floor, pound holes into the lid by driving a nail with a hammer through the lid.
4. Place the jar on its side.
5. Spread the gravel out on the bottom of the jar so it will be concentrated towards the back of the jar as in the diagram.

Lid   Gravel

6. Place the ferns, mosses, lichens and liverworts over the gravel.
7. Pour some water in (do not put in so much that it covers the back portion of the arrangement).
8. Place a dried twig in the jar.

9. Place a small turtle or frog in the jar.

10. Feed the turtle or frog insects or turtle food every other day.

11. Cover the jar with the punctured lid.

12. Place the terrarium in an area where light is weak.

Comparing and observing — How does the life found in the aquarium differ from that found in the desert and/or bog terrariums?

Classifying — What kinds of conditions do the fish, turtle, frog, or lizard have to have in order to survive in their particular habitats?

Observing — What kinds of conditions do the bog plants require in order to grow well?

Observing — What kinds of food do the fish, the lizards, or the turtle eat?

Hypothesizing — What do you think would happen to the turtle if you left him in the desert habitat, or to the lizard if you put him in the bog habitat?

OPEN-ENDED QUESTIONS

1. What experiment would you do to find out what happens to plants when grown under different environmental conditions?

2. What other kinds of surroundings or environments could you make through the use of mayonnaise jars?

3. What does the "environment" have to do with the kinds of organisms found in it?

4. Can you name some organisms that are able to live in many different surroundings?

5. What would happen to a fern plant if it were transplanted to a desert region?

6. What would happen to a penguin if it were taken to live in a desert?

7. What would happen to a primitive human being if he were suddenly brought to a large city?

8. What statements can you make about the effect of "environment" on a living thing?

How Do Animals Affect Their Environment?   (3-6)

CONCEPTS

Living things are dependent upon one another for food.

In general, the smaller the animal, the greater the number present in a community.

Larger animals may consume many small animals in order to satisfy their
   need for food.

The stronger, better-adapted animals survive.

When the supply of food does not equal the demand in an environment, a
   change of some kind must occur in the numbers and/or types of organisms
   present in it.

Water plants are important to an aquatic community.

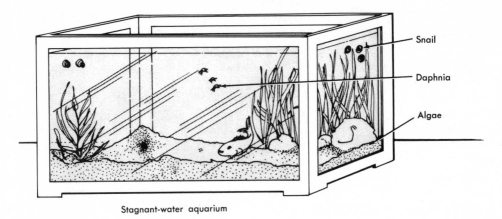

Stagnant-water aquarium

MATERIALS

Aquarium	2 or more Daphnia
Water from a swamp or lake	Rocks
Green algae	2-6 small fish
2-6 snails	

Processes	**Pupil Discovery Activity**
	1. Obtain an aquarium containing some water from a swamp or lake, green algae, snails, Daphnia, rocks, and a small fish. Assemble the material as indicated in the diagram. You now have a *microcosm*, a small world environment. You are not to add anything to the microcosm.
Hypothesizing	What function do you think the plants serve in it?
Hypothesizing	What changes would you expect to take place tomorrow? in a week? in a month?
Observing	2. Observe and record what the animals eat.
Inferring	What does the plant do for the animals in the aquarium?
Inferring	Where does the plant get its food?
Hypothesizing	What might cause the fish to die?

Teacher's Note: The fish may die if there is not sufficient oxygen dissolved in the water or a sufficient food supply.

	If one of the fish dies, allow it to remain in the aquarium.
Observing	3. Observe carefully what happens to the fish after it is dead.
Inferring	What effect did the dead fish have on the number of small animals in the aquarium?
Inferring	What evidence do you have from the microcosm that one animal may be dependent on another for food?
Inferring	Why did the number of organisms start to decrease just after you set up the microcosm?
Inferring	Why did they later increase?
Inferring	What effect can the death of an animal have on the microcosm?
Inferring	Why is it usually true that the bigger the animal, the fewer of them there are in a particular area?

OPEN-ENDED QUESTIONS

1. What would you do to make a microcosm using a land environment instead of a water environment?
2. Why is it important for the numbers of wildlife to be kept in balance?

How Is Life Affected by Variations in Temperature? (4-6)

CONCEPTS

A warm temperature is more beneficial to life than a cold temperature.
There are maximum and minimum temperatures that living things can stand.
Most animals tend to be more active when the temperature is warm.
Some animals are cold-blooded, and others are warm-blooded.
Fish and frogs are cold-blooded animals. Their body temperature is about the same as the environment around them.

MATERIALS

4 quart jars	Paper towels
Thermometer	Candle
Ice cubes	Match
Polliwogs or goldfish	Tripod
Jar of ants	Plastic wrap
Bean seeds	

DISCUSSION

What do you think would happen if you were to place goldfish in cold water? What could you do to find out?

Processes	**Pupil Discovery Activity**

PART I   *Goldfish or Polliwogs*

1. Obtain two jars of water, several ice cubes, two goldfish or polliwogs, and a thermometer.
2. Place the ice cubes in one of the jars of water. Keep the other at room temperature.

Observing
3. Place one goldfish or polliwog in each jar and observe the activity.

Ice cubes

Polliwogs

Collecting data
4. After 15 minutes, note the temperature of each container and record it.

Observing
5. Note the activity of the goldfish or polliwog in each jar.

Comparing
    Explain what you see and compare it with your first observation.

Hypothesizing
    What types of animals are more active in warm environments?

Designing an investigation
    What could you do to find out?

PART II   *Ants*

1. Obtain ants, a candle, tripod, a match, and 2 jars. Place some ants in each jar. Place one jar in a refrigerator and keep the other at room temperature.

Observing
2. After half an hour, observe the activity of the ants in each jar.

Hypothesizing
    What do you think would happen if a jar with some ants in it were heated gently with a candle?

3. Place a jar of ants on a tripod over a lighted candle.

Inferring
    What effect does a change in temperature have on ants?

PART III

Hypothesizing

Designing an
investigation

Plant Seeds

1. What do you think would be the effect of different temperatures on plants?
   What could you do to find out?

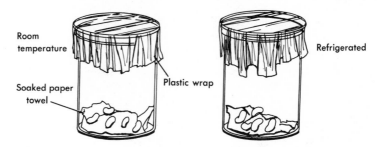

Room temperature   Refrigerated

Soaked paper towel   Plastic wrap

2. Obtain two jars. Place water-soaked paper towels in the bottom of the two jars. Add bean seeds to each jar. Cover with plastic wrap.
3. Place one of the jars in a refrigerator and leave the other at room temperature.

Observe

4. Each day check on what is happening in the experiment and record your observations as indicated below:

   Date you wet them: _____
   Cold temperature environment: _____
   Room temperature: _____
   Date sprouted: _____
   Rate of growth: _____

Comparing

5. At the end of a week, remove the seeds from the jars and measure them to determine which group grew faster.

Observing
Inferring

Explain what you see.
What effect does a change in temperature have on the sprouting seeds?

OPEN-ENDED QUESTIONS

1. What would happen in winter if you placed a plant outside?
2. Lizards and snakes are cold-blooded animals.
   How active do you think they would be on a cold day?
3. Why do you think some people grow plants in a greenhouse?
4. How fast do you think plants would grow in a temperature of 200°F?
5. What other experiments can you think of to do with plants or animals which might show the effects of temperature?

How Do Earthworms Change the Soil?   (2-6)

CONCEPTS

Earthworms loosen soil so that it is more easily aerated.
Earthworms loosen the soil, helping to conserve water.
Earthworms are active in the dark and avoid light.
Earthworms eat the organic material in the soil.

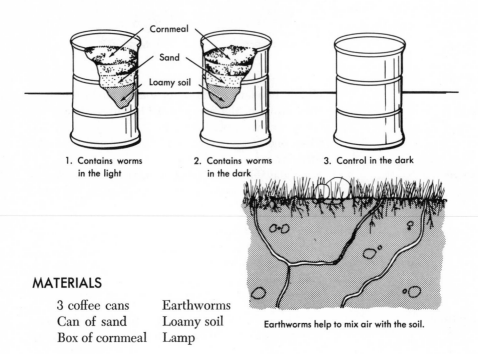

Cornmeal
Sand
Loamy soil

1. Contains worms in the light
2. Contains worms in the dark
3. Control in the dark

Earthworms help to mix air with the soil.

MATERIALS

3 coffee cans	Earthworms
Can of sand	Loamy soil
Box of cornmeal	Lamp

DISCUSSION

Why are earthworms important?
Where do earthworms live?
How do earthworms affect the soil?
How do you think earthworms react to light?
What can you do to find out the answers to some of these questions?

Processes

Pupil Discovery Activity

1. Obtain three coffee cans and fill each two-thirds full with loose loamy soil.
2. Add some earthworms to two of the cans.
3. To all three cans add about an inch of sand and on top of this about one-half inch of cornmeal.

4. Place one of the cans with worms near a window. Place a lamp near it which can be turned on at night.
5. Place the other two cans in the dark.
6. Add a small amount of water at room temperature to the cans every other day.

Observing

7. Observe the cans each day to note if any changes have taken place.
Record in your notebook what happens.

Comparing

8. After 4 days, compare the cans and determine what is different about the can you kept in the light compared with the two you kept in the dark.

Inferring

What was the purpose of the can without worms?

Inferring

Why do you think the soil was moistened with water?

Inferring

What conclusion can you make about the sensitivity of worms to light and dark?

Inferring

Which of the cans seems to hold water better?

Inferring

Why do you think they did?

Inferring

What do you think happened to the water in the soil containing the worms?

Inferring

How do you think worms help conserve water in soil?

Summarizing

How do worms condition the soil?

OPEN-ENDED QUESTIONS

1. Why do you not see many worms on the lawns during the daytime?
2. Why do you think the cornmeal was placed on top of the soil?
3. How do you think worms help to conserve our soil?
4. Why was there less moisture in the soil without worms?
5. What caused the soil with the cornmeal to change in appearance?
6. What would you do in order to raise worms to sell to fishermen?
7. What can you do to determine the kind of soil in which worms will grow best?

How May the Unwise Use of Various Substances Endanger Your Health and Safety?

(K-6)

CONCEPTS

Sink and toilet cleaners contain strong chemical materials which may injure the skin severely if used carelessly.

Some dry cleaning compounds are flammable (burn) and may give off dangerous fumes.

Most germ killers are extremely dangerous if taken internally.

Many insect sprays are poisonous to humans as well as to insects.

Paint removers often burn or give off dangerous fumes.

Household ammonia is poisonous and should be kept in a safe place, not in the medicine cabinet.

The poison label is a skull (skeleton head) with cross bones.

Bleaches should be used in the home with extreme caution.

All poisons should be kept "out of reach" of children. They can be used by adults, but with caution.

MATERIALS

Empty containers with poison or warning labels on them:

Bleach bottle	Sink and toilet cleaner cans
Aspirin bottle	Paint remover can
Medicine bottles	Can of insect spray
Gasoline can	—
Iodine bottle	Jar of insects
Ammonia bottle	Piece of cloth

DISCUSSION

What is the symbol placed on bottles to indicate they contain poisons?

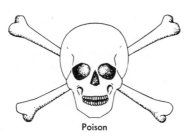

Poison

Teacher's Note: Display an enlarged picture of skull and crossbones or draw it on the board. A colored skull and crossbones would be very effective. Also place many of the containers suggested in the materials on your desk.

Where should the word "poison" be placed on the board?

Why do you think these bottles were placed on the desk?

Teacher's Note: Point to the poison label on the bottles. Explain the reasons for each label. Some poison labels will also have antidotes listed on them. Discuss the purpose of the antidote with the class. Discuss the terms— flammable, antiseptic, bleach, ammonia and medicine.

Processes

PART I

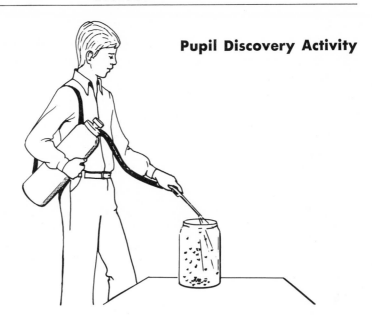

Pupil Discovery Activity

Hypothesizing

Observing
Inferring

1. Obtain a jar of insects and a can of insect spray.
   What do you think will happen to the insects when they are sprayed?
2. Spray the insects and observe.
   What do you think the spray would do to you?
   Where should these sprays be kept?

PART II

Hypothesizing

Observing
Inferring

1. Pour some bleach on a piece of cloth. Allow it to stand for several hours.
   What do you think will happen to the material on which the bleach was poured?
2. After two days, have the children note results.
   What does this tell you about bleaches and other chemicals used around the house?

PART III

1. Place iodine on a leaf or skin of a fruit and allow it to stand for several hours.

Hypothesizing	What do you think the iodine will do to the leaf?
	2. Examine it after several hours.
Observing	What happened?

Teacher's Note: Point out that iodine is a medicine, but it may be harmful to the skin if used for too long on the same spot. Iodine also is very poisonous.

Inferring	What rule or rules would you make to follow in regard to medicines and the places they should be kept in the home?

Teacher's Note: Explain that chemicals and medicines kept in the medicine cabinets may be dangerous if not used properly, and children should not use any medicines unless their parents are there to help them.

PART IV

Observing	1. Display the following cans: paint thinner, gasoline, kerosene, and cigarette lighter fluid.

Teacher's Note: It may be a good idea to have the children describe the smells these materials give off.

Comparing	What do all of these have in common?
	2. Write the word "flammable" on the board and ask the children to explain what it means.
	What rule can you make in regard to the use and storage of flammable chemicals?

Teacher's Note: Point out they should never be used near fires. Gasoline should particularly never be used to start a fire. It is extremely dangerous to pour gasoline from a container onto a fire because the fire will travel right up the gasoline being poured to the container itself and may cause an explosion and burning.

Inferring	Why should you not play with chemicals you know nothing about?
Inferring	From what you observed with the insect spray, why should your parents wash their hands after using an insect spray?
Inferring	Why should you not get things from the medicine cabinet in the dark?
Inferring	Why is gasoline very dangerous?
Hypothesizing	How can you protect babies and small children from the dangers of medicines and chemicals?
Hypothesizing	What can you do to protect your family from the

dangers of these various substances and make your home a safer place?

OPEN-ENDED QUESTIONS

1. What do you think bleach would do to leather or skin?

What Do Plants Need in Order to Grow?   (1-6)

Teacher's Note: In the primary grades it is suggested that the class be broken up into groups. Each group should be assigned to test the effect of only one of the variables listed below, such as water or light.

CONCEPTS

Plants need food in order to grow.
Plants need water in order to grow.
Plants need light in order to grow.
Too much water may kill some plants.

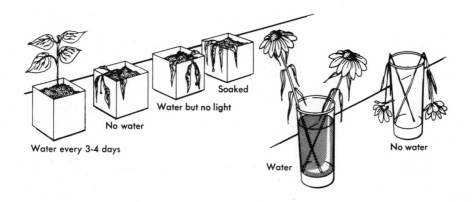

MATERIALS

Seeds (pea, bean, or lima)
8 small milk cartons
Topsoil

DISCUSSION

What do plants need in order to grow?
If you were going to raise some plants from seeds, what could you do?
If you wanted to find out how light affects plants, what could you do?
If you wanted to find out how water affects plants, what could you do?

Processes	Pupil Discovery Activity
	1. Obtain 8 small milk cartons, topsoil, and bean seeds.
	2. Punch 4 small holes in the bottom of 6 of the cartons to allow for drainage. Leave 2 cartons intact.
	3. Fill all 8 cartons with topsoil.
	4. Plant 3 seeds in each carton one inch deep. Cover the seeds with soil and pack the soil down with your hand.
	5. Water all cartons so soil is damp but not soaking and continue to water them every 2 or 3 days until plants are a few inches high.
	6. After the seeds sprout, keep the 2 cartons left intact filled with water so the soil is always soaked.
	7. After the plants sprout, stop watering 2 of your 6 cartons.
	8. Water regularly 2 other cartons, but place them in a dark place where they get no light.
	9. Keep the other 2 cartons in a well lighted place, and water regularly. This is your control.
	10. Observe and record your observations daily.
Hypothesizing	What do you think will happen to the plants being soaked?
Hypothesizing	What do you think will happen to the plants not being watered?
Hypothesizing	What do you think will happen to the plants which are in the dark?
Hypothesizing	What do you think will happen to the plants kept in a lighted room and watered regularly?
	Two weeks later, answer the following:
Comparing	Which plants appear to be the most healthy?
Observing	What happened to the plants that were kept soaked?
Collecting and organizing data	What happened to the plants you did not water?
Observing	What happened to the plants kept in a dark place and not exposed to light?
Observing	What happened to the plants kept in a lighted room and watered regularly?
Inferring	What do plants need in order to grow well?

OPEN-ENDED QUESTIONS

1. Why are cut flowers placed in water?
2. What would happen if they were not placed in water?
3. Do all plants need soil, air and water? Explain.
4. Of what importance are plants to man?
5. Under what conditions do plants grow best in your house?
6. What other factors influence healthy plant life?

EVOLUTION

What Are Fossils and Fossil Beds?   (3-6)

CONCEPTS

A fossil is any remains or evidence of previous life.

A fossil may have been buried in mud, covered by sand, volcanic ash, or other material, or frozen in ice or soil.

Some types of fossils are actual remains found in ice, amber, asphalt pits, oil shale, coal, and other carbonaceous remains.

Other fossils are petrified wood, and casts, including tracks, molds, and coprolites (hardened feces).

Fossil beds occur in areas containing sedimentary deposits. These are areas where soil has washed or blown over the organism.

MATERIALS

2 ice trays	Model of an animal or a cutout of an
Fruit such as cherries and grapes	animal
Water	Several sheets of paper
Soil	Actual fossils if available
Small cardboard box	Pictures of fossils if available

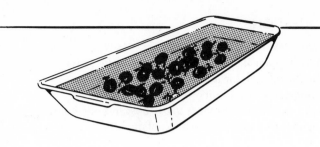

Processes

PART I

Pupil Discovery Activity

Teacher's Note: This activity should be done in groups of five.

1. Obtain two ice trays, fruit, water, and soil.
2. Place some fruit in an ice tray and put the tray in the freezing compartment of a refrigerator.
3. Place soil and water in another ice tray and add some fruit to it. Put the tray in the freezing compartment of the refrigerator.
4. Place some of the same kind of fruit in the refrigerator on a shelf and in the classroom on a shelf.

Hypothesizing — What do you think will happen to the fruit in the water in the ice tray?

Hypothesizing — What do you think will happen to the fruit in the soil and water in the ice tray?

Hypothesizing — What do you think will happen to the fruit on the shelf in the refrigerator?

Hypothesizing — What do you think will happen to the fruit on the shelf in the classroom?

Hypothesizing — How long do you think the fruit will last (be preserved) in each place?

Observing — 5. Take your ice trays out each day and record what you see in them.

Communicating — 6. Record information about the fruit in the refrigerator and on the shelf.

Observing — What has happened to the fruit in each instance?

Observing — How long did the fruit last in each instance?

Hypothesizing — If an animal were to die in Alaska or in the Artic and was covered by snow and ice, what do you think would happen to that animal?

Some years ago, part of a mammoth (an animal

which looks like an elephant) was found buried in
the ice in Siberia.

Inferring

What does this tell you about the area?
What do we call the remains of an animal or plant
from an earlier geological period?

Teacher's Note: Explain terms when necessary. Point
out to the children that this is one way that fossils
are formed.

PART II

1. Obtain soil and a small cardboard box.
2. Add water to the soil, making mud that is fairly
   thick. Place it in the bottom of the small cardboard
   box. Smooth it out; press your hand in the mud so
   that you get a good impression. Cover the mud
   with a layer of sand several inches deep.

Hypothesizing

What do you think will happen to the impression of
your hand?

3. After two or three days, carefully remove the sand.

Observing

What has happened to the impression of your hand?

Inferring

What would you call this impression?

Inferring

What kinds of impressions similar to this help
geologists find out about life in previous geological
times?

Inferring

In what types of materials do you find imprints such
as these?

Inferring

Where could you find imprints such as these?

Teacher's Note: Point out that this is another way in
which fossils are formed. If possible, have some fossils and pictures of different kinds of fossils in the
classroom. The children can examine and discuss
them and discover more information.

PART III

1. Obtain a model of an animal or a cutout of an ani-
   mal and cover it with several sheets of paper.
   What have you made?
   What would each layer of paper be in nature?

Applying

What do you think would happen to the animal?
What do you think a fossil bed is?

Inferring

Why do you think a fossil bed usually must have
several layers of soil in it?

OPEN-ENDED QUESTIONS

1. Where would you expect to find fossils?
2. Why are more fossils not found?
3. Explain why you could or could not expect to find fossils in the area in which you live?
4. What evidence is there that fossils are being formed today?
5. What information can you discover from fossils?

How Can a Fossil Be Made?   (K-6)

CONCEPTS

A fossil is any remain, impression, or trace of an animal or plant of a former geological age.

Fossils can be found in sedimentary rock.

Sedimentary rock is formed from mud and silt.

Organisms whose fossils are uncovered lived and died in a period when the layers were laid down in which their remains are found.

Older layers of rocks have fossils which are unlike the animals and plants now living.

Teacher's Note: If possible, hold up some examples of fossils, or show pictures of fossils. Show pictures of extinct animals. Ask the children how man knows that these animals existed if they are no longer present on earth.

MATERIALS

Pictures of fossils and extinct animals	Shells
Fossils	Vaseline
Plaster of paris	Cardboard
Assorted leaves	Water

DISCUSSION

What is a fossil?
Where could you find a fossil?

Processes   **Pupil Discovery Activity**

1. Obtain some plaster of paris, vaseline, a leaf or shell, and a piece of cardboard.

Designing an
investigation

2. What could you do with these materials to make an imprint of a leaf or shell?

3. Mix a small amount of water with about 3 table-spoons of plaster of paris until the plaster is smooth and fairly thick.

4. Coat the leaf with vaseline and place the leaf on about ¼ inch of plaster. Press the leaf gently into the plaster. Let the plaster and leaf dry on the window sill.

5. Remove the leaf.

Comparing

What have you made?

Teacher's Explanation: Point out that the plaster would be like small particles of dirt (sediment) dropped by a river and that it takes millions of years to make hard rock out of sediment.

Inferring

6. How do fossils enable man to tell the kinds of life on earth before written history?

Summarizing

7. What evidence is there that life has changed in a million years?

Inferring

Why?

OPEN-ENDED QUESTIONS

1. What other things could you use to make imprints?
2. Where does man get the oil he uses in his car?

APPENDICES

A Comparative Chart of Elementary Science Curriculum Projects*

PROJECT	ADDRESS AND TELEPHONE	SUPPORT
AAAS Commission on Science Education (AAAS)	AAAS 1515 Massachusetts Ave., N.W. Washington, D.C. 20005 (202) DU7-7171	American Association for the Advancement of Science/National Science Foundation
Conceptually Oriented Program in Elementary Science (COPES)	New York University 4 Washington Place New York, N.Y. 10003 (212) SP7-2000	New York University/U.S. Office of Education
Elementary School Science Project (ESSP)	Science Education Department University of Illinois 805 West Pennsylvania Ave. Urbana, Illinois 61801 (207) 333-3090	University of Illinois/National Science Foundation
Elementary School Science Project Utah State University (ESSP–USU)	Physics Department Utah State University Logan, Utah 84321 (801) 752-4100, ext. 698 or 466	Utah State University/National Science Foundation
Elementary Science Advisory and Research Project	Elementary Science Advisory Ctr. Ketchum 306W, Univ. of Colo. Boulder, Colorado 80302	University of Colorado/U.S. Office of Education/Rocky Mountain Educational Laboratory/Educational Services, Inc.
Elementary Science Study (ESS)	Educational Services, Incorporated 55 Chapel Street Newton, Massachusetts 02160 (617) 969-7100, ext. 504	Educational Services Inc./National Science Foundation/(also some small grants for short-term efforts—Peace Corps, Cardozo Model School District)
Flint Hills Elementary Science Program Development Project	Kansas State Teachers College Emporia, Kansas 66801 (316) DI2-1342	Flint Hills Educational Research and Development Association/Title III, ESEA, U.S. Office of Education
K–12 Science Design	Curriculum Coordination Office Las Cruces School District No. 2 301 West Amador Avenue Las Cruces, New Mexico 88001 (505) 524-2894	Las Cruces School District No. 2
Minnesota Mathematics and Science Teaching Project (MINNEMAST)	MINNEMAST 720 Washington Ave., S.E. Minneapolis, Minnesota 55414 (617) 373-3522	University of Minnesota/National Science Foundation/U.S. Office of Education
Oakleaf Individualized Elementary School Science	Research and Development Center 160 N. Craig St. University of Pittsburgh Pittsburgh, Pennsylvania 15213 (412) 683-8640	Learning Research and Development Center/Baldwin Whitehall School District/U.S. Office of Education
Pennsylvania Science in Action Program	Science Education Advisor Office Bureau of General and Academic Education, Box 911 Harrisburg, Pennsylvania 17126 (717) 787-7320	Department of Public Instruction, Commonwealth of Pennsylvania/ State Funds/NDEA, Title III
Minneapolis Reorganized Science Curriculum K–12	Minneapolis Reorganized Science Curriculum 807 N. E. Broadway Minneapolis, Minnesota 55413	Minneapolis Public Schools, Special School District No. 1, Minneapolis, Minnesota
School Science Curriculum Project (SSCP)	School Science Curriculum Project 805 West Pennsylvania Ave. University of Illinois Urbana, Ill. 61801 (217) 333-4230	University of Illinois, Department of Secondary and Continuing Education/National Science Foundation
Science Curriculum Improvement Study (SCIS)	Lawrence Hall of Science University of California Berkeley, California 94720 (415) 845-6000, ext. 4541	University of California, Berkeley/ National Science Foundation
Special Materials Science Project (SMSP)	Mahopac Board of Education 42 Stevenson Ave. Peekskill, N.Y. 10566 (914) PE7-2241	Mahopac Board of Education/Title I, ESEA, U.S. Office of Education

*J. David Lockhard, *The Instructor,* Vol. LXVII, No. 5 (Jan., 1968), pp. 52-53.

APPENDIX A

PURPOSE OF PROJECT	MATERIALS ALREADY PRODUCED
Broad concerns for science education at all levels including curriculum development for grades K-16 and teacher preparation	Science—a process approach in seven volumes plus Commentary for teachers; equipment kits for Parts One through Seven, numerous articles, and several teacher-training films
An understanding of the nature of matter at various levels of sophistication, grades K-6	First draft of teacher's manual for teaching the conservation of energy scheme and test materials
To develop and write astronomy materials that reflect the structure of the subject as it is viewed by professional astronomers, grades 5-9	Pupil's book and teacher's guide with the following titles: Charting the universe, The universe in motion, Gravitation, The message of starlight, The life story of a star, and Galaxies and the universe
To provide qualitative and quantitative experiments for children from five to seven, which can be understood in terms of their experiences, grades K-2	Science for first grade, a manual for teachers; Concept prerequisite and development test specimen set and Science for second grade, a manual for teachers
Exploration of new patterns for facilitating children's work in the elementary science curriculum and of modifying content and style of available materials accordingly; grades K-6 (also for preschool children)	Guides for elementary school teachers, the first to be Science equipment in the elementary school
Development of more meaningful science materials; open-ended rather than teacher- or textbook-directed investigations are emphasized; various fields of science, grades K-8	Units with teacher's guides and kits on: Behavior of mealworms, 6; Gases and "airs," 5-8; Growing seeds, K-3; Small things, 5; Microgardening, 4-7; Bones, 4-6; Mirror cards, 1-7; Curious gerbils; Light and shadows, K-3; Attribute games and problems, K-8; Butterflies, 1-4; Batteries and bulbs, 5-8; Ice cubes, 5-6; Primary balancing, Changes, 1-4; Drops, streams, and containers, primary; Euglena, 6-8; Rocks and charts, 3-5; Eggs and tadpoles, K-8; films; a newsletter
Development of an exemplary instructional program in science with emphasis on a program of studies for upper (6-8) grades	Field Guide to Geology of East Central Kansas and a general information pamphlet
To study curricula in science and to develop a design to meet the district's needs, grades 1-12	Resource units for Grade 1 through Grade 9; covers such topics as health, the earth, machines, animals, energy, weather, light, conservation, biology, chemistry, magnetism and electricity
To produce coordinated mathematics and science curriculum for grades K-6, and organized materials for in-service teacher education	Minnemast reports, Mathematics: Units I-XXV; Science: Units K-1 through 2-6
Objectives are stated in terms of expected student performance in a laboratory setting; diagnostic tests with objects used to find out what each student can or cannot do, K-6	Units on Discrimination; Sorting and classification; Observation and measurement; Magnetism; and Light
To assist in in-service workshops where resource teachers are prepared to develop and implement programs for their own school systems, grades K-college	Unit booklets on Microbiology and a "Science in Action" series on: A guide for teaching science measurement; Simple machines; Force, energy and power; Simple plants and animals; Insects and spiders; Problems of space travel; Astronomy; Vertebrates; Ecology; Meteorology; Physiology; and Basic electricity
Reorganization of the former science curriculum into an integrated science curriculum, K-12, with classroom teacher resource materials and evaluative tools	K-12 Overview—1961; K-12 Handbook—1961; Kdg. Supplement—1962; Grade 1 Supplement—1962; Grade 2 Supplement—1962; Grade 3 Supplement—1962; Grade 4 Supplement—1965; Grade 5 Supplement—1964; Grade 6 Supplement—1964; Also supplements for grades 7-10
To design science curricula for grades 4-9, and the development of specific teaching materials	Units on: Running water and river development, 5-8; Beans and biology, 6-9; Motion, photographs and pendulums, 4-6; short interval timer, The construction of fifty-gallon and thirty-gallon aquariums, Hatchet planimeter pendulum.
To develop a complete and integrated curriculum rather than self-contained teaching units; SCIS stresses concepts and phenomena, with process learnings an implicit by-product; physical and life sciences, grades K-6; sequential rather than graded	Units titled: Materials objects; Organisms; Interaction; Measurement; Subsystems; Relativity; Temperature; and several explanatory films
To develop a program of science activities for educationally deprived children in grades 6-7; to design activities to stimulate and interest educationally deprived children; to develop kits to accompany science activities	Units under project Alpha I—Grade 6; Observing and recording; Measurement; Natural history; A study in ecology; Variation and nature; The spectrum. Project Alpha II—Grade 7: Observation and measurement; Metric measurement; Electricity; Tiny things

PROJECT	PRESENT AND/OR FUTURE ACTIVITIES	
AAAS Commission on Science Education (AAAS)	Commercial editions of first three parts as well as revised kits of equipment and supplies are being developed; future plans include	revision and extension of evaluations, in-service training programs, supplying consultants to schools, producing additional films
Conceptually Oriented Program in Elementary Science (COPES)	Final draft of materials mentioned, development of a proposal for grant funds from the U.S. Office	of Education for support after September 1967
Elementary School Science Project (ESSP)	Revision of certain books; concentration upon broad evaluation	questions related to this and other course content improvement projects
Elementary School Science Project Utah State University (ESSP–USU)	Kindergarten lessons and third- and fourth-grade teachers manuals; production of teacher-training films; using summers to write	third- and fourth-grade materials and winters to test lessons and produce films
Elementary Science Advisory and Research Project	Further guides for elementary school teachers on Patterns and colors, Use of native dyes, Batteries and bulbs, Use of school gardens;	practical courses for in-service teachers, summer school courses and observational learning and teaching
Elementary Science Study (ESS)	Over 50 units being prepared for trial teaching; continued work on existing units as well as initiation	of new ones; summer programs in teacher education
Flint Hills Elementary Science Program Development Project	Field guides to flora and fauna of East Central Kansas; film and slide sets of the geology of the state of Kansas with concentra-	tion on the earth and biological sciences; development of teaching guides and related materials
K–12 Science Design	Curriculum content for grades 10-12; updating of existing materials by the teachers who wrote the original design	
Minnesota Mathematics and Science Teaching Project (MINNEMAST)	Ten integrated science-mathematics units for K-1; future plans include	curriculum materials for integrated science-mathematics, 2-6
Oakleaf Individualized Elementary School Science	Additional lessons drawn from AAAS program, SCIS program, and Dr. Novak's science series; lessons are then rewritten and adapted for the individualized	laboratory; aim is to produce about 1,000 laboratory lessons which develop to the process and content objectives
Pennsylvania Science in Action Program	"Science in Action" series unit on Heat, light and sound; more intensive workshop experience on	consultative assistance at the local level; conference to begin development of behavioral objectives
Minneapolis Reorganized Science Curriculum K–12	Additional material for grades 7-9; constant updating of supplement materials for K-10; more resource	units at each grade level; work on an evaluative program
School Science Curriculum Project (SSCP)	Additional units on: Control—feedback; Planaria; From chick to chick; Ninsect game; Classification; Running water; Aquarium; Drosophila; Flies; Ferns and mosses; Matter and electricity; Writing systems autolab; Snail	island; "Why is a ninsect"; Fresh water aquarium; Energy; A little arithmetic with your science; Densitometer; Constructing weights; Hand microtome; Incubator; Oxygen blue bottle; Humidity sensor
Science Curriculum Improvement Study (SCIS)	A life science program; A physical science program; tests; science reading series XVI-XX; recordings	for the teacher VI-IX; course overview book; development of a teacher educational program
Special Materials Science Project (SMSP)	Revision of as well as additional activities for present Alpha I and Alpha II; tentatively. Alpha III (8)	and Alpha IV (9), all subject to financial support approval

Elementary Science Courses of Study: Grades

STATE	DATE	TITLE	DATE	COST	ADDRESS
Alabama	1–6	Elementary Science	1965	–	Dept. of Education Montgomery, Ala. 36104
California	K–8	Science Curriculum Development in the Elementary School	1964	.35	State Dept. of Education Bureau of Textbooks 721 Capitol Mall Sacramento, Calif. 95814
Delaware	K–6	Elementary Science Guide	1965	–	P.O. Box 869 Wilmington, Del. 19899
Florida	3–6	Today's Science in Tomorrow's World	1965	.75	Administration Building 1410 N.E. 2nd Ave.
	1–6	Elementary Science	1964	1.00	Miami, Fla. 33132
Georgia	1–3	Science for Georgia	1965	2.00	Department of Education
	4–6	Schools—Vol. I, Vol. II		2.00	State Office Building Atlanta, Ga. 30334
Idaho	K–12	Science Program for Idaho Falls Public Schools	1964	–	State House Boise, Idaho
Illinois	K–8	Lincolnwood Science Guide	1965	1.00	Lincolnwood Schools 6855 N. Crawford Lincolnwood, Ill. 60645
Indiana	K–3	Primary Science Guide	1966	–	210 East Columbus Drive
	4–6	Elementary Science Guide	1963	1.50	East Chicago, Ind. 46312
Iowa	K–3	Science for Iowa Schools	1965	–	State Dept. of Public Instruc-
	4–6		1966	–	tion, State Office Building Des Moines, Iowa 50319
Louisiana	Prim.	Teaching Primary Science, Vol. I, II, III	1962	2.00 each	Acadia Parish School Board P.O. Box 308 Crawley, La. 70526
Maryland	1–2	Elementary Curriculum	1965	2.00	St. Mary's County Board of
	3–4	Guide, Science Vol. I,			Education
	5–6	Vol. II, Vol. III			Leonardtown, Md. 20650
Michigan	K–6	An overview of the Elem. School Curriculum	1964	2.50	Lansing Schools 3426 South Cedar Street Lansing, Mich. 48910
New Hampshire	1–6	Elementary Science Guide	1961	–	State Dept. of Education Concord, N.H. 03301
New Mexico	1–6	Science Outline	1961	–	Director of Instruction Grants, N.M. 87020
New York	K–3	Science K–3	1965	.50	Publications Dist.
	4–6	Science 4–6	1966	.50	Finance Sec.-State Ed. Dept.
	K–12	What Science Is	1961	.25	Albany, N.Y. 12224
	K–2	Science K–2	1966	1.50	Bd. of Education Pub. Office
	K–6	Science K–6 (7 units)	1958	.50 each	110 Livingston St. Brooklyn, N.Y. 11201
North Dakota	K–3	Elementary Science Handbook	1961	1.50	Dept. of Public Instruction Bismarck, N.D. 58501
Ohio	K–3	Primary Manual	1963	4.50	Bd. of Education
	4–6	Intermediate Manual	1962	4.50	608 E. McMillan Street Cincinnati, Ohio 45206
Pennsylvania	K–12	Tri-Cycle Science Curriculum	1965	–	Plymouth Whitemarsh School District Plymouth Meeting, Pa. 19462
South Carolina	1–6	Guide for Teaching of Science	1962	–	1429 Senate St. Columbia, S.C. 29201
West Virginia	1–6	Science—A Sourcebook for Elementary Teachers	1961	–	Dept. of Education Charleston, W.Va. 25305

Source: National Science Teachers Association: Compiled Bibliography, 1965, & Courses of Science.

Commercial Suppliers of Science Kits

American Basic Science Club,
Inc.
501 East Crockett St.
San Antonio, Tex. 78202

Atomic Accessories, Inc.
811 West Merrick Rd.
Valley Stream, N.Y. 11580

Atomic Corp. of America
14725 Arminita St.
Panorama City, Calif. 91402

Baird-Atomic, Inc.
33 University Rd.
Cambridge, Mass. 02138

Barnett Instrument Co.
Kraft St.
Clarksville, Tenn. 37040

Cambosco Scientific Co.
37 Antwerp St.
Boston, Mass. 02135

Carolina Biological Supply Co.
Burlington, N.C. 27215

Central Scientific Co.
1700 Irving Park Rd.
Chicago, Ill. 60613

Clay-Adams, Inc.
141 East 25th St.
New York, N.Y. 10010

Creative Playthings
P.O. Box 1100
Princeton, N.J. 08540

W. H. Curtin & Co.
Box 14
New Orleans, La. 70101

Denoyer-Geppert Co.
5235-5259 Ravenswood Ave.
Chicago, Ill. 60640

Dumville Manufacturing Co.
Box 5595
Washington, D.C. 20016

Eckert Mineral Research, Inc.
110 East Main St.
Florence, Colo. 81226

Edmund Scientific Corp.
101 E. Gloucester Pike
Barrington, N.J. 08007

Fisher Scientific Co.
620 Fisher Building
Pittsburgh, Pa. 15219

General Biological Supply
House
8200 South Hoyne Ave.
Chicago, Ill. 60620

General Electric Co.
1001 Broad St.
Utica, N.Y. 13501

A. C. Gilbert Co.
Erector Square
New Haven, Conn.

Irving Science Labs
2052 Hillside Ave.
New Hyde Park, N.Y. 11040

Laboratory Furniture Co.
Old Country Rd.
Mineola, N.Y. 11501

Labosco, Inc.
Lombard, Ill. 60148

Lafayette Radio
165-08 Liberty Ave.
Jamaica, N.Y. 11433

Arthur S. LaPine & Co.
6001 South Knox Ave.
Chicago, Ill. 60629

Living Science Labs
1605 Jericho Tpke.
New Hyde Park, N.Y. 11040

Macalaster Scientific Corp.
253 Norfolk Ave.
Cambridge, Mass. 02139

F. A. Owens Publishing Co.
Dansville, N.Y. 11437

Paco Electronic Co.
70-31 84th St.
Glendale, N.Y. 11227

Philco TechRep Division
P.O. Box 4730
Philadelphia, Pa. 19134

Product Design Co.
2796 Middlefield Rd.
Redwood City, Calif. 94063

Research Scientific Supplies,
Inc.
Dept. ST8
126 West 23rd St.
New York, N.Y. 10011

Science Education Products
2796 Middlefield Rd.
Redwood City, Calif. 94063

Science Electronics, Inc.
195 Massachusetts Ave.
Cambridge, Mass. 02129

Science Service
1719 U St., NW
Washington, D.C. 20009

Sesco, Inc.
1312 South 13th St.
Vincennes, Ind. 47591

APPENDIX D

Supplies, Equipment, and Materials from Community Sources

DIME STORE

balloons
balls
candles
compasses (magnetic)
cotton (absorbent)
dyes
flashlights
glues and paste
inks
magnifying glasses
marbles
matches
mechanical toys
mirrors
mouse traps
scissors
sponges
thermometers

DRUGSTORE

acids (HCL, etc.)
adhesive tape
alcohol (rubbing)
bottles
canned heat
carbon tetrachloride
castor oil
cigar boxes
cold cream
corks
cotton
forceps
heat-resistant nursing bottles
hydrogen peroxide
iodine
limewater
medicine droppers
mercury
pipe cleaners
rubber stoppers
soda bicarbonate
spatulas
straws
sulfur

ELECTRICAL APPLIANCE SHOP

bell wire
burned-out fuses and
  light bulbs
dry cells
electric fans
electric hotplates
flashlights
flashlight bulbs
friction tape
magnets
  (from old appliances)
old radios
soldering iron
sun lamp
worn out extension cords,
  electrical appliances

FABRIC SHOP

cardboard tubes
cheesecloth
flannel
knitting needles
leather
needles
netting
silk thread
spools
scraps of different kinds of
  materials

FARM OR DAIRY

birds' nests
bottles
clay
containers
dry ice
gravel
hay or straw
humus
insects
leaves
lodestone
loam
rocks
sand
seeds

FIRE DEPARTMENT

samples of material used to
  extinguish various types of
  fire
water pumping equipment

GARDEN SUPPLY STORE

bulbs (crocus, tulips, etc.)
fertilizers
flower pots
garden hose
garden twine
growing plants
labels
lime
seed catalogs
seeds
sprinkling cans
spray guns
trowels and other garden tools

GAS STATION

batteries
ball bearings
cans
copper tubing
gasoline
gears
gear transmissions
grease
inner tubes
jacks
maps
old wet-cell batteries
pulleys
tools
valves from tires
wheels

GROCERY STORE

ammonia
baking soda
borax
candles
carbon tetrachloride
  (carbona)
cellophane
clothespins
cornstarch
corrugated cardboard boxes
fruits
matches
paper bags
paraffin
plastic wrapping
salt
sponges
sugar
tinfoil
vegetables

vinegar
wax
waxed paper

HARDWARE STORE

brace and bits
cement
chisels
clocks
dry-cell batteries
electric push buttons, lamps,
  and sockets
extension cords
files
flashlights
fruit jars
glass cutters
glass funnels
glass friction rods
glass tubing
hammers
hard rubber rods
insulated copper wire
lamp chimneys
metal and metal scraps
nails
nuts and bolts
paints and varnishes
plaster of Paris
pulleys
sandpaper
saws
scales
scrap lumber
screening
screwdrivers
screws

steel wool
thermometers
  (indoor and outdoor)
tin snips
toy electric motors
turpentine
wheelbarrow
window glass
  (broken pieces will do)
wire
yardsticks

MACHINE SHOP

ball bearings
iron filings
iron rods
magnets
nuts and bolts
screws
scrap metals
wire

MEDICAL AND DENTAL OFFICES AND HOSPITALS

all kinds of chemicals
corks
flasks
funnels
glass tubing
hard lenses
litmus paper
microscopes
models, such as teeth
rubber sheeting
rubber tubing
rubber stoppers
test tubes

test tube holders
thermometers
tongue depressors

MUSIC SHOP

broken string and drum heads
musical instruments
pitch pipes
tuning forks

PET SHOP

air pumps
animals
animal cages
aquariums
ant houses
birds
cages
fish
insects
nets (butterfly, fish, etc.)
plastic tubing
strainers
terrariums

RESTAURANT OR DINER

bones (chicken, etc.)
bottles
cans (coffee, 5 gallons)
drums (ice cream)
dry ice
five gallon cans (oil)
food coloring
gallon jars (wide-mouthed,
  pickles, mayonnaise, etc.)
gallon jugs (vinegar)
pie tins

This is only a partial list of the places in the community that are possible sources of items for a science program in the elementary school. Other sources that should not be overlooked are local factories, the janitor of the school, the school cafeteria, radio and television repair shops, florists' shops, the other teachers in the school, the junior and senior high school science teachers, etc. The materials are there; it just takes a little looking.

There are times, though, when in spite of the most careful searching, certain pieces of equipment or supplies are just not obtainable from local sources; also, there are many things that schools should buy from scientific supply houses. A partial list of some of the selected, reliable, scientific supply houses serving elementary schools is given in Appendix E.

Selected Sources of Scientific Equipment, Supplies, Models, Living Things, and Collections

American Optical Instrument Div.
Eggert and Sugar Roads
Buffalo, N.Y. 14215

Bausch & Lomb, Inc.
85737 Bausch Street
Rochester, N.Y. 14602

Bioscope Manufacturing Co.
Box 1492
Tulsa, Okla. 74101

Corning Glass Works
Building 8, 4th Floor
Corning, N.Y. 14830

Cenco Scientific Company
2600 South Kostner Avenue
Chicago, Ill. 60623

    3232 Eleventh Avenue
    Birmingham, Ala. 35201

    6610 Stillwell Street
    Houston, Tex. 77017

    6446 Telegraph Road
    Los Angeles, Calif. 90022

    237 Sheffield Street
    Mountainside, N.J. 07092

    3241 East Jackson
    Phoenix, Ariz. 85034

    1040 Martin Avenue
    Santa Clara, Calif. 95052

    160 Washington Street
    Somerville, Mass. 02143

    6910 East Twelfth Street
    Tulsa, Okla. 74115

Central Scientific Co.
1700 Irving Park Rd.
Chicago, Ill. 60613

Clay-Adams Co.
141 E. 25th St.
New York, N.Y. 10010

Denoyer-Geppert Co.
5235 Ravenswood Ave.
Chicago, Ill. 60640

Edmond Scientific Co.
Barrington, N.J. 08007

Educational Services, Inc.
108 Water St.
Watertown, Mass. 02172

Farquhar Transparent Globes
5007 Warrington Avenue
Philadelphia, Pa. 19143

Hubbard Scientific Company
Box 105
Northbrook, Ill. 60062

Ideal School Supply Company
11004 S. Lavergne Avenue
Oak Lawn, Ill. 60453

Jewel Aquarium Company
5005 W. Armitage Avenue
Chicago, Ill. 60639

Kimtec, Inc.
3625 Westheimer
Houston, Tex. 77027

La Pine Scientific Co.
6001 South Knox Ave.
Chicago, Ill. 60629

Models of Industry
2804 Tenth St.
Berkeley, Calif. 91501

New York Scientific
  Supply Co.
28 W. 30th St.
New York, N.Y. 10001

A. J. Nystrom and Co.
3333 Elston Ave.
Chicago, Ill. 60618

Ohaus Scale Corporation
1050 Commerce Avenue
Union, N.J. 07033

Science Associates
401 N. Broad St.
Philadelphia, Pa. 19108

Science Kit
2299 Military Rd.
Tonowanda, N.Y. 10003

Science Materials Center
59 Fourth Ave.
New York, N.Y. 10003

E. H. Sheldon Equipment Co.
716 Nims Street
Muskegon, Mich.

Standard Science Supply Co.
1232 N. Paulina St.
Chicago, Ill. 60622

Stansi Manufacturing Co.
1231 N. Honore St.
Chicago, Ill. 60623

Testa Manufacturing Co.
10126 E. Rush Street
S. El Monte, Calif. 91733

Trippensee Planetarium Co.
2200 S. Hamilton
Saginaw, Mich. 48602

Turtox Service Dept.
General Supply House
8200 South Hoyne Avenue
Chicago, Ill. 60620

Viking Importers
113 S. Edgemont St.
Los Angeles, Calif. 90004

Ward's Natural Science
  Establishment, Inc.
3000 E. Ridge Rd.
Rochester, N.Y. 14622

Welch Scientific Co.
7300 N. Linder Avenue
Skokie, Ill. 60076

609 West 51st Street
New York, N.Y. 10019

Selected References for the Teacher or School Professional Library

PROFESSIONAL BOOKS IN ELEMENTARY SCHOOL SCIENCE

Blough, Glenn O. and Julius Schwartz. *Elementary School Science and How to Teach It,* Third edition (New York: Holt, Rinehart & Winston, 1964).

Burnett, R. Will. *Teaching Science in the Elementary School* (New York: Holt, Rinehart & Winston, Inc., 1957), 540 pp.

Craig, Gerald S. *Science for the Elementary Teacher* (Boston: Ginn and Company, 1966).

Crouse, William Harry. *Understanding Science,* Revised edition (New York: McGraw-Hill Book Co., Inc., 1956).

Croxton, W. C. *Science in the Elementary School* (New York: McGraw-Hill Book Co., Inc., 1937), 454 pp.

Freeman, Kenneth, Thomas I. Dowling, Nan Lacy, and James S. Tippet. *Helping Children Understand Science* (New York: Holt, Rinehart & Winston, Inc., 1958), 314 pp.

Gega, Peter C. *Science in Elementary Education* (New York: John Wiley & Sons, Inc., 1966).

Greenlee, Julian. *Better Teaching Through Elementary Science* (Dubuque, Iowa: William C. Brown Company, Publishers, 1954), 204 pp.
Teaching Science to Children, Revised edition (Dubuque, Iowa: William C. Brown Company, Publishers, 1955), 195 pp.

Hubler, Clark. *Working with Children in Science* (Boston: Houghton Mifflin Company, 1957), 425 pp.

Kambly, Paul E. and John E. Suttle. *Teaching Elementary School Science* (New York: The Ronald Press Company, 1963).

Kuslan, Louis I. and A. Harris Stone. *Teaching Children Science: An Inquiry Approach* (Belmont, Calif.: Wadsworth Publishing Co., 1968).

Lewis, June E. and Irene C. Potter. *The Teaching of Science in the Elementary School* (Englewood Cliffs, N.J.: Prentice-Hall, Inc., 1961).

Navarra, John G. and Joseph Zaffarone. *Science Today for the Elementary School Teacher* (Evanston, Ill.: Harper & Row, Publishers, 1959), 470 pp.

Piltz, Alber, and Robert Sund. *Creative Teaching of Science in the Elementary School* (Boston: Allyn and Bacon, 1968).

Renner, John W. and William B. Regan. *Teaching Science in the Elementary School* (New York: Harper and Row, 1968).

Tannenbaum, Harold and Nathan Stillman. *Science Education for Elementary School Teachers* (Boston: Allyn and Bacon, Inc., 1960), 339 pp.

Victor, Edward. *Science for the Elementary School* (New York: The Macmillan Company, 1965); *and* Marjorie E. Lerner. *Readings in Science Education for the Elementary School* (New York: The Macmillan Company, 1967).

Wells, Harrington. *Elementary Science Education* (New York: McGraw-Hill Book Co., Inc., 1951), 333 pp.

PSYCHOLOGY OF LEARNING AND SCIENCE EDUCATION

Almy, Millie, Edward Chittenden, and Paula Miller. *Young Children's Thinking* (New York: Teachers College Press, 1966).

Ausubel, David P. *The Psychology of Meaningful Verbal Learning* (New York: Grune and Stratton, 1963).

Bruner, J. S. *The Process of Education* (Cambridge: Harvard University, 1960).

Bruner, Jerome. *Learning about Learning: A Conference Report* (Washington: United States Government Printing Office, 1966).

Flavell, J. H. *The Developmental Psychology of Jean Piaget* (Princeton: D. Van Nostrand, 1963).

Ford, G. W. (ed.). *The Structure of Knowledge and the Curriculum* (Chicago: Rand McNally, 1964).

Cagné, R. M. *The Conditions of Learning* (New York: Holt, Rinehart and Winston, 1965).

Hunt, J. McV. *Intelligence and Experience* (New York: The Ronald Press, 1961).

Inhelder, Barbel, and Jean Piaget. *The Growth of Logical Thinking from Childhood to Adolescence* (New York: Basic Books, 1958).

Navarra, John G. *The Development of Scientific Concepts in a Young Child* (New York: Teachers College, Columbia University, 1955).

Passow, A. Harry, and Robert R. Leeper (eds.). *Intellectual Development: Another Look* (Washington, D.C.: Association for Supervision and Curriculum Development, 1964).

Piaget, Jean. *The Child's Conception of Number* (London: Routledge & Kegan Paul, Ltd., 1963); *and* Barbel Inhelder. *The Child's Conception of Space* (trans. F. J. Langdon and J. L. Lunzer) (London: Routledge and Kegan Paul, Ltd., 1963).

Ripple, R. and V. Rockcastle. *Piaget Rediscovered* (Ithaca: Cornell University Press, 1964).

Smith, Herbert A. "Educational Research Related to Science Instruction for the Elementary and Junior High School: A Review and Commentary," *Journal of Research in Science Teaching,* I (1963), p. 199.

Vygotsky, L. *Thought and Language* (New York: John Wiley and Sons, 1962).

Wann, Kenneth D., Miriam Selchen Dorn, and Elizabeth Ann Liddle. *Fostering Intellectual Development in Young Children* (New York: Teachers College Press, Columbia University, 1962).

SCIENCE EDUCATION PAMPHLETS AND BULLETINS

Alexander, Uhlman S. *Supervision for Quality Education in Science* (Washington, D.C.: U.S. Dept. of Health, Education, and Welfare, Government Printing Office, 1963).

Ashley, Tracy H., et al. *An Administrator's Guide to Elementary School Science Program.* Association of Public School Systems, 525 W. 120 St., New York 27, N.Y., 1960.

Ashley, Tracy H. and Paul Blackwood. *Teaching Elementary School Science,* Bulletin No. 4 (Suggestions for Classroom Teachers), (Washington, D.C.: U.S. Office of Education, 1948).

Aylesworth, Thomas G. *Planning for Effective Science Teaching* (Columbus, Ohio: American Education Publications, 1963).

Blough, Glenn O. *It's Time for Better Elementary School Science.* (Washington, D.C.: National Science Teachers Association, 1958).

Leadership for Science in the Elementary Schools (California Association for Supervision and Curriculum Development, 1960).

Looking Ahead in Science (California State Dept. of Education, 1960).

Craig, Gerald S. *What Research Says to the Teacher Series—Science in the Elementary School* (Washington, D.C.: Department of Classroom Teachers, N.E.A., 1957).

Dunfee, Maxine. *Elementary School Science: A Guide to Current Research* (Washington, D.C.: Association for Supervision and Curriculum Development, 1967).

Education and the Spirit of Science (Washington, D.C.: Educational Policies Commission, N.E.A., 1966).

Fitzpatrick, F. L. *Policies for Science Education* (New York: Teachers College, Columbia University, 1960).

Goodlad, John I., Renata von Stoephasius, and M. Frances Klein. *The Changing School Curriculum* (New York: Fund for the Advancement of Education, August 1966).

Guidelines for the Development of Programs in Science Instruction (Washington, D.C.: Association for Supervision and Curriculum Development, 1966).

Harbeck, Mary Blatt (ed.). *A Sourcebook for Science Supervisors* (Washington, D.C.: National Science Supervisors Association, N.E.A., 1967).

Hochman, Vivienne and Mildred Greenwald. *Science Experiences in Early Childhood Education* (New York: Bank St. Publication, 1953).

Laboratories in the Classroom: New Horizon in Science Education (N.Y.: Science Materials Center, 1960).

The New Science (Washington, D.C.: American Association for the Advancement of Science, 1963).

Richardson, John S. (ed.) *Perspectives in Science Education Series* (Columbus, Ohio: Charles E. Merrill Publishing Co., 1967).

Shapp, Martha. *Planning and Organizing Science Programs for Elementary Schools* (New York: The Grolier Society Incorporated, 1959).

Theory Into Action in Science Curriculum Development (Washington, D.C.: National Science Teachers Association, 1964).

Zaffroni, Joseph. *New Developments in Elementary School Science* (Washington, D.C.: National Science Teachers Association, 1963).

Zim, Herbert S. *Science for Children and Teachers* (Washington, D.C.: Association for Childhood Education International, 1953).

Note: Additional science education books, pamphlets and bulletins are available from science curriculum projects. Write directly to the projects at the addresses listed in appendix A. Government publications in the field of education are listed in a special catalog available from the Superintendent of Documents, U.S. Government Printing Office, Washington, D.C. 20402.

EXPERIMENTS, DEMONSTRATION, AND CONSTRUCTION REFERENCES

FOR TEACHERS AND CHILDREN

Arey, Charles K. *Science Experiences for Elementary School* (New York: Teachers College, Columbia University, 1942).

Ashbaugh, B. and Muriel Beuschlein. *Things to Do in Science and Conservation* (Danville, Ill.: Interstate Printers, 1960).

Atkin, J. Myron and R. Will Burnett. Elementary School Science Activities Series: *Air, Winds and Weather; Electricity and Magnetism; Working with Animals; Working with Plants* (New York: Holt, Rinehart & Winston, Inc., 1960).

Baker, Tunis. *Baker Science Packets.* Educational Science Packet, 42 Carolin Rd., Upper Montclair, N.J., 1952.

Beeler, Nelson F. and Franklyn M. Bramley. *Experiments in Chemistry* (1952); *Experiments with Airplane Instruments* (1953); *More Experiments in Science* (1960) (New York: Thomas Y. Crowell Company).

Berger, Melvin and Frank Clark. *Science and Music* (New York: Whittlesey House, 1961).

Blackwood, Paul E. (ed.) *How and Why Wonder Books* (Columbus, Ohio: Charles E. Merrill Publishing Co.). (Explorations in the fields of science. Titles include: *Weather; Electricity; Rocks and Minerals; Rockets and Missiles; Beginning Science; Our Earth; The Microscope; Science Experiments; The Human Body;* and many more.)

Blough, Glenn O. and Marjorie H. Campbell. *Making and Using Classroom Science Materials in the Elementary School* (New York: Dryden Press, 1954).

Branley, Franklyn M. *Experiments in the Principles of Space Travel* (New York: Thomas Y. Crowell Company, 1955). (Also other titles.)

Challand, Helen J. and Elizabeth R. Brandt. *Science Activities from A to Z.* (Chicago: Children's Press, 1963).

Cooper, Elizabeth K. *Science on the Shores and Banks* (1960); *Science in Your Own Back Yard* (1960) (New York: Harcourt, Brace & World).

De Vries, L. *The Book of Experiments* (New York: The Macmillan Co., 1959).

Frank, Annette and Tillie S. Pine. *Science Experiences Related to the Social Studies.* (New York: 69 Bank Street Publication, 1955).

Freeman, Mae and Ira M. *Fun With Chemistry* (1944); *Fun With Science* (1956); *Fun With Scientific Experiments* (1960) (New York: Random House, Inc.).

Herbert, Don. *Mr. Wizard's Science Secrets* (New York: Popular Mechanics, 1953); *Mr. Wizard's Experiments for Young Scientists* (New York: Doubleday & Company, Inc., 1959).

Hone, Elizabeth, et al. *Teaching Elementary Science: A Sourcebook for Elementary Science* (New York: Harcourt, Brace & World, Inc., 1962).

Leavitt, Jerome and John Juntsberber. *Fun-Time Terrariums and Aquariums* (Chicago: Children's Press, 1961).

Lemming, Joseph. *The Real Book of Science Experiments* (Garden City: Doubleday and Company, Inc., 1954).

Lewellyn, John. *Boy Scientist* (New York: Simon and Schuster, Inc., 1954).

Lynde, Carlton J. *Science Experiences With Home Equipment* (1955); *Science Experiences With Inexpensive Equipment* (1956); *Science Experiments With Ten-Cent Store Equipment* (1955) (New York: D. Van Nostrand Co., Inc.)

Microscope Experiments for Elementary and High School (El Monte, Calif.: Test Manufacturing Co., 1960).

Milgrom, Harry (ed.). *Matter, Energy and Change* (Holt, Rinehart & Winston, Inc., 1961).

National Science Teachers Association. *Science Teaching Today Series:* Vol. 1, Water; Vol. 2, Air; Vol. 3, Fuels and Fire; Vol. 4, Heat; Vol. 5, Magnetism and Electricity; Vol. 6, Sounds; Vol. 7, Light and Color (Washington, D.C., 1954).
Investigating Science With Children Series: Vol. 1, Living Things; Vol. 2, The Earth; Vol. 3, Atoms and Molecules; Vol. 4, Motion; Vol. 5, Energy in Waves; Vol. 6, Space (Darien, Conn.: Teachers Publishing Co., 1964).

Nelson, Leslie W. and George C. Lorbeer. *Science Activities for Elementary School Children* (Dubuque, Iowa: William C. Brown Company, Publishers, 1967).

Newbury, N. F. and H. A. Armstrong. *The Young Experimenter* (New York: Sterling Publishing Co., Inc., 1960).

Parker, Bertha. *Science Experiences, Elementary School* (Evanston, Ill.: Harper & Row, Publishers, 1958).

Partridge, J. A. *Natural Science Through the Season* (New York: The Macmillan Company, 1955).

Podendorf, Illa. *The True Book of Science Experiments* (1954); *Discovering Science on Your Own* (1962); *101 Science Experiments* (1960) (Chicago: Children's Press).

Selsam, Millicent E. *Underwater Zoos* (New York: William Morrow & Co., Inc., 1961).

Sheckles, Mary. *Building Children's Science Concepts* (New York: Teachers College, Columbia University, 1958).

Straight, G. M. *Company Science Experiments* (New York: Hart Publishing Co., 1957).

Swezey, Kenneth M. *After Dinner Science* (New York: Whittlesey House, 1948).

Tannenbaum, Beulah and Myra Stilman. *Understanding Light* (New York: Whittlesey House, 1960).

Thaw, Richard F. and John E. Morlan. *Experiences and Demonstrations in Elementary Physical Science* (Dubuque, Iowa: Wm. C. Brown Co. Inc., 1964).

UNESCO, *UNESCO Source Book for Science Teaching* (UNESCO Publications Center, 801 Third Ave., New York, N.Y., 1962).

Vessel, M. F. and H. Wong. *How to Stimulate Your Science Programs: A Guide to Simple Science Activities Series* (San Francisco: Fearon Publishers, 1959).

Visner, Harold and Adelaide Hechtlinger. *Simple Science Experiments for the Elementary Grades* (Palisades, N.J.: Franklin Publishing Co., 1960).

Children and teachers can keep abreast with the rapid development in research in science and science education by referring to the following periodicals. They provide the most information and are an invaluable supplement to science textbooks.

(T)—teacher oriented   (C)—child oriented

American Biology Teacher. The National Association of Biology Teachers, 19 S. Jackson St., Danville, Ill. 61832 (Monthly) (T)

American Forests. The American Forestry Association, 919 17th St. N.W., Washington, D.C. (Monthly) (T)

The American Journal of Physics. American Association of Physics Teachers, 57 E. 55th St., New York, N.Y. 10022 (Monthly) (T)

The Aquarium. Innes Publishing Co., Philadelphia, Pa. 19107 (Monthly) (C&T)

Audubon Magazine. The National Audubon Society, 1130 Fifth Ave., New York, N.Y. 10028 (Bimonthly) (C&T)

Biology & General Science Digest. W. M. Welch Co., 1515 Sedgwick St., Chicago, Ill. (Free) (T)

Chemistry. Science Service, 1719 16 St. N.W., Washington, D.C. 20009 (Monthly) (T)

Cornell Rural School Leaflets. New York State College of Agriculture, Ithaca, N.Y. 14850 (Quarterly) (T)

Current Science and Aviation. American Education Publications, Education Center, Columbus, Ohio 43216 (Weekly during the school year) (T&C)

Geotimes. American Geological Institute, 1515 Massachusetts Ave. N.W., Washington, D.C. (Monthly) (T)

Grade Teacher. Educational Publishing Co., Darien, Conn. 06820 (Monthly Sept.–June) (T)

Journal of Chemical Education. Business and Publication Office, 20th & Northampton Sts., Easton, Pa. 18042 (Monthly) (T)

Journal of Research in Science Teaching. John Wiley and Sons, 605 Third Ave., New York, N.Y. 10016 (T)

Junior Astronomer. Benjamin Adelman, 4211 Colie Dr., Silver Springs, Md. (C&T) 20906

Junior Natural History. American Museum of Natural History, New York, N.Y. 10024 (Monthly) (C&T)

Monthly Evening Sky Map. Box 213, Clayton, Mo. 63105 (Monthly) (C&T)

My Weekly Reader. American Education Publications, Education Center, Columbus, Ohio (Weekly during the school year) 43216

National Geographic. National Geographic Society, 1146 Sixteenth St. N.W., Washington, D.C. (Monthly) (C&T)

Natural History. American Museum of Natural History, 79th St. and Central Park West, New York, N.Y. 10024 (Monthly) (C&T)

Nature Magazine. American Nature Association, 1214 15th St. N.W., Washington, D.C. (Monthly Oct. to May and bimonthly June to Sept.) (C&T)

Our Dumb Animals. Massachusetts Society for the Prevention of Cruelty to Animals, Boston, Mass. 02115 (Monthly) (C&T)

Outdoors Illustrated. National Audubon Society, 1000 Fifth Ave., New York, N.Y. (Monthly) (C&T)

Physics and Chemistry Digest. W. M. Welch Co., 1515 Sedgwich St., Chicago, Ill. (Free) (T)

Physics Today. American Institute of Physics, 335 E. 45 St., New York, N.Y. 10017 (Monthly) (T)

Popular Science Monthly. Popular Science Publishing Co., 335 Lexington Ave., New York 17, N.Y. 10016 (Monthly) (C&T)

School Science and Mathematics. Central Association Science and Mathematics Teachers, P.O. Box 48, Oak Park, Ill. 60305 (Monthly 9 times a year) (T)

Readers Guide to Oceanography. Woods Hole Oceanographic Institute, Woods Hole, Mass. 02543 (Monthly) (T)

Science. American Association for the Advancement of Science, 1515 Massachusetts Ave. N.W., Washington, D.C. 20025 (T)

Science Digest, 959 8th Ave., New York, N.Y. 10019 (Monthly) (T)

Science Education. Science Education Inc., C. M. Pruitt, University of Tampa, Tampa, Fla. 33606 (5 times yearly) (T)

Science Newsletter. Science Service, Inc., 1719 N. Street N.W., Washington, D.C. 20036 (Weekly) (T)

Science and Children. National Science Teachers Association, Washington, D.C. 20036 (Monthly 8 times a year) (C&T)

Scientific American. 415 Madison Ave., New York, N.Y. 10017 (Monthly) (T)

Scientific Monthly. The American Association for the Advancement of Science, 1515 Massachusetts Ave., Washington, D.C. 20005 (Monthly) (T)

Space Science. Benjamin Adelman, 4211 Colie Dr., Silver Springs, Md. 20906 (Monthly—during school year) (Formerly *Junior Astronomer*) (C&T)

Science Teacher. National Science Teachers' Association, National Education Association, 1201 16 St. N.W., Washington, D.C. 20036 (Monthly—Sept.–May) (T)

Science World. Scholastic Magazines, Inc., 50 W. 44 St., New York, N.Y. 10036 (T&C)

Sky and Telescope. Sky Publishing Corp., Harvard College Observatory, Cambridge, Mass. 02138 (Monthly) (C&T)

Tomorrow's Scientists. National Science Teachers Association, Washington, D.C. 20036 (8 issues per year) (T)

UNESCO Courier. The UNESCO Publications Center, 801 3rd Ave., New York, N.Y. 10022 (Monthly) (T)

Weatherwise. American Meteorological Society, 3 Joy St., Boston, Mass. 02108 (Monthly) (T)

Sources of Free and Inexpensive Science Materials

Air Age Education
100 E. 42 St.
New York, N.Y. 10017

Aluminum Co. of America
818 Gulf Bldg.
Pittsburgh, Pa. 15219

American Can Co.
100 Park Ave.
New York, N.Y. 10013

American Cancer Society
521 W. 57 St.
New York, N.Y. 10019

American Corp. (Americana
Encyclopedia)
4606 East-West Hwy.
Washington, D.C. 20014

American Dental Association
222 E. Superior St.
Chicago, Ill. 60611

American Forest Products
Industries, Inc.
1816 North St. N.W.
Washington, D.C. 20006

American Gas Ass'n.
Educational Services Bureau
429 Lexington Ave.
New York, N.Y. 10017

American Geological Inst.
2101 Constitution Ave.
Washington, D.C. 20037

American Heart Ass'n.
44 E. 23 St.
New York, N.Y. 10010

American Iron & Steel Inst.
150 E. 42 St.
New York, N.Y. 10017

American Medical Association
535 Dearborn St.
Chicago, Ill. 60610

American National Red Cross
National Hq.
Washington, D.C. 20013

American Petroleum Institute
50 W. 50 St.
New York, N.Y. 10020

American Telephone &
Telegraph
195 Broadway
New York, N.Y. 10007

Animal Welfare Institute
270 Park Ave.
New York, N.Y. 10017

Association of American
Railroads
Transportation Bldg.
Washington, D.C. 20006

Automobile Manufacturer's
Association
New Center Bldg.
Detroit, Mich. 48202

Beuschlein, Muriel and
James Saunders
*Free and Inexpensive Teach-
ing Materials for Science
Education*
Chicago Teachers College
Chicago, Ill.

Bristol-Myers Prod. Division
45 Rockefeller Plaza
New York, N.Y. 10020

Chrysler Corp. Educational
Services
P.O. Box 1919
Detroit, Mich. 48231

Collier and Son (Collier's
Encyclopedia)
640 Fifth Ave.
New York, N.Y. 10019

Columbia University Press
(Columbia Encyclopedia)
2960 Broadway
New York, N.Y. 10027

Compton and Co.
(Compton Pictured
Encyclopedia)
1000 N. Dearborn St.
Chicago, Ill. 60610

Consolidated Edison Co.
4 Irving Place
New York, N.Y. 10003

Denoyer Geppert Co.
5235 Ravenswood Ave.
Chicago, Ill. 60640

DuPont de Nemours
Information Division
Wilmington, Del. 19801

Educational Research Bureau
1129 Vermont Ave. N.W.
Washington, D.C. 20005

E.S.I. (Educational Services,
Inc.)
108 Water St.
Watertown, Mass. 02172

Educators Association Inc.
Volume Library
307 Fifth Ave.
New York, N.Y. 10001

Educator's Progress Service
Randolph, Wisconsin
(Educator's Guides to: Free
Films, Free Filmstrips, Free
Science Materials)

Educator's Mutual Insurance
Co.
Lancaster, Pa. 17604

Encyclopædia Britannica, Inc.
425 N. Michigan Ave.
Chicago, Ill. 60611

Field Enterprises
(World Book and Childcraft
Encyclopedia)
510 Merchandise Mart Plaza
Chicago, Ill. 60654

Ford Motor Co.
Public Relations Office
3000 Schaefer Rd.
Dearborn, Mich. 48126

Frontier Press (Lincoln
Library)
Lafayette Bldg.
Buffalo, N.Y. 14103

General Electric Co.
1 River Rd.
Schenectady, N.Y. 12306

General Motors Corp.
General Motors Bldg.
Detroit, Mich. 48202

Grolier Society Co.
(Grolier Encyclopedia, Book
of Knowledge, Programmed
Learning), 2 W. 45 St.
New York, N.Y. 10036

National Association of
Audubon Societies
1775 Broadway
New York, N.Y. 10019

National Association of
Manufacturers
2 E. 48 St.
New York, N.Y. 10017

National Aviation Education
Council
1025 Connecticut Ave., N.W.
Washington, D.C. 20006

National Aeronautics & Space
Administration
Washington, D.C. 20502

National Coal Association
15 & H Sts. N.W.
Washington, D.C. 20005

National College of Education
(Records of the Children's
School)
Evanston, Ill.

National Canners Association
1133 20 St. N.W.
Washington, D.C. 20036

National Dairy Council
111 N. Canal St.
Chicago, Ill. 60606

National Foundation, Inc.
301 E. 42 St.
New York, N.Y. 10017

National Geographic Society
16 & M Sts.
Washington, D.C. 20036

National Wildlife Federation
232 Carrol St. N.W.
Washington, D.C. 20012

Pan American World Airways
28-81 Bridge Plaza North
Long Island City, N.Y. 11101

Proctor and Gamble,
Education Dept.
Cincinnati, Ohio 45202

Science Service
1719 N St. N.W.
Washington, D.C. 20036

Sears, Roebuck and Co.
(*Our Wonderful World
Encyclopedia*)
925 S. Homan Ave.
Chicago, Ill. 60624

Field Enterprises Educational
Corp.
(*Sources of Free and
Inexpensive Educational
Materials*)
510 Merchandise Mart Plaza
Chicago, Ill. 60654

Standard Oil Co.
Education Dept.
30 Rockefeller Plaza
New York, N.Y. 10020

Standard Oil Co. of California
Education Dept.
225 Bush St.
San Francisco, Calif. 94104

Swift & Co.
Agricultural Research Dept.
Chicago, Ill. 60690

Union Carbide & Carbon
Corp.
30 E. 42 St.
New York, N.Y. 10017

United Fruit Corp.
Pier 3, North River
New York, N.Y. 10006

United States Atomic Energy
Comm.
Public Information Service
1901 Constitution Ave.
Washington, D.C. 20545

United States Dept. of
Commerce
Weather Bureau Publ. Sect.
Washington, D.C. 20235

United States Dept. of Health,
Education, & Welfare
Printing Office
Washington, D.C. 20203

United States Steel Corp.
71 Broadway
New York, N.Y. 10004

Westinghouse Electric Corp.
Gateway Center
401 Liberty Ave.
Pittsburgh, Pa. 15222

Elementary Science Textbook Publishers

PUBLISHER	SERIES	AUTHOR(S)	GRADES	COPYRIGHT DATE
Allyn & Bacon, Inc. 470 Atlantic Ave. Boston, Mass. 02210	Exploring Science	Thurber & Durkee	1–6	1966
American Book Co. 55 Fifth Ave. New York, N.Y. 10003	Thinking Ahead in Science	Jacobson, et. al.	1–6	1968
Ginn and Co. Statler Building Back Bay P.O. 191 Boston, Mass. 02117	Science for You	Craig, et. al.	1–6	1966
Harcourt, Brace & World 757 Third Ave. New York, N.Y. 10017	Concepts in Science	Brandwein, et. al.	1–6	1970
Harper and Row 2500 Crawford Ave. Evanston, Ill. 60201	Today's Basic Science	Navarra & Zaffroni	1–6	1963
D. C. Heath and Co. 285 Columbus Ave. Boston, Mass. 02116	Heath Science Series	Herman & Schneider	K–6	1968
Holt, Rinehart & Winston 383 Madison Ave. New York, N.Y. 10017	Science: A Modern Approach	Fischler, et. al.	1–6	1966
Laidlaw Brothers Thatcher & Madison Sts. River Forest, Ill. 60305	The Laidlaw Science Series	Smith, et. al.	1–6	1965
The Macmillan Company 866 Third Ave. New York, N.Y. 10022	Science for Tomorrow's World	Barnard, et. al.	1–6	1966
Charles E. Merrill Publishing Company 1300 Alum Creek Drive Columbus, Ohio 43216	Discovering Science	Piltz, et. al.	K–6	1970
Scott, Foresman and Co. 1900 E. Lake Ave. Glenview, Ill. 60025	Basic Science Program	Blough, et. al.	1–6	1968
L. W. Singer Co. 501 Madison Avenue New York, N.Y. 10022	Science through Discovery	MacCracken, et. al.	1–6	1968
Steck-Vaugh Co. Box 2028 Austin, Tex. 78767	Science Series— Worktexts	Ware, et. al.	1–6	1965

Supplementary Science Book Publishers

Abelard-Schuman Ltd.
6 W. 57 St.
New York, N.Y. 10019

Benefic Press
10300 W. Roosevelt Rd.
Westchester, Ill. 60153

Blaisdell Publishing Co.
275 Wyman St.
Waltham, Mass. 02154

William C. Brown Co.
135 S. Locust St.
Dubuque, Iowa 52001

Children's Press, Inc.
1224 W. Van Buren St.
Chicago, Ill. 60607

Cornell University Press
124 Roberts Pl.
Ithaca, N.Y. 14850

Coward-McCann, Inc.
200 Madison Ave.
New York, N.Y. 10016

Thomas Y. Crowell Co.
201 Park Ave.
New York, N.Y. 10003

The John Day Co., Inc.
200 Madison Ave.
New York, N.Y. 10016

Doubleday & Co., Inc.
501 Franklin Ave.
Garden City, N.Y. 11530

E. P. Dutton & Co., Inc.
201 Park Ave. S.
New York, N.Y. 10003

Follet Publishing Co.
1010 W. Washington Blvd.
Chicago, Ill. 60607

Golden Press, Inc.
850 Third Ave.
New York, N.Y. 10022

Grossett & Dunlap, Inc.
51 Madison Ave.
New York, N.Y. 10022

Holiday House, Inc.
18 E. 56 St.
New York, N.Y. 10022

Houghton Mifflin Co.
110 Tremont St.
Boston, Mass. 02107

Alfred A. Knopf, Inc.
501 Madison Ave.
New York, N.Y. 10022

J. B. Lippincott Co.
East Washington Square
Philadelphia, Pa. 19105

Little, Brown and Co.
34 Beacon St.
Boston, Mass. 02106

Lothrop, Lee and Shepard
Co., Inc.
381 Park Ave. S.
New York, N.Y. 10016

McGraw-Hill Book Co.
Webster Division
Manchester Rd.
Manchester, Mo. 63011

Melmont Publishers, Inc.
1224 W. Van Buren St.
Chicago, Ill. 60607

William Morrow and Co., Inc.
425 Park Ave. S.
New York, N.Y. 10016

Prentice-Hall, Inc.
Englewood Cliffs, N.J. 07632

G. P. Putnam's Sons
200 Madison Avenue
New York, N.Y. 10016

Random House, Inc.
457 Madison Ave.
New York, N.Y. 10022

Ronald Press Co.
79 Madison Ave.
New York, N.Y. 10016

Silver Burdett Co.
Park Ave. and Columbia Rd.
Morristown, N.J. 07960

Simon and Schuster, Inc.
630 Fifth Ave.
New York, N.Y. 10020

Time, Inc.
Time & Life Bldg.
Rockefeller Center
New York, N.Y. 10020

D. Van Nostrand Co., Inc.
120 Alexander St.
Princeton, N.J. 08540

The Viking Press, Inc.
625 Madison Ave.
New York, N.Y. 10022

Ward's Natural Science
Establishment
Box 1712
Rochester, N.Y. 14603

Franklin Watts, Inc.
575 Lexington Ave.
New York, N.Y. 10022

John Wiley and Sons, Inc.
605 Third Ave.
New York, N.Y. 10016

Science Education Film Distributors

(PRODUCERS AND DISTRIBUTORS OF FILMS. CATALOGS SENT UPON REQUEST.)

Audio-Visual School Service
114 E. 31 St.
New York, N.Y. 10016

Bailey Films, Inc.
6509 De Longpre Ave.
Hollywood, Calif. 90028

Bell Telephone Co.
Film Library
Refer to local business office

Cenco Educational Films
1800 Foster Ave.
Chicago, Ill. 60640

Churchill-Wexler Film
    Producers
801 N. Steward St.
Los Angeles, Calif. 90008

Coast Visual Education Co.
5620 Hollywood Blvd.
Hollywood, Calif. 90028

Communication Films
870 Monterey Pass Rd.
Monterey, Calif. 91754

Coronet Instructional Films
65 E. South Water St.
Chicago, Ill. 60601

Curriculum Materials Corp.
1319 Vine St.
Philadelphia, Pa. 19107

De Vry Corp.
1111 Armitage Ave.
Chicago, Ill. 60603

Walt Disney Productions
Educational Film Dept.
477 Madison Ave.
New York, N.Y. 10022

Educational Horizons
3015 Delores St.
Los Angeles, Calif. 90065

Encyclopædia Britannica
    Films
425 N. Michigan Ave.
Chicago, Ill. 60611

Eye Gate House, Inc.
146-01 Archer Ave.
Jamaica, N.Y. 11453

Family Films, Inc.
5823 Santa Monica Blvd.
Hollywood, Calif. 90028

Film Associates of California
11014 Santa Monica Blvd.
Hollywood, Calif. 90025

Filmstrip House, Inc.
432 Park Ave. S.
New York, N.Y. 10007

Film Strip-of-the-Month Club,
    Inc.
355 Lexington Ave.
New York, N.Y. 10017

Gateway Productions, Inc.
1859 Paivell St.
San Francisco, Calif. 94111

The Jam Handy Organization
2821 E. Grand Blvd.
Detroit, Mich. 48211

International Film Bureau,
    Inc.
332 S. Michigan Ave.
Chicago, Ill. 60604

Fred Lasse Productions
245 Oak St.
Itasca, Ill. 60143

McGraw-Hill Text Films
330 W. 42 St.
New York, N.Y. 10036

Moody Institute of Science
11428 Santa Monica Blvd.
Los Angeles, Calif. 90025

Nasco
Fort Atkinson, Wisc. 53538

National Audubon Society
Photo and Film Dept.
1130 Fifth Avenue
New York, N.Y. 10028

National Educational
    Television Film Service—
    Audio Visual Center
Indiana University
Bloomington, Indiana 47401

National Geographic Society
1145 16 St. N.W.
Washington, D.C. 20036

Official Films, Inc.
724 Fifth Ave.
New York, N.Y. 10019

Park Films
288 N. Almont Dr.
Beverly Hills, Calif.

Resources for Education, Inc.
63 Fourth Ave.
Mt. Vernon, N.Y.

Society for Visual Education,
    Inc.
1345 Diversey Pkway.
Chicago, Ill. 60614

Tabletopper Productions
11 E. 6th St.
Carson City, Nevada 89701

United World Films, Inc.
1445 Park Ave.
New York, N.Y. 10029

Young America Films
McGraw-Hill Text Films
    Dept.
330 W. 42 St.
New York, New York 10036

Professional Societies For
Science Teachers and Supervisors

American Association for
  the Advancement of Science
1515 Massachusetts Ave., N.W.
Washington, D.C. 20005

American Association of Physics Teachers
335 E. 45th St.
New York, N.Y. 10017

American Chemical Society
Chemical Education Division
1155 Sixteenth St., N.W.
Washington, D.C. 20036

American Nature Study Society
(No permanent headquarters.
Current officers listed in
Nature Teaching Tips.)

American Nature Study Society
(No permanent headquarters.)

Association for Supervision
  and Curriculum Development
1201 Sixteenth St., N.W.
Washington, D.C. 20036

Central Association of Science
  and Mathematics Teachers
(No permanent headquarters.
Current officers listed in
School Science and Mathematics.)

National Association of Biology Teachers
1420 N Street, N.W.
Washington, D.C. 20005

National Association for Research
  in Science Teaching
(No permanent headquarters.)

National Association of Geology Teachers
(No permanent headquarters.
Current officers listed in
Journal of Geological Education.)

National Science Teachers Association
1201 Sixteenth St., N.W.
Washington, D.C. 20036

Requirements For Various Animals

FOOD AND WATER	RABBITS	GUINEA PIGS	HAMSTERS	MICE	RATS
Daily					
pellets / or / grain	rabbit pellets: keep dish half full	corn, wheat, or oats: keep dish half full	large dog pellets: one or two		canary seeds or oats:
green or leafy vegetables, lettuce, cabbage and celery tops / or	4-5 leaves	2 leaves	1½ tablespoon 1 leaf	2 teaspoons ⅛-¼ leaf	3-4 teaspoons ¼ leaf
grass, plantain, lambs' quarters, clover, alfalfa / or	2 handfuls	1 handful	½ handful	—	—
hay, if water is also given carrots	2 medium	1 medium			
Twice a week					
apple (medium) iodized salt (if not contained in pellets)	½ apple or salt block	¼ apple	⅛ apple	½ core and seeds	1 core
corn, canned or fresh, once or twice a week	½ ear	sprinkle over lettuce or greens ¼ ear	sprinkle over lettuce or greens 1 tablespoon 1/3 ear	¼ tablespoon or end of ear	½ tablespoon or end of ear
water	should always be available			necessary only if lettuce or greens are not provided	

*Source: Grace K. Pratt, *How To . . . Care For Living Things in the Classroom* (Washington, D.C.: NSTA, 1965), p. 9.

FOOD AND WATER PLANTS	GOLDFISH	GUPPIES
Daily		
dry commercial food	1 small pinch	1 very small pinch; medium size food for adults; fine size food for babies
Twice a week		
shrimp – dry – or another kind of dry fish food	4 shrimp pellets, or 1 small pinch	dry shrimp food or other dry food: 1 very small pinch
Two or three times a week tubifex worms	enough to cover ½ area of a dime	enough to cover ⅛ area of a dime
Add enough "conditioned" water to keep tank at required level	allow one gallon per inch of fish add water of same temperature as that in tank – at least 65°F	allow ¼–½ gallon per adult fish add water of same temperature as that in tank – 70–80°F
Plants cabomba, anacharis, etc.	should always be available	

	NEWTS	FROGS
Daily		
small earthworms or mealworms	1–2 worms	2–3 worms
or tubifex worms	enough to cover ½ area of a dime	enough to cover ¾ area of a dime
or raw chopped beef	enough to cover a dime	enough to cover a dime
water	should always be available at same temperature as that in tank or room temperature	

FOOD AND WATER PLANTS (FOR FISH)	WATER TURTLES	LAND TURTLES	SMALL TURTLES
Daily			
worms or night crawlers or tubifex or blood worms and/or	1 or 2	1 or 2	¼ inch of tiny earthworm
raw chopped beef or meat and fish-flavored dog or cat food	½ teaspoon	½ teaspoon	enough to cover ½ area of a dime
fruit and vegetables fresh		¼ leaf lettuce or 6–10 berries or 1–2 slices peach, apple, tomato, melon or 1 tablespoon corn, peas, beans	
dry ant eggs, insects, or other commercial turtle food			1 small pinch
water	¾ of container	always available at room temperature; should be ample for swimming and submersion large enough for shell	half to ¾ of container

APPENDIX K

AAAS Classroom Observation Rating Form (CORF)

ITEMS RELATED TO TEACHER RESPONSES, ACTIONS, AND PLANNING.

BEHAVIOR A	TIME INTERVALS					
	2	4	6	8	10	T
1. Teacher *responds* to explanations *with questions*						
2. Teacher keeps an *open mind* to student responses						
3. Teacher directs student thinking with *new situation*						
4. Teacher asks students to *refine responses*						
5. Teacher *questions* explanations that *do not fit* into the *child's experience*						
6. Teacher directs *vocabulary building* from experience						
7. Teacher *recognizes the limitations of one experience* for the understanding of all students						
8. Teacher *evaluates* student performance on basis of *what students are able to do*						
9. Teacher poses questions which *provoke thinking*						
10. Teacher directs questions at *different experience levels*						
11. Teacher *probes for basis for incorrect response* before telling student he is wrong						
12. Teacher asks *student to more fully explain* a complex or unclear response						
13. Teacher periodically *reviews and summarizes progress*						

BEHAVIOR B	TIME INTERVALS					
	2	4	6	8	10	T
1. Teacher *agrees or disagrees* with explanations						
2. Teacher accepts *only* the answer he *deems correct*						
3. Teacher *abandons hope* by saying "you don't get it", etc.						
4. Teacher *accepts first response*						
5. Teacher *accepts* responses that fit *his own experience*						
6. Teacher *presents vocabulary* before experience						
7. Teacher *assumes that one experience is satisfactory* for understanding of all students						
8. Teacher *evaluates* student *performance* on basis of *what students say* or on basis of *what he assumes they can do*						
9. Teacher poses questions which *get desired responses*						
10. Teacher directs questions at *common level*						
11. Teacher *tells student he is wrong* and asks for another response						
12. Teacher *accepts any response*						
13. Teacher moves through lesson with *no attention to review or summary*						

BEHAVIOR A

	TIME INTERVALS					
	2	4	6	8	10	T
14. Teacher *commends work well done*						
15. Teacher *gives help willingly*						
16. Teacher *anticipates* and *recognizes individual needs and abilities*						
17. Teacher works *with students at their own rate of* speed						
18. *Procedures planned and well organized*						
19. Evidence of *large number of students being involved*						
20. Evidence that *lesson is paced* to include "going off on a tangent" when this is called for						
21. Evidence that *illustrations* of an idea are selected progressively from *simpler to less obvious*						
22. Teacher works *to involve many children in discussions*						
23. Evidence that *teacher has objectives* of lesson *clearly in mind*						
24. *Students grouped for small group* or *individual* activity						
25. *Students grouped for lecture* activity						
26. *Needed materials readily available*						
27. Teacher *depends sparingly on guide* to conduct the lesson						

BEHAVIOR B

	TIME INTERVALS					
	2	4	6	8	10	T
14. Teacher is *hypercritical*						
15. Teacher *leaves students entirely on their own*						
16. Teacher *works with students as one*						
17. Teacher sets common pace for all						
18. *Procedures without plan or organization*						
19. *Teacher only involved*						
20. Teacher *narrows the lesson* only to the subject at hand						
21. Teacher *assumes* that because the students saw the point in a simple illustration, *they will see it again*						
22. Activity chiefly a dialogue between *teacher* and a *few students* or *one student*						
23. *No goals* or objectives evident						
24. *No grouping* evident						
25. *Lecture activity predominates* the lesson						
26. *Materials inadequate or poorly organized*						
27. Teacher *refers constantly to guide*						

INDEX

# indicates discovery laboratory activity.